TWENTIETH
CENTURY
CRITICISM

TWENTIETH CENTURY CRITICISM

The Major Statements

Edited by

William J. Handy

Max Westbrook

Fp THE FREE PRESS
A Division of Macmillan Publishing Co., Inc.
NEW YORK

The Free Press
A Division of Macmillan Publishing Co., Inc
866 Third Avenue, New York, N.Y. 10022

Library of Congress Catalog Card Number: 73-3898

Printed in the United States of America

printing number
1 2 3 4 5 6 7 8 9 10

Library of Congress Cataloging in Publication Data

Handy, William J   comp.
     Twentieth century criticism.

     Includes bibliographies.
     1. Criticism--Addresses, essays, lectures. I. West-
brook, Max Roger, 1927-   joint comp. II. Title.
PN94.H3   801'.95'0904   73-3898
ISBN 0-02-913710-1

Copyright Acknowledgements

Booth, Wayne C. "Telling and Showing." From *The Rhetoric of Fiction* by Wayne
     C. Booth. Reprinted by permission of the author and the University of Chicago
     Press.

Bowron, Bernard, Leo Marx and Arnold Rose. "Literature and Covert Culture."
     From American Quarterly, Winter, 1957, copyright 1957, Trustees of the University
     of Pennsylvania. Reprinted by permission of the authors and the publishers.

Brooks, Cleanth. "The Language of Paradox." Reprinted by permission of the author.

Burke, Kenneth. "Psychology and Form." Reprinted by permission of the author.

Chase, Richard. "Notes on the Study of Myth." From *Partisan Review*, Vol. 13, No. 3.
     Copyright 1946 by *Partisan Review*. Reprinted by permission of Frances W. Chase,
     Executor of the Estate of Richard Chase.

Contents

PART 2 *Genre Criticism*

PART 3 *Archetypal Criticism*

PART 4 *Historical Criticism*

PART 5 *Interdisciplinary Criticism*

Preface

The organizing principle of this book follows from the conviction that there are four major types of literary criticism which have a distinct philosophical base. We believe that Formalist Criticism is grounded in the Kantian and Coleridgian tradition, with important contributions from the Imagists and the New Critics; that the foundations of Genre Criticism are located in the philosophy of Aristotle, more recognizably in *The Poetics*; that Archetypal Criticism is founded, centrally, in C. G. Jung's theory of "The Archetypes of the Collective Unconscious"; and that the theoretical base of Historical Criticism is best articulated in Taine's monumental study, *The History of English Literature*. In addition to these four types of criticism, there are numerous critics who share a common belief in the necessity of moving from one base to another as suggested by the task at hand. Their profound differences notwithstanding, the critics represented in the fifth section of this book believe that literature should be related to the other arts and to intellectual disciplines, especially the social sciences; and they are, in this sense, Interdisciplinary Critics.

Each of the first four sections begins with the appropriate philosophical foundation. Since the Interdisciplinary Critic does not work from a central philosophical position, the fifth section begins with a classic essay in the field which discusses and demonstrates the method.

Our major effort in selecting essays has been to identify the essay which is seminal to a given critic and to the position with which he is associated. The penultimate essay in each of the first four sections is an example of the current directions of the respective schools of criticism. Since the current direction in criticism generally is interdisciplinary, we have given more space to contemporary essays in the section of Interdisciplinary Criticism. The concluding essay in each section is a representative essay in the practice of criticism which not only illustrates the theory of a given approach but at the same time provides a sustained test of that theory on the common ground of Shakespearean tragedy.

While emphasizing distinct kinds of criticism, we believe also that all significant critical movements possess a single purpose which transcends their separation into irreconcilable camps. Critics of different allegiance live in the same world, respond to the same literature, and profess the same intention: the elucidation of the literature. Kenneth Burke, for example, is at once formalist and archetypal; T. S. Eliot is a formalist who relates his critical vision to the literary history and archetypal consciousness; Lionel Trilling's awareness of the ways that history can be made to work in literature is formalistic as well as historical; and Northrop Frye is represented—quite comfortably we feel—in both the Genre and the Archetypal sections.

Some of our editorial decisions—the inclusion of three or four essays which are more helpful than "major," the omission of a few standard choices—are pedagogically motivated. While paying primary attention to the material, and not hesitating to include the most demanding essays, we have kept in mind the student's need to learn what criticism is rather than merely to read comments about criticism.

Our own introductions have a special devotion to this cause. Instead of tracing the history of each movement, instead of emphasizing the differences within a movement, we have concentrated on defining the central principles of the best critics in each school. The introductions are written in sympathy with the type of criticism under discussion, sometimes even to the style employed, and the topics selected for explanation are the ones we felt most beneficial to the student. The critical essays themselves are allowed to stand without editorial comment.

The essays selected represent a balanced attention to poetry, fiction, drama, and culture while centering on theoretical and practical criticism. Our chief hope is that these selections and this arrangement will help the student to see and to be responsible for the theoretical implications of what he says about the meaning of a word in a poem, that is, to become a more perceptive reader.

Biographical Sketches

Formalist Criticism

Samuel Taylor Coleridge, poet, critic, literary theorist, was unquestionably one of the strongest influences in the shaping of modern literary criticism. He was born in Devon, England in 1772 and died in 1834. He was educated at Christ's Hospital and at Jesus College, Cambridge. With Wordsworth he composed the *Lyrical Ballads* with its famous "Preface" and Coleridge's "The Ancient Mariner." His chief contribution to literary criticism is contained in *The Biographia Literaria*, 1817, which was influential in introducing German aesthetic theory to England.

Immanuel Kant, 18th century German philosopher, is generally considered to be the philosophical source of formalist criticism. He was born (1724), educated, and taught in Königsberg, Prussia. From 1770 until his death in 1804 he lectured as professor of logic and metaphysics at the University of Königsberg. His three monumental works appeared within a ten year period: the *Critique of Pure Reason* in 1781, the *Critique of Practical Reason* in 1788, and the *Critique of Judgment* in 1790. The latter work is one of the foundation documents in modern literary theory as well as in the history of aesthetics.

T. M. Greene was born in 1897 in Constantinople. He received his Ph.D. at the University of Edinburgh in 1924, his LL.D. in 1947 and his L.H.D. in 1953. He taught philosophy at Princeton beginning in 1923, and later at Stanford, Yale, Rice Institute, Scripps College and at the American University at Beirut, among others. His famous work is *The Arts and the Art of Criticism*, 1940. He is co-editor of *Liberal Education Re-examined*, 1943, and is the author of *Our Cultural Heritage*, 1956; *Liberalism*, 1957; and *Moral Aesthetic and Religious Insight*, 1957.

F. S. Flint was a minor British poet who was associated with the Imagist movement. Ezra Pound's *Des Imagistes*, 1913, the first anthology of Imagist poems, contained five of Flint's poems. He was born in 1885 in London. His education was limited to the common school and a workingman's night school in London. In March, 1909, Flint and a group of young poets, including T. E. Hulme and John Gould Fletcher, all of whom shared a "dissatisfaction with English poetry as it is being written," began a series of Thursday evening meetings in a London Soho restaurant. This was the beginning of the Imagist movement.

Ezra Pound, American poet and literary critic, is generally considered together with T. E. Hulme as the co-founder of Imagism. After completing his Ph.D. at the University of Pennsylvania, he moved to Europe where he became the London editor of *Poetry*, 1913, and the *Little Review*, 1917–1919. His poetic works include: *Personae* and *Cantos*; his literary criticism: *Make It New*; *ABC of Reading*; *Polite Essays*; *Literary Essays*. He had a profound influence as a teacher and critic on several well-known writers, including T. S. Eliot and Ernest Hemingway.

I. A. Richards, British literary critic, is associated with the beginnings of the New Criticism. His *Principles of Literary Criticism*, 1924; *Science and Poetry*, 1925; and *Practical Criticism*, 1929, are generally regarded as foundation works for New Criticism. He was a University Lecturer at Harvard from 1939 to 1944 and Professor of English from 1944 to 1963. His critical writing was a strong influence on the theory and practice of Cleanth Brooks.

T. S. Eliot, whose monumental poem, "The Wasteland" (1922), became the strongest influence on the poetry of the first half of the twentieth century, also exerted a notable influence on modern literary criticism. He was born in St. Louis, Missouri in 1888 and died a British citizen in 1965. He was educated at Harvard, the Sorbonne, and Oxford. He returned to America briefly to lecture at Harvard while continuing his graduate study. His criticism includes *The Sacred Wood* (1920), a collection of essays; *For Launcelot Andrews* (1928), another collection of essays. His *Selected Essays* (1932) contains his famous statement of the "objective correlative," the key to his poetic expressionism and "The Metaphysical Poets," one of the country's major political statements.

John Crowe Ransom, one of America's foremost modern poets and literary critics, is perhaps the leading theorist of the new criticism movement. As founder and senior fellow of the School of Letters at Kenyon College, he invited the leading critics of the day to conduct classes each summer in the theoretical and practical criticism of literature. As Editor of the *Kenyon Review* from 1939 until 1959, he advanced the new critical movement by dedicating a leading literary journal to its cause. And as author of two major critical works, *The World's Body*, 1939, and *The New Criticism*, 1941, he established the principles underlying the theory and practice of new criticism. He was born in Pulaski, Tennessee, educated at Vanderbilt University, Oxford University (as a Rhodes Scholar) and at Christ's College. He was professor of English at Vanderbilt from 1927–37 and at Kenyon from 1937–58.

Cleanth Brooks is one of the foremost spokesmen for new criticism and its later version, "formalism," the name associated with the movement after the publication of Brooks' essay, "The Formalist Critic," published in the Kenyon Review, 1950. His *Understanding Poetry* (1938), edited in collaboration with Robert Penn Warren, has had a profound influence on the teaching of poetry in the universities. The work, a critical anthology, contained, along with a statement of critical convictions, some of the best practical criticism of individual poems that the new criticism had produced. He was born in Murray, Kentucky, educated at Vanderbilt University, where he was a pupil under John Crowe Ransom, at Tulane University and at Oxford, where he was a Rhodes Scholar. His criticism includes: *Modern Poetry and the Tradition* (1939); *The Well-Wrought Urn* (1947); *William Faulkner: The Yoknapatawpha Country*

(1963); and *Literary Criticism: A Short History*, in collaboration with W. K. Wimsatt, 1957. His latest book, *A Shaping Joy: Studies in the Writer's Craft*, appeared in 1971.

Mark Schorer was the first of the formalist critics to apply the theory and practice of the movement to the criticism of fiction in his essay, "Technique As Discovery." He is Professor of English at Berkeley and a one-time fellow of the School of Letters at Indiana University (formerly at Kenyon College). He is the author of *William Blake: The Politics of Vision*, 1946; *Sinclair Lewis* (a biography), 1961; *D. H. Lawrence*, 1968; and *The World We Imagine: Selected Essays*, 1968.

Joseph Frank was born in 1918 in New York City, He was a member of the editorial staff of the Bureau of National Affairs in Washington, D.C. and a Fulbright Fellow in Europe. He is the author of *The Widening Gyre*, 1963; and the editor of *A Primer of Ignorance*, 1967, and *Horizons of a Philosopher*, 1963.

Robert Heilman has written the best formalist criticism of drama in two full length studies of individual Shakespeare plays: *This Great Stage: Image and Structure in King Lear* (1948), and *Magic in the Web: Action and Language in Othello* (1956). He was born in Philadelphia in 1906, educated at Lafayette College, Ohio State University and Harvard. He is a professor of English at the University of Washington, Seattle. His latest work is *The Iceman, The Arsonist, and The Troubled Agent: Tragedy and Melodrama on the Modern Stage*, 1973.

Genre Criticism

Aristotle (384–322 B.C.), the great Greek philosopher, was born in Macedonia. He was a student under Plato at Athens, where he remained for twenty years. Subsequently he lectured to scholars at the Lyceum in Athens for thirteen years. His works have survived in the main as summaries and notes of his oral lectures. His most famous treatises are his "Logic," the science of reasoning; his "Ethics," an introduction to moral philosophy; his "Metaphysics," on the nature of being; and his "Poetics," one of the foundation documents of subsequent literary theory.

Elder Olson is one of the leading genre critics of the Chicago School of Criticism. He is the co-author with R. S. Crane of a major work in literary theory, *Critics and Criticism* (1952); the author of *Tragedy and the Theory of Drama* (1961); and *The Theory of Comedy* (1968). His work in practical criticism, *The Poetry of Dylan Thomas* (1954), brought him the award for the best critical book on poetry given by the Academy of American Poets. He is a professor of English at the University of Chicago. He was born in Chicago and educated through the completion of the Ph.D. degree at the University of Chicago.

R. S. Crane was a professor of English at the University of Chicago, and one of the chief spokesmen and founders of the Chicago School of Criticism, which bases its theory and practice on the treatises of Aristotle. He is the author of works on literary criticism: *Critics and Criticism*, which he co-authored with Elder Olson (1952); *Language of Criticism and the Structure of Poetry* (1953); *The Idea of Humanities, and Other Essays Critical and Historical* (1967); and *Critical and Historical Principles of Literary History* (1971). He was born in Tecumseh, Michigan in 1886 and educated at the University of Michigan, the University of Pennsylvania and Northwestern University. He died in 1967.

Northrop Frye is universally recognized as one of the century's outstanding literary theorists. His best known work, *Anatomy of Criticism* (1957), is unquestionably one of the masterpieces of literary scholarship and the book which more than any other laid the groundwork for the archetypal or mythopoetic approach to literary study. Other critical works include: *Fearful Symmetry: A Study of William Blake* (1947); *Fables of Identity* (1963); *The Well-Tempered Critic* (1963); *T. S. Eliot* (1963); *The Educated Imagination* (1964); *A Natural Perspective: The Development of Shakespearean Comedy and Romance* (1965); *The Modern Century* (1967); and *The Critical Path: An Essay on the Social Context of Literary Criticism* (1971). He is Professor of English Literature at the University of Toronto. He was born in Quebec in 1912 and was educated at Toronto, Oxford and Queen's University.

Wayne Booth is one of the later critics of the Chicago School to receive national attention, primarily for his outstanding book on the literary criticism of fiction, *The Rhetoric of Fiction*, 1961. He is a professor of English at the University of Chicago and a fellow of the School of Letters at Indiana University. He was born in Utah in 1921 and was educated at Brigham Young University, and at the University of Chicago where he received his Ph.D. in 1950. In 1967 he edited *The Knowledge Most Worth Having*.

Archetypal Criticism

C. G. Jung, the great Swiss psychiatrist, was born in 1875 and educated at Basel and at Zurich where he received his M.D. degree in 1902. He was a physician in the Psychiatric Clinic at Zurich from 1900–9 and a lecturer in psychology from 1905–13, a professor of psychology at Zurich 1933–41 and a professor of medical psychology at Basel, 1943. His revolutionary work was *Psychology of the Unconscious* (1921). He is the author of *Psychological Types* (1923); *Two Essays on Analytical Psychology* (1928); *Modern Man in Search of a Soul* (1933); *Psychology and Religion* (1938); *The Integration of the Personality* (1940); *Essays on a Science of Mythology*, with C. Kerenyi (1949): *The Structure and Dynamics of the Psyche* (Eng. tr., 1960), among others. He died in 1961.

Northrop Frye. (See under Genre section).

Richard Chase, born in New Hampshire in 1914, was educated at Dartmouth and at Columbia University where he was a professor of English until his death in 1962. He is the author of *Quest for Myth* (1949); *Herman Melville* (1949);

Emily Dickinson (1951); *The American Novel and its Tradition* (1957); *The Democratic Vista* (1958); and *Walt Whitman* (1961).

Philip Wheelwright was born in 1901 and educated through the Ph.D. at Princeton. He taught at Princeton and at Dartmouth and Pomona Colleges and is presently Professor Emeritus in philosophy at the University of California at Riverside. His works include: *A Critical Introduction to Ethics* (1935); *The Burning Fountain* (1954); *The Way of Philosophy* (1954); and *Metaphor and Reality* (1962).

Kenneth Burke is a literary critic whose critical interests are both archetypal and formalist. He was a lecturer at the New School for Social Research (1937). He taught literature and criticism at Bennington College from 1943–62. He was a senior fellow of the School of Letters at Kenyon College (1950) and at Indiana University (1952 and 1958). His works on literary criticism include: *Counter-Statement* (1931); *The Philosophy of Literary Form* (1941); *A Grammar of Motives* (1945); and *Language as Symbolic Action* (1966). He was born in Pittsburgh, Pennsylvania in 1897 and attended Ohio State University (1916–17) and Columbia University (1917–18).

Leslie Fiedler is a literary critic whose writing has emphasized the criticism of the American culture. He teaches literature at the State University of New York at Buffalo. He was a fellow of the School of Letters at Indiana University (1953) and the Kenyon Review Fellow in Criticism (1956–7). He is the author of critical works which include: *An End to Innocence* (1955); *Love and Death in the American Novel* (1960); *No! In Thunder* (1960); and *Collected Essays* (1971). He was born in Newark, New Jersey and educated at New York University and the University of Wisconsin.

Herbert Weisinger, Professor of English at Michigan State University (1944–66) and now teaching at the State University of New York at Stony Brook, is the author of works on criticism and mythology. His works include: *Tragedy and the Paradox of the Fortunate Fall* (1953); and *The Agony and the Triumph, Papers on the Use and Abuse of Myth* (1964). He was born in Brooklyn in 1913 and educated at Brooklyn College and the University of Michigan.

Historical Criticism

Hippolyte Taine (1828–93) is the great nineteenth century literary critic and historian. His *History of English Literature* (1856–9) is one of the foundation documents for the subsequent study of literary history.

Edmund Wilson, in addition to being one of the century's better known literary critics, was also a poet, playwright and journalist. His works include: *Discordant Encounters* (1926), dialogues and plays; *Poets, Farewell!* (1929), a collection of poems; *Axel's Castle* (1931), and *The Triple Thinkers* (1938), a literary history and criticism; *The Scrolls from the Dead Sea* (1955), literary scholarship; *The American Earthquake* (1958); and *The Bit Between My Teeth* (1965). He was born in 1895, educated at Princeton and died in 1972.

A. S. P. Woodhouse was a Canadian scholar who has published chiefly in the field of literary history. He is the author of *Puritanism and Liberty* (1938); *The Poet and His Faith* (1965); and *The Heavenly Muse* (1972). He was Professor of English Literature at the University of Toronto. He was born in Ontario, Canada in 1895 and educated at Harvard and Arcadia Universities. He died in 1969.

Bruce Harkness is the author of works on literary history and criticism, including: *Conrad's Heart of Darkness* (1960), and *Conrad's Secret Sharer* (1962). He is currently Professor and Dean of Arts and Science at Kent State University in Ohio. He was born in Beaver Dam, Wisconsin in 1923 and educated through the Ph.D. at the University of Chicago.

Roy Harvey Pearce is one of the major spokesmen for the historical approach to literature, especially the history of ideas school of Johns Hopkins University. He is the author of works on American literary history and criticism, including: *Colonial American Writing* (1950); *The Savages of America* (1953); *The Continuity of American Poetry* (1961); and *Historicism Once More* (1969). He was a professor of English at Ohio State University from 1954–63 and is currently Professor of English at the University of California. He was born in Chicago and educated at UCLA and Johns Hopkins University.

Lionel Trilling is one of America's outstanding critics of literature and culture Probably his best known work is *The Liberal Imagination* (1950), which reveals his lifelong interest in sociological as well as historical criticism. His famous essay, "The Sense of the Past" is one of the key chapters in that collection. Other of his works include: *Matthew Arnold* (1939); *E. M. Forster* (1943); *The Opposing Self* (1955); *A Gathering of Fugitives* (1956); and *Beyond Culture: Essays on Literature and Learning* (1965). He was born and educated in New York City (Columbia University). He is Professor of English at Columbia and a Senior Fellow of the School of Letters.

Richard Ellman is probably best known for his monumental biography, *James Joyce* (1959), which won the National Book Award in 1960. Other of his works on literary history and criticism include: *Yeats: The Man and the Masks* (1948); *The Identity of Yeats* (1954); *Eminent Domain* (1967); and *Ulysses on the Liffey* (1972). He is a professor of English at Northwestern University. He was selected as the Kenyon Review Fellow in Criticism in 1955. He was born in Highland Park, Michigan in 1918 and educated at Yale University.

Jane H. Jack is a Tutor and Lecturer in English at St. Anne's College, Oxford, England. She holds an M.A. from Edinburgh and a B.Litt. degree from Oxford.

Interdisciplinary Criticism

Bernard Bowron was born in Berkeley, California in 1913. He attended the University of California and Harvard, where he received his Ph.D. in 1948. At present he is a professor of English at the University of Minnesota.

Leo Marx, born in 1919 in New York City, was educated at Harvard (Ph.D. 1950). He is the author of *The Machine in the Garden* (1964), and the editor of *The Americanness of Walt Whitman* (1960). He is Professor of English and American Studies at Amherst College.

Arnold M. Rose was educated at the University of Chicago where he received his Ph.D. in sociology, in 1946. He taught at Bennington College, Washington University, and at the University of Minnesota at Minneapolis. He is the author of *Theory and Method in the Social Sciences* (1954). He died in 1968.

Herbert Read is a British literary critic whose critical interests are varied and manifold. His writings reveal his interest in formalist, archetypal, sociological and psychological approaches to literature. They include: *Art and Society* (1937); *Collected Essays in Literary Criticism* (1938); *The Philosophy of Modern Art* (1952); *Icon and Idea* (1965); *Poetry and Experience* (1967); and *The Cult of Sincerity* (1969). He was born in England and educated at the University of Leeds. He was Professor of Fine Arts at the University of Edinburgh (1931–1933). He died in 1968.

Nathan Scott, Jr. is Professor of Theology and Literature at the Divinity School, University of Chicago. He is the author of works on theology, culture, and modern literary criticism which include: *Modern Literature and the Religious Frontier* (1958); *The Tragic Vision and the Christian Faith* (1957); *Albert Camus* (1962); *The Climate of Faith in Modern Literature* (1964); *Samuel Beckett* (1965); and *The Unquiet Vision: Mirrors of Man in Existentialism* (1969). He was born in Cleveland, Ohio and educated at the University of Michigan, *Union Theological Seminary* and Columbia University.

Claude Levi-Strauss is Professor of Anthropology at the College de France in Paris. He was a visiting professor at the New School for Social Research (1942–45). He is the author of works on anthropology: *La Vie Familiale et Social des Indiens Nambikwara* (1948); *Les Structures Élémentaires de la Parenté* (1949); *Anthropologie Structurale* (1958); and *Le Totemisme Aujourd'hui* (1962).

Susan Sontag is an author and film director. Her chief contribution to literary criticism is her book, *Against Interpretation* (1966). Her novels include: *The Benefactor* (1963), and *Death Kit* (1967). She is the author of a screenplay, *Duet for Cannibals* (1970), and a critical work, *Styles of Radical Will* (1969). In 1966 she was the recipient of the George Polk Memorial Award for contributions toward better appreciation of theatre, motion pictures and literature.

Anthony Schillaci is a professor of Metaphysics, Philosophy of Art and Liturgy at Aquinas Institute, River Forest, Illinois. He is the author of *Movies and Morals* (1968), and co-editor of *Films Deliver* (1970). He has taught courses in film aesthetics, the history of film, and filmmaking in various American universities.

Ernest Jones, born in 1879, was a leading follower of Sigmund Freud. His many works include: *Addresses on Psycho-analysis* (1921); *Hamlet and Oedipus* (1949); *Essays in Applied Psycho-analysis* (1951); and *Free Associations* (1959). He died in London in 1958.

PART 1

Formalist Criticism

Central to Formalist Criticism is the work of John Crowe Ransom and his contemporaries, critics like Richard Blackmur, I. A. Richards, William Empson, Robert Heilman, Yvor Winters, T. S. Eliot, and Ransom's famous pupils like Cleanth Brooks and Allen Tate. In their contributions to the understanding of the poem's structure and its intention as a symbolic form of man's experience, they offered varied and even at times contradictory accounts. But in their conviction that the poem possessed a distinct and radically different structure and intention from logical prose, they were in complete agreement. What was agreed upon in each instance was the principle that the poem's function was to formulate the concrete character of human experience, what Ransom called the "bodiness of the world" in his catechizing work on literary aesthetics, *The World's Body*. For all of these theorists, as well as Ransom, the world's body was something to be celebrated and with as much "ontological" justification as the scientists had celebrated the world's skeleton, that is, its underlying principles.

The impulse to *abstraction* the New Critics saw as the scientific impulse; the impulse to *concretion* they claimed for poetry. As Ransom insisted, "the sciences deal almost entirely with structures, which are scientific structures; but poetic structures differ radically from these, and it is that difference which defines them. The ontological materials are different, and are such as to fall outside the possible range of science." The fundamental language unit of science, they pointed out, was the concept, but the differentia of poetry they asserted to be the image. As Ransom wrote in *The New Criticism*:

> Science deals exclusively in pure symbols, but art deals essentially, though not exclusively, in iconic signs. This makes at once a sharp formal or technical distinction between the two forms of discourse; but one would think it must become at once a philosophical distinction also.

The passage calls attention, however obliquely, to the character of the image as "iconic." And further, "art deals essentially, though not exclusively, in iconic signs." The "not exclusively" points to Ransom's insistence that a "logical core" is also an essential part of the poem's structure. New Criticism developed a minor schism at this point, Ransom and Winters holding to the necessity for the logical or cognitive aspect of poetic apprehension, while Brooks became the spokesman for those who held an "organicist's" view—namely that the poem was an organic composition of its images.

But in either case the image was seen as "iconic" or in Suzanne Langer's term "presentational" in character. The interchangeable use of the terms "image" and "icon" may be seen in Herbert Read's title *Icon and Idea* for his work on poetic theory or in W. K. Wimsatt's *The Verbal Icon*. The opposition suggested in each case reflects the intention of these critics, not merely to make what Ransom had called the "ontological" distinction between science and poetry, but to explore the particular characteristics which differentiated the poetic image or icon from the scientific language unit, the abstract concept. In *The World's Body,* Ransom wrote:

> [The image] cannot be dispossessed of a primordial freshness which idea can never claim. An idea is derivative and tamed. The image is in the natural or wild state and it has to be discovered there, not put there, obeying its own law and none of ours. We think we can lay hold of image and take it captive, but the docile captive is not the real image but only the idea, which is the image with its character beaten out of it.

Ransom, more than any other modern theorist, continually sought to ground his critical theory in philosophical aesthetics, chiefly that of Immanuel Kant. And he continually sought out his philosophical contemporaries for their verification of his observations on his theory of poetry, aestheticians like Eliseo Vivas, Charles Morris, and T. M. Greene. In one of his major essays, "Criticism as Pure Speculation," Ransom wrote:

> A chasm, perhaps an abyss, separates the critic and the aesthetician ordinarily, if the books in the library are evidence. But the authority of criticism depends on its coming to terms with aesthetics, and the authority of literary aesthetics depends on its coming to terms with criticism. Mr. Greene is an aesthetician, and his department is philosophy, but he has subscribed in effect to this thesis.

And it should be noted, perhaps because both are Kantians, that Professor Greene does support Ransom's theory. In discussing the nature of the image, Greene wrote:

> The perfect literary image is the very opposite of a scientific illustration or a diagram, for it is at once individualized and immediately expressive of the universals it was created to evoke.

3

And in another assertion which again gives support to Ransom's position, Greene wrote:

> We never succeed in specifying the particular save in terms that define the *type* or *class* of things to which it belongs. Perceptual immediacy and discursive language are incompatible.

In just such pronouncements can be seen the deepest convictions of formalism. And by the mid 1940's, criticism applying formalist convictions to fiction and drama began to appear in the literary quarterlies, criticism like Joseph Frank's "Spatial Form in Modern Fiction," Mark Schorer's "Technique as Discovery," and Robert Heilman's *Understanding Drama*. The writers in each instance saw that such assertions as Ransom's and Greene's concerning the poetic image applied as well to fiction and drama. The application here was to the *scene*, which in its presentational character was shown to function with the same "presentational immediacy" as did the image and icon in poetry.

The task, then, for the Formalist Critic of fiction and drama became essentially that of the New Critic of poetry: to attend to the complexity of meaning embodied in a particular scene in the same way that the critic of poetry attended to the manifold of meaning in the poetic image. Ransom stated the problem for the practice of poetry criticism and suggested the nature of the critical approach to the poem when he wrote:

> The image which is not remarkable in any particular property is marvellous in its assemblage of many properties, a manifold of properties, like a mine or field, something to be explored for the properties. [*The World's Body*]

And for the Formalist Critic, the problem for fiction and drama criticism was viewed as essentially the same: to discover by sensitive reading, by what Eliseo Vivas called "rapt attention on the object," those meanings which inhere in the presentational units of fiction and drama. Form here, just as in poetry, was thus regarded by the Formalist Critic as "presentational" or "non-discursive." Style in fiction and drama, in its most fundamental sense, became for the Formalist Critic the unique way that a novelist or dramatist gives form to his concrete presentations. In each case meaning was seen to be "embodied" in the indirect form of fictional and dramatic style that constituted the essential art of the writer concerned.

Thus it was the New Critic, whose focus was the lyric poem, who established the approach to be taken by the Formalist Critic of fiction and drama: the discovery and disclosure of meaning in the presentational scenes which define the "ontological" structure of the novel or play.

Bibliography

Blackmur, R. P. "A Burden for Critics." *Hudson Review,* I (Summer, 1948), pp. 170–85.

Blackmur, R. P. *Language as Gesture.* New York: Harcourt, Brace and Co., 1952.

Brooks, Cleanth. "My Credo: Formalist Critics." *Kenyon Review,* XIII (1951), pp. 72–81.

————*Modern Poetry and the Tradition.* Chapel Hill, N.C.: University of North Carolina Press, 1939.

————"The Poem as Organism." *English Institute Essays,* 1940. New York: Columbia University Press, 1941, pp. 20–41.

————"The Poet's Fancy." *New Republic,* LXXXV (November 13, 1935), pp. 26–27.

————and Robert Penn Warren, eds. *Understanding Poetry.* New York: Henry Holt and Company, Inc., 1938.

————*The Well-Wrought Urn.* New York: Reynal & Hitchcock, 1947.

Burke, Kenneth. *Counter-Statement.* New York: Harcourt, Brace and Co., 1931.

Cassirer, Ernest. *An Essay on Man.* New Haven, Conn.: Yale University Press, 1944.

Eliot, T. S. *After Strange Gods: A Primer of Modern Heresy.* New York: Harcourt, Brace and Co., 1934.

————*The Sacred Wood.* London: Metheun and Company, Ltd., 1920.

————*Selected Essays:* 1917–1932. London: Faber and Faber, Ltd., 1932.

————*The Use of Poetry and the Use of Criticism.* Cambridge, Mass.: Harvard University Press, 1933.

Empson, William. *Seven Types of Ambiguity.* New York: New Directions, 1947.

Erlich, Victor. *Russian Formalism: History, Doctrine.* The Hague: Mouton, 1965.

Greene, Theodore Meyer. *The Arts and the Art of Criticism.* Princeton, N.J.: Princeton University Press, 1940.

Handy, William J. *Kant and the Southern New Critics.* Austin, Texas: University of Texas Press, 1963.

Heilman, Robert B. *This Great Stage.* Baton Rouge, La.: Louisiana State University Press, 1948.

Kant, Immanuel. *The Critique of Aesthetic Judgment.* Translated by J. H. Bernard. London: Macmillan & Company, Ltd., 1931.

Krieger, Murray. "After the New Criticism." *Massachusetts Review,* IV (1962), pp. 183–205.

————*The New Apologists for Poetry.* Minneapolis, Minn.: University of Minnesota Press, 1956.

Langer, Susanne. *Philosophy in a New Key.* Cambridge, Mass.: Harvard University Press, 1942.

Moorman, Charles. "The Vocabulary of the New Criticism." *American Quarterly,* IX (1957), pp. 180–84.

Oxenhandler, Neal. "Ontological Criticism in America and France." *Modern Language Review,* LV (1960), pp. 17–23.

Pound, Ezra. *The ABC of Reading.* New Haven, Conn.: Yale University Press, 1934. *How to Read.* London: D. Harmsworth, 1931.

Ransom, John Crowe. "Criticism as Pure Speculation." In *The Intent of the Critic.* Edited by D. A. Stauffer. Princeton, N.J.: Princeton University Press, 1941.

————,'The Literary Criticism of Aristotle." *Kenyon Review,* X (1948), pp. 382–402.

————*The New Criticism*. New York: New Directions, 1941.

————*The World's Body*. New York: Charles Scribner's Sons, 1938.

Read, Herbert. *Icon and Idea*. Cambridge, Mass.: Harvard University Press, 1956.

Read, Herbert, ed. *Speculations, by T. E. Hulme*. Kegan Paul; Harcourt, 1924; 1936.

Richards, I. A. *Practical Criticism*. New York: Harcourt, Brace and Co., 1929.

————*Principles of Literary Criticism*. New York: Harcourt, Brace and Co., 1925.

————*Science and Poetry*. New York: W. W. Norton and Co., 1926.

Sister Mary Janet. "Poetry as Knowledge in the New Criticism." *Western Humanities Review*, XVI (1962), pp. 199–210.

Spender, Stephen. "The Making of a Poem," *Partisan Review*, XIII (1946), pp. 294–308.

Spilka, Mark. "The Necessary Stylist: A New Critical Revision." *Modern Fiction Studies*, VI (1960), pp. 283–97.

Tate, Allen. *Reason in Madness: Critical Essays*. New York: G. P. Putnam's Sons, 1941.

Vivas, Eliseo. *Creation and Discovery: Essays in Criticism and Aesthetics*. New York: The Noonday Press, Inc., 1955.

————"Literature and Knowledge." *Sewanee Review*, LX (1952), pp. 561–92.

————"The Objective Correlative of T. S. Eliot." *American Bookman*, I (1944), pp. 7–18.

Warren, R. P. "Pure and Impure Poetry." *Kenyon Review*, V (1943), pp. 228–54.

————*The Rime of the Ancient Mariner: An Essay*. New York: Reynal & Hitchcock, 1946.

Wellek, Rene. *In Concepts of Criticism*. Edited by Stephen G. Nichols, Jr. New Haven, Conn.: Yale University Press, 1963, pp. 54–68; 353–60.

————and Austin Warren. *Theory of Literature*. New York: Harcourt, Brace and Co., 1949.

Wimsatt, W. K., Jr. and Monroe C. Beardsley. "The Affective Fallacy." *Sewanee Review*, LVII (1949), pp. 31–55.

————"The Intentional Fallacy." *Sewanee Review*, LIV (1946), pp. 455–88.

Wimsatt, W. K., Jr. *The Verbal Icon*. Lexington Ky.: The University of Kentucky Press, 1954.

Winters, Yvor. *In Defense of Reason*. Denver Colo.: Swallow Press and W. Morrow and Company, 1947.

Biographia Literaria

SAMUEL COLERIDGE

But if the definition sought for be that of a *legitimate* poem, I answer, it must be one, the parts of which mutually support and explain each other; all in their proportion harmonizing with, and supporting the purpose and known influences of metrical arrangement. The philosophic critics of all ages coincide with the ultimate judgment of all countries, in equally denying the praises of a just poem, on the one hand, to a series of striking lines or distiches, each of which, absorbing the whole attention of the reader to itself, becomes disjoined from its context, and forms a separate whole, instead of a harmonizing part; and on the other hand, to an unsustained composition, from which the reader collects rapidly the general result unattracted by the component parts. The reader should be carried forward, not merely or chiefly by the mechanical impulse of curiosity, or by a restless desire to arrive at the final solution; but by the pleasureable activity of mind excited by the attractions of the journey itself. Like the motion of a serpent, which the Egyptians made the emblem of intellectual power; or like the path of sound through the air;—at every step he pauses and half recedes, and from the retrogressive movement collects the force which again carries him onward. *Praecipitandus est liber spiritus*,[1] says Petronius most happily. The epithet, *liber*, here balances the preceding verb; and it is not easy to conceive more meaning condensed in fewer words.

But if this should be admitted as a satisfactory character of a poem, we have still to seek for a definition of poetry. The writings of Plato, and Jeremy Taylor, and Burnet's Theory of the Earth, furnish undeniable proofs that poetry of the highest kind may exist without metre, and even without the contra-

[1] [The free spirit must be brought down.]

distinguishing objects of a poem. The first chapter of Isaiah—(indeed a very large portion of the whole book)—is poetry in the most emphatic sense; yet it would be not less irrational than strange to assert, that pleasure, and not truth was the immediate object of the prophet. In short, whatever specific import we attach to the word, Poetry, there will be found involved in it, as a necessary consequence, that a poem of any length neither can be, nor ought to be, all poetry. Yet if an harmonious whole is to be produced, the remaining parts must be preserved in keeping with the poetry; and this can be no otherwise effected than by such a studied selection and artificial arrangement, as will partake of one, though not a peculiar property of poetry. And this again can be no other than the property of exciting a more continuous and equal attention than the language of prose aims at, whether colloquial or written.

My own conclusions on the nature of poetry, in the strictest use of the word, have been in part anticipated in some of the remarks on the Fancy and Imagination in the early part of this work. What is poetry?—is so nearly the same question with, what is a poet?—that the answer to the one is involved in the solution of the other. For it is a distinction resulting from the poetic genius itself, which sustains and modifies the images, thoughts, and emotions of the poet's own mind.

The poet, described in ideal perfection, brings the whole soul of man into activity, with the subordination of its faculties to each other according to their relative worth and dignity. He diffuses a tone and spirit of unity, that blends, and (as it were) *fuses*, each into each, by that synthetic and magical power, to which I would exclusively appropriate the name of Imagination. This power, first put in action by the will and understanding, and retained under their irremissive, though gentle and unnoticed, control, *laxis effertur habenis,* reveals itself in the balance or reconcilement of opposite or discordant qualities; of sameness, with difference; of the general with the concrete; the idea with the image; the individual with the representative; the sense of novelty and freshness with old and familiar objects; a more than usual state of emotion with more than usual order.

From *Critique of Judgment*

IMMANUEL KANT

THE FACULTIES OF THE MIND WHICH CONSTITUTE GENIUS

Of certain products which are expected, partly at least, to stand on the footing of fine art, we say they are *soul*less; and this, although we find nothing to censure in them as far as taste goes. A poem may be very pretty and elegant, but is soulless. A narrative has precision and method, but is soulless. A speech on some festive occasion may be good in substance and ornate withal, but may be soulless. Conversation frequently is not devoid of entertainment, but yet soulless. Even of a woman we may well say, she is pretty, affable, and refined, but soulless. Now what do we here mean by "soul"?

"*Soul*" (*Geist*) in an aesthetical sense, signifies the animating principle in the mind. But that whereby this principle animates the psychic substance (*Seele*)— the material which it employs for that purpose—is that which sets the mental powers into a swing that is final, i.e. into a play which is self-maintaining and which strengthens those powers for such activity.

Now my proposition is that this principle is nothing else than the faculty of presenting *aesthetic ideas*. But, by an aesthetic idea I mean that representation of the imagination which induces much thought, yet without the possibility of any definite thought whatever, i.e. *concept*, being adequate to it, and which language, consequently, can never get quite on level terms with or render completely intelligible.—It is easily seen, that an aesthetic idea is the counterpart (pendant) of a *rational idea*, which, conversely, is a concept, to which no *intuition* (representation of the imagination) can be adequate.

The imagination (as a productive faculty of cognition) is a powerful agent for creating, as it were, a second nature out of the material supplied to it by actual nature. It affords us entertainment where experience proves too commonplace; and we even use it to remodel experience, always following, no doubt, laws that are based on analogy, but still also following principles which have a higher seat in reason (and which are every whit as natural to us as those followed by the understanding in laying hold of empirical nature). By this means we get a sense of our freedom from the law of association (which attaches to the empirical employment of the imagination), with the result that the material can be borrowed by us from nature in accordance with that law, but be worked up by us into something else—namely, what surpasses nature.

Such representation of the imagination may be termed *ideas*. This is partly because they at least strain after something lying out beyond the confines of experience, and so seek to approximate to a presentation of rational concepts (i.e. intellectual ideas), thus giving to these concepts the semblance of an object-ive reality. But, on the other hand, there is this most important reason, that no concept can be wholly adequate to them as internal intuitions. The poet essays the task of interpreting to sense the rational ideas of invisible beings, the kingdom of the blessed, hell, eternity, creation &c. Or, again, as to things of which examples occur in experience, e.g. death, envy, and all vices, as also love, fame, and the like, transgressing the limits of experience he attempts with the aid of an imagination which emulates the display of reason in its attainment of a maximum, to body them forth to sense with a completeness of which nature affords no parallel; and it is in fact precisely in the poetic art that the faculty of aesthetic ideas can show itself to full advantage. This faculty, however, regarded solely on its own account, is properly no more than a talent (of the imagination).

If, now, we attach to a concept a representation of the imagination belonging to its presentation, but inducing solely on its own account such a wealth of thought as would never admit of comprehension in a definite concept, and, as a consequence, giving aesthetically an unbounded expansion to the concept itself, then the imagination here displays a creative activity, and it puts the faculty of intellectual ideas (reason) into motion—a motion, at the instance of a repre-sentation, towards an extension of thought, that, while germane, no doubt, to the concept of the object, exceeds what can be laid hold of in that representation or clearly expressed.

Those forms which do not constitute the presentation of a given concept itself, but which, as secondary representations of the imagination, express the derivatives connected with it, and its kinship with other concepts, are called (aesthetic) *attributes* of an object, the concept of which, as an idea of reason, cannot be adequately presented. In this way Jupiter's eagle, with the lightning in its claws, is an attribute of the mighty king of heaven, and the peacock of its stately queen' They do not, like *logical attributes*, represent what lies in our concepts of the sublimity and majesty of creation, but rather something else—something that gives the imagination an incentive to spread its flight over a whole host of kindred representations that provoke more thought than admits of expression in a concept determined by words. They furnish an *aesthetic idea*, which serves the above rational idea as a substitute for logical presentation, but with the proper function, however, of animating the mind by opening out for it a prospect into a field of kindred representations stretching beyond its ken.

But it is not alone in the arts of painting or sculpture, where the name of attribute is customarily employed, that fine art acts in this way; poetry and rhetoric also derive the soul that animates their works wholly from the aesthetic attributes of the objects—attributes which go hand in hand with the logical, and give the imagination an impetus to bring more thought into play in the matter, though in an undeveloped manner, than allows of being brought within the embrace of a concept, or, therefore, of being definitely formulated in language'—For the sake of brevity I must confine myself to a few examples only. When the great king expresses himself in one of his poems by saying:

> Oui, finissons sans trouble, et mourons sans regrets,
> En laissant l'Univers comblé de nos bienfaits.
> Ainsi l'Astre du jour, au bout de sa carrière,
> Répand sur l'horizon une douce lumière,
> Et les derniers rayons qu'il darde dans les airs
> Sont les derniers soupirs qu'il donne à l'Univers;

he kindles in this way his rational idea of a cosmopolitan sentiment even at the close of life, with the help of an attribute which the imagination (in remembering all the pleasures of a fair summer's day that is over and gone—a memory of which pleasures is suggested by a serene evening) annexes to that representation, and which stirs up a crowd of sensations and secondary representations for which no expression can be found. On the other hand, even an intellectual concept may serve, conversely, as attribute for a representation of sense, and so animate the latter with the idea of the supersensible; but only by the aesthetic factor subjectively attaching to the consciousness of the supersensible being employed for the purpose. So, for example, a certain poet says in his description of a beautiful morning: "The sun arose, as out of virtue rises peace." The consciousness of virtue, even where we put ourselves only in thought in the position of a virtuous man, diffuses in the mind a multitude of sublime and tranquillizing feelings, and gives a boundless outlook into a happy future, such as no expression within the compass of a definite concept completely attains.

In a word, the aesthetic idea is a representation of the imagination, annexed to a given concept, with which, in the free employment of imagination, such a multiplicity of partial representations are bound up, that no expression indicating a definite concept can be found for it—one which on that account allows a concept to be supplemented in thought by much that is indefinable in words, and the feeling of which quickens the cognitive faculties, and with language, as a mere thing of the letter, binds up the spirit (soul) also.

THE JUDGMENT OF TASTE IS AESTHETIC

If we wish to discern whether anything is beautiful or not, we do not refer the representation of it to the Object by means of understanding with a view to cognition, but by means of the imagination (acting perhaps in conjunction with understanding) we refer the representation to the Subject and its feeling of pleasure or displeasure. The judgment of taste, therefore, is not a cognitive judgment, and so not logical, but is aesthetic—which means that it is one whose determining ground *cannot be other than subjective*. Every reference of representations is capable of being objective, even that of sensations (in which case it signifies the real in an empirical representation). The one exception to this is the feeling of pleasure or displeasure. This denotes nothing in the object, but is a feeling which the Subject has of itself and of the manner in which it is affected by the representation.

To apprehend a regular and appropriate building with one's cognitive faculties, be the mode of representation clear or confused, is quite a different thing from being conscious of this representation with an accompanying sensation of delight. Here the representation is referred wholly to the Subject, and what is more to its feeling of life—under the name of the feeling of pleasure or displeasure—and this forms the basis of a quite separate faculty of discriminating and estimating, that contributes nothing to knowledge. All it does is to compare the given representation in the Subject with the entire faculty of representations of which the mind is conscious in the feeling of its state. Given representations in a judgment may be empirical, and so aesthetic; but the judgment which is pronounced by their means is logical, provided it refers them to the Object. Conversely, be the given representations even rational, but referred in a judgment solely to the Subject (to its feeling), they are always to that extent aesthetic.

THE BEAUTIFUL IS THAT WHICH, APART FROM CONCEPTS, IS REPRESENTED AS THE OBJECT OF A UNIVERSAL DELIGHT[1]

This definition of the beautiful is deducible from the foregoing definition of it as an object of delight apart from any interest. For where any one is conscious that his delight in an object is with him independent of interest, it is inevitable that he should look on the object as one containing a ground of delight for all men. For, since the delight is not based on any inclination of the Subject (or on any other deliberate interest), but the Subject feels himself completely *free* in respect of the liking which he accords to the object, he can find as reason for his delight no personal conditions to which his own subjective self might alone be party. Hence he must regard it as resting on what he may also presuppose in every other person; and therefore he must believe that he has reason for demanding a similar delight from every one. Accordingly he will speak of the beautiful as if beauty were a quality of the object and the judgment logical (forming a cognition of the Object by concepts of it); although it is only aesthetic, and contains merely a reference of the representation of the object to the Subject;

---

[1] The definition of taste here relied upon is that it is the faculty of estimating the beautiful. But the discovery of what is required for calling an object beautiful must be reserved for the analysis of judgments of taste. In my search for the moments to which attention is paid by this judgment in its reflection, I have followed the guidance of the logical functions of judging (for a judgment of taste always involves a reference to understanding). I have brought the moment of quality first under review, because this is what the aesthetic judgment on the beautiful looks to in the first instance.

—because it still bears this resemblance to the logical judgment, that it may be presupposed to be valid for all men. But this universality cannot spring from concepts. For from concepts there is no transition to the feeling of pleasure or displeasure (save in the case of pure practical laws, which, however, carry an interest with them; and such an interest does not attach to the pure judgment of taste). The result is that the judgment of taste, with its attendant consciousness of detachment from all interest, must involve a claim to validity for all men, and must do so apart from universality attached to Objects, i.e. there must be coupled with it a claim to subjective universality.

THE CONDITION OF THE NECESSITY ADVANCED BY A JUDGMENT OF TASTE IS THE IDEA OF A COMMON SENSE

Were judgments of taste (like cognitive judgments) in possession of a definite objective principle, then one who in his judgment followed such a principle would claim unconditioned necessity for it. Again, were they devoid of any principle, as are those of the mere taste of sense, then no thought of any necessity on their part would enter one's head. Therefore they must have a subjective principle, and one which determines what pleases or displeases, by means of feeling only and not through concepts, but yet with universal validity. Such a principle, however, could only be regarded as a *common sense*. This differs essentially from common understanding, which is also sometimes called common sense (*sensus communis*): for the judgment of the latter is not one by feeling, but always one by concepts, though usually only in the shape of obscurely represented principles.

The judgment of taste, therefore, depends on our presupposing the existence of a common sense. (But this is not to be taken to mean some external sense, but the effect arising from the free play of our powers of cognition. Only under the presupposition, I repeat, of such a common sense, are we able to lay down a judgment of taste.

On Kant's *Critique of Judgment*

THEODORE M. GREENE

There remain to be considered two other aspects of human experience to which men have always attached great importance, the appreciation and creation of beauty and the discovery of scientific truth. Kant seeks in the *Critique of Judgment* to relate these experiences to one another on the ground that each is clearly distinguishable both from our ordinary consciousness of objects and from morality, each involves pleasure as an essential ingredient, and each throws new light upon the interrelation of the phenomenal and noumenal worlds. This attempt to discover what the two experiences have in common is less illuminating, however, than are his highly suggestive interpretations of each experience in turn.

His study of the aesthetic experience starts off as usual with an analysis of its unique characteristics. The judgment of taste is, first, disinterested. This does not mean that a beautiful[1] object is uninteresting—on the contrary, it interests us profoundly—but merely that it awakens in us no desire, moral or sensuous, to do anything with reference to it other than contemplate it and enjoy it. It does not arouse our appetites nor call forth our moral approval or condemnation but merely delights us in being what it is. Secondly, the judgment of taste is at once universal and non-conceptual. It is universal in being not merely an expression of private preference but in laying claim to universal acceptance. To say that an object is beautiful is to suggest that others possessed of taste will agree with this judgment, always provided that the judgment has

---

[1] The use of the word "beauty" should not lead the reader to suppose that Kant is conceiving of the object of the aesthetic experience more narrowly than does the modern student of aesthetics. Such a term as "the aesthetically satisfying" might be employed as a synonym for "the beautiful," as he uses it.

been correctly made. In short, we look upon beauty as though it were objective and possessed of a character of its own, and as though our aesthetic judgments might be true or false. Yet beauty, unlike truth and goodness, is not objective in the sense of being susceptible to analysis and proof. No intellectual criterion of beauty can be found and judgments of taste cannot be tested according to objective standards. We cannot approach a work of art with a clear idea in mind of what constitutes beauty and measure it in terms of this idea, for beauty does not lend itself to such conceptual treatment.

By this characterization of taste, Kant disassociated himself from the explanations of the beautiful, current in his day—the sensationalist, which identified it with the sensuously pleasant, and the rationalist, which regarded it as the object of confused thought. The aesthetic experience is, he insists, unique, however hard it may be accurately to describe it. It is "the feeling of purposiveness without the idea of purpose", the sense of meaning without conceptual definition of what is meant, the awareness of finality or completeness without an intellectual realization of what was aimed at or achieved.

Now this paradoxical nature of taste calls for an explanation. How are we to account for the fact that beauty, though not a quality of the sensuously apprehended object, and though not apprehended conceptually but merely "felt," occasions, none the less, judgments of taste which carry with them the implication that beauty is the same for all, an object of necessary satisfaction to all who are aesthetically sensitive? Kant explains this paradox first in terms of man's faculties of cognition and then, more illuminatingly, in terms of his noumenal nature.

The first solution rests on his earlier analysis of our cognitive activity. In our ordinary awareness of physical objects the faculty of imagination (whereby the temporally successive impressions are presented to consciousness all at once) and the faculty of understanding (whereby the relation of these impressions to one another is apprehended) co-öperate to produce intelligent perception. In the aesthetic experience these same faculties are aroused by the object called beautiful to a more harmonious and complete activity than is occasioned by ordinary objects. The feeling of this greater and unexpected harmony is aesthetic pleasure. And, since all men's cognitive faculties are essentially alike, what gives me aesthetic enjoyment may be expected to do the same for others. The communicability of our delight in beauty is thus explained and the paradox of taste is psychologically resolved.

The metaphysical solution is developed by Kant in answer to the question: How are we to interpret the beauty of nature and the creations of artistic genius? Genius, says Kant, baffles mere scientific explanation. For though the genius employs a definite technique, the value of his work lies not primarily in its technical excellence but in its "spirit"; though nature is his model, he does not copy nature slavishly; and though each work of art which he produces is an expression of his artistic insight, he is himself more often than not unaware of what he meant to say until, in the finished product, it has said itself. Such unique activity can be accounted for only in terms of inspiration. Genius is the vehicle of a supra-individual force whose comings and goings the artist himself can only partially control. Works of art are phenomenal expressions of the noumenal realm of value. Beauty, like goodness, is born in mysterious fashion, and its discovery by genius is not to be explained solely in terms of psychological and physical antecedents. It is created; yet not, like goodness, by an act of will and through the agency of reason, but rather through the spontaneous activity of our noumenal nature. And since all genuine works of art are perfect and complete, they may well be regarded as the most adequate expressions of noumenal value which the phenomenal world affords.

This account of genius at once suggests a more illuminating explanation of the universality and communicability of taste. May it not be the super-sensible or noumenal in each of us which, though in most cases too feeble to produce great art, yet makes possible our apprehension and enjoyment of the beauty which genius has created? Genius, moreover, provides us with the key for natural beauty. For nature is not beautiful to the aesthetically untutored mind; the artist teaches us to find beauty in it and in so doing opens up to us a new and deeply satisfying approach to nature. In the aesthetic experience natural objects are apprehended not as embodiments of universal law, but, on the analogy of art, concretely, each object being regarded as complete and perfect in itself. The understanding still clings, in science, to the mechanical interpretation of nature; our aesthetic sense meanwhile releases us from this conceptual yoke and, calling upon us to view nature from within rather than from without, opens our eyes to a beauty which the scientist cannot see. This new experience does not of itself justify the definite assertion that natural beauty has been created by nature for our special benefit, but it does enable us to envisage nature as the phenomenal embodiment of the selfsame noumenal reality, or "super-sensible substrate," as Kant now calls it, which, in creative genius and aesthetic insight, stirs the human soul.

On Imagism

F. S. FLINT AND EZRA POUND

IMAGISME*

Some curiosity has been aroused concerning *Imagisme,* and as I was unable to find anything definite about it in print, I sought out an *imagiste,* with intent to discover whether the group itself knew anything about the "movement". I gleaned these facts.

The *imagistes* admitted that they were contemporaries of the Post Impressionists and the Futurists; but they had nothing in common with these schools. They had not published a manifesto. They were not a revolutionary school; their only endeavour was to write in accordance with the best tradition, as they found it in the best writers of all time,—in Sappho, Catullus, Villon. They seemed to be absolutely intolerant of all poetry that was not written in such endeavour, ignorance of the best tradition forming no excuse. They had a few rules, drawn up for their own satisfaction only, and they had not published them. They were:

1. Direct treatment of the "thing," whether subjective or objective.

2. To use absolutely no word that did not contribute to the presentation.

3. As regarding rhythm: to compose in sequence of the musical phrase, not in sequence of a metronome.

By these standards they judged all poetry, and found most of it wanting. They held also a certain "Doctrine of the Image," which they had not com-

* Editor's Note—In response to many requests for information regarding *Imagism* and the *Imagistes,* we publish this note by Mr. Flint, supplementing it with further exemplification by Mr. Pound. It will be seen from these that *Imagism* is not necessarily associated with Hellenic subjects, or with *vers libre* as a prescribed form.

mitted to writing; they said that it did not concern the public, and would provoke useless discussion.

The devices whereby they persuaded approaching poetasters to attend their instruction were:

1. They showed him his own thought already splendidly expressed in some classic (and the school musters altogether a most formidable erudition).
2. They re-wrote his verses before his eyes, using about ten words to his fifty.

Even their opponents admit of them—ruefully—"At least they do keep bad poets from writing!"

I found among them an earnestness that is amazing to one accustomed to the usual London air of poetic dilettantism. They consider that Art is all science, all religion, philosophy and metaphysic. It is true that *snobisme* may be urged against them; but it is at least *snobisme* in its most dynamic form, with a great deal of sound sense and energy behind it; and they are stricter with themselves than with any outsider.

F. S. Flint

A FEW DON'TS BY AN IMAGISTE

An "Image" is that which presents an intellectual and emotional complex in an instant of time. I use the term "complex" rather in the technical sense employed by the newer psychologists, such as Hart, though we might not agree absolutely in our application.

It is the presentation of such a "complex" instantaneously which gives that sense of sudden liberation; that sense of freedom from time limits and space limits; that sense of sudden growth, which we experience in the presence of the greatest works of art.

It is better to present one Image in a lifetime than to produce voluminous works.

All this, however, some may consider open to debate. The immediate necessity is to tabulate A LIST OF DON'TS for those beginning to write verses. But I can not put all of them into Mosaic negative.

To begin with, consider the three rules recorded by Mr. Flint, not as dogma —never consider anything as dogma—but as the result of long contemplation, which, even if it is some one else's contemplation, may be worth consideration.

Pay no attention to the criticism of men who have never themselves written a notable work. Consider the discrepancies between the actual writing of the Greek poets and dramatists, and the theories of the Graeco-Roman grammarians, concocted to explain their metres.

LANGUAGE

Use no superfluous word, no adjective, which does not reveal something.

Don't use such an expression as "dim lands *of peace*." It dulls the image.

It mixes an abstraction with the concrete. It comes from the writer's not realizing that the natural object is always the *adequate* symbol.

Go in fear of abstractions. Don't retell in mediocre verse what has already been done in good prose. Don't think any intelligent person is going to be deceived when you try to shirk all the difficulties of the unspeakably difficult art of good prose by chopping your composition into line lengths.

What the expert is tired of today the public will be tired of tomorrow.

Don't imagine that the art of poetry is any simpler than the art of music, or that you can please the expert before you have spent at least as much effort on the art of verse as the average piano teacher spends on the art of music.

Be influenced by as many great artists as you can, but have the decency either to acknowledge the debt outright, or to try to conceal it.

Don't allow "influence" to mean merely that you mop up the particular decorative vocabulary of some one or two poets whom you happen to admire. A Turkish war correspondent was recently caught red-handed babbling in his dispatches of "dove-gray" hills, or else it was "pearl-pale," I can not remember.

Use either no ornament or good ornament.

RHYTHM AND RHYME

Let the candidate fill his mind with the finest cadences he can discover, preferably in a foreign language so that the meaning of the words may be less likely to divert his attention from the movement; e.g., Saxon charms, Hebridean Folk Songs, the verse of Dante, and the lyrics of Shakespeare—if he can dissociate the vocabulary from the cadence. Let him dissect the lyrics of Goethe coldly into their component sound values, syllables long and short, stressed and unstressed, into vowels and consonants.

It is not necessary that a poem should rely on its music, but if it does rely on its music that music must be such as will delight the expert.

Let the neophyte know assonance and alliteration, rhyme immediate and delayed, simple and polyphonic, as a musician would expect to know harmony and counterpoint and all the minutiae of his craft. No time is too great to give to these matters or to any one of them, even if the artist seldom have need of them.

Don't imagine that a thing will "go" in verse just because it's too dull to go in prose.

Don't be "viewy"—leave that to the writers of pretty little philosophic essays. Don't be descriptive; remember that the painter can describe a landscape much better than you can, and that he has to know a deal more about it.

When Shakespeare talks of the "Dawn in russet mantle clad" he presents something which the painter does not present. There is in this line of his nothing that one can call description; he presents.

Consider the way of the scientists rather than the way of an advertising agent for a new soap.

The scientist does not expect to be acclaimed as a great scientist until he has *discovered* something. He begins by learning what has been discovered already. He goes from that point onward. He does not bank on being a charming fellow personally. He does not expect his friends to applaud the results of his freshman class work. Freshmen in poetry are unfortunately not confined to a definite and recognizable class room. They are "all over the shop." Is it any wonder "the public is indifferent to poetry?"

Don't chop your stuff into separate *iambs*. Don't make each line stop dead at the end, and then begin every next line with a heave. Let the beginning of the next line catch the rise of the rhythm wave, unless you want a definite longish pause.

In short, behave as a musician, a good musician, when dealing with that phase of your art which has exact parallels in music. The same laws govern, and you are bound by no others.

Naturally, your rhythmic structure should not destroy the shape of your words, or their natural sound, or their meaning. It is improbable that, at the start, you will be able to get a rhythm-structure strong enough to affect them very much, though you may fall a victim to all sorts of false stopping due to line ends and caesurae.

The musician can rely on pitch and the volume of the orchestra. You can not. The term harmony is misapplied to poetry; it refers to simultaneous sounds of different pitch. There is, however, in the best verse a sort of residue of sound which remains in the ear of the hearer and acts more or less as an organ-base. A rhyme must have in it some slight element of surprise if it is to give pleasure; it need not be bizarre or curious, but it must be well used if used at all.

Vide further Vildrac and Duhamel's notes on rhyme in "*Technique Poetique.*"

That part of your poetry which strikes upon the imaginative *eye* of the reader will lose nothing by translation into a foreign tongue; that which appeals to the ear can reach only those who take it in the original.

Consider the definiteness of Dante's presentation, as compared with Milton's rhetoric. Read as much of Wordsworth as does not seem too unutterably dull.

If you want the gist of the matter go to Sappho, Catullus, Villon, Heine when he is in the vein, Gautier when he is not too frigid; or, if you have not the tongues, seek out the leisurely Chaucer. Good prose will do you no harm, and there is good discipline to be had by trying to write it.

Translation is likewise good training, if you find that your original matter "wobbles" when you try to rewrite it. The meaning of the poem to be translated can not "wobble."

If you are using a symmetrical form, don't put in what you want to say and then fill up the remaining vacuums with slush.

Don't mess up the perception of one sense by trying to define it in terms of another. This is usually only the result of being too lazy to find the exact word. To this clause there are possibly exceptions.

The first three simple proscriptions* will throw out nine-tenths of all the

*Noted by Mr. Flint.

bad poetry now accepted as standard and classic; and will prevent you from many a crime of production.

". . . *Mais d'abord il faut etre un poete,*" as MM. Duhamel and Vildrac have said at the end of their little book, "*Notes sur la Technique Poetique*"; but in an American one takes that at least for granted, otherwise why does one get born upon that august continent!

Ezra Pound

Pseudo-Statements

I. A. RICHARDS

The business of the poet, as we have seen, is to give order and coherence, and so freedom, to a body of experience. To do so through words which act as its skeleton, as a structure by which the impulses which make up the experience are adjusted to one another and act together. The means by which words do this are many and varied. To work them out is a problem for linguistic psychology, that embarrassed young heir to philosophy. What little can be done shows already that most critical dogmas of the past are either false or nonsense. A little knowledge is not here a danger, but clears the air in a remarkable way.

Roughly and inadequately, even in the light of present knowledge, we can say that words work in the poem in two main fashions. As sensory stimuli and as (in the *widest* sense) symbols. We must refrain from considering the sensory side of the poem, remarking only that it is *not* in the least independent of the other side, and that it has for definite reasons prior importance in most poetry. We must confine ourselves to the other function of words in the poem, or rather, omitting much that is of secondary relevance, to one form of that function, let me call it *pseudo-statement*.

It will be admitted—by those who distinguish between scientific statement, where truth is ultimately a matter of verification as this is understood in the laboratory, and emotive utterance, where "truth" is primarily acceptability *by* some attitude, and more remotely is the acceptability of this attitude itself— that it is *not* the poet's business to make scientific statements. Yet poetry has constantly the air of making statements, and important ones; which is one reason why some mathematicians cannot read it. They find the alleged statements to be *false*. It will be agreed that their approach to poetry and their expectations from it are mistaken. But what exactly is the other, the right, the poetic, approach and how does it differ from the mathematical?

The poetic approach evidently limits the framework of possible consequences into which the pseudo-statement is taken. For the scientific approach this framework is unlimited. Any and every consequence is relevant. If any of the consequences of a statement conflicts with acknowledged fact then so much the worse for the statement. Not so with the pseudo-statement when poetically approached. The problem is—just how does the limitation work? One tempting account is in terms of a supposed universe of discourse, a world of make-believe, of imagination, of recognized fictions common to the poet and his readers. A pseudo-statement which fits into this system of assumptions would be regarded as "poetically true"; one which does not, as "poetically false." This attempt to treat "poetic truth" on the model of general "coherence theories" is very natural for certain schools of logicians but is inadequate, on the wrong lines from the outset. To mention two objections, out of many; there is no means of discovering what the "universe of discourse" is on any occasion, and the kind of coherence which must hold within it, supposing it to be discoverable, is not an affair of logical relations. Attempt to define the system of propositions into which

O Rose, thou art sick!

must fit, and the logical relations which must hold between them if it is to be "poetically true"; the absurdity of the theory becomes evident.

We must look further. In the poetic approach the relevant consequences are not logical or to be arrived at by a partial relaxation of logic. Except occasionally and by accident logic does not enter at all. They are the consequences which arise through our emotional organization. The acceptance which a pseudo-statement receives is entirely governed by its effects upon our feelings and attitudes. Logic only comes in, if at all, in subordination, as a servant to our emotional response. It is an unruly servant, however, as poets and readers are constantly discovering. A pseudo-statement is "true" if it suits and serves some attitude or links together attitudes which on other grounds are desirable. This kind of "truth" is so opposed to scientific "truth" that it is a pity to use so similar a word, but at the present it is difficult to avoid the malpractice.[1]

This brief analysis may be sufficient to indicate the fundamental disparity and opposition between pseudo-statements as they occur in poetry and statements as they occur in science. A pseudo-statement is a form of words which is justified entirely by its effect in releasing or organizing our impulses and attitudes (due regard being had for the better or worse organizations of these *inter se*); a statement, on the other hand, is justified by its truth, *i.e.*, its correspondence, in a highly technical sense, with the fact to which it points.

---

[1] A pseudo-statement, as I use the term, is not necessarily false in any sense. It is merely a form of words whose scientific truth or falsity is irrelevant to the purpose at hand.

"Logic" in this paragraph is, of course, being used in a limited and conventional, or popular sense.

Statements true and false alike do, of course, constantly touch off attitudes and action. Our daily practical existence is largely guided by them. On the whole true statements are of more service to us than false ones. None the less we do not and, at present, cannot order our emotions and attitudes by true statements alone. Nor is there any probability that we ever shall contrive to do so. This is one of the great new dangers to which civilization is exposed. Countless pseudo-statements—about God, about the universe, about human nature, the relations of mind to mind, about the soul, its rank and destiny— pseudo-statements which are pivotal points in the organization of the mind, vital to its well-being, have suddenly become, for sincere, honest and informal minds, impossible to believe as for centuries they have been believed.[2] The accustomed incidences of the modes of believing are changed irrecoverably; and the knowledge which has displaced them is not of a kind upon which an equally fine organization of the mind can be based.

This is the contemporary situation. The remedy, since there is no prospect of our gaining adequate knowledge, and since indeed it is fairly clear that genuine knowledge cannot meet this need, is to cut our pseudo-statements free from that kind of belief which is appropriate to verified statements. So released they will be changed, of course, but they can still be the main instruments by which we order our attitudes to one another and to the world. This is not a desperate remedy, for, as poetry conclusively shows, even the most important among our attitudes can be aroused and maintained without any believing of a factual or verifiable order entering in at all. We need no such beliefs, and indeed we must have none. If we are to read *King Lear*. Pseudo-statements to which we attach no belief and statements proper, such as science provides, cannot conflict. It is only when we introduce inappropriate kinds of believing into poetry that danger arises. To do so is from this point of view a profanation of poetry.

Yet an important branch of criticism which has attracted the best talents from prehistoric times until today consists of the endeavour to persuade men that the functions of science and poetry are identical, or that the one is a "higher form" of the other, or that they conflict and we must choose between them.

The root of this persistent endeavour has still to be mentioned; it is the same as that from which the Magical View of the world arose. If we give to a pseudo-statement the kind of unqualified acceptance which belongs by right only to certified scientific statements—and those judgments of the routine of perception and action from which science derives—, if we can contrive to do this, the impulses and attitudes with which we respond to it gain a notable stability and vigour. Briefly, if we can contrive to believe poetry, then the world *seems*,

---

[2] For the mind I am considering here, the question "Do I believe *x*?" is no longer the same. Not only the "What" that is to be believed but the "How" of the believing has changed— through the segregation of science and its clarification of the techniques of proof. This is the danger; and the remedy suggested is a further differentiation of the "Hows." To these differences correspond differences in the sense of "is so" and "being" where, as is commonly the case, "is so" and "being" assert believings. As we admit this, the world that "is" divides into worlds commensurable in respect of so-called "degrees of reality." Yet, and this is all-important, these worlds have an order, with regard to one another, which is the order of the mind; and inter- ference between them imperils sanity.

while we do so, to be transfigured. It used to be comparatively easy to do this, and the habit has become well established. With the extension of science and the neutralization of nature it has become difficult as well as dangerous. Yet it is still alluring; it has many analogies with drug-taking. Hence the endeavours of the critics referred to. Various subterfuges have been devised along the lines of regarding Poetic Truth as figurative, symbolic; or as more immediate, as a truth of Intuition transcending human knowledge; or as a higher form of the same truth as reason yields. Such attempts to use poetry as a denial or as a corrective of science are very common. One point can be made against them all: they are never worked out in detail. There is no equivalent of Mill's *Logic* expounding any of them. The language in which they are framed is usually a blend of obsolete psychology and emotive exclamations.

The long-established and much-encouraged habit of giving to emotive utterances—whether pseudo-statements simple, or looser and larger wholes taken as saying something figuratively—the kind of assent which we give to unescapable facts, has for most people debilitated a wide range of their responses. A few scientists, caught young and brought up in the laboratory, are free from it; but then, as a rule, they pay no *serious* attention to poetry. For most men the recognition of the neutrality of nature brings about—through this habit—a divorce from poetry. They are so used to having their responses propped up by beliefs, however vague, that when those shadowy supports are removed they are no longer able to respond. Their attitudes to so many things have been forced in the past, over-encouraged. And when the world-picture ceases to assist there is a collapse. Over whole tracts of natural emotional response we are today like a bed of dahlias whose sticks have been removed. And this effect of the neutralization of nature is only in its beginnings. However, human nature has a prodigious resilence. Love poetry seems able to out-play psycho-analysis.

A sense of desolation, of uncertainty, of futility, of the groundlessness of aspirations, of the vanity of endeavour, and a thirst for a life-giving water which seems suddenly to have failed, are the signs in consciousness of this necessary reorganization of our lives.[3] Our attitudes and impulses are being compelled to become self-supporting; they are being driven back upon their biological justification, made once again sufficient to themselves. And the only impulses which seem strong enough to continue unflagging are commonly so crude that,

---

[3] My debt to *The Waste Land* here will be evident. The original footnote seems to have puzzled Mr. Eliot and some other readers. Well it might! In saying, though, that he "had effected a complete severance between his poetry and all beliefs" I was referring not to the poet's own history, but to the technical detachment of the poetry. And the way in which he then seemed to me to have "realized what might otherwise have remained a speculative possibility" was by finding a new order through the contemplation and exhibition of disorder.

"Yes! Very funny this terrible thing is. A man that is born falls into a dream like a man falls into the sea. If he tries to climb out into the air as inexperienced people endeavour to do, he drowns—*nicht wahr?* . . . No! I tell you! The way is to the destructive element submit yourself, and with the exertions of your hands and feet in the water make the deep, deep, sea keep you up. So if you ask me how to be? In the destructive element immerse . . . that was the way." *Lord Jim*, p. 216. Mr. Eliot's later verse has sometimes shown still less "dread of the unknown depths." That, at least, seems in part to explain to me why *Ash Wednesday* is better poetry than even the best sections of *The Waste Land*.

to more finely developed individuals, they hardly seem worth having. Such people cannot live by warmth, food, fighting, drink, and sex alone. Those who are least affected by the change are those who are emotionally least removed from the animals. As we shall see at the close of this essay, even a considerable poet may attempt to find relief by a reversion to primitive mentality.

It is important to diagnose the disease correctly and to put the blame in the right quarter. Usually it is some alleged "materialism" of science which is denounced. This mistake is due partly to clumsy thinking, but chiefly to relics of the Magical View. For even if the Universe were "spiritual" all through (whatever that assertion might mean; all such assertions are probably nonsense), that would not make it any more accordant to human attitudes. It is not what the universe is made of but how it works, the law it follows, which makes knowledge of it incapable of spurring on our emotional responses, and further, the nature of knowledge itself makes it inadequate. The contact with things which we therein establish is too sketchy and indirect to help us. We are beginning to know too much about the bond which unites the mind to its object in knowledge[4] for that old dream of a perfect knowledge which would guarantee perfect life to retain its sanction. What was thought to be pure knowledge, we see now to have been shot through with hope and desire, with fear and wonder; and these intrusive elements indeed gave it all its power to support our lives. In knowledge, in the "How?" of events, we can find hints by which to take advantage of circumstances in our favour and avoid mischances. But we cannot get from it a *raison d'être* or a justification of more than a relatively lowly kind of life.

The justification, or the reverse, of any attitude lies, not in the object, but in itself, in its serviceableness to the whole personality. Upon its place in the whole system of attitudes, which is the personality, all its worth depends. This is true equally for the subtle, finely compounded attitudes of the civilized individual as for the simpler attitudes of the child.

In brief, the imaginative life is its own justification; and this fact must be faced, although sometimes—by a lover, for example—it may be very difficult to accept. When it is faced, it is apparent that all the attitudes to other human beings and to the world in all its aspects, which have been serviceable to humanity, remain as they were, as valuable as ever. Hesitation felt in admitting this is a measure of the strength of the evil habit I have been describing. But many of these attitudes, valuable as ever, are, now that they are being set free, more difficult to maintain, because we still hunger after a basis in belief.

APPENDIX

Two chief words seem likely occasions of misunderstanding in the above: and they have in fact misled some readers. One is *Nature*, the other is *Belief*.

---

[4] Verifiable scientific knowledge, of course. Shift the sense of "knowledge" to include hope and desire and fear as well as reference, and what I am saying would no longer be true. But the relevant sense of "true" would have changed too. Its sanction would no longer be verifiability.

Nature is evidently as variable a word as can be used. Its senses range from the mere inconclusive THAT, in which we live and of which we are a part, to whatever would correspond to the most detailed and interconnected account we could attain of this. Or we omit ourselves (and other minds) and make Nature *either* what influences us (in which case we should not forget our metabolism), *or* an object we apprehend (in which case there are as many Natures as there are types of apprehension we care to distinguish). And what is "natural" to one culture is strange and artificial to another. (See *Mencius on the Mind,* chap. III.) More deceptively, the view here being inseparable from the eye, and this being a matter of habitual speculation, we may talk, as we think, the same language, and yet put very different things into Nature, and what we then find will not be unconnected with what we have put in.

I have attempted some further discussion of these questions in Chapters VI and VII of *Coleridge on Imagination.*

Belief. Two "beliefs" may differ from one another: (1) In their objects (2) In their statements or expressions (3) In their modes (4) In their grounds (5) In their occasions (6) In their connections with other "beliefs" (7) In their links with possible action (8) And in other ways. Our chief evidence usually for the beliefs of other people (and often for our own) must be some statement or other expression. But very different beliefs may fittingly receive the same expression. Most words used in stating any speculative opinion are as ambiguous as "Belief"; and yet by such words belief-objects must be distinguished.

But in the case of "belief" there is an additional difficulty. Neither it nor its partial synonyms suggest the great variety of attitudes (3) that are commonly covered (and confused) by the term. They are often treated as though they were mere variations in degree. Of what? Of belief, it would be said. But this is no better than the parallel trick of treating varieties of love as a mere more or less only further differentiated by their objects. Such crude over-simplifications distort the structure of the mind, and, although favourite suasive devices with some well-intentioned teachers, are disastrous.

There is an ample field here awaiting a type of dispassionate inquiry which it has seldom received. A world threatened with ever more and more leisure should not be too impatient of important and explorable subtleties.

Meanwhile, as with "Nature," misunderstandings should neither provoke nor surprise. I should not be much less at my reader's mercy if I were to add notes doubling the length of this little book. On so vast a matter, even the largest book could contain no more than a sketch of how things have seemed to be sometimes to the writer.

Tradition and the Individual Talent

T. S. ELIOT

In English writing we seldom speak of tradition, though we occasionally apply its name in deploring its absence. We cannot refer to "the tradition" or to "a tradition"; at most, we employ the adjective in saying that the poetry of So-and-so is "traditional" or even "too traditional." Seldom, perhaps, does the word appear except in a phrase of censure. If otherwise, it is vaguely approbative, with the implication, as to the work approved, of some pleasing archaeological reconstruction. You can hardly make the word agreeable to English ears without this comfortable reference to the reassuring science of archaeology.

Certainly the word is not likely to appear in our appreciations of living or dead writers. Every nation, every race, has not only its own creative, but its own critical turn of mind; and is even more oblivious of the shortcomings and limitations of its critical habits than of those of its creative genius. We know, or think we know, from the enormous mass of critical writing that has appeared in the French language the critical method or habit of the French; we only conclude (we are such unconscious people) that the French are "more critical' than we, and sometimes even plume ourselves a little with the fact, as if the French were the less spontaneous. Perhaps they are; but we might remind ourselves that criticism is as inevitable as breathing, and that we should be none the worse for articulating what passes in our minds when we read a book and feel an emotion about it, for criticizing our own minds in their work of criticism. One of the facts that might come to light in this process is our tendency to insist, when we praise a poet, upon those aspects of his work in which he least resembles any one else. In these aspects or parts of his work we pretend to find what is individual, what is the peculiar essence of the man. We dwell with satisfaction upon the poet's difference from his predecessors, especially his immediate predecessors; we endeavour to find something that can be isolated in order to be enjoyed. Whereas if we approach a poet without this prejudice we shall often find that not only the best, but the most individual parts of his work may be those in which the dead poets, his ancestors, assert their immortality most vigorously. And I do not mean the impressionable period of adolescence, but the period of full maturity.

Yet if the only form of tradition, of handing down, consisted in following the ways of the immediate generation before us in a blind or timid adherence to its successes, "tradition" should positively be discouraged. We have seen many such simple currents soon lost in the sand; and novelty is better than repetition. Tradition is a matter of much wider significance. It cannot be inherited, and if you want it you must obtain it by great labour. It involves, in the first place, the historical sense, which we may call nearly indispensable to any one who would continue to be a poet beyond his twenty-fifth year; and the historical sense involves a perception, not only of the pastness of the past, but of its presence; the historical sense compels a man to write not merely with his own generation in his bones, but with a feeling that the whole of the literature of Europe from Homer and within it the whole of the literature of his own country has a simultaneous existence and composes a simultaneous order. This historical sense, which is a sense of the timeless as well as of the temporal and of the timeless and of the temporal together, is what makes a writer traditional. And it is at the same time what makes a writer most acutely conscious of his place in time, of his own contemporaneity.

No poet, no artist of any art, has his complete meaning alone. His significance, his appreciation is the appreciation of his relation to the dead poets and artists. You cannot value him alone; you must set him, for contrast and comparison, among the dead. I mean this as a principle of aesthetic, not merely historical, criticism. The necessity that he shall conform, that he shall cohere, is not onesided; what happens when a new work of art is created is something that happens simultaneously to all the works of art which preceded it. The existing monuments form an ideal order among themselves, which is modified by the introduction of the new (the really new) work of art among them. The existing order is complete before the new work arrives; for order to persist after the supervention of novelty, the *whole* existing order must be, if ever so slightly, altered; and so the relations, proportions, values of each work of art toward the whole are readjusted; and this is conformity between the old and the new. Whoever has approved this idea of order, of the form of European, of English literature will not find it preposterous that the past should be altered by the present as much as the present is directed by the past. And the poet who is aware of this will be aware of great difficulties and responsibilities.

In a peculiar sense he will be aware also that he must inevitably be judged by the standards of the past. I say judged, not amputated, by them; not judged to be as good as, or worse or better than, the dead; and certainly not judged by the canons of dead critics. It is a judgment, a comparison, in which two things are measured by each other. To conform merely would be for the new work not really to conform at all; it would not be new, and would therefore not be a work of art. And we do not quite say that the new is more valuable because it fits in; but its fitting in is a test of its value—a test, it is true, which can only be slowly and cautiously applied, for we are none of us infallible judges of conformity. We say: it appears to conform, and is perhaps individual, or it appears individual, and many conform; but we are hardly likely to find that it is one and not the other.

To proceed to a more intelligible exposition of the relation of the poet to the past: he can neither take the past as a lump, an indiscriminate bolus, nor can he form himself wholly on one or two private admirations, nor can he form himself wholly upon one preferred period. The first course is inadmissible, the second is an important experience of youth, and the third is a pleasant and highly desirable supplement. The poet must be very conscious of the main current, which does not at all flow invariably through the most distinguished reputations. He must be quite aware of the obvious fact that art never improves, but that the material of art is never quite the same. He must be aware that the mind of Europe—the mind of his own country—a mind which he learns in time to be much more important than his own private mind—is a mind which changes, and that this change is a development which abandons nothing *en route*, which does not superannuate either Shakespeare, or Homer, or the rock drawing of the Magdalenian draughtsmen. That this development, refinement perhaps, complication certainly, is not, from the point of view of the artist, any improvement. Perhaps not even an improvement from the point of view of the psychologist or not to the extent which we imagine; perhaps only in the end based upon a complication in economics and machinery. But the difference between the present and the past is that the conscious present is an awareness of the past in a way and to an extent which the past's awareness of itself cannot show.

Some one said: "The dead writers are remote from us because we *know* so much more than they did." Precisely, and they are that which we know.

I am alive to a usual objection to what is clearly part of my programme for the *métier* of poetry. The objection is that the doctrine requires a ridiculous amount of erudition (pedantry), a claim which can be rejected by appeal to the lives of poets in any pantheon. It will even be affirmed that much learning deadens or perverts poetic sensibility. While, however, we persist in believing that a poet ought to know as much as will not encroach upon his necessary receptivity and necessary laziness, it is not desirable to confine knowledge to whatever can be put into a useful shape for examinations, drawing-rooms, or the still more pretentious modes of publicity. Some can absorb knowledge, the more tardy must sweat for it. Shakespeare acquired more essential history from Plutarch than most men could from the whole British Museum. What is to be insisted upon is that the poet must develop or procure the consciousness of the past and that he should continue to develop this consciousness throughout his career.

What happens is a continual surrender of himself as he is at the moment to something which is more valuable. The progress of an artist is a continual self-sacrifice, a continual extinction of personality.

There remains to define this process of depersonalization and its relation to the sense of tradition. It is this depersonalization that art may be said to approach the condition of science. I, therefore, invite you to consider, as a suggestive analogy, the action which takes place when a bit of finely filiated platinum is introduced into a chamber containing oxygen and sulphur dioxide.

II

Honest criticism and sensitive appreciation are directed not upon the poet but upon the poetry. If we attend to the confused cries of the newspaper critics and the *susurrus* of popular repetition that follows, we shall hear the names of poets in great numbers; if we seek not Blue-book knowledge but the enjoyment of poetry, and ask for a poem, we shall seldom find it. I have tried to point out the importance of the relation of the poem to other poems by other authors, and suggested the conception of poetry as a living whole of all the poetry that has ever been written. The other aspect of this Impersonal theory of poetry is the relation of the poem to its author. And I hinted, by an analogy, that the mind of the mature poet differs from that of the immature one not precisely in any valuation of "personality," not being necessarily more interesting, or having "more to say," but rather by being a more finely perfected medium in which special, or very varied, feelings are at liberty to enter into new combinations.

The analogy was that of the catalyst. When the two gases previously mentioned are mixed in the presence of a filament of platinum, they form sulphurous acid. This combination takes place only if the platinum is present; nevertheless the newly formed acid contains no trace of platinum, and the platinum itself is apparently unaffected; has remained inert, neutral, and unchanged. The mind of the poet is the shred of platinum. It may partly or exclusively operate upon the experience of the man himself; but, the more perfect the artist, the more completely separate in him will be the man who suffers and the mind which creates; the more perfectly will the mind digest and transmute the passions which are its material.

The experience, you will notice, the elements which enter the presence of the transforming catalyst, are of two kinds: emotions and feelings. The effect of a work of art upon the person who enjoys it is an experience different in kind from any experience not of art. It may be formed out of one emotion, or may be a combination of several; and various feelings, inhering for the writer in particular words or phrases or images, may be added to compose the final result. Or great poetry may be made without the direct use of any emotion whatever: composed out of feelings solely. Canto XV of the *Inferno* (Brunetto Latini) is a working up of the emotion evident in the situation; but the effect, though single as that of any work of art, is obtained by considerable complexity of detail. The last quatrain gives an image, a feeling attaching to an image, which "came," which did not develop simply out of what precedes, but which was probably in suspension in the poet's mind until the proper combination arrived for it to add itself to. The poet's mind is in fact a receptacle for seizing and storing up numberless feelings, phrases, images, which remain there until all the particles which can unite to form a new compound are present together.

If you compare several representative passages of the greatest poetry you see how great is the variety of types of combination, and also how completely any semi-ethical criterion of "sublimity" misses the mark. For it is not the "greatness," the intensity, of the emotions, the components, but the intensity of the artistic process, the pressure, so to speak, under which the fusion takes place, that counts. The episode of Paolo and Francesca employs a definite emotion, but the intensity of the poetry is something quite different from whatever intensity in the supposed experience it may give the impression of. It is no more intense, furthermore, than Canto XXVI, the voyage of Ulysses, which has not the direct dependence upon an emotion. Great variety is possible in the process of transmutation of emotion: the murder of Agamemnon, or the agony of Othello, gives an artistic effect apparently closer to a possible original than the scenes from Dante. In the *Agamemnon,* the artistic emotion approximates to the emotion of an actual spectator; in *Othello* to the emotion of the protagonist himself. But the difference between art and the event is always absolute; the combination which is the murder of Agamemnon is probably as complex as that which is the voyage of Ulysses. In either case there has been a fusion of elements. The ode of Keats contains a number of feelings which have nothing particular to do with the nightingale, but which the nightingale, partly, perhaps, because of its attractive name, and partly because of its reputation, served to bring together.

The point of view which I am struggling to attack is perhaps related to the metaphysical theory of the substantial unity of the soul: for my meaning is, that the poet has, not a "personality" to express, but a particular medium, which is only a medium and not a personality, in which impressions and experiences combine in peculiar and unexpected ways. Impressions and experiences which are important for the man may take no place in the poetry, and those which become important in the poetry may play quite a negligible part in the man, the personality.

I will quote a passage which is unfamiliar enough to be regarded with fresh attention in the light—or darkness—of these observations:

> *And now methinks I could e'en chide myself*
> *For doating on her beauty, though her death*
> *Shall be revenged after no common action.*
> *Does the silkworm expend her yellow labours*
> *For thee? For thee does she undo herself?*
> *Are lordships sold to maintain ladyships*
> *For the poor benefit of a bewildering minute?*
> *Why does yon fellow falsify highways,*
> *And put his life between the judge's lips,*
> *To refine such a thing—keeps horse and men*
> *To beat their valours for her? . . .*

In this passage (as is evident if it is taken in its context) there is a combination of positive and negative emotions: an intensely strong attraction toward beauty and an equally intense fascination by the ugliness which is contrasted with it and which destroys it. This balance of contrasted emotion is in the dramatic situation to which the speech is pertinent, but that situation alone is inadequate to it. This is, so to speak, the structural emotion, provided by the drama. But the whole effect, the dominant tone, is due to the fact that a number of floating feelings, having an affinity to this emotion by no means superficially evident, have combined with it to give us a new art emotion.

It is not in his personal emotions, the emotions provoked by particular events in his life, that the poet is in any way remarkable or interesting. His particular emotions may be simple, or crude, or flat. The emotion in his poetry will be a very complex thing, but not with the complexity of the emotions of people who have very complex or unusual emotions in life. One error, in fact, of eccentricity in poetry is to seek for new human emotions to express; and in this search for novelty in the wrong place it discovers the perverse. The business of the poet is not to find new emotions, but to use the ordinary ones and, in working them up into poetry, to express feelings which are not in actual emotions at all. And emotions which he has never experienced will serve his turn as well as those familiar to him. Consequently, we must believe that "emotion recollected in tranquillity" is an inexact formula. For it is neither emotion, nor recollection, nor, without distortion of meaning, tranquillity. It is a concentration, and a new thing resulting from the concentration, of a very great number of experiences which to the practical and active person would not seem to be experiences at all; it is a concentration which does not happen consciously or of deliberation. These experiences are not "recollected," and they finally unite in an atmosphere which is "tranquil" only in that it is a passive attending upon the event. Of course this is not quite the whole story. There is a great deal, in the writing of poetry, which must be conscious and deliberate. In fact, the bad poet is usually unconscious where he ought to be conscious, and conscious where he ought to be unconscious. Both errors tend to make him "personal." Poetry is not a turning loose of emotion, but an escape from emotion; it is not the expression of personality, but an escape from personality. But, of course, only those who have personality and emotions know what it means to want to escape from these things.

III

ὁ δὲ νοῦς ἴσως θειότερόν τι χαί ἀπαθές ἐστιν

This essay proposes to halt at the frontier of metaphysics or mysticism, and confine itself to such practical conclusions as can be applied by the responsible person interested in poetry. To divert interest from the poet to the poetry is a laudable aim: for it would conduce to a juster estimation of actual poetry, good and bad. There are many people who appreciate the expression of sincere emotion in verse, and there is a smaller number of people who can appreciate technical excellence. But very few know when there is an expression of *significant* emotion, emotion which has its life in the poem and not in the history of the poet. The emotion of art is impersonal. And the poet cannot reach this impersonality without surrendering himself wholly to the work to be done. And he is not likely to know what is to be done unless he lives in what is not merely the present, but the present moment of the past, unless he is conscious, not of what is dead, but of what is already living.

The Metaphysical Poets

T. S. ELIOT

By collecting these poems[1] from the work of a generation more often named than read, and more often read than profitably studied, Professor Grierson has rendered a service of some importance. Certainly the reader will meet with many poems already preserved in other anthologies, at the same time that he discovers poems such as those of Aurelian Townshend or Lord Herbert of Cherbury here included. But the function of such an anthology as this is neither that of Professor Saintsbury's admirable edition of Caroline poets nor that of the *Oxford Book of English Verse*. Mr. Grierson's book is in itself a piece of criticism and a provocation of criticism; and we think that he was right in including so many poems of Donne, elsewhere (though not in many editions) accessible, as documents in the case of "metaphysical poetry." The phrase has long done duty as a term of abuse or as the label of a quaint and pleasant taste. The question is to what extent the so-called metaphysicals formed a school (in our own time we should say a "movement"), and how far this so-called school or movement is a digression from the main current.

Not only is it extremely difficult to define metaphysical poetry, but difficult to decide what poets practise it and in which of their verses. The poetry of Donne (to whom Marvell and Bishop King are sometimes nearer than any of the other authors) is late Elizabethan, its feeling often very close to that of Chapman. The "courtly" poetry is derivative from Jonson, who borrowed liberally from the Latin; it expires in the next century with the sentiment and witticism of Prior. There is finally the devotional verse of Herbert, Vaughan,

---

[1] *Metaphysical Lyrics and Poems of the Seventeenth Century:* Donne to Butler. Selected and edited, with an Essay, by Herbert J. C. Grierson (Oxford: Clarendon Press. London: Milford).

and Crashaw (echoed long after by Christina Rossetti and Francis Thompson); Crashaw, sometimes more profound and less sectarian than the others, has a quality which returns through the Elizabethan period to the early Italians. It is difficult to find any precise use of metaphor, simile, or other conceit, which is common to all the poets and at the same time important enough as an element of style to isolate these poets as a group. Donne, and often Cowley, employ a device which is sometimes considered characteristically "metaphysical"; the elaboration (contrasted with the condensation) of a figure of speech to the farthest stage to which ingenuity can carry it. Thus Cowley develops the commonplace comparison of the world to a chess-board through long stanzas (*To Destiny*), and Donne, with more grace, in *A Valediction*, the comparison of two lovers to a pair of compasses. But elsewhere we find, instead of the mere explication of the content of a comparison, a development by rapid association of thought which requires considerable agility on the part of the reader.

> *On a round ball*
> *A workman that hath copies by, can lay*
> *An Europe, Afrique, and an Asia,*
> *And quickly make that, which was nothing, All,*
> > *So doth each teare,*
> > *Which thee doth weare,*
> *A globe, yea, world by that impression grow,*
> *Till thy tears mixt with mine doe overflow*
> *This world, by waters sent from thee, my heaven dissolved so.*

Here we find at least two connexions which are not implicit in the first figure, but are forced upon it by the poet: from the geographer's globe to the tear, and the tear to the deluge. On the other hand, some of Donne's most successful and characteristic effects are secured by brief words and sudden contrasts:

> *A bracelet of bright hair about the bone,*

where the most powerful effect is produced by the sudden contrast of associations of "bright hair" and of "bone." This telescoping of images and multiplied associations is characteristic of the phrase of some of the dramatists of the period which Donne knew: not to mention Shakespeare, it is frequent in Middleton, Webster, and Tourneur, and is one of the sources of the vitality of their language.

Johnson, who employed the term "metaphysical poets," apparently having Donne, Cleveland, and Cowley chiefly in mind, remarks of them that "the most heterogeneous ideas are yoked by violence together." The force of this impeachment lies in the failure of the conjunction, the fact that often the ideas are yoked but not united; and if we are to judge of styles of poetry by their abuse, enough examples may be found in Cleveland to justify Johnson's condemnation. But a degree of heterogeneity of material compelled into unity by the operation of the poet's mind is omnipresent in poetry. We need not select for illustration such a line as:

> *Notre âme est un trois-mâts cherchant son Icarie;*

we may find it in some of the best lines of Johnson himself (*The Vanity of Human Wishes*):

> *His fate was destined to a barren strand,*
> *A petty fortress, and a dubious hand;*
> *He left a name at which the world grew pale,*
> *To point a moral, or adorn a tale.*

where the effect is due to a contrast of ideas, different in degree but the same in principle, as that which Johnson mildly reprehended. And in one of the finest poems of the age (a poem which could not have been written in any other age), the *Exequy* of Bishop King, the extended comparison is used with perfect success: the idea and the simile become one, in the passage in which the Bishop illustrates his impatience to see his dead wife, under the figure of a journey:

> *Stay for me there; I will not faile*
> *To meet thee in that hollow Vale.*
> *And think not much of my delay;*
> *I am already on the way,*
> *And follow thee with all the speed*
> *Desire can make, or sorrows breed.*
> *Each minute is a short degree,*
> *And ev'ry houre a step towards thee.*
> *At night when I betake to rest,*
> *Next morn I rise nearer my West*
> *Of life, almost by eight houres sail,*
> *Than when sleep breath'd his drowsy gale . . .*
> *But heark! My Pulse, like a soft Drum*
> *Beats my approach, tells* Thee *I come;*
> *And slow howere my marches be,*
> *I shall at last sit down by Thee.*

(In the last few lines there is that effect of terror which is several times attained by one of Bishop King's admirers, Edgar Poe.) Again, we may justly take these quatrains from Lord Herbert's Ode, stanzas which would, we think, be immediately pronounced to be of the metaphysical school:

> *So when from hence we shall be gone,*
> *And be no more, nor you, nor I,*
> *As one another's mystery,*
> *Each shall be both, yet both but one.*
>
> *This said, in her up-lifted face,*
> *Her eyes, which did that beauty crown,*
> *Were like two starrs, that having faln down,*
> *Look up again to find their place:*
>
> *While such a moveless silent peace*
> *Did seize on their becalmed sense,*
> *One would have thought some influence*
> *Their ravished spirits did possess.*

There is nothing in these lines (with the possible exception of the stars, a simile not at once grasped, but lovely and justified) which fits Johnson's general observations on the metaphysical poets in his essay on Cowley. A good deal resides in the richness of association which is at the same time borrowed from and given to the word "becalmed"; but the meaning is clear, the language simple and elegant. It is to be observed that the language of these poets is as a rule simple and pure; in the verse of George Herbert this simplicity is carried as far as it can go—a simplicity emulated without success by numerous modern poets. The *structure* of the sentences, on the other hand, is sometimes far from simple, but this is not a vice; it is a fidelity to thought and feeling. The effect, at its best, is far less artificial than that of an ode by Gray. And as this fidelity induces variety of thought and feeling, so it induces variety of music. We doubt whether, in the eighteenth century, could be found two poems in nominally the same metre, so dissimilar as Marvell's *Coy Mistress* and Crashaw's *Saint Teresa;* the one producing an effect of great speed by the use of short syllables, and the other an ecclesiastical solemnity by the use of long ones:

> *Love, thou art absolute sole lord*
> *Of life and death.*

If so shrewd and sensitive (though so limited) a critic as Johnson failed to define metaphysical poetry by its faults, it is worth while to inquire whether we may not have more success by adopting the opposite method: by assuming that the poets of the seventeenth century (up to the Revolution) were the direct and normal development of the precedent age; and, without prejudicing their case by the adjective "metaphysical," consider whether their virtue was not something permanently valuable, which subsequently disappeared but ought not to have disappeared. Johnson has hit, perhaps by accident, on one of their peculiarities, when he observes that "their attempts were always analytic"; he would not agree that, after the dissociation, they put the material together again in a new unity.

It is certain that the dramatic verse of the later Elizabethan and early Jacobean poets expresses a degree of development of sensibility which is not found in any of the prose, good as it often is. If we except Marlowe, a man of prodigious intelligence, these dramatists were directly or indirectly (it is at least a tenable theory) affected by Montaigne. Even if we except also Jonson and Chapman, these two were notably erudite, and were notably men who incorporated their erudition into their sensibility: their mode of feeling was directly and freshly altered by their reading and thought. In Chapman especially there is a direct sensuous apprehension of thought, or a recreation of thought into feeling, which is exactly what we find in Donne:

> *in this one thing, all the discipline*
> *Of manners and of manhood is contained;*
> *A man to join himself with th' Universe*
> *In his main sway, and make in all things fit*
> *One with that All, and go on, round as it;*

> *Not plucking from the whole his wretched part,*
> *And into straits, or into nought revert,*
> *Wishing the complete Universe might be*
> *Subject to such a rag of it as he;*
> *But to consider great Necessity.*

We compare this with some modern passage:

> *No, when the fight begins within himself,*
> *A man's worth something. God stoops o'er his head,*
> *Satan looks up between his feet—both tug—*
> *He's left, himself, i' the middle; the soul wakes*
> *And grows. Prolong that battle through his life!*

It is perhaps somewhat less fair, though very tempting (as both poets are concerned with the perpetuation of love by offspring), to compare with the stanzas already quoted from Lord Herbert's Ode the following from Tennyson:

> *One walked between his wife and child,*
> *With measured footfall firm and mild,*
> *And now and then he gravely smiled.*
> > *The prudent partner of his blood*
> > *Leaned on him, faithful, gentle, good,*
> > *Wearing the rose of womanhood.*
> *And in their double love secure,*
> *The little maiden walked demure,*
> *Pacing with downward eyelids pure.*
> *These three made unity so sweet,*
> *My frozen heart began to beat,*
> *Remembering its ancient heat.*

The difference is not a simple difference of degree between poets. It is something which had happened to the mind of England between the time of Donne or Lord Herbert of Cherbury and the time of Tennyson and Browning; it is the difference between the intellectual poet and the reflective poet. Tennyson and Browning are poets, and they think; but they do not feel their thought as immediately as the odour of a rose. A thought to Donne was an experience; it modified his sensibility. When a poet's mind is perfectly equipped for its work, it is constantly amalgamating disparate experience; the ordinary man's experience is chaotic, irregular, fragmentary. The latter falls in love, or reads Spinoza, and these two experiences have nothing to do with each other, or with the noise of the typewriter or the smell of cooking; in the mind of the poet these experiences are always forming new wholes.

We may express the difference by the following theory: The poets of the seventeenth century, the successors of the dramatists of the sixteenth, possessed a mechanism of sensibility which could devour any kind of experience. They are simple, artificial, difficult, or fantastic, as their predecessors were; no less nor more than Dante, Guido Cavalcanti, Guinizelli, or Cino. In the seventeenth century a dissociation of sensibility set in, from which we have never recovered; and this dissociation, as is natural, was aggravated by the influence of the two most powerful poets of the century, Milton and Dryden. Each of these men performed certain poetic functions so magnificently well that the magnitude of the effect concealed the absence of others. The language went on and in some respects improved; the best verse of Collins, Gray, Johnson, and even Goldsmith satisfies some of our fastidious demands better than that of Donne or Marvell or King. But while the language became more refined, the feeling became more crude. The feeling, the sensibility, expressed in the *Country Churchyard* (to say nothing of Tennyson and Browning) is cruder than that in the *Coy Mistress.*

The second effect of the influence of Milton and Dryden followed from the first, and was therefore slow in manifestation. The sentimental age began early in the eighteenth century, and continued. The poets revolted against the ratiocinative, the descriptive; they thought and felt by fits, unbalanced; they reflected. In one or two passages of Shelley's *Triumph of Life,* in the second *Hyperion,* there are traces of a struggle toward unification of sensibility. But Keats and Shelley died, and Tennyson and Browning ruminated.

After this brief exposition of a theory—too brief, perhaps, to carry conviction—we may ask, what would have been the fate of the "metaphysical" had the current of poetry descended in a direct line from them, as it descended in a direct line to them? They would not, certainly, be classified as metaphysical. The possible interests of a poet are unlimited; the more intelligent he is the better; the more intelligent he is the more likely that he will have interests: our only condition is that he turn them into poetry, and not merely meditate on them poetically. A philosophical theory which has entered into poetry is established, for its truth or falsity in one sense ceases to matter, and its truth in another sense is proved. The poets in question have, like other poets, various faults. But they were, at best, engaged in the task of trying to find the verbal equivalent for states of mind and feeling. And this means both that they are more mature, and that they wear better, than later poets of certainly not less literary ability.

It is not a permanent necessity that poets should be interested in philosophy, or in any other subject. We can only say that it appears likely that poets in our civilization, as it exists at present, must be *difficult.* Our civilization comprehends great variety and complexity, and this variety and complexity, playing upon a refined sensibility, must produce various and complex results. The poet must become more and more comprehensive, more allusive, more indirect, in order to force, to dislocate if necessary, language into his meaning. (A brilliant and extreme statement of this view, with which it is not requisite to associate oneself, is that of M. Jean Epstein, *La Poésie d'aujourd'hui.*) Hence we get something which looks very much like the conceit—we get, in fact, a method curiously similar to that of the "metaphysical poets," similar also in its use of obscure words and of simple phrasing.

> *O géraniums diaphanes, guerroyeurs sortilèges,*
> *Sacrilèges monomanes!*
> *Emballages, dévergondages, douches! O pressoirs*
> *Des vendanges des grands soirs!*
> *Layettes aux abois,*
> *Thyrses au fond des bois!*
> *Transfusions, représailles,*
> *Relevailles, compresses et l'éternal potion,*
> *Angélus! n'en pouvoir plus*
> *De débâcles nuptiales! de débâcles nuptiales!*

The same poet could write also simply:

> *Elle est bien loin, elle pleure,*
> *Le grand vent se lamente aussi . . .*

Jules Laforgue, and Tristan Corbière in many of his poems, are nearer to the "school of Donne" than any modern English poet. But poets more classical than they have the same essential quality of transmuting ideas into sensations, of transforming an observation into a state of mind.

> *Pour l'enfant, amoureux de cartes et d'estampes,*
> *L'univers est égal à son vaste appétit.*
> *Ah, que le monde est grand à la clarté des lampes!*
> *Aux yeux du souvenir que le monde est petit!*

In French literature the great master of the seventeenth century—Racine—and the great master of the nineteenth—Baudelaire—are in some ways more like each other than they are like any one else. The greatest two masters of diction are also the greatest two psychologists, the most curious explorers of the soul. It is interesting to speculate whether it is not a misfortune that two of the greatest masters of diction in our language, Milton and Dryden, triumph with a dazzling disregard of the soul. If we continued to produce Miltons and Drydens it might not so much matter, but as things are it is a pity that English poetry has remained so incomplete. Those who object to the "artificiality" of Milton or Dryden sometimes tell us to "look into our hearts and write." But that is not looking deep enough; Racine or Donne looked into a good deal more than the heart. One must look into the cerebral cortex, the nervous system, and the digestive tracts.

May we not conclude, then, that Donne, Crashaw, Vaughan, Herbert and Lord Herbert, Marvell, King, Cowley at his best, are in the direct current of English poetry, and that their faults should be reprimanded by this standard rather than coddled by antiquarian affection? They have been enough praised in terms which are implicit limitations because they are "metaphysical" or "witty," "quaint" or "obscure," though at their best they have not these attributes more than other serious poets. On the other hand, we must not reject the criticism of Johnson (a dangerous person to disagree with) without having mastered it, without having assimilated the Johnsonian canons of taste. In reading the celebrated passage in his essay on Cowley we must remember that by wit he clearly means something more serious than we usually mean today; in his criticism of their versification we must remember in what a narrow discipline he was trained, but also how well trained; we must remember that Johnson tortures chiefly the chief offenders, Cowley and Cleveland. It would be a fruitful work, and one requiring a substantial book, to break up the classification of Johnson (for there has been none since) and exhibit these poets in all their difference of kind and of degree, from the massive music of Donne to the faint, pleasing tinkle of Aurelian Townshend—whose *Dialogue between a Pilgrim and Time* is one of the few regrettable omissions from the excellent anthology of Professor Grierson.

Poetry: A Note on Ontology

JOHN CROWE RANSOM

A poetry may be distinguished from a poetry by virtue of subject-matter, and subject-matter may be differentiated with respect to its ontology, or the reality of its being. An excellent variety of critical doctrine arises recently out of this differentiation, and thus perhaps criticism leans again upon ontological analysis as it was meant to do by Kant. The recent critics remark in effect that some poetry deals with things, while some other poetry deals with ideas. The two poetries will differ from each other as radically as a thing differs from an idea.

The distinction in the hands of critics is a fruitful one. There is apt to go along with it a principle of valuation, which is the consequence of a temperament, and therefore basic. The critic likes things and intends that his poet shall offer them: or likes ideas and intends that he shall offer them: and approves him as he does the one or the other. Criticism cannot well go much deeper than this. The critic has carried to the last terms his analysis of the stuff of which poetry is made, and valued it frankly as his temperament or his need requires him to value it.

So philosophical a critic seems to be highly modern. He is; but this critic as a matter of fact is peculiarly on one side of the question. (The implication is unfavourable to the other side of the question.) He is in revolt against the tyranny of ideas, and against the poetry which celebrates ideas, and which may be identified—so far as his usual generalization may be trusted—with the hateful poetry of the Victorians. His bias is in favour of the things. On the other hand the critic who likes Victorian verse, or the poetry of ideas, has probably not thought of anything of so grand a simplicity as electing between the things and the ideas, being apparently not quite capable of the ontological distinction. Therefore he does not know the real or constitutional ground of his liking, and may somewhat ingenuously claim that his predilection is for those poets who give him inspiration, or comfort, or truth, or honest metres, or something else equally "worth while." But Plato, who was not a modern, was just as clear as we are about the basic distinction between the ideas and the things, and yet stands far apart from the aforesaid conscious modern in passionately preferring the ideas over the things. The weight of Plato's testimony would certainly fall on the side of the Victorians, though they may scarcely have thought of calling him as their witness. But this consideration need not conclude the hearing.

1. PHYSICAL POETRY

The poetry which deals with things was much in favour a few years ago with the resolute body of critics. And the critics affected the poets. If necessary, they became the poets, and triumphantly illustrated the new mode. The Imagists were important figures in the history of our poetry, and they were both theorists and creators. It was their intention to present things in their thinginess, or *Dinge* in their *Dinglichkeit*; and to such an extent had the public lost its sense of *Dinglichkeit* that their redirection was wholesome. What the public was inclined to seek in poetry was ideas, whether large ones or small ones, grand ones or pretty ones, certainly ideas to live by and die by, but what the Imagists identified with the stuff of poetry was, simply, things.

Their application of their own principle was sufficiently heroic, though they scarcely consented to be as extreme in the practice as in the theory. They had artistic talent, every one of the original group, and it was impossible that they should make of poetry so simple an exercise as in doctrine they seemed to think it was. Yet Miss Lowell wrote a poem on *Thompson's Lunch Room, Grand Central Station*; it is admirable if its intention is to show the whole reach of her courage. Its detail goes like this:

> Jagged greenwhite bowls of pressed glass
> Rearing snow-peaks of chipped sugar
> Above the lighthouse-shaped castors
> Of gray pepper and gray-white salt.

For most of us as for the public idealist, with his "values," this is inconsequential. Unhappily it seems that the things as things do not necessarily interest us, and that in fact we are not quite constructed with the capacity for a disinterested interest. But it must be noted even here that the things are on their good behaviour, looking rather well, and arranged by lines into something approaching a military formation. More technically, there is cross-imagery in the snow-peaks of sugar, and in the lighthouse-shaped castors, and cross-imagery involves association, and will presently involve dissociation and thinking. The metre is but a vestige, but even so it means something, for metre is a powerful intellectual determinant marshalling the words and, inevitably, the things.

The *Dinglichkeit* of this Imagist specimen, or the realism, was therefore not pure. But it was nearer pure than the world was used to in poetry, and the exhibit was astonishing.

For the purpose of this note I shall give to such poetry, dwelling as exclusively as it dares upon physical things, the name Physical Poetry. It is to stand opposite to that poetry which dwells as firmly as it dares upon ideas.

But perhaps thing *versus* idea does not seem to name an opposition precisely. Then we might phrase it a little differently: image *versus* idea. The idealistic philosophies are not sure that things exist, but they mean the equivalent when they refer to images. (Or they may consent to perceptions; or to impressions, following Hume, and following Croce, who remarks that they are pre-intellectual and independent of concepts. It is all the same, unless we are extremely technical.) It is sufficient if they concede that image is the raw material of idea. Though it may be an unwieldy and useless affair for the idealist as it stands, much needing to be licked into shape, nevertheless its relation to idea is that of a material cause, and it cannot be dispossessed of its priority.

It cannot be dispossessed of a primordial freshness, which idea can never claim. An idea is derivative and tamed. The image is in the natural or wild state, and it has to be discovered there, not put there, obeying its own law and none of ours. We think we can lay hold of image and take it captive, but the docile captive is not the real image but only the idea, which is the image with its character beaten out of it.

But we must be very careful: idealists are nothing if not dialectical. They object that an image in an original state of innocence is a delusion and cannot exist, that no image ever comes to us which does not imply the world of ideas, there is "no percept without a concept." There is something in it. Every property discovered in the image is a universal property, and nothing discovered in the image is marvellous in kind though it may be pinned down historically or statistically as a single instance. But there is this to be understood too: the image which is not remarkable in any particular property is marvellous in its assemblage of many properties, a manifold of properties, like a mine or a field, something to be explored for the properties; yet science can manage the image, which is infinite in properties, only by equating it to the one property with which the science is concerned: for science at work is always *a science*, and committed to a special interest. It is not by refutation but by abstraction that science destroys the image. It means to get its "value" out of the image, and we may be sure that it has no use for the image in its original state of freedom. People who are engrossed with their pet "values" become habitual killers. Their game is the images, or the things, and they acquire the ability to shoot them as far off as they can be seen, and do. It is thus that we lose the power of imagination, or whatever faculty it is by which we are able to contemplate things as they are in their rich and contingent materiality. But our dreams reproach us, for in dreams they come alive again. Likewise our memory; which makes light of our science by recalling the images in their panoply of circumstance and with their morning freshness upon them.

It is the dream, the recollection, which compels us to poetry, and to deliberate aesthetic experience. It can hardly be argued, I think, that the arts are constituted automatically out of original images, and arise in some early age of innocence. (Though Croce seems to support this view, and to make art a pre-adult stage of experience.) Art is based on second love, not first love. In it we make a return to something which we had wilfully alienated. The child is occupied mostly with things, but it is because he is still unfurnished with systematic ideas, not because he is a ripe citizen by nature and comes along already trailing clouds of glory. Images are clouds of glory for the man who has discovered that ideas are a sort of darkness. Imagism, that is, the recent historical movement, may resemble a naïve poetry of mere things, but we can read the theoretical pronouncements of Imagists, and we can learn that Imagism is motivated by a distaste for the systematic abstractedness of thought. It presupposes acquaintance with science; that famous activity which is "constructive" with respect to the tools of our economic role in this world, and destructive with respect to nature. Imagists wish to escape from science by immersing themselves in images.

Not far off the simplicity of Imagism was, a little later, the subtler simplicity of Mr. George Moore's project shared with several others, in behalf of "pure poetry." In Moore's house on Ebury Street they talked about poetry, with an after-dinner warmth if not an early-morning discretion, and their tastes agreed almost perfectly and reinforced one another. The fruit of these conversations was the volume *Pure Poetry*. It must have been the most exclusive anthology of English poetry that had yet appeared, since its room was closed to all the poems that dallied visibly with ideas, so that many poems that had been coveted by all other anthologists do not appear there. Nevertheless the book is delicious, and something more deserves to be said for it.

First, that "pure poetry" is a kind of Physical Poetry. Its visible content is a thing-content. Technically, I suppose, it is effective in this character if it can exhibit its material in such a way that an image or set of images and not an idea must occupy the foreground of the reader's attention. Thus:

> Full fathom five thy father lies
> Of his bones are coral made.

Here it is difficult for anybody (except the perfect idealist who is always theoretically possible and who would expect to take a return from anything whatever) to receive any experience except that of a very distinct image, or set of images. It has the configuration of image, which consists in being sharp of edges, and the modality of image, which consists in being given and non-negotiable, and the density, which consists in being full, a plenum of qualities. What is to be done with it? It is pure exhibit; it is to be contemplated; perhaps it is to be enjoyed. The art of poetry depends more frequently on this faculty than on any other in its repertory; the faculty of presenting images so whole and clean that they resist the catalysis of thought.

And something else must be said, going in the opposite direction. "Pure poetry," all the same, is not as pure as it is claimed to be, though on the whole it is Physical Poetry. (All true poetry is a phase of Physical Poetry.) It is not as pure as Imagism is, or at least it is not as pure as Imagism would be if it lived up to its principles; and in fact it is significant that the volume does not contain any Imagist poems, which argues a difference in taste somewhere. Imagism may take trifling things for its material; presumably it will take the first things the poet encounters, since "importance" and "interest" are not primary qualities which a thing possesses but secondary or tertiary ones which the idealist attributes to it by virtue of his own requirements. "Pure poetry" as Moore conceives it, and as the lyrics of Poe and Shakespeare offer it, deals with the more dramatic materials, and here dramatic means human, or at least capable of being referred to the critical set of human interests. Employing this sort of material the poet cannot exactly intend to set the human economists in us actually into motion, but perhaps he does intend to comfort us with the fleeting sense that it is potentially our kind of material.

In the same way "pure poetry" is nicely metred, where Imagism was free. Technique is written on it. And by the way the anthology contains no rugged anonymous Scottish ballad either, and probably for a like reason: because it would not be technically finished. Now both Moore and de la Mare are accomplished conservative artists, and what they do or what they approve may be of limited range but it is sure to be technically admirable, and it is certain that they understand what technique in poetry is though they do not define it. Technique takes the thing-content and metres and orders it. Metre is not an original property of things. It is artificial, and conveys the sense of human control, even if it does not wish to impair the thinginess of the things. Metric is a science, and so far as we attend to it we are within the scientific atmosphere. Order is the logical arrangement of things. It involves the dramatic "form" which selects the things, and brings out their appropriate qualities, and carries them through a systematic course of predication until the total impression is a unit of logic and not merely a solid lump of thing-content. The "pure poems" which Moore admires are studied, though it would be fatal if they looked studious. A sustained effort of ideation effected these compositions. It is covered up, and communicates itself only on a subliminal plane of consciousness. But experienced readers are quite aware of it; they know at once what is the matter when they encounter a realism shamelessly passing for poetry, or a well-planned but blundering poetry.

As critics we should have every good will toward Physical Poetry: it is the basic constituent of any poetry. But the product is always something short of a pure or absolute existence, and it cannot quite be said that it consists of nothing but physical objects. The fact is that when we are more than usually satisfied with a Physical Poetry our analysis will probably disclose that it is more than usually impure.

II. PLATONIC POETRY

The poetry of ideas I shall denominate: Platonic Poetry. This also has grades of purity. A discourse which employed only abstract ideas with no images would be a scientific document and not a poem at all, not even a Platonic poem. Platonic Poetry dips heavily into the physical. If Physical Poetry tends to employ some ideation surreptitiously while still looking innocent of idea, Platonic Poetry more than returns the compliment, for it tries as hard as it can to look like Physical Poetry, as if it proposed to conceal its medicine, which is the idea to be propagated, within the sugar candy of objectivity and *Dinglich-keit*. As an instance, it is almost inevitable that I quote a famous Victorian utterance:

> The year's at the spring
> And day's at the morn;
> Morning's at seven;
> The hill-side's dew-pearled;
> The lark's on the wing;
> The snail's on the thorn:
> God's in his heaven—
> All's right with the world!

which is a piece of transparent homiletics; for in it six pretty, co-ordinate images are marched, like six little lambs to the slaughter, to a colon and a powerful text. Now the exhibits of this poetry in the physical kind are always large, and may take more of the attention of the reader than is desired, but they are meant mostly to be illustrative of the ideas. It is on this ground that idealists like Hegel detect something unworthy, like a pedagogical trick, in poetry after all, and consider that the race will abandon it when it has outgrown its childishness and is enlightened.

The ablest arraignment of Platonic Poetry that I have seen, as an exercise which is really science but masquerades as poetry by affecting a concern for physical objects, is that of Mr. Allen Tate in a series of studies recently in *The New Republic*.[1] I will summarize, Platonic Poetry is allegory, a discourse in things, but on the understanding that they are translatable at every point into ideas. (The usual ideas are those which constitute the popular causes, patriotic, religious, moral, or social.) Or Platonic Poetry is the elaboration of ideas as such, but in proceeding introduces for ornament some physical properties after the style of Physical Poetry; which is rhetoric. It is positive when the poet believes in the efficacy of the ideas. It is negative when he despairs of their efficacy, because they have conspicuously failed to take care of him, and utters his personal wail:

> I fall upon the thorns of life! I bleed!

This is "Romantic Irony," which comes at occasional periods to interrupt the march of scientific optimism. But it still falls under the category of Platonism; it generally proposes some other ideas to take the place of those which are in vogue.

But why Platonism? To define Platonism we must remember that it is not

---

[1] "Three Types of Poetry." Reprinted in *Reactionary Essays* (1936). Reprinted in *On the Limits of Poetry* (1948). [*Editor's Note.*]

the property of the historical person who reports dialogues about it in an Academy, any more than "pure poetry" is the property of the talkers who describe it from a house on Ebury Street. Platonism, in the sense I mean, is the name of an impulse that is native to us all, frequent, tending to take a too complete possession of our minds. Why should the spirit of mortal be proud? The chief explanation is that modern mortal is probably a Platonist. We are led to believe that nature is rational and that by the force of reasoning we shall possess it. I have read upon high authority: "Two great forces are persistent in Plato: the love of truth and zeal for human improvement." The forces are one force. We love to view the world under universal or scientific ideas to which we give the name truth; and this is because the ideas seem to make not for right-eousness but for mastery. The Platonic view of the world is ultimately the predatory, for it reduces to the scientific, which we know. The Platonic Idea becomes the Logos which science worships, which is the Occidental God, whose minions we are, and whose children, claiming a large share in His powers for patrimony.

Now the fine Platonic world of ideas fails to coincide with the original world of perception, which is the world populated by the stubborn and con-tingent objects, and to which as artists we fly in shame. The sensibility mani-fested by artists makes fools of scientists, if the latter are inclined to take their special and quite useful form of truth as the whole and comprehensive article. A dandified pagan worldling like Moore can always defeat Platonism; he does it every hour; he can exhibit the savour of his fish and wines, the fragrance of his coffee and cigars, and the solidity of the images in his favourite verse. These are objects which have to be experienced, and cannot be reported, for what is their simple essence that the Platonist can abstract? Moore may sound mystical but he is within the literal truth when he defends "pure poetry" on the ground that the things are constant, and it is the ideas which change—changing according to the latest mode under which the species indulges its grandiose expectation of subjugating nature. The things are constant in the sense that the ideas are never emancipated from the necessity of referring back to them as their original; and the sense that they are not altered nor diminished no matter which ideas may take off from them as a point of departure. The way to obtain the true *Dinglichkeit* of a formal dinner or a landscape or a beloved person is to approach the object as such, and in humility; then it unfolds a nature which we are unprepared for if we have put our trust in the simple idea which at-tempted to represent it.

The special antipathy of Moore is to the ideas as they put on their moral complexion, the ideas that relate everything to that insignificant centre of action, the human "soul" in its most Platonic and Pharisaic aspect. Nothing can darken perception better than a repetitive moral earnestness, based on the reputed superiority and higher destiny of the human species. If morality is the code by which we expect the race to achieve the more perfect possession of nature, it is an incitement to a more heroic science, but not to aesthetic experience, nor religious; if it is the code of humility, by which we intend to know nature as nature is, that is another matter; but in an age of science morality is inevitably for the general public the former; and so transcendent a morality as the latter is now unheard of. And therefore:

> O love, *they* die in yon rich sky,
>> *They* faint on hill or field or river;
> *Our* echoes roll from soul to soul,
>> And grow forever and forever.

The italics are mine. These lines conclude an otherwise innocent poem, a candidate for the anthology, upon which Moore remarks: "The Victorian could never reconcile himself to finishing a poem without speaking about the soul, and the lines are particularly vindinctive." Vindinctive is just. By what right did the Laureate exult in the death of the physical echoes and call upon his love to witness it, but out of the imperiousness of his savage Platonism? Plato himself would have admired this ending, and considered that it redeemed an otherwise vicious poem.

Why do persons who have ideas to promulgate risk the trial by poetry? If the poets are hired to do it, which is the polite conception of some Hegelians, why do their employers think it worth the money, which they hold in public trust for the cause? Does a science have to become a poetry too? A science is the less effective as a science when it muddies its clear waters with irrelevance, a sermon becomes less cogent when it begins to quote the poets. The moralist, the scientist, and the prophet of idealism think evidently that they must establish their conclusions in poetry, though they reach these conclusions upon quite other evidence. The poetry is likely to destroy the conclusions with a sort of death by drowning, if it is a free poetry.

When that happens the Platonists may be cured of Platonism. There are probably two cures, of which this is the better. One cure is by adversity, by the failure of the ideas to work, on account of treachery or violence, or the contingencies of weather, constitution, love, and economics; leaving the Platonist defeated and bewildered, possibly humbled, but on the other hand possibly turned cynical and worthless. Very much preferable is the cure which comes by education in the fine arts, erasing his Platonism more gently, leading him to feel that that is not a becoming habit of mind which dulls the perceptions.

The definition which some writers have given to art is: the reference of the idea to the image. The implication is that the act is not for the purpose of honest comparison so much as for the purpose of proving the idea by image. But in the event the idea is not disproved so much as it is made to look ineffective and therefore foolish. The ideas will not cover the objects upon which they are imposed, they are too attenuated and threadlike; for ideas have extension and objects have intension, but extension is thin while intension is thick.

There must be a great deal of genuine poetry which started in the poet's mind as a thesis to be developed, but in which the characters and the situations have developed faster than the thesis, and of their own accord. The thesis disappears; or it is recaptured here and there and at the end, and lodged sententiously with the reader, where every successive reading of the poem will dislodge it again. Like this must be some plays, even some play out of Shakespeare, whose thesis would probably be disentangled with difficulty out of the crowded pageant; or some narrative poem with a moral plot but much pure detail; perhaps some "occasional" piece by a Laureate or official person, whose purpose is compromised but whose personal integrity is saved by his wavering between the sentiment which is a public duty and the experience which he has in his own right; even some proclaimed allegory, like Spenser's, unlikely as that may seem, which does not remain transparent and everywhere translatable into idea but makes excursions into the territory of objectivity. These are hybrid performances. They cannot possess beauty of design, though there may be a beauty in detailed passages. But it is common enough, and we should be grateful. The mind is a versatile agent, and unexpectedly stubborn in its determination not really to be hardened in Platonism. Even in an age of science like the nineteenth century the poetic talents are not so loyal to its apostolic zeal as they and it suppose, and do not deserve the unqualified scorn which it is fashionable to offer them, now that the tide has turned, for their performance is qualified.

But this may be not stern enough for concluding a note on Platonic Poetry. I refer again to that whose Platonism is steady and malignant. This poetry is an imitation of Physical Poetry, and not really a poetry. Platonists practise their bogus poetry in order to show that an image will prove an idea, but the literature which succeeds in this delicate mission does not contain real images but illustrations.

III. METAPHYSICAL POETRY

"Most men," Mr. Moore observes, "read and write poetry between fifteen and thirty and afterwards very seldom, for in youth we are attracted by ideas, and modern theory being concerned almost exclusively with ideas we live on duty, liberty, and fraternity as chameleons are said to live on light and air, till at last we turn from ideas to things, thinking that we have lost our taste for poetry, unless, perchance, we are classical scholars."

Much is conveyed in this characteristic sentence, even in proportion to its length. As for the indicated chronology, the cart is put after the horse, which is its proper sequence. And it is pleasant to be confirmed in the belief that many men do recant from their Platonism and turn back to things. But it cannot be exactly a *volte-face,* for there are qualifications. If pure ideas were what these men turn from, they would have had no poetry at all in the first period, and if pure things were what they turn to, they would be having not a classical poetry but a pure imagism, if such a thing is possible, in the second.

The mind does not come unscathed and virginal out of Platonism. Onto-logical interest would have to develop curiously, or wastefully and discontinuously, if men through their youth must cultivate the ideas so passionately that upon its expiration they are done with ideas forever and ready to become as little (and pre-logical) children. Because of the foolishness of idealists are ideas to be taboo for the adult mind? And, as critics, what are we to do with those poems (like *The Canonization* and *Lycidas*) which could not obtain admission by Moore into the anthology but which very likely are the poems we cherish beyond others?

The reputed "innocence" of the aesthetic moment, the "knowledge without desire" which Schopenhauer praises, must submit to a little scrutiny, like anything else that looks too good to be true. We come into this world as aliens come into a land which they must conquer if they are to live. For native endowment we have an exacting "biological" constitution which knows precisely what it needs and determines for us our inevitable desires. There can be no certainty that any other impulses are there, for why should they be? They scarcely belong in the biological picture. Perhaps we are simply an efficient animal species, running smoothly, working fast, finding the formula of life only too easy, and after a certain apprenticeship piling up power and wealth far beyond the capacity of our appetites to use. What will come next? Perhaps poetry, if the gigantic effort of science begins to seem disproportionate to the reward, according to a sense of diminishing returns. But before this pretty event can come to pass, it is possible that every act of attention which is allowed us is conditioned by a gross and selfish interest.

Where is innocence then? The aesthetic moment appears as a curious moment of suspension; between the Platonism in us, which is militant, always sciencing and devouring, and a starved inhibited aspiration towards innocence which, if it could only be free, would like to respect and know the object as it might of its own accord reveal itself.

The poetic impulse is not free, yet it holds out stubbornly against science for the enjoyment of its images. It means to reconstitute the world of perceptions. Finally there is suggested some such formula as the following:

Science gratifies a rational or practical impulse and exhibits the minimum of perception. Art gratifies a perceptual impulse and exhibits the minimum of reason.

Now it would be strange if poets did not develop many technical devices for the sake of increasing the volume of the percipienda or sensibilia. I will name some of them.

First Device: metre. Metre is the most obvious device. A formal metre impresses us as a way of regulating very drastically the material, and we do not stop to remark (that is, as readers) that it has no particular aim except some nominal sort of regimentation. It symbolizes the predatory method, like a sawmill which intends to reduce all the trees to fixed unit timbers, and as business men we require some sign of our business. But to the Platonic censor in us it gives a false security, for so long as the poet appears to be working faithfully at his metrical engine he is left comparatively free to attend lovingly to the things that are being metered, and metering them need not really hurt them. Metre is the gentlest violence he can do them, if he is expected to do some violence.

Second Device: fiction. The device of the fiction is probably no less important and universal in poetry. Over every poem which looks like a poem is a sign which reads: This road does not go through to action: fictitious. Art always sets out to create an "aesthetic distance" between the object and the subject, and art takes pains to announce that it is not history. The situation treated is not quite an actual situation, for science is likely to have claimed that field, and exiled art; but a fictive or hypothetical one, so that science is less greedy and perception may take hold of it. Kant asserted that the aesthetic judgment is not concerned with the existence or non-existence of the object, and may be interpreted as asserting that it is so far from depending on the object's existence that it really depends on the object's non-existence. Sometimes we have a certain melancholy experience. We enjoy a scene which we receive by report only, or dream, or meet with in art; but subsequently find ourselves in the presence of an actual one that seems the very same scene; only to discover that we have not now the power to enjoy it, or to receive it aesthetically, because the economic tension is upon us and will not indulge us in the proper mood. And it is generally easier to obtain our aesthetic experience from art than from nature, because nature is actual, and communication is forbidden. But in being called fictive or hypothetical the art-object suffers no disparagement. It cannot be true in the sense of being actual, and therefore it may be despised by science. But it is true in the sense of being fair or representative, in permitting the "illusion of reality"; just as Schopenhauer discovered that music may symbolize all the modes of existence in the world; and in keeping with the customary demand of the readers of fiction proper, that it shall be "true to life." The defenders of art must require for it from its practitioners this sort of truth, and must assert of it before the world this dignity. If jealous science succeeds in keeping the field of history for its own exclusive use, it does not therefore annihilate the arts, for they reappear in a field which may be called real though one degree removed from actuality. There the arts perform their function with much less interference, and at the same time with about as much fidelity to the phenomenal world as history has.

Third Device: tropes. I have named two important devices; I am not prepared to offer the exhaustive list. I mention but one other kind, the device which comprises the figures of speech. A proper scientific discourse has no intention of employing figurative language for its definitive sort of utterance. Figures of speech twist accidence away from the straight course, as if to intimate astonishing lapses of rationality beneath the smooth surface of discourse, inviting perceptual attention, and weakening the tyranny of science over the senses. But I skip the several easier and earlier figures, which are timid, and stop on the climactic figure, which is the metaphor: with special reference to its consequence, a poetry which once in our history it produced in a beautiful and abundant exhibit, called Metaphysical Poetry.

And what is Metaphysical Poetry? The term was added to the official vocabulary of criticism by Johnson, who probably took it from Pope, who probably took it from Dryden, who used it to describe the poetry of a certain school of poets, thus: "He [John Donne] affects the metaphysics, not only in his satires, but in his amorous verses, where nature only should reign. . . . In this Mr. Cowley has copied him to a fault." But the meaning of metaphysical which was common in Dryden's time, having come down from the Middle Ages through Shakespeare, was simply: supernatural; *miraculous*. The context of the Dryden passage indicates it.

Dryden, then, noted a miraculism in poetry and repudiated it; except where it was employed for satire, where it was not seriously intended and had the effect of wit. Dryden himself employs miraculism wittily, but seems rather to avoid it if he will be really committed by it; he may employ it in his translations of Ovid, where the responsibility is Ovid's and not Dryden's, and in an occasional classical piece where he is making polite use of myths well known to be pagan errors. In his "amorous" pieces he finds the reign of nature sufficient, and it is often the worse for his amorous pieces. He is not many removes from a naturalist. (A naturalist is a person who studies nature not because he loves it but because he wants to use it, approaches it from the standpoint of common sense, and sees it thin and not thick.) Dryden might have remarked that Donne himself had a change of heart and confined his miraculism at last to the privileged field of a more or less scriptural revelation. Perhaps Dryden found his way to accepting Milton because Milton's miraculism was mostly not a contemporary sort but classical and scriptural, pitched in a time when the age of miracles had not given way to the age of science. He knew too that Cowley had shamefully recanted from his petty miraculism, which formed the conceits, and turned to the scriptural or large order of miraculism to write his heroic (but empty) verses about David; and had written a Pindaric ode in extravagant praise of "Mr. Hobs," whose naturalistic account of nature seemed to render any other account fantastic if not contrary to the social welfare.

Incidentally, we know how much Mr. Hobbes affected Dryden too, and the whole of Restoration literature. What Bacon with his disparagement of poetry had begun, in the cause of science and protestantism, Hobbes completed. The name of Hobbes is critical in any history that would account for the chill which settled upon the poets at the very moment that English poetry was attaining magnificently to the fullness of its powers. The name stood for common sense and naturalism, and the monopoly of the scientific spirit over the mind. Hobbes was the adversary, the Satan, when the latter first intimidated the English poets. After Hobbes his name is legion.

"Metaphysics," or miraculism, informs a poetry which is the most original and exciting, and intellectually perhaps the most seasoned, that we know in our literature, and very probably it has few equivalents in other literatures. But it is evident that the metaphysical effects may be large-scale or they may be small-scale. (I believe that generically, or ontologically, no distinction is to be made between them.) If Donne and Cowley illustrate the small-scale effects, Milton will illustrate the large-scale ones, probably as a consequence of the fact that he wrote major poems. Milton, in the *Paradise Lost*, told a story which was heroic and miraculous in the first place. In telling it he dramatized it, and allowed the scenes and characters to develop of their own native energy. The virtue of a long poem on a "metaphysical" subject will consist in the dramatization or substantiation of all the parts, the poet not being required to devise fresh miracles on every page so much as to establish the perfect "naturalism" of the material upon which the grand miracle is imposed. The *Paradise Lost* possesses this virtue nearly everywhere:

Thus *Adam* to himself lamented loud
Through the still Night, not now, as ere man fell,
Wholsom and cool, and mild, but with black Air
Accompanied, with damps and dreadful gloom,
Which to his evil Conscience represented
All things with double terror: On the ground
Outstrecht he lay, on the cold ground, and oft
Curs'd his Creation, Death as oft accus'd
Of tardie execution, since denounc't
The day of his offence. Why comes not Death,
Said hee, with one thrice acceptable stroke
To end me?

This is exactly the sort of detail for a large-scale metaphysical work, but it would hardly serve the purpose with a slighter and more naturalistic subject: with "amorous" verses. For the critical mind Metaphysical Poetry refers perhaps almost entirely to the so-called "conceits" that constitute its staple. To define the conceit is to define small-scale Metaphysical Poetry.

It is easily defined, upon a little citation. Donne exhibits two conceits, or two branches of one conceit in the familiar lines:

Our hands were firmly cemented
By a fast balm which thence did spring;
Our eye-beams twisted, and did thread
Our eyes upon one double string.

The poem which follows sticks to the topic; it represents the lovers in precisely that mode of union and no other. Cowley is more conventional yet still bold in the lines:

Oh take my Heart, and by that means you'll prove
　　Within, too stor'd enough of love:
Give me but yours, I'll by that change so thrive
　　That Love in all my parts shall live.
So powerful is this my change, it render can,
My outside Woman, and your inside Man.

A conceit originates in a metaphor; and in fact the conceit is but a metaphor if the metaphor is meant; that is, if it is developed so literally that it must be meant, or predicated so baldly that nothing else can be meant. Perhaps this will do for a definition.

Clearly the seventeenth century had the courage of its metaphors, and imposed them imperially on the nearest things, and just as clearly the nineteenth century lacked this courage, and was half-heartedly metaphorical, or content with similes. The difference between the literary qualities of the two periods is the difference between the metaphor and the simile. (It must be admitted that this like other generalizations will not hold without its exceptions.) One period was pithy and original in its poetic utterance, the other was prolix and predictable. It would not quite commit itself to the metaphor even if it came upon one. Shelley is about as vigorous as usual when he says in *Adonais:*

> Thou young Dawn,
> Turn all thy dew to splendour . . .

But splendour is not the correlative of dew, it has the flat tone of a Platonic idea, while physically it scarcely means more than dew with sunshine upon it. The seventeenth century would have said: "Turn thy dew, which is water, into fire, and accomplish the transmutation of the elements." Tennyson in his boldest lyric sings:

> Come into the garden, Maud,
> For the black bat, night, has flown.

and leaves us unpersuaded of the bat. The predication would be complete without the bat, "The black night has flown," and a flying night is not very remarkable. Tennyson is only affecting a metaphor. But later in the same poem he writes:

> The red rose cries, "She is near, she is near";
> And the white rose weeps, "She is late";
> The larkspur listens, "I hear, I hear";
> And the lily whispers, "I wait."

and this is a technical conceit. But it is too complicated for this author, having a plurality of images which do not sustain themselves individually. The flowers stand for the lover's thoughts, and have been prepared for carefully in an earlier stanza, but their distinctness is too arbitrary, and these are like a schoolgirl's made-up metaphors. The passage will not compare with one on a very similar situation in *Green Candles,* by Mr. Humbert Wolfe:

> "I know her little foot," gray carpet said:
> "Who but I should know her light tread?"
> "She shall come in," answered the open door,
> "And not," said the room, "go out any more."

Wolfe's conceit works and Tennyson's does not, and though Wolfe's performance seems not very daring or important, and only pleasant, he employs the technique of the conceit correctly: he knows that the miracle must have a basis of verisimilitude.

Such is Metaphysical Poetry; the extension of a rhetorical device; as one of the most brilliant successes in our poetry, entitled to long and thorough examination; and even here demanding somewhat by way of a more ontological criticism. I conclude with it.

We may consult the dictionary, and discover that there is a miraculism or supernaturalism in a metaphorical assertion if we are ready to mean what we say, or believe what we hear. Or we may read Mr. Hobbes, the naturalist, who was very clear upon it: "II. The second cause of absurd assertions I ascribe to the giving of names of 'bodies' to 'accidents,' or of 'accidents' to 'bodies,' as they do that say 'faith is infused' or 'inspired,' when nothing can be 'poured' or 'breathed' into anything but body . . . and that 'phantasms' are 'spirits,' etc." Translated into our present terms, Hobbes is condemning the confusion of single qualities with whole things; or the substitution of concrete images for simple ideas.

Specifically, the miraculism arises when the poet discovers by analogy an identity between objects which is partial, though it should be considerable, and proceeds to an identification which is complete. It is to be contrasted with the simile, which says "as if" or "like," and is scrupulous to keep the identification partial. In Cowley's passage above, the lover is saying, not for the first time in this literature: "She and I have exchanged our hearts." What has actually been exchanged is affections, and affections are only in a limited sense the same as hearts. Hearts are unlike affections in being engines that pump blood and form body; and it is a miracle if the poet represents the lady's affection as rendering her inside into man. But he succeeds, with this mixture, in depositing with us the image of a very powerful affection.

From the strict point of view of literary criticism it must be insisted that the miraculism which produces the humblest conceit is the same miraculism which supplies to religions their substantive content. (This is said to assert the dignity not of the conceits but of the religions.) It is the poet and nobody else who gives to the God a nature, a form, faculties, and a history; to the God, most comprehensive of all terms, which, if there were no poetic impulse to actualize or "find" Him, would remain the driest and deadest among Platonic ideas, with all intension sacrificed to infinite extension. The myths are conceits, born of metaphors. Religions are periodically produced by poets and destroyed by naturalists. Religion depends for its ontological validity upon a literary understanding, and that is why it is frequently misunderstood. The metaphysical poets, perhaps like their spiritual fathers the mediaeval Schoolmen, were under no illusions about this. They recognized myth, as they recognized the conceits, as a device of expression; its sanctity as the consequence of its public or social importance.

But whether the topics be Gods or amorous experiences, why do poets resort to miraculism? Hardly for the purpose of controverting natural fact or scientific theory. Religion pronounces about God only where science and philosophy is negative; for a positive is wanted, that is, a God who has his being in the physical world as well as in the world of principles and abstractions. Likewise with the little secular enterprises of poetry. Not now are the poets so brave, not for a very long time have they been so brave, as to dispute the scientists on what they call their "truth"; though it is a pity that the statement cannot be turned round. Poets will concede that every act of science is legitimate, and has its efficacy. The metaphysical poets of the seventeenth century particularly admired the methodology of science, and in fact they copied it, and their phrasing is often technical, spare, and polysyllabic, though they are not repeating actual science but making those metaphorical substitutions that are so arresting.

The intention of Metaphysical Poetry is to complement science, and improve discourse. Naturalistic discourse is incomplete, for either of two reasons. It has the minimum of physical content and starves the sensibility, or it has the maximum, as if to avoid the appearance of evil, but is laborious and pointless. Platonic Poetry is too idealistic, but Physical Poetry is too realistic and realism is tedious and does not maintain interest. The poets therefore introduce the psychological device of the miracle. The predication which it permits is clean and quick but it is not a scientific predication. For scientific predication concludes an act of attention but miraculism initiates one. It leaves us looking, marvelling, and revelling in the thick *dinglich* substance that has just received its strange representation.

Let me suggest as a last word, in deference to a common Puritan scruple, that the predication of Metaphysical Poetry is true enough. It is not true like history, but no poetry is true in that sense, and only a part of science. It is true in the pragmatic sense in which some of the generalizations of science are true: it accomplishes precisely the sort of representation that it means to. It suggests to us that the object is perceptually or physically remarkable, and we had better attend to it.

Irony as a Principle of Structure

CLEANTH BROOKS

One can sum up modern poetic technique by calling it the rediscovery of metaphor and the full commitment to metaphor. The poet can legitimately step out into the universal only by first going through the narrow door of the particular. The poet does not select an abstract theme and then embellish it with concrete details. On the contrary, he must establish the details, must abide by the details, and through his realization of the details attain to whatever general meaning he can attain. The meaning must issue from the particulars; it must not seem to be arbitrarily forced upon the particulars. Thus, our conventional habits of language have to be reversed when we come to deal with poetry. For here it is the tail that wags the dog. Better still, here it is the tail of the kite—the tail that makes the kite fly—the tail that renders the kite more than a frame of paper blown crazily down the wind.

The tail of the kite, it is true, seems to negate the kite's function: it weights down something made to rise; and in the same way, the concrete particulars with which the poet loads himself seem to deny the universal to which he aspires. The poet wants to "say" something. Why, then, doesn't he say it directly and forthrightly? Why is he willing to say it only through his metaphors? Through his metaphors, he risks saying it partially and obscurely, and risks not saying it at all. But the risk must be taken, for direct statement leads to abstraction and threatens to take us out of poetry altogether.

The commitment to metaphor thus implies, with respect to general theme, a principle of indirection. With respect to particular images and statements, it implies a principle of organic relationship. That is, the poem is not a collection of beautiful or "poetic" images. If there really existed objects which were somehow intrinsically "poetic," still the mere assemblage of these would not give us a poem. For in that case, one might arrange bouquets of these poetic images and thus create poems by formula. But the elements of a poem are related to each other, not as blossoms juxtaposed in a bouquet, but as the blossoms are related to the other parts of a growing plant. The beauty of the poem is the flowering of the whole plant, and needs the stalk, the leaf, and the hidden roots.

If this figure seems somewhat highflown, let us borrow an analogy from another art: the poem is like a little drama. The total effect proceeds from all the elements in the drama, and in a good poem, as in a good drama, there is no waste motion and there are no superfluous parts.

In coming to see that the parts of a poem are related to each other organically, and related to the total theme indirectly, we have come to see the importance of *context*. The memorable verses in poetry—even those which seem somehow intrinsically "poetic"—show on inspection that they derive their poetic quality from their relation to a particular context. We may, it is true, be tempted to say that Shakespeare's "Ripeness is all" is poetic because it is a sublime thought, or because it possesses simple eloquence; but that is to forget the context in which the passage appears. The proof that this is so becomes obvious when we contemplate such unpoetic lines as "vitality is all," "serenity is all," "maturity is all,"—statements whose philosophical import in the abstract is about as defensible as that of "ripeness is all." Indeed, the commonplace word "never" repeated five times becomes one of the most poignant lines in *Lear,* but it becomes so because of the supporting context. Even the "meaning" of any particular item is modified by the context. For what is said is said in a particular situation and by a particular dramatic character.

The last instances adduced can be most properly regarded as instances of "loading" from the context. The context endows the particular word or image or statement with significance. Images so charged become symbols; statements so charged become dramatic utterances. But there is another way in which to look at the impact of the context upon the part. The part is modified by the pressure of the context.

Now the *obvious* warping of a statement by the context we characterize as "ironical." To take the simplest instance, we say "this is a fine state of affairs," and in certain contexts the statement means quite the opposite of what it purports to say literally. This is sarcasm, the most obvious kind of irony. Here a complete reversal of meaning is effected: effected by the context, and pointed, probably, by the tone of voice. But the modification can be most important even though it falls far short of sarcastic reversal and it need not be underlined by the tone of voice at all. The tone of irony can be effected by the skillful disposition of the context. Gray's *Elegy* will furnish an obvious example.

> Can storied urn or animated bust
> Back to its mansion call the fleeting breath?
> Can Honour's voice provoke the silent dust,
> Or Flatt'ry soothe the dull cold ear of death?

In its context, the question is obviously rhetorical. The answer has been implied in the characterization of the breath as fleeting and of the ear of death as dull and cold. The form is that of a question, but the manner in which the question has been asked shows that it is no true question at all.

These are obvious instances of irony, and even on this level, much more poetry is ironical than the reader may be disposed to think. Many of Hardy's poems and nearly all of Housman's, for example, reveal irony quite as definite and overt as this. Lest these examples, however, seem to specialize irony in the direction of the sardonic, the reader ought to be reminded that irony, even in its obvious and conventionally recognized forms, comprises a wide variety of modes: tragic irony, self-irony, playful, arch, mocking, or gentle irony, etc. The body of poetry which may be said to contain irony in the ordinary senses of the term stretches from *Lear*, on the one hand, to "Cupid and Campaspe Played," on the other.

What indeed would be a statement wholly devoid of an ironic potential—a statement that did not show any qualification of the context? One is forced to offer statements like "Two plus two equals four," or "The square on the hypotenuse of a right triangle is equal to the sum of the squares on the two sides." The meaning of these statements is unqualified by any context; if they are true, they are equally true in any possible context.[1] These statements are properly abstract, and their terms are pure denotations. (If "two" or "four" actually happened to have connotations for the fancifully minded, the connotations would be quite irrelevant: they do not participate in the meaningful structure of the statement.)

But connotations are important in poetry and do enter significantly into the structure of meaning which is the poem. Moreover, I should claim also—as a corollary of the foregoing proposition—that poems never contain abstract statements. That is, any "statement" made in the poem bears the pressure of the context and has its meaning modified by the context. In other words, the statements made—including those which appear to be philosophical generalizations—are to be read as if they were speeches in a drama. Their relevance, their propriety, their rhetorical force, even their meaning, cannot be divorced from the context in which they are imbedded.

The principle I state may seem a very obvious one, but I think that it is nonetheless very important. It may throw some light upon the importance of the term *irony* in modern criticism. As one who has certainly tended to over-use the term *irony* and perhaps, on occasion, has abused the term, I am closely concerned here. But I want to make quite clear what that concern is: it is not to justify the term *irony* as such, but rather to indicate why modern critics are

[1] This is not to say, of course, that such statements are not related to a particular "universe of discourse." They are indeed, as are all statements of whatever kind. But I distinguish here between "context" and "universe of discourse." "Two plus two equals four" is not dependent on a special dramatic context in the way in which a "statement" made in a poem is. Compare "two plus two equals four" and the same "statement" as contained in Housman's poem:

> —To think that two and two are four
> And neither five nor three
> The heart of man has long been sore
> And long 'tis like to be.

so often tempted to use it. We have doubtless stretched the term too much, but it has been almost the only term available by which to point to a general and important aspect of poetry.

Consider this example: The speaker in Matthew Arnold's "Dover Beach" states that the world, "which seems to lie before us like a land of dreams . . . hath really neither joy nor love nor light. . . ." For some readers the statement will seem an obvious truism. (The hero of a typical Hemingway short story or novel, for example, will say this, though of course in a rather different idiom.) For other readers, however, the statement will seem false, or at least highly questionable. In any case, if we try to "prove" the proposition, we shall raise some very perplexing metaphysical questions, and in doing so, we shall certainly also move away from the problems of the poem and, finally, from a justification of the poem. For the lines are to be justified in the poem in terms of the context: the speaker is standing beside his loved one, looking out of the window on the calm sea, listening to the long withdrawn roar of the ebbing tide, and aware of the beautiful delusion of moonlight which "blanches" the whole scene. The "truth" of the statement, and of the poem itself, in which it is imbedded, will be validated, not by a majority report of the association of sociologists, or a committee of physical scientists, or of a congress of metaphysicians who are willing to stamp the statement as proved. How is the statement to be validated? We shall probably not be able to do better than to apply T. S. Eliot's test: does the statement seem to be that which the mind of the reader can accept as coherent, mature, and founded on the facts of experience? But when we raise such a question, we are driven to consider the poem as drama. We raise such further questions as these: Does the speaker seem carried away with his own emotions? Does he seem to oversimplify the situation? Or does he, on the other hand, seem to have won to a kind of detachment and objectivity? In other words, we are forced to raise the question as to whether the statement grows properly out of a context; whether it acknowledges the pressures of the context; whether it is "ironical"—or merely callow, glib, and sentimental.

I have suggested elsewhere that the poem which meets Eliot's test comes to the same thing as I. A. Richards' "poetry of synthesis"—that is, a poetry which does not leave out what is apparently hostile to its dominant tone and which, because it is able to fuse the irrelevant and discordant, has come to terms with itself and is invulnerable to irony. Irony, then, in this further sense, is not only an acknowledgment of the pressures of a context. Invulnerability to irony is the stability of a context in which the internal pressures balance and mutually support each other. The stability is like that of the arch: the very forces which are calculated to drag the stones to the ground actually provide the principle of support—a principle in which thrust and counterthrust become the means of stability.

In many poems the pressures of the context emerge in obvious ironies. Marvell's "To His Coy Mistress" or Raleigh's "Nymph's Reply" or even Gray's "Elegy" reveal themselves as ironical, even to readers who use irony strictly in the conventional sense.

But can other poems be subsumed under this general principle, and do they show a comparable basic structure? The test case would seem to be presented by the lyric, and particularly the simple lyric. Consider, for example, one of Shakespeare's songs:

> Who is Silvia: what is she
>   That all our swains commend her?
> Holy, fair, and wise is she;
>   The heavens such grace did lend her,
> That she might admired be.
>
> Is she kind as she is fair?
>   For beauty lives with kindness.
> Love doth to her eyes repair,
>   To help him of his blindness,
> And, being help'd, inhabits there.
>
> Then to Silvia let us sing,
>   That Silvia is excelling;
> She excels each mortal thing
>   Upon the dull earth dwelling:
> To her let us garlands bring.

On one level the song attempts to answer the question "Who is Silvia?" and the answer given makes her something of an angel and something of a goddess. She excels each mortal thing "Upon the dull earth dwelling." Silvia herself, of course, dwells upon that dull earth, though it is presumably her own brightness which makes it dull by comparison. (The dull earth, for example, yields bright garlands which the swains are bringing to her.) Why does she excel each mortal thing? Because of her virtues ("Holy, fair, and wise is she"), and these are a celestial gift. She is heaven's darling ("The heavens such grace did lend her").

Grace, I suppose, refers to grace of movement, and some readers will insist that we leave it at that. But since Silvia's other virtues include holiness and wisdom, and since her grace has been lent from above, I do not think that we can quite shut out the theological overtones. Shakespeare's audience would have found it even more difficult to do so. At any rate, it is interesting to see what happens if we are aware of these overtones. We get a delightful richness, and we also get something very close to irony.

The motive for the bestowal of grace—that she might admired be—is oddly untheological. But what follows is odder still, for the love that "doth to her eyes repair" is not, as we might expect, Christian "charity" but the little pagan god Cupid ("Love doth to her eyes repair, / To help him of his blindness.") But if Cupid lives in her eyes, then the second line of the stanza takes on another layer of meaning. "For beauty lives with kindness" becomes not merely a kind of charming platitude—actually often denied in human experience. (The Petrarchan lover, for example, as Shakespeare well knew, frequently found a beautiful and *cruel* mistress.) The second line, in this context, means also that the love god lives with the kind Silvia, and indeed has taken these eyes that sparkle with kindness for his own.

Is the mixture of pagan myth and Christian theology, then, an unthinking confusion into which the poet has blundered, or is it something wittily combined? It is certainly not a confusion, and if blundered into unconsciously, it is a happy mistake. But I do not mean to press the issue of the poet's self-consciousness (and with it, the implication of a kind of playful irony). Suffice it to say that the song is charming and delightful, and that the mingling of elements is proper to a poem which is a deft and light-fingered attempt to suggest the quality of divinity with which lovers perennially endow maidens who are finally mortal. The touch is light, there is a lyric grace, but the tone is complex, nonetheless.

I shall be prepared, however, to have this last example thrown out of court since Shakespeare, for all his universality, was a contemporary of the metaphysical poets, and may have incorporated more of their ironic complexity than is necessary or normal. One can draw more innocent and therefore more convincing examples from Wordsworth's Lucy poems.

> She dwelt among the untrodden ways
>   Beside the springs of Dove,
> A maid whom there were none to praise
>   And very few to love;
>
> A violet by a mossy stone
>   Half hidden from the eye!
> Fair as a star, when only one
>   Is shining in the sky.
>
> She lived unknown, and few could know
>   When Lucy ceased to be;
> But she is in her grave, and, oh,
>   The difference to me.

Which is Lucy really like—the violet or the star? The context in general seems to support the violet comparison. The violet, beautiful but almost unnoticed, already half hidden from the eye, is now, as the poem ends, completely hidden in its grave, with none but the poet to grieve for its loss. The star comparison may seem only vaguely relevant—a conventional and here a somewhat anomalous compliment. Actually, it is not difficult to justify the star comparison: to her lover's eyes, she is the solitary star. She has no rivals, nor would the idea of rivalry, in her unselfconscious simplicity, occur to her.

The violet and the star thus balance each other and between themselves define the situation: Lucy was, from the viewpoint of the great world, unnoticed, shy, modest, and half hidden from the eye, but from the standpoint of her lover, she is the single star, completely dominating that world, not arrogantly like the sun, but sweetly and modestly, like the star. The implicit contrast is that so often developed ironically by John Donne in his poems where the lovers, who amount to nothing in the eyes of the world, become, in their own eyes, each the other's world—as in "The Good-Morrow," where their love makes "one little room an everywhere," or as in "The Canonization," where the lovers drive into the mirrors of each other's eyes the "towns, countries, courts"—which make up the great world; and thus find that world in themselves. It is easy to imagine how Donne would have exploited the contrast between the violet and the star, accentuating it, developing the irony, showing how the violet was really like its antithesis, the star, etc.

Now one does not want to enter an Act of Uniformity against the poets. Wordsworth is entitled to his method of simple juxtaposition with no underscoring of the ironical contrast. But it is worth noting that the contrast with its ironic potential is there in his poem. It is there in nearly all of Wordsworth's successful lyrics. It is certainly to be found in "A slumber did my spirit seal."

> A slumber did my spirit seal;
>   I had no human fears:
> She seemed a thing that could not feel
>   The touch of earthly years.
>
> No motion has she now, no force;
>   She neither hears nor sees,
> Rolled round in earth's diurnal course,
>   With rocks, and stones, and trees.

The lover's insensitivity to the claims of mortality is interpreted as a lethargy of spirit—a strange slumber. Thus the "human fears" that he lacked are apparently the fears normal to human beings. But the phrase has a certain pliability. It could mean fears *for* the loved one as a mortal human being; and the lines that follow tend to warp the phrase in this direction: it does not occur to the lover that he needs to fear for one who cannot be touched by "earthly years." We need not argue that Wordsworth is consciously using a witty device, a purposed ambiguity; nor need we conclude that he is confused. It is enough to see that Wordsworth has developed, quite "normally," let us say, a context calculated to pull "human fears" in opposed directions, and that the slightest pressure of attention on the part of the reader precipitates an ironical effect.

As we move into the second stanza, the potential irony almost becomes overt. If the slumber has sealed the lover's spirit, a slumber, immersed in which he thought it impossible that his loved one could perish, so too a slumber has now definitely sealed *her* spirit: "No motion has she now, no force; / She neither hears nor sees." It is evident that it is her unnatural slumber that has waked him out of his. It is curious to speculate on what Donne or Marvell would have made of this.

Wordsworth, however, still does not choose to exploit the contrast as such. Instead, he attempts to suggest something of the lover's agonized shock at the loved one's present lack of motion—of his response to her utter and horrible inertness. And how shall he suggest this? He chooses to suggest it, not by saying that she lies as quiet as marble or as a lump of clay; on the contrary, he attempts to suggest it by imagining her in violent motion—violent, but imposed motion, the same motion indeed which the very stones share, whirled about as they are in earth's diurnal course. Why does the image convey so powerfully the sense of something inert and helpless? Part of the effect, of course, resides in the fact that a dead lifelessness is suggested more sharply by an object's being whirled about by something else than by an image of the object in repose. But there are other matters which are at work here: the sense of the girl's falling back into the clutter of things, companioned by things chained like a tree to one particular spot, or by things completely inanimate, like rocks and stones. Here, of course, the concluding figure leans upon the suggestion made in the first stanza, that the girl once seemed something not subject to earthly limitations at all. But surely, the image of the whirl itself is important in its suggestion of something meaningless—motion that mechanically repeats itself. And there is one further element: the girl, who to her lover seemed a thing that could not feel the touch of earthly years, is caught up helplessly into the empty whirl of the earth which measures and makes time. She is touched by and held by earthly time in its most powerful and horrible image. The last figure thus seems to me to summarize the poem—to offer to almost every facet of meaning suggested in the earlier lines a concurring and resolving image which meets and accepts and reduces each item to its place in the total unity.

Wordsworth, as we have observed above, does not choose to point up specifically the ironical contrast between the speaker's former slumber and the loved one's present slumber. But there is one ironical contrast which he does stress: this is the contrast between the two senses in which the girl becomes insulated against the "touch of earthly years." In the first stanza, she "could not feel / The touch of earthly years" because she seemed divine and immortal. But in the second stanza, now in her grave, she still does not "feel the touch of earthly years," for, like the rocks and stones, she feels nothing at all. It is true that Wordsworth does not repeat the verb "feels"; instead he writes "She neither *hears* nor *sees*." But the contrast, though not commented upon directly by any device of verbal wit, is there nonetheless, and is bound to make itself felt in any sensitive reading of the poem. The statement of the first stanza has been literally realized in the second, but its meaning has been ironically reversed.

Ought we, then, to apply the term *ironical* to Wordsworth's poem? Not necessarily. I am trying to account for my temptation to call such a poem ironical—not to justify my yielding to the temptation—least of all to insist that others so transgress. Moreover, Wordsworth's poem seems to me admirable, and I entertain no notion that it might have been more admirable still had John Donne written it rather than William Wordsworth. I shall be content if I can make a much more modest point: namely, that since both Wordsworth and Donne are poets, their work has at basis a similar structure, and that the dynamic structure—the pattern of thrust and counterthrust—which we associate with Donne has its counterpart in Wordsworth. In the work of both men, the relation between part and part is organic, which means that each part modifies and is modified by the whole.

Yet to intimate that there are potential ironies in Wordsworth's lyric may seem to distort it. After all, is it not simple and spontaneous? With these terms we encounter two of the critical catchwords of the nineteenth century, even as *ironical* is in danger of becoming a catchword of our own period. Are the terms *simple* and *ironical* mutually exclusive? What after all do we mean by *simple* or by *spontaneous?* We may mean that the poem came to the poet easily and even spontaneously: very complex poems may—indeed have—come just this way. Or the poem may seem in its effect on the reader a simple and spontaneous utterance: some poems of great complexity possess this quality. What is likely to cause trouble here is the intrusion of a special theory of composition. It is fairly represented as an intrusion since a theory as to how a poem is written is being allowed to dictate to us how the poem is to be read. There is no harm in thinking of Wordsworth's poem as simple and spontaneous unless these terms deny complexities that actually exist in the poem, and unless they justify us in reading the poem with only half our minds. A slumber ought not to seal the *reader's* spirit as he reads this poem, or any other poem.

I have argued that irony, taken as the acknowledgment of the pressures of context, is to be found in poetry of every period and even in simple lyrical poetry. But in the poetry of our own time, this pressure reveals itself strikingly. A great deal of modern poetry does use irony as its special and perhaps its characteristic strategy. For this there are reasons, and compelling reasons. To cite only a few of these reasons: there is the breakdown of a common symbolism; there is the general scepticism as to universals; not least important, there is the depletion and corruption of the very language itself, by advertising and by the mass-produced arts of radio, the moving picture, and pulp fiction. The modern poet has the task of rehabilitating a tired and drained language so that it can convey meanings once more with force and with exactitude. This task of qualifying and modifying language is perennial; but it is imposed on the modern poet as a special burden. Those critics who attribute the use of ironic techniques to the poet's own bloodless sophistication and tired scepticism would be better advised to refer these vices to his potential readers, a public corrupted by Hollywood and the Book of the Month Club. For the modern poet is not addressing simple primitives but a public sophisticated by commercial art.

At any rate, to the honour of the modern poet be it said that he has frequently succeeded in using his ironic techniques to win through to clarity and passion. Randall Jarrell's "Eighth Air Force" represents a success of this sort.

> If, in an odd angle of the hutment,
> A puppy laps the water from a can
> Of flowers, and the drunk sergeant shaving
> Whistles *O Paradiso!*—shall I say that man
> Is not as men have said: a wolf to man?
>
> The other murderers troop in yawning;
> Three of them play Pitch, one sleeps, and one
> Lies counting missions, lies there sweating

Till even his heart beats: One; One; One.
O murderers! . . . Still, this is how it's done:

This is a war. . . . But since these play, before they die,
Like puppies with their puppy; since, a man,
I did as these have done, but did not die—
I will content the people as I can
And give up these to them: Behold the man!

I have suffered, in a dream, because of him,
Many things; for this last saviour, man,
I have lied as I lie now. But what is lying?
Men wash their hands, in blood, as best they can:
I find no fault in this just man.

There are no superfluous parts, no dead or empty details. The airmen in their hutment are casual enough and honest enough to be convincing. The raw building is domesticated: there are the flowers in water from which the mascot, a puppy, laps. There is the drunken sergeant, whistling an opera aria as he shaves. These "murderers," as the poet is casually to call the airmen in the next stanza, display a touching regard for the human values. How, then, can one say that man is a wolf to man, since these men "play before they die, like puppies with their puppy." But the casual presence of the puppy in the hutment allows us to take the stanza both ways, for the dog is a kind of tamed and domesticated wolf, and his presence may prove on the contrary that the hutment is the wolf den. After all, the timber wolf plays with its puppies.

The second stanza takes the theme to a perfectly explicit conclusion. If three of the men play pitch, and one is asleep, at least one man is awake and counts himself and his companions murderers. But his unvoiced cry "O murderers" is met, countered, and dismissed with the next two lines: ". . . Still this is how it's done: / This is a war. . ."

The note of casuistry and cynical apology prepares for a brilliant and rich resolving image, the image of Pontius Pilate, which is announced specifically in the third stanza:

I will content the people as I can
And give up these to them: behold the man!

Yet if Pilate, as he is first presented, is a jesting Pilate, who asks "What is truth?" it is a bitter and grieving Pilate who concludes the poem. It is the integrity of Man himself that is at stake. Is man a cruel animal, a wolf, or is he the last saviour, the Christ of our secular religion of humanity?

The Pontius Pilate metaphor, as the poet uses it, becomes a device for tremendous concentration. For the speaker (presumably the young airman who cried "O murderers") is himself the confessed murderer under judgment, and also the Pilate who judges, and, at least as a representative of man, the saviour whom the mob would condemn. He is even Pilate's better nature, his wife, for the lines "I have suffered, in a dream, because of him, / Many things" is merely a rearrangement of *Matthew* 27:19, the speech of Pilate's wife to her husband. But this last item is more than a reminiscence of the scriptural scene. It reinforces the speaker's present dilemma. The modern has had high hopes for man; are the hopes merely a dream? Is man incorrigible, merely a cruel beast? The speaker's present torture springs from that hope and from his reluctance to dismiss it as an empty dream. This Pilate is even harder-pressed than was the Roman magistrate. For he must convince himself of this last saviour's innocence. But he has lied for him before. He will lie for him now.

> Men wash their hands in blood, as best they can:
> I find no fault in this just man.

What is the meaning of "Men wash their hands in blood, as best they can"? It can mean: Since my own hands are bloody, I have no right to condemn the rest. It can mean: I know that man can love justice, even though his hands are bloody, for there is blood on mine. It can mean: Men are essentially decent: they try to keep their hands clean even if they have only blood in which to wash them.

None of these meanings cancels out the others. All are relevant, and each meaning contributes to the total meaning. Indeed, there is not a facet of significance which does not receive illumination from the figure.

Some of Jarrell's weaker poems seem weak to me because they lean too heavily upon this concept of the goodness of man. In some of them, his approach to the theme is too direct. But in this poem, the affirmation of man's essential justness by a Pilate who contents the people as he washes his hands in blood seems to me to supply every qualification that is required. The sense of self-guilt, the yearning to believe in man's justness, the knowledge of the difficulty of so believing—all work to render accurately and dramatically the total situation.

It is easy at this point to misapprehend the function of irony. We can say that Jarrell's irony pares his theme down to acceptable dimensions. The theme of man's goodness has here been so qualified that the poet himself does not really believe in it. But this is not what I am trying to say. We do not ask a poet to bring his poem into line with our personal beliefs—still less to flatter our personal beliefs. What we do ask is that the poem dramatize the situation so accurately, so honestly, with such fidelity to the total situation that it is no longer a question of our beliefs, but of our participation in the poetic experience. At his best, Jarrell manages to bring us, by an act of imagination, to the most penetrating insight. Participating in that insight, we doubtless become better citizens. (One of the "uses" of poetry, I should agree, is to make us better citizens.) But poetry is not the eloquent rendition of the citizen's creed. It is not even the accurate rendition of his creed. Poetry must carry us beyond the abstract creed into the very matrix out of which, and from which, our creeds are abstracted. That is what "The Eighth Air Force" does. That is what, I am convinced, all good poetry does.

For the theme in a genuine poem does not confront us as abstraction—that is, as one man's generalization from the relevant particulars. Finding its proper symbol, defined and refined by the participating metaphors, the theme becomes a part of the reality in which we live—an insight, rooted in and growing out of concrete experience, many-sided, three-dimensional. Even the resistance to generalization has its part in this process—even the drag of the particulars away from the universal—even the tension of opposing themes—play their parts. The kite properly loaded, tension maintained along the kite string, rises steadily *against* the thrust of the wind.

Technique as Discovery

MARK SCHORER

I

Modern criticism, through its exacting scrutiny of literary texts, has demonstrated with finality that in art beauty and truth are indivisible and one. The Keatsian overtones of these terms are mitigated and an old dilemma solved if for beauty we substitute form, and for truth, content. We may, without risk of loss, narrow them even more, and speak of technique and subject matter. Modern criticism has shown us that to speak of content as such is not to speak of art at all, but of experience; and that it is only when we speak of the *achieved* content, the form, the work of art as a work of art, that we speak as critics. The difference between content, or experience, and achieved content, or art, is technique.

When we speak of technique, then, we speak of nearly everything. For technique is the means by which the writer's experience, which is his subject matter, compels him to attend to it; technique is the only means he has of discovering, exploring, developing his subject, of conveying its meaning, and, finally, of evaluating it. And surely it follows that certain techniques are sharper tools than others, and will discover more; that the writer capable of the most exacting technical scrutiny of his subject matter, will produce works with the most satisfying content, works with thickness and resonance, works which reverberate, works with maximum meaning.

We are no longer able to regard as seriously intended criticism of poetry which does not assume these generalizations; but the case for fiction has not yet been established. The novel is still read as though its content has some value in itself, as though the subject matter of fiction has greater or lesser value in itself, and as though technique were not a primary but a supplementary element, capable perhaps of not unattractive embellishments upon the surface of the subject, but hardly of its essence. Or technique is thought of in blunter terms from those which one associates with poetry, as such relatively obvious matters as the arrangement of events to create plot; or, within plot, of suspense and climax; or as the means of revealing character motivation, relationship, and development; or as the use of point of view, but point of view as some nearly arbitrary device for the heightening of dramatic interest through the narrowing or broadening of perspective upon the material, rather than as a means toward the positive definition of theme. As for the resources of language, these, somehow, we almost never think of as a part of the technique of fiction—language as used to create a certain texture and tone which in themselves state and define themes and meanings; or language, the counters of our ordinary speech, as forced, through conscious manipulation, into all those larger meanings which our ordinary speech almost never intends. Technique in fiction, all this is a way of saying, we somehow continue to regard as merely a means of organizing material which is "given" rather than as the means of exploring and defining the values in an area of experience which, for the first time *then,* are being given.

Is fiction still regarded in this odd, divided way because it is really less tractable before the critical suppositions which now seem inevitable to poetry? Let us look at some examples: two well-known novels of the past, both by writers who may be described as "primitive," although their relative innocence of technique is of a different sort—Defoe's *Moll Flanders* and Emily Bronte's *Wuthering Heights;* and three well-known novels of this century—*Tono Bungay,* by a writer who claimed to eschew technique; *Sons and Lovers,* by a novelist who, because his ideal of subject matter ("the poetry of the immediate present") led him at last into the fallacy of spontaneous and unchangeable composition, in effect eschewed technique; and *A Portrait of the Artist as a Young Man,* by a novelist whose practice made claims for the supremacy of technique beyond those made by anyone in the past or by anyone else in this century.

Technique in fiction is, of course, all those obvious forms of it which are usually taken to be the whole of it, and many others; but for the present purposes, let it be thought of in two respects particularly: the uses to which language, as language, is put to express the quality of the experience in question; and the uses of point of view not only as a mode of dramatic delimitation, but more particularly, of thematic definition. Technique is really what T. S. Eliot means by "convention"—any selection, structure, or distortion, any form or rhythm imposed upon the world of action; by means of which—it should be added—our apprehension of the world of action is enriched or renewed. In this sense, everything is technique which is not the lump of experience itself, and one cannot properly say that a writer has no technique or that he eschews technique, for, being a writer, he cannot do so. We can speak of good and bad technique, of adequate and inadequate, of technique which serves the novel's purpose, or disserves.

II

In the prefatory remarks to *Moll Flanders*, Defoe tells us that he is not writing fiction at all, but editing the journals of a woman of notorious character, and rather to instruct us in the necessities and the joys of virtue than to please us. We do not, of course, take these professions seriously, since nothing in the conduct of the narrative indicates that virtue is either more necessary or more enjoyable than vice. On the contrary, we discover that Moll turns virtuous only after a life of vice has enabled her to do so with security; yet it is precisely for this reason that Defoe's profession of didactic purpose has interest. For the actual morality which the novel enforces is the morality of any commercial culture, the belief that virtue pays—in worldly goods. It is a morality somewhat less than skin deep, having no relation to motives arising from a sense of good and evil, least of all, of evil-*in*-good, but exclusively from the presence or absence of food, drink, linen, damask, silver, and time-pieces. It is the morality of measurement, and without in the least intending it, *Moll Flanders* is our classic revelation of the mercantile mind: the morality of measurement, which Defoe has completely neglected to measure. He fails not only to evaluate this material in his announced way, but to evaluate it at all. His announced purpose is, we admit, a pious humbug, and he meant us to read the book as a series of scandalous events; and thanks to his inexhaustible pleasure in excess and exaggeration, this element in the book continues to amuse us. Long before the book has been finished, however, this element has also become an absurdity; but not half the absurdity as that which Defoe did not intend at all—the notion that Moll could live a rich and full life of crime, and yet, repenting, emerge spotless in the end. The point is, of course, that she has no moral being, nor has the book any moral life. Everything is external. Everything can be weighed, measured, handled, paid for in gold, or expiated by a prison term. To this, the whole texture of the novel testifies: the bolts of goods, the inventories, the itemized accounts, the landlady's bills, the lists, the ledgers: all this, which taken together comprises what we call Defoe's method of circumstantial realism.

He did not come upon that method by any deliberation: it represents precisely his own world of value, the importance of external circumstance to Defoe. The point of view of Moll is indistinguishable from the point of view of her creator. We discover the meaning of the novel (at unnecessary length, without economy, without emphasis, with almost none of the distortions or the advantages of art) in spite of Defoe, not because of him. Thus the book is not the true chronicle of a disreputable female, but the true allegory of an impoverished soul—the author's; not an anatomy of the criminal class, but of the middle class. And we read it as an unintended comic revelation of self and of a social mode. Because he had no adequate resources of technique to separate himself from his material, thereby to discover and to define the meanings of his material, his contribution is not to fiction but to the history of fiction, and to social history.

The situation in *Wuthering Heights* is at once somewhat the same and yet very different. Here, too, the whole novel turns upon itself, but this time to its estimable advantage; here, too, is a revelation of what is perhaps the author's world of value, but this time, through what may be an accident of technique, the revelation is meaningfully accomplished. Emily Bronte may merely have stumbled upon the perspectives which define the form and the theme of her book. Whether she knew from the outset, or even at the end, what she was doing, we may doubt; but what she did and did superbly we can see.

We can assume, without at all becoming involved in the author's life but merely from the tone of somnambulistic excess which is generated by the writing itself, that this world of monstrous passion, of dark and gigantic emotional and nervous energy, is for the author, or was in the first place, a world of ideal value; and that the book sets out to persuade us of the moral magnificence of such unmoral passion. We are, I think, expected, in the first place, to take at their own valuation these demonic beings, Heathcliff and Cathy: as special creatures, set apart from the cloddish world about them by their heightened capacity for feeling, set apart, even, from the ordinary objects of human passion as, in their transcendental, sexless relationship, they identify themselves with an uncompromising landscape and cosmic force. Yet this is absurd, as much of the detail that surrounds it ("Other dogs lurked in other recesses") is absurd. The novelist Emily Bronte had to discover these absurdities to the girl Emily; her technique had to evaluate them for what they were, so that we are persuaded that it is not Emily who is mistaken in her estimate of her characters, but they who are mistaken in their estimate of themselves. The theme of the moral magnificence of unmoral passion is an impossible theme to sustain, and what interests us is that it was device—and this time, mere, mechanical device—which taught Emily Bronte that, the needs of her temperament to the contrary, all personal longing and reverie to the contrary, perhaps—that this was indeed not at all what her material must mean as art. Technique objectifies.

To lay before us the full character of this passion, to show us how it first comes into being and then comes to dominate the world about it and the life that follows upon it, Emily Bronte gives her material a broad scope in time, lets it, in fact, cut across three generations. And to manage material which is so extensive, she must find a means of narration, points of view, which can encompass that material, and, in her somewhat crude concept of motive, justify its telling. So she chooses a foppish traveller who stumbles into this world of passionate violence, a traveller representing the thin and conventional emotional life of the far world of fashion, who wishes to hear the tale: and for her teller she chooses, almost inevitably, the old family retainer who knows everything, a character as conventional as the other, but this one representing not the conventions of fashion, but the conventions of the humblest moralism. What has happened is, first, that she has chosen as her narrative perspective those very elements, conventional emotion and conventional morality, which her hero and heroine are meant to transcend with such spectacular magnificence; and second, that she has permitted this perspective to operate throughout a long period of time. And these two elements compel the novelist to see what her unmoral passions come to. Moral magnificence? Not at all; rather, a devastating spectacle of human waste; ashes. For the time of the novel is carried on long enough to show Heathcliff at last an emptied man, burned out by his fever ragings, exhausted and will-less, his passion meaningless at last. And it goes even a little further, to Lockwood, the fop, in the graveyard, sententiously contemplating headstones. Thus in the end the triumph is all on the side of the cloddish world, which survives.

Perhaps not all on that side. For, like Densher at the end of *The Wings of the Dove,* we say, and surely Hareton and the second Cathy say, "We shall never be again as we were!" But there is more point in observing that a certain body of materials, a girl's romantic daydreams, have, through the most conventional devices of fiction, been pushed beyond their inception in fancy to their meanings, their conception as a written book—that they, that is, are not at all as they were.

III

Technique alone objectifies the materials of art; hence technique alone evaluates those materials. This is the axiom which demonstrates itself so devastatingly whenever a writer declares, under the urgent sense of the importance of his materials (whether these are autobiography, or social ideas, or personal passions)—whenever such a writer declares that he cannot linger with technical refinements. That art will not tolerate such a writer H. G. Wells handsomely proves. His enormous literary energy included no respect for the techniques of his medium, and his medium takes its revenge upon his bumptiousness. "I have never taken any very great pains about writing. I am outside the hierarchy of conscious and deliberate writers altogether. I am the absolute antithesis of Mr. James Joyce . . . Long ago, living in close conversational proximity to Henry James, Joseph Conrad, and Mr. Ford Madox Heuffer, I escaped from under their immense artistic preoccupations by calling myself a journalist." Precisely. And he escaped—he disappeared—from literature into the annals of an era.

Yet what confidence! "Literature," Wells said, "is not jewelry, it has quite other aims than perfection, and the more one thinks of 'how it is done' the less one gets it done. These critical indulgences lead along a fatal path, away from every natural interest towards a preposterous emptiness of technical effort, a monstrous egotism of artistry, of which the later work of Henry James is the monumental warning. 'It,' the subject, the thing or the thought, has long since disappeared in these amazing works; nothing remains but the way it has been 'manipulated.' " Seldom has a literary theorist been so totally wrong; or what we learn as James grows for us and Wells disappears, is that without what he calls "manipulation," there *is* no "it," no "subject" in art. There is again only social history.

The virtue of the modern novelist—from James and Conrad down—is not only that he pays so much attention to his medium, but that, when he pays most, he discovers through it a new subject matter, and a greater one. Under the "immense artistic preoccupations" of James and Conrad and Joyce, the form of the novel changed, and with the technical change, analogous changes took place in substance, in point of view, in the whole conception of fiction. And the final lesson of the modern novel is that technique is not the secondary thing that it seemed to Wells, some external machination, a mechanical affair, but a deep and primary operation; not only that technique *contains* intellectual and moral implications, but that it *discovers* them. For a writer like Wells, who wished to give us the intellectual and the moral history of our times, the lesson is a hard one: it tells us that the order of intellect and the order of morality do not exist at all, in art, except as they are organized in the order of art.

Wells's ambitions were very large. "Before we have done, we will have all life within the scope of the novel." But that is where life already is, within the scope of the novel; where it needs to be brought is into novels. In Wells we have all the important topics in life, but no good novels. He was not asking too much of art, or asking that it include more than it happily can; he was not asking anything of it—as art, which is all that it can give, and that is everything.

A novel like *Tono Bungay,* generally thought to be Wells's best, is therefore instructive. "I want to tell—*myself,*" says George, the hero, "and my impressions of the thing as a whole"—the thing as a whole being the collapse of traditional British institutions in the twentieth century. George "tells himself" in terms of three stages in his life which have rough equivalents in modern British social history, and this is, to be sure, a plan, a framework; but it is the framework of Wells's abstract thinking, not of his craftsmanship, and the primary demand which one makes of such a book as this, that means be discovered whereby the dimensions of the hero contain the experiences he recounts, is never met. The novelist flounders through a series of literary imitations—from an early Dickensian episode, through a kind of Shavian interlude, through a Conradian episode, to a Jules Vernes vision at the end. The significant failure is in that end, and in the way that it defeats not only the entire social analysis of the bulk of the novel, but Wells's own ends as a thinker. For at last George finds a purpose in science. "I decided that in power and knowledge lay the salvation of my life, the secret that would fill my need; that to these things I would give myself."

But science, power and knowledge, are summed up at last in a destroyer. As far as one can tell Wells intends no irony, although he may here have come upon the essence of the major irony in modern history. The novel ends in a kind of meditative rhapsody which denies every value that the book had been aiming toward. For of all the kinds of social waste which Wells has been describing, this is the most inclusive, the final waste. Thus he gives us in the end not a novel, but a hypothesis; not an individual destiny, but a theory of the future; and not his theory of the future, but a nihilistic vision quite opposite from everything that he meant to represent. With a minimum of attention to the virtues of technique, Wells might still not have written a good novel; but he would at any rate have established a point of view and a tone which would have told us what he meant.

To say what one means in art is never easy, and the more intimately one is implicated in one's material, the more difficult it is. If, besides, one commits fiction to a therapeutic function which is to be operative not on the audience but on the author, declaring, as D. H. Lawrence did, that "One sheds one's sicknesses in books, repeats and presents again one's emotions to be master of them," the difficulty is vast. It is an acceptable theory only with the qualification that technique, which objectifies, is under no other circumstances so imperative. For merely to repeat one's emotions, merely to look into one's heart and write, is also merely to repeat the round of emotional bondage. If our books are to be exercises in self-analysis, then technique must—and alone can—take the place of the absent analyst.

Lawrence, in the relatively late Introduction to his *Collected Poems,* made that distinction of the amateur between his "real" poems and his "composed" poems, between the poems which expressed his demon directly and created their own form "willy-nilly," and the poems which, through the hocus pocus of technique, he spuriously put together and could, if necessary, revise. His belief in a "poetry of the immediate present," poetry in which nothing is fixed, static, or final, where all is shimmeriness and impermanence and vitalistic essence, arose from this mistaken notion of technique. And from this notion, an unsympathetic critic like D. S. Savage can construct a case which shows Lawrence driven "concurrently to the dissolution of personality and the dissolution of art." The argument suggests that Lawrence's early, crucial novel, *Sons and Lovers,* is another example of meanings confused by an impatience with technical resources.

The novel has two themes: the crippling effects of a mother's love on the emotional development of her son; and the "split" between kinds of love, physical and spiritual, which the son develops, the kinds represented by two young women, Clara and Miriam. The two themes should, of course, work together, the second being, actually, the result of the first: this "split" is the "crippling." So one would expect to see the novel developed, and so Lawrence, in his famous letter to Edward Garnett, where he says that Paul is left at the end with the "drift towards death," apparently thought he had developed it. Yet in the last few sentences of the novel, Paul rejects his desire for extinction and turns towards "the faintly humming, glowing town," to life—as nothing in his previous history persuades us that he could unfalteringly do.

The discrepancy suggests that the book may reveal certain confusions between intention and performance.

The first of these is the contradiction between Lawrence's explicit character-izations of the mother and father and his tonal evaluations of them. It is a problem not only of style (of the contradiction between expressed moral epithets and the more general texture of the prose which applies to them) but of point of view. Morel and Lawrence are never separated, which is a way of saying that Lawrence maintains for himself in this book the confused attitude of his character. The mother is a "proud, *honourable* soul," but the father has a "small, *mean* head." This is the sustained contrast; the epithets are characteristic of the whole; and they represent half of Lawrence's feelings. But what is the other half? Which of these characters is given his real sympathy—the hard self-righteous, aggressive, demanding mother who comes through to us, or the simple, direct, gentle, downright, fumbling, ruined father? There are two attitudes here. Lawrence (and Morel) loves his mother, but he also hates her for compelling his love; and he hates his father with the true Freudian jealousy, but he also loves him for what he is in himself, and he sympathizes more deeply with him because his wholeness has been destroyed by the mother's domination, just as his, Lawrence-Morel's, has been.

This is a psychological tension which disrupts the form of the novel and obscures its meaning, because neither the contradiction in style nor the confusion in point of view is made to right itself. Lawrence is merely repeating his emotions, and he avoids an austerer technical scrutiny of his material because it would compel him to master them. He would not let the artist be stronger than the man.

The result is that, at the same time that the book condemns the mother, it justifies her; at the same time that it shows Paul's failure, it offers rationalizations which place the failure elsewhere. The handling of the girl, Miriam, if viewed closely, is pathetic in what it signifies for Lawrence, both as man and artist. For Miriam is made the mother's scape-goat, and in a different way from the way that she was in life. The central section of the novel is shot through with alternate statements as to the source of the difficulty: Paul is unable to love Miriam wholly, and Miriam can love only his spirit. The contradictions appear sometimes within single paragraphs, and the point of view is never adequately objectified and sustained to tell us which is true. The material is never seen as material; the writer is caught in it exactly as firmly as he was caught in his experience of it. "That's how women are with me," said Paul. "They want me like mad, but they don't want to belong to me". So he might have said, and believed it; but at the end of the novel, Lawrence is still saying that, and himself believing it.

For the full history of this technical failure, one must read *Sons and Lovers* carefully and then learn the history of the manuscript from the book called *D. H. Lawrence: A Personal Record,* by one E. T., who was Miriam in life. The basic situation is clear enough. The first theme—the crippling effects of the mother's love—is developed right through to the end; and then suddenly, in the last few sentences, turns on itself, and Paul gives himself to life, not death. But all the way through, the insidious rationalizations of the second theme have crept in to destroy the artistic coherence of the work. A "split" would occur in Paul; but as the split is treated, it is superimposed upon rather than developed in support of the first theme. It is a rationalization made from it. If Miriam is made to insist on spiritual love, the meaning and the power of theme one are reduced; yet Paul's weakness is disguised. Lawrence could not separate the investigating analyst, who must be objective, from Lawrence, the subject of the book; and the sickness was not healed, the emotion not mastered, the novel not perfected. All this, and the character of a whole career, would have been altered if Lawrence had allowed his technique to discover the fullest meaning of his subject.

A Portrait of the Artist as a Young Man, like *Tono Bungay* and *Sons and Lovers,* is autobiographical, but unlike these it analyzes its material rigorously, and it defines the value and the quality of its experience not by appended comment or moral epithet, but by the texture of the style. The theme of *A Portrait,* a young artist's alienation from his environment, is explored and evaluated through three different styles and methods as Stephen Dedalus moves from childhood through boyhood into maturity. The opening pages are written in something like the stream of consciousness of *Ulysses,* as the environment impinges directly on the consciousness of the infant and the child, a strange, opening world which the mind does not yet subject to questioning, selection, or judgment. But this style changes very soon, as the boy begins to explore his surroundings, and as his sensuous experience of the world is enlarged, it takes on heavier and heavier rhythms and a fuller and fuller body of sensuous detail, until it reaches a crescendo of romantic opulence in the emotional climaxes which mark Stephen's rejection of domestic and religious values. Then gradually the style subsides into the austerer intellectuality of the final sections, as he defines to himself the outlines of the artistic task which is to usurp his maturity.

A highly self-conscious use of style and method defines the quality of experience in each of these sections, and, it is worth pointing out in connection with the third and concluding section, the style and method evaluate the experience. What has happened to Stephen is, of course, a progressive alienation from the life around him as he progressed in his initiation into it, and by the end of the novel, the alienation is complete. The final portion of the novel, fascinating as it may be for the developing aesthetic creed of Stephen-Joyce, is peculiarly bare. The life experience was not bare, as we know from *Stephen Hero;* but Joyce is forcing technique to comment. In essence, Stephen's alienation is a denial of the human environment; it is a loss; and the austere discourse of the final section, abstract and almost wholly without sensuous detail or strong rhythm, tells us of that loss. It is a loss so great that the texture of the notation-like prose here suggests that the end is really all an illusion, that when Stephen tells us and himself that he is going forth to forge in the smithy of his soul the uncreated conscience of his race, we are to infer from the very quality of the icy, abstract void he now inhabits, the implausibility of his aim. For *Ulysses* does not create the conscience of the race; it creates our consciousness.

In the very last two or three paragraphs of the novel, the style changes once more, reverts from the bare, notative kind to the romantic prose of Stephen's adolescence. "Away! Away! The spell of arms and voices: the white arms of roads, their promise of close embraces and the black arms of tall ships that stand against the moon, their tale of distant nations. They are held out to say: We are alone—come." Might one not say that the austere ambition is founded on adolescent longing? That the excessive intellectual severity of one style is the counterpart of the excessive lyric relaxation of the other? And that the final passage of *A Portrait* punctuates the illusory nature of the whole ambition?

For *Ulysses* does not create a conscience. Stephen, in *Ulysses,* is a little older, and gripped now by guilt, but he is still the cold young man divorced from the human no less than the institutional environment. The environment of urban life finds a separate embodiment in the character of Bloom, and Bloom is as lost as Stephen, though touchingly groping for moorings. Each of the two is weakened by his inability to reach out, or to do more than reach out to the other. Here, then, is the theme again, more fully stated, as it were in counter-point.

But if Stephen is not much older, Joyce is. He is older as an artist not only because he can create and lavish his Godlike pity on a Leopold Bloom, but also because he knows now what both Stephen and Bloom mean, and *how much*, through the most brilliant technical operation ever made in fiction, they can be made to mean. Thus *Ulysses*, through the imaginative force which its techniques direct, is like a pattern of concentric circles, with the immediate human situation at its centre, this passing on and out to the whole dilemma of modern life, this passing on and out beyond that to a vision of the cosmos, and this to the mythical limits of our experience. If we read *Ulysses* with more satisfaction than any other novel of this century, it is because its author held an attitude toward technique and the technical scrutiny of subject matter which enabled him to order, within a single work and with superb coherence, the greatest amount of our experience.

IV

In the United States during the last twenty-five years, we have had many big novels but few good ones. A writer like James T. Farrell apparently assumes that by endless redundancy in the description of the surface of American Life, he will somehow write a book with the scope of *Ulysses*. Thomas Wolfe apparently assumed that by the mere disgorging of the raw material of his experience he would give us at last our epic. But except in a physical sense, these men have hardly written novels at all.

The books of Thomas Wolfe were, of course, journals, and the primary role of his publisher in transforming these journals into the semblance of novels is notorious. For the crucial act of the artist, the unique act which is composition, a sympathetic editorial blue pencil and scissors were substituted. The result has excited many people, especially the young, and the ostensibly critical have observed the prodigal talent with the wish that it might have been controlled. Talent there was, if one means by talent inexhaustible verbal energy, excessive response to personal experience, and a great capacity for auditory imitativeness, yet all of this has nothing to do with the novelistic quality of the written result; until the talent is controlled, the material organized, the content achieved, there is simply the man and his life. It remains to be demonstrated that Wolfe's conversations were any less interesting as novels than his books which is to say that his books are without interest as novels. As with Lawrence, our response to the books is determined, not by their qualities as novels, but by our response to him and his qualities as a temperament.

This is another way of saying that Thomas Wolfe never really knew what he was writing *about*. Of Time and the River is merely a euphemism for Of a

Man and his Ego. It is possible that had his conception of himself and of art included an adequate respect for technique and the capacity to pursue it, Wolfe would have written a great novel on his true subject—the dilemma of romantic genius; it was his true subject, but it remains his undiscovered subject, it is the subject which *we* must dig out for him, because he himself had neither the lamp nor the pick to find it in and mine it out of the labyrinths of his experience. Like Emily Bronte, Wolfe needed a point of view beyond his own which would separate his material and its effect.

With Farrell, the situation is opposite. He knows quite well what his subject is and what he wishes to tell us about it, but he hardly needs the novel to do so. It is significant that in sheer clumsiness of style, no living writer exceeds him, for his prose is asked to perform no service beyond communication of the most rudimentary kind of fact. For his ambitions, the style of the newspaper and the lens of the documentary camera would be quite adequate, yet consider the diminution which Leopold Bloom, for example, would suffer, if he were to be viewed from these, the technical perspectives of James Farrell. Under the eye of this technique, the material does not yield up enough; indeed, it shrinks.

More and more writers in this century have felt that naturalism as a method imposes on them strictures which prevent them from exploring through all the resources of technique the full amplifications of their subjects, and that thus it seriously limits the possible breadth of aesthetic meaning and response. James Farrell is almost unique in the complacency with which he submits to the blunt techniques of naturalism; and his fiction is correspondingly repetitive and flat.

That naturalism had a sociological and disciplinary value in the nineteenth century is obvious; it enabled the novel to grasp materials and make analyses which had eluded it in the past, and to grasp them boldly; but even then it did not tell us enough of what, in Virginia Woolf's phrase, is "really real," nor did it provide the means to the maximum of reality coherently contained. Even the Flaubertian ideal of objectivity seems, today, an unnecessarily limited view of objectivity, for as almost every good writer of this century shows us, it is quite as possible to be objective about subjective states as it is to be objective about the circumstantial surfaces of life. Dublin, in *Ulysses*, is a moral setting: not only a city portrayed in the naturalistic fashion of Dickens' London, but also a map of the modern psyche with its oblique and baffled purposes. The second level of reality in no way invalidates the first, and a writer like Joyce shows us that, if the artist truly respects his medium, he can be objective about both at once. What we need in fiction is a devoted fidelity to every technique which will help us to discover and to evaluate our subject matter, and more than that, to discover the amplifications of meaning of which our subject matter is capable.

Most modern novelists have felt this demand upon them. André Gide allowed one of his artist-heroes to make an observation which considerably resembles an observation we have quoted from Wells. "My novel hasn't got a subject . . . Let's say, if you prefer it, it hasn't got *one* subject . . . 'A slice of life,' the naturalist school said. The great defect of that school is that it always cuts its slice in the same direction; in time, lengthwise. Why not in breadth? Or in depth? As for me I should like not to cut at all. Please understand; I should like to put everything into my novel." Wells, with his equally large blob of potential material, did not know how to cut it to the novel's taste; Gide cut, of course—in every possible direction. Gide and others. And those "cuts" are all the new techniques which modern fiction has given us. None, perhaps, is more important than that inheritance from French symbolism which Huxley, in the glittering wake of Gide, called "the musicalization of fiction." Conrad anticipated both when he wrote that the novel "must strenuously aspire to the plasticity of sculpture, to the colour of painting, and to the magic suggestiveness of music—which is the art of arts," and when he said of that early but wonderful piece of symbolist fiction, *Heart of Darkness,* "It was like another art altogether. That sombre theme had to be given a sinister resonance, a tonality of its own, a continued vibration that, I hoped, would hang in the air and dwell on the ear after the last note had been struck." The analogy with music, except as a metaphor, is inexact, and except as it points to techniques which fiction can employ as fiction, not very useful to our sense of craftsmanship. It has had an approximate exactness in only one work, Joyce's final effort, and an effort unique in literary history, *Finnegan's Wake,* and here, of course, those readers willing to approach the "ideal effort" Joyce demands, discovering an inexhaustible wealth and scope, are most forcibly reminded of the primary importance of technique to subject, and of their indivisibility.

The techniques of naturalism inevitably curtail subject and often leave it in its original area, that of undefined social experience. Those of our writers who, stemming from this tradition, yet, at their best, achieve a novelistic definition of social experience—writers like the occasional Sherwood Anderson, William Carlos Williams, the occasional Erskine Caldwell, Nathanael West, and Ira Wolfert in *Tucker's People,* have done so by pressing naturalism far beyond itself, into positively gothic distortions. The structural machinations of Dos Passos and the lyrical interruptions of Steinbeck are the desperate manoeuvres of men committed to a method of whose limitations they despair. They are our symbolists *manqué,* who end as allegorists.

Our most accomplished novels leave no such impression of desperate and intentional struggle, yet their precise technique and their determination to make their prose work in the service of their subjects have been the measure of their accomplishment. Hemingway's *The Sun Also Rises* and Wescott's *The Pilgrim Hawk* are works of art not because they may be measured by some external, neo-classic notion of form, but because their forms are so exactly equivalent with their subjects, and because the evaluation of their subjects exists in their styles.

Hemingway has recently said that his contribution to younger writers lay in a certain necessary purification of the language; but the claim has doubtful value. The contribution of his prose was to his subject, and the terseness of style for which his early work is justly celebrated is no more valuable, as an end in itself, than the baroque involutedness of Faulkner's prose, or the cold elegance of Wescott's. Hemingway's early subject, the exhaustion of value, was perfectly investigated and invested by his bare style, and in story after story, no meaning at all is to be inferred from the fiction except as the style itself suggests that there is no meaning in life. This style, more than that, was the perfect technical substitute for the conventional commentator; it expresses and it measures that peculiar morality of the stiff lip which Hemingway borrowed from athletes. It is an instructive lesson, furthermore, to observe how the style breaks down when Hemingway moves into the less congenial subject matter of social affirmation: how the style breaks down, the effect of verbal economy as mute suffering is lost, the personality of the writer, no longer protected by the objectification of an adequate technique, begins its offensive intrusion, and the entire structural integrity slackens. Inversely, in the stories and the early novels, the technique was the perfect embodiment of the subject and it gave that subject its astonishing largeness of effect and of meaning.

One should correct Buffon and say that style is the subject. In Wescott's *Pilgrim Hawk*, a novel which bewildered its many friendly critics by the apparent absence of subject, the subject, the story, is again in the style itself. This novel, which is a triumph of the sustained point of view, is only bewildering if we try to make a story out of the narrator's observations upon others; but if we read his observations as oblique and unrecognized observations upon himself the story emerges with perfect coherence, and it reverberates with meaning, is as suited to continuing reflection as the greatest lyrics.

The rewards of such respect for the medium as the early Hemingway and the occasional Wescott have shown may be observed in every good writer we have. The involutions of Faulkner's style are the perfect equivalent of his involved structures, and the two together are the perfect representation of the moral labyrinths he explores, and of the ruined world which his novels repeatedly invoke and in which these labyrinths exist. The cultivated sensuosity of Katherine Anne Porter's style has charm in itself, of course, but no more than with these others does it have aesthetic value in itself; its values lie in the subtle means by which sensuous details become symbols, and in the way that the symbols provide a network which is the story, and which at the same time provides the writer and us with a refined moral insight by means of which to test it. When we put such writers against a writer like William Saroyan, whose respect is reserved for his own temperament, we are appalled by the stylistic irresponsibility we find in him, and by the almost total absence of theme, or defined subject matter, and the abundance of unwarranted feeling. Such a writer inevitably becomes a sentimentalist because he has no means by which to measure his emotion. Technique, at last, is measure.

These writers, from Defoe to Porter, are of unequal and very different talent, and technique and talent are, of course, after a point, two different things. What Joyce gives us in one direction, Lawrence, for all his imperfections as a technician, gives us in another, even though it is not usually the direction of art. Only in some of his stories and in a few of his poems, where the demands of technique are less sustained and the subject matter is not autobiographical, Lawrence, in a different way from Joyce, comes to the same aesthetic fulfilment. Emily Bronte, with what was perhaps her intuitive grasp of the need to establish a tension between her subject matter and her perspective upon it, achieves a similar fulfilment; and, curiously, in the same way and certainly by intuition alone, Hemingway's early work makes a moving splendour from nothingness.

And yet, whatever one must allow to talent and forgive in technique, one risks no generalization in saying that modern fiction at its best has been peculiarly conscious of itself and of its tools. The technique of modern fiction, at once greedy and fastidious, achieves as its subject matter not some singleness, some topic or thesis, but the whole of the modern consciousness. It discovers the complexity of the modern spirit, the difficulty of personal morality, and the fact of evil—all the untractable elements under the surface which a technique of the surface alone can not approach. It shows us—in Conrad's words, from *Victory*—that we all live in an "age in which we are camped like bewildered travellers in a garish, unrestful hotel," and while it puts its hard light on our environment, it penetrates, with its sharp weapons, the depths of our bewilderment. These are not two things, but only an adequate technique can show them as one. In a realist like Farrell, we have the environment only, which we know from the newspapers; in a subjectivist like Wolfe, we have the bewilderment only, which we record in our own diaries and letters. But the true novelist gives them to us together, and thereby increases the effect of each, and reveals each in its full significance.

Elizabeth Bowen, writing of Lawrence, said of modern fiction, "We want the naturalistic surface, but with a kind of internal burning. In Lawrence every bush burns." But the bush burns brighter in some places than in others, and it burns brightest when a passionate private vision finds its objectification in exacting technical search. If the vision finds no such objectification, as in Wolfe and Saroyan, there is a burning without a bush. In our committed realists, who deny the resources of art for the sake of life, whose technique forgives both innocence and slovenliness—in Defoe and Wells and Farrell, there is a bush but it does not burn. There, at first glance, the bush is only a bush; and then, when we look again, we see that, really, the thing is dead.

Spatial Form in Modern Literature

JOSEPH FRANK

Modern Anglo-American poetry received its initial impetus from the Imagist movement of the years directly preceding and following the First World War. Imagism was important not so much for any actual poetry written by Imagist poets—no one knew quite what an Imagist poet was—but rather because it opened the way for later developments by its clean break with sentimental Victorian verbiage. The critical writings of Ezra Pound, the leading theoretician of Imagism, are an astonishing farrago of acute aesthetic perceptions thrown in among a series of boyishly naughty remarks whose chief purpose is to *épater le bourgeois*. But Pound's definition of the image, perhaps the keenest of his perceptions, is of fundamental importance for any discussion of modern literary form.

"An 'Image,'" Pound wrote, "is that which presents an intellectual and emotional complex in an instant of time." The implications of this definition should be noted: an image is defined not as a pictorial reproduction but as a unification of disparate ideas and emotions into a complex presented spatially in an instant of time. Such a complex does not proceed discursively, in unison with the laws of language, but strikes the reader's sensibility with an instantaneous impact. Pound stresses this aspect by adding, in the next paragraph, that only the *instantaneous* presentation of such complexes gives "that sense of sudden liberation; that sense of freedom from time limits and space limits; that sense of sudden growth, which we experience in the presence of the greatest works of art."

At the very outset, therefore, modern poetry advocates a poetic method in direct contradiction to Lessing's analysis of language. And if we compare Pound's definition of the image with Eliot's description of the psychology of the poetic process, we can see clearly how profoundly this conception has influenced our modern idea of the nature of poetry. For Eliot, the distinctive quality of a poetic sensibility is its capacity to form new wholes, to fuse seemingly disparate experiences into an organic unity. The ordinary man, Eliot writes, "falls in love, or reads Spinoza, and these two experiences have nothing to do with each other, or with the noise of the typewriter or the smell of cooking; in the mind of the poet these experiences are always forming new wholes." Pound had attempted to define the image in terms of its aesthetic attributes; Eliot, in this passage, is describing its psychological origin; but the result in a poem would be the same in both cases.

Such a view of the nature of poetry immediately gave rise to numerous problems. How was more than one image to be included in a poem? If the chief value of an image was its capacity to present an intellectual and emotional complex simultaneously, linking images in a sequence would clearly destroy most of their efficacy. Or was the poem itself one vast image, whose individual components were to be apprehended as a unity? But then it would be necessary to undermine the inherent consecutiveness of language, frustrating the reader's normal expectation of a sequence and forcing him to perceive the elements of the poem as juxtaposed in space rather than unrolling in time.

This is precisely what Eliot and Pound attempted in their major works. Both poets, in their earlier work, had still retained some elements of conventional structure. Their poems were looked upon as daring and revolutionary chiefly because of technical matters, like the loosening of metrical pattern and the handling of subjects ordinarily considered nonpoetic. Perhaps this is less true of Eliot than of Pound, especially the Eliot of the more complex early works like *Prufrock, Gerontion* and *Portrait of a Lady;* but even here, although the sections of the poem are not governed by syntactical logic, the skeleton of an implied narrative structure is always present. The reader of *Prufrock* is swept up in a narrative movement from the very first lines:

> Let us go then, you and I,
> When the evening . . .

And the reader, accompanying Prufrock, finally arrives at their mutual destination:

> In the room the women come and go
> Talking of Michelangelo.

At this point the poem becomes a series of more or less isolated fragments, each stating some aspect of Prufrock's emotional dilemma. But the fragments are now localized and focused on a specific set of circumstances, and the reader can organize them by referring to the implied situation. The same method is employed in *Portrait of a Lady,* while in *Gerontion* the reader is specifically told that he has been reading the "thoughts of a dry brain in a dry season"—the stream of consciousness of "an old man in a dry month, being read to by a boy, waiting for the rain." In both poems there is a perceptible framework around which the seemingly disconnected passages of the poem can be organized.

This was one reason why Pound's *Mauberley* and Eliot's early work were first regarded, not as forerunners of a new poetic form, but as latter-day *vers de société*—witty, disillusioned, with a somewhat brittle charm, but lacking that quality of "high seriousness' which Matthew Arnold had brandished as the touchstone of poetic excellence. These poems were considered unusual mainly because *vers de société* had long fallen out of fashion, but there was little difficulty in accepting them as an entertaining departure from the grand style of the nineteenth century.

In the *Cantos* and *The Waste Land,* however, it should have been clear that a radical transformation was taking place in aesthetic structure; but this transformation has been touched on only peripherally by modern critics. R. P. Blackmur comes closest to the central problem while analyzing what he calls Pound's "anecdotal" method. The special form of the *Cantos,* Blackmur explains, "is that of the anecdote begun in one place, taken up in one or more other places, and finished, if at all, in still another. This deliberate disconnectedness, this art of a thing continually alluding to itself, continually breaking off short, is the method by which the *Cantos* tie themselves together. So soon as the reader's mind is concerted with the material of the poem, Mr. Pound deliberately disconcerts it, either by introducing fresh and disjunct material or by reverting to old and, apparently, equally disjunct material."

Blackmur's remarks apply equally well to *The Waste Land,* where syntactical sequence is given up for a structure depending on the perception of relationships between disconnected word-groups. To be properly understood, these word-groups must be juxtaposed with one another and perceived simultaneously. Only when this is done can they be adequately grasped; for, while they follow one another in time, their meaning does not depend on this temporal relationship. The one difficulty of these poems, which no amount of textual exegesis can wholly overcome, is the internal conflict between the time-logic of language and the space-logic implicit in the modern conception of the nature of poetry.

Aesthetic form in modern poetry, then, is based on a space-logic that demands a complete reorientation in the reader's attitude toward language. Since the primary reference of any word-group is to something inside the poem itself, language in modern poetry is really reflexive. The meaning-relationship is completed only by the simultaneous perception in space of word-groups that have no comprehensible relation to each other when read consecutively in time. Instead of the instinctive and immediate reference of words and word-groups to the objects or events they symbolize and the construction of meaning from the sequence of these references, modern poetry asks its readers to suspend the process of individual reference remporarily until the entire pattern of internal references can be apprehended as a unity.

It would not be difficult to trace this conception of poetic form back to Mallarmé's ambition to create a language of "absence" rather than of presence —a language in which words negated their objects instead of designating them; nor should one overlook the evident formal analogies between *The Waste Land* and the *Cantos* and Mallarmé's *Un Coup de Dés.* Mallarmé, indeed, dislocated the temporality of language far more radically than either Eliot or Pound has ever done; and his experience with *Un Coup de Dés* showed that this ambition of modern poetry has a necessary limit. If pursued with Mallarmé's relentlessness, it culminates in the self-negation of language and the creation of a hybrid pictographic "poem" that can only be considered a fascinating historical curiosity. Nonetheless, this conception of aesthetic form, which may be formulated as the principle of reflexive reference, has left its traces on all of modern poetry. And the principle of reflexive reference is the link connecting the aesthetic development of modern poetry with similar experiments in the modern novel.

For a study of aesthetic form in the modern novel, Flaubert's famous county fair scene in *Madame Bovary* is a convenient point of departure. This scene has been justly praised for its mordant caricature of bourgeois pomposity, its portrayal—unusually sympathetic for Flaubert—of the bewildered old servant, and its burlesque of the pseudo-romantic rhetoric by which Rodolphe woos the sentimental Emma. At present, however, it is enough to notice the method by which Flaubert handles the scene—a method we might as well call cinematographic since this analogy comes immediately to mind.

As Flaubert sets the scene, there is action going on simultaneously at three levels; and the physical position of each level is a fair index to its spiritual significance. On the lowest plane, there is the surging, jostling mob in the street, mingling with the livestock brought to the exhibitions. Raised slightly above the street by a platform are the speechmaking officials, bombastically reeling off platitudes to the attentive multitudes. And on the highest level of all, from a window overlooking the spectacle, Rodolphe and Emma are watching the proceedings and carrying on their amorous conversation in phrases as stilted as those regaling the crowds. Albert Thibaudet has compared this scene to the mediaeval mystery play, in which various related actions occur simultaneously on different stage levels; but this acute comparison refers to Flaubert's intention rather than to his method. "*Everything should sound simultaneously*," Flaubert later wrote, in commenting on this scene; "one should hear the bellowing of cattle, the whispering of the lovers, and the rhetoric of the officials all at the same time."

But since language proceeds in time, it is impossible to approach this simultaneity of perception except by breaking up temporal sequence. And this is exactly what Flaubert does. He dissolves sequence by cutting back and forth between the various levels of action in a slowly rising crescendo until—at the climax of the scene—Rodolphe's Chateaubriandesque phrases are read at almost the same moment as the names of prize winners for raising the best pigs. Flaubert takes care to underline this satiric similarity by exposition as well as by juxtaposition—as if afraid the reflexive relations of the two actions might not be grasped: "From magnetism, by slow degrees, Rodolphe had arrived at affinities, and while M. le Président was citing Cincinnatus at his plow, Diocletian planting his cabbages and the emperors of China ushering in the new year with sowing-festivals, the young man was explaining to the young woman that these irresistible attractions sprang from some anterior existence."

This scene illustrates, on a small scale, what we mean by the spatialization of form in a novel. For the duration of the scene, at least, the time-flow of the narrative is halted; attention is fixed on the interplay of relationships within the immobilized time-area. These relationships are juxtaposed independently of the progress of the narrative, and the full significance of the scene is given only by the reflexive relations among the units of meaning. In Flaubert's scene, however, the unit of meaning is not, as in modern poetry, a word-group or a fragment of an anecdote; it is the totality of each level of action taken as an integer. The unit is so large that each integer can be read with an illusion of complete understanding, yet with a total unawareness of what Thibaudet calls the "dialectic of platitude" interweaving all levels and finally linking them together with devastating irony.

In other words, the adoption of spatial form in Pound and Eliot resulted in the disappearance of coherent sequence after a few lines; but the novel, with its larger unit of meaning, can preserve coherent sequence within the unit of meaning and break up only the time-flow of narrative. Because of this difference readers of modern poetry are practically forced to read reflexively to get any literal sense, while readers of a novel like *Nightwood,* for example, are led to expect narrative sequence by the deceptive normality of language sequence within the unit of meaning. But this does not affect the parallel between aesthetic form in modern poetry and the form of Flaubert's scene. Both can be properly understood only when their units of meaning are apprehended reflexively in an instant of time.

Flaubert's scene, although interesting in itself, is of minor importance to his novel as a whole and is skilfully blended back into the main narrative structure after fulfilling its satiric function. But Flaubert's method was taken over by James Joyce and applied on a gigantic scale in the composition of *Ulysses.* Joyce composed his novel of a vast number of references and cross references that relate to each other independently of the time sequence of the narrative. These references must be connected by the reader and viewed as a whole before the book fits together into any meaningful pattern. Ultimately, if we are to believe Stuart Gilbert, these systems of reference form a complete picture of practically everything under the sun, from the stages of man's life and the organs of the human body to the colours of the spectrum; but these structures are far more important for Joyce, as Harry Levin has remarked, than they could ever possibly be for the reader. And while students of Joyce fascinated by his erudition, have usually applied themselves to exegesis, our problem is to inquire into the perceptual form of his novel.

Joyce's most obvious intention in *Ulysses* is to give the reader a picture of Dublin seen as a whole—to re-create the sights and sounds, the people and places, of a typical Dublin day, much as Flaubert had re-created his *comice agricole.* And like Flaubert, Joyce aimed at attaining the same unified impact, the same sense of simultaneous activity occurring in different places. As a matter of fact, Joyce frequently makes use of the same method as Flaubert (cutting back and forth between different actions occurring at the same time) and he usually does so to obtain the same ironic effect. But Joyce faced the additional problem of creating this impression of simultaneity for the life of a whole teeming city, and of maintaining it—or rather of strengthening it— through hundreds of pages that must be read as a sequence. To meet this problem Joyce was forced to go far beyond what Flaubert had done. Flaubert had still maintained a clear-cut narrative line except in the county fair scene; but Joyce breaks up his narrative and transforms the very structure of his novel into an instrument of his aesthetic intention.

Joyce conceived *Ulysses* as a modern epic. And in the epic, as Stephen Dedalus tells us in *The Portrait of the Artist as a Young Man,* "the personality of the artist, at first sight a cry or a cadence and then a fluid and lambent narrative, finally refines itself out of existence, impersonalizes itself, so to speak . . . the artist, like the God of creation, remains within or beyond or above his handiwork, invisible, refined out of existence, indifferent, paring his finger-nails." The epic is thus synonymous for Joyce with the complete self-effacement of the author; and with his usual uncompromising rigour Joyce carries this implication further than anyone had previously dared.

For Joyce assumes—what is obviously not true—that all his readers are Dubliners, intimately acquainted with Dublin life and the personal history of his characters. This allows him to refrain from giving any direct information about his characters and thus betraying the presence of an omniscient author. What Joyce does, instead, is to present the elements of his narrative—the relations between Stephen and his family, between Bloom and his wife, between Stephen and Bloom and the Dedalus family—in fragments, as they are thrown out unexplained in the course of casual conversation or as they lie embedded in the various strata of symbolic reference. The same is true of all the allusions to Dublin life and history, and to the external events of the twenty-four hours during which the novel takes place. All the factual background summarized for the reader in an ordinary novel must here be reconstructed from fragments, sometimes hundreds of pages apart, scattered through the book. As a result, the reader is forced to read *Ulysses* in exactly the same manner as he reads modern poetry, that is, by continually fitting fragments together and keeping allusions in mind until, by reflexive reference, he can link them to their complements.

Joyce desired in this way to build up in the reader's mind a sense of Dublin as a totality, including all the relations of the characters to one another and all the events that enter their consciousness. The reader is intended to acquire this sense as he progresses through the novel, connecting allusions and references spatially and gradually becoming aware of the pattern of relationships. At the conclusion it might almost be said that Joyce literally wanted the reader to become a Dubliner. For this is what Joyce demands: that the reader have at hand the same instinctive knowledge of Dublin life, the same sense of Dublin as a huge, surrounding organism, that the Dubliner possesses as a birthright. It is this birthright that, at any one moment of time, gives the native a knowledge of Dublin's past and present as a whole; and it is only such knowledge that would enable the reader, like the characters, to place all the references in their proper context. This, it should be realized, is the equivalent of saying that Joyce cannot be read—he can only be reread. A knowledge of the whole is essential to an understanding of any part; but unless one is a Dubliner such knowledge can be obtained only after the book has been read, when all the references are fitted into their proper places and grasped as a unity. The burdens placed on the reader by this method of composition may well seem insuperable. But the fact remains that Joyce, in his unbelievably laborious fragmentation of narrative structure, proceeded on the assumption that a unified spatial apprehension of his work would ultimately be possible.

In a far more subtle manner than in either Joyce or Flaubert, the same principle of composition is at work in Marcel Proust. Since Proust himself tells us that his novel will have imprinted on it "a form which usually remains invisible, the form of Time," it may seem strange to speak of Proust in connection with spatial form. He has almost invariably been considered the novelist of time par excellence—the literary interpreter of that Bergsonian "real time" intuited by the sensibility, as distinguished from the abstract, chronological time of the conceptual intelligence. To stop at this point, however, is to miss what Proust himself considered the deepest significance of his work.

Oppressed and obsessed by a sense of the ineluctability of time and the evanescence of human life, Proust was suddenly, he tells us, visited by certain quasi-mystical experiences (described in detail in the last volume of his book, *Le Temps Retrouvé*). These experiences provided him with a spiritual technique for transcending time, and thus enabled him to escape time's domination. Proust believed that these transcendent, extratemporal moments contained a clue to the ultimate nature of reality; and he wished to translate these moments to the level of aesthetic form by writing a novel. But no ordinary narrative, which tried to convey their meaning indirectly through exposition and description, could really do them justice. For Proust desired, through the medium of his novel, to communicate to the reader the full impact of these moments as he had felt them himself.

To define the method by which this is accomplished, we must first understand clearly the precise nature of the Proustian revelation. Each such experience was marked by a feeling that "the permanent essence of things, usually concealed, is set free and our true self, which had long seemed dead but was not dead in other ways, awakes, takes on fresh life as it receives the celestial nourishment brought to it." This celestial nourishment consists of some sound, or odour, or other sensory stimulus, "sensed anew, simultaneously in the present and the past."

But why should these moments seem so overwhelmingly valuable that Proust calls them celestial? Because, Proust observes, imagination ordinarily can operate only on the past; the material presented to imagination thus lacks any sensuous immediacy. At certain moments, however, the physical sensations of the past came flooding back to fuse with the present; and Proust believed that in these moments he grasped a reality "real without being of the present moment, ideal but not abstract." Only in these moments did he attain his most cherished ambition—"to seize, isolate, immobilize for the duration of a lightning flash" what otherwise he could not apprehend, "namely: a fragment of time in its pure state." For a person experiencing this moment, Proust adds, the word "death" no longer has meaning. "Situated outside the scope of time, what could he fear from the future?"

The significance of this experience, though obscurely hinted at throughout the book, is made explicit only in the concluding pages, which describe the final appearance of the narrator at the reception of the Princesse de Guermantes. And the narrator decides to dedicate the remainder of his life to re-creating these experiences in a work of art. This work will differ essentially from all others because, at its root, will be a vision of reality refracted through an extra-temporal perspective. This decision, however, should not be confused with the Renaissance view of art as the guarantor of immortality, nor with the late nineteenth-century cult of art for art's sake (though Proust has obvious affinities with both traditions, and particularly with the latter). It was not the creation of a work of art per se that filled Proust with a sense of fulfilling a prophetic mission; it was the creation of a work of art that should stand as a monument to his *personal* conquest of time. His own novel was to be at once the vehicle through which he conveyed his vision and the *concrete experience* of that vision expressed in a form that compelled the world (the reader) to re-experience its exact effect on Proust's own sensibility.

The prototype of this method, like the analysis of the revelatory moment, appears during the reception at the Princesse de Guermantes'. The narrator has spent years in a sanatorium and has lost touch almost completely with the fashionable world of the earlier volumes; now he comes out of his seclusion to attend the reception. Accordingly, he finds himself bewildered by the changes in social position, and the even more striking changes in character and personality, among his former friends. No doubt these pages paint a striking picture of the invasion of French society by the upper bourgeoisie, and the gradual breakdown of all social and moral standards caused by the First World War; but, as the narrator takes great pains to tell us, this is far from being the most important theme of this section of the book. Much more crucial is that, almost with the force of a blow, these changes jolt the narrator into a consciousness of the passage of time. He tries painfully to recognize old friends under the masks that, he feels, the years have welded to them. And when a young man addresses him respectfully instead of familiarly, he realizes suddenly that, without being aware of it, he too has assumed a mask—the mask of an elderly gentleman. The narrator now begins to understand that in order to become conscious of time it has been necessary for him to absent himself from his accustomed environment (in other words, from the stream of time acting on that environment) and then to plunge back into the stream again after a lapse of years. In so doing he finds himself presented with two images—the world as he had formerly known it and the world, transformed by time, that he now sees before him. When these two images become juxtaposed, the narrator discovers that the passage of time may suddenly be experienced through its visible effects.

Habit is a universal soporific, which ordinarily conceals the passage of time from those who have gone their accustomed ways. At any one moment of time the changes are so minute as to be imperceptible. "Other people," Proust writes, "never cease to change places in relation to ourselves. In the imperceptible, but eternal march of the world, we regard them as motionless in a moment of vision, too short for us to perceive the motion that is sweeping them on. But we have only to select in our memory two pictures taken of them at different moments, close enough together however for them not to have altered in themselves—perceptibly, that is to say—and the difference between the two pictures is a measure of the displacement that they have undergone in relation to us." By comparing these two images in a moment of time, the passage of time can be experienced concretely through the impact of its visible effects on the sensibility. And this discovery provides the narrator with a method that, in T. S. Eliot's phrase, is an "objective correlative" to the visionary apprehension of the fragment of "pure time" intuited in the revelatory moment.

When the narrator discovers this method of communicating his experience of the revelatory moment, he decides, as we have already observed, to incorporate it in a novel. But the novel the narrator undertakes to write has just been finished by the reader; and its form is controlled by the method that he has outlined in its concluding pages. In other words, the reader is substituted for the narrator and is placed by the author throughout the book in the same position as that occupied by the narrator before his own experience at the reception of the Princesse de Guermantes. This is done by the discontinuous presentation of character—a simple device which nonetheless is the clue to the form of Proust's vast structure.

Every reader soon notices that Proust does not follow any of his characters continuously through the whole course of his novel. Instead, they appear and reappear in various stages of their lives. Hundreds of pages sometimes go by between the time they are last seen and the time they reappear; and when they do turn up again, the passage of time has invariably changed them in some decisive way. Rather than being submerged in the stream of time and intuiting a character progressively, in a continuous line of development, the reader is confronted with various snapshots of the characters "motionless in a moment of vision" taken at different stages in their lives; and in juxtaposing these images he experiences the effects of the passage of time exactly as the narrator had done. As Proust has promised, therefore, he does stamp his novel indelibly with the form of time; but we are now in a position to understand exactly what he meant by this engagement.

To experience the passage of time, Proust had learned, it was necessary to rise above it and to grasp both past and present simultaneously in a moment of what he called "pure time." But "pure time," obviously, is not time at all—it is perception in a moment of time, that is to say, space. And, by the discontinuous presentation of character Proust forces the reader to juxtapose disparate images spatially, in a moment of time, so that the experience of time's passage is communicated directly to his sensibility. Ramon Fernandez has acutely stressed this point in some remarks on Proust and Bergson. "Much attention has been given to the importance of time in Proust's work," he writes, "but perhaps it has not been sufficiently noted that he gives time the value and characteristics of space . . . in affirming that the different parts of time reciprocally exclude and remain external to each other." And he adds that, while Proust's method of making contact with his *durée* is quite Bergsonian (that is, springing from the interpenetration of the past with the present), "the reactions of his intelligence on his sensibility, which determine the trajectory of his work, would orient him rather toward a *spatialisation* of time and memory."

There is a striking analogy here between Proust's method and that of his beloved Impressionist painters; but this analogy goes far deeper than the usual comments about the "impressionism" of Proust's style. The Impressionist painters juxtaposed pure tones on the canvas, instead of mixing them on the palette, in order to leave the blending of colours to the eye of the spectator. Similarly, Proust gives us what might be called pure views of his characters— views of them "motionless in a moment of vision" in various phases of their lives—and allows the sensibility of the reader to fuse these views into a unity. Each view must be apprehended by the reader as a unit; and Proust's purpose is achieved only when these units of meaning are referred to each other reflexively in a moment of time. As with Joyce and the modern poets, spatial form is also the structural scaffolding of Proust's labyrinthine masterpiece.

The Sight Pattern in King Lear

ROBERT BECHTOLD HEILMAN

Gloucester's blindness is by no means a chance product of bitter vengeful-ness, interchangeable with any other punitive mutilation that might have satisfied his tormentors. Like that of Oedipus, it is wholly in harmony with the aesthetic and moral context; it is the centre of a whole family of cross references. Its ironic relationship to Gloucester's own defect of insight is clear enough. But that relationship is not merely left to inference; it is carefully established by the sight pattern, which not only tells us a good deal about Gloucester but is used to help qualify all the main characters in the play.

Gloucester's tragic flaw is a special kind of lack of insight. Gloucester is not a stupid man, but he is a man who does not ask enough questions, who takes evidence at its face value, who confounds appearance and substance. He is the man of the world, the sophisticate, as we might say, who has the naïveté ironically inseparable from the type.[1] His whole history is consistent. Long before the time of the play he enjoyed an adulterous liaison of which Edmund was the fruit—a liaison which indicated that he viewed sex morality entirely as a man of the world. His unperceptive worldliness is the opening note of the play: in the first few lines he talks to Kent with jaunty wit about his escapade with Edmund's mother—even, it appears, within earshot of Edmund. Gloucester does not take the trouble to go beneath the surface, he falls in with whatever is going on about him: this is his way of avoiding responsibility. When Edmund makes a specious case against Edgar (I.ii), Gloucester falls right in with Edmund's plans; he shows what we come to recognize as his characteristic suggestibility, and he dodges the responsibility of finding out what lies behind the superficial

---

[1] There is an excellent analysis of Gloucester in Granville Barker's *Prefaces*, I, 313 ff.

evidence. Lear's strange conduct and what he supposes to be that of Edgar elicit from him little more than startled exclamations; he wants to charge these distresses up to the "late eclipses in the sun and moon" (I.ii, 112)[2]—a convenient way of evading moral inquiry (very significantly, this astrological habit of mind is shared by no one else in the play). *Eclipses,* at the same time, is one of the hints of the *darkness* in which the now sound-eyed Gloucester is regularly operating. The light in which he sees things lights up only the surface of the world. It is quite consistent that he is inclined to get on with the new political regime: he plainly has his doubts about the way in which things are going, but that a principle is involved, a principle on which he should take a stand, simply does not occur to him. He falls in again. He regrets Cornwall's stocking Lear's follower, Kent (II.ii, 147 ff.); but he himself contributes to the infuriation of Lear by his efforts to "fix it up" between him and Cornwall. "You know the fiery quality of the Duke," he tells Lear (II.iv, 93), and, more maddeningly for Lear, "I would have all well betwixt you" (II.iv, 121). Gloucester hopes that he can "do business with" Cornwall; despite his genuine discomfort, he inclines toward the status quo. The *de facto,* the immediate, the circumscribing world hypnotize him: he cannot question. Yet Gloucester is not unalterably a bandwagon man; he can rise to become a tragic figure, and finally, shocked into a new alertness, he undertakes the commitment to Lear which is his ruin in the practical world whose creature he has been, but at the same time the salvation of his soul. But his spiritual awakening is very subtly managed; there is a fine stroke in the ambiguity of the terms in which Gloucester tells Edmund that he intends to aid Lear (III.iii). There is no doubt whatever that he pities Lear and realizes—note his phrase, "this unnatural dealing" (III.iii, 1)—at last that more is involved than political bad taste. But it is also true that he has been abused and mistreated by the usurpers, and that he says, "These injuries the King now bears will be revenged home; there's part of a power already footed; we must incline to the King" (III.iii, 11–13). He is waking up to the moral state of affairs, but in his consciousness there is also some hint that to be pro-Lear may be a good thing; and he is at least in part manoeuvring toward the comfortable stream of history. Gloucester does not consciously seek evil, or deliberately hunt for feather beds; it is simply that he is tragically slow in seeing what is implied in the situations in which he finds himself.

His being blinded, then, is an ironic completion of his career (III.vii). The symbolic reverberations of the scene are virtually unmistakable; yet Shakespeare does not leave the perception of them to chance. In fact, almost as if intent upon making us see them,[3] Shakespeare continues with this material which is fresh

---

[2] The line numbers are the standard ones which appear in the Globe, Arden, Kittredge, and other editions. Except for the passages which are not in the folios, I am using the folio readings almost entirely. My authority is Leo Kirschbaum, *The True Text of King Lear* (Baltimore, 1945).

[3] There is an early comment upon the relationship among various sight passages in G. G. Gervinus, *Shakespeare Commentaries,* tr. F. E. Bunnett (London and New York, 1892), p. 633. Bradley says that the play "purges the soul's sight by blinding that of the eyes" (*op. cit.,* p. 327). In *The Fool: His Social and Literary History* (London, 1935), Enid Welsford suggests that the sight pattern has a structural relationship to the play as a whole (pp. 263–64). Paul Kreider gives an

in our minds and devotes the very next scene (IV.i) to Gloucester. When the Old Man says, "You cannot see your way" (IV.i, 17), Gloucester replies:

> I have no way and therefore want no eyes;
> I stumbled when I saw.   (18–19)

Thus the symbolism becomes explicit: Gloucester here summarizes his whole career. With eyes he did not see, but now, blind, he has come a long way—far enough even to see into himself. He is beginning to master the eternal human problem. And he goes on:

> Ah, dear son Edgar,
> .   .   .   .
> Might I but live to see thee in my touch,
> I'ld say I had eyes again!   (21–24)

Though he can now only touch Edgar, he *sees* him—that is, the truth about him—as he did not see him before. And seeing Edgar is itself a symbol of understanding, so that, if Edgar were again restored to him, he could feel that he had eyes—that is, the power for which eyes are a symbol. Thus all the evidence of drama and language points to the conclusion that Gloucester's *hamartia* is, as we have said, failure to see essential things. Furthermore, it seems clear, this failure is meant to be evidenced in the original adultery which Coleridge[4] regards as Gloucester's originating moral misdeed. Near the end the philosophical Edgar, speaking of Gloucester, says to Edmund, "The dark and vicious place where thee he got/Cost him his eyes" (V.iii, 172–73). A reader sensitive to the symbolic pattern can hardly read *dark* as a mere rhetorical flourish or didactic cliché, especially when it is juxtaposed with "Cost him his eyes"; the place was *dark* because years before, Gloucester was exhibiting a characteristic failure to see what his deed involved. The unity of his career as it is symbolized in the sight pattern, is further supported by the bitter lines of

---

encyclopaedic record of all the uses of words of seeing and allied terms in the play (*Repetition in Shakespeare's Plays,* pp. 194–214). J. I. M. Stewart, in "The Blinding of Gloucester," *Review of English Studies,* XXI (1945), 264–70, defends the blinding of Gloucester upon the stage as the culmination of the sight symbolism in the play. After all this, Charles Olson, in *Call Me Ishmael* (New York, 1947), expresses surprise that the sight symbolism has not been observed. Although Olson's perception of the blindness paradox is not new, he adds new details in relating it to the language of the play (pp. 49–50).

    Professor Kreider's account, which I discovered long after my own analysis was finished, does both a service and a disservice to this kind of criticism. The service is its heroic completeness; it is well, in an analysis of language patterns, to collect every possible example of contributory words. But it is very important to eliminate words that do not have a fairly demonstrable function, and I feel that Professor Kreider has somewhat neglected this side of his critical process. As for his interpretation: he believes that the function of the sight words is merely to unify the Gloucester and Lear plots; but it is questionable whether the words could have this effect without having a symbolic function. I think that Professor Kreider senses the existence of such a function, for he speaks twice of Lear's "spiritual blindness" (pp. 195, 196), once of his "faulty moral vision" (p. 212), and again of "situations demonstrative of both moral and physical sight or blindness" (p. 213), but these phrases, I believe, exhaust his analysis of meaning. He seems unaware of the irony and paradox which are the heart of the pattern.

[4] *Coleridge's Shakespearean Criticism,* I, 57.

Gloucester near the end of the scene quoted above (IV.i), when he is making his arrangements to be guided by "Tom":

> Let the superfluous and lust-dieted man,
> That slaves your ordinance, that will not see
> Because he does not feel, feel your pow'r quickly.[5]
>
> (IV.i, 68–70)

At first glance we may take Gloucester's word to be an invoking of divine wrath against common types of evildoer. Actually, however, Gloucester is describing himself: he was "lust-dieted" and he "slaved" (i.e., contemned) divine ordinance; he would not see because he did not feel; and he has now felt—the repetition of the verb points to his sharpened sensibility—divine power. He understands himself wholly: the blind man has come to insight.

The irony of Gloucester's final condition is exactly paralleled by the irony of his earlier actions as a man with good eyes. Just when he most fails to see where he is going, he feels, like Oedipus, most shrewd and observant. The sight pattern points the issues for us. While he is being made to see things as Edmund wishes Gloucester feels that he is detecting the truth: "Let's see," he demands of Edmund three times (I.ii, 35, 45)—and he does not see. Again, ". . . if it be nothing, I shall not need spectacles" (35–36). Spectacles are a symbol of what he does need: Shakespeare hits upon the characteristic human frailty by which the denial of a deficiency actually announces the deficiency. It is altogether logical, then, that Edmund's next move against Edgar takes place *at night* (II.i): the physical darkness betokens Gloucester's failure to see into what is going on. The actors in the nocturnal setting, indeed, represent more than one phase of a human plight: Gloucester victimizes and Edgar is victimized—he flees at night —because of the same kind of unseeingness.[6] It is a meaningful, not merely a rhetorical, irony when Edmund calls, "Light, ho, here!/. . . Torches, torches! . . ." (33–34): those who want light least can call for it most loudly. Then Gloucester enters—how? ". . . with torches" (38)—the agent of light, but a kind of light—a physical reality like his eyes—that does him no good; it is inner illumination that he needs. It is at the end of this scene, finally, that Regan and Cornwall come to Gloucester's castle. They come, then, at night, a fact which we might easily pay no attention to if Shakespeare did not twice remind us of it. Edmund tells Edgar that Cornwall is coming, "now, i' th' night" (26); and then Regan's words add emphasis, "out of season, threading darkey'd night"—a phrase full of suggestion of things not seen and things not meant to be seen. Regan's thus coming into the sight pattern nicely amplifies the moral context:

---

[5] The echoes from one part of the play to another, which, as we shall see, are extraordinarily frequent, are illustrated by the fact that these last two speeches of Gloucester are reminders of the imaginary sins of which Edgar, as Tom, has given so full an account. Though a servingman, Tom appears to have been well off materially ("superfluous"); he "serv'd the lust of my mistress' heart" ("lust-dieted") and "did the act of darkness with her"; and he swore oaths "in the sweet face of heaven" (III.iv, 87–92).

[6] Cf. Edmund's way of reassuring Edgar: "You have now the good advantage of the night" (24).

Regan joins Edmund among those who utilize the dark. These must always have a Gloucester—the not-seeing, or, better, the late-seeing.

For gradually Gloucester comes to see—in practical terms, too late. The first glimmerings come to him in III.iii, when he tells Edmund of his decision to aid Lear. But even now, as we have seen, his motives are not altogether clear, and he is still in the dark about Edmund. In giving practical form to the allegiance to Lear upon which he has resolved, Gloucester again acts in the darkness of the night. In III.iv he hunts up Lear in the stormy night, just as he hunted for Edgar at night in II.i. This time he finds what he is looking for, and at the same time, so to speak, finds himself. The scene of his arrival on the heath is full of imaginative connections with other scenes. Just before Gloucester enters, the Fool says: "Now a little fire in a wild field were like an old lecher's heart— a small spark, all the rest on's body cold. Look, here comes a walking fire" (III.iv, 116–19). Since the play has opened with an account of Gloucester's lechery, it seems more than an accident that the Fool is given this particular simile just at the moment of Gloucester's entrance; we can hardly avoid reading it as a direct announcement of Gloucester. In another sense, too, the Fool's language is appropriate: Gloucester's heart has up until now been indeed but a "small spark," and, on the field of Lear's desolate situation, Gloucester's help is hardly more than "a little fire." Just at the moment when the Fool announces "a walking fire," Gloucester enters, significantly, "with a torch" (120). It is the only other time the play mentions lights. This time we feel that the torch is not ironic but symbolizes the first dim stage of enlightenment: Gloucester is no longer blindly confident as he travels the way of the world, and he exhibits a growing sympathy with Lear and a moderation of his attitude to Edgar, whom he once called villain repeatedly (II.i, 79 ff.) but of whom he now speaks in regret rather than anger (III.iv, 171 ff.). As I have said, he finds himself. In III.vi he warns Lear of the plot against his life. Just when Gloucester is at last taking a stand which can have very serious consequences, whether or not he can foresee them entirely, Edmund's plot against him matures. The very first threat against him is Goneril's "Pluck out his eyes" (III.vii, 5)—the eyes which have given Gloucester so limited a perception as to make him partially adjust himself to Goneril's own regime. He is arrested; then follows the "trial" scene; and his eyes are put out. He is deprived of the organs which he once used so superficially. Yet this happens just as he is at last coming to real insight.

The fifty lines of dialogue which accompany the gouging out of Gloucester's eyes are full of verbal commentary upon what is happening and its meaning. Cornwall is brutally direct: "Upon these eyes of thine I'll set my foot" (68). There is a minor tension between the horrifyingly fierce wit of Regan, "One side will mock another. Th' other too!" (71) and the dying sally of the Servant who has attacked Cornwall and has been stabbed from the rear by Regan, "My lord, you have one eye left/To see some mischief on him" (81–82)—which is at once a reminder of Gloucester's torture and yet the proffering of such comfort as may come from a slender hope of requital for the torturer. Repeatedly Cornwall betrays a mad passion to cut off the seeing process (68, 72), especially at the moment when, fatally wounded, he puts out Gloucester's second eye.

"Lest it see more, prevent it" (83). Each remark of his picks up a *see* from the preceding speaker: he is frenzied by the thought, which hardly takes clear form in his mind, of what Gloucester has seen.

Cornwall's ferocity here is in excellent contrast with his bathetically considerate dismissal, a little earlier, of Edmund, who is almost equally callous. Even this dismissal is done in terms of the sight imagery. It is just after Goneril has called "Pluck out his eyes" that Cornwall speaks thus to Edmund, "The revenges we are bound to take upon your traitorous father are not fit for your beholding" (7–8). Such considerateness sets off, also, the real, costly compassion which Gloucester has for Lear: and this is the heart of the scene—the growing insight of Gloucester. Gloucester is defensive at first, perhaps a little uncertain; but at last he recognizes the moment of decision. Questioned, he answers Regan, "Because I would not see thy cruel nails/Pluck out his poor old eyes; . . ." (56–57), his words ironically anticipating his own fate. He even becomes consciously prophetic, "But I shall see/The winged vengeance overtake such children" (65–66). The former peacemaker, once a little in awe of Gloucester, has thrown off his old character. Then Gloucester, "dark and comfortless" (85) as in the earlier night scenes, begs Edmund—who is physically absent now as he was spiritually deficient before, and whose physical absence Gloucester cannot see just as before he could not detect his spiritual shortcoming—to "enkindle all the sparks of nature" (86) to avenge him: Edmund is to be both a fire and a light. Instead, Gloucester ironically receives from Regan his climactic enlightenment: it was Edmund who "made the overture" (89) of Gloucester's treason, that is, laid it open to the eyes of Goneril and Regan. Yet the real climax comes in Gloucester's answer. Gloucester does not dwell on Edmund's treachery; in fact, he does not refer to Edmund at this moment or ever again. From now on, he is concerned about his own dreadful mistake and the wrong he has done Edgar. His words are,

> O my follies! then Edgar was abus'd.
> Kind gods, forgive me that, and prosper him!   (91–92)

Gloucester has leapt immediately to the truth about Edgar, as he might have done when Edmund first made his accusation. Then, he avoided the hard work of consulting Edgar's life—the true image of his character. Now, in his act of inference we see that his imagination—long dulled, or perhaps never active—is at work: insight comes to him. He whom Cornwall calls an "eyeless villain" (96) sees at last.

The blinding of Gloucester is at once an act of vengeance by the tyrants, an expiatory suffering by Gloucester,[7] and an ironic commentary upon human

---

[7] Some commentators are extraordinarily unwilling to see any sort of moral continuity in the play. Typical of these is George Brandes, who regards the opening scene as a lazy borrowing, full of incredible actions. Hence he can describe the "ruin of the moral world" as consisting in all the disasters to people of noble character. In Gloucester's experience all he sees is that "he who is merciful . . . , taking the suffering and injured under his roof, has the loss of his eyes for his reward" (*William Shakespeare: A Critical Study,* tr. by Archer and others [New York, 1898], II, 141). The ruin of the moral world comes about, however, not through the efficacy of evil, against innocent victim or tragic hero with *hamartia,* but through a general acquiescence in or rationalization of evil.

experience. In this final character it transcends the concocted irony which at first glance the coincidence of Gloucester's coming to insight and his being blinded might be mistaken for. The irony is not a put-up effect but is inseparable from a profound writer's attitude to his materials. "Out, vile jelly!/Where is thy lustre now?" (83–84)—Cornwall's words of triumph imply, as the speeches of Shakespeare's villains often do, more than he suspects. What Cornwall does not know is that Gloucester now sees better than he has ever seen; perhaps the final guarantee of his insight is his loss of outward sight. The vile jelly, the material seeing, had but caught reflections from the outer surfaces of life; as long as these were available to him, the seeing Gloucester was spiritually blind. The sisters and Cornwall cut him off from this outer world, which, as we know, circumscribed his vision; hence their fury is self-defeating, for they give him what their general conduct has already prepared him for—inward vision. His physical and material loss is spiritual gain: he who would find his life must lose it.

This is a basic paradox of the play. It is one of a series of paradoxes which, developed by the patterns, are the main structural determinants of *King Lear*. To have eyes, and to see not, is to be at the mercy of evil, and thus to aid evil. Not to see is not to understand: the sight pattern prepares us for the study of evil that finds its main treatment in the madness pattern.

It still remains for blind Gloucester to see one spiritual truth—that he must "bear/Affliction till it do cry out itself/'Enough, enough,' . . ." (IV.vi, 75–77). To this realization he is brought by Edgar, whose insight into his father enables him to defeat Gloucester's suicide—and the despair which makes Gloucester attempt suicide (IV.vi). Gloucester, indeed, provides a test for the kind of sight which his sons exhibit.[8] Shortly before the battle, for instance, Regan tells us all in one breath about a double errand of Edmund. Since the blind Gloucester evokes too much popular compassion, Edmund has gone

> In pity of his misery, to dispatch
> His nighted life; moreover, to descry
> The strength o' th' enemy.   (IV.v, 12–14)

Edmund has a purely practical vision which is a logical extension of his father's worldliness:[9] he sees that a blind man is dangerous to his side—the *pity* repre-

---

[8] Others are measured, also, by the way in which they look at him. Albany becomes a more clearly outlined character because of the shock with which he receives the news of the blinding of Gloucester (IV.ii, 72 ff.). Regan, on whose hard practical view of things more remains to be said, regards the blindness merely as an unfortunate source of popular indignation (IV.v, 8–10), and suggests to Oswald that it may be profitable to cut off "that blind traitor" (IV.v, 37–38). Hence to Oswald "that eyeless head" is only a possible source of advancement (IV.vi, 231–32). Oswald also belongs to the blind.

[9] See Chapter I, p. 34. Later Edmund looks at Lear in the same hard, pragmatic way. He has sequestered Lear, he tells Albany, lest the aged king "pluck the common bosom on his side/ And turn our impress'd lances in our eyes" (V.iii, 49–50). *Pluck* and *eyes* recall the blinding scene; we remember, also, that at the blinding scene the "common bosom," in the form of the Servant, revolted against Cornwall. Edmund's realism here makes it highly unlikely that we are to take literally Regan's statement that Edmund has gone to dispatch his father "in pity of his misery." Harbage does take it literally (*op. cit.*, p. 66), but Bradley calls it a "lie" (*op. cit.*, p. 299).

sents the only moment of hypocrisy in Regan since the opening scene—and goes with equal dispassionateness to kill him and to reconnoiter the enemy. He is the same coolly rational person that he was at the beginning of the play; we have a further hint at the nature of the evil with which the play is concerned.

In the scene of Gloucester's attempted suicide Edgar performs an ultimate act of love—protecting his father against himself, normally a function performed by parent for child. At the same time he sees a practical problem with a new skill.[10] Now the special significance of this scene lies in its being an almost exact duplicate of II.ii, in which Edmund tricks his father into believing that Edgar is plotting against him. Thus we have another of the play's structural echoes, a reciprocal enlightenment by two related parts. The two scenes show two different kinds of practical insight at work. In each scene a son deceives a blind father: Edmund an emotionally and morally blind father, for his own profit; Edgar, a physically blind father, in the interest of that father's spiritual self-mastery. The parallelism enters into the details. Whereas Edgar really protects his father against himself, Edmund *pretends* to do just that! ". . . if you violently proceed against him, mistaking his purpose, it would make a great gap in your own honour . . ." (I.ii, 89–92). Each son lets Gloucester believe that he is having his own way and controlling the situation. Even Gloucester's credulity appears with a certain consistency, a consistency which, as we shall see later, sheds light on Gloucester's position with respect to religion: in the first scene, he attributes troubles to eclipses; in the latter, his salvation to super-natural forces. But the nicest tie of all is in the radical opinion which Edmund attributes to Edgar, that "fathers declining, the father should be as ward to the son, and the son manage his revenue" (I.ii, 77–79). That is exactly the situation in Act IV: Gloucester has declined and is ward to Edgar. Edmund's practical insight enabled him to fool Gloucester completely: in the midst of apparently bright light, Gloucester was in real darkness. But now Edgar's insight has brought Gloucester out of the darkness of despair; his later dark world is illuminated by the light of love. The basic paradox of sight is amplified.

Blindness, then, is treated from two sides; on one side the blind person is an agent who brings on his own tragic catastrophe; on the other, he is the object of good or evil conduct by others who, as they mould him, exhibit their own way of looking at life. Each pattern points to the problem of values.

Gloucester, we have seen, is imposed upon, whereas Lear imposes; and this relationship we should keep clear. But what one imposes on other people is also a reflection of one's insight—insight into the implications of what one does, and into those upon whom one imposes something. Lear's problem, then, we might

---

[10] The sight pattern is used specifically to exhibit the once gullible Edgar as the possessor of a new resourcefulness. After he has killed Oswald, he says, "Let's see his pockets; . . . Let us see" (IV.vi, 261–63)—the very words Gloucester used in I.ii just before reading the forged letter signed "Edgar." Then Edgar finds and reads the letter in which Goneril encourages Edmund to kill Albany; with this knowledge Edgar goes on to plot successfully the overthrow of Edmund. First he plans to "strike the sight/ Of the death-practis'd Duke" (283–84) with Goneril's letter.

also expect to be underlined by the sight pattern,[11] and it is; and the applicability of the same poetic terms to both protagonists is one evidence of thematic kinship between them and thus of the unity of the play.

Lear, of course, is treated primarily in terms of the understanding, and the paradox of his wisdom is that it is concomitant with madness—a stroke of genius that raises the whole problem of the uses and limits of rationalism. But the madness pattern is enriched by the support of the sight pattern, which exhibits Lear as progressing, not from a blind sight to a seeing blindness, like Gloucester, but from an unwillingness to see, through a period of gradual anguished enlightenment, to a final passionate struggle to see. Early in the play Lear, blinded by anger, orders Kent, "Out of my sight!" (I.i, 159); there is more than chance in these words, for Kent picks them up immediately with, "See better, Lear, and let me still remain/The true blank of thine eye" (160–61). Kent sees what is involved; Lear does not. His vision called in question, Lear swears, ironically, by Apollo—the god of light; and Kent retorts, ". . . by Apollo, . . ./ Thou swear'st thy gods in vain" (162–63); both invoke the power of light, and Kent obeys only on an oath by Jupiter, the overriding absolute (181). Now, in another example of Shakespeare's regular use of parallelism of scenes, this episode is replayed, as it were, with variations, late in the play, where the effect combines irony and pathos: at the end of the play, Lear can hardly recognize Kent physically, as before he could not "see" Kent's moral quality and ordered him out of his sight. "Mine eyes are not o' th' best," he says, and "This' a dull sight" and "I'll see that straight" (V.iii, 279, 282, 287). Kent cannot comfort and aid Lear now just as, though he was willing enough, he could not give him needed help at the beginning. Suitably Kent comments, "All's cheerless, dark, and deadly" (290). The meaning of Lear's words extends far beyond the immediate context; they call into play again the paradox of experience embodied in Gloucester's history: he who is sure of his sight needs to question it, but he with a sense of "dull sight" in the world may see sharply within.

For if Lear is not clear about physical identities, he is now fairly straight about moral identities: he comes both to recognize Cordelia and to know what she stands for. The treatment of the Lear-Cordelia relationship forges a still more powerful sight link between first and final scenes. In Act I Lear says,

> . . . for we
> Have no such daughter, nor shall ever see
> That face of hers again.   (I.i, 265–67)

---

[11] In the experience of Lear there is of course no such event as the blinding of Gloucester to focus the sight pattern, and it is possible simply to read the language of sight in a literal and restricted sense. But the sight symbolism in the presentation of Gloucester, where it is explicit, can hardly be kept from transferring itself also to the passages by or concerning Lear. As Robert Penn Warren says, "Once the symbolic import of an image is established for our minds, that image cannot in its workings upon us elsewhere in the poem be disencumbered of that import, whether or not we are consciously defining it. The criterion for such full rather than restricted interpretation is consistency with the central symbolic import and, insofar as it is possible to establish the fact, with the poet's basic views as drawn from external sources" (*op. cit.*, pp. 89–90). We cannot establish Shakespeare's views from external sources, but the sight symbolism, as it appears in the Lear passages, is exactly consistent with "the central symbolic import." Besides,

He is, as we have said, banishing a part of himself, determining to be blind. But, as Lear is bitterly enlightened, the face becomes a symbol of the sole value worth having, and Lear not only comes to want to see that face again but at the end passionately studies it, searching for a sign of life. "Lend me a looking-glass," he cries (V.iii, 261); it is to be for him a mirror of physical life, and a mirror of the life of the spirit. His words also recall the joke of the Fool, "For there was never yet fair woman but she made mouths in a glass" (III.ii, 35–36). But this fair woman, far from looking at herself, can make no kind of sign for others to see. Just before he dies, Lear strains frantically, possibly convinced that he does see life:[12]

> Do you see this? Look on her, look, her lips!
> Look there, look there!   (V.iii, 310–11)

The frenzied searching of the face which he had once said he would never see again is a symbol of how his seeing, and the impulses that direct his seeing, have improved. Once he tossed light away; now, in the darkness of Act V, he seeks—and perhaps finds, for a moment—the illuminating love which came to Gloucester in his blindness. "Look up," Edgar says (312), but the time for looking has given way to sightless death.[13]

Between these opening and closing scenes there is, in Lear's experience, an unremitting stress upon darkness, a stress which permits us to feel still further the effects of the sight pattern. Always we are reminded of the tragic failure to see the truth in time—the failure of those who had the power of sight but did not use it. "So out went the candle, and we were left darkling," says the Fool in apparent jest[14] (I.iv, 237); yet *darkling* is rich in overtones. It is at this time in the play that—with Shakespeare's usual irony—Lear is beginning to regain his lost vision. In a few seconds he asks, of himself,

---

there is in the Lear passages the fact of recurrence which draws our attention to the existence of a sight pattern.

[12] Bradley, Granville-Barker, and Chambers agree that Lear dies in the ecstasy of thinking that Cordelia is alive (see Chambers, *op. cit.*, pp. 44–45). Chambers has observed the relationship between the first-act and fifth-act episodes which I am here discussing (p. 43).

[13] The sight pattern suggests that at the end the search for understanding animates even the supporting characters. "O, see, see!" cries Albany (V.iii, 304) as Lear stoops over Cordelia's body, just before his dying speech. Edgar, who earlier describes Lear as a "side-piercing sight" (IV.vi, 85; this is in direct contrast with Edmund's attitude to Lear), asks, when Lear has demanded a looking glass to determine whether Cordelia is breathing, "[Is this an] image of that horror?" (V.iii, 264). In his search for understanding he sees the episode as a likeness to the end of the world. His final words addressed to Lear, it may be worth noting, echo his words to Gloucester just after Gloucester's imaginary leap from Dover cliff. His words to Lear are, "Look up"; but Lear is dead. His words to Gloucester are, "Do but look up" (IV.vi, 59); Gloucester replies, "Alack, I have no eyes!" (60). The request to Gloucester has of course a quite literal meaning in the context: look at the height from which you have fallen. But the symbolic overtones are audible: see better what the moral situation is. And Gloucester, though he must mention his blindness, is seeing better. Perhaps, in speaking similarly to Lear at the end, Edgar, who is characteristically hopeful and encouraging, has some idea that Lear may be "brought around."

[14] Dr. Carl Hense wrote, in 1856, ". . . the point is, that the light of the moral world has now ceased to shine, and the darkness incessantly increases" (Furness, p. 460).

> Where are his eyes?
> Either his notion weakens, his descernings
> Are lethargied— (247–49);

his words are almost the equivalent of Gloucester's "I stumbled when I saw." "Alack, the night comes on," Gloucester says (II.iv, 303)—the night which is the penalty for blindness, even though a little light is now coming through to the blind. Lear swears, "Darkness and devils" (I.iv, 273), and Edgar carries the hint a bit further with remarks on the "prince of darkness" (III.iv, 148; vi, 7–8). In a distraught world even casual phrases reflect the kind of ill it suffers from, for it is the darkness, the failure to see, that is diabolical.[15] Lear asks where his eyes have been; then he swears, as it were, by the very blindness that is the source of the evil. These words are spoken in the storm and dark night— it is notable how much important action takes place in the dark night[16]—and then Lear falls gradually into mental darkness. Yet this darkness, instead of being a merciful blotting out of evil sights, brings with it paradoxically a new intensity of imaginative illumination. Like Gloucester, Lear sees better when normal faculties are gone. A terrible darkness and a terrible light coincide. Shakespeare makes this point explicitly in terms of the sight imagery: he has the physician tell Cordelia that his medicine "Will close the eye of anguish" (IV.iv, 15). Sleeping will cut off a burning vision—yet help restore a normal sight which cannot discern much less than anguish. Still, after this protracted dark night,[17] it is peculiarly right that almost the first words of Lear, after his restorative sleep, are, "Fair daylight?" (IV.vii, 52). At one level, of course, the words convey incredulity and sense of relief. But his inquiry opens a group of lines which symbolize the change in his power of seeing. He continues:

> I should e'en die with pity,
> To see another thus. I know not what to say.
> I will not swear these are my hands. Let's see,
>
> .   .   .   .
>
> *Cor.*   O, look upon me, sir,
> And hold your hands in benediction o'er me. (53–58)

He can see compassionately; he can inquire—"Let's see"—instead of insisting upon his own correctness with proud obstinacy (we recall that Gloucester, when he said, "Let's see," was being gulled, and Edgar used the same words when he was skilfully managing a situation); and he can look upon Cordelia, whom once he wanted never to see again. Of what she stands for, he will not lose sight again; yet in seeing her he will have to go through a final agony.

What must man see? How shall he see? Shakespeare constantly labored at

---

[15] Cf. Gloucester's later remark on what Lear "in hell-black night endur'd" (III.vii. 60).

[16] The chief of these are II.i, II.iv, III.i, ii, iii, iv, v, vi. It is possible, also, that the action of II.ii, in which Oswald is "in the dark," takes place before daybreak.

[17] Perhaps, after the continued stress upon darkness, it is not wholly fantastic to suggest that Lear's phrase in his second speech in the play—"our darker purpose" (I.i, 37)—can be read as containing, besides its literal meaning, a mild anticipation of things to come.

the question, and in a sense he came early to a specific problem of modern civilization, which from his time to ours has been casting old insights overboard and looking for replacements. At times the problem phrases itself for Shakespeare as the problem of innocence, to which he devoted himself more than once. Innocence—not seeing enough—may itself be a gateway to evil. Othello and Desdemona are the primary innocents. Gloucester and Edgar act on a different plane, of course, yet a little more of the serpent in either would have been practically useful to both. But in Shakespeare there is an unfailing use of counterpoint: there is always the glance at the other extreme. If failure to see is dangerous, seeing too well may be fatal: the lost souls in *King Lear* are those who see too well. Goneril and Regan have freed themselves of the old insights and learned to look sharply at the immediate world; they see nothing of spirit, but they miss few of the close facts of experience. There may therefore be more content than we normally assume in the hyperbolic assurance made to Lear by the sharp-eyed Goneril—she who later shrieks, as her sentence upon Gloucester, "Pluck out his eyes!"—that she loves him "dearer than eyesight" (I.i, 57)— the words which actually introduce the sight pattern in the play. What kind of eyesight that is is exactly defined by a subsequent phrase applied by Cordelia to her sisters, "still-soliciting eye" (234), and by Goneril's own words to Regan, "You see how full of changes his age is. The observation we have made of it hath not been little"[18] (291–92). That is, they see what the situation is and know how to manage it; indeed, they see things only too clearly. But the deficiencies of their shrewd kind of observation are not left merely to inference: Shakespeare points directly at them in Albany's "How far your eyes may pierce I cannot tell" (I.iv, 368) and in the Fool's ditty, "Fathers that wear rags/Do make their children blind" (II.iv, 48–49). Even these casual lines call our attention to a myopia that has spread ironically through a society. Yet the sisters' deficiency of sight is a very special case, for it is they who especially practice a realistic looking at things; here is one first suggestion of a counterpoint to the paradox of the blinded Gloucester who has insight—namely, the paradox of blindness in those who see too well.

To say that one's way of seeing things is an index of character is a truism; yet the truism lights up with poetic energy when it becomes identified with the patterns in *King Lear*.[19] When he comes to understand her (she "Look'd black upon me," he says—II.iv, 162), Lear curses Goneril thus: "You nimble lightnings, dart your blinding flames/Into her scornful eyes!" (II.iv, 167–68). This packed speech not only places Goneril more clearly in the system of meanings of the play (her "scornful eyes" symbolize her view of the moral values assumed by Lear and the others), but also sets up a double irony: it is not she who is blinded (she is already *blind*), but Gloucester who is blinded by her, and not she,

---

[18] In the second sentence, the *not* is from the Qq. Some editors stress the change in prose in the last twenty-five lines of I.i as a symbolic accompaniment of the change to the sisters' dispassionate calculations.

[19] Oswald's insolence creeps into his facial expression. Lear exclaims, "Do you bandy looks with me, you rascal?" (I.iv, 91).

but Lear himself, who is exposed to the lightning.[20] The irony takes a new tack a few lines later when Lear, speaking to Regan of Goneril, compares the sisters: "Her eyes are fierce; but thine/Do comfort and not burn" (II.iv, 175 76). But these fierce eyes, which Lear will soon find that Regan shares, do not look ahead: they do not sense retribution. In the imaginary trial scene in the farmhouse, Edgar says, "Look, where he stands and glares! Want'st thou eyes at trial, madam?" (III.vi, 25–26) that is, can you not see the foul fiend? A minute later Lear reinvokes the original symbol for his inevitable recantation of trust in Regan's kindness: her "warp'd looks proclaim/What store her heart is made on"[21] (III.vi, 56–57).

What comes of scornful and fierce eyes and warped looks? The distortion of experience which they bring to the minds behind them must ultimately incapacitate those minds. It is beautifully ironic that just when Albany has emerged from what we may assume to be a difficult conflict of loyalties and has come to see Goneril as she is, Goneril should sneer at him as a man "Who hast not in thy brows an eye discerning/Thine honour from thy suffering" (IV.ii, 52–53). We recognize the human pattern: Goneril wants Albany to be blind, for it is to her convenience that he do not see many things: yet the reassuring conviction that he is blind—which takes the paradoxical form of an accusation —serves for the first time to dull her practical sight: she does not detect in him a moral ally of the opposing forces. Or to put it another way: the great difficulty of true perception appears in the clear-sighted evil person's inability to recognize goodness in another; from such a failure may come insuperable danger. In fact, Goneril and her sister have got caught in a complex of self-betrayals, chief of

---

[20] Thus there is an unaccented lightning pattern, which really is an elaboration of the darkness-and-light pattern. In the storm Lear cries:

> You sulph'rous and thought-executing fires,
> Vaunt-couriers of oak-cleaving thunderbolts,
> Singe my white head! And thou, all-shaking thunder,
> Strike flat. . . .   (III.ii, 4–7)

Again, "Rumble thy bellyful! Spit, fire! spout, rain!" (III.ii, 14). If the storm symbolizes Lear's emotional suffering, the lightning is also excess of light—the new knowledge which is a part of the anguish he undergoes. The pattern is also used to help define the quality of the tragic protagonist, to indicate the apparent disproportion of nemesis to deed which characterizes tragedy. Cordelia asks, after the storm,

> Was this a face
> . . . .
> To stand against the deep dread-bolted thunder?
> In the most terrible and nimble stroke
> Of quick cross lightning?   (IV.vii, 31–35)

Before this, Gloucester, in his first partisan lines, extended the lightning pattern to characterize Goneril and Regan and suggest their future. It is after commenting on "such a storm as his bare head/ In hell-black night endur'd" (III.vii, 59–60) that he assures the sisters, "But I shall see/ The winged vengeance overtake such children" (III.vii, 65–66). Thunder and lightning are the agents of divine justice.

[21] This expression of relationship between manner of looking (seeing) and feeling prepares for Gloucester's subsequent line, which I have already discussed, on the man "that will not see/ Because he does not feel" (IV.i. 69–70).

which is their passion for Edmund: at the end all they can see is each other. The sight pattern demonstrates that his new turn is a logical continuation of the path they have already travelled. Regan suspects Goneril: "She gave strange eliads and most speaking looks/To noble Edmund" (IV.v, 25–26): the hard, realistic eye engages in love play. When Regan intimates that she may marry Edmund, Goneril retorts, "That eye that told you so look'd but asquint" (V.iii, 72). Without knowing it Goneril, who often phrases keen truths, actually summarizes, in this speech which comes close to the end, what the play has been saying about Regan and herself. One kind of eyesight was very dear to them; yet those who trust only to the outer eye and deny the inner find themselves, at the end, looking asquint.[22]

Shakespeare has found in sight a flexibly responding symbol for the problems which arise in connection with the point of view from which man judges the meaning of experience. He enriches his commentary on the problems by another use of his symbolic pattern, which heightens the contrast between the sisters and Cordelia. They look hard, scornful, fierce. But as early as Act I Cordelia can say she leaves "with wash'd eyes" (I.i, 271)—in tears, perhaps, but also cleansed of any mote that might deflect her clear view of her sisters.[23] Later her eyes are wet with tears; the tears which denote sympathy are themselves a way of looking at experience. Gloucester condemns the man who "will not see/ Because he does not feel"; shortly after his speech, Cordelia exemplifies the human being who sees because she does feel (IV.iii, 20). She feels compassion and cries; the tears come from the eyes; feeling and seeing are identified. Lear urges her not to cry (IV.vii, 71; V.iii, 23); and he constantly fights his own tears (II.iv, 280 ff.; IV.vi, 199–201). For a king, tears would be a surrender, a way of seeing failure, giving comfort to the point of view of those in control. With dry eyes he will observe what he missed before. And in resisting one impulse to cry he makes a self-criticism that has a double value: he threatens to "pluck out," if they weep again, his "old fond eyes" (I.iv, 323–24). As it turns out, it is not his eyes that are plucked out, but Gloucester's—because he did not finally surrender, but did show compassion to a public enemy. But the eyes which are "fond" because they would weep[24] have already been "fond" in another way: we are reminded again of Lear's original blindness.

---

[22] It may be pushing the evidence too far to suggest that, after the bodies of Goneril and Regan are brought out on the stage, Albany's words, "Cover their faces" (V.iii, 242) are, besides a command for the usual mantling of the dead, a reminder of what these faces especially contained—frowns, dark looks, scornful glances, lustful expressions. It is only twenty lines later that Lear begins studying Cordelia's face for signs of life, and fifty lines after this first calling for a glass that he dies, all his attention focused on Cordelia's face.

[23] This interpretation is made by W. L. Phelps in his edition of *King Lear* (the Yale Shakespeare [New Haven, 1917], p. 131).

[24] Weeping becomes not only necessary but obligatory after the death of Cordelia. Lear cries:

> Howl, howl, howl, howl! O, you are men of stone.
> Had I your tongues and eyes, I'ld use them so
> That heaven's vault should crack.   (V.iii, 257–59)

He wants them to show grief, of course; but what is also implied is that they should show insight into what Cordelia stood for.

By a full and varied use of all the functions of men's eyes Shakespeare has achieved a rich, multivalued symbolic expression of man's moral make-up. Kent, whose detachment and courage are set forth in the sight imagery,[25] uses a proverbial saying for a comment on Lear's ironic fate.

> Good King, that must approve the common saw,
> Thou out of heaven's benediction com'st
> To the warm sun!   (II.ii, 167–69)

The king's experience, that is, burns him; but the sun is light, also, and Lear, by suffering, receives illumination. Lear at first not only sees Cordelia in the wrong light, but encourages Burgundy to do likewise; the terms in which Cordelia and France comment upon Burgundy's view of Cordelia indicate that he is looking at her from the wrong point of view: his "regards" are "Aloof from th' entire point"[26] (I.i, 243). That is, his seeing is directed by the wrong values —a matter which other patterns to which we shall come make much of. This line, then, and that of Kent's have a choral value; and the aptness of the symbol appears in its ability to be used chorally.[27]

An effective chorus is never a flat statement which comes up with a two-plus-two-equals-four about the figures on the stage. It needs to be integral with the design, and wholly unselfconscious, and for that reason it comes best as a speech which belongs primarily to its own dramatic context but which, by its identification with the pattern of which the reader has become aware, transcends the context and becomes an imaginative commentary upon the whole world of the drama. When the Gentleman speaks of "impetuous blasts, with eyeless rage" (III.i, 8), surely his words "eyeless rage" suggest the essence of various actions—primarily the unseeing passion of Lear, but also that of Gloucester, and that of Cornwall to come, and of the sisters still later: rages

[25] The lines quoted in the text and in this note are spoken by Kent after he has been put into the stocks by Regan and Cornwall. Kent comments drily, "Nothing almost sees miracles/ But misery" (II.ii, 172–73). The passage as a whole contains some effective implied irony. Kent uses the sun as a metaphor for Lear's suffering (167–69), then prays to it as a bringer of light by which he may read Cordelia's letter (170–72), and then, with day coming on, calls for the darkness of sleep: "Take vantage, heavy eyes, not to behold/ This shameful lodging" (178–79). The darkness prayed for is different from the darkness of some of the other characters: it is desired because of a courageous unwillingness to dwell upon immediate ills.

[26] Mr. Ransom's article on Shakespeare's use of Latinate English (see Chapter I, note 5) encourages me in the suspicion that Shakespeare has embedded a number of bilingual puns in the lines which accompany Burgundy's rejection and France's acceptance of Cordelia. Just after Cordelia speaks of a "still-soliciting eye" France says,

> Love's not love
> When it is mingled with *regards* that stands
> Aloof from th'entire point.   (I.i, 241–43)

Cordelia says of Burgundy that "*respects* of fortune are his love" (251), and France, addressing Cordelia as "most lov'd *despis'd*" (254), comments that neglect has strangely kindled his love to "inflam'd *respect*" (258). The words which I have italicized are all derived from words of seeing, which the educated would certainly recognize.

[27] It is perhaps well to add a final assurance that there are many uses of words of seeing and of allied terms in *King Lear* which have no symbolic overtones but are restricted to their immediate literal meaning. There is an example at IV.iii, 19.

which are retribution and which call forth further retribution. When Edgar tells Gloucester that he can no longer look down the supposed cliff lest "the deficient sight/Topple down headlong" (IV.vi, 23–24), we can only think of the "deficient sight" that causes disaster throughout the play, and of those whom it has indeed toppled down headlong. When the Fool wittily exclaims, "All that follow their noses are led by their eyes but blind men . . ."[28] (II.iv, 68–70), the very fact that he makes his statement as a general truth strengthens the reminder that in the world of the play there are few that follow their eyes, or that have eyes to follow. Lear and Gloucester are blind to the meaning of those phenomena which betoken the presence of evil; Edmund, Goneril, and Regan to the existence of moral barriers to the consummation of their ambitions. But the blind man cannot be tricked by his eyes; whereas those who pride themselves on clear sight may be misled both by the world they seem to control and by the appearance of well-being within themselves. And after so much rage, so many reversals, so much agony, so much searching for truth, it is fitting for Edgar to close by saying, "We that are young/Shall never see so much . . ." An epoch has passed; the next stage in the cycle will be quieter and less searching.

What the sight pattern never lets us forget is the importance of man's way of looking at the world: the problem is not, "How shall the world be saved?" but "How shall the world be seen?" And since seeing implies understanding, the sight pattern brings us at least to the threshold of the larger question, "How shall the world be understood?" That question is the special material of the madness pattern, in which Lear dominates. The sight and madness patterns work together creatively: they build up a reservoir of unformulated but powerful impressions which, when channeled by such a summary line as Gloucester's " 'Tis the time's plague, when madmen lead the blind" (IV.i, 46), release through it immense poetic force.

---

[28] This is one of the points at which the smell pattern and the sight pattern work together. We shall come to many more examples of such collaborations.

PART 2

Genre
Criticism

Any critic who concentrates on formal distinctions in literature may be called, in the loose sense of the term, a Genre Critic. Typical distinctions are poetry, fiction, and drama; lyric and narrative; character types and kinds of stories; epic, tragedy, and comedy; and sub-genres such as the epistolary novel, comedy of manners, and impromptu theatre. On philosophical grounds, however, Genre Criticism is associated with the inductive method. The centre of the movement is the Chicago School, a group of critics whose theory of literature is based in Aristotle. The Chicago Critics are individuals, but the study of Genre Criticism, in any sense of the term, is best begun with a study of Aristotle and of their use of the inductive method as a foundation for literary criticism. The inductive method of Aristotle makes no pretence of metaphysical innocence. The method is not inductive merely or purely, in the manner of the idealized scientist who is supposed to approach a piece of work with his head innocent of all possible conclusions, all expectations. The distinction between induction and deduction, in fact, is often an oversimplification; and in order to understand the Aristotelean base of the Genre Critic it is necessary first to realize that method, whether inductive or deductive or something else, comes after ontology, not before. Unless method is understood in its proper role, the Genre Critic will be misread as a mechanical scholar who compiles, for example, the characteristics of the Horatian Ode and then, list in hand, reads other odes hunting for analogues.

Both Plato and Aristotle were intensely interested in principles and experience, in deduction and induction. And both knew perfectly well what Descartes, several centuries later, did not know: man cannot become a pure and innocent observer. The act of observation cannot take place apart from ideas. Ideas are necessary, practical, and they will not be shunted aside to wait until called. To choose a method is to make a metaphysical commitment, and Aristotle and the Genre Critics who ground their approach in his philosophy have always understood this quite clearly.

Aristotle's commitment is usually described, informally but accurately, as his attempt to get the real and the actual closer together than seemed possible in Plato's system. It was not easy to do. Plato's argument that the idea of a table is neither created nor destroyed by carpenters is a convincing argument. Man's consciousness of the principle by which a table stands rather than falls is one thing; man's use or nonuse of the principle is also one thing; but the existence of the principle is independent of man's consciousness and action. It may be difficult to say where the idea *is* when man has no knowledge of the principle of table legs and has never seen a table; but it is just as difficult to say where the idea *is* when you have a table right in front of you. And it is certainly awkward—as Berkeley was to find out—to maintain the position that an idea exists only when man is aware of it and ceases to exist if man is not aware of it. Still, Aristotle was a scientist, and his study of nature convinced him that a philosophy accurate to the world would have to show an intimate connection between idea and object.

The solution Aristotle finally came up with is called the doctrine of inherent forms. There is still a distinction between the real and the actual, as in Plato, but Aristotle believed the real to be inherent within the actual or physical structure of the object. The standard example is that of the acorn, which contains in its actual make-up the potential of the oak tree. The oak tree, in turn, is said to contain in its actual make-up the potential of lumber. Or one could draw examples from chemistry: inherent structure determines the capacity of lead to cause cohesion (and thus become a part of paint), or of carbon tetrachloride to reject oily substances (and thus become a part of soap). The doctrine of inherent forms, in short, is a doctrine which holds that the physical make-up of substances is a potential which constitutes idea.

It is in the step from metaphysics to aesthetics, however, that the Genre Critics have encountered their most difficult problem. The doctrine of inherent forms was developed from a study of the physical world, and it was not meant for artificial things like poems; but if the real is grounded in actual objects, the artificial is left in an embarrassing association with the unreal. Even if literature is artificial, it is not artificial in the sense of being private or in the sense of being arbitrary. A poem has no base that corresponds to the atomic structure of physical matter, but the power of the poem—for poet and reader—does have an objective status somewhere. The identity of that status is debated among Genre Critics, and while the argument goes forward there in the background is the enormous prestige of the metaphysical doctrine of inherent forms.

The major figures of Genre Criticism have defined their positions by the way they handle this problem. One important approach associates literature with a practical ethic that is reasoned rather than arbitrary and therefore objective rather than merely man-made. The most characteristic direction calls for an emphasis on style or eloquence, with rhetoric as the base in the objective world. A third answer, most significantly represented by Northrop Frye, is a combination of Genre Criticism and Archetypal Criticism; and here the archetypes themselves are held to be "universal forms," not make-believe merely, which explains, by the way, why Northrop Frye may be called, on substantive grounds, both a Genre Critic and an Archetypal Critic. Frye advocates the doctrine of inherent forms and the scientific method associated with it; but the form that he finds to be inherent is the paradigmatic structure of the archetypes.

But regardless of the method by which an individual Genre Critic finds for literature a base in the objective world, he does believe that he is working with objective materials. R. S. Crane, for example, believes that plot works on the audience as a type of rhetoric or dramatic reasoning, a "shaping force." Crane's analysis of the problem of empathy in *Macbeth* is a brilliant instance of the Genre Critic at work. In less capable hands, the method may become offensively systematic, especially to a beginning student. How, I have been asked in class, can a rigorous analysis reveal "the odour of the rose"? It's a good question and deserves an answer.

Knowledge, for Aristotle, was based on systematic analysis, as distinguished from the unsystematic or chaotic. If the subject under study is whimsical, the study itself should be systematic, not whimsical. If the subject is poetry, an imaginative use of metaphor and story, the study itself should still be systematic, not metaphorical and fictive.

The New Critic, because of his Platonic-Kantian base, in part, agrees. Criticism, he feels, should not be another poem, but the critical method for poetry is different in kind from, most notably, the scientific method; and the difference thus indicated is ontological.

For Plato, the real could not be captured in any physical instance. No table contains the principle by which a table may be balanced and made to stand. The principle exists apart from any and all actual tables and is neither created nor destroyed by man's use or nonuse or consciousness. The relation between the real and the actual, therefore, is always oblique, indirect, metaphorical, imaginative, and never literal. It follows, for the Formalist Critic, that any analysis which attempts to capture the *ding an sich* of a poem will fall into a methodology that is contrary to the nature of poetry. The Formalist Critic will stress the difference between the poem and the necessarily inadequate critique of the poem, and he will be rigorous himself in explicative studies of language and structure; but he will feel that he is working "by indirections to find directions out." A good critic, of course, must be an educated man; but theories of tragedies tend to become preconceptions, the Formalist Critic feels, and to prejudice the reading of *Hamlet* or the particular tragedy in hand.

For the Genre Critic, this is a blunder. He argues that knowledge of a thing cannot be discovered by working within the framework of the thing itself. To know the object (or poem) is to know it in the world, by a system which contains it. *Hamlet* will not provide a system by which we may have knowledge of *Hamlet*; a concept of tragedy, or of drama, is required.

Thus one of the strengths of the Genre Critic is his ability to make distinctions and connections. He will be quick to distinguish types of literature from one another. He will discriminate carefully among questions of viewpoint. And he will make his distinctions with an inductive open-mindedness. But his goal is to understand the original and individual poem by reading it in the contexts which enable the words to become a poem in the world rather than remain unformed and private.

Bibliography

Crane, R. S. "The Critical Monism of Cleanth Brooks." *Modern Philology*, XLV (1948), pp. 226–45.

———— *et al.*, ed. *Critics and Criticism: Ancient and Modern*. Chicago: University of Chicago Press, 1957.

Crane, R. S. "Interpretation of Texts and the History of Ideas." *College English*, II (1941), pp. 755–65.

————*The Languages of Criticism and the Structure of Poetry*. Toronto: University of Toronto Press, 1953.

————"Literature, Philosophy, and the History of Ideas." *Modern Philology*, III (1954), pp. 73–83.

————"Observations on a Story by Hemingway." In *Introduction to Literature*. Edited by Louis Locke, William M. Gibson, and George Arms. New York: Holt, Rinehart and Winston, 1967, pp. 409–17.

————"Questions and Answers in the Teaching of Literature." In *The Idea of the Humanities and Other Essays, Critical and Historical*. Chicago: University of Chicago Press, 1967, pp. 176–93.

Farmer, Norman K., Jr. "A Theory of Genre for Seventeenth-Century Poetry." *Genre*, III (1970), pp. 293–317.

Frye, Northrop. *The Anatomy of Criticism: Four Essays*. Princeton, N.J.: Princeton University Press, 1957.

———— *Fables of Identity*. New York: Harcourt, Brace and World, Inc., 1963.

————*The Well-Tempered Critic*. Bloomington, Ind.: Indiana University Press, 1963.

Keast, W. R., ed. *Seventeenth-Century English Poetry: Modern Essays in Criticism*. New York: Oxford University Press, 1962.

Maclean, Norman. "An Analysis of a Lyric Poem." *University of Kansas City Review*, VIII (1942), pp. 202–09.

McKeon, Richard. "Aristotle's Conception of Language and the Arts of Language." *Classical Philology*, XLI (1946), pp. 193–206; XLII (1947), pp. 21–50.

———— *Freedom and History*. New York: Noonday Press, 1952.

————"The Philosophic Bases of Art and Criticism." *Modern Philology*, XLI (1943), pp. 65–87; XLII (1944), pp. 129–71.

Olson, Elder. *Aristotle's Poetics and English Literature: A Collection of Critical Essays*. Chicago: University of Chicago Press, 1965.

————"The Poetic Method of Aristotle: Its Powers and Limitations." *English Institute Essays: 1951* (1952), pp. 70–94.

————*The Poetry of Dylan Thomas*. Chicago: University of Chicago Press, 1962.

————" 'Sailing to Byzantium' : Prolegomena to a Poetics of the Lyric." *University Review*, VIII (1942), pp. 209–19.

————*The Theory of Comedy*. Bloomington, Ind.: Indiana University Press, 1968.

————*Tragedy and the Theory of Drama*. Detroit: Wayne State University Press, 1961.

Scholes, Robert, ed. *Approaches to the Novel: Materials for a Poetics*. San Francisco: Chandler Publishing Company, 1966 (revised edition).

————*The Fabulators*. New York: Oxford University Press, 1967.

———— and Robert Kellogg *The Nature of Narrative*. New York: Oxford University Press, 1966.

Sacks, Sheldon. *Fiction and the Shape of Belief*. Berkeley: University of California Press, 1964.

Vance, William L. "Romance in *The Octopus*." *Genre*, III (1970), pp. 111–36.

Warner, A. Wick. "The 'Political' Philosophy of Logical Empricism." *Philosophical Studies*, II (1951), pp. 49–56.

Weinberg, Bernard. "From Aristotle to Pseudo-Aristotle." *Comparative Literature*, V (1953), pp. 97–104.

————"Scaliger versus Aristotle on Poetics." *Modern Philology*, XXXIX (1942), pp. 337–60.

Wimsatt, W. K., Jr. "The Chicago Critics." *Comparative Literature*, V (1953), pp. 50–74.

Wright, Austin McGiffert. *The American Short Story in the Twenties*. Chicago: University of Chicago Press, 1961.

Zaslove, Jerald. "Fiction Extended: The Genre of Apocalypse and Dead Ends." *Genre*, III (1970), pp. 17–39.

from *Aristotle's Poetics*

TRANSLATED BY LEON GOLDEN

I

Let us discuss the art of poetry, itself, and its species, describing the character of each of them, and how it is necessary to construct plots if the poetic composition is to be successful and, furthermore, the number and kind of parts to be found in the poetic work, and as many other matters as are relevant. Let us follow the order of nature, beginning with first principles.

Now epic poetry, tragedy, comedy, dithyrambic poetry, and most forms of flute and lyre playing all happen to be, in general, imitations, but they differ from each other in three ways: either because the imitation is carried on by different means or because it is concerned with different kinds of objects or because it is presented, not in the same, but in a different manner.

For just as some artists imitate many different objects by using colour and form to represent them (some through art, others only through habit), other artists imitate through sound, as indeed, in the arts mentioned above; for all these accomplish imitation through rhythm and speech and harmony, making use of these elements separately or in combination. Flute playing and lyre playing, for example, use harmony and rhythm alone; and this would also be true of any other arts (for example, the art of playing the shepherd's pipe) that are similar in character to these. Dancers imitate by using rhythm without harmony, since they imitate characters, emotions, and actions by rhythms that are arranged into dance-figures.

The art that imitates by words alone, in prose and in verse, and in the latter case, either combines various meters or makes use of only one, has been nameless up to the present time. For we cannot assign a common name to the mimes of Sophron and Xenarchus and the Socratic dialogues; nor would we have a name for such an imitation if someone should accomplish it through trimeters or elegiacs or some other such meter, except that the public at large by joining the term "poet" to a meter gives writers such names as "elegiac poets" and "epic poets." Here the public classifies all those who write in meter as poets and completely misses the point that the capacity to produce an imitation is the essential characteristic of the poet. The public is even accustomed to apply the name "poet" to those who publish a medical or scientific treatise in verse, although Homer has nothing at all in common with Empedocles except the meter. It is just to call Homer a poet, but we must consider Empedocles a physicist rather than a poet.

And in the same way, if anyone should create an imitation by combining all the meters as Chairemon did when he wrote *The Centaur,* a rhapsody composed by the use of all the meters, he must also be designated a poet. Concerning these matters let us accept the distinctions we have just made.

There are some arts that use all the means that have been discussed, namely, rhythm and song and meter, as in the writing of dithyrambs and nomic poetry[1] and in tragedy and comedy. A difference is apparent here in that some arts use all the various elements at the same time, whereas others use them separately. These, then, are what I call the differences in the artistic means through which the imitation is accomplished.

II

Artists imitate men involved in action and these must either be noble or base since human character regularly conforms to these distinctions, all of us being different in character because of some quality of goodness or evil. From this it follows that the objects imitated are either better than or worse than or like the norm. We find confirmation of this observation in the practice of our painters. For Polygnotus represents men as better, Pauson as worse, and Dionysius as like the norm.[2] It is clear that each of the above-mentioned forms of imitation will manifest differences of this type and will be different through its choosing, in this way, a different kind of object to imitate. Even in dancing, flute-playing, and lyre-playing it is possible for these differences to exist, and they are seen also in prose, and in verse that does not make use of musical accompaniment, as is shown by the fact that Cleophon represents men like the norm, Homer as better, and both Hegemon the Thasian (who was the first writer of parodies) and Nicochares, the author of the *Deiliad,* as worse.[3] The

---

[1] The dithyramb was originally a choral ode sung in honour of Dionysus, whereas nomic poetry was originally concerned with texts taken from the epic and was presented with a flute or lyre accompaniment.

[2] Polygnotus was one of the great painters of the fifth century B.C. Neither Pauson nor Dionysius are identified with certainty.

[3] Not much is known about the poets other than Homer mentioned here. Cleophon was a dramatic or epic writer; a small fragment of a parody of Hegemon of Thasos is preserved in Athenaeus; we have no further certain information about Nicochares.

same situation is found in dithyrambic and nomic poetry,[4] as we see in the way Timotheus and Philoxenus handled the Cyclops theme.[5] It is through the same distinction in objects that we differentiate comedy from tragedy, for the former takes as its goal the representation of men as worse, the latter as better, than the norm.

III

There is, finally, a third factor by which we distinguish imitations, and that is the manner in which the artist represents the various types of object. For, using the same means and imitating the same kinds of object, it is possible for the poet on different occasions to narrate the story (either speaking in the person of one of his characters as Homer does or in his own person without changing roles)[6] or to have the imitators performing and acting out the entire story.

As we said at the beginning, imitations are to be distinguished under these three headings: means, object, and manner. Thus, in one way, Sophocles is the same kind of imitative artist as Homer, since they both imitate noble men; but in another sense, he resembles Aristophanes, since they both imitate characters as acting and dramatizing the incidents of the story. It is from this, some tell us, that these latter kinds of imitations are called "dramas" because they present characters who "dramatize" the incidents of the plot.

By the way, it is also for this reason that the Dorians claim to be the originators of both tragedy and comedy. The Megarians—both those in Megara itself, who assert that comedy arose when democracy was established among them, and those Megarians in Sicily, who point out that their poet Epicharmus far antedates Chionides and Magnes[7]—claim to have originated comedy; in addition, some of the Dorians in the Peloponnesus claim to be the originators of tragedy. As proof of their contentions, they cite the technical terms they use for these art forms: for they say that they call the towns around their city *komai*, but that the Athenians call their towns *demoi*. By this they argue that the root of the name "comedian" is not derived from *komazein* [the word for "revelling"] but from *komai* [their word for the towns] that the comic artists visited in their wanderings after they had been driven in disgrace from the city. In support of their claim to be the originators of "drama," they point out that

---

[4] There is a lacuna in the text at this point where the name of another writer of nomic poetry was probably mentioned.

[5] Timotheus was a dithyrambic poet who lived in Miletus from 450–360 B.C.; Philoxenus was a dithyrambic poet who lived in Cythera from 436 to 380 B.C.

[6] The translation given of this phrase is based on the traditional text, which has been accepted by Butcher, Hardy, and Kassel. On philosophical and linguistic grounds, Bywater prefers to emend the text of the passage so that it reads as follows: "Given both the same means and the same kind of object for imitation, one may either (1) speak at one moment in narrative and at another in an assumed character, as Homer does; or (2) one may remain the same throughout, without any such change; or (3) the imitators may represent the whole story dramatically, as though they were actually doing the things described," (p. 7).

[7] Not much is known, in addition to what Aristotle tells us in the *Poetics*, about these three comic writers who lived in the early part of the fifth century B.C.

the word for "doing" is *dran* in their dialect, whereas Athenians use the word *prattein* for this concept.

Concerning the number and kind of distinctions that characterize "imitations," let us accept what has been said above.

IV

Speaking generally, the origin of the art of poetry is to be found in two natural causes. For the process of imitation is natural to mankind from childhood on: Man is differentiated from other animals because he is the most imitative of them, and he learns his first lessons through imitation, and we observe that all men find pleasure in imitations. The proof of this point is what actually happens in life. For there are some things that distress us when we see them in reality, but the most accurate representations of these same things we view with pleasure—as, for example, the forms of the most despised animals and of corpses. The cause of this is that the act of learning is not only most pleasant to philosophers but, in a similar way, to other men as well, only they have an abbreviated share in this pleasure. Thus men find pleasure in viewing representations because it turns out that they learn and infer what each thing is—for example, that this particular object is that kind of object; since if one has not happened to see the object previously, he will not find any pleasure in the imitation *qua* imitation but rather in the workmanship or colouring or something similar.

Since imitation is given to us by nature, as are harmony and rhythm (for it is apparent that meters are parts of the rhythms), men, having been naturally endowed with these gifts from the beginning and then developing them gradually, for the most part, finally created the art of poetry from their early improvisations.

Poetry then diverged in the directions of the natural dispositions of the poets. Writers of greater dignity imitated the noble actions of noble heroes; the less dignified sort of writers imitated the actions of inferior men, at first writing invectives as the former writers wrote hymns and encomia. We know of no "invective" by poets before Homer, although it is probable that there were many who wrote such poems; but it is possible to attribute them to authors who came after Homer—for example, the *Margites* of Homer himself, and other such poems. In these poems, the fitting meter came to light, the one that now bears the name "iambic" [i.e., invective] because it was originally used by men to satirize each other. Thus, of our earliest writers, some were heroic and some iambic poets. And just as Homer was especially the poet of noble actions (for he not only handled these well but he also made his imitations dramatic), so also he first traced out the form of comedy by dramatically presenting not invective but the ridiculous. For his *Margites* has the same relation to comedy as the *Iliad* and *Odyssey* have to tragedy. But when tragedy and comedy began to appear, poets were attracted to each type of poetry according to their individual natures, one group becoming writers of comedies in place of iambics, and the other, writers of tragedies instead of epics because these genres were of greater importance and more admired than the others.

Now then, the consideration of whether or not tragedy is by now sufficiently developed in its formal elements, judged both in regard to its essential nature and in regard to its public performances, belongs to another discussion. What is relevant is that it arose, at first, as an improvisation (both tragedy and comedy are similar in this respect) on the part of those who led the dithyrambs, just as comedy arose from those who led the phallic songs that even now are still customary in many of our cities. Tragedy, undergoing many changes (since our poets were developing aspects of it as they emerged), gradually progressed until it attained the fulfilment of its own nature. Aeschylus was the first to increase the number of actors from one to two; he also reduced the role of the chorus and made the dialogue the major element in the play. Sophocles increased the number of actors to three and introduced scene painting. Then tragedy acquired its magnitude. Thus by developing away from a satyr-play of short plots and absurd diction, tragedy achieved, late in its history, a dignified level. Then the iambic meter took the place of the tetrameter. For the poets first used the trochaic tetrameter because their poetry was satyric and very closely associated with dance; but when dialogue was introduced, nature itself discovered the appropriate meter. For the iambic is the most conversational of the meters— as we see from the fact that we speak many iambs when talking to each other, but few [dactylic] hexameters, and only when departing from conversational tone. Moreover, the number of episodes was increased. As to the other elements by which, we are told, tragedy was embellished, we must consider them as having been mentioned by us. For it would probably be an enormous task to go through each of these elements one by one.

V

As we have said, comedy is an imitation of baser men. These are characterized not by every kind of vice but specifically by "the ridiculous," which is a subdivision of the category of "deformity." What we mean by "the ridiculous" is some error or ugliness that is painless and has no harmful effects. The example that comes immediately to mind is the comic mask, which is ugly and distorted but causes no pain.

Now then, the successive changes in the history of tragedy and the men who brought them about have been recorded; but the analogous information about the history of comedy is lacking because the genre was not treated, at the beginning, as a serious art form. It was only recently that the archons began to grant choruses to the comic poets; until then, the performers were all volunteers. And it was only after comedy had attained some recognizable form that we began to have a record of those designated as "comic poets." Who introduced masks or prologues, who established the number of actors, and many other matters of this type, are unknown. The creation of plots came first from Sicily, where it is attributed to Epicharmus and Phormis; and it was first

Crates among the Athenian poets who departed from iambic [or invective] poetry and began to write speeches and plots of a more universal nature.

Now epic poetry follows the same pattern as tragedy insofar as it is the imitation of noble subjects presented in an elevated meter. But epic differs from tragedy in that it uses a single meter, and its manner of presentation is narrative. And further, there is a difference in length. For tragedy attempts, as far as possible, to remain within one circuit of the sun or, at least, not depart from this by much. Epic poetry, however, has no limit in regard to time, and differs from tragedy in this respect; although at first the poets proceeded in tragedy in the same way as they did in epic. Some of the parts of a poem are common to both tragedy and epic, and some belong to tragedy alone. Therefore, whoever can judge what is good and bad in tragedy can also do this in regard to epic. For whatever parts epic poetry has, these are also found in tragedy; but, as we have said, not all of the parts of tragedy are found in epic poetry.

VI

We shall speak about the form of imitation that is associated with hexameter verse and about comedy later. Let us now discuss tragedy, bringing together the definition of its essence that has emerged from what we have already said. Tragedy is, then, an imitation of a noble and complete action, having the proper magnitude;[8] it employs language that has been artistically enhanced by each of the kinds of linguistic adornment, applied separately in the various parts of the play; it is presented in dramatic, not narrative form, and achieves, through the representation of pitiable and fearful incidents, the catharsis of such pitiable and fearful incidents. I mean by "language that has been artistically enhanced," that which is accompanied by rhythm and harmony and song; and by the phrase "each of the kinds of linguistic adornment applied separately in the various parts of the play," I mean that some parts are accomplished by meter alone and others, in turn, through song.

And since [in drama] agents accomplish the imitation by acting the story out, it follows, first of all, that the arrangement of the spectacle should be, of necessity, some part of the tragedy as would be melody and diction, also; for these are the means through which the agents accomplish the imitation. I mean by diction the act, itself, of making metrical compositions, and by melody, what is completely obvious. Since the imitation is of an action and is accomplished by certain agents, the sort of men these agents are is necessarily dependent upon their "character" and "thought." It is, indeed, on the basis of these two considerations that we designate the quality of actions, because the two natural causes of human action are thought and character. It is also in regard

---

[8] There is no word in the Greek text for "proper" but I have followed the practice of several other translators who add a modifier to the term "magnitude" where it is logically warranted. The term "representation" has also been added to the final clause of this sentence because of Aristotle's insistence that the pleasure of tragedy is achieved *through imitation* (Ch. XIV, 11. 15–6). See L. Golden, "Catharsis," *TAPA*, XCIII (1962), 58.

to these that the lives of all turn out well or poorly. For this reason we say that tragic plot is an imitation of action.

Now I mean by the plot the arrangement of the incidents, and by character that element in accordance with which we say that agents are of a certain type; and by thought I mean that which is found in whatever things men say when they prove a point or, it may be, express a general truth. It is necessary, therefore, that tragedy as a whole have six parts in accordance with which, as a genre, it achieves its particular quality. These parts are plot, character, diction, thought, spectacle, and melody. Two of these parts come from the means by which the imitation is carried out; one from the manner of its presentation, and three from the objects of the imitation. Beyond these parts there is nothing left to mention. Not a few poets, so to speak, employ these parts; for indeed, every drama [theoretically has] spectacle, character, plot, diction, song, and thought.

The most important of these parts is the arrangement of the incidents; for tragedy is not an imitation of men, *per se,* but of human action and life and happiness and misery. Both happiness and misery consist in a kind of action; and the end of life is some action, not some quality.[9] Now according to their characters men have certain qualities; but according to their actions they are happy or the opposite. Poets do not, therefore, create action in order to imitate character; but character is included on account of the action. Thus the end of tragedy is the presentation of the individual incidents and of the plot; and the end is, of course, the most significant thing of all. Furthermore, without action tragedy would be impossible, but without character it would still be possible. This point is illustrated both by the fact that the tragedies of many of our modern poets are characterless, and by the fact that many poets, in general, experience this difficulty. Also, to take an example from our painters, Zeuxis illustrates the point when compared to Polygnotus; for Polygnotus is good at incorporating character into his painting, but the work of Zeuxis shows no real characterization at all. Furthermore, if someone arranges a series of speeches that show character and are well-constructed in diction and thought, he will not, by this alone, achieve the end of tragedy; but far more will this be accomplished by the tragedy that employs these elements rather inadequately but, nevertheless, has a satisfactory plot and arrangement of incidents. In addition to the arguments already given, the most important factors by means of which tragedy exerts an influence on the soul are parts of the plot, the reversal, and the recognition. We have further proof of our view of the importance of plot in the fact that those who attempt to write tragedies are able to perfect diction and character before the construction of the incidents, as we see, for example, in nearly all of our early poets.

The first principle, then, and to speak figuratively, the soul of tragedy, is the plot; and second in importance is character. A closely corresponding situation exists in painting. For if someone should paint by applying the most beautiful colours, but without reference to an overall plan, he would not please us as much as if he had outlined the figure in black and white. Tragedy, then,

---

[9] The text is corrupt here. The translation follows an emendation suggested by Vahlen and accepted by Bywater and Hardy.

is an imitation of an action; and it is, on account of this, an imitation of men acting.

Thought is the third part of tragedy and is the ability to say whatever is pertinent and fitting to the occasion, which, in reference to the composition of speeches, is the essential function of the arts of politics and rhetoric. As proof of this we point out that our earlier poets made their characters speak like statesmen, and our contemporary poets make them speak like rhetoricians. Now character is that part of tragedy which shows an individual's purpose by indicating, in circumstances where it is not clear, what sort of things he chooses or rejects. Therefore those speeches do not manifest character in which there is absolutely nothing that the speaker chooses or rejects. Thought we find in those speeches in which men show that something is or is not, or utter some universal proposition.

The fourth literary part is diction, and I mean by diction, as has already been said, the expression of thoughts through language which, indeed, is the same whether in verse or prose.

Of the remaining parts, melody is the greatest of the linguistic adornments; and spectacle, to be sure, attracts our attention but is the least artistic and least essential part of the art of poetry. For the power of tragedy is felt even without a dramatic performance and actors. Furthermore, for the realization of spectacle, the art of the costume designer is more effective than that of the poet.

VII

Now that we have defined these terms, let us discuss what kind of process the arrangement of incidents must be, since this is the first and most important element of tragedy. We have posited that tragedy is the imitation of a complete and whole action having a proper magnitude.[10] For it is possible for something to be a whole and yet not have any considerable magnitude. To be a whole is to have a beginning and a middle and an end. By a "beginning" I mean that which is itself not, by necessity, after anything else but after which something naturally is or develops. By an "end" I mean exactly the opposite: that which is naturally after something else, either necessarily or customarily, but after which there is nothing else. By a "middle" I mean that which is itself after something else and which has something else after it. It is necessary, therefore, that well-constructed plots not begin by chance, anywhere, nor end anywhere, but that they conform to the distinctions that have been made above.

Furthermore, for beauty to exist, both in regard to a living being and in regard to any object that is composed of separate parts, not only must there be a proper arrangement of the component elements, but the object must also be of a magnitude that is not fortuitous. For beauty is determined by magnitude and order; therefore, neither would a very small animal be beautiful (for one's view of the animal is not clear, taking place, as it does, in an almost unperceived length of time), nor is a very large animal beautiful (for then one's view does

---

[10] For the phrase "proper magnitude" see Ch. VI, f.n. 8.

not occur all at once, but, rather, the unity and wholeness of the animal are lost to the viewer's sight as would happen, for example, if we should come across an animal a thousand miles in length). So that just as it is necessary in regard to bodies and animals for there to be a proper magnitude—and this is the length that can easily be perceived at a glance—thus, also, there must be a proper length in regard to plots, and this is one that can be easily taken in by the memory. The limit of length in regard to the dramatic contests and in terms of the physical viewing of the performance is not a matter related to the art of poetry. For if it were necessary for a hundred tragedies to be played, they would be presented by timing them with water clocks as we are told happened on some occasions in the past. The limit, however, that is set in regard to magnitude by the very nature of the subject itself is that whatever is longer (provided it remains quite clear) is always more beautiful. To give a general rule, we say that whatever length is required for a change to occur from bad fortune to good or from good fortune to bad through a series of incidents that are in accordance with probability or necessity, is a sufficient limit of magnitude.

VIII

A plot is a unity not, as some think, merely if it is concerned with one individual, for in some of the many and infinitely varied things that happen to any one person, there is no unity. Thus, we must assert, there are many actions in the life of a single person from which no overall unity of action emerges. For this reason all those poets seem to have erred who have written a *Heracleid* and a *Theseid* and other poems of this type; for they think that since Heracles was one person it is appropriate for his story to be one story. But Homer, just as he was superior in other respects, also seems to have seen this point well, whether through his technical skill or his native talent, since in making the *Odyssey* he did not include all the things that ever happened to Odysseus. (For example, it happened that Odysseus was wounded on Parnassus and that he feigned madness at the time of the call to arms; but between these two events there is no necessary or probable relation.) Homer, rather, organized the *Odyssey* around one action of the type we have been speaking about and did the same with the *Iliad*. Necessarily, then, just as in other forms of imitation, one imitation is of one thing, so also, a plot, since it is an imitation of an action, must be an imitation of an action that is one and whole. Moreover, it is necessary that the parts of the action be put together in such a way that if any one part is transposed or removed, the whole will be disordered and disunified. For that whose presence or absence has no evident effect is no part of the whole.

IX

It is apparent from what we have said that it is not the function of the poet to narrate events that have actually happened, but rather, events such as might occur and have the capability of occurring in accordance with the laws of probability or necessity. For the historian and the poet do not differ by their writing in prose or verse (the works of Herodotus might be put into verse but they would, nonetheless, remain a form of history both in their metrical and prose versions). The difference, rather, lies in the fact that the historian narrates events that have actually happened, whereas the poet writes about things as they might possibly occur. Poetry, therefore, is more philosophical and more significant than history, for poetry is more concerned with the universal, and history more with the individual. By the universal I mean what sort of man turns out to say or do what sort of thing according to probability or necessity—this being the goal poetry aims at, although it gives individual names to the characters whose actions are imitated. By the individual I mean a statement telling, for example, "what Alcibiades did or experienced."

Now then, this point has already been made clear in regard to comedy; for the comic poets, once they have constructed the plot through probable incidents, assign any names that happen to occur to them, and they do not follow the procedure of the iambic poets who write about specific individuals. In regard to tragedy, however, our poets cling to the names of the heroes of the past on the principle that whatever is clearly capable of happening is readily believable. We cannot be sure that whatever has not yet happened is possible; but it is apparent that whatever has happened is also capable of happening for, if it were not, it could not have occurred. Nevertheless in some tragedies one or two of the names are well known and the rest have been invented for the occasion; in others not even one is well-known, for example, Agathon's *Antheus*,[11] since in this play both the incidents and the names have been invented, and nonetheless they please us. Thus we must not seek to cling exclusively to the stories that have been handed down and about which our tragedies are usually written. It would be absurd, indeed, to do this since the well-known plots are known only to a few, but nevertheless please everyone. It is clear then from these considerations that it is necessary for the poet to be more the poet of his plots than of his meters, insofar as he is a poet because he is an imitator and imitates human actions. If the poet happens to write about things that have actually occurred, he is no less the poet for that. For nothing prevents some of the things that have actually occurred from belonging to the class of the probable or possible, and it is in regard to this aspect that he is the poet of them.

Of the simple plots and actions the episodic are the worst; and I mean by episodic a plot in which the episodes follow each other without regard for the laws of probability or necessity. Such plots are constructed by the inferior poets because of their own inadequacies and by the good poets because of the actors. For since they are writing plays that are to be entered in contests (and so stretch the plot beyond its capacity) they are frequently forced to distort the sequence of action.

Since the imitation is not only a complete action but is also of fearful and pitiable incidents, we must note that these are intensified when they occur

---

[11] Agathon was a late fifth-century B.C. tragic poet whose work has not survived except in fragments. He appears, prominently, in Plato's *Symposium*.

unexpectedly, yet because of one another. For there is more of the marvellous in them if they occur this way than if they occurred spontaneously and by chance. Even in regard to coincidences, those seem to be most astonishing that appear to have some design associated with them. We have an example of this in the story of the statue of Mitys in Argos killing the man who caused Mitys' death by falling upon him as he was a spectator at a festival.[12] The occurrence of such an event, we feel, is not without meaning and thus we must consider plots that incorporate incidents of this type to be superior ones.

X

Plots are divided into the simple and the complex, for the actions of which the plots are imitations are naturally of this character. An action that is, as has been defined, continuous and unified I call simple when its change of fortune arises without reversal and recognition, and complex when its change of fortune arises through recognition or reversal or both. Now these aspects of the plot must develop directly from the construction of the plot, itself, so that they occur from prior events either out of necessity or according to the laws of probability. For it makes quite a difference whether they occur *because* of those events or merely *after* them.

XI

Reversal is the change of fortune in the action of the play to the opposite state of affairs, just as has been said; and this change, we argue, should be in accordance with probability and necessity. Thus, in the *Oedipus* the messenger comes to cheer Oedipus and to remove his fears in regard to his mother; but by showing him who he actually is he accomplishes the very opposite effect. And in *Lynceus,* Lynceus is being led away to die and Danaus is following to kill him; but it turns out, because of the action that has taken place, that Danaus dies and Lynceus is saved. Recognition, as the name indicates, is a change from ignorance to knowledge, bringing about either a state of friendship or one of hostility on the part of those who have been marked out for good fortune or bad. The most effective recognition is one that occurs together with reversal, for example, as in the *Oedipus*. There are also other kinds of recognition for, indeed, what we have said happens, in a way, in regard to inanimate things, even things of a very casual kind; and it is possible, further, to "recognize" whether someone has or has not done something. But the type of recognition that is especially a part of the plot and the action is the one that has been mentioned. For such a recognition and reversal will evoke pity or fear, and we have defined tragedy as an imitation of actions of this type; and furthermore, happiness and misery will appear in circumstances of this type. Since this kind of recognition is of persons, some recognitions that belong to this class will

---

[12] I have followed Butcher's, Hardy's, and Bywater's interpretation of this passage. Others, however, understand the phrase to mean "when he was looking at the statue."

merely involve the identification of one person by another when the identity of the second person is clear; on other occasions it will be necessary for there to be a recognition on the part of both parties: for example, Iphigenia is recognized by Orestes from her sending of the letter; but it is necessary that there be another recognition of him on her part.

Now then, these are two parts of the plot, reversal and recognition, and there is also a third part, suffering. Of these, reversal and recognition have been discussed; the incident of suffering results from destructive or painful action such as death on the stage, scenes of very great pain, the infliction of wounds, and the like.

XII

The parts of tragedy that we must view as formal elements we have discussed previously; looking at the quantitative aspect of tragedy and the parts into which it is divided in this regard, the following are the distinctions to be made: prologue, episode, exode, and the choral part, which is divided into parode and stasimon. These are commonly found in all plays, but only in a few are found songs from the stage and *kommoi*. The prologue is the complete section of a tragedy before the parode of the chorus; an episode is the complete section of a tragedy between complete choric songs; the exode is the complete section of a tragedy after which there is no song of the chorus. Of the choral part, the parode is the entire first speech of the chorus, the stasimon is a song of the chorus without anapests and trochees, and a *kommos* is a lament sung in common by the chorus and the actors. The parts of tragedy that we must view as formal elements we have discussed previously; the above distinctions have been made concerning the quantitative aspect of tragedy, and the parts into which it is divided in this regard.

XIII

What goals poets must aim at, what difficulties they must be wary of when constructing their plots, and how the proper function of tragedy is accomplished are matters we should discuss after the remarks that have just been made.

Since the plots of the best tragedies must be complex, not simple, and the plot of a tragedy must be an imitation of pitiable and fearful incidents (for this is the specific nature of the imitation under discussion), it is clear, first of all, that unqualifiedly good human beings must not appear to fall from good fortune to bad; for that is neither pitiable nor fearful; it is, rather, repellent. Nor must an extremely evil man appear to move from bad fortune to good fortune for that is the most untragic situation of all because it has none of the necessary requirements of tragedy; it both violates our human sympathy and contains nothing of the pitiable or fearful in it. Furthermore, a villainous man should not appear to fall from good fortune to bad. For, although such a plot would be in accordance with our human sympathy, it would not contain the necessary elements of pity and fear; for pity is aroused by someone who undeservedly falls into misfortune, and fear is evoked by our recognizing that it is someone like ourselves who encounters this misfortune (pity, as I say, arising for the former reason, fear for the latter). Therefore the emotional effect of the situation just mentioned will be neither pitiable nor fearful. What is left, after our considerations, is someone in between these extremes. This would be a person who is neither perfect in virtue and justice, nor one who falls into misfortune through vice and depravity; but rather, one who succumbs through some miscalculation. He must also be a person who enjoys great reputation and good fortune, such as Oedipus, Thyestes, and other illustrious men from similar families. It is necessary, furthermore, for the well-constructed plot to have a single rather than a double construction, as some urge, and to illustrate a change of fortune not from bad fortune to good but, rather, the very opposite, from good fortune to bad, and for this to take place not because of depravity but through some great miscalculation on the part of the type of person we have described (or a better rather than a worse one).

A sign of our point is found in what actually happens in the theatre. For initially, our poets accepted any chance plots; but now the best tragedies are constructed about a few families, for example, about Alcmaeon, Oedipus, Orestes, Meleager, Thyestes, Telephon, and any others who were destined to experience, or to commit, terrifying acts. For as we have indicated, artistically considered, the best tragedy arises from this kind of plot. Therefore, those critics make the very mistake that we have been discussing who blame Euripides because he handles the material in his tragedies in this way, and because many of his plots end in misfortune. For this is, indeed, the correct procedure, as we have said. The very great proof of this is that on the stage and in the dramatic contests such plays appear to be the most tragic, if they are properly worked out; and Euripides, even if, in other matters he does not manage things well, nevertheless appears to be the most tragic of the poets. The second ranking plot, one that is called first by some, has a double structure of events, as in the *Odyssey*, ending in opposite ways for the better and worse characters. It seems to be first on account of the inadequacy of the audience. For our poets trail along writing to please the tastes of the audience. But this double structure of events involves a pleasure that is not an appropriate pleasure of tragedy but rather of comedy. For in comedy, whoever are the greatest enemies in the story —for example, Orestes and Aegisthus—becoming friends at the end, go off together, and no one is killed by anyone.

XIV

Pity and fear can arise from the spectacle and also from the very structure of the plot, which is the superior way and shows the better poet. The poet should construct the plot so that even if the action is not performed before spectators, one who merely hears the incidents that have occurred both shudders and feels pity from the way they turn out. That is what anyone who hears the plot of the *Oedipus* would experience. The achievement of this effect through the spectacle does not have much to do with poetic art and really belongs to the business of producing the play. Those who use the spectacle to create not the fearful but only the monstrous have no share in the creation of tragedy; for we should not seek every pleasure from tragedy but only the one proper to it.

Since the poet should provide pleasure from pity and fear through imitation, it is apparent that this function must be worked into the incidents. Let us try to understand what type of occurrences appear to be terrifying and pitiable. It is, indeed, necessary that any such action occur either between those who are friends or enemies to each other, or between those who have no relationship, whatsoever, to each other. If an enemy takes such an action against an enemy, there is nothing pitiable in the performance of the act or in the intention to perform it, except the suffering itself. Nor would there be anything pitiable if neither party had any relationship with the other. But whenever the tragic incidents occur in situations involving strong ties of affection—for example, if a brother kills or intends to kill a brother or a son a father or a mother a son or a son a mother or commits some equally terrible act—there will be something pitiable. These situations, then, are the ones to be sought. Now, it is not possible for a poet to alter completely the traditional stories. I mean, for example, the given fact that Clytemnestra dies at the hands of Orestes, and Eriphyle at the hands of Alcmaeon; but it is necessary for the poet to be inventive and skilful in adapting the stories that have been handed down. Let us define more clearly what we mean by the skilful adaptation of a story. It is possible for the action to occur, as our early poets handled it, with the characters knowing and understanding what they are doing, as indeed Euripides makes Medea kill her children. It is also possible to have the deed done with those who accomplish the terrible deed in ignorance of the identity of their victim, only later recognizing the relationship as in Sophocles' *Oedipus*. The incident, here, is outside the plot, but we find an example of such an incident in the play itself, in the action of Astydamas' *Alcmaeon* or of Telegonus in the *Wounded Odysseus;*[13] and there is further a third type in addition to these that involves someone who intends to commit some fatal act through ignorance of his relationship to another person but recognizes this relationship before doing it. Beyond these possibilities, there is no other way to have an action take place. For it is necessary either to do the deed or not and either knowingly or in ignorance.

Of these possibilities, the case in which one knowingly is about to do the deed and does not is the worst; for it is repellent and not tragic because it lacks the element of suffering. Therefore, no one handles a situation this way, except rarely; for example, in the *Antigone,* Haemon is made to act in this way toward Creon. To do the deed knowingly is the next best way. Better than this is the case where one does the deed in ignorance and after he has done it recognizes his relationship to the other person. For the repellent aspect is not present, and the recognition is startling. But the most effective is the final type, for example,

[13] Astydamas was a fourth-century B.C. poet; the *Wounded Odysseus* may have been a play by Sophocles.

in the *Cresphontes,* where Merope is going to kill her son and does not, but, on the contrary, recognizes him, and in the *Iphigenia,* where a sister is involved in a similar situation with a brother, and in the *Helle,* where a son who is about to surrender his mother recognizes her.[14]

It is for this reason that, as we have said previously, tragedies are concerned with a few families. For proceeding not by art, but by trial and error, poets learned how to produce the appropriate effect in their plots. They are compelled, therefore, to return time and again to that number of families in which these terrifying events have occurred. We have now spoken sufficiently about the construction of the incidents and of what type the plot must be.

XV

In regard to character, there are four points to be aimed at. First and foremost, character should be good. If a speech or action has some choice connected with it, it will manifest character, as has been said, and the character will be good if the choice is good. Goodness is possible for each class of individuals. For, both a woman and a slave have their particular virtues even though the former of these is inferior to a man, and the latter is completely ignoble. Second, character must be appropriate. For it is possible for a person to be manly in terms of character, but it is not appropriate for a woman to exhibit either this quality or the intellectual cleverness that is associated with men. The third point about character is that it should be like reality, for this is different from making character virtuous and making it appropriate, as we have defined these terms. The fourth aspect of character is consistency. For even if it is an inconsistent character who is the subject of the imitation (I refer to the model that suggested the kind of character being imitated), it is nevertheless necessary for him to be consistently inconsistent. We have an example of unnecessarily debased character in the figure of Menelaus in the *Orestes,* of unsuitable and inappropriate character in the lament of Odysseus in the *Scylla* and the speech of Melanippe, and of inconsistency of character in *Iphigenia at Aulis* where the heroine's role as a suppliant does not fit in with her character as it develops later in the play.

In character, as in the construction of the incidents, we must always seek for either the necessary or the probable, so that a given type of person says or does certain kinds of things, and one event follows another according to necessity or probability. Thus, it is apparent that the resolutions of the plots should also occur through the plot itself and not by means of the *deus ex machina,* as in the *Medea,* and also in regard to the events surrounding the departure of the fleet in the *Iliad.* The *deus ex machina* must be reserved for the events that lie outside the plot, either those that happened before it that are not capable of being known by men, or those that occur after that need to be announced and spoken of beforehand. For we grant to the gods the power of seeing all things.

[14] The *Cresphontes* and the *Iphigenia,* the former no longer extant, are plays by Euripides. We have no further information concerning the *Helle.*

There should, then, be nothing improbable in the action; but if this is impossible, it should be outside the plot as, for example, in Sophocles' *Oedipus*.

Because tragedy is an imitation of the nobler sort of men it is necessary for poets to imitate the good portrait painters. For even though they reproduce the specific characteristics of their subjects and represent them faithfully, they also paint them better than they are. Thus, also, the poet imitating men who are prone to anger or who are indifferent or who are disposed in other such ways in regard to character makes them good as well, even though they have such characteristics, just as Agathon[15] and Homer portray Achilles.

It is necessary to pay close attention to these matters and, in addition, to those that pertain to the effects upon an audience that follow necessarily from the nature of the art of poetry. For, indeed, it is possible frequently to make mistakes in regard to these. We have spoken sufficiently about these matters in our published works.

XVI

What we mean by "recognition" we have indicated previously. Of the kinds of recognition that occur, there is one, first of all, that is least artistic, which poets mainly use through the poverty of their inspiration. This is the form of recognition that is achieved through external signs; some of these are birthmarks, for example, "the spearhead which the Earth-born are accustomed to bear," or the "stars" such as Carcinus wrote about in his *Thyestes*. Then there are characteristics that we acquire after birth. Of these some are found on the body, for example, scars; and others are external to the body, such as necklaces, and as another example, the ark through which the recognition is accomplished in the *Tyro*. It is also possible to employ these recognitions in better and worse ways; for example, Odysseus was recognized through his scar in one way by the nurse and in another way by the swineherds. Now those recognitions are less artistic that depend on signs as proof, as well as all that are similar to these; but those that derive from the reversal of action, as in the Bath Scene of the *Odyssey,* are better.

In second place come those recognitions that have been contrived for the occasion by the poet and are therefore inartistic. For example, the way Orestes in the *Iphigenia* makes known that he is Orestes; for Iphigenia made herself known through the letter, but he himself says what the poet wishes him to say but not what the plot requires. Therefore this type of recognition is rather close to the error that has already been mentioned; for it would have been just as possible for him to carry tokens with him. Another example of this type of recognition is the use of the "voice of the shuttle" in the *Tereus* of Sophocles.

The third type arises from our being stimulated by something that we see to remember an event that has an emotional significance for us. This type of recognition occurs in the *Cyprioe* of Dicaeogenes where the sight of the painting

---

[15] I have followed Butcher, Hardy, and Bywater in reading the name of the tragic poet here. Other scholars accept a manuscript reading of the word meaning "good."

brings forth tears, and also in the story of Alcinous where Odysseus hears the lyre player and, reminded of his past fortunes, weeps; in both instances, it was by their emotional reactions that the characters were recognized.

The fourth type of recognition occurs through reasoning, for example, in the *Choéphoroe* it is achieved by the deduction: Someone like me has come; there is no one resembling me except Orestes; he, therefore, has come. Another recognition of this type was suggested by Polyidus the Sophist in regard to Iphigenia; for it was reasonable for Orestes to infer that, since his sister was sacrificed, he was also going to be sacrificed. Again, in the *Tydeus* of Theodectes, the deduction is made that he who had come to find a son was, himself, to perish. Another example is in the *Phinidae* where the women, when they had seen the place, inferred their destiny: that since they had been exposed there, they were fated to die there.

There is also a type of composite recognition from false reasoning on the part of another character, for example, in the story of Odysseus, the False Messenger; for he said that he would know the bow that he had not seen, but it is false reasoning to suppose through this that he *would* recognize it again (as if he had seen it before).

The best recognition is the one that arises from the incidents themselves, striking us, as they do, with astonishment through the very probability of their occurrence as, for example, in the action of the *Oedipus* of Sophocles and in the *Iphigenia*, where it is reasonable for the heroine to wish to dispatch a letter. Such recognitions, alone, are accomplished without contrived signs and necklaces. The second best type of recognition is the one that is achieved by reasoning.

The Poetic Method of Aristotle:
Its Powers and Limitations

ELDER OLSON

"No especial recognition [writes A. E. Taylor] is given in Aristotle's own classification to the Philosophy of Art. Modern students of Aristotle have tried to fill in the omission by adding artistic creation to contemplation as a third fundamental form of mental activity, and thus making a threefold division of Philosophy into Theoretical, Practical, and Productive. The object of this is to find a place in the classification for Aristotle's famous *Poetics* and his *Rhetoric*. But the admission of the third division of Science has no warrant in the text of Aristotle, nor are the *Poetics* and *Rhetoric,* properly speaking, a contribution to Philosophy. They are intended as collections of practical rules for the composition of a pamphlet or a tragedy, not as a critical examination of the canons of literary taste."[1]

The problems touched upon in the passage just cited are important, for they involve the entire scheme of the Aristotelian sciences and the role of poetics within that scheme, and even raise the question whether the treatise on poetics is of philosophical character. They bear directly, therefore, on the whole matter of Aristotle's poetic method; and they illustrate not merely how questions of the powers and limitations of a method are dependent upon interpretation of the method but also how that interpretation, in turn, is dependent upon our interpretation of the larger scheme. With all respect to A. E. Taylor, I should like to look into these problems a little. I shall do so by considering (1) what knowledge, especially scientific knowledge, meant for Aristotle; (2) how, consequently, the subject of an art would be handled by him; (3) how all these

---

[1] A. E. Taylor, *Aristotle*, London, n.d., p. 19. See also pp. 88–90.

considerations affect the structure of the *Poetics;* (4) the consequent powers and limitations of his poetic method.

For Aristotle, all animals are capable of knowledge in some sense; the character of that knowledge, however, varies according to the object of knowledge, the nature of what is known, the faculties involved, and the end of the knowledge. Thus, all animals have at least one sense, that of touch, which tells them about the tangible,[2] and those with more senses have additional channels of information.[3] But the knowledge provided by sensation is of the fact alone, and is instantial only;[4] that is, it is knowledge, let us say, that this particular flame is hot, but not that flame generally is hot or why flame is hot. Some animals have memory, and so can supplement present sensation by past sensations; and man, moreover, is capable not merely of supplementing present sensation by past but also of so unifying memory that several memories of the same thing have a single effect; this capacity Aristotle calls *empeiria,* experience. Experience is also knowledge of a kind, and is similar to art and science; but art and science are, strictly speaking, produced out of experience, rather than identical with it. For experience is knowledge of individuals, while art and science are knowledge of universals, and although in reference to action and production (the sphere of which is the individual) men of experience alone succeed better than those who have theory without experience, experience provides knowledge of the fact, whereas artistic and scientific knowledge is of the cause.[5]

But scientific knowledge is not constituted simply by knowledge of universal and cause. Sensation, which gives particular information, is not scientific, but neither is intuition; if reference of individual to universal were all, intuition would be scientific knowledge, induction would be the solitary scientific process, and science would consist of scientific principles only. We moderns tend to classify the sciences as inductive or deductive; Aristotle thought that all sciences are both, in the sense that principles achieved through induction are utilized to demonstrate, through causal reasoning, the inherence of attributes in a subject.[6] Hence, for him scientific knowledge is a matter neither of mere generality nor of mere specificity, but is knowledge of cause as appropriate to (or, we might say, as commensurate or simultaneous with) the inherence of attribute in subject.[7] For example, the figure *ABC* has its internal angles equal to a straight angle; it has this attribute, not *qua* this individual triangle of wood or *qua* plane figure or *qua* isosceles triangle, but simply *qua* triangle, and the cause is the appropriate cause of the inherence of this attribute in the subject (triangle), in which it inheres primarily.[8] On this conception, the subject

---

[2] *De anima,* iii. 12. 434b 13–15. In order to avoid multiplying references I shall merely give the first that comes to mind, except when there is a special point in doing otherwise.

[3] *Analytica posteriora,* i. 18. 81a 36.

[4] *Physica,* i. 5. 189a 7, *Met.* i. 1. 981b 10 ff.

[5] *Metaphysica,* i. 1. 980a 21–981b9; *An. post.* i. 13. 22 ff.; 31. 87b 27 ff.

[6] *Loc. cit.*; see also *Phys.* i. 1. 184a 9 ff., *An. post.* i. 1. 71a ff.; ii. 19.

[7] *An. post.* i. 13. 15 ff.

[8] *Ibid.,* i. 9. 76a 3 ff.

matter of a science is neither determined by a subject simply, nor by an attribute or group of attributes simply, but by a subject as possessing certain attributes which inhere in it primarily. Thus, for Aristotle science is not single and all-comprehending; there are several different sciences, according to the inherence of different attributes in different subjects through different causes, and these sciences must necessarily differ in their principles.[9]

In a very general sense the methods of these sciences will be the same, for all will depend upon principles intuitively derived from experience of particulars, and all will be concerned with proof, via cause, of the inherence of attributes in a subject;[10] but more specifically their methods will differ, for as subjects differ, attributes and proofs of their inherence will differ:[11] not all causes will be relevant,[12] not all definitions will be constructed in the same way,[13] directions of proof will differ,[14] principles will differ in number and accuracy,[15] demonstration will be inappropriate to inexact subject matters concerned with probabilities,[16] probable reasoning will be inappropriate to exact subject matters concerned with necessary attributes,[17] and so forth. Again, not all questions relating to a given object are relevant to the science of that object, but only those which relate to that object as falling under a single universal. For example, not all questions relating to geometrical figures are geometrical questions, but only those which form premises for the theorems of geometry or its subaltern sciences, such as optics.[18] A single object, let us say, poetry, can fall under a whole variety of sciences, but not all questions raised concerning it are "poetical"; some will be metaphysical, some ethical, some political, and so forth. Distinguished as the sciences are in this general scheme, they have also a basic communion, for all are connected through the common axioms of demonstration and the common disciplines such as dialectic.[19]

We have, thus, a body of sciences distinct from each other in subject matter, problems, and methods, but still interconnected. Aristotle divides the sciences into three groups, the theoretical, the practical, and the productive, or "poetic," sciences; he not only makes this division explicitly a number of times (although Taylor has strangely failed to find warrant for it),[20] but makes many correlative distinctions, such as the numerous ones between "knowing," "doing," and "making,"[21] and as a matter of fact the very foundations of his method demand this primary distinction.[22]

[9] *Ibid.*, i. 9. 75b 37 ff.; i. 10. 76a 37 ff.; i. 28. 87a 38 ff.

[10] *Ibid.*, ii. 19. 100b 1–18.   [11] *Ibid.*, i. 32. 88a 17–88b 29.

[12] *De an.* i. 1. 403a 25–403b 17.   [13] *Phys.* ii. 2.

[14] *Met.* vii. 7. 1032a 25; *Phys.* ii. 9. 200a 15.   [15] *An. post.* i. 27.

[16] *Nicomachean ethics*, i. 3. 1094b 23–27.   [17] 1094b 28.

[18] *An. post.* i. 7. 75a 37–75b 20; i. 12. 77a 40 ff.   [19] *Ibid.*, i. 11. 77a 26 ff.

[20] *E.g.*, *Met.* i. 1. 982a 1; vi. 1. 1025b 21, 1025b 26; ix, 2. 1046b 3.

[21] *Nic. eth.* vi. 4. 1140a 1; also 3. 1139b–4. 1140a 24.

[22] Since art is distinct from theoretical science (*ibid.*, vi. 3) and since making and acting are different (1140a 16), and since these distinctions go back radically to the distinction of the sciences in terms of causes, which in turn rests on the subject-attribute-cause formulation of scientific knowledge, the very pivot of the Aristotelian philosophy.

The theoretical sciences—metaphysics, mathematics, and physics—differ as they may in certain respects from each other, are alike in that they involve necessary propositions and have knowledge as their end. In the practical sciences of ethics and politics, knowledge is subordinate to action—one knows what virtue is in order to act virtuously[23]—and in the productive sciences, which are the arts, whether useful or fine, the end is neither knowledge nor action, but the product to be produced. As the practical sciences are less exact than the theoretical, so the productive are less exact than the practical; for sciences are more exact as they involve fewer elements[24] and are less dependent upon other sciences[25]—thus, arithmetic is more exact than geometry—whereas the practical sciences derive many propositions from the theoretical, and in turn the productive derive propositions from both theoretical and practical sciences.

The *Poetics* is so sharply determined in its problems and method by the fact that it is a treatise of productive science that we may well occupy ourselves briefly with some considerations concerning the scope and structure of such science. In the first place, is scientific knowledge of poetry possible? Not, we must answer, if it is a matter of the accidental or the incidental. There is no science of the accidental for Aristotle:[26] science is concerned only with what happens always or for the most part, with what is necessary or probable;[27] hence, to ask whether a science is possible is to ask whether some subject can be found in which attributes inhere, and that not accidentally. Hence, poetic science cannot center in the artist or the producer; for, although art has a natural basis in man, nature does not produce art, and artistic activity is not a necessary attribute of man. Again, the activity itself cannot serve as the subject, for it does not contain its principle in itself; it is for the sake of the product and is determined by the product. The distinction between doing and making is precisely that in doing the activity contains its own end (Happiness, the end of virtue, is an activity and not a quality for Aristotle), whereas in making the end is a product produced over and above the activity—that is, the productive action is for the sake of the product. The ethical and political sciences are possible because ethical and political activities contain as principles their own ends; but a science of artistic capacity or activity, apart from consideration of the product, is not. We are left, thus, with the product itself as a possible subject.

Moreover, according to Aristotle all art is concerned with coming into being, that is,

> with contriving and considering how something may come into being which is capable of either being or not being and whose origin is in the maker, not in the thing made; for art is concerned neither with things that are or come into being by necessity nor with things that do so in accordance with nature, since these latter have their origin in themselves.[28]

[23] *Ibid.*, i. 3. 1095a 5.
[25] *Met.* i. 2. 982a 25 ff.
[27] *Met.* vi. 2. 1027a 20–21.

[24] *An. post.* i. 27. 87a 33.
[26] *Ibid.*, vi. 2. 1026b 24–1027a 28.
[28] *Nic. eth.* vi. 4. 1040a 10–16 (Oxford tr.).

What is made by the artist is neither the form nor the matter, but the *synolon*, the *concretum*. For instance, the sculptor makes neither the marble which is his material nor the human form which he gives it, but the statue, which is the human form imposed upon marble; and the ironworker makes neither the iron nor the spherical form, but the iron sphere, a *concretum* of form and matter.[29] In art a form in the mind of the artist is imposed upon his medium, to produce the artistic composite;[30] and the productive process may be divided into two parts, which are, as it were, of contrary direction. The first proceeds from the form to be produced to the first thing which can be produced; this is reasoning. The second proceeds from the first thing which can be produced to the form itself; this is making.[31] For example, if a shoe is to be produced—a certain kind of composite—then parts must be stitched or nailed together; but first there must be the requisite parts, and these will have to be cut and prepared, and so forth to the first thing that can be done. All this is reasoning; but the process from the terminus of the reasoning to the final production of the form is making. Now, art according to Aristotle is a state concerned with making, involving a true course of reasoning; and it is precisely this reasoning universalized, the rationale of art or production, which is in a sense scientific knowledge of the productive kind; the reasoning part, that is, not the making part; for the latter is not knowledge, but production in accordance with knowledge, and it depends rather upon skill and experience. By "course of reasoning" Aristotle means, naturally, not the psychological processes of the individual artist, for these are incidental to the individual and cannot be formulated, but the course that would be followed in correct, true, and appropriate reasoning about making a given product. Since the arts propose not productions merely but also productions excellent of their kind—for example, the sculptor seeks to make not merely a statue but also a good statue—such reasoning will have to include not merely the "nature" of the thing intended but its "excellence" as well.[32]

The scope of any productive science, therefore, is the rational part of production centering in, and indeed based upon, the nature of the product; and the structure of such science may be described as hypothetical regressive reasoning, taking for its starting-point, or principle, the artistic whole which is to be produced and proceeding through the various parts of the various kinds to be assembled.[33] The reasoning is hypothetical because it is based upon hypotheses: If such and such a work, which is a whole, is to be produced, then such and such parts must be assembled in such and such a way; and if the work is to have excellence as a whole, then the parts must be of such and such a kind and quality. The reasoning is regressive because it works backward from the whole, which is to exist, to the parts which must have existence previous to that of the whole. Since the reasoning is based upon a definition of a certain whole as its principle and since that definition must be arrived at in some fashion, any productive science must consist of two main parts: inductive reasoning

---

[29] *Met.* vii. 8. 1033a 23–1033b 11.

[30] 7. 1032a 32.

[31] 1032b 15 ff.

[32] *Poetics*, i. 1447a 10:

[33] *De partibus animalium*, i. 1. 639b 24 ff.; *De generatione et corruptione*, ii. 11. 337b 14 ff.

toward its principle, and deductive reasoning from its principle.[34] One part must make possible the formulation of the whole; the other must determine the parts according to that formulation.

On examination, the *Poetics* clearly follows this general pattern. Chapters i–v are concerned with establishing the definition of tragedy, which is given in chapter vi; chapters vi–xxii resolve tragedy into its proper parts; chapters xxiii–xxiv offer a treatment of epic based upon that of tragedy; and the final chapters conclude with critical problems relative to both forms.

The definition on which everything centers, thus, is no mere statement of the meaning of a term or name, as we ordinarily think of definition nowadays;[35] it is a statement of the nature of a whole produced by a certain art; and it is introduced, not merely to clarify meanings a little but much more importantly, to serve as the principle of the art and hence as the basis of all reasoning. And because it is a definition of a thing produced by art, it must differ sharply from a mathematical or physical definition. Mathematical definitions treat of forms as abstracted from matter and hence do not include the matter;[36] I do not, for instance, include "brazen" or "wooden" or anything of the sort in my definition of sphere or cube. Physical definitions—dealing with natural things—must include matter;[37] for physical things are composites of matter and form; hence physical terms, as Aristotle repeatedly reminds us, are like the term "snub"—for "snub" involves not merely nose or merely concavity, but both—a nose (matter) which is concave (form).[38] The things of art—also composites—must also be defined through matter and form. But natural things have a natural matter and are in a natural genus, whereas artificial things are not; hence, while natural things are defined by a two-part definition consisting of genus (matter) and difference (form), artificial things must be defined by enumeration and differentiation of the various causes which make them what they are. These will still group themselves into two parts, matter and form: the one part will state what has been organized as matter; the other will state the working or effect or power *(dynamis)* which is their form. For, as Aristotle says, things must be defined through their working or power;[39] thus, a definition of a hand as a certain organization of bones, veins, and tissues would be incomplete, for it would leave out manual power, which is the form of the hand and the end to which these elements are organized, and such a definition would fit a dead hand as well, although a dead hand is really a hand in name only.[40]

The argument leading to the definition may be stated as follows. Assuming that certain arts are imitative (and this is strictly assumed, not proven, for it is not a proposition which belongs to poetics, but to some other science), specific forms of these arts must be specific forms of imitation. To imitate implies a matter or medium (means) in which one imitates, some form (object) which one imitates, and a certain way (manner) in which one imitates. Thus, considered

[34] *Supra*, n. 6.

[35] *An. post.* ii. 10. 93b 28–94a 3.

[36] *Met.* vii. 10.

[37] *Phys.* ii. 2.

[38] 194a 4–6.

[39] *Pol.* i. 2. 1253a 24.

[40] See, *e.g.*, *Met.* vii. 10. 1035b 25; *Meteórologica*, iv. 12. 389b 26.

as imitation, every imitation must involve means, object, and manner, and therefore imitations must differ as they involve different means, objects, or manners. Hence, in chapter i Aristotle differentiates a certain body of arts which involve related media (words, rhythm, tune) according to specific differences of the media involved; in chapter ii, according to objects imitated; and in chapter iii, according to the manners of imitation. As he shows,[41] no one of these lines of differentiation is sufficient to discriminate a given art; according to manner alone, comedy and tragedy are indifferentiable; according to object alone, epic would be indifferentiable from tragedy; while according to the means alone, the imitative poet is not distinguishable from the scientist who writes verse treatises. All three lines of differentiation must therefore be used simultaneously; no one is peculiar, but all three collectively are peculiar, to a given art.[42] These lines of differentiation are in fact causes, in the technical sense in which Aristotle speaks of causes as the answers we give when we are asked "Why is this thing what it is?"[43] For if we are asked, let us say, "why is this thing a tragedy?" we respond, "because it is in a certain medium, because it imitates a certain object, and because it does this in a certain manner."

Yet this causal account is still incomplete; for, to continue the example, tragedy is not really owing to these differentiations, although if they did not exist, tragedy would not.[44] A saw, for instance, does not exist simply because of its metal, or because of the saw-maker, or because of a certain shape, although without these the saw would not exist. These are conditions of its existence, and necessary ones; but it exists primarily because it has a certain function, sawing. And the existence of tragedy results primarily from its effect or power; these other things are for the sake of that. Compare the case of the saw just mentioned. Why is a saw such as it is? To effect cutting in a certain way; and if so, a certain shape and material are required, and an artisan must compound them. This fourth, or final, cause must be found for the various arts under consideration; chapters iv–v are devoted to it. Since for Aristotle what each thing is when fully developed is its nature, and since the nature of each thing is its end and is best and self-sufficient,[45] he achieves the final cause by recounting the origin and development of poetry. This is a history in terms of the successive final causes which imitative poetry has had; each phase involves a different final cause, and in each that cause is shown as governing the other elements of poetry.

Thus, in the first phase, human instinct for imitation for the sake of the pleasure and knowledge derived from imitation, whether we ourselves imitate or merely observe imitations, is the originating cause; and since man has also an instinct for tune and rhythm, it is natural that imitation in words, melody, and rhythm should result.[46] But instinct is perfectly uniform and consequently

---

[41] *Manner*, 1448a 25 ff.; *object*, 1448a 7 ff.; *means*, 1447b 17 ff.

[42] *An. post.* ii. 13, esp. 96a 32. See also 96b 15–24, and for important remarks on differentiational procedure, *De part. an.* i. 2–4, and *Met.* vii. 12. On species, see *ibid.*, x. 8.

[43] *Phys.* ii. 3; ii. 7; *Met.* v. 2; vii. 17; *De part. an.* i. 1. 639b 12 ff.

[44] *Phys.* ii. 9. 200a 5–200b 10.   [45] *Politica*, i. 2. 1252b 32 ff.

[46] *Poet.* 4. 1448b 4–24.

cannot account for variation in poetry; and in the second phase, in which poetry diversifies, as poets imitate either noble or ignoble actions and characters, the cause of the diversification lies in the moral nature of the imitator himself.[47] In the third phase, forms desirable in themselves are developed; here we have art proper.[48] Poetry thus passes through phases in which its functions, or final causes, are instinctive, ethical, and artistic. In the first, moreover, the means is developed;[49] in the second, objects of imitation are differentiated, and the means is adjusted to these;[50] in the third, manner is developed, and, art forms such as comedy and tragedy having now come into being, these are improved and perfected by alterations and accommodations of their parts.[51] Taylor, among many others, has said that Aristotle's theory of *katharsis* was intended to answer Plato's charges against poetry;[52] but it is much more accurate to observe that Plato never conceives of poetry as developing into this third phase and that Aristotle's proper answer lies here: it is one thing to imitate the low and vicious through inclinations of one's character; quite another to imitate them for artistic purposes.

The causal account now complete, Aristotle "collects," as he says,[53] the four causes into the famous definition. The specific problem is now to discover what parts, of what kind and number, are requisite for a whole of the sort just defined. If tragedy is dramatic in manner, there must be spectacle; if the means are as described, there must be diction and music; and if the object imitated is an action of a certain kind *(spoudaios,* or serious), there must be plot and hence (since action is discriminated in terms of character and thought) character and thought also. But a whole, for Aristotle, does not simply have a certain number of parts but has them in a certain ordering; one part will be determined by another until the principal part is reached, which determines all.[54] Consequently, to determine this ordering he establishes the relative importance of the parts, arguing that plot is the principal part, the "soul" of tragedy; and one may observe in passing that those who attack this view have never answered the arguments here and, perhaps, have never quite conceived of plot itself as it is here conceived.

If tragedy is a whole, and if plot is its primary part, and if a whole has its characteristics according to its primary part, plot must be investigated; for if that is not whole and entire and beautiful, the tragedy also will not be. Aristotle's treatment of plot is governed by three primary considerations: that it, too, is a whole, and a whole of a certain kind; that it is to be a beautiful whole; and that it is to have a certain effect or function. Plot is a whole of the sort that has beginning, middle, and end; has its parts complete and ordered; is not only of some magnitude, but of a magnitude such that it is beautiful; has a certain unity, in this instance a unity achieved by conjunction; and is continuous. Moreover, since actions, as con-

---

[47] 1448b 25.

[48] 1449a 5 ff.

[49] 1448b 24.

[50] 1448b 26–32.

[51] 1449b 10–31.

[52] *Aristotle*, pp. 88–90.

[53] απολαβοντεσ

[54] *Met.* v. 26, esp. 1024a 1 ff.

tinuities, are simple or complex according as they are or are not differentiable into distinctive parts, plot also must be simple or complex, the latter kind having as its parts reversal, discovery, or both. These matters, resulting from the specification of metaphysical doctrines of "whole," "part," and so forth to the case of plot, occupy chapters vii–xi. But plot is not merely to be whole and beautiful, but is to have a particular effect or power (upon the emotions); the true form of the tragic plot, thus, is precisely to have this effect; hence, Aristotle examines the nature of the tragic protagonist and the tragic deed, which are the conditions of the tragic effect (chapters xiii–xiv). Development of these conditions brings the treatment of plot as principal part to a close, and the remaining parts are discussed in the order of their importance. Finally, since tragedy includes the parts of epic, epic can be dealt with in terms of its similarities or dis-similarities to tragedy, and the two forms can be compared, and critical questions organized and resolved.

The method of the *Poetics,* thus, is precisely the method of productive science or art as Aristotle conceives it, and as such determined by the entire body of the philosophy of which it is a part. The degree of this dependency can be seen in the fact that, as Aristotle brought all his doctrines of method to bear on the subject matter of poetry, it was necessary, in the foregoing analysis to explain his procedure by reference to most of his extant works. A more thorough-going analysis would, I believe, establish that dependency more clearly and fully, in proportion as it clarified Aristotle's procedure; conversely, apart from such consideration of the philosophy as a whole, not merely the argument of the *Poetics* but even the doctrines, indeed, even individual concepts, such as those of imitation, plot, and *katharsis,* become unintelligible.

In order to illustrate this last point, as well as to exhibit some further aspects of Aristotle's method, let me briefly consider the case of plot. If I may be bold enough to say what I really think, I shall say that Aristotle's conception of plot is unique in the history of criticism and that in the innumerable discussions of "plot" from his day to our own, his conception is never again attached to the term *mythos* or any of its synonyms, such as *fabula, argumentum, argumento, favola, fable,* fable, plot, *Handlung,* and the like.

Critical discussions of "plot" since Aristotle have turned, I think, on several different conceptions. First, "plot" sometimes has the meaning of the material, whether historical or legendary, which is given poetic treatment; in this sense the various Oedipuses and Fausts are said to have the same plot. Again, "plot" often means a tissue of metaphorical or exemplary events or actions used as vehicle for didactic statement. Thus, we have all heard of the "plot" of *The Faerie Queene* and the "plot" of Richardson's *Pamela,* although the former is really sustained allegorical metaphor and the latter a series of *exempla*; and in ages when poetry is conceived of as didactic only—for example, in the greater part of the medieval period—this meaning becomes the principal, if not the exclusive, one. Again, "plot" has meant the sequence of events simply, without regard to the moral agencies involved in the actions; this is the sense in which you tell the "plot" of a movie, and in this sense *Romeo and Juliet* and "Pyramus and Thisbe" (in *A Midsummer Night's Dream*) are said so have the same general plot, although one is serious and the other comic travesty. Again, "plot" can mean such events as are narrated, or as are represented upon the stage; this is the sense, I think, in which most European critics of the sixteenth and seventeenth centuries employed the term. Finally, there is "plot" in the sense of a string of occasions invented, *ficelle*-fashion, for the manifestation of character and thought and even the use of special diction. This is the conception which E. M. Forster and Ortega y Gasset entertain when they speak of plot as a mere spine, skeleton, or armature, something as arbitrary as the string upon which we string beads.[55] I submit that these conceptions of plot are not equivalent to Aristotle's, that they stem from conceptions of poetry very different from Aristotle's, and that, even if plot should appear as important in any of them, it would hardly be in the sense in which Aristotle thought of plot as important.

For Aristotle was not concerned with everything which we should call poetry, and also he was concerned with some things that we should no longer call poetry. It will not do even to say that he was concerned with tragedy, epic, and comedy, for the significance of these terms has altered since his day. He thought of epic as the *Iliad* and the *Odyssey* and whatever had the same form—not as the sort of epic that Aratus and Nicander were to produce; of tragedy as poetry similar to the *Oedipus* of Sophocles, not to the *Oedipus* of Seneca or *The White Devil*. While he says repeatedly that the arts imitate nature, he means that the causes and productive processes of artificial objects resemble those which nature would have evolved had the products been natural and not artificial; he does not mean that all artificial objects are imitations in the sense in which he thinks tragedy is an imitation.[56]

In brief: he had observed that certain kinds of art had developed to a stage at which they were produced and appreciated for their own sake; that these forms happened to be (he uses the verb *tuxanousi*) imitative of human actions, in the sense that they simulated human actions, and that not simply, but human actions of different kinds, as serious or ludicrous, affecting us differently according to such differences of kind. The point is not that everything which has been or might be called poetry imitates human action, but that certain forms of poetry undoubtedly do; and it is these that he is discussing. Now, if actions are serious or ludicrous according to the degree in which they involve happiness or misery, and if happiness and misery are functions of the moral characters of the persons involved, the imitative action, or plot, cannot consist of events simply, or actions simply, but of activity of a certain moral quality, such that it produces a particular emotional effect; that is, the kind of action includes the kind of moral choice made, just as the moral choice includes the kind of reasoning and moral principles upon which the choice is made. Plot, therefore, in such imitative forms, is a system of morally differentiated activities or actions; as such, it is indubitably the primary part of such constructions, since it actualizes and completes and gives form to all the other parts, which are related to it as matter to form. But it is primary only in this conception of it, and only in this

[55] See, *e.g.*, Ortega y Gasset, *Notes on the Novel* (pub. together with *The Dehumanization of Art*, Princeton, 1948), pp. 65, 82, 87–88.

[56] *Phys.* ii. 8. 199a 8–19. Note Aristotle's careful statement at *Poet.* 1447a 13–16.

conception of poetry; and these conceptions are in turn dependent upon the whole body of the Aristotelian philosophy. To separate them from that philosophy is to lose not merely their scientific justification but their very significance as well.

What, then, are the powers and limitations of Aristotle's poetic method? I think that after a fashion we have been discussing them all along. There are some limitations which are almost invariably brought out—that the *Poetics* is a fragment, that portions of that fragment present certain textual difficulties, that Aristotle could have been cognizant of only very few literary forms and of these only to the degree of development which they had reached by his day, and so forth. I regard these "limitations" as trivial. Any philosophic method which is worthy of the name is not one which produces merely passive results, but one through which we may actively inquire, prove, and know; and if Aristotle offers a genuine philosophic method, anyone truly possessed of that method will be able to supply these deficiencies, real or supposed, with the authority of the master himself, for the authority should derive, not from the person, but from the method.

But there are two other kinds of limitation, much more real and important, although neither impairs the soundness of method or of doctrine. One stems from the method of the *Poetics* proper, the other from the general method of Aristotle; both originate in the fact that to adopt a given method is to be able to do certain things and not to be able to do certain others. The *Poetics* cannot be viewed, without serious distortion of it, as exhausting all questions pertinent to the arts, or even to all of the poetic arts. Of the problems which confront artist or critic, some are peculiar to the individual work, and, as accidental, are not amenable to scientific treatment. Some relate to the artistic faculty or process, some to the psychology of audiences, some to the social and political functions of art, some to the nature of what is imitated, and so forth; while Aristotle can handle such questions, it cannot be under poetic science, but under some other science or faculty. We can grasp something of these limitations, I think, by reflecting on a single point which I do not remember anyone ever to have made about the *Poetics*; that while the center of everything here is imitation, Aristotle in fact never tells us how to imitate; never tells us how to make likenesses of this or that action, this or that character. He tells us that characters must be likenesses, but never how to give them likeness—as he tells us that actions must be necessary or probable, but not how to make them necessary or probable. In fact he presupposes all such things, as he does the natural capacity, skill, and knowledge of the artist, and they do not enter into the art of poetics as he conceives it, although inevitably they must go into the making of any poem. In the *Poetics* he is concerned only with the nature of the forms at which the artist must aim and the causes of success and failure in terms of these. The treatise is not a treatise of the whole poetic art or craft, but of as much of it as can be scientific knowledge of a kind; indeed, it is only the beginnings and principles even of poetic science, for it must be extended to keep commensurate with the generation and development of new forms. To sum up on this point: from the modern point of view the primary limitation is the scope itself of the *Poetics*; and to see that, you have only to look at the first and last paragraphs of the work, in which Aristotle respectively states and restates his program of problems, and ask yourselves whether these questions exhaust all the possible questions of art.

As for the kind of limitation arising from Aristotle's general method, that is, that of his philosophy itself: I mean by this that he is limited, precisely as every philosopher is limited, by the questions which he raises, by the kind of solution he requires for them, and by the devices of inquiry and proof which he employs; and since, as I have already suggested, such limitations are necessarily inherent in any single philosophy, it is our part to be aware of the limitations and of the powers of any one system. This is a view of which I cannot attempt in a moment or two to persuade you; let me therefore make a few large statements, more in illustration of my meaning than anything else.

Let me say that by this second half of the twentieth century I think that we should have learned a few things about philosophy, and about criticism too, since that is also philosophy. We should have learned, for instance, that every philosophy is limited by the problems which it raises and that every philosophic problem is limited by the terms in which it is couched. We should have learned, after all the labors of logicians, that there are many different ways of making propositions and that there are many senses of the terms "truth" and "falsity." We should have learned, after the many kinds of proofs and demonstrations offered to us, that there are many kinds, that there are many kinds of valid logics, as there are many valid geometries and algebras; and we should be wise enough to conclude that perhaps there are many valid—I say, "valid"—philosophies. We should be too wise to accept any one philosophy as exhausting the whole of truth, and too wise to conclude that therefore every philosophy is false or that we must make a patchwork of philosophies without consideration of the diverse methods which they entail. We should, in short, be wise enough to consider the diverse valid philosophies only as instruments, all with various powers and limitations, and valuable relatively to the kinds of questions to which they are directed.

The conception of mimetic poetry which underlies the *Poetics* is that in these arts the center and principle of all is human beings doing and experiencing things which are humanly interesting and affecting. For Aristotle that humanity is prime: that happiness or misery, that activity serious or laughable, every other part of the poem must serve so as to set it before us as powerfully and vividly as possible; and every part must be beautiful in itself as it can be consistently with the whole. Insofar as they permit of scientific treatment, questions proper to the synthesis of such objects are the whole concern of the *Poetics*; as new forms of mimetic art emerge, the theory can be extended to cover them as well—provided that the extension is by one who has sufficient knowledge of and skill in Aristotle's method. In this sense Aristotle can be said to have developed not only a permanently true but also an indefinitely operable poetic method. But we cannot legitimately expect it to solve all problems that might be raised concerning all forms of art; especially not when the questions posed, the answers demanded, and the method postulated are all of an order alien to Aristotle's own.

The Multiplicity of Critical Languages

R. S. CRANE

What I would propose, then, as a major premise of these lectures, is that literary criticism is not, and never has been, a single discipline, to which successive writers have made partial and never wholly satisfactory contributions but rather a collection of distinct and more or less incommensurable "frameworks" or "languages," within any one of which a question like that of poetic structure necessarily takes on a different meaning and receives a different kind of answer from the meaning it has and the kind of answer it is properly given in any of the rival critical languages in which it is discussed.[1] It is not a sufficient objection to this view of criticism that it has rarely been entertained even by the most self-conscious of critics. For the diversities of language we are here concerned with are matters of assumed principle, definition, and method, such as are not likely to show themselves, save indirectly, on the surface of a critic's discourse, and hence not likely, even in controversy, to force themselves on his attention. They pertain rather to what he thinks *with* than to what he thinks *about*—to the implicit structure and rationale of his argument as a whole than to the explicit doctrines he is attempting to state. And both the reality and the importance of the diversities have been further disguised, in the criticism of our European tradition, by the persistence of a large body of terms and commonplaces—like the word "structure" itself or "poetry" or "tragedy" or "plot" —the verbal identity of which in different critics tends effectually to conceal

---

[1] For other statements, in somewhat different terms, of this view, see *Critics and Criticism: Ancient and Modern*, ed. R. S. Crane (Chicago, 1952), pp. 5–12, 148–49, 174–75, 463–545, 546–52. See also Richard McKeon, "Philosophy and Method," *Journal of Philosophy*, XLVIII (1951), 653–82; "Semantics, Science, and Poetry," *Modern Philology*, XLIX (1952), 145–59; and *Freedom and History* (New York, 1952).

the often sharp oppositions of principle and method that separate their discussions from one another. It takes some effort after all to realize that a writer may not be talking about the same things I am, or reasoning about them in the same way, merely because he happens to use the same customary formulae in the statement of his points! The true state of affairs, however, often reveals itself whenever, on being confronted with an extreme clash of doctrines between two obviously serious and intelligent critics employing the same vocabulary, we undertake to pry into the hidden structures of definitions and assumptions which their respective arguments presuppose.

An illuminating case is the attempt of Mr. L. C. Knights, in his well-known essay on "How Many Children Had Lady Macbeth?", to correct what he regards as the errors imposed on readers of Shakespeare by A. C. Bradley's classic lectures on *Shakespearean Tragedy*.[2] The most damaging of these, he tells us, is the dogma that Shakespeare was "pre-eminently a great 'creator of characters'" and that the main task, consequently, of students of the plays consists in laying bare the marvellous insights into human nature in crisis which the tragedies, in particular, embody. Eminent critic as Bradley was—so the argument runs—he did a grave disservice to Shakespeare when he devoted so many of his pages to detailed psychological and moral analyses of the characters of the plays, to the exclusion of any serious concern with their language and verse, and especially when he continued the bad tradition of writing about Shakespeare's *dramatis personae* as if they were real persons whose lives could be properly thought of as extending beyond the plays in which they are involved. To write thus, according to Mr. Knights, is to disregard the essential fact, which has been revealed to us by C. H. Rickword, that the "characters" of a drama or novel, as well as its "plot," have no existence except as "precipitates" from the reader's memory of the successive words he has read and that, as such, they are mere critical "abstractions" to which we can attend only at the cost of impoverishing our "total response" to the work. And it is also to forget that a play of Shakespeare is not a drama simply but a "dramatic poem," the end of which is "to communicate a rich and controlled experience by means of words"; and accordingly that the only profitable approach to it must be by way of "an exact and sensitive study of the quality of the verse, of the rhythm and imagery, of the controlled associations of the words and their emotional and intellectual force, in short by an exact and sensitive study of Shakespeare's handling of language."

I have selected this controversy because it seems to me a comparatively easy one to resolve in the terms of my hypothesis. Let us suppose that we are critics for whom the primary object of concern is something we call "poetry" and let us further suppose that we have defined "poetry" in such a way as to make it distinct from "drama" in the sense in which an ordinary prose play depicting "real" characters in action is drama, and that we have, moreover, conceived of a poem, of whatever sort, as essentially a certain definitive arrangement of words, or rather as the sum total of emotional and intellectual responses—

[2] See *Explorations*, pp. 1–18, and especially pp. 1, 4, 10.

corresponding to the experience the poet wished to communicate—which this arrangement of words is calculated to evoke in the mind of a properly trained reader. It would then follow, naturally enough, that in writing of one of Shakespeare's plays, we would direct attention, as Mr. Knights does, mainly to its key words and metaphors and the pattern of associated and contrasted meanings these suggest, and would be no less convinced than he is that "to stress in the conventional way character or plot or any of the other abstractions that can be made, is to impoverish the total response to the poetry." It would be unthinkable, indeed, for us to take any other line. But now let us suppose that we have started with concepts and terms of quite a different sort. We have taken as the genus of our subject-matter not "poetry" or "poetic drama" but "Shakespearean tragedy" (in which "poetry" in Mr. Knight's sense is one of the technical means) and have identified this, not with a specific art form or with a particular kind of effect to be produced in audiences, but with a certain imaginative conception in the mind of the poet—the conception of "the tragic aspect of life" which Shakespeare sought to embody dramatically in different ways, but always in terms of actions issuing from and expressing moral character, in *Hamlet, Othello, King Lear,* and *Macbeth.* Wouldn't it follow from this that our central problem in discussing the plays would now be, as it was for Bradley, the recovery for each of them of what was in Shakespeare's mind when he wrote it, so that, as Bradley said, the action and the personages engaged in it "may assume in our imaginations a shape a little less unlike the shape they wore in the imagination of their creator"?[3] And wouldn't it also follow that in effecting such a recovery, we would be justified in concentrating on the characters as the main source of "the tragic fact" and in considering them not as "abstractions" from the words of the plays as finally written but as the concrete semblances of real men and women, each with a being more or less independent of the particular actions he performs in the completed drama, which they undoubtedly were for the imagination of the poet who conceived them? It would be unthinkable, once more, given the scheme of terms we have chosen to use in discussing the tragedies, that we should take any other line.

What I have been saying, in short, is that the opposition between Bradley and Mr. Knights on the issue of the nature and importance of character in drama is not at all an opposition of the kind which requires us to assume that if one of the two propositions is true, the other must be false. It would be such an opposition only if the two propositions were answers to the same question about the same object; and we have seen that this is not the case, inasmuch as Bradley is talking about the plays as reflections of their author's imaginative view of what is tragic in life, whereas Mr. Knights is talking about them as effects in the right reader of certain determinate arrangements of words on the printed page. It is therefore possible to affirm without contradiction both that the characters of Shakespeare are individual men and women possessed of a reality analogous to that of living people and that they are merely (in Rickword's phrase) "precipitates from the memory" that have "emotive valency"

---

[3] A. C. Bradley, *Shakespearean Tragedy* (2nd ed., London, 1929), p. 1.

only "in solution."[4] The opposition, in other words—though this is largely concealed by the similarities in vocabulary—is not one of conflicting interpretations of the same facts, to be settled by an appeal to a common body of evidence, but of two distinct worlds of discourse, in which the "facts" cited by each critic in support of his position have been determined differently for the two of them by their prior decisions to constitute the subject-matter of Shakespearean criticism in essentially different terms.

It should be clear from this example that the real subject-matter of any critic can never be accurately defined by noting merely that he is talking about such things as dramatic poetry or tragedy or Shakespearean tragedy or *Macbeth*. His real subject-matter is not any of these things in itself (whatever that may mean), nor is it necessarily any of these things as conceived by us or by any of the other critics whose errors are being exposed. Rather it is simply that aspect, or those aspects, of his indicated subject upon which our attention is focused by the semantic and logical constitution of his discourse; it is what, in short, he has thus *taken* his subject to be. And the range of possible critical subject-matters, in this sense, that may lie hidden under the various familiar names for literary entities is extraordinarily great. This is only to be expected, perhaps, when we consider that the typical subjects of criticism are such as lend themselves peculiarly to diverse and shifting modes of consideration. Although they have a basis in human nature, they are not invariant natural phenomena but contingent human constructions, so that their "true" character is always relative, as that of the objects of physical science is not, to what men have designed or thought them to be; and that character, besides, has often been affected, in the course of history, by the very attempts of theorizing critics to say what it is. They differ, moreover, from such artificial products as dwelling houses, automobiles, and atomic bombs in having a far wider variety of significant uses and hence in permitting a much greater diversity of interpretations and of criteria for judging their success or failure. It is little wonder, therefore, that critics in all periods—writing under the influence of varying practical aims or philosophic preoccupations—should have felt free to constitute literature or poetry or any of their individual monuments as widely discrepant kinds of things, the differing natures of which are bound to be reflected, in many subtle but decisive ways, in the differing structures of terms they employ in making statements about them.

I know of no historian or theorist of criticism who has succeeded in exhibiting the full range of such differences, but it is clearly much greater than our usual classifications of critical approaches—for example, as historical, biographical, psychological, aesthetic, moral, sociological, and the like—would suggest. It is common, thus, to say that both Longinus and Coleridge are psychological critics; but the subject-matter of Longinus, in the sense of that which gives determinate reference and intelligibility to his propositions and arguments, is a certain general quality of writing, amenable to art, the character of which is

---

[4] Quoted by Knights, *Explorations*, p. 4.

best described in terms of its effect on readers, whereas the subject-matter of Coleridge (when he talks about "poetry") is primarily the manifestation in poems of a natural power inherent in poets and best described in terms of the mental faculty in which it resides—"that synthetic and magical power," as he calls it, "to which we have exclusively appropriated the name of imagination."[5] And so also with many of the general words which critics themselves have used to designate the subjects or characteristics of subjects they are engaged in discussing—it can never be safely assumed in advance that their common use by two different critics is a sign that these critics have constituted the effective subject-matters of their discussions in the same way, so that it is possible to make direct comparisons between their conclusions and to say that one is more nearly adequate to the real state of affairs than the other. The term "imitation" is of crucial importance, as we all know, for the discussion of poetry in both Plato and Aristotle; but whereas for Plato it is a universal and unifying term applicable not only to art but to human actions and knowledge and to the natural world itself and hence a term that brings the objects of criticism into organic relationship, in the dialogues, with all other objects, its function for Aristotle, on the contrary, is that of a differentiating term by which poetry, or rather a certain class of poems, is distinguished from nature, action, and knowledge, and constituted, for the purposes of the *Poetics,* as a body of concrete objects presupposing peculiar principles of construction and subject to evaluation in ways not relevant to either actions or propositions.[6] This is a radical difference in subject-matter between the two philosophers, in the light of which it is surely not fair to Plato to say that Aristotle "refuted" his condemnation of poetry in *The Republic* or fair to Aristotle to say that Plato took a sounder view than he did of the relation between poetry and morals. Or consider, again, the discussions of "metaphysical poetry" in Dr. Johnson and Mr. Ransom. In spite of the fact that Mr. Ransom writes in full awareness of Johnson's use of the term and that both critics refer to some of the same seventeenth-century poets, the real object of discussion in the two is only nominally identical, the object envisaged by Johnson being a historically determinate "race" of poets in the generation before Dryden, to whom he attributes certain excesses and defects in the light of his general criteria for poetry of any kind, whereas the object of concern for Mr. Ransom, as constituted in the terms of his essay, is strictly not a particular school of poets at all but a universal kind of poetry, the nature of which is determined, in his definition, by the opposition he established between it and the two contrasting extremes of "physical poetry" on the one hand and "Platonic poetry" on the other.[7] One term, again, but two subject-matters that overlap at no essential point; and though we may prefer, with Mr. Ransom, to use the name "metaphysical poetry" in a more honorific sense that it has in Johnson, we must not allow ourselves to suppose that we are honouring the same thing.

[5] *Biographia literaria,* ed. J. Shawcross (Oxford, 1907), II, 12.

[6] See McKeon, in *Critics and Criticism,* pp. 149–68.

[7] See his "Poetry: A Note in Ontology," in *The World's Body* (New York, 1938), pp. 111–42.

This will suffice as an indication of one basis of divergence among critical languages, of which we shall see a good many other examples as we proceed in these lectures. A critical language, however, is more than a finite set of basic and often implicit definitions which, as a conceptual scheme of a determinate sort, constitutes its literary objects as the particular subject-matter that is being talked about. It is also a special set of assumptions as to how the principles and distinctions needed in the discussion are to be derived and as to how they may be used to give valid and relevant knowledge concerning whatever the subject-matter is taken to be. There can be no critical writing that makes coherent sense which does not rest upon such a double commitment; but the two aspects are so related that what literature or poetry or any poem is for a given critic may be conditioned quite as much by his preference among possible ways of investigating or arguing about subjects of this sort as his selection of a method of inquiry or demonstration is conditioned by what he assumes literature or poetry to be.

Of the various differences of basic method discernible in the history of criticism, I can deal here, illustratively, with only one. It is a difference that emerges clearly enough when we contrast the procedure of a critic like Mr. Ransom in his essays on poetry with the procedure of Longinus in his attempt to construct an art of the "sublime." Such an art is possible, Longinus argues, because the "sublime" exists as a concrete effect or quality actually achieved and hence achievable in language—an effect, quite distinct from that of rhetorical persuasion, which we all experience whenever, in reading works of poetry, philosophy, oratory, or history, we come upon a passage that transports us out of ourselves and makes us, in a sense, one with the writer or speaker. For the art which Longinus envisages, this empirically verifiable effect, the nature of which can be defined in general terms by distinguishing it from its various possible opposites (turgidity, frigidity, and *parenthyrson*), becomes the end to be sought and hence the starting-point or first principle of his inquiry. That inquiry, since its object is a practical one, must follow an *a posteriori* course from the nature of the effect to be achieved to its necessary causes or conditions in what a writer must do if he wishes to attain "sublimity" of utterance; and the problem is solved when Longinus has discriminated the five essential sources of "sublime" effects in literature (noble conception, strong emotion, and a proper employment of figures, diction, and rhythmic and harmonic composition), has demonstrated that these exhaust the possible causes, and has shown for each that it is a means conducive to the end desired.[8]

Strikingly different from this is Mr. Ransom's procedure in the argument that serves to support his well-known contention that any good poem is a composite of a "logical structure" and an "irrelevant local texture," the first being a prerequisite of the second though only very loosely determinative of it. If we ask why we must accept this as a description of what the objects of poetic criticism are, one answer that might be given is that it works in practice. We have only to read Marvell's "To His Coy Mistress," for example, to see that

---

[8] See Elder Olson, in *Critics and Criticism*, pp. 235–59.

behind the poem is "an easy argument to the effect that a lover, after pointing out the swift passage of time, reasons with his mistress that they had better love at once," but that the poem itself gives us "a good deal more than we had hoped for"—that the detail of its various parts has assumed "a good deal more of independent character than could possibly have been predicted" from a consideration of the "logical argument" alone.[9] This, however, is not altogether satisfactory; for it is clear that much of what, in Mr. Ransom's analysis of Marvell's poem, is "irrelevant texture" (in other words, "poetry" as distinguished from "prose") would at once become part of the "logical structure" had he only made his paraphrase of the "argument" a bit more precise—for example, by qualifying the lover as "impatient" and "witty" and the mistress as "coy"; and it is equally clear that the poem could be satisfactorily analysed, as it has been, in terms of many other pairs of contrary terms than the one he has seen fit to employ. The important question, therefore, is why we must accept this particular opposition of "logical structure" and "irrelevant texture" as a necessary formulation of the nature of this and all other poems.

The necessity is plainly not of the same order as that which leads from Longinus' isolation and definition of the "sublime" as an effect possible in language to his distinction of noble conception and strong emotion as the two "natural" conditions of its existence in any piece of writing. It is not, that is to say, the hypothetical necessity that joins, in practical experience and the arts, something taken as an end with the means requisite for its achievement, but rather, we may suspect, the kind of necessity that compels us, once we have granted the premises of a given argument, to assent to whatever conclusions are drawn from them. And our suspicion that the necessity behind Mr. Ransom's analysis of poetry is of this dialectical sort is confirmed when we examine the foundations of his poetic theory as set forth especially in the essays collected in *The World's Body*.[10] For here we discover, at the basis of all his reasoning about particular literary questions (for example, in the discussion of "metaphysical poetry" already referred to), a general hypothesis or supposition concerning man and his possible relations to the world of concrete things, according to which the fundamental opposition in human life is between the impulse to use, take, and "devour" things in the interest of conceptual knowledge and practical or "economic" action and the impulse to contemplate and love things in all their "wild" particularity for their own sake. This is the starting-point of all his speculations; and from the structure of primary terms and relations thus fixed upon he proceeds to generate, by strictly logical disjunction and equation, a whole series of more particular oppositions—between "idea" and "image" ("An idea is derivative and tamed. The image is in the natural or wild state, and it has to be discovered there, not put there, obeying its own law and none of ours"); between science, as one extreme, and religion, manners, and art, as the other; between poetry "of the feelings" (in which "the subject does not really propose to lose himself in the object") and "metaphysical poetry" (which, starting with feelings, tends to "objectify these imaginatively into external

[9] John Crowe Ransom, *The New Criticism* (Norfolk, Conn., 1941), pp. 270–71.

[10] See especially pp. 36–38, 41–46, 111–42, 181–83, 195–211, 278–95.

actions"); and so on. The two original impulses, and all their derivatives, remain in dialectical opposition throughout, but in such a manner that the two must be present somehow, and in some ratio of one to the other, in any human act or production. Science and art are thus necessarily contraries but not wholly exclusive of one another: "Science gratifies a rational or practical impulse and exhibits the minimum of perception. Art gratifies a perceptual impulse and exhibits the minimum of reason." And so with poetry. "The poetic impulse is not free"—there must be some element of "science" in it if only in its metre—"yet it holds out stubbornly against science for the enjoyment of its images." A poem must be therefore, by necessary inference from the preceding argument if from nothing else, a composite of "logical structure" (since we must have some concepts if we are to grasp anything) and of "irrelevant texture" (since the differentia of poetry is that it gives us, in opposition to science, the "world's body" rather than merely ideas about it).

Here then are two sharply contrasting methods of deriving critical principles and solving critical problems; and it is easy to see that much will depend upon which of them a critic chooses. The one is a "matter of fact" method (as Hume would say) that seeks to render an account of empirically distinguishable literary phenomena in terms of their essential and distinctive causes of production. Its starting-point is always some literary form or actuality that has been and hence can be achieved by art (whatever other prerequisites may be involved), and its procedure consists in reasoning back from this to the necessary and sufficient conditions of its existence or of its existence in the best possible state. The distinctions it looks for and employs are distinctions of "nature" rather than of "reason" inasmuch as their relevance is determined not by the exigencies of the critic's hypothesis but by some kind of inductive consideration of the particular phenomena he is studying: for example, of the various kinds of wholes that poets may construct (as in Aristotle's differentiations of tragedy, comedy, and epic), or of the different elements necessary to the production of an effect or of a work of a certain kind (as in Longinus' analysis of the sources of the "sublime" or Aristotle's discrimination of plot, character, thought, diction, melody, and spectacle as the constitutive parts of tragedies), or of the alternative devices or procedures available to poets with a view to certain ends (as in the modern distinction between symbolic and literal modes of representation in the novel), or of distinguishable factors in the responses of audiences (as in Johnson's resolution of the general conditions of literary pleasure into "truth" and "variety"). And it is characteristic of the method that it prefers multiple and overlapping classifications of literary things to classification on the basis of a single principle of division to which all of the particular distinctions developed in the critic's discourse may be referred.

The second method is in most respects the contrary of this. It is that "other scientific method"—to quote Hume again—"where a general abstract principle is first established, and is afterwards branched out into a variety of inferences and conclusions" which are then made to apply to the immediate subject in hand.[11] Its starting-point is always something laid down as a basic truth from

---

[11] *An Enquiry Concerning the Principles of Morals*, Section I.

which, if it is granted, consequences can be inferred by logical equation and opposition that are assumed to be appropriate in some way to literature or poetry through one or another or some combination of its causes in the minds or creative processes of writers, in the language they use, in the things or actions they represent, or in the effects their works are capable of having on readers. The essential first step is therefore to fix upon some kind of general structure discernible in things or actions or mental faculties or symbolic expressions (for example, the creative powers of God, the universal relations of man and nature, the character of discourse or of science, the nature of metaphor or synecdoche, the operations of the libido, the manifestations of primitive myth and ritual) which can be taken as a model or analogue in the discussion and which, being simpler or better known than poetry, can be used to supply the critic with principles and distinctions wherewith to mark off poetry from other things or to assimilate it to them and ultimately to make statements about the structures and values of individual poems. In the procedure thus determined, once the "general abstract principle" is established or the model chosen, the basic oppositions it makes possible necessarily persist, in however qualified or disguised forms, throughout the critic's discourse, with the result that his account of poetry, no matter how sharply he may wish to set it apart, is always framed in patterns of terms that can be applied with more or less equal relevance to other things (as we have seen in Mr. Ransom). This cannot be avoided, but at the same time it is possible for a critic who uses this method to employ it in two different ways: either reductively, by arguing that the literary object he is concerned with is "nothing but" the more simple or general model to which it is referred (as in much contemporary psychoanalytic and "archetypal" criticism), or constructively, by retaining the basic oppositions afforded by the model but showing that they are inevitably particularized and qualified as they manifest themselves in more differentiated forms (as, for the most part, in Mr. Ransom). In both of its two modes, finally, it is a method that can be described, in contrast with the other method, either as hypothetical, in the sense that its starting-point is a general supposition chosen more or less arbitrarily for its assumed explanatory powers; or as dialectical, in the sense both that the relevance of its initial premises is something to be granted rather than established inductively by inspection of concrete literary phenomena and that it proceeds typically by dialectical devices of division and composition; or as "abstract," in the sense that its essential distinctions (like the Marxist conception of the "inner contradictions" in capitalism) are "relations of ideas" or distinctions of "reason" rather than of "nature."

Any critic who wants to make coherent sense about literary questions must evidently choose between these two methods of procedure, even if he remains unconscious that he is making the choice; and as he chooses the one or the other so will what he is talking about, under the name of "tragedy" or what not, be one kind of thing or another, and few of the statements he may make about it will have the same meaning or possess equal validity in the two cases. For clearly what may be true of tragedy, or of any tragedy, when "tragedy" is taken, in the first method of consideration, as a name for a particular species of concrete artistic productions that are distinguished, among other things, by having such-and-such a plot-form as a necessary condition of producing such-and-such an effect, will not be true, or true in the same sense, when "tragedy" is taken, in the second method of consideration, as the name of a universal attitude or "vision" of life the distinctive nature of which is defined in dialectical opposition to another similarly universal attitude or "vision" of life for which the word "comedy" is thought to be the appropriate symbol.[24] And so with any other literary thing that is susceptible of formulation in either "matter of fact" or "abstract" terms; it must inevitably suffer a change of nature in passing from the one language to the other—so inescapable, in criticism, is the mutal interdependence of the subject-matter the critic actually talks about and the method of inquiry and argument by which it is constituted for him in his discussion.

Myth, Fiction, and Displacement

NORTHROP FRYE

"Myth" is a conception which runs through many areas of contemporary thought: anthropology, psychology, comparative religion, sociology, and several others. What follows is an attempt to explain what the term means in literary criticism today. Such an explanation must begin with the question: Why did the term ever get into literary criticism? There can be only one legitimate answer to such a question: because myth is and has always been an integral element of literature, the interest of poets in myth and mythology having been remarkable and constant since Homer's time.

There are two broad divisions of literary works, which may be called the fictional and the thematic. The former comprises works of literature with internal characters, and includes novels, plays, narrative poetry, folk tales, and everything that tells a story. In thematic literature the author and the reader are the only characters involved: this division includes most lyrics, essays, didactic poetry and oratory. Each division has its own type of myth, but we shall be concerned here with only the fictional part of literature, and with myth in its more common and easily recognized form as a certain kind of narrative.

When a critic deals with a work of literature, the most natural thing for him to do is to freeze it, to ignore its movement in time and look at it as a completed pattern of words, with all its parts existing simultaneously. This approach is common to nearly all types of critical techniques: here new and old-fashioned critics are at one. But in the direct experience of literature, which is something distinct from criticism, we are aware of what we may call the persuasion of continuity, the power that keeps us turning the pages of a novel and that holds us in our seats at the theatre. The continuity may be logical, or pseudo-logical, or psychological, or rhetorical: it may reside in the surge and thunder of epic verse or in some donkey's carrot like the identity of the murderer in a detective story or the first sexual act of the heroine in a romance. Or we may feel afterwards that the sense of continuity was pure illusion, as though we had been laid under a spell.

The continuity of a work of literature exists on different rhythmical levels. In the foreground, every word, every image, even every sound made audibly or inaudibly by the words, is making its tiny contribution to the total movement. But it would take a portentous concentration to attend to such details in direct experience: they belong to the kind of critical study that is dealing with a simultaneous unity. What we are conscious of in direct experience is rather a series of larger groupings, events and scenes that make up what we call the story. In ordinary English the word "plot" means this latter sequence of gross events. For a term that would include the total movement of sounds and images, the word "narrative" seems more natural than "plot," though the choice is a matter of usage and not of inherent correctness. Both words translate Aristotle's *mythos,* but Aristotle meant mainly by *mythos* what we are calling plot: narrative, in the above sense, is closer to his *lexis.* The plot, then, is like the trees and houses that we focus our eyes on through a train window: the narrative is more like the weeds and stones that rush by in the foreground.

We now run into a curious difficulty. Plot, Aristotle says, is the life and soul of tragedy (and by implication of fiction generally): the essence of fiction, then, is plot or imitation of action, and characters exist primarily as functions of the plot. In our direct experience of fiction we feel how central is the importance of the steady progression of events that holds and guides our attention. Yet afterwards, when we try to remember or think about what we have seen, this sense of continuity is one of the most difficult things to recapture. What stands out in our minds is a vivid characterization, a great speech or striking image, a detached scene, bits and pieces of unusually convincing realization. A summary of a plot, say of a Scott novel, has much the same numbing effect on a hearer as a summary of last night's dream. That is not how we remember the book; or at least not why we remember it. And even with a work of fiction that we know thoroughly, such as *Hamlet,* while we keep in mind a sequence of scenes, and know that the ghost comes at the beginning and the duel with Laertes at the end, still there is something oddly discontinuous about our possession of it. With the histories this disappearance of continuity is even more striking. *The Oxford Companion to English Literature* is an invaluable reference work largely because it is so good at summarizing all the fictional plots that one has forgotten, but here is its summary of *King John*:

The play, with some departures from historical accuracy, deals with various events in King John's reign, and principally with the tragedy of young Arthur. It ends with the death of John at Swinstead Abbey. It is significant that no mention of Magna Carta appears in it. The tragic quality of the play, the poignant grief of Constance, Arthur's mother, and the political

complications depicted, are relieved by the wit, humour, and gallantry of
the Bastard of Faulconbridge.

This is, more or less, how we remember the play. We remember Faulconbridge
and his great speech at the end; we remember the death scene of Prince Arthur;
we remember Constance; we remember nothing about Magna Carta; we
remember in the background the vacillating, obstinate, defiant king. But what
happened in the play? What were the incidents that made it an imitation of an
action? Does it matter? If it doesn't matter, what becomes of the principle that
that characters exist for the sake of the action, the truth of which we felt so
vividly while watching the play? If it does matter, are we going to invent some
silly pedantic theory of unity that would rule out *King John* as legitimate
drama?

Whatever the final answer, we may tentatively accept the principle that, in
the direct experience of fiction, continuity is the centre of our attention; our
later memory, or what I call the possession of it, tends to become discontinuous.
Our attention shifts from the sequence of incidents to another focus: a sense of
what the work of fiction was all *about,* or what criticism usually calls its theme.
And we notice that as we go on to study and reread the work of fiction, we tend,
not to reconstruct the plot, but to become more conscious of the theme, and to
see all incidents as manifestations of it. Thus the incidents themselves tend to
remain, in our critical study of the work, discontinuous, detached from one
another and regrouped in a new way. Even if we know it by heart this is still
true, and if we are writing or lecturing on it, we usually start with something
other than its linear action.

Now in the conception "theme," as in the conception "narrative," there are
a number of distinguishable elements. One of them is "subject," which criticism
can usually express by some kind of summarized statement. If we are asked
what Arthur Miller's *The Crucible* is about, we say that it is about—that is, its
subject is—the Salem witch trials. Similarly, the subject of *Hamlet* is Hamlet's
attempt at revenge on an uncle who has murdered his father and married his
mother. But the Olivier movie of *Hamlet* began with the statement (quoted from
an unreliable memory): "This is the story of a man who could not make up
his mind." Here is a quite different conception of theme: it expresses the theme
in terms of what we may call its allegorical value. To the extent that it is an
adequate statement of the theme of *Hamlet,* it makes the play into an allegory
and the chief character into a personification of Indecision. In his illuminating
study of *The Ancient Mariner,* Robert Penn Warren says that the poem is written
out of, and about, the general belief that the truth is implicit "in the poetic act
as such, that the moral concern and the aesthetic concern are aspects of the
same activity, the creative activity, and that this activity is expressive of the
whole mind" (italicized in the original). Here again is allegorization, of a kind
that takes the theme to be what Aristotle appears to have meant primarily by
dianoia, the "thought" or sententious reflexion that the poem suggests to a
meditative reader.

It seems to me that a third conception of "theme" is possible, less abstract than the subject and more direct than an allegorical translation. It is also, however, a conception for which the primitive vocabulary of contemporary criticism is ill adapted. Theme in this third sense is the *mythos* or plot examined as a simultaneous unity, when the entire shape of it is clear in our minds. In *Anatomy of Criticism* I use *dianoia* in this sense: an extension of Aristotle's meaning, no doubt, but in my opinion a justifiable one. The theme, so considered, differs appreciably from the moving plot: it is the same in substance, but we are now concerned with the details in relation to a unity, not in relation to suspense and linear progression. The unifying factors assume a new and increased import-ance, and the smaller details of imagery, which may escape conscious notice in direct experience, take on their proper significance. It is because of this difference that we find our memory of the progression of events dissolving as the events regroup themselves around another centre of attention. Each event or incident, we now see, is a manifestation of some underlying unity, a unity that it both conceals and reveals, as clothes do the body in *Sartor Resartus*.

Further, the plot or progress of events as a whole is also a manifestation of the theme, for the same story (i.e., theme in our sense) could be told in many different ways. It is, of course, impossible to say how extensive the changes in detail would have to be before we had a different theme, but they can be surprisingly extensive. Chaucer's *Pardoner's Tale* is a folk tale that started in India and must have reached Chaucer from some West-European source. It also stayed in India, where Kipling picked it up and put it into the *Second Jungle Book*. Everything is different—setting, details, method of treatment—yet I think any reader, on whatever level of sophistication, would say that it was recognizably the same "story"—story as theme, that is, for the linear progression is what is different. More often we have only smaller units in common, of a kind that students of folklore call motifs. Thus in Hawthorne's *The Marble Faun* we have the motif of the two heroines, one dark and one light, that we have in *Ivanhoe* and elsewhere; in *Lycidas* we have the motif of the "sanguine flower inscrib'd with woe," the red or purple flower that turns up everywhere in pastoral elegy, and so on. These smaller units I have elsewhere called archetypes, a word which has been connected since Plato's time with the sense of a pattern or model used in creation.

In most works of fiction we are at once aware that the *mythos* or sequence of events which holds our attention is being shaped into a unity. We are con-tinually, if often unconsciously, attempting to construct a larger pattern of simultaneous significance out of what we have so far read or seen. We feel confident that the beginning implies an end, and that the story is not like the soul in natural theology, starting off at an arbitrary moment in time and going on forever. Hence we often keep on reading even a tiresome novel "to see how it turns out." That is, we expect a certain point near the end at which linear suspense is resolved and the unifying shape of the whole design becomes conceptually visible. This point was called *anagnorisis* by Aristotle, a term for which "recognition" is a better rendering than "discovery." A tragic or comic plot is not a straight line: it is a parabola following the shapes of the mouths on the conventional masks. Comedy has a U-shaped plot, with the action sinking into deep and often potentially tragic complications, and then suddenly turning upward into a happy ending. Tragedy has an inverted U, with the action rising in crisis to a peripety and then plunging downward to catastrophe through a series of recognitions, usually of the inevitable consequences of previous acts. But in both cases what is recognized is seldom anything new; it is something which has been there all along, and which, by its reappearance or manifestation, brings the end into line with the beginning.

Recognition, and the unity of theme which it manifests, is often symbolized by some kind of emblematic object. A simple example is in the sixteenth-century play, *Gammer Gurton's Needle,* the action of which is largely a great to-do over the loss of the needle, and which ends when a clown named Hodge gets it stuck in his posterior, bringing about what *Finnegans Wake* would call a culious epiphany. Fans, rings, chains and other standard props of comedy are emblematic talismans of the same kind. Nearly always, however, such an emblem has to do with the identification of a chief character. Birthmarks and their symbolic relatives have run through fiction from Odysseus' scar to the scarlet letter, and from the brand of Cain to the rose tattoo. In Greek romance and its descendants we have infants of noble birth exposed on a hillside with birth-tokens beside them; they are found by a shepherd or farmer and brought up in a lower station of life, and the birth-tokens are produced when the story has gone on long enough. In more complex fiction the emblem may be an oblique comment on a character, as with Henry James's golden bowl; or, if it is only a motif, it may serve as what T. S. Eliot calls an objective correlative.

In any case, the point of recognition seems to be also a point of identification, where a hidden truth about something or somebody emerges into view. Besides the emblem, the hero may discover who his parents or children are, or he may go through some kind of ordeal (*basanos*) that manifests his true character, or the villain may be unmasked as a hypocrite, or, as in a detective story, identified as a murderer. In the Chinese play *The Chalk Circle* we have almost every possible form of recognition in the crucial scene. A concubine bears her master a son and is then accused of having murdered him by the wife, who has murdered him herself, and who also claims the son as her own. The concubine is tried before a foolish judge and condemned to death, then tried again before a wise one, who performs an experiment in a chalk circle resembling that of the judgment of Solomon in the Bible, and which proves that the concubine is the mother. Here we have: (a) the specific emblematic device which gives the play its name; (b) an ordeal or test which reveals character; (c) the reunion of the mother with her rightful child; and (d) the recognition of the true moral natures of concubine and wife. There are several other elements of structural importance, but these will do to go on with.

So far, however, we have been speaking of strictly controlled forms, like comedy, where the end of the linear action also manifests the unity of the theme. What shall we find if we turn to other works where the author has just let his imagination go? I put the question in the form of this very common phrase because of the way that it illustrates a curious critical muddle. Usually, when we think of "imagination" psychologically, we think of it in its Renaissance sense as a faculty that works mainly by association and outside the province of judgment. But the associative faculty is not the creative one, though the two are frequently confused by neurotics. When we think of imagination as the power that produces art, we often think of it as the designing or structural principle in creation, Coleridge's "esemplastic" power. But imagination in this sense, left to itself, can only design. Random fantasy is exceedingly rare in the arts, and most of what we do have is a clever simulation of it. From primitive cultures to the *tachiste* and action paintings of today, it has been a regular rule that the uninhibited imagination, in the structural sense, produces highly conventionalized art.

This rule implies, of course, that the main source of inhibitions is the need to produce a credible or plausible story, to come to terms with things as they are and not as the story-teller would like them to be for his convenience. Removing the necessity for telling a credible story enables the teller to concentrate on its structure, and when this happens, characters turn into imaginative projections, heroes becoming purely heroic and villains purely villainous. That is, they become assimilated to their functions in the plot. We see this conventionalizing of structure very clearly in the folk tale. Folk tales tell us nothing credible about the life or manners of any society; so far from giving us dialogue, imagery or complex behavior, they do not even care whether their characters are men or ghosts or animals. Folk tales are simply abstract story-patterns, uncomplicated and easy to remember, no more hampered by barriers of language and culture than migrating birds are by customs officers, and made up of interchangeable motifs that can be counted and indexed.

Nevertheless, folk tales form a continuum with other literary fictions. We know, vaguely, that the story of Cinderella has been retold hundreds of thousands of times in middle-class fiction, and that nearly every thriller we see is a variant of Bluebeard. But it is seldom explained why even the greatest writers are interested in such tales: why Shakespeare put a folk-tale motif into nearly every comedy he wrote; why some of the most intellectualized fiction of our day, such as the later works of Thomas Mann, are based on them. Writers are interested in folk tales for the same reason that painters are interested in still-life arrangements: because they illustrate essential principles of storytelling. The writer who uses them then has the technical problem of making them sufficiently plausible or credible to a sophisticated audience. When he succeeds, he produces, not realism, but a distortion of realism in the interests of structure. Such distortion is the literary equivalent of the tendency in painting to assimilate subject-matter to geometrical form, which we see both in primitive painting and in the sophisticated primitivism of, say, Léger or Modigliani.

What we see clearly in the folk tale we see less clearly in popular fiction. If we want incident for its own sake, we turn from the standard novelists to adventure stories, like those of Rider Haggard or John Buchan, where the action is close to if not actually across the boundary of the credible. Such stories are not looser or more flexible than the classical novels, but far tighter. Gone is all sense of the leisurely acquiring of incidental experience, of exploring all facets of a character, of learning about a specific society. A hazardous enterprise is announced at the beginning and everything is rigorously subordinated to that. In such works, while characters exist for the sake of the action, the two aspects of the action which we have defined as plot and theme are very close together. The story could hardly have been told in any other narrative shape, and our attention has so little expanding to do when it reaches the recognition that we often feel that there would be no point in reading it a second time. The subordination of character to linear action is also a feature of the detective story, for the fact that one of the characters is capable of murder is the concealed clue on which every detective story turns. Even more striking is the subordinating of moral attitude to the conventions of the story. Thus in Robert Louis Stevenson's tale, *The Body-Snatcher*, which is about the smuggling of corpses from cemeteries into medical classrooms, we read of bodies being "exposed to uttermost indignities before a class of gaping boys," and much more to the same effect. It is irrelevant to inquire whether this is really Stevenson's attitude to the use of cadavers in medical study or whether he expects it to be ours. The more sinister the crime can be felt to be, the more thrilling the thriller, and the moral attitude is being deliberately talked up to thicken the atmosphere.

The opposite extreme from such conventionalized fiction is represented by Trollope's *Last Chronicle of Barset*. Here the main story line is a kind of parody of a detective novel—such parodies of suspense are frequent in Trollope. Some money has been stolen, and suspicion falls on the Reverend Josiah Crawley, curate of Hogglestock. The point of the parody is that Crawley's character is clearly and fully set forth, and if you imagine him capable of stealing money you are simply not attending to the story. The action, therefore, appears to exist for the sake of the characters, reversing Aristotle's axiom. But this is not really true. Characters still exist only as functions of the action, but in Trollope the "action" resides in the huge social panorama that the linear events build up. Recognition is continuous: it is in the texture of characterization, the dialogue and the comment itself, and needs no twist in the plot to dramatize a contrast between appearance and reality. And what is true of Trollope is roughly true of most mimetic fiction between Defoe and Arnold Bennett. When we read Smollett or Jane Austen or Dickens, we read them for the sake of the texture of characterization, and tend to think of the plot, when we think of it at all, as a conventional, mechanical, or even (as occasionally in Dickens) absurd contrivance included only to satisfy the demands of the literary market.

The requirement of plausibility, then, has the apparently paradoxical effect of limiting the imagination by making its design more flexible. Thus in a Dutch realistic interior the painter's ability to render the sheen of satin or the varnish of a lute both limits his power of design (for a realistic painter cannot, like Braque or Juan Gris, distort his object in the interest of pictorial composition) and yet makes that design less easy to take in at a glance. In fact we often "read" Dutch pictures instead of looking at them, absorbed by their technical virtuosity but unaffected by much conscious sense of their total structure.

By this time the ambiguity in our word "imagination" is catching up with us. So far we have been using it in the sense of a structural power which, left to itself, produces rigorously predictable fictions. In this sense Bernard Shaw spoke of the romances of Marie Corelli as illustrating the triumph of imagination over mind. What is implied by "mind" here is less a structural than a reproductive power, which expresses itself in the texture of characterization and imagery. There seems no reason why this should not be called imagination too: in any case, in reading fiction there are two kinds of recognition. One is the continuous recognition of credibility, fidelity to experience, and of what is not so much lifelikeness as life-liveliness. The other is the recognition of the identity of the total design, into which we are initiated by the technical recognition in the plot.

The influence of mimetic fiction has thrown the main emphasis in criticism on the former kind of recognition. Coleridge, as is well known, intended the climax of the *Biographia Literaria* to be a demonstration of the "esemplastic" or structural nature of the imagination, only to discover when the great chapter arrived that he was unable to write it. There were doubtless many reasons for this, but one was that he does not really think of imagination as a constructive power at all. He means by imagination what we have called the reproductive power, the ability to bring to life the texture of characterization and imagery. It is to this power that he applies his favorite metaphor of an organism, where the unity is some mysterious and elusive "vitality." His practical criticism of work he admires is concerned with texture: he never discusses the total design, or what we call the theme, of a Shakespeare play. It is really fancy which is his "esemplastic" power, and which he tends to think of as mechanical. His conception of fancy as a mode of memory, emancipated from time and space and playing with fixities and definites, admirably characterizes the folk tale, with its remoteness from society and its stock of interchangeable motifs. Thus Coleridge is in the tradition of critical naturalism, which bases its values on the immediacy of contact between art and nature that we continuously feel in the texture of mimetic fiction.

There is nothing wrong with critical naturalism, as far as it goes, but it does not do full justice to our feelings about the total design of a work of fiction. We shall not improve on Coleridge, however, by merely reversing his perspective, as T. E. Hulme did, and giving our favorable value-judgments to fancy, wit, and highly conventionalized forms. This can start a new critical trend, but not develop the study of criticism. In the direct experience of a new work of fiction we have a sense of its unity which we derive from its persuasive continuity. As the work becomes more familiar, this sense of continuity fades out, and we tend to think of it as a discontinuous series of episodes, held together by something which eludes critical analysis. But that this unity is available for critical study as well seems clear when it emerges as a unity of "theme," as we call it, which we can study all at once, and to which we are normally initiated by some crucial recognition in the plot. Hence we need a supplementary form of criticism which can examine the total design of fiction as something which is neither mechanical nor of secondary importance.

By a myth, as I said at the beginning, I mean primarily a certain type of story. It is a story in which some of the chief characters are gods or other beings larger in power than humanity. Very seldom is it located in history: its action takes place in a world above or prior to ordinary time, *in illo tempore,* in Mircea Eliade's phrase. Hence, like the folk tale, it is an abstract story-pattern. The characters can do what they like, which means what the story-teller likes: there is no need to be plausible or logical in motivation. The things that happen in myth are things that happen only in stories; they are in a self-contained literary world. Hence myth would naturally have the same kind of appeal for the fiction writer that folk tales have. It presents him with a ready-made framework, hoary with antiquity, and allows him to devote all his energies to elaborating its design. Thus the use of myth in Joyce or Cocteau, like the use of folk tale in Mann, is parallel to the use of abstraction and other means of emphasizing design in contemporary painting; and a modern writer's interest in primitive fertility rites is parallel to a modern sculptor's interest in primitive woodcarving.

The differences between myth and folk tale, however, also have their importance. Myths, as compared with folk tales, are usually in a special category of seriousness: they are believed to have "really happened," or to have some exceptional significance in explaining certain features of life, such as ritual. Again, whereas folk tales simply interchange motifs and develop variants, myths show an odd tendency to stick together and build up bigger structures. We have creation myths, fall and flood myths, metamorphosis and dying-god myths, divine-marriage and hero-ancestry myths, etiological myths, apocalyptic myths; and writers of sacred scriptures or collectors of myth like Ovid tend to arrange these in a series. And while myths themselves are seldom historical, they seem to provide a kind of containing form of tradition, one result of which is the obliterating of boundaries separating legend, historical reminiscence, and actual history that we find in Homer and the Old Testament.

As a type of story, myth is a form of verbal art, and belongs to the world of art, and unlike science, it deals, not with the world that man contemplates, but with the world that man creates. The total form of art, so to speak, is a world whose content is nature but whose form is human; hence when it "imitates" nature it assimilates nature to human forms. The world of art is human in perspective, a world in which the sun continues to rise and set long after science has explained that its rising and setting are illusions. And myth, too, makes a systematic attempt to see nature in human shape: it does not simply roam at large in nature like the folk tale.

The obvious conception which brings together the human form and the natural content in myth is the god. It is not the connexion of the stories of Phaethon and Endymion with the sun and moon that makes them myths, for we could have folk tales of the same kind: it is rather their attachment to the body of stories told about Apollo and Artemis which gives them a canonical place in the growing system of tales that we call a mythology. And every developed mythology tends to complete itself, to outline an entire universe in which the "gods" represent the whole of nature in humanized form, and at the same time show in perspective man's origin, his destiny, the limits of his power, and the extension of his hopes and desires. A mythology may develop by accretion, as in Greece, or by rigorous codifying and the excluding of unwanted material, as in Israel; but the drive toward a verbal circumference of human experience is clear in both cultures.

The two great conceptual principles which myth uses in assimilating nature to human form are analogy and identity. Analogy establishes the parallels between human life and natural phenomena, and identity conceives of a "sun-god" or a "tree-god." Myth seizes on the fundamental element of design offered by nature—the cycle, as we have it daily in the sun and yearly in the seasons—and assimilates it to the human cycle of life, death, and (analogy again) rebirth. At the same time the discrepancy between the world man lives in and the world he would like to live in develops, a dialectic in myth which, as in the New Testament and Plato's *Phaedo,* separates reality into two contrasting states, a heaven and a hell.

Again, myths are often used as allegories of science or religion or morality: they may arise in the first place to account for a ritual or a law, or they may be *exempla* or parables which illustrate a particular situation or argument, like the myths in Plato or Achilles' myth of the two jars of Zeus at the end of the Iliad. Once established in their own right, they may then be interpreted dogmatically or allegorically, as all the standard myths have been for centuries, in innumerable ways. But because myths are stories, what they "mean" is inside them, in the implications of their incidents. No rendering of any myth into conceptual language can serve as a full equivalent of its meaning. A myth may be told and retold: it may be modified or elaborated, or different patterns may be discovered in it; and its life is always the poetic life of a story, not the homiletic life of some illustrated truism. When a system of myths loses all connexion with belief, it becomes purely literary, as Classical myth did in Christian Europe. Such a development would be impossible unless myths were inherently literary in structure. As it makes no difference to that structure whether an interpretation of the myth is believed in or not, there is no difficulty in speaking of a Christian mythology.

Myth thus provides the main outlines and the circumference of a verbal universe which is later occupied by literature as well. Literature is more flexible than myth, and fills up this universe more completely: a poet or novelist may work in areas of human life apparently remote from the shadowy gods and gigantic story-outlines of mythology. But in all cultures mythology merges insensibly into, and with, literature. The Odyssey is to us a work of literature, but its early place in the literary tradition, the importance of gods in its action, and its influence on the later religious thought of Greece, are all features common to literature proper and to mythology, and indicate that the difference between them is more chronological than structural. Educators are now aware that any effective teaching of literature has to recapitulate its history and begin, in early childhood, with myths, folk tales and legends.

We should expect, therefore, that there would be a great many literary works derived directly from specific myths, like the poems by Drayton and Keats about Endymion which are derived from the myth of Endymion. But the study of the relations between mythology and literature is not confined to such one-to-one relationships. In the first place, mythology as a total structure, defining as it does a society's religious beliefs, historical traditions, cosmologic speculations—in short, the whole range of its verbal expressiveness—is the matrix of literature, and major poetry keeps returning to it. In every age poets who are thinkers (remembering that poets think in metaphors and images, not in propositions) and are deeply concerned with the origin or destiny or desires of mankind—with anything that belongs to the larger outlines of what literature can express—can hardly find a literary theme that does not coincide with a myth. Hence the imposing body of explicitly mythopoeic poetry in the epic and encyclopaedic forms which so many of the greatest poets use. A poet who accepts a mythology as valid for belief, as Dante and Milton accepted Christianity, will naturally use it; poets outside such a tradition turn to other mythologies as suggestive or symbolic of what might be believed, as in the adaptations of Classical or occult mythological systems made by Goethe, Victor Hugo, Shelley, or Yeats.

Similarly, the structural principles of a mythology, built up from analogy and identity, become in due course the structural principles of literature. The absorption of the natural cycle into mythology provides myth with two of these structures; the rising movement that we find in myths of spring or the dawn, of birth, marriage and resurrection, and the falling movement in myths of death, metamorphosis, or sacrifice. These movements reappear as the structural principles of comedy and tragedy in literature. Again, the dialectic in myth that projects a paradise or heaven above our world and a hell or place of shades below it reappears in literature as the idealized world of pastoral and romance and the absurd, suffering, or frustrated world of irony and satire.

The relation between myth and literature, therefore, is established by studying the genres and conventions of literature. Thus the convention of the pastoral elegy in *Lycidas* links it to Virgil and Theocritus, and thence with the myth of Adonis. Thus the convention of the foundling plot, which is the basis of *Tom Jones* and *Oliver Twist,* goes back to Menandrine comedy formulas, thence to Euripides, and so back to such myths as the finding of Moses and Perseus. In myth criticism, when we examine the theme or total design of a fiction, we must isolate that aspect of the fiction which is conventional, and held in common with all other works of the same category. When we begin, say, *Pride and Prejudice,* we can see at once that a story which sustains that particular mood or tone is most unlikely to end in tragedy or melodrama or mordant irony or romance. It clearly belongs to the category represented by the word "comedy," and we are not surprised to find in it the conventional features of comedy, including a foolish lover, with some economic advantages, encouraged by one of the parents, a hypocrite unmasked, misunderstandings between the chief characters eventually cleared up and happy marriages for those who deserve them. This conventional comic form is in *Pride and Prejudice* somewhat as the sonata form is in a Mozart symphony. Its presence there does not account for any of the merits of the novel, but it does account for its conventional, as distinct from its individual, structure. A serious interest in structure, then, ought naturally to lead us from *Pride and Prejudice* to a study of the comic form which it exemplifies, the conventions of which have presented much the same features from Plautus to our own day. These conventions in turn take us back into myth. When we compare the conventional plot of a play of Plautus with the Christian myth of a son appeasing the wrath of a father and redeeming his bride, we can see that the latter is quite accurately described, from a literary point of view, as a divine comedy.

Whenever we find explicit mythologizing in literature, or a writer trying to indicate what myths he is particularly interested in, we should treat this as confirmatory or supporting evidence for our study of the genres and conventions he is using. Meredith's *The Egoist* is a story about a girl who narrowly escapes marrying a selfish man, which makes many references, both explicitly and indirectly in its imagery, to the two best known myths of female sacrifice, the stories of Andromeda and Iphigeneia. Such allusions would be pointless or unintelligible except as indications by Meredith of an awareness of the conventional shape of the story he is telling. Again, it is as true of poetry as it is of myth that its main conceptual elements are analogy and identity, which reappear in the two commonest figures of speech, the simile and the metaphor. Literature, like mythology, is largely an art of misleading analogies and mistaken identities. Hence we often find poets, especially young poets, turning to myth because of the scope it affords them for uninhibited poetic imagery. If Shakespeare's *Venus and Adonis* had been simply a story about a willing girl and an unwilling boy, all the resources of analogy and identity would have been left unexplored: the fanciful imagery appropriate to the mythical subject would have been merely tasteless exaggeration. Especially is this true with what may be called sympathetic imagery, the association of human and natural life:

> No flower was nigh, no grass, herb, leaf, or weed,
> But stole his blood and seem'd with him to bleed.

The opposite extreme from such deliberate exploiting of myth is to be found in the general tendency of realism or naturalism to give imaginative life and coherence to something closely resembling our own ordinary experience. Such realism often begins by simplifying its language, and dropping the explicit connexions with myth which are a sign of an awareness of literary tradition. Wordsworth, for example, felt that in his day Phoebus and Philomela were getting to be mere trade slang for the sun and the nightingale, and that poetry would do better to discard this kind of inorganic allusion. But, as Wordsworth himself clearly recognized, the result of turning one's back on explicit myth can only be the reconstructing of the same mythical patterns in more ordinary words:

> Paradise, and groves
> Elysian, Fortunate Fields—like those of old
> Sought in the Atlantic Main—why should they be
> A history only of departed things,
> Or a mere fiction of what never was?
> For the discerning intellect of Man,

> When wedded to this goodly universe
> In love and holy passion, shall find these
> A simple produce of the common day.

To this indirect mythologizing I have elsewhere given the name of displacement. By displacement I mean the techniques a writer uses to make his story credible, logically motivated or morally acceptable—lifelike, in short. I call it displacement for many reasons, but one is that fidelity to the credible is a feature of literature that can affect only content. Life presents a continuum, and a selection from it can only be what is called a *tranche de vie:* plausibility is easy to sustain, but except for death life has little to suggest in the way of plausible conclusions. And even a plausible conclusion does not necessarily round out a shape. The realistic writer soon finds that the requirements of literary form and plausible content always fight against each other. Just as the poetic metaphor is always a logical absurdity, so every inherited convention of plot in literature is more or less mad. The king's rash promise, the cuckold's jealousy, the "lived happily ever after" tag to a concluding marriage, the manipulated happy endings of comedy in general, the equally manipulated ironic endings of modern realism—none of these was suggested by any observation of human life or behavior: all exist solely as story-telling devices. Literary shape cannot come from life; it comes only from literary tradition, and so ultimately from myth. In sober realism, like the novels of Trollope, the plot, as we have noted, is often a parody plot. It is instructive to notice, too, how strong the popular demand is for such forms as detective stories, science fiction, comic strips, comic formulas like the P. G. Wodehouse stories, all of which are as rigorously conventional and stylized as the folk tale itself, works of pure "esemplastic" imagination, with the recognition turning up as predictably as the caesura in minor Augustan poetry.

One difficulty in proceeding from this point comes from the lack of any literary term which corresponds to the word "mythology." We find it hard to conceive of literature as an order of words, as a unified imaginative system that can be studied as a whole by criticism. If we had such a conception, we could readily see that literature as a whole provides a framework or context for every work of literature, just as a fully developed mythology provides a framework or context for each of its myths. Further, because mythology and literature occupy the same verbal space, so to speak, the framework or context of every work of literature can be found in mythology as well, when its literary tradition is understood. It is relatively easy to see the place of a myth in a mythology, and one of the main uses of myth criticism is to enable us to understand the corresponding place that a work of literature has in the context of literature as a whole.

Putting works of literature in such a context gives them an immense reverberating dimension of significance. (If anyone is worrying about value-judgments, I should add that establishing such a context tends to make the genuine work of literature sublime and the pinchbeck one ridiculous.) This reverberating significance, in which every literary work catches the echoes of all other works of its type in literature, and so ripples out into the rest of literature and thence into life, is often, and wrongly, called allegory. We have allegory when one literary work is joined to another, or to a myth, by a certain interpretation of meaning rather than by structure. Thus *The Pilgrim's Progress* is related allegorically to the Christian myth of redemption, and Hawthorne's story, *The Bosom Serpent*, is related allegorically to various moral serpents going back to the Book of Genesis. Arthur Miller's *The Crucible*, already mentioned, deals with the Salem witch trials in a way that suggested McCarthyism to most of its original audience. This relation in itself is allegorical. But if *The Crucible* is good enough to hold the stage after McCarthyism has become as dead an issue as the Salem trials, it would be clear that the theme of *The Crucible* is one which can always be used in literature, and that any social hysteria can form its subject matter. Social hysteria, however, is the content and not the form of the theme itself, which belongs in the category of the purgatorial or triumphant tragedy. As so often happens in literature, the only explicit clue to its mythical shape is provided by the title.

To sum up. In the direct experience of a new work of literature, we are aware of its continuity or moving power in time. As we become both more familiar with and more detached from it, the work tends to break up into a discontinuous series of felicities, bits of vivid imagery, convincing characterization, witty dialogue, and the like. The study of this belongs to what we have called critical naturalism or continuous recognition, the sense of the sharply focused reproduction of life in the fiction. But there was a feeling of unity in the original experience which such criticism does not recapture. We need to move from a criticism of "effects" to what we may call a criticism of causes, specifically the formal cause which holds the work together. The fact that such unity is available for critical study as well as for direct experience is normally symbolized by a crucial recognition, a point marking a real and not merely apparent unity in the design. Fictions like those of Trollope which appeal particularly to critical naturalism often play down or even parody such a device, and such works show the highest degree of displacement and the least conscious or explicit relationship to myth.

If, however, we go on to study the theme or total shape of the fiction, we find that it also belongs to a convention or category, like those of comedy and tragedy. With the literary category we reach a dead end, until we realize that literature is a reconstructed mythology, with its structural principles derived from those of myth. Then we can see that literature is in a complex setting what a mythology is in a simpler one: a total body of verbal creation. In literature, whatever has a shape has a mythical shape, and leads us toward the center of the order of words. For just as critical naturalism studies the counterpoint of literature and life, words and things, so myth criticism pulls us away from "life" toward a self-contained and autonomous literary universe. But myth, as we said at the beginning, means many things besides literary structure, and the world of words is not so self-contained and autonomous after all.

Telling and Showing

WAYNE C. BOOTH

"Action, and tone, and gesture, the smile of the lover,
the frown of the tyrant, the grimace of the buffoon,—all
must be told [in the novel], for nothing can be shown.
Thus, the very dialogue becomes mixed with the narration; for he must not only tell what the characters
actually said, in which his task is the same as that of the
dramatic author, but must also describe the tone, the
look, the gesture, with which their speech was accompanied,—telling, in short, all which, in the drama, it
becomes the province of the actor to express."

—SIR WALTER SCOTT

"Authors like Thackeray, or Balzac, say, or H. G. Wells
. . . are always *telling* the reader what happened instead
of showing them the scene, telling them what to think
of the characters rather than letting the reader judge for
himself or letting the characters do the telling about one
another. I like to distinguish between novelists that *tell*
and those [like Henry James] that *show*."

—JOSEPH WARREN BEACH

"The only law that binds the novelist throughout,
whatever course he is pursuing, is the need to be consistent on *some* plan, to follow the principle he has
adopted."

—PERCY LUBBOCK

"A novelist can shift his view point if it comes off, and it came off with Dickens and Tolstoy."

—E. M. FORSTER

AUTHORITATIVE "TELLING" IN EARLY NARRATION

One of the most obviously artificial devices of the storyteller is the trick of going beneath the surface of the action to obtain a reliable view of a character's mind and heart. Whatever our ideas may be about the natural way to tell a story, artifice is unmistakably present whenever the author tells us what no one in so-called real life could possibly know. In life we never know anyone but ourselves by thoroughly reliable internal signs, and most of us achieve an all too partial view even of ourselves. It is in a way strange, then, that in literature from the very beginning we have been told motives directly and authoritatively without being forced to rely on those shaky inferences about other men which we cannot avoid in our own lives.

"There was a man in the land of Uz, whose name was Job; and that man was perfect and upright, one that feared God, and eschewed evil." With one stroke the unknown author has given us a kind of information never obtained about real people, even about our most intimate friends. Yet it is information that we must accept without question if we are to grasp the story that is to follow. In life if a friend confided his view that *his* friend was "perfect and upright," we would accept the information with qualifications imposed by our knowledge of the speaker's character or of the general fallibility of mankind. We could never trust even the most reliable of witnesses as completely as we trust the author of the opening statement about Job.

We move immediately in Job to two scenes presented with no privileged information whatever: Satan's temptation of God and Job's first losses and lamentations. But we conclude the first section with another judgment which no real event could provide for any observer: "In all this Job sinned not, nor charged God foolishly." How do we know that Job sinned not? Who is to pronounce on such a question? Only God himself could know with certainty whether Job charged God foolishly. Yet the author pronounces judgment, and we accept his judgment without question.

It might at first appear that the author does not require us to rely on his unsupported word, since he gives us the testimonial of God himself, conversing with Satan, to confirm his view of Job's moral perfection. And after Job has been pestered by his three friends and has given his own opinion about his experience, God is brought on stage again to confirm the truth of Job's view. But clearly the reliability of God's statements ultimately depends on the author himself; it is he who names God and assures us that this voice is truly His.

This form of artificial authority has been present in most narrative until recent times. Though Aristotle praises Homer for speaking in his own voice less than other poets, even Homer writes scarcely a page without some kind of direct clarification of motives, of expectations, and of the relative importance of events. And though the gods themselves are often unreliable, Homer—the Homer we know—is not. What he tells us usually goes deeper and is more accurate than anything we are likely to learn about real people and events. In the opening lines of the *Iliad,* for example, we are told, under the half-pretence of an invocation, precisely what the tale is to be about: "the anger of Peleus' son Achilleus and its devastation."[1] We are told directly that we are to care more about the Greeks than the Trojans. We are told that they were "heroes" with "strong souls." We are told that it was the will of Zeus that they should be "the delicate feasting of dogs." And we learn that the particular conflict between Agamemnon, "the lord of men," and "brilliant" Achilles was set on by Apollo. We could never be sure of any of this information in real life, yet we are sure as we move through the *Iliad* with Homer constantly at our elbow, controlling rigorously our beliefs, our interests, and our sympathies. Though his commentary is generally brief and often disguised as simile, we learn from it the precise quality of every heart; we know who dies innocent and who guilty, who foolish and who wise. And we know, whenever there is any reason for us to know, what the characters are thinking: "the son of Tydeus pondered doubt-fully/. . . . Three times in his heart and spirit he pondered turning . . . (Book VIII, 11. 167–169).

In the *Odyssey* Homer works in the same explicit and systematic way to keep our judgments straight. Though E. V. Rieu is no doubt correct in calling Homer an "impersonal" and "objective" author, in the sense that the life of the real Homer cannot be discovered in his work,[2] Homer "intrudes" deli-berately and obviously to insure that our judgment of the "heroic," "resource-ful," "admirable," "wise" Odysseus will be sufficiently favorable. "Yet all the gods were sorry for him, except Poseidon, who pursued the heroic Odysseus with relentless malice till the day when he reached his own country."

Indeed, the major justification of the opening scene in the palace of Zeus is not as mere exposition of the facts of Odysseus' plight. What Homer requires of us is sympathetic involvement in that plight, and Athene's opening reply to Zeus provides authoritative judgment on what is to follow. "It is for Odysseus that my heart is wrung—the wise but unlucky Odysseus, who has been parted so long from all his friends and is pining on a lonely island far away in the middle of the seas." To her accusation of neglect, Zeus replies, "How could I ever forget the admirable Odysseus? He is not only the wisest man alive but has been the most generous in his offerings. . . . It is Poseidon . . . who is so implacable towards him. . . ."

When we come to Odysseus' enemies, the poet again does not hesitate either to speak in his own person or to give divine testimony. Penelope's suitors must look bad to us; Telemachus must be admired. Not only does Homer dwell on Athene's approval of Telemachus, he lays on his own direct judgments with

---

[1] Trans. Richmond Lattimore (Chicago, 1951). All quotations are from this translation.

[2] The *Odyssey,* trans. E. V. Rieu (Penguin ed., 1959), p. 10. The quotations that follow are from Rieu's translation, Books I–IV. Different translations give different emphases to Homer's moral judgments, and some use less forceful epithets than does Rieu. But no translator has been able to portray a neutral Homer.

bright colors. The "insolent," "swaggering," and "ruffianly" suitors are contrasted to the "wise" (though almost helplessly young) Telemachus and the "good" Mentor. "Telemachus now showed his good judgment." Mentor "showed his good will now by rising to admonish his compatriots." We seldom encounter the suitors without some explicit attack by the poet: "This was their boastful way, though it was they who little guessed how matters really stood." And whenever there might be some doubt about where a character stands, Homer sets us straight: " 'My Queen,' replied Medon, who was by no means a villain. . . ." Hundreds of pages later, when Medon is spared from Odysseus' slaughter, we can hardly be surprised.

The result of all this direct guidance, when it is joined with Athene's divine attestation that the gods "have no quarrel" with Telemachus and have settled that he "shall come home safe," is to leave us, as we enter upon Odysseus' first adventure in Book Five, perfectly clear about what we should hope for and what fear; we are unambiguously sympathetic toward the heroes and contemptuous of the suitors. It need hardly be said that another poet, working with the same episodes but treating them from the suitors' point of view, could easily have led us into the same adventures with radically different hopes and fears.[3]

Direct and authoritative rhetoric of the kind we have seen in Job and in Homer's works has never completely disappeared from fiction. But as we all know, it is not what we are likely to find if we turn to a typical modern novel or short story.

> Jim had a great trick that he used to play w'ile he was travelin'. For instance, he'd be ridin' on a train and they'd come to some little town like, well, like, we'll say, like Benton. Jim would look out of the train window and read the signs on the stores.
>
> For instance, they'd be a sign, "Henry Smith, Dry Goods." Well, Jim would write down the name and the name of the town and when he got to wherever he was goin' he'd mail back a postal card to Henry Smith at Benton and not sign no name to it, but he'd write on the card, well, somethin' like "Ask your wife about that book agent that spent the afternoon last week," or "Ask your Missus who kept her from gettin' lonesome the last time you was in Carterville." And he'd sign the card, "A Friend."
>
> Of course, he never knew what really come of none of these jokes, but he could picture what probably happened and that was enough . . . . Jim was a card.

Most readers of Lardner's "Haircut" (1926) have recognized that Lardner's opinion of Jim is radically different here from the speaker's. But no one in the story has said so. Lardner is not present to say so, not, at least, in the sense that

---

[3] Some readers may fear at this point that I am stumbling blindfold into the "affective fallacy." I try to meet their legitimate concern in chaps. iii–v.

Homer is present in his epics. Like many other modern authors, he has effaced himself, renounced the privilege of direct intervention, retreated to the wings and left his characters to work out their own fates upon the stage.

> In sleep she knew she was in her bed, but not the bed she had lain down in a few hours since, and the room was not the same but it was a room she had known somewhere. Her heart was a stone lying upon her breast outside of her; her pulses lagged and paused, and she knew that something strange was going to happen, even as the early morning winds were cool through the lattice. . . .
>
> Now I must get up and go while they are all quiet. Where are my things? Things have a will of their own in this place and hide where they like. . . . Now what horse shall I borrow for this journey I do not mean to take? . . . Come now, Graylie, she said, taking the bridle, we must outrun Death and the Devil. . . .

The relation between author and spokesman is more complex here. Katherine Anne Porter's Miranda ("Pale Horse, Pale Rider" [1936]) cannot be simply classified, like Lardner's barber, as morally and intellectually deficient; the ironies at work among character, author, and reader are considerably more difficult to describe. Yet the problem for the reader is essentially the same as in "Haircut." The story is presented without comment, leaving the reader without the guidance of explicit evaluation.

Since Flaubert, many authors and critics have been convinced that "objective" or "impersonal" or "dramatic" modes of narration are naturally superior to any mode that allows for direct appearances by the author or his reliable spokesman. Sometimes, as we shall see in the next three chapters, the complex issues involved in this shift have been reduced to a convenient distinction between "showing," which is artistic, and "telling," which is inartistic. "I shall not *tell* you anything," says a fine young novelist in defense of his art. "I shall allow you to eavesdrop on my people, and sometimes they will tell the truth and sometimes they will lie, and you must determine for yourself when they are doing which. You do this every day. Your butcher says, 'This is the best,' and you reply, 'That's *you* saying it.' Shall my people be less the captive of their desires than your butcher? I can *show* much, but show only. . . . You will no more expect the novelist to tell you precisely *how* something is said than you will expect him to stand by your chair and hold your book."[4]

But the changed attitudes toward the author's voice in fiction raise problems that go far deeper than this simplified version of point of view would suggest. Percy Lubbock taught us forty years ago to believe that "the art of fiction does not begin until the novelist thinks of his story as a matter to be *shown*, to be so exhibited that it will tell itself."[5] He may have been in some sense right—but to say so raises more questions than it answers.

[4] Mark Harris, "Easy Does It Not," in *The Living Novel*, ed. Granville Hicks (New York, 1957), p. 117.

[5] *The Craft of Fiction* (London, 1921), p. 62.

Why is it that an episode "told" by Fielding can strike us as more fully realized than many of the scenes scrupulously "shown" by imitators of James or Hemingway? Why does some authorial commentary ruin the work in which it occurs, while the prolonged commentary of *Tristram Shandy* can still enthral us? What, after all, does an author do when he "intrudes" to "tell" us something about his story? Such questions force us to consider closely what happens when an author engages a reader fully with a work of fiction; they lead us to a view of fictional technique which necessarily goes far beyond the reductions that we have sometimes accepted under the concept of "point of view."

TWO STORIES FROM THE "DECAMERON"

Our task will be simpler if we begin with some stories written long before anyone worried very much about cleaning out the rhetorical impurities from the house of fiction. The stories in Boccaccio's *Decameron,* for example, seem extremely simple—perhaps even simple-minded and inept—if we ask of them the questions which many modern stories invite us to ask. It is bad enough that the characters are what we call two-dimensional, with no revealed depths of any kind, what is much worse, the "point of view" of the narrator shifts among them with a total disregard for the kind of technical focus or consistency generally admired today. But if we read these stories in their own terms, we soon discover a splendid and complex skill underlying the simplicity of the effect.

The material of the ninth story of the fifth day is in itself conventional and shallow indeed. There was once a young lover, Federigo, who impoverished himself courting a chaste married woman, Monna Giovanna. Rejected, he withdrew to a life of poverty, with only a beloved falcon remaining of all his former possessions. The woman's husband died. Her son, who had grown fond of Federigo's falcon, became seriously ill and asked Monna to obtain the falcon for his comfort. She reluctantly went to Federigo to request the falcon. Federigo was overwhelmed with excitement by her visit, and he was determined, in spite of his poverty, to entertain her properly. But his cupboard was bare, so he killed the falcon and served it to her. They discovered their misunderstanding, and the mother returned empty-handed to her boy, who soon died. But the childless widow, impressed by Federigo's generous gesture in offering his falcon, chose him for her second husband.

Such a story, reduced in this way to a bare outline, could have been made into any number of fully realized plots with radically different effects. It could have been a farce, stressing Federigo's foolish extravagance, his ridiculous antics in trying to think of something to serve his beloved for breakfast, and the absurdity of the surprise ending. It could have been a meditative or a comic piece on the ironical twists of fate, emphasizing the transformation in Monna from proud resistance to quick surrender—something on the order of Christopher Fry's *A Phoenix Too Frequent* as derived from Petronius. It could have been a sardonic tale written from the point of view of the husband and son who, like the falcon, must be killed off, as it were, to make the survivors happy. And so on.

As it is, every stroke is in a direction different from these. The finished tale is designed to give the reader the greatest possible pleasure in the sympathetic comedy of Monna's and Federigo's deserved good fortune, to make the reader delight in this instance of the announced theme for all the tales told on the fifth day: "good fortune befalling lovers after divers direful or disastrous adventures."[6] Though one never views these characters or their "direful or disastrous adventures" in anything like a tragic light, and though, in fact, one laughs at the excesses of Federigo's passion and at his willingness to pursue it even to poverty, our laughter must always be sympathetic. Much as Federigo deserves his disasters, in the finished tale he also deserves the supreme good fortune of winning Monna.

To insure our pleasure in such an outcome—a pleasure which might have been mild indeed considering that there are nine other tales attempting something like the same effect—the two main characters must be established with great precision. First the heroine, Monna Giovanna, must be felt to be thoroughly worthy of Federigo's "extravagant" love. In a longer, different kind of story, this might have been done by showing her in virtuous action; one could take whatever space were required for episodes dramatizing her as worthy of Federigo's fantastic devotion. But here economy is at least as important as precision. And the economical method of imposing her virtues on the reader is for the narrator to *tell* us about them, supporting his telling with some judiciously chosen, and by modern standards very brief and unrealistic, episodes. These can be of two kinds, either in the form of what James was later to call "going behind" to reveal the true workings of the heroine's mind and heart or in the form of overt action. Thus, the narrator begins by describing her as the "fairest" and "most elegant," and as "no less virtuous than fair." In a simple story of this kind, her beauty and elegance require for validation no more than Federigo's dramatized passion. Our belief in her virtue, however—certainly in Boccaccio a more unlikely gift than beauty and elegance—is supported both by her sustained chastity in the face of his courtship and, far more important, by the quality of what is revealed whenever we enter her thoughts.

> Whereupon the lady was silent a while, bethinking her what she should do. She knew that Federigo had long loved her, and had never had so much as a single kind look from her: wherefore she said to herself:—How can I send or go to beg of him this falcon, which by what I hear is the best that ever flew, and moreover is his sole comfort? And how could I be so unfeeling as to seek to deprive a gentleman of the one solace that is now left him? And so, albeit she very well knew that she might have the falcon for the asking, she was perplexed, and knew not what to say, and gave her son no answer. At length, however, the love she bore the boy carried the day, and she made up her mind, for his contentment . . . to go herself and fetch him the falcon.

[6] Trans. J. M. Rigg (Everyman ed., 1930). All quotations are from this edition.

The interest in this passage lies of course in the moral choice that it presents and in the effect upon our sentiments that is implicit in that choice. Though the choice is in one respect a relatively trivial one, it is far more important than most choices faced by the characters who people Boccaccio's world. Dramatized at greater length, it could in fact have been made into the central episode for the story—though the story that resulted would be a far different one from what we now have. As it is treated here, the choice is given precisely the degree of importance it should have in the whole. Because we experience Monna's thoughts and feelings at first hand, we are forced to agree with the narrator's assessment of her great worth. She is not simply virtuous in conventional matters like chastity, but she is also capable of moral delicacy in more fundamental matters: unlike the majority of Boccaccio's women, she is above any casual manipulation of her lover for her own purposes. Even this delicacy, admirable in itself, can be overridden by a more important value, "the love she bore the boy." Yet all this is kept strictly serviceable to our greater interest in Federigo and the falcon; there is never any question of our becoming sidetracked into deep psychological or sentimental involvement with her as a person.

Because the narrator has *told* us what to think of her, and then *shown* her briefly in support of his claims, all the while keeping our sympathy and admiration carefully subordinated to the comic effect of the whole, we can move to the most important episode with our expectations clear and—in their own kind —intense. We can move to Monna's relatively long and wonderfully delicate speech to Federigo requesting the falcon, with our hopes centered clearly on the "good fortune" of their ultimate union.

If all this skilful presentation of the admirable Monna is to succeed, we must see Federigo himself as an equally admirable, though not really heroic, figure. Too much moral stature will spoil the comedy; too little will destroy our desire for his success. It is not enough to show his virtues through his actions; his only admirable act is the gift of the falcon and that might be easily interpreted in itself as a further bit of foolish extravagance. Unless the story is to be lengthened unduly with episodes showing that he is worthy, in spite of his extravagance, the narrator must give us briefly and directly the necessary information about his true character. He is therefore described, unobtrusively but in terms that only an omniscient narrator could use with success, as "gallant," "full of courtesy," "patient," and most important of all, as "more in love than ever before"; the world of *his* desires is thus set off distinctly from the world of many of the other tales, where love is reduced for comic purposes to lust.

These completely straightforward statements of the narrator's opinions are supported by what we see of Federigo's own mind. His comic distress over not having anything to feed his beloved visitor, and his unflinching sacrifice of the bird, are rendered in intimate detail, with frequent—though by modern standards certainly shallow—inside views; his poverty "was brought home to him," he was "distressed beyond measure," he "inwardly" cursed "his evil fortune." "Sorely he longed that the lady might not leave his house altogether unhonoured, and yet to crave help of his own husbandman was more than his pride could brook." All this insures that the wonderful comedy of the breakfast will be the comedy of sympathetic laughter: we are throughout completely in favor of Federigo's suit. And our favor is heightened by the method of presenting the scene of discovery. "No sooner had Federigo apprehended what the lady wanted, than, *for grief that 'twas not in his power to serve her* . . . he fell a-weeping . . . ." At first Monna supposed that " 'twas only because he was loath to part with the brave falcon that he wept." We might have made the same mistake but for the author's help provided in the clause I have italicized.

Once we have become assured of his character in this way, Federigo's speeches, like Monna Giovanna's, become the equivalent of inside views, because we know that everything he says is a trustworthy reflection of his true state of mind. His long speech of explanation about the falcon serves, as a result, to confirm all we have learned of him; when he concludes, "I doubt I shall never know peace of mind more," we believe in his sincerity, though of course we know with complete certainty, and have known from the beginning, that the story is to end with "good fortune."

Having seen this much, we need little more. To make Monna the heiress as provided in the will, her son must die in a passage only one or two lines longer than the one or two lines earlier given to the death of the husband. Her "inward commendation" of Federigo's "magnanimity" leads her to the decision to marry him rather than a wealthy suitor: "I had rather have a man without wealth than wealth without a man." Federigo is a man, as we know by now. Though his portrait is conventional, "flat," "two-dimensional," it includes everything we need. We can thus accept without irony the narrator's concluding judgment that married to such a wife he lived happily to the end of his days. Fiammetta's auditors all "praised God that He had worthily rewarded Federigo."

If we share in the pleasure of seeing the comic but worthy hero worthily rewarded, the reason is thus not to be found in any inherent quality of the materials but rather in the skilful construction of a living plot out of materials that might have been used in many different ways. The deaths of the husband and son, which in the finished version are merely conveniences for Federigo's exaltation, would in any truly impartial account occupy considerably more space than Federigo's anxiety over not having anything to serve his mistress. Treated impartially, the boy's death would certainly be dramatized as fully as the mother's hesitation about troubling Federigo for his falcon. But the demands of this plot are for a technique that wins us to Federigo's side.

Quite obviously this technique cannot be judged by modern standards of consistency; the story could not have been written from a consistent point of view without stretching it to three times its present length and thereby losing its taut comic force. To tell it entirely through Federigo's eyes would require a much longer introductory section, and the comedy of the visit to fetch the falcon would be partially lost if we did not see more of the preparation for it than Federigo can possibly be aware of. Yet since it is primarily Federigo's story, to see it through Monna's eyes would require a great deal of manipulation and extension. Such conjectural emendations are in a way absurd, since they almost certainly would never have occurred to Boccaccio. But they help to make emphatic the great gap that separates Boccaccio's technique from the more obviously rigorous methods we have come to look for. In this story there is no important revelation of truth, no intensity of illusion, no ironic complexity, no prophetic vision, no rich portrayal of moral ambiguities. There is some incidental irony, it is true, but the greatness of the whole resides in unequivocal intensity not of illusion but of comic delight produced in extraordinarily brief compass.

Any temptation we might have to attribute its success to unconscious or accidental primitivism can be dispelled by looking at the radically different experience offered by other tales. Since his different effects are based on different moral codes, Boccaccio can never assume that his readers will hold precisely the correct attitudes as they approach any one story. He certainly does not assume that his readers will approve of the license of his most licentious tales. Even Dionco, the most lewd of all the ten narrators, must spend a good deal of energy manipulating us into the camp of those who can laugh with a clear conscience at his bawdy and often cruel stories. In the potentially distressing tale of how the holy man, Rustico, debauches the young and innocent Alibech by teaching her how to put the devil in hell (third day, tenth tale), great care is taken with the character and ultimate fate of the simple-minded girl in order to lead us to laugh at conduct that in most worlds, including the world in which Boccaccio lived, would be considered cruel and sacrilegious rather than comic.

If Dioneo, the lusty young courtier, must use care with his rhetoric in a bawdy tale, Fiammetta, the lovely lady, must use even more when she comes to praise infidelity. On the seventh day the subject is "the tricks which, either for love or for their deliverance from peril, ladies have heretofore played their husbands, and whether they were by the said husbands detected, or no." In "The Falcon" Fiammetta worked to build admiration for the virtue of Federigo and Monna Giovanna; she now (fifth tale) employs a different rhetoric. Since her task is to insure our delight in the punishment of a justifiably jealous husband, her commentary tells us directly what is borne out by our views of the husband's mind: he is "a poor creature, and of little sense" who deserves what he gets. More important, she prefaces the story with a little oration, about one-seventh of the length of the whole story, setting our values straight: "For which reason, to sum up, I say that a wife is rather to be commended than censured, if she take her revenge upon a husband that is jealous without cause."

In support of this general argument, the whole tale is manipulated in such a way as to make the reader desire the comic punishment of the husband. Most of it is seen through the eyes of the woman, with great stress on her comic suffering at the hands of the great bullying fool. The climax is his full punishment, in the form of a clever, lashing speech from his wife. Few readers can feel that he has received anything but what he deserves when Fiammetta concludes that the cuckold's wife has now earned her "charter of indulgence."

These extremes by no means exhaust the variety of norms that we are led to accept by the shifting rhetoric as we move through the *Decameron*. The standards of judgment change so radically, in fact, that it is difficult to discern any figure in Boccaccio's carpet.[7] I shall try later on to deal with some of the issues raised when an author heightens specific effects at the expense of his general notions of moral truth or reality. What is important here is to recognize the radical inadequacy of the telling-showing distinction in dealing with the practice of this one author. Boccaccio's artistry lies not in adherence to any one supreme manner of narration but rather in his ability to order various forms of telling in the service of various forms of showing.

THE AUTHOR'S MANY VOICES

In the next three chapters I shall look in detail at some of the more important arguments for authorial objectivity or impersonality. Most of these call for eliminating certain overt signs of the author's presence. As we might expect, however, one man's objectivity is another man's bête noire. If we are to have any degree of clarity as we make our way through attacks on the author's voice, we must have some preliminary notion of the variety of forms that voice can take, both in fiction and in attacks on fiction. What is it, in fact, that we might expunge if we attempted to drive the author from the house of fiction?

First, we must erase all direct addresses to the reader, all commentary in the author's own name. When the author of the *Decameron* speaks to us directly, in both the introduction and conclusion, whatever illusion we may have had that we are dealing immediately with Fiammetta and her friends is shattered. An astonishing number of authors and critics since Flaubert have agreed that such direct, unmediated commentary will not do. And even those authors who would allow it have often, like E. M. Forster, forbidden it except on certain limited subjects.[8]

But what, really, is "commentary"? If we agree to eliminate all personal intrusions of the kind used by Fielding, do we then agree to expunge less obtrusive comment? Is Flaubert violating his own principles of impersonality when he allows himself to tell us that in such and such a place one finds the worst Neufchatel cheeses of the entire district, or that Emma was "incapable of understanding what she didn't experience, or of recognizing anything that wasn't expressed in conventional terms"?[9]

---

[7] Erich Auerbach, for example, complains that he can find no basic moral attitude and no clear approach to reality lying back of all the tales. So long as he considers what Boccaccio does "for the sake of the comic effect," he has nothing but praise for his "critical sense" of the world, "firm yet elastic in perspective, which, without abstract moralizing, allots phenomena their specific, carefully nuanced moral value" (*Mimesis: The Representation of Reality in Western Literature* [Berne, 1946], trans. Willard Trask [Anchor Books ed., 1957], p. 193). It is only on the level of the most general qualities, common to all the stories despite the differing needs of the moment, that Auerbach encounters difficulties and complains of the "vagueness and uncertainty" of Boccaccio's "early humanism" (p. 202). Auerbach's account is invaluable in showing how Boccaccio's style, in so far as it is common to all of the tales, serves as a kind of rhetoric convincing the reader of the reality of his world.

[8] Forster would not allow the author to take "the reader into his confidence about his characters," since "intimacy is gained but at the expense of illusion and nobility." But he allows the author to take the reader into his confidence "about the universe" (*Aspects of the Novel* [London, 1927], pp. 111–12).

[9] *Madame Bovary*, trans. Francis Steegmuller (New York, 1957), p. 80.

Even if we eliminate all such explicit judgments, the author's presence will be obvious on every occasion when he moves into or out of a character's mind—when he "shifts his point of view," as we have come to put it. Flaubert tells us that Emma's little attention to Charles were "never, as he believed, for his sake . . . but for her own, out of exasperated vanity" (p. 69). It is clearly Flaubert who constructs this juxtaposition of Emma's motive with Charles' belief about the motive, and the same obtrusive "voice" is evident whenever a new mind is introduced. When Emma's father bids farewell to Emma and Charles, he remembers "his own wedding, his own earlier days. . . . He, too, had been very happy. . . . He felt dismal, like a stripped and empty house" (pp. 34–35). This momentary shift to Rouault is Flaubert's way of providing us with an evaluation of the marriage and a sense of what is to come. If we are troubled by all reminders of the author's presence, we shall be troubled here.

But if we are to object to this, why not go the next step and object to all inside views, not simply those that require a shift in point of view. In life such views are not to be had. The act of providing them in fiction is itself an obtrusion by the author.[10]

For that matter, we must object to the reliable statements of any dramatized character, not just the author in his own voice, because the act of narration as performed by even the most highly dramatized narrator is itself the author's presentation of a prolonged "inside view" of a character. When Fiammetta says "the love she bore the boy carried the day," she is giving us a reliable inside view of Monna, and she is also giving a view of her own evaluation of events. Both are reminders of the author's controlling hand.

But why stop here? The author is present in every speech given by any character who has had conferred upon him, in whatever manner, the badge of reliability. Once we know that God is God in Job, once we know that Monna speaks only truth in "The Falcon," the authors speak whenever God and Monna speak. Introducing the great Doctor Larivière, Flaubert says:

> He belonged to that great surgical school created by Bichat—that genera-
> tion, now vanished, of philosopher-practitioners, who cherished their art
> with fanatical love and applied it with enthusiasm and sagacity. Everyone
> in his hospital trembled when he was angry; and his students so revered
> him that the moment they set up for themselves they imitated him as much
> as they could . . . . Disdainful of decorations . . . hospitable, generous, a

---

[10] Such obtrusions are especially obvious in narration that purports to be historical. And yet intelligent men were until quite recently able to read ostensibly historical accounts, like the Bible, packed with such illicit entries into private minds, with no distress whatever. For us it may seem strange that the writers of the Gospels should claim so much knowledge of what Christ is feeling and thinking. "Moved with pity, he stretched out his hand and touched him" (Mark 1:41). "And Jesus, perceiving in himself that power had gone forth from him . . ." (5:30). Who reported to the authors these internal events? Who told them what occurs in the Garden, when everyone but Jesus is asleep? Who reported to them that Christ prays to God to "let this cup pass"? Such questions, like the question of how Moses could have written an account of his own death and burial, may be indispensable in historical criticism, but they can easily be overdone in literary criticism.

father to the poor, practicing Christian virtues although an unbeliever, he might have been thought of as a saint if he hadn't been feared as a devil because of the keenness of his mind [pp. 363–364].

This unambiguous bestowal of authority contributes greatly to the power of the next few pages, in which Larivière judges for us everything that we see. But helpful as he is, he must go—if the author's voice is a fault.

Even here we cannot stop, though many of the critics of the author's voice have stopped here. We can go on and on, purging the work of every recognizably personal touch, every distinctive literary allusion or colourful metaphor, every pattern of myth or symbol; they all implicitly evaluate. Any discerning reader can recognize that they are imposed by the author.[11]

Finally, we might even follow Jean-Paul Sartre and object, in the name of "durational realism," to all evidences of the author's meddling with the natural sequence, proportion, or duration of events. Earlier authors, Sartre says, tried to justify "the foolish business of story-telling by ceaselessly bringing to the reader's attention, explicitly or by allusion, the existence of an author." The existentialist novels, in contrast, will be "toboggans, forgotten, unnoticed," hurling the reader "into the midst of a universe where there are no witnesses." Novels should "exist in the manner of things, of plants, of events, and not at first like products of man."[12] If this is so, the author must never summarize, never curtail a conversation, never telescope the events of three days into a paragraph. "If I pack six months into a single page, the reader jumps out of the book" (p. 229).

Sartre is certainly right in claiming that all these things are signs of the author's manipulating presence. In *The Brothers Karamazov*, for example, the story of Father Zossima's conversion could logically be placed anywhere. The events of Zossima's story took place long before the novel begins; unless they are to be placed at the beginning, which is out of the question, there is no natural reason for giving them in one place rather than another. Wherever they are placed, they will call attention to the author's selecting presence, just as Homer is glaringly present to us whenever the *Odyssey* takes one of its many leaps back and forth over a nineteen-year period. It is not accident but Dostoevski's careful choice that gives us Zossima's story as the sequel to Ivan's dream of the Grand Inquisitor. It is intended as a judgment on the values implied by that dream, just as everything that happens to Ivan afterward is an explicit criticism of his own ideas. Since the sequence is obviously not dictated by anything other than the author's purposes, it betrays the author's voice, and according to Sartre, it presumably will not do.

But, as Sartre woefully admits (see chap. iii, below), even with all these

---

[11] Speaking of Joyce's *Ulysses*, Edmund Wilson once complained that as soon as "we are aware of Joyce himself systematically embroidering on his text," packing in puzzles, symbols, and puns, "the illusion of the dream is lost" ("James Joyce," *Axel's Castle* [New York, 1931], p. 235).

[12] "Situation of the Writer in 1947," *What Is Literature?* trans. Bernard Frechtman (London, 1950), p. 169.

forms of the author's voice expunged, what we have left will reveal to us a shameful artificiality. Unless the author contents himself with simply retelling The Three Bears or the story of Oedipus in the precise form in which they exist in popular accounts—and even so there must be some choice of *which* popular form to tell—his very choice of what he tells will betray him to the reader. He chooses to tell the tale of Odysseus rather than that of Circe or Polyphemus. He chooses to tell the cheerful tale of Monna and Federigo rather than a pathetic account of Monna's husband and son. He chooses to tell the story of Emma Bovary rather than the potentially heroic tale of Dr. Larivière. The author's voice is as passionately revealed in the decision to write the *Odyssey,* "The Falcon," or *Madame Bovary* as it is in the most obtrusive direct comment of the kind employed by Fielding, Dickens, or George Eliot. Everything he *shows* will serve to *tell*; the line between showing and telling is always to some degree an arbitrary one.

In short, the author's judgment is always present, always evident to anyone who knows how to look for it. Whether its particular forms are harmful or serviceable is always a complex question, a question that cannot be settled by any easy reference to abstract rules. As we begin now to deal with this question, we must never forget that though the author can to some extent choose his disguises, he can never choose to disappear.

Toward a More Adequate Criticism
of Poetic Structure: Macbeth

R. S. CRANE

In these attempts, as should be clear from what I have said, we shall be making a pretty complete break with the tradition of practical criticism discussed in the last two lectures—a tradition in which it has always been necessary, before individual works of poetic art can be analyzed or judged, to conceive of poetry as a homogeneous whole and to define its nature in some kind of dialectical relation to other modes of discourse and thought. We shall not need, for our purposes, to commit ourselves to any of the numerous and apparently inconsistent theories of poetry, tragedy, lyric, or the like, based on such a presupposition, which this tradition has developed. We shall not need to worry, as so many contemporaries have done, about how poetry differs from science or prose, or about what its mission is in the modern world. We shall not need to decide in advance of our studies of poems whether poetry in general is best defined as a kind of language or a kind of subject-matter; whether its end is pleasure or some species of knowledge or practical good; whether its proper domain includes all the kinds of imaginative writing or only some of these; whether it is most closely akin to rhetoric and dialectic or to ritual, myth, or dream; or whether it is or is not a separable element in prose fiction and drama. Nor shall we need to assume that all good poems have "themes" or that poetic expression is always indirect, metaphorical, and symbolic. Not merely would such speculative commitments be useless to us, given our empirical starting-point, but they would be fatal, in proportion as we allowed our analyses to be directed by them, to our very effort, since they would inevitably blind us to all those aspects of our problem which our particular doctrine of poetry failed to take into account.

I do not mean that we shall not have to make some assumptions of our own, but only that these need not and ought not to be particularized assumptions about the intrinsic nature and necessary structure of our objects considered as a unitary class of things. We shall have to assume that any poetic work, like any other production of human art, has, or rather is, a definite structure of some kind which is determined immediately by its writer's intuition of a form to be achieved in its materials by the right use of his medium, and, furthermore, that we can arrive at some understanding of what this form actually is and use our understanding as a principle in the analysis and criticism of the work. We shall have to come to some agreement, moreover, as to what we will mean by "poetic works"; but here again the fewer specifications we impose on ourselves in advance the better. It will be sufficient for all our purposes if we begin, simply, by taking as "poems" or "works of literary art" all those kinds of productions which have been commonly called such at different times, but without any supposition that, because these have the same name, they are all "poems" or "works of literary art" in the same fundamental structural sense— that the art necessary to write *The Divine Comedy* or *The Faerie Queene* is the same art, when viewed in terms of its peculiar principles of form, as the art which enabled Shakespeare to write *King Lear* and *Othello*. And for such productions we shall need to assume, in addition, only one common characteristic: that they are all works which, in one degree or another, justify critical consideration primarily for their own sake, as artistic structures, rather than merely for the sake of the knowledge or wisdom they express or the practical utility we may derive from them, though either or both of these other values may be importantly involved in any particular case.

The problem of structure, for any individual work of this kind, is the problem—to give it its most general statement—of how the material nature of the work is related to its formal nature, when we understand by form that principle, or complex of principles, which gives to the subject-matter the power it has to affect our opinions and emotions in a certain definite way such as would not have been possible had the synthesizing principle been of a different kind. The question, as I have said, is primarily one of fact and cause; and it is answered, for a given work, when we have made as intelligible as we can the fashion in which its material elements of whatever kind—words, images, symbols, thoughts, character-traits, incidents, devices of representation—are made to function in relation to a formal whole which we can warrantably assert was the actual final cause of its composition. By "actual final cause" I mean simply a cause without the assumption of which, as somehow effective in the writing, the observable characteristic of the parts, their presence in the poem, their arrangement and proportioning, and their interconnections cannot be adequately understood. In discovering what this shaping principle is in any work we must make use of such evidence as there may be concerning the history of its conception and writing, including any statements the writer may have made about his intentions. Our task, however, is not to explain the writer's activity but the result thereof; our problem is not psychological but artistic; and hence the causes that centrally concern us are the internal causes of which the only sufficient evidence is the work itself as a completed product. What we want to know is not the actual process but the actual rationale of the poem's construction in terms of the poetic problems the writer faced and the reasons which determined his solutions. And in looking for these we shall assume that if the poem holds together as an intelligibly effective whole, in which a certain form is realized in a certain matter which never before had this form, the result can be understood fully only by supposing that such and such problems were involved and were solved by the writer in accordance with reasons which, in part at least, we can state; and this clearly does not commit us to holding that the problems and reasons we uncover in our analysis, as necessarily implied by the completed poem, must have presented themselves to the writer explicitly as such in a continuous movement of self-conscious deliberation; it will be sufficient if we can show that the poem could hardly have been written as it is or have the effect it does on our minds had the writer not done, somehow or at some time, what these particular problems and reasons dictate.

We can never, of course, know such things directly, but only by inference from the consequences of the conceived form, whether of the whole or of any of its parts, in the details of the completed work; and there can be no such inference except by way of hypotheses which both imply and are implied by the observable traits of the work. There are, however, hypotheses and hypotheses, and the character of those we shall have to make is determined by the nature of our problem. We propose to consider poems as unique existent things the structural principles of which are to be discovered, rather than as embodiments of general truths about the structure of poetry already adequately known. Hence our procedure must be the reverse of that procedure by way of preferred paradigms or models of structure which we have seen to be so characteristic of contemporary practical criticism. Our task is not to show the reflection in poems of complex or "ironical" attitudes, interactions of prose and poetry or of logical structure and irrelevant texture, patterns of ritual drama, or basic mythical themes, on the assumption that if the poem is a good poem it will inevitably have whichever of these or other similarly derived general structures we happen to be interested in finding examples of; it is rather the task of making formal sense out of any poetic work before us on the assumption that it may in fact be a work for whose peculiar principles of structure there are nowhere any usable parallels either in literary theory or in our experience of other works. The hypotheses we have to make, therefore, will not be of the fixed and accredited kind which scientists employ only when their problem is not to find out something still unknown but to "demonstrate" a classic experiment to beginners, but rather of the tentative kind—to be modified or rejected altogether at the dictation of the facts—which are the proper means to any serious inductive inquiry. They will be particular working hypotheses for the investigation of the structures of individual poems, not general hypotheses about such things as poetry or "poetic drama" in which the specific nature of the individual structures to be examined is already assumed.

We must also distinguish between critical hypotheses in the strict sense and interpretative hypotheses concerning the details of literary works in their material aspects. It is not one of our presuppositions that "form" in poetry is "meaning"; we should hold, rather, that meaning is something involved in poems as a necessary, but not sufficient, condition of the existence in them of poetic form, and hence that the recovery of meaning is an essential prerequisite to the discovery of form though not in itself such a discovery. Before we can understand a poem as an artistic structure we must understand it as a grammatical structure made up of successive words, sentences, paragraphs, and speeches which give us both meanings in the ordinary sense of that term and signs from which we may infer what the speakers, whether characters or narrators, are like and what they are thinking, feeling, or doing. The great temptation for critics who are not trained and practising scholars is to take this understanding for granted or to think that it may easily be obtained at second hand by consulting the works of scholars. This is an illusion, just as it is an illusion in scholars to suppose that they can see, without training in criticism, all the problems which their distinctive methods are fitted to solve. The ideal would be that all critics should be scholars and all scholars critics; but, although there ought to be the closest correlation of the two functions in practice, they are nevertheless distinct in nature and in the kinds of hypotheses to which they lead. The hypotheses of interpretation are concerned with the meanings and implications in texts that result from their writers' expressive intentions in setting down particular words and constructions and arranging these in particular sequences. Such meanings and implications, indeed, are forms, of which words and sentences are the matter; but they are forms of a kind that can appear in any sort of discourse, however unpoetic. They are to be interpreted by resolving the forms into the elements which poems share with the common speech or writing and the common thought and experience of the times when they were written; and this requires the use of techniques and principles quite different from any that poetic theory can afford: the techniques and principles of historical grammar, of the analysis and history of ideas, of the history of literary conventions, manners, and so on, and the still more general techniques and principles, seldom methodized, by which we construe characters and actions in everyday life.

The hypotheses of criticism, on the contrary, are concerned with the shaping principles, peculiar to the poetic arts, which account in any work for the power of its grammatical materials, in the particular ordering given to these, to move our opinions and feelings in such-and-such a way. They will be of two sorts according as the questions to which they are answers relate to the principles by which poetic works have been constructed as wholes of certain definite kinds or to the reasons which connect a particular part of a given work, directly or indirectly, with such a principle by way of the poetic problems it set for the writer at this point. And there can be no good practical criticism in this mode in which both sorts are not present; for although the primary business of the critic is with the particulars of any work he studies down to its minuter details of diction and rhythm, he can never exhibit the artistic problems involved in these or find other than extra-poetic reasons for their solutions without the guidance of an explicit definition of the formal whole which they have made possible.

A single work will suffice to illustrate both kinds of critical hypotheses as well as the relation between them, and I will begin by considering what idea of the governing form of *Macbeth* appears to accord best with the facts of that play and the sequence of emotions it arouses in us. I need not say again why it seems to me futile to look for an adequate structural formula for *Macbeth* in any of the more "imaginative" directions commonly taken by recent criticism; I shall assume, therefore, without argument, that we have to do, not with a lyric "statement of evil" or an allegory of the workings of sin in the soul and the state or a metaphysical myth of destruction followed by recreation or a morality play with individualized characters rather than types,[1] but simply with an imitative tragic drama based on historical materials. To call it an imitative tragic drama, however, does not carry us very far; it merely limits roughly the range of possible forms we have to consider. Among these are the contrasting plot-forms embodied respectively in *Othello* and in *Richard III*: the first a tragic plot-form in the classic sense of Aristotle's analysis in *Poetics* 13; the second a plot-form which Aristotle rejected as non-tragic but which appealed strongly to tragic poets in the Renaissance—a form of serious action designed to arouse moral indignation for the deliberately unjust and seemingly prospering acts of the protagonist and moral satisfaction at his subsequent ruin. The plot-form of *Macbeth* clearly involves elements which assimilate it now to the one and now to the other of both these kinds. The action of the play is twofold, and one of its aspects is the punitive action of Malcolm, Macduff, and their friends which in the end brings about the protagonist's downfall and death. The characters here are all good men, whom Macbeth has unforgivably wronged, and their cause is the unqualifiedly just cause of freeing Scotland from a bloody tyrant and restoring the rightful line of kings. All this is made clear in the representation not only directly through the speeches and acts of the avengers but indirectly by those wonderfully vivid devices of imagery and general thought in which modern critics have found the central value and meaning of the play as a whole; and our responses, when this part of the action is before us, are such as are clearly dictated by the immediate events and the poetic commentary: we desire, that is, the complete success of the counter-action and this as speedily as possible before Macbeth can commit further horrors. We desire this, however —and that is what at once takes the plot-form out of the merely retributive class—not only for the sake of humanity and Scotland but also for the sake of Macbeth himself. For what most sharply distinguishes our view of Macbeth from that of his victims and enemies is that, whereas they see him from the outside only, we see him also, throughout the other action of the play—the major action—from the inside, as he sees himself; and what we see thus is a moral spectacle the emotional quality of which, for the impartial observer, is not too far removed from the tragic *dynamis* specified in the *Poetics*. This is not

[1] See *The Languages of Criticism and the Structure of Poetry* (University of Toronto Press, 1953), pp. 7–8.

to say that the main action of *Macbeth* is not significantly different, in several respects, from the kind of tragic action which Aristotle envisages. The change is not merely from good to bad fortune, but from a good state of character to a state in which the hero is almost, but not quite, transformed into a monster; and the tragic act which initiates the change, and still more the subsequent unjust acts which this entails, are acts done—unlike Othello's killing of Desdemona—in full knowledge of their moral character. We cannot, therefore, state the form of this action in strictly Aristotelian terms, but the form is none the less one that involves, like tragedy in Aristotle's sense, the arousal and catharsis of painful emotions for, and not merely with respect to, the protagonist —emotions for which the terms pity and fear are not entirely inapplicable.

Any adequate hypothesis about the structure of *Macbeth,* then, would have to take both of these sets of facts into account. For both of the views we are given of the hero are true: he is in fact, in terms of the nature and objective consequences of his deeds, what Macduff and Malcolm say he is throughout Acts IV and V, but he is also—and the form of the play is really the interaction of the two views in our opinions and emotions—what we ourselves see him to be as we witness the workings of his mind before the murder of Duncan, then after the murder, and finally when, at the end, all his illusions and hopes gone, he faces Macduff. He is one who commits monstrous deeds without becoming wholly a monster, since his knowledge of the right principle is never altogether obscured, though it is almost so in Act IV. We can understand such a person and hence feel fear and pity of a kind for him because he is only doing upon a grander scale and with deeper guilt and more terrifying consequences for himself and others what we can, without too much difficulty, imagine ourselves doing, however less extremely, in circumstances generally similar. For the essential story of *Macbeth* is that of a man, not naturally depraved, who has fallen under the compulsive power of an imagined better state for himself which he can attain only by acting contrary to his normal habits and feelings; who attains this state and then finds that he must continue to act thus, and even worse, in order to hold on to what he has got; who persists and becomes progressively hardened morally in the process; and who then, ultimately, when the once alluring good is about to be taken away from him, faces the loss in terms of what is left of his original character. It is something like this moral universal that underlies, I think, and gives emotional form to the main action of *Macbeth*. It is a form that turns upon the difference between what seemingly advantageous crime appears to be in advance to a basically good but incontinent man and what its moral consequences for such a man inevitably are; and the catharsis is effected not merely by the man's deserved overthrow but by his own inner suffering and by his discovery, before it is too late, of what he had not known before he began to act. If we are normal human beings we must abhor his crimes; yet we cannot completely abhor but must rather pity the man himself, and even when he seems most the monster (as Macbeth does in Act IV) we must still wish for such an outcome as will be best, under the circumstances, not merely for Scotland but for him.

But if this, or something close to it, is indeed the complex emotional structure intended in *Macbeth,* then we have a basis for defining with some precision the various problems of incident, character, thought, imagery, diction, and representation which confronted Shakespeare in writing the play, and hence a starting-point for discussing, in detail, the rationale of its parts.[2] Consider— to take only one instance—the final scene. In the light of the obvious consequences of the form I have attributed to the play as a whole, it is not difficult to state what the main problems at this point are. If the catharsis of the tragedy is to be complete, we must be made to feel both that Macbeth is being killed in a just cause and that his state of mind and the circumstances of his death are such as befit a man who, for all his crimes, has not altogether lost our pity and goodwill. We are of course prepared for this double response by all that has gone before, and, most immediately, in the earlier scenes of Act V, by the fresh glimpses we are given of the motivation of the avengers and by Macbeth's soliloquies. But it will clearly be better if the dual effect can be sustained until the very end; and this requires, on the one hand, that we should be vividly reminded once more of Macbeth's crimes and the justified hatred they have caused and of the prospect of a new and better time which his death holds out for Scotland, and, on the other hand, that we should be allowed to take satisfaction, at last, in the manner in which Macbeth himself behaves. The artistic triumph of the scene lies in the completeness with which both problems are solved: the first in the words and actions of Macduff, the speeches about young Siward, and Malcolm's closing address; the second by a variety of devices, both of invention and of representation, the appropriateness of which to the needed effect can be seen if we ask what we would not want Macbeth to do at this moment. We want him to be killed, as I have said, for his sake no less than that of Scotland; but we would not want him either to seek out Macduff or to flee the encounter when it comes or to "play the Roman fool"; we would not want him to show no recognition of the wrongs he has done Macduff or, when his last trust in the witches has gone, to continue to show fear or to yield or to fight with savage animosity; and he is made to do none of these things, but rather the contraries of all of them, so that he acts in the end as the Macbeth whose praises we have heard in the second scene of the play. And I would suggest that the cathartic effect of these words and acts is reinforced indirectly, in the representation, by the analogy we can hardly help drawing between his conduct now and the earlier conduct of young Siward, for of Macbeth too it can be said that "he parted well and paid his score"; the implication of this analogy is surely one of the functions, though not the only one, which the lines about Siward are intended to serve.

Such are the kinds of hypotheses we shall need to make if we are to have critical knowledge of the shaping principles of poetic works or of the artistic reasons governing the character and interrelation of their parts. They are working suppositions which, as I have said, both imply and are implied by the particulars of the works for which they are constructed; and they can never be

---

[2] See, in addition to what follows, Wayne C. Booth, *Journal of General Education,* VI (1951), 21–25. For a somewhat similar discussion of an episode in *King Lear,* cf. Maclean, in *Critics and Criticism,* pp. 595–615.

made well by any critic who is not naturally sensitive to such particulars and in the habit of observing them closely. These, however, though indispensable, are not sufficient conditions. It never happens in any inquiry into matters of fact that the particulars we observe determine their own meaning automatically; the concrete or the individual is never intelligible except through the general and the abstract; and if we are to allow the facts to speak for themselves, we must in some fashion supply them with a language in which to talk. Hypotheses, in short, are not made out of nothing, but presuppose on the part of the inquirer who forms them a systematic body of concepts relative to the subject-matter with which he is dealing. The critic who proposes to explore hypothetically the structures of individual poems is in the same predicament; he must bring to his task, inescapably, general ideas about poetic structure, or he can never construct a workable hypothesis about the structure of any poem.

Hence the crucial importance for the practical critic of poetic forms, in the sense we are now giving to this term, of the kind of analytic of poetry which was outlined earlier in this lecture. From the point of view of the criticism of individual poems, the concepts and distinctions involved in that analytic differ from those which most contemporary critics have been content to use: they supply, not a unified set of terms for constituting structural patterns in poems (like Mr. Heilman's formula for "poetic drama" or the theories that make all good poetry a species of "ironical" or "paradoxical" structure), but a great variety of terms designating distinct and alternative principles, devices, and functions in poetry from which the critic need select only such combinations as appear to be relevant to the poems he is examining. What he thus acquires are not hypotheses ready formed but elements out of which he may form such hypotheses as the facts of his poems seem to warrant—in short, knowledge of structural possibilities only, resting on inductive inquiry into the principles poets have actually used in building poems and hence expanding with the development and progressive differentiation of poetry itself, so that he brings to the discussion of individual poems merely conceptual materials for framing pertinent questions about them without any predetermination of the substance of his answers, much as a physician uses the alternatives given him by medical theory in diagnosing symptoms in one of his patients. In the other mode of criticism the relation of theory to a particular poem is the relation of a previously selected idea or pattern of structure to its embodiment or reflection in a given work; here the relation is one of many known possibilities of structural patterning in poetry to the actualization in the poem examined of some one or more of these.

A critic using the first type of theory might argue somewhat as follows, for example, about the structure of Gray's *Elegy*. We must assume, he might say, the language of poetry being what it is, that the principle of structure in any good poem is a principle of balancing and harmonizing discrepant connotations, attitudes, and meanings; we must look therefore for a structure of this kind in Gray's poem or be content to relegate it to an inferior class of poetry; and our quest, indeed, is not in vain, for when we examine the text in the light of our general hypothesis of "ironical" structure, we quickly find that all the details of the *Elegy* can be subsumed under the theme of a continuous contrast of two modes of burial—in the church itself and in the church-yard—in which, as in all good poetry, opposing meanings are finally resolved.[3] A critic, however, whose theory was of the second type, would proceed in an altogether different way. He would have no favourite hypothesis of structure as such, but would know merely that among short poems which, like the *Elegy*, evoke in us serious emotions, the shaping principle may be of several essentially distinct types, each of them generating distinct artistic problems for the poet; and he would use this knowledge as a basis for asking himself some such questions as these: Is what happens in the *Elegy* best explained by supposing, as the other critic has clearly done, that the poem is intended to be read as an emotionalized argument in verse (whether about modes of burial or something else), the personal qualities of the speaker and the setting of his meditation being simply devices for enforcing the unifying dialectic? Or is the poem better read—better, that is, with respect to the actual shaping principle of its construction—as an imitative lyric? And if it is this latter kind of structure, is the form one in which the speaker is conceived as being merely moved in a certain way by his situation (as in Gray's "Ode on a Distant Prospect of Eton College"), or as acting in a certain manner in relation to it (as in Marvell's "To His Coy Mistress"), or as deliberating morally in a certain state of mind on what is for him a serious issue in life? Weighing these possibilities (which give us perhaps the major forms which short serious imitative poems can have), our second critic would probably conclude that it is the last possibility which best explains both the constructed matter and the arrangement of the *Elegy* and the peculiar quality of the emotions which Gray's words and rhythms arouse in us. He might then describe the *Elegy* as an imitative lyric of moral choice rather than of action or of mood, representing a situation in which a virtuous, sensitive, and ambitious young man of undistinguished birth confronts the possibility of his death while still to "Fortune and to Fame unknown," and eventually, after much disturbance of mind (hinted at in the Swain's description of him), reconciles himself to his probable fate by reflecting that none of the rewards of successful ambition can "sooth the dull cold ear of Death," which comes as inevitably to the great as to the obscure; that a life passed "far from the madding crowd's ignoble strife," though circumscribing the exercise of virtue and talent, may yet be a means of preserving innocence; and that he can at any rate look forward to—what all men desire as a minimum—living on in the memory of at least one friend, while his merits and frailties alike repose "in trembling hope" on the bosom of his Father and his God.[4] Something like this, I think (pedantic as any brief statement of it must sound), is the answer our second critic would give; but the point is that in arriving at it he would be using his theory of possible principles of structure in short poems simply to furnish him with the distinctions he needs if he is not to substitute a structure of his own for the structure Gray achieved.

The more extensive and discriminating such general knowledge, therefore,

[3] Cleanth Brooks, *The Well Wrought Urn*, pp. 96–113.

[4] I borrow here the substance and many of the words of a note of mine in *Critics and Criticism*, p. 99.

the better the critic's hypotheses are likely to be. But it is also the nature of this kind of theoretical knowledge to be always inadequate, though in varying degrees, to the particulars we use it to illuminate. We can never know in advance all the possibilities, and we can never, consequently, form a hypothesis about a work of any artistic complexity or even about many simpler works without making a shorter or longer inductive leap from the words and sentences before us to the peculiar combination of universals which define their poetic form. And that is why, in this mode of criticism, we can make no separation except analytically between theory and application, the latter being possible only if the former already exists at least up to a certain point and the former being constantly refined and enlarged as we proceed with the latter.

Application, however, is our main problem here, and its success depends upon the extent to which the universal terms of our hypotheses and the perceived and felt particulars of the texts for which they are constructed can be made to fit together. The general conditions are two: first, our ability to keep our explanatory formulae fluid and to submit them to constant revisions in principle or in detail before we transform them into conclusions; and, second, our willingness to use systematically what has been called "the method of multiple working hypotheses."[5] We have to remember, that is, that the value of a hypothesis is always relative, not merely to the facts it is intended to explain, but to all the other variant hypotheses which the same facts might suggest if only we gave them a chance; that the best hypothesis is simply the best among several possible hypotheses, relevant to the same work or problem, with which we have actually compared it; and that unless we make such comparisons a regular part of our procedure, we always court the danger of missing either slightly or altogether what our author was really attempting to do.

There are also, in addition to these very general rules, several more particular criteria. Our aim is an explanation and judgment of poetic works in terms of their structural causes; hence, in the first place, the necessity of so framing our hypotheses that they are not descriptive formulae merely but clearly imply practical artistic consequences, in what the writers must or cannot or might well do in the act of writing, for the details of the works they are being used to explain; that is the character, for example, of Aristotle's definition of tragic plot-form in *Poetics* 13, and I have tried to impart a similar character to the statements above about *Macbeth*. The ideal is to have a central principle of explanation that will enable us to see precisely the functional relations between all the particular problems a writer has attempted to solve and the form of his work as a whole, even though we may have to conclude, in some cases, that the relation is a very tenuous one. In the second place, our aim is an explanation and judgment in terms adapted as closely as possible to the peculiar structure and power of the work before us; hence the necessity of trying to go beyond formulae that imply the work as a whole or any of its parts only generically;

---

[5] By T. C. Chamberlin, in a paper with this title, first published in *Science*, Old Series, XV (1890), 92–96; reprinted in the *Journal of Geology*, XXXIX (1931), 155–65. The "method of multiple working hypotheses" is contrasted with "the method of the ruling theory" and "the method of the working hypothesis."

as when, for instance, we neglect to distinguish between the different material structures possible in lyrics and treat a particular lyric without regard to such distinctions, or as when we discuss a work like Jane Austen's *Emma* merely as a comedy, failing to see how little this can tell us about its distinctive comic construction. In the third place, we aspire to completeness of explanation; and this means that in framing a hypothesis about any work we must consider everything in the text as significant evidence that involves in any way a free choice on the writer's part between possible alternative things to be done with his materials or ways of doing them at any point. The hypothesis must therefore be complex rather than simple; it must recognize that the same parts may have different functions, including that of mere adornment; and, above all, it cannot be arrived at by giving a privileged position, on *a priori* grounds, to a particular variety of signs of artistic intention, in a complex work, to the exclusion of other and often conflicting signs of the same thing. This last is conspicuously the error of those interpreters of *Macbeth* who have inferred the central form of that play chiefly from the thought and imagery that serve to emphasize the "unnatural" character of the hero's crimes and the inevitability of a just retribution, without attempting to correlate with this the many signs, both in the construction of the plot and in its extraordinarily artful representation, of the distinctive moral quality of Macbeth's actions when these are seen from the inside. There will always be incompleteness in any hypothesis, moreover, or in any criticism that follows its use, that leaves out of account, as one of the crucial facts, the peculiar sequence of emotions we feel when we read the work unbiased by critical doctrine; for, as we have seen, the most important thing about any poetic production is the characteristic power it has to affect us in this definite way rather than that.[6] Completeness, however, is impossible without coherence; hence our hypotheses, in the fourth place, must aim at a maximum of internal unity, on the assumption that, although many works are episodic and although many predominantly imitative works, for example, also have didactic or topical parts, this can best be seen if we begin by presuming that literary artists usually aim at creating wholes.

The only proof there can be of a hypothesis about any particular thing lies in its power of completeness and coherence of explanation within the limits of the data it makes significant—and this always relatively to the other hypotheses pertinent to the same data with which it has been compared. We must be guided, however, in choosing among alternative hypotheses, by a further criterion—the classic criterion of economy: that that hypothesis is the best, other things being equal, which requires the fewest supplementary hypotheses to make it work or which entails the least amount of explaining away; it is no recommendation, thus, for Mr. Knights's interpretation of *Macbeth* that he has to say of the emotion aroused in most readers as well as in Bradley by Macbeth's soliloquies in Act V, that this is mere "conventional 'sympathy for the hero,' " which ought not to be allowed to distort that dialectical system of values in the play that is for him "the pattern of the whole."[7] And we must be careful,

[6] Cf. Keast, in *Critics and Criticism*, pp. 131–36.

[7] *Explorations*, p. 36. Cf. above, pp. 33–34.

further, not to construe our "data" in too narrow a sense and so be satisfied with hypotheses that clearly conflict with facts external to the works we are considering but relevant nevertheless to their interpretation; I mean not only such particular evidences as we can often find of writers' intentions—for example, Coleridge's statements about the kind of poem he designed *The Rime of the Ancient Mariner* to be—but also such general probabilities with respect to the works of a given period or genre or with respect to poetic works of any kind or age as are supplied by either our historical knowledge or our common sense. It is not likely, for instance, that a Shakespearean tragedy intended for the popular stage should really have a kind of basic structure which practising playwrights of any time would find it difficult or impossible to make effective for their audiences.[8] Nor is it ever a sensible thing in a critic to cultivate indifference to common opinion about the works he is discussing. The opinion may be wrong or, as often happens, it may need to be corrected and refined; but in such conflicts—at least when they involve the larger aspects and effects of works— the burden of proof is on him. For the secrets of art are not, like the secrets of nature, things lying deeply hid, inaccessible to the perception and under- standing of all who have not mastered the special techniques their discovery requires. The critic does, indeed, need special techniques, but for the sake of building upon common sense apprehensions of his objects, not of supplanting these; and few things have done greater harm to the practice and repute of literary criticism in recent times than the assumption that its discoveries, like those of the physical sciences, must gain in importance and plausibility as they become more and more paradoxical in the ancient sense of that word: as if—to adapt a sharp saying of Professor Frank Knight about social studies—now that everybody is agreed that natural phenomena are not like works of art, the business of criticism must be to show that works of art are like natural pheno- mena.

It remains, finally, to consider the bearing of all this on judgments of poetic value. And the first thing to observe is that, if our hypothesis concerning the shaping principle of any work is adequate, it will give us a basis for saying with some precision (as my example of Act V of *Macbeth* will perhaps suggest) what are the necessities which such a form imposes on any artist whose aim is its successful realization in his materials. Some of them will be necessities common to all self-contained poetic works of no matter what kind, such as the necessity, if the parts are to cohere, of devices for effecting continuity from beginning through middle to end; others will be more and more specific necessities determined by the nature of the form we assume to have been intended, such as the necessity, if a comic effect like that of *Tom Jones* is to be obtained, of keeping the ridiculous mistakes of the hero from obscuring the sympathetic traits that make us wish him ultimate good fortune. These will all be conse- quences inferable from our basic definition of the form, and our primary task will be to trace them, in detail, throughout the particulars of the work at all its levels from plot or lyric situation down to the imagery and words. A kind of

---

[8] Cf. Keast, in *Critics and Criticism*, pp. 135–37.

judgment of value will thus emerge in the very process of our analysis: if the writer has indeed done, somehow, all the essential things he would need to do on the assumption that he is actually writing the kind of work we have defined, then to that extent the work is good, or at least not artistically bad; and we should have to use very little rhetoric in addition to make this clear. But this is only half of the problem, for it is true of most mediocre writers that they usually do, in some fashion, a great part or all of the things their particular forms require, but do little more besides. The crucial question, therefore, concerns not so much the necessities of the assumed form as its possibilities. What is it that the writer might have done, over and above the minimum requirements of his task, which he has not done, or what is it that we have not expected him to do which he has yet triumphantly accomplished? These are the things our analyses ought peculiarly to attend to if they are to be adequate to their objects.

The possible in this sense, as distinguished from the necessary, is that which tends to perfect—to warrant praise of a positive rather than a merely negative kind. We can know it in two ways: by having our minds stored with memories of what both the most and the least perfect of artists have done when confronted with similar problems of invention, representation, and writing; and by considering theoretically the conditions under which any particular effect aimed at in a given work might be better or worse achieved—by asking, for instance, what would in general make a predicament like that of Tom Jones on the discovery of his first affair with Molly seem most completely comic, and then discussing the episode, as it is actually developed by Fielding, in these terms.[9] Both methods are comparative, but the comparisons, if they are not to result in unfair impositions on the writer whose work we are considering, must take account of the fact that the desirable or admirable in literature is never something absolute but is always relative, in any given part of a work, to the requirements of the over-all form and to the function of the part as only one part along with many others: forgetting this, we should make the mistake of Mr. Joyce Cary's critic and demand neatness where clumsiness is what "belongs," vividness and particularity where faintness and generality are needed, doing more than is done when this would be doing too much.

The judgments of value we should thus be trying to make would for this reason always be judgments in kind, grounded on a prior definition of the writer's problems as problems peculiar, at least in their concrete determination, to the formal nature of the work he is writing. They would also be judgments in terms of intentions—what is it that the writer aimed to do here and how well has he succeeded in doing it?—but the intentions we should take as principles would not be those, except accidentally, which the writer had stated explicitly before or after writing or those which can be defined for the writer by saying that he must have intended to write this work because this is what he has written. The common objections to criticism based on "intention" in either of these senses are unanswerable. They do not hold, however, when we identify intention with the hypothesized form of a poetic work and then consider how

---

[9] Cf. Crane, *ibid.*, pp. 639–40.

fully what we know of the necessities and possibilities of this form are achieved in the work, on the assumption that, if the work shows any serious concern with art at all, the writer must have wished or been willing to be judged in this way. There is nothing unfair to the writer in such an approach, inasmuch as we are not engaged in a judicial process of bringing his work under a previously formulated general theory of literary value but in a free inquiry whose aim is simply the discovery of those values in his work—among them, we always hope, unprecedented values—which he has been able to put there. They will always be values incident to the relation between the form of the work and its matter at all of its structural levels; and it will be appropriate to interpret what we find in terms of a distinction between three classes of works considered from this point of view: works that are well conceived as wholes but contain few parts the formal excellence of which remains in our memory or invites us to another reading; works that are rich in local virtues but have only a loose or tenuous over-all form; and works that satisfy Coleridge's criterion for a poem, that it aims at "the production of as much immediate pleasure in parts, as is compatible with the largest sum of pleasure in the whole."[10] These last are the few relatively perfect productions in the various literary kinds, and as between the other two we shall naturally prefer the second to the first.

---

[10] *Coleridge's Shakespearean Criticism*, ed. T. M. Raysor (London, 1930), II, 66–67; cf. *Biographia literaria*, II, 9–10.

PART 3

Archetypal Criticism

Here is a story that has happened countless times. One person phones another, a sister or brother perhaps, and says slowly, trying not to shock, that Father is dead. The typical reaction is "No," meaning "I do not want father to be dead," meaning "I love my father and would feel disloyal to accept without protest the news of his death." But the meaning beyond all others is "No, I do not believe it. His death is not real to me. I do not feel it."

An Archetypal Critic, in the strict sense, is a critic who believes that when the temporal touches the permanent—as in the death of your father—the intellect cannot discover or shape the experience. The "No" to the death of a Father may be taken quite literally: Father is not dead; a sense of his being alive is present and real; there is no sense of his being dead. Factual messages about cardiac arrest will say something to the intellect, but they will not banish from the memory a thousand pictures that are still alive, pictures that are part of the past and present, of *being*.

What we must do is put on a play. And talking about the play will not do the job. We must get up on a stage and become actors, carrying props, wearing costumes, saying prepared lines. We must have, in short, a funeral. And when the funeral is ended, the intellect can then record the experience now made real to the being: "Yes, my father is dead."

The inadequacy of the intellect and the primacy of another way of knowing, the Archetypal Critic believes, is illustrated in all qualitative experience: birth, puberty, marriage; encounters with the reality presented in stories of Christ, Satan, Eden, Heaven, and Hell; the journeys in actual life which bring one face to face with the unconscious, like the wise old man who gives cryptic advice, the earth mother, and so on. Such experiences can only be accommodated by the play, by the action of the whole self.

A wedding, for example, should be a qualitative change, a reconstruction of two separate individuals into a single being, and thus an instance of the temporal in touch with the permanent, the marriage of two mortals recreating the original marriage of the sun with the earth. A merely legal procedure will not cause such a reconstruction; the father of the bride may not simply tell the groom to take her, she is yours. A special language is required, and the father's role is to act out the giving by walking down an aisle with his daughter and handing her over to the groom, not a signature or a symbol merely, but the daughter herself, who acts out her part in the play by leaving the side of her father and joining hands with the groom.

On descriptive grounds, anyone who likes to identify and analyze such stories may be called an Archetypal Critic. And critics of whatever propensity who write on "The Pardoner's Tale" or Blake's poetry or Faulkner's *The Bear* will necessarily discuss archetypal themes. But writing about archetypal themes does not make one an Archetypal Critic, just as close analysis of imagery does not make one a Formalist Critic, analysis of genres does not make one a Genre Critic, and attention to history does not make one an Historical Critic. On ontological grounds, a theory of literature is founded in a theory of reality.

Critics who are ontologically archetypal disagree with one another, of course, but there is a fundamental and characteristic belief in the primordial energy of the original founding of the world. In so far as we symbolize or intellectualize or primly domesticate the original, in so far do we lose contact with our self and with our world. When we civilize the original gods and reduce their power and lust and caprice to mere goodness, then do we construct an imaginary and intellectual god, one that has no touch with the power and lust and caprice within ourselves and within the world. A philosophy that denies the wild and nonrational variety of man and his gods, the Archetypal Critic believes, has lost touch with reality.

In careless hands, this belief is treated as anti-intellectualism; but disciplined thinkers, like C. G. Jung, praise the intellect for its splendid empirical capacities and insist that it is the monopoly of the intellect and not the intellect itself which is to be deprecated. There is a way of knowing that is more profound than the intellectual. D. H. Lawrence calls it "blood knowledge" or "bone knowledge," by which he means knowledge gained when the whole person is actively engaged in his world. Such knowledge is illustrated in the play we call a funeral, the play we call a marriage, or even in the simple touch of someone who is loved, provided the act of touching surpasses the conventional or mechanical and includes the whole of self and place.

After the ceremony has acted our whole being back into harmony with our whole world, then the intellect can perform its empirical function, analysis *after* the act. But for all its fine analytical capacities, the intellect cannot generate, cannot tap the primordial powers of original creation, cannot, as Whitman put it, "start with the sun." Most of us, the Archetypal Critic believes, are like T. S. Eliot's Gerontion and have lost our "sight, smell, hearing, taste and touch," have lost, that is, the ability to recreate the original act. Instead of founding a world, we make a financial investment in a brick veneer stereotype, in the right part of town, where we turn on the air conditioner and sit before a television set, wondering what went wrong.

As indicated by the relevance of such themes to present problems, there is reason to believe that Archetypal Criticism is the most recent of the major movements in criticism; and yet it is also the oldest, for its characteristic stories appear in cultures of incredible diversity and have been studied for centuries. This pervasiveness may be cited as support for those who believe that archetypes have an objective status. This pervasiveness may also create a problem for those who seek to understand. Archetypal patterns occur among ancients and moderns, in formal theology and the Beat Movement, in Plato and contemporary customs of dress and music, and leave us asking questions rather than enjoying the wealth of material. What is a rite? What is a myth? And what is the relation between the two? Why is it that most of the standard books are works of anthropology or psychology rather than literary criticism? Are there new archetypes? Is there archetypal content in stories of intellectualized and disenfranchised American idealists like Lambert Strether and Quentin Compson? Or does the emphasis on ancient cultures imply that all archetypes have already been found?

Whatever his answers may be, the devotee will cite the confusing wealth of material as support for his belief that archetypes are something we cannot get along without. Modern man's allegiance to a demythologized practicality, he believes, has led to an impractical loss of purpose.

But the most compelling invitation to further study comes from the literature itself. Writers do not ignore the power of the archetype. Nor do they merely repeat the ancient story. Instead, they search, like Nathaniel Hawthorne in his attic or Ernest Hemingway at a bull fight or Ralph Ellison in New York City; and the stories they create seem to be contemporaneous in the telling and yet archetypal in their power.

Bibliography

Bloom, Harold. *Shelley's Mythmaking*. New Haven, Conn.: Yale University Press, 1959.

Bodkin, Maud. *Archetypal Patterns in Poetry*. New York: Vintage Books, 1958.

Burke, Kenneth. *The Philosophy of Literary Form*. Baton Rouge, La.: Louisiana State University Press, 1941.

Caillois, Roger. *Man and the Sacred*. Translated by Meyer Barash. Glencoe, Illinois: Free Press, 1959.

Campbell, Joseph. *The Hero With a Thousand Faces*. New York: Pantheon Books, 1949.

Chase, Richard. *Quest for Myth*. Baton Rouge, La.: Louisiana State University Press, 1949.

Cornford, F. M. *The Origin of the Attic Comedy*. London: Edward Arnold, 1914.

Douglas, W. W. "The Meanings of 'Myth' in Modern Criticism," *Modern Philology*, L (1953), pp. 232–42.

Durkheim, Emile. *The Elementary Forms of the Religious Life*. Translated by Joseph Ward Swain. London: Allen and Unwin, 1915.

Eliade, Mircea. *Cosmos and History: The Myth of the Eternal Return*. Translated by Willard R. Trask. New York: Harper Torchbooks, 1949, 1954, 1959.

———*The Sacred and the Profane*. Translated by Willard R. Trask. New York: Harper and Rowe, 1961.

Fergusson, Francis. *The Idea of a Theater*. Princeton, N.J.: Princeton University Press, 1949.

Franklin, H. Bruce. *The Wake of the Gods: Melville's Mythology*. Stanford: Stanford University Press, 1963.

Frazer, Sir James. *The Golden Bough: A Study in Magic and Religion*. New York: Macmillan, 1922, 1940.

Freud, Sigmund. *Totem and Taboo*. Translated by A. A. Brill. New York: Moffat, Yard and Co., 1918.

Fromm, Erich. *The Forgotten Language: An Introduction to the Understanding of Dreams, Myths and Fairy Tales*. New York: Holt, Rinehart and Winston, Inc., 1951.

Frye, Northrop. *The Anatomy of Criticism*. Princeton, N.J.: Princeton University Press, 1957.

———*The Educated Imagination*. Bloomington, Ind.: Indiana University Press, 1964.

———*Fables of Identity*. New York: Harcourt, Brace and World, Inc., 1963.

———*Fearful Symmetry: A Study of Blake*. Princeton, N.J.: Princeton University Press, 1947.

Gaster, Theodor. *Thespis: Ritual, Myth and Drama in The Ancient Near East*. Garden City, N.Y.: Doubleday and Co., Inc., 1950.

Gennep, Arnold Van. *The Rites of Passage*. Translated by Monica B. Vizedom and Gabrielle L. Caffee. London: Routledge and Kegan Paul, 1960.

Harrison, Jane. *Themis*. Cambridge, Mass.: Cambridge University Press, 1912.

Hoffman, Daniel G. *Form and Fable in American Fiction*. New York: Oxford University Press, 1961.

Hyman, Stanley Edgar. *The Tangled Bank*. New York: Atheneum, 1962.

Jones, Ernest. *Essays in Applied Psycho-Analysis*. London: Hogarth Press, 1951, Vol. 2.

Jung, Carl Gustav. *Modern Man in Search of a Soul*. New York: Harcourt, Brace and World, Inc., 1956.

———*Psyche and Symbol*. Garden City, N.Y.: Doubleday and Co., Inc., 1958.

Krieger, Murray. "After the New Criticism," *Massachusetts Review*, IV (1962), pp. 183–205.

Langer, Susanne. *Philosophy in a New Key*. New York: New American Library, 1948.

———*Problems of Art*. New York: Charles Scribner's Sons, 1957.

Lawrence, D. H. *Apocalypse*. New York: The Viking Press, 1931, 1960.

———*Studies in Classic American Literature*. Garden City, N.Y.: Doubleday, 1953 (c1951).

Levy-Bruhl, Lucien. *Primitive Mentality*. Translated by Lilian A. Clare. London: George Allen and Unwin, 1923.

Lewis, R. W. B. *The American Adam: Innocence, Tragedy and Tradition in the Nineteenth Century*. Chicago: The University of Chicago Press, 1955.

Malinowski, Bronislaw. *Myth in Primitive Psychology*. London: K. Paul, Trench, Trubner, 1926.

Murray, Gilbert. *The Rise of the Greek Epic*. London: Oxford University Press, 4th Ed., 1934.

Murray, Henry A., ed. *Myth and Myth-Making*. New York: Braziller, 1960.

Ohmann, Richard, ed. *The Making of Myth*. New York: G. P. Putnam's Sons, 1962.

Radin, Paul. *Primitive Religion*. New York: Viking, 1937.

———*The Trickster*. New York: Philosophical Library, 1956.

Raglan, Lord. *The Hero*. London: Watts, 1949.

Rougemont, Denis De. *Love in the Western World*. Translated by Montgomery Belgion. New York: Pantheon, 1956.

Sebeok, Thomas A., ed. *Myth: A Symposium*. Bloomington, Ind.: Indiana University Press, 1955.

Shumaker, Wayne. *Literature and the Irrational*. Englewood Cliffs, N.J.: Prentice-Hall, Inc., 1960.

Slote, Bernice, ed. *Myth and Symbol*. Lincoln, Neb.: University of Nebraska Press, 1963.

Slote, Bernice, James E. Miller and Karl Shapiro. *Start With the Sun*. Lincoln, Neb.: University of Nebraska Press, 1960.

Vickery, John B. "*The Golden Bough:* Impact and Archetype." *Virginia Quarterly Review*, XXXIX (1963), pp. 37–57.

———*Myth and Literature: Contemporary Theory and Practice*. Lincoln, Neb.: University of Nebraska Press, 1966.

Weisinger, Herbert. *The Agony and the Triumph: Papers on the Use and Abuse of Myth*. East Lansing, Mich.: Michigan State University Press, 1953.

Wellek, Rene and Austin Warren. *Theory of Literature*. New York: Harcourt, Brace and World, Inc., 1956, pp. 179–183.

Whalley, George. *The Poetic Process*. London: Routledge and Kegan Paul, 1953.

Wheelwright, Philip. *The Burning Fountain*. Bloomington, Ind.: Indiana University Press, 1954.

———*Metaphor and Reality*. Bloomington, Ind.: Indiana University Press, 1962.

Wimsatt, W. K., Jr. and Cleanth Brooks. *Literary Criticism: A Short History*. New York: Alfred A. Knopf, Inc., 1957, pp. 708–720.

Archetypes of the Collective Unconscious

C. G. JUNG

The hypothesis of a collective unconscious belongs to the class of ideas that people at first find strange but soon come to possess and use as familiar conceptions. This has been the case with the concept of the unconscious in general. After the philosophical idea of the unconscious, in the form presented chiefly by Carus and von Hartmann, had gone down under the overwhelming wave of materialism, leaving hardly a ripple behind it, it gradually reappeared in the scientific domain of medical psychology.

At first the concept of the unconscious was limited to denoting the state of repressed or forgotten contents. Even with Freud, who makes the unconscious— at least metaphorically—take the stage as the acting subject, it is really nothing but the gathering place of forgotten and repressed contents, and has a functional significance thanks only to these. For Freud, accordingly, the unconscious is of an exclusively personal nature,[1] although he was aware of its archaic and mythological thought-forms.

A more or less superficial layer of the unconscious is undoubtedly personal. I call it the *personal unconscious*. But this personal unconscious rests upon a deeper layer, which does not derive from personal experience and is not a personal acquisition but is inborn. This deeper layer I call the *collective unconscious*. I have chosen the term "collective" because this part of the unconscious is not individual but universal; in contrast to the personal psyche, it has contents and modes of behavior that are more or less the same everywhere and in all individuals. It is, in other words, identical in all men and thus constitutes a

[1] In his later works Freud differentiated the basic view mentioned here. He called the instinctual psyche the "id," and his "superego" denotes the collective consciousness, of which the individual is partly conscious and partly unconscious (because it is repressed).

common psychic substrate of a suprapersonal nature which is present in every one of us.

Psychic existence can be recognized only by the presence of contents that are *capable of consciousness*. We can therefore speak of an unconscious only insofar as we are able to demonstrate its contents. The contents of the personal unconscious are chiefly the *feeling-toned complexes,* as they are called; they constitute the personal and private side of psychic life. The contents of the collective unconscious, on the other hand, are known as *archetypes*.

The term "archetype" occurs as early as Philo Judaeus,[2] with reference to the *Imago Dei* (God-image) in man. It can also be found in Irenaeus, who says: "The creator of the world did not fashion these things directly from himself but copied them from archetypes outside himself."[3] In the *Corpus Hermeticum,*[4] God is called *to archetypon phôs* (archetype of light). The term occurs several times in Dionysius the Areopagite, as for instance in *De caelesti hierachia,* II, 4: "immaterial Archetypes,"[5] and in *De divinis nominibus,* I, 6: "Archetypal stone."[6] The term "archetype" is not found in St. Augustine, but the idea of it is. Thus in *De diversis quaestionibus LXXXIII* he speaks of "ideas . . . which themselves are not formed . . . which are contained in the divine intelligence."[7] "Archetype" is an explanatory paraphrase of the Platonic *eidos*. For our purposes this term is apposite and helpful, because it tells us that so far as the collective unconscious contents are concerned we are dealing with archaic or—I would say—primordial types, that is, with universal images that have existed since the remotest times. The term *"représentations collectives,"* used by Lévy-Bruhl to denote the symbolic figures in the primitive view of the world, could easily be applied to unconscious contents as well, since it means practically the same thing. Primitive tribal lore is concerned with archetypes that have been modified in a special way. They are no longer contents of the unconscious, but have already been changed into conscious formulae taught according to tradition, generally in the form of esoteric teachings. This last is a typical means of expression for the transmission of collective contents originally derived from the unconscious.

Another well-known expression of the archetypes is myth and fairy tale. But here too we are dealing with forms that have received a specific stamp

[2] *De opificio mundi,* I, 69.

[3] *Adversus haereses,* II, 7, 5: "Mundi fabricator non a semetipso fecit haec, sed de alienis archetypis transtulit."

[4] Walter Scott, *Hermetica* (Oxford, 1924–36; 4 vols.).

[5] In Jacques Paul Migne, *Patrologiae cursus completus* (Greek series, *PG*), Paris, 1857–66, 166 vols., vol. 3, col. 144.

[6] *Ibid.,* vol. 3, col. 595.

[7] Jacques Paul Migne, *Patrologiae cursus completus* (Latin series, *PL*) Paris, 1844–64, 221 vols., vol. 40, col. 30. "Archetype" is used in the same way by the alchemists, as in the "Tractatus aureus" of Hermes Trismegistus (*Theatrum chemicum,* Ursel and Strasbourg, IV, 1613, p. 718: "As God [contains] all the treasure of his godhead . . . hidden in himself as in an archetype [*in se tamquam archetypo absconditum*] . . . in like manner Saturn carries the similitudes of metallic bodies hiddenly in himself." In the "Tractatus de igne et sale" of Vigenerus (*Theatr. chem.,* VI, 1661, p. 3), the world is "ad archetypi sui similitudinem factus" (made after the likeness of its archetype) and is therefore called the "magnus homo" (the "homo maximus" of Swedenborg).

and have been handed down through long periods of time. The term "arche-type" thus applies only indirectly to the *"représentations collectives,"* since it designates only those psychic contents which have not yet been submitted to conscious elaboration and are therefore an immediate datum of psychic experi-ence. In this sense there is a considerable difference between the archetype and the historical formula that has evolved. Especially on the higher levels of esoteric teaching the archetypes appear in a form that reveals quite unmistak-ably the critical and evaluating influence of conscious elaboration. Their immediate manifestation, as we encounter it in dreams and visions, is much more individual, less understandable, and more naïve than in myths, for example. The archetype is essentially an unconscious content that is altered by becoming conscious and by being perceived, and it takes its color from the individual consciousness in which it happens to appear.[8]

What the word "archetype" means in the nominal sense is clear enough, then, from its relations with myth, esoteric teaching, and fairy tale. But if we try to establish what an archetype is *psychologically,* the matter becomes more complicated. So far mythologists have always had recourse to solar, lunar, meteorological, vegetal, and various other ideas of the kind. The fact that myths are first and foremost psychic phenomena that reveal the nature of the soul is something they have absolutely refused to see until now. Primitive man is not much interested in objective explanations of the obvious, but he has an imperative need—or rather, his unconscious psyche has an irresistible urge—to assimilate all outer sense experiences to inner, psychic events. It is not enough for the primitive to see the sun rise and set; this external observation must at the same time be a psychic happening: the sun in its course must represent the fate of a god or hero who, in the last analysis, dwells nowhere except in the soul of man. All the mythologized processes of nature, such as summer and winter, the phases of the moon, the rainy seasons, and so forth, are in no sense allegories[9] of these objective experiences; rather they are symbolic expressions of the inner, unconscious drama of the psyche which becomes accessible to man's consciousness by way of projection—that is, mirrored in the events of nature. The projection is so fundamental that it has taken several thousand years of civilization to detach it in some measure from its outer object. In the case of astrology, for instance, this age-old *"scientia intuitiva"* came to be branded as rank heresy because man had not yet succeeded in making the psychological description of character independent of the stars. Even today, people who still believe in astrology fall almost without exception for the old superstitious assumption of the influence of the stars. And yet anyone who can calculate a horoscope should know that, since the days of Hipparchus of Alexandria, the spring-point has been fixed at 0° Aries, and that the zodiac

[9] An allegory is a paraphrase of a conscious content, whereas a symbol is the best possible expression for an unconscious content whose nature can only be guessed, because it is still unknown.

[8] One must, for the sake of accuracy, distinguish between "archetype" and "archetypal ideas." The archetype as such is a hypothetical and irrepresentable model, something like the "pattern of behavior" in biology. Cf. *On the Nature of the Psyche* [this volume, p. 37].

on which every horoscope is based is therefore quite arbitrary, the spring-point having gradually advanced, since then, into the first degrees of Pisces, owing to the precession of the equinoxes.

Primitive man impresses us so strongly with his subjectivity that we should really have guessed long ago that myths refer to something psychic. His knowledge of nature is essentially the language and outer dress of an unconscious psychic process. But the very fact that this process is unconscious gives us the reason why man has thought of everything except the psyche in his attempts to explain myths. He simply didn't know that the psyche contains all the images that have ever given rise to myths, and that our unconscious is an acting and suffering subject with an inner drama which primitive man rediscovers, by means of analogy, in the processes of nature both great and small.[10]

"The stars of thine own fate lie in thy breast,"[11] says Seni to Wallenstein— a dictum that should satisfy all astrologers if we knew even a little about the secrets of the heart. But for this, so far, men have had little understanding. Nor would I dare to assert that things are any better today.

Tribal lore is always sacred and dangerous. All esoteric teachings seek to apprehend the unseen happenings in the psyche, and all claim supreme authority for themselves. What is true of primitive lore is true in even higher degree of the ruling world religions. They contain a revealed knowledge that was originally hidden, and they set forth the secrets of the soul in glorious images. Their temples and their sacred writings proclaim in image and word the doctrine hallowed from of old, making it accessible to every believing heart, every sensitive vision, every farthest range of thought. Indeed, we are compelled to say that the more beautiful, the more sublime, the more comprehensive the image that has evolved and been handed down by tradition, the further removed it is from individual experience. We can just feel our way into it and sense something of it, but the original experience has been lost.

Why is psychology the youngest of the empirical sciences? Why have we not long since discovered the unconscious and raised up its treasure-house of eternal images? Simply because we had a religious formula for everything psychic—and one that is far more beautiful and comprehensive than immediate experience. Though the Christian view of the world has paled for many people, the symbolic treasure-rooms of the East are still full of marvels that can nourish for a long time to come the passion for show and new clothes. What is more, these images—be they Christian or Buddhist or what you will—are lovely, mysterious, and richly intuitive. Naturally, the more familiar we are with them the more does constant usage polish them smooth, so that what remains is only banal superficiality and meaningless paradox. The mystery of the Virgin Birth, or the *homoousia* of the Son with the Father, or the Trinity which is nevertheless not a triad—these no longer lend wings to any philosophical fancy. They have stiffened into mere objects of belief. So it is not surprising if the religious need, the believing mind, and the philosophical speculations of the educated European

[10] Cf. my papers on the divine child and the Kore [*Coll. Works,* Vol. 9, Pt. I] and Kerényi's complementary essays in *Essays on a Science of Mythology* [Bollingen Series XXII, New York, 1949].

[11] [Schiller, *Piccolomini*, II, 6.]

are attracted by the symbols of the East—those grandiose conceptions of divinity in India and the abysms of Taoist philosophy in China—just as once before the heart and mind of the men of antiquity were gripped by Christian ideas. There are many Europeans who began by surrendering completely to the influence of the Christian symbol until they landed themselves in a Kierke-gaardian neurosis, or whose relation to God, owing to the progressive impoverishment of symbolism, developed into an unbearably sophisticated I-You relationship—only to fall victims in their turn to the magic and novelty of Eastern symbols. This surrender is not necessarily a defeat; rather it proves the receptiveness and vitality of the religious sense. We can observe much the same thing in the educated Oriental, who not infrequently feels drawn to the Christian symbol or to the science that is so unsuited to the Oriental mind, and even develops an enviable understanding of them. That people should succumb to these eternal images is entirely normal, in fact it is what these images are for. They are meant to attract, to convince, to fascinate, and to overpower. They are created out of the primal stuff of revelation and reflect the ever-unique experience of divinity. That is why they always give man a premonition of the divine while at the same time safeguarding him from immediate experience of it. Thanks to the labors of the human spirit over the centuries, these images have become embedded in a comprehensive system of thought that ascribes an order to the world, and are at the same time represented by a mighty, far-spread, and venerable institution called the Church.

I can best illustrate my meaning by taking as an example the Swiss mystic and hermit, Brother Nicholas of Flüe,[12] who has recently been canonized. Probably his most important religious experience was the so-called Trinity Vision, which preoccupied him to such an extent that he painted it, or had it painted, on the wall of his cell. The painting is still preserved in the parish church at Sachseln. It is a mandala divided into six parts, and in the center is the crowned countenance of God. Now we know that Brother Klaus investigated the nature of his vision with the help of an illustrated devotional booklet by a German mystic, and that he struggled to get his original experience into a form he could understand. He occupied himself with it for years. This is what I call the "elaboration" of the symbol. His reflections on the nature of the vision, influenced as they were by the mystic diagrams he used as a guiding thread, inevitably led him to the conclusion that he must have gazed upon the Holy Trinity itself—the *summum bonum,* eternal love. This is borne out by the "expurgated" version now in Sachseln.

The original experience, however, was entirely different. In his ecstasy there was revealed to Brother Klaus a sight so terrible that his own countenance was changed by it—so much so, indeed, that people were terrified and felt afraid of him. What he had seen was a vision of the utmost intensity. Woelflin,[13] our oldest source, writes as follows:

---

[12] Cf. my "Brother Klaus" (*Coll. Works,* Vol. 11).

[13] Heinrich Woelflin, also called by the Latin form Lupulus, born 1470, humanist and director of Latin studies at Bern. Cited in Fritz Blanke, *Bruder Klaus von Flüe* (Zurich, 1948), pp. 92 f.

"All who came to him were filled with terror at the first glance. As to the cause of this, he himself used to say that he had seen a piercing light resembling a human face. At the sight of it he feared that his heart would burst into little pieces. Therefore, overcome with terror, he instantly turned his face away and fell to the ground. And that was the reason why his face is now terrible to others."

This vision has rightly been compared[14] with the one in Revelation 1:13ff., that strange apocalyptic Christ-image, which for sheer gruesomeness and singularity is surpassed only by the monstrous seven-eyed lamb with seven horns (Rev. 5:6 f.). It is certainly very difficult to see what is the relationship between this figure and the Christ of the gospels. Hence Brother Klaus's vision was interpreted in a quite definite way by the earliest sources. In 1508, the humanist Karl Bovillus (Charles de Bouelles) wrote to a friend:

I wish to tell you of a vision which appeared to him in the sky, on a night when the stars were shining and he stood in prayer and contemplation. He saw the head of a human figure with a terrifying face, full of wrath and threats.[15]

This interpretation agrees perfectly with the modern amplification furnished by Revelation 1:13.[16] Nor should we forget Brother Klaus's other visions, for instance, of Christ in the bearskin, of God the Father and God the Mother, and of himself as the Son. They exhibit features which are very undogmatic indeed.

Traditionally this great vision was brought into connection with the Trinity picture in the church at Sachseln, and so, likewise, was the wheel symbolism in the so-called "Pilgrim's Tract."[17] Brother Klaus, we are told, showed the picture of the wheel to a visiting pilgrim. Evidently this picture had preoccupied him for some time. Blanke is of the opinion that, contrary to tradition, there is no connection between the vision and the Trinity picture.[18] This skepticism seems to me to go too far. There must have been some reason for Brother Klaus's interest in the wheel. Visions like the one he had often cause mental confusion and disintegration (witness the heart bursting "into little pieces"). We know from experience that the protective circle, the mandala, is the traditional antidote for chaotic states of mind. It is therefore only too clear why Brother Klaus was fascinated by the symbol of the wheel. The interpretation of the terrifying vision as an experience of God need not be so wide of the mark either. The connection between the great vision and the Trinity picture, and of both with the wheel symbol, therefore seems to me very probable on psychological grounds.

[14] *Ibid.*, p. 94.

[15] *Ein gesichte Bruder Clausen ynn Schweytz und seine deutunge* (Wittemberg, 1528), p. 5. Cited in Alban Stoeckli, O. M. Cap., *Die Visionen des seligen Bruder Klaus* (Einsiedeln, 1933), p. 34.

[16] M. B. Lavaud, O.P. (*Vie Profonde de Nicolas de Flue,* Fribourg, 1942) gives just as apt a parallel with a text from the *Horologium sapientae* of Henry Suso, where the apocalyptic Christ appears as an infuriated and wrathful avenger, very much in contrast to the Jesus who preached the Sermon on the Mount.

[17] *Ein nutzlicher und loblicher Tractat von Bruder Claus und einem Pilger* (Nuremberg, 1488).

[18] Blanke, *op. cit.*, pp. 95 ff.

This vision, undoubtedly fearful and highly perturbing, which burst like a volcano upon his religious view of the world, without any dogmatic prelude and without exegetical commentary, naturally needed a long labor of assimilation in order to fit it into the total structure of the psyche and thus restore the disturbed psychic balance. Brother Klaus came to terms with his experience on the basis of dogma, then firm as a rock; and the dogma proved its powers of assimilation by turning something horribly alive into the beautiful abstraction of the Trinity idea. But the reconciliation might have taken place on a quite different basis provided by the vision itself and its unearthly actuality—much to the disadvantage of the Christian conception of God and no doubt to the still greater disadvantage of Brother Klaus himself, who would then have become not a saint but a heretic (if not a lunatic) and would probably have ended his life at the stake.

This example demonstrates the use of the dogmatic symbol: it formulates a tremendous and dangerously decisive psychic experience, fittingly called an "experience of the Divine," in a way that is tolerable to our human understanding, without either limiting the scope of the experience or doing damage to its overwhelming significance. The vision of divine wrath, which we also meet in Jakob Böhme, ill accords with the God of the New Testament, the loving Father in heaven, and for this reason it might easily have become the source of an inner conflict. That would have been quite in keeping with the spirit of the age—the end of the fifteenth century, the time of Nicholas Cusanus, whose formula of the "*complexio oppositorum*" actually anticipated the schism that was imminent. Not long afterwards the Yahwistic conception of God went through a series of rebirths in Protestantism. Yahweh is a God-concept that contains the opposites in a still undivided state.

Brother Klaus put himself outside the beaten track of convention and habit by leaving his home and family, living alone for years, and gazing deep into the dark mirror, so that the wondrous and terrible boon of original experience befell him. In this situation the dogmatic image of divinity that had been developed over the centuries worked like a healing draught. It helped him to assimilate the fatal incursion of an archetypal image and so escape being torn asunder. Angelus Silesius was not so fortunate; the inner conflict tore him to pieces, because in his day the stability of the Church that dogma guarantees was already shattered.

Jakob Böhme, too, knew a God of the "Wrath-fire," a real *Deus absconditus*. He was able to bridge the profound and agonizing contradiction on the one hand by means of the Christian formula of Father and Son, and embody it speculatively in his view of the world—which, though Gnostic, was in all essential points Christian. Otherwise he would have become a dualist. On the other hand it was undoubtedly alchemy, long brewing the union of opposites in secret, that came to his aid. Nevertheless the opposition has left obvious traces in the mandala appended to his *XL Questions concerning the Soul*,[19] showing the nature of the divinity. The mandala is divided into a dark and a light half,

[19] London, 1647.

and the semicircles that are drawn round them, instead of joining up to form a ring, are turned back to back.[20]

Dogma takes the place of the collective unconscious by formulating its contents on a grand scale. The Catholic way of life is completely unaware of psychological problems in this sense. Almost the entire life of the collective unconscious has been channeled into the dogmatic archetypal ideas and flows along like a well-controlled stream in the symbolism of creed and ritual. It manifests itself in the inwardness of the Catholic psyche. The collective unconscious, as we understand it today, was never a matter of "psychology," for before the Christian Church existed there were the antique mysteries, and these reach back into the gray mists of neolithic prehistory. Mankind has never lacked powerful images to lend magical aid against all the uncanny things that live in the depths of the psyche. Always the figures of the unconscious were expressed in protecting and healing images and in this way were expelled from the psyche into cosmic space.

The iconoclasm of the Reformation, however, quite literally made a breach in the protective wall of sacred images, and since then one image after another has crumbled away. They became dubious, for they conflicted with awakening reason. Besides, people had long since forgotten what they meant. Or had they really forgotten? Could it be that men had never really known what they meant, and that only in recent times did it occur to the Protestant part of mankind that actually we haven't the remotest conception of what is meant by the Virgin Birth, the divinity of Christ, and the complexities of the Trinity? It almost seems as if these images had just lived, and as if their living existence had simply been accepted without question and without reflection, much as everyone decorates Christmas trees or hides Easter eggs without ever knowing what these customs mean. The fact is that archetypal images are so packed with meaning in themselves that people never think of asking what they really do mean. That the gods die from time to time is due to man's sudden discovery that they do not mean anything, that they are made by human hands, useless idols of wood and stone. In reality, however, he has merely discovered that up till then he has never thought about his images at all. And when he starts thinking about them, he does so with the help of what he calls "reason"—which in point of fact is nothing more than the sum total of all his prejudices and myopic views.

The history of Protestantism has been one of chronic iconoclasm. One wall after another fell. And the work of destruction was not too difficult once the authority of the Church had been shattered. We all know how, in large things as in small, in general as well as in particular, piece after piece collapsed, and how the alarming poverty of symbols that is now the condition of our life came about. With that the power of the Church has vanished too—a fortress robbed of its bastions and casemates, a house whose walls have been plucked away, exposed to all the winds of the world and to all dangers.

Although this is, properly speaking, a lamentable collapse that offends our sense of history, the disintegration of Protestantism into nearly four hundred

---

[20] Cf. my "Study in the Process of Individuation" (*Coll. Works,* Vol. 9, pt. I).

denominations is yet a sure sign that the restlessness continues. The Protestant is cast out into a state of defenselessness that might well make the natural man shudder. His enlightened consciousness, of course, refuses to take cognizance of this fact, and is quietly looking elsewhere for what has been lost to Europe. We seek the effective images, the thought-forms, that satisfy the restlessness of heart and mind, and we find the treasures of the East.

There is no objection to this, in and for itself. Nobody forced the Romans to import Asiatic cults in bulk. If Christianity had really been—as so often described—"alien" to the Germanic tribes, they could easily have rejected it when the prestige of the Roman legions began to wane. But Christianity had come to stay, because it fits in with the existing archetypal pattern. In the course of the centuries, however, it turned into something its founder might well have wondered at had he lived to see it; and the Christianity of Negroes and other dark-skinned converts is certainly an occasion for historical reflections. Why, then, should the West not assimilate Eastern forms? The Romans too went to Eleusis, Samothrace, and Egypt in order to get themselves initiated. In Egypt there even seems to have been a regular tourist trade in this commodity.

The gods of Greece and Rome perished from the same disease as did our Christian symbols: people discovered then, as today, that they had no thoughts whatever on the subject. On the other hand, the gods of the strangers still had unexhausted mana. Their names were weird and incomprehensible and their deeds portentously dark—something altogether different from the hackneyed *chronique scandaleuse* of Olympus. At least one couldn't understand the Asiatic symbols, and for this reason they were not banal like the conventional gods. The fact that people accepted the new as unthinkingly as they had rejected the old did not become a problem at that time.

Is it becoming a problem today? Shall we be able to put on, like a new suit of clothes, ready-made symbols grown on foreign soil, saturated with foreign blood, spoken in a foreign tongue, nourished by a foreign culture, interwoven with foreign history, and so resemble a beggar who wraps himself in kingly raiment, a king who disguises himself as a beggar? No doubt this is possible. Or is there something in ourselves that commands us to go in for no mummeries, but perhaps even to sew our garment ourselves?

I am convinced that the growing impoverishment of symbols has a meaning. It is a development that has an inner consistency. Everything that we have not thought about, and that has therefore been deprived of a meaningful connection with our developing consciousness, has got lost. If we now try to cover our nakedness with the gorgeous trappings of the East, as the theosophists do, we would be playing our own history false. A man does not sink down to beggary only to pose afterwards as an Indian potentate. It seems to me that it would be far better stoutly to avow our spiritual poverty, our symbollessness, instead of feigning a legacy to which we are not the legitimate heirs at all. We are, surely, the rightful heirs of Christian symbolism, but somehow we have squandered this heritage. We have let the house our fathers built fall into decay, and now we try to break into Oriental palaces that our fathers never knew. Anyone who has lost the historical symbols and cannot be satisfied with substitutes is certainly in a very difficult position today: before him there yawns the void, and he turns away from it in horror. What is worse, the vacuum gets filled with absurd political and social ideas, which one and all are distinguished by their spiritual bleakness. But if he cannot get along with these pedantic dogmatisms, he sees himself forced to be serious for once with his alleged trust in God, though it usually turns out that his fear of things going wrong if he did so is even more persuasive. This fear is far from unjustified, for where God is closest the danger seems greatest. It is dangerous to avow spiritual poverty, for the poor man has desires, and whoever has desires calls down some fatality on himself. A Swiss proverb puts it drastically: "Behind every rich man stands a devil, and behind every poor man two."

Just as in Christianity the vow of worldly poverty turned the mind away from the riches of this earth, so spiritual poverty seeks to renounce the false riches of the spirit in order to withdraw not only from the sorry remnants—which today call themselves the Protestant Church—of a great past, but also from all the allurements of the odorous East; in order, finally, to dwell with itself alone, where, in the cold light of consciousness, the blank barrenness of the world reaches to the very stars.

We have inherited this poverty from our fathers. I well remember the confirmation lessons I received at the hands of my own father. The catechism bored me unspeakably. One day I was turning over the pages of my little book, in the hope of finding something interesting, when my eye fell on the paragraphs about the Trinity. This interested me at once, and I waited impatiently for the lessons to get to that section. But when the longed-for lesson arrived, my father said: "We'll skip this bit; I can't make head or tail of it myself." With that my last hope was laid in the grave. I admired my father's honesty, but this did not alter the fact that from then on all talk of religion bored me to death.

Our intellect has achieved the most tremendous things, but in the meantime our spiritual dwelling has fallen into disrepair. We are absolutely convinced that even with the aid of the latest and largest reflecting telescope, now being built in America, men will discover behind the farthest nebulae no fiery empyrean; and we know that our eyes will wander despairingly through the dead emptiness of interstellar space. Nor is it any better when mathematical physics reveals to us the world of the infinitely small. In the end we dig up the wisdom of all ages and peoples, only to find that everything most dear and precious to us has already been said in the most superb language. Like greedy children we stretch out our hands and think that, if only we could grasp it, we would possess it too. But what we possess is no longer valid, and our hands grow weary from the grasping, for riches lie everywhere, as far as the eye can reach. All these possessions turn to water, and more than one sorcerer's apprentice has been drowned in the waters called up by himself—if he did not first succumb to the saving delusion that *this* wisdom was good and *that* was bad. It is from these adepts that there come those terrifying invalids who think they have a prophetic mission. For the artificial sundering of true and false wisdom creates a tension in the psyche, and from this there arises a loneliness and a craving like that of the morphine addict, who always hopes to find companions in his vice.

When our natural inheritance has been dissipated, then the spirit too, as Heraclitus says, has descended from its fiery heights. But when spirit becomes heavy it turns to water, and with Luciferian presumption the intellect usurps the seat where once the spirit was enthroned. The spirit may legitimately claim the *patria potestas* over the soul; not so the earth-born intellect, which is man's sword or hammer, and not a creator of spiritual worlds, a father of the soul. Hence Ludwig Klages[21] and Max Scheler[22] were moderate enough in their attempts to rehabilitate the spirit, for both were children of an age in which the spirit was no longer up above but down below, no longer fire but water.

Therefore the way of the soul in search of its lost father—like Sophia seeking Bythos—leads to the water, to the dark mirror that reposes at its bottom. Whoever has elected for the state of spiritual poverty, the true heritage of Protestantism carried to its logical conclusion, goes the way of the soul that leads to the water. This water is no figure of speech, but a living symbol of the dark psyche. I can best illustrate this by a concrete example, one out of many:

A Protestant theologian often dreamed the same dream: *He stood on a mountain slope with a deep valley below, and in it a dark lake. He knew in the dream that something had always prevented him from approaching the lake. This time he resolved to go to the water. As he approached the shore, everything grew dark and uncanny, and a gust of wind suddenly rushed over the face of the water. He was seized by a panic fear, and awoke.*

This dream shows us the natural symbolism. The dreamer descends into his own depths, and the way leads him to the mysterious water. And now there occurs the miracle of the pool of Bethesda: an angel comes down and touches the water, endowing it with healing power. In the dream it is the wind, the *pneuma*, which bloweth whither it listeth. Man's descent to the water is needed in order to evoke the miracle of its coming to life. But the breath of the spirit rushing over the dark water is uncanny, like everything whose cause we do not know—since it is not ourselves. It hints at an unseen presence, a numen to which neither human expectations nor the machinations of the will have given life. It lives of itself, and a shudder runs through the man who thought that "spirit" was merely what he believes, what he makes himself, what is said in books, or what people talk about. But when it happens spontaneously it is a spookish thing, and primitive fear seizes the naïve mind. The elders of the Elgonyi tribe in Kenya gave me exactly the same description of the nocturnal god whom they call the "maker of fear." "He comes to you," they said, "like a cold gust of wind, and you shudder, or he goes whistling round in the tall grass"—an African Pan who glides among the reeds in the haunted noontide hour, playing on his pipes and frightening the shepherds.

Thus, in the dream, the breath of the *pneuma* frightened another pastor, a shepherd of the flock, who in the darkness of the night trod the reed-grown

---

[21] [Cf. *Der Geist als Widersacher der Seele* (Leipzig, 1929–32, 3 vols.).]

[22] [Cf., e.g., *Die Stellung des Menschen im Kosmos* (Darmstadt, 1928).]

shore in the deep valley of the psyche. Yes, that erstwhile fiery spirit has made a descent to the realm of nature, to the trees and rocks and the waters of the psyche, like the old man in Nietzsche's *Zarathustra,* who, wearied of humankind, withdrew into the forest to growl with the bears in honor of the Creator.

We must surely go the way of the waters, which always tend downward, if we would raise up the treasure, the precious heritage of the father. In the Gnostic hymn to the soul,[23] the son is sent forth by his parents to seek the pearl that fell from the King's crown. It lies at the bottom of a deep well, guarded by a dragon, in the land of the Egyptians—that land of fleshpots and drunkenness with all its material and spiritual riches. The son and heir sets out to fetch the jewel, but forgets himself and his task in the orgies of Egyptian worldliness until a letter from his father reminds him what his duty is. He then sets out for the water and plunges into the dark depths of the well, where he finds the pearl on the bottom, and in the end offers it to the highest divinity.

This hymn, ascribed to Bardesanes, dates from an age that resembled ours in more than one respect. Mankind looked and waited, and it was a *fish*— "*levatus de profundo*" (drawn from the deep)[24]—that became the symbol of the savior, the bringer of healing.

As I wrote these lines, I received a letter from Vancouver, from a person unknown to me. The writer is puzzled by his dreams, which are always about water: "Almost every time I dream it is about water: *either I am having a bath, or the water closet is overflowing, or a pipe is bursting, or my home has drifted down to the water's edge, or I see an acquaintance about to sink into water, or I am trying to get out of water, or I am having a bath and the tub is about to overflow,*" etc.

Water is the commonest symbol for the unconscious. The lake in the valley is the unconscious, which lies, as it were, underneath consciousness, so that it is often referred to as the "subconscious," usually with the pejorative connotation of an inferior consciousness. Water is the "valley spirit," the water dragon of Tao, whose nature resembles water—a *yang* embraced in the *yin.* Psychologically, therefore, water means spirit that has become unconscious. So the dream of the theologian is quite right in telling him that down by the water he could experience the working of the living spirit like a miracle of healing in the pool of Bethesda. The descent into the depths always seems to precede the ascent. Thus another theologian[25] dreamed that *he saw on a mountain a kind of Castle of the Grail. He went along a road that seemed to lead straight to the foot of the mountain and up it. But as he drew nearer he discovered to his great disappointment that a chasm separated him from the mountain, a deep, darksome gorge with underworldly water rushing along the bottom. A steep path led downwards and toilsomely climbed up again on the other side. But the prospect looked uninviting,* and the dreamer awoke. Here again the dreamer, thirsting for the shining heights, had first to descend into the dark depths, and

---

[23] M. R. James (tr.), *Apocryphal New Testament* (Oxford, 1924), pp. 411–15.

[24] Augustine, *Confessions,* Lib. XIII, cap. XXI.

[25] The fact that it was another theologian who dreamed this dream is not so surprising, since priests and clergymen have a professional interest in the motif of "ascent." They have to speak of it so often that the question naturally arises as to what they are doing about their own spiritual ascent.

this proves to be the indispensable condition for climbing any higher. The prudent man avoids the danger lurking in these depths, but he also throws away the good which a bold but imprudent venture might bring.

The statement made by the dream meets with violent resistance from the conscious mind, which knows "spirit" only as something to be found in the heights. "Spirit" always seems to come from above, while from below comes everything that is sordid and worthless. For people who think in this way, spirit means highest freedom, a soaring over the depths, deliverance from the prison of the chthonic world, and hence a refuge for all those timorous souls who do not want to become anything different. But water is earthy and tangible, it is also the fluid of the instinct-driven body, blood and the flowing of blood, the odor of the beast, carnality heavy with passion. The unconscious is the psyche that reaches down from the daylight of mentally and morally lucid consciousness into the nervous system that for ages has been known as the "sympathetic." This does not govern perception and muscular activity like the cerebrospinal system, and thus control the environment; but, though functioning without sense-organs, it maintains the balance of life and, through the mysterious pathways of sympathetic excitation, not only gives us knowledge of the inner-most life of other beings but also has an inner effect upon them. In this sense it is an extremely collective system, the operative basis of all *participation mystique,* whereas the cerebrospinal function reaches its high point in separating off the specific qualities of the ego, and only apprehends surfaces and externals —always through the medium of space. It experiences everything as an outside, whereas the sympathetic system experiences everything as an inside.

The unconscious is commonly regarded as a sort of incapsulated fragment of our most personal and intimate life—something like what the Bible calls the "heart" and considers the source of all evil thoughts. In the chambers of the heart dwell the wicked blood-spirits, swift anger and sensual weakness. This is how the unconscious looks when seen from the conscious side. But consciousness appears to be essentially an affair of the cerebrum, which sees everything sepa-rately and in isolation, and therefore sees the unconscious in this way too, regarding it outright as *my* unconscious. Hence it is generally believed that anyone who descends into the unconscious gets into a suffocating atmosphere of egocentric subjectivity, and in this blind alley is exposed to the attack of all the ferocious beasts which the caverns of the psychic underworld are supposed to harbor.

True, whoever looks into the mirror of the water will see first of all his own face. Whoever goes to himself risks a confrontation with himself. The mirror does not flatter, it faithfully shows whatever looks into it; namely, the face we never show to the world because we cover it with the *persona,* the mask of the actor. But the mirror lies behind the mask and shows the true face.

This confrontation is the first test of courage on the inner way, a test sufficient to frighten off most people, for the meeting with ourselves belongs to the more unpleasant things that can be avoided so long as we can project everything negative into the environment. But if we are able to see our own shadow and can bear knowing about it, then a small part of the problem has already been solved: we have at least brought up the personal unconscious. The shadow is a living part of the personality and therefore wants to live with it in some form. It cannot be argued out of existence or rationalized into harmlessness. This problem is exceedingly difficult, because it not only challenges the whole man, but reminds him at the same time of his helplessness and ineffectuality. Strong natures—or should one rather call them weak?—do not like to be reminded of this, but prefer to think of themselves as heroes who are beyond good and evil, and to cut the Gordian knot instead of untying it. Nevertheless, the account has to be settled sooner or later. In the end one has to admit that there are problems which one simply cannot solve on one's own resources. Such an admission has the advantage of being honest, truthful, and in accord with reality, and this prepares the ground for a compensatory reaction from the collective unconscious: you are now more inclined to give heed to a helpful idea or intuition, or to notice thoughts which had not been allowed to voice themselves before. Perhaps you will pay attention to the dreams that visit you at such moments, or will reflect on certain inner and outer occurrences that take place just at this time. If you have an attitude of this kind, then the helpful powers slumbering in the deeper strata of man's nature can come awake and intervene, for helplessness and weakness are the eternal problem of mankind. To this problem there is also an eternal answer, otherwise it would have been all up with humanity along ago. When you have done everything that could possibly be done, the only thing that remains is what you could still do if only you knew it. But how much do we know of ourselves? Precious little, to judge by experience. Hence there is still a great deal of room left for the unconscious. Prayer, as we know, calls for a very similar attitude and therefore has much the same effect.

The necessary and needful reaction from the collective unconscious expresses itself in archetypally formed ideas. The meeting with oneself is, at first, the meeting with one's own shadow. The shadow is a tight passage, a narrow door, whose painful constriction no one is spared who goes down to the deep well. But one must learn to know oneself in order to know who one is. For what comes after the door is, surprisingly enough, a boundless expanse full of unprecedented uncertainty, with apparently no inside and no outside, no above and no below, no here and no there, no mine and no thine, no good and no bad. It is the world of water, where all life floats in suspension; where the realm of the sympathetic system, the soul of everything living, begins; where I am indivisibly this *and* that; where I experience the other in myself and the other-than-myself experiences me.

No, the collective unconscious is anything but an incapsulated personal system; it is sheer objectivity, as wide as the world and open to all the world. There I am the object of every subject, in complete reversal of my ordinary consciousness, where I am always the subject that has an object. There I am utterly one with the world, so much a part of it that I forget all too easily who I really am. "Lost in oneself" is a good way of describing this state. But this self is the world, if only a consciousness could see it. That is why we must know who we are.

The unconscious no sooner touches us than we *are* it—we become unconscious of ourselves. That is the age-old danger, instinctively known and feared by primitive man, who himself stands so very close to this pleroma. His consciousness is still uncertain, wobbling on its feet. It is still childish, having just emerged from the primal waters. A wave of the unconscious may easily roll over it, and then he forgets who he was and does things that are strange to him. Hence primitives are afraid of uncontrolled emotions, because consciousness breaks down under them and gives way to possession. All man's strivings have therefore been directed towards the consolidation of consciousness. This was the purpose of rite and dogma; they were dams and walls to keep back the dangers of the unconscious, the "perils of the soul." Primitive rites consist accordingly in the exorcizing of spirits, the lifting of spells, the averting of the evil omen, propitiation, purification, and the production by sympathetic magic of helpful occurrences.

It is these barriers, erected in primitive times, that later became the foundations of the Church. It is also these barriers that collapse when the symbols become weak with age. Then the waters rise and boundless catastrophes break over mankind. The religious leader of the Taos pueblo, known as the Loco Tenente Gobernador, once said to me: "The Americans should stop meddling with our religion, for when it dies and we can no longer help the sun our Father to cross the sky, the Americans and the whole world will learn something in ten years' time, for then the sun won't rise any more." In other words, night will fall, the light of consciousness is extinguished, and the dark sea of the unconscious breaks in.

Whether primitive or not, mankind always stands on the brink of actions it performs itself but does not control. The whole world wants peace and the whole world prepares for war, to take but one example. Mankind is powerless against mankind, and the gods, as ever, show it the ways of fate. Today we call the gods "factors" which comes from *facere*, "to make." The makers stand behind the wings of the world-theater. It is so in great things as in small. In the realm of consciousness we are our own masters; we seem to be the "factors" themselves. But if we step through the door of the shadow we discover with terror that we are the objects of unseen factors. To know this is decidedly unpleasant, for nothing is more disillusioning than the discovery of our own inadequacy. It can even give rise to primitive panic, because, instead of being believed in, the anxiously guarded supremacy of consciousness—which is in truth one of the secrets of human success—is questioned in the most dangerous way. But since ignorance is no guarantee of security, and in fact only makes our insecurity still worse, it is probably better despite our fear to know where the danger lies. To ask the right question is already half the solution of a problem. At any rate we then know that the greatest danger threatening us comes from the unpredictability of the psyche's reactions. Discerning persons have realized for some time that external historical conditions, of whatever kind, are only occasions, jumping-off grounds, for the real dangers that threaten our lives. These are the present politicosocial delusional systems. We should not regard them causally, as necessary consequences of external conditions, but as decisions precipitated by the collective unconscious.

The problem is not new, for all ages before us have believed in gods in some form or other. Only an unparalleled impoverishment of symbolism could enable us to rediscover the gods as psychic factors, that is, as archetypes of the unconscious. No doubt this discovery is hardly credible at present. To be convinced, we need to have the experience pictured in the dream of the theologian, for only then do we experience the self-activity of the spirit moving over the waters. Since the stars have fallen from heaven and our highest symbols have paled, a secret life holds sway in the unconscious. That is why we have a psychology today, and why we speak of the unconscious. All this would be quite superfluous in an age or culture that possessed symbols. Symbols are spirit from above, and under those conditions the spirit is above too. Therefore it would be a foolish and senseless undertaking for such people to wish to experience or investigate an unconscious that contains nothing but the silent, undisturbed sway of nature. Our unconscious, on the other hand, hides living water, spirit that has become nature, and that is why it is disturbed. Heaven has become for us the cosmic space of the physicists, and the divine empyrean a fair memory of things that once were. But "the heart glows," and a secret unrest gnaws at the roots of our being. In the words of the *Völuspa* we may ask:

> What murmurs Wotan over Mimir's head?
> Already the spring boils . . .

Our concern with the unconscious has become a vital question for us—a question of spiritual being or nonbeing. All those who have had an experience like that mentioned in the dream know that the treasure lies in the depths of the water and will try to salvage it. As they must never forget who they are, they must on no account imperil their consciousness. They will keep their standpoint firmly anchored to the earth, and will thus—to preserve the metaphor—become fishers who catch with hook and net what swims in the water. There may be consummate fools who do not understand what fishermen do, but the latter will not mistake the timeless meaning of their action, for the symbol of their craft is many centuries older than the still unfaded story of the Grail. But not every man is a fisherman. Sometimes this figure remains arrested at an early, instinctive level, and then it is an otter, as we know from Oskar Schmitz's fairy tales.[26]

Whoever looks into the water sees his own image, but behind it living creatures soon loom up; fishes, presumably, harmless dwellers of the deep—harmless, if only the lake were not haunted. They are water beings of a peculiar sort. Sometimes a nixie gets into the fisherman's net, a female, half-human fish.[27]

Nixies are entrancing creatures:

> Half drew she him,
> Half sank he down
> And nevermore was seen.

[26] [The "Fischottermärchen" in *Märchen aus dem Unbewussten* (Munich, 1932), pp. 14ff., 43ff.]

[27] Cf. Paracelsus, *De vita longa* (1562), and my commentary in "Paracelsus as a Spiritual Phenomenon" (to be pub. in *Coll. Works*, Vol. 15. Cf. *Paracelsica*, Zurich, 1942).

The nixie is an even more instinctive version of a magical feminine being whom I call the *anima*. She can also be a siren, *melusina* (mermaid),[28] wood-nymph, Grace, or Erlking's daughter, or a lamia or succubus, who infatuates young men and sucks the life out of them. Moralizing critics will say that these figures are projections of soulful emotional states and are nothing but worthless fantasies. One must admit that there is a certain amount of truth in this. But is it the whole truth? Is the nixie really nothing but a product of moral laxity? Were there not such beings long ago, in an age when dawning human consciousness was still wholly bound to nature? Surely there were spirits of forest, field and stream long before the question of moral conscience ever existed. What is more, these beings were as much dreaded as adored, so that their rather peculiar erotic charms were only one of their characteristics. Man's consciousness was then far simpler, and his possession of it absurdly small. An unlimited amount of what we now feel to be an integral part of our psychic being disports itself merrily for the primitive in projections ranging far and wide.

The word "projection" is not really appropriate, for nothing has been cast out of the psyche; rather, the psyche has attained its present complexity by a series of acts of introjection. Its complexity has increased in proportions to the despiritualization of nature. An alluring nixie from the dim bygone is today called an "erotic fantasy," and she may complicate our psychic life in a most painful way. She comes upon us just as a nixie might; she sits on top of us like a succubus; she changes into all sorts of shapes like a witch, and in general displays an unbearable independence that does not seem at all proper in a psychic content. Occasionally she causes states of fascination that rival the best bewitchment, or unleashes terrors in us not to be outdone by any manifestation of the devil. She is a mischievous being who crosses our path in numerous transformations and disguises, playing all kinds of tricks on us, causing happy and unhappy delusions, depressions and ecstasies, outbursts of affect, etc. Even in a state of reasonable introjection the nixie has not laid aside her roguery. The witch has not ceased to mix her vile potions of love and death; her magic poison has been refined into intrigue and self-deception, unseen though none the less dangerous for that.

But how do we dare to call this elfin being the "anima"? Anima means soul and should designate something very wonderful and immortal. Yet this was not always so. We should not forget that this kind of soul is a dogmatic conception whose purpose it is to pin down and capture something uncannily alive and active. The German word *Seele* is closely related, via the Gothic form *saiwalō*, to the Greek word *aiolos*, which means "quick-moving," "change-ful of hue," "twinkling," something like a butterfly—*psychē* in Greek—which reels drunkenly from flower to flower and lives on honey and love. In Gnostic typology the *anthropos psychikos*, "psychic man," is inferior to the *pneumatikos*,

[28] Cf. the picture of the adept in *Liber mutus* (La Rochelle, 1677) (fig. 13 in *The Practice of Psychotherapy, Coll. Works*, Vol. 16, p. 320). He is fishing, and has caught a nixie. His *soror mystica*, however, catches birds in her net, symbolizing the animus. The idea of the anima often turns up in the literature of the 16th and 17th centuries, for instance in Richardus Vitus, Aldrovandus, and the commentator of the *Tractatus aureus*. Cf. "The Enigma of Bologna" in my *Mysterium Coniunctionis* (to be pub. as *Coll. Works*, Vol. 14. Cf. Swiss edn., Zurich, 1956ff.)

"spiritual man," and finally there are wicked souls who must roast in hell for all eternity. Even the quite innocent soul of the unbaptized newborn babe is deprived of the contemplation of God. Among primitives, the soul is the magic breath of life (hence the term "anima"), or a flame. An uncanonical saying of our Lord's aptly declares: "Whoso is near unto me is near to the fire." For Heraclitus the soul at the highest level is fiery and dry, because *psyché* as such is closely akin to "cool breath"—*psychein* means "to breathe," "to blow"; *psychros* and *psychos* mean "cold," "chill," "damp."

Being that has soul is living being. Soul is the living thing in man, that which lives of itself and causes life. Therefore God breathed into Adam a living breath, that he might live. With her cunning play of illusions the soul lures into life the inertness of matter that does not want to live. She makes us believe incredible things, that life may be lived. She is full of snares and traps, in order that man should fall, should reach the earth, entangle himself there, and stay caught, so that life should be lived; as Eve in the garden of Eden could not rest content until she had convinced Adam of the goodness of the forbidden apple. Were it not for the leaping and twinkling of the soul, man would rot away in his greatest passion, idleness.[29] A certain kind of reasonableness is its advocate, and a certain kind of morality adds its blessing. But to have soul is the whole venture of life, for soul is a life-giving demon who plays his elfin game above and below human existence, for which reason—in the realm of dogma—he is threatened and propitiated with superhuman punishments and blessings that go far beyond the possible deserts of human beings. Heaven and hell are the fates meted out to the soul and not to civilized man, who in his nakedness and timidity would have no idea of what to do with himself in a heavenly Jerusalem.

The anima is not the soul in the dogmatic sense, not an *anima rationalis,* which is a philosophical conception, but a natural archetype that satisfactorily sums up all the statements of the unconscious, of the primitive mind, of the history of language and religion. It is a "factor" in the proper sense of the word. Man cannot make it; on the contrary, it is always the a priori element in his moods, reactions, impulses, and whatever else is spontaneous in psychic life. It is something that lives of itself, that makes us live; it is a life behind consciousness that cannot be completely integrated with it, but from which, on the contrary, consciousness arises. For, in the last analysis, psychic life is for the greater part an unconscious life that surrounds consciousness on all sides—a notion that is sufficiently obvious when one considers how much unconscious preparation is needed, for instance, to register a sense-impression.

Although it seems as if the whole of our unconscious psychic life could be ascribed to the anima, she is yet only one archetype among many. Therefore, she is not characteristic of the unconscious in its entirety. She is only one of its aspects. This is shown by the very fact of her femininity. What is not-I, not masculine, is most probably feminine, and because the not-I is felt as not belonging to me and therefore as outside me, the anima-image is usually projected upon women. Either sex is inhabited by the opposite sex up to a

[29] La Rochefoucauld, Pensées DLX. Quoted in *Symbols of Transformation* (*Coll. Works,* Vol. 5, p. 174).

point, for, biologically speaking, it is simply the greater number of masculine genes that tips the scales in favor of masculinity. The ¦smaller number of feminine genes seems to form a feminine character, which usually remains unconscious because of its subordinate position.

With the archetype of the anima we enter the realm of the gods, or rather the realm that metaphysics has reserved for itself. Everything the animal touches becomes numinous—unconditional, dangerous, taboo, magical. She is the serpent in the paradise of the harmless man with good resolutions and still better intentions. She affords the most convincing reasons for not prying into the unconscious, an occupation that would break down our moral inhibitions and unleash forces that had better been left unconscious and undisturbed. As usual, there is something in what the anima says; for life in itself is not good only, it is also bad. Because the anima wants life, she wants both good and bad. These categories do not exist in the elfin realm. Bodily life as well as psychic life have the impudence to get along much better without conventional morality, and they often remain the healthier for it.

The anima believes in the *kalon kagathon,* the "beautiful and the good," a primitive conception that antedates the discovery of the conflict between aesthetics and morals. It took more than a thousand years of Christian differentiation to make it clear that the good is not always the beautiful and the beautiful not necessarily good. The paradox of this marriage of ideas troubled the ancients as little as it does the primitives. The anima is conservative and clings in the most exasperating fashion to the ways of earlier humanity. She likes to appear in historic dress, with a predilection for Greece and Egypt. In this connection we would mention the classic anima stories of Rider Haggard and Pierre Benoît. The Renaissance dream known as the *Ipnerotomachia* of Poliphilo,[30] and Goethe's *Faust,* likewise reach deep into antiquity in order to find *le vrai mot* for the situation. Poliphilo conjured up Queen Venus; Goethe, Helen of Troy. Aniela Jaffé[31] has sketched a lively picture of the anima in the age of Biedermeier and the Romantics. If you want to know what happens when the anima appears in modern society, I can warmly recommend John Erskine's *Private Life of Helen of Troy.* She is not a shallow creation, for the breath of eternity lies over everything that is really alive. The anima lives beyond all categories, and can therefore dispense with blame as well as with praise. Since the beginning of time, man, with his wholesome animal instinct, has been engaged in combat with his soul and its demonism. If the soul were uniformly dark it would be a simple matter. Unfortunately this is not so, for the anima can appear also as an angel of light, a psychopomp who points the way to the highest meaning, as we know from *Faust.*

If the encounter with the shadow is the "apprentice-piece" in the individual's development, then that with the anima is the "masterpiece." The relation with the anima is again a test of courage, an ordeal by fire for the spiritual and moral

---

[30] Cf. *The Dream of Poliphilo* (Bollingen Series XXV; New York, 1950), ed. by Linda Fierz-David.

[31] "Bilder und Symbole aus E. T. A. Hoffmanns Der Goldene Topf; in Jung's *Gestaltungen des Unbewussten* (Zurich, 1950).

forces of man. We should never forget that in dealing with the anima we are dealing with psychic facts which have never been in man's possession before, since they were always found "outside" his psychic territory, so to speak, in the form of projections. For the son, the anima is hidden in the dominating power of the mother, and sometimes she leaves him with a sentimental attachment that lasts throughout life and seriously impairs the fate of the adult. On the other hand, she may spur him on to the highest flights. To the men of antiquity the anima appeared as a goddess or a witch, while for medieval man the goddess was replaced by the Queen of Heaven and Mother Church. The desymbolized world of the Protestant produced first an unhealthy sentimentality and then a sharpening of the moral conflict, which, because it was so unbearable, led logically to Nietzsche's "beyond good and evil." In centers of civilization this state shows itself in the increasing insecurity of marriage. The American divorce rate has been reached, if not exceeded, in many European countries, which proves that the anima projects herself by preference on the opposite sex, thus giving rise to magically complicated relationships. This fact, largely because of its pathological consequences, has led to the growth of modern psychology, which in its Freudian form cherishes the belief that the essential cause of all disturbances is sexuality—a view that only exacerbates the already existing conflict.[32] There is a confusion here between cause and effect. The sexual disturbance is by no means the cause of neurotic difficulties, but is, like these, one of the pathological effects of a maladaptation of consciousness, as when consciousness is faced with situations and tasks to which it is not equal. Such a person simply does not understand how the world has altered, and what his attitude would have to be in order to adapt to it.

In dealing with the shadow or anima it is not sufficient just to know about these concepts and to reflect on them. Nor can we ever experience their content by feeling our way into them or by appropriating other people's feelings. It is no use at all to learn a list of archetypes by heart. Archetypes are complexes of experience that come upon us like fate, and their effects are felt in our most personal life. The anima no longer crosses our path as a goddess, but, it may be, as an intimately personal misadventure, or perhaps as our best venture. When, for instance, a highly esteemed professor in his seventies abandons his family and runs off with a young red-headed actress, we know that the gods have claimed another victim. This is how demonic power reveals itself to us. Until not so long ago it would have been an easy matter to do away with the young woman as a witch.

In my experience there are very many people of intelligence and education who have no trouble in grasping the idea of the anima and her relative auton-omy, and can also understand the phenomenology of the animus in women. Psychologists have more difficulties to overcome in this respect, probably because they are under no compulsion to grapple with the complex facts peculiar to the psychology of the unconscious. If they are doctors as well, their somato-psychological thinking gets in the way, with its assumption that psychological

---

[32] I have expounded my views at some length in "Psychology of the Transference" (*Coll. Works,* Vol. 16).

processes can be expressed in intellectual, biological, or physiological terms. Psychology, however, is neither biology nor physiology nor any other science than just this knowledge of the psyche.

The picture I have drawn of the anima so far is not complete. Although she may be the chaotic urge to life, something strangely meaningful clings to her, a secret knowledge or hidden wisdom, which contrasts most curiously with her irrational elfin nature. Here I would like to refer again to the authors already cited. Rider Haggard calls She "Wisdom's Daughter"; Benoît's Queen of Atlantis has an excellent library that even contains a lost book of Plato. Helen of Troy, in her reincarnation, is rescued from a Tyrian brothel by the wise Simon Magus and accompanies him on his travels. I purposely refrained from mentioning this thoroughly characteristic aspect of the anima earlier, because the first encounter with her usually leads one to infer anything rather than wisdom.[33] This aspect appears only to the person who comes to grips with her seriously. Only then, when this hard task has been faced,[34] does he come to realize more and more that behind all her cruel sporting with human fate there lies something like a hidden purpose which seems to reflect a superior knowledge of life's laws. It is just the most unexpected, the most terrifyingly chaotic things, which reveal a deeper meaning. And the more this meaning is recognized, the more the anima loses her impetuous and compulsive character. Gradually breakwaters are built against the surging of chaos, and the meaningful divides itself from the meaningless. When sense and nonsense are no longer identical, the force of chaos is weakened by their subtraction; sense is then endued with the force of meaning, and nonsense with the force of meaningless. In this way a new cosmos arises. This is not a new discovery in the realm of medical psychology, but the age-old truth that out of the richness of a man's experience there comes a teaching which the father can pass on to the son.[35]

In elfin nature wisdom and folly appear as one and the same; and they *are* one and the same as long as they are acted out by the anima. Life is crazy and meaningful at once. And when we do not laugh over the one aspect and speculate about the other, life is exceedingly drab, and everything is reduced to the littlest scale. There is then little sense and little nonsense either. When you come to think about it, nothing has any meaning, for when there was nobody to think, there was nobody to interpret what happened. Interpretations are only for those who don't understand; it is only the things we don't understand that have any meaning. Man woke up in a world he did not understand, and that is why he tries to interpret it.

Thus the anima and life itself are meaningless in so far as they offer no interpretation. Yet they have a nature that can be interpreted, for in all chaos there is a cosmos, in all disorder a secret order, in all caprice a fixed law, for

[33] I am referring here to literary examples that are generally accessible and not to clinical material. These are quite sufficient for our purpose.

[34] I.e., coming to terms with the contents of the collective unconscious in general. This is *the* great task of the integration process.

[35] A good example is the little book by Gustav Schmaltz, *Östliche Weisheit und Westliche Psychotherapie* (Stuttgart, 1951).

everything that works is grounded on its opposite. It takes man's discriminating understanding, which breaks everything down into antinomial judgments, to recognize this. Once he comes to grips with the anima, her chaotic capriciousness will give him cause to suspect a secret order, to sense a plan, a meaning, a purpose over and above her nature, even—we might almost be tempted to say —to "postulate" such a thing, though this would not be in accord with the truth. For in actual reality we do not have at our command any power of cool reflection, nor does any science or philosophy help us, and the traditional teachings of religion do so only to a limited degree. We are caught and entangled in aimless experience, and the judging intellect with its categories proves itself powerless. Human interpretation fails, for a turbulent life-situation has arisen that refuses to fit any of the traditional meanings assigned to it. It is a moment of collapse. We sink into a final depth—Apuleius calls it "a kind of voluntary death." It is a surrender of our own powers, not artificially willed but forced upon us by nature; not a voluntary submission and humiliation decked in moral garb but an utter and unmistakable defeat crowned with panic fear of demoralization. Only when all props and crutches are broken, and no cover from the rear offers even the slightest hope of security, does it become possible for us to experience an archetype that up till then had lain hidden behind the meaningful nonsense played out by the anima. This is the *archetype of meaning*, just as the anima is the *archetype of life itself*.

It always seems to us as if meaning—compared with life—were the younger event, because we assume, with some justification, that we assign it of ourselves, and because we believe, equally rightly no doubt, that the great world can get along without being interpreted. But how do we assign meaning? From what source, in the last analysis, do we derive meaning? The forms we use for assigning meaning are historical categories that reach back into the mists of time—a fact we do not take sufficiently into account. Interpretations make use of certain linguistic matrices that are themselves derived from primordial images. From whatever side we approach this question, everywhere we find ourselves confronted with the history of language, with images and motifs that lead straight back to the primitive wonder-world.

Take, for instance, the word "idea." It goes back to the *eîdos* concept of Plato, and the eternal ideas are primordial images stored up *en hyperouranioi topoi* (in a supracelestial place) as eternal, transcendent forms. The eye of the seer perceives them as "*imagines et lares*," or as images in dreams and revelatory visions. Or let us take the concept of energy, which is an interpretation of physical events. In earlier times it was the secret fire of the alchemists, or phlogiston, or the heat-force inherent in matter, like the "primal warmth" of the Stoics, or the Heraclitean *pȳr aei zōon* (ever-living fire), which borders on the primitive notion of an all-pervading vital force, a power of growth and magic healing that is generally called *mana*.

I will not go on needlessly giving examples. It is sufficient to know that there is not a single important idea or view that does not possess historical antecedents. Ultimately they are all founded on primordial archetypal forms whose concreteness dates from a time when consciousness did not *think*, but only *perceived*.

"Thoughts" were objects of inner perception, not thought at all, but sensed as external phenomena—seen or heard, so to speak. Thought was essentially revelation, not invented but forced upon us or bringing conviction through its immediacy and actuality. Thinking of this kind precedes the primitive ego-consciousness, and the latter is more its object than its subject. But we ourselves have not yet climbed the last peak of consciousness, so we also have a pre-existent thinking, of which we are not aware so long as we are supported by traditional symbols—or, to put it in the language of dreams, so long as the father or the king is not dead.

I would like to give you an example of how the unconscious "thinks" and paves the way for solutions. It is the case of a young theological student, whom I did not know personally. He was in great straits because of his religious beliefs, and about this time he dreamed the following dream:[36]

He was standing in the presence of a handsome old man dressed entirely in black. *He knew it was the* white *magician. This personage had just addressed him at considerable length, but the dreamer could no longer remember what it was about. He had only retained the closing words: "And for this we need the help of the* black *magician." At that moment the door opened and in came another old man exactly like the first, except that he was dressed in* white. *He said to the white magician, "I need your advice," but threw a sidelong, questioning look at the dreamer, whereupon the white magician answered: "You can speak freely, he is an innocent." The black magician then began to relate his story. He had come from a distant land where something extraordinary had happened. The country was ruled by an old king who felt his death near. He—the king—had sought out a tomb for himself. For there were in that land a great number of tombs from ancient times, and the king had chosen the finest for himself. According to legend, a virgin had been buried in it. The king caused the tomb to be opened, in order to get it ready for use. But when the bones it contained were exposed to the light of day, they suddenly took on life and changed into a black horse, which at once fled into the desert and there vanished. The black magician had heard of this story and immediately set forth in pursuit of the horse. After a journey of many days, always on the tracks of the horse, he came to the desert and crossed to the other side, where the grasslands began again. There he met the horse grazing, and there also he came upon the find on whose account he now needed the advice of the white magician. For he had found the lost keys of paradise, and he did not know what to do with them. At this exciting moment the dreamer awoke.*

In the light of our earlier remarks the meaning of the dream is not hard to guess: the old king is the ruling symbol that wants to go to its eternal rest, and in the very place where similar "dominants" lie buried. His choice falls, fittingly enough, on the grave of the anima, who lies in the death trance of a Sleeping Beauty so long as the king is alive—that is, so long as a valid principle (prince or *princeps*) regulates and expresses life. But when the king draws to his

[36] I have already used this dream in "The Phenomenology of the Spirit in Fairytales" (*Coll. Works*, Vol. 9, pt. I), par. 398, and in "Psychology and Education" (*Coll. Works*, Vol. 17), pp. 117ff., as an example of a "big" dream, without commenting on it more closely.

end,[37] she comes to life again and changes into a black horse, which in Plato's parable stands for the unruliness of the passions. Anyone who follows this horse comes into the desert, into a wild land remote from men—an image of spiritual and moral isolation. But there lie the keys of paradise.

Now what is paradise? Clearly, the Garden of Eden with its two-faced tree of life and knowledge and its four streams. In the Christian version it is also the heavenly city of the Apocalypse, which, like the Garden of Eden, is conceived as a mandala. But the mandala is a symbol of individuation. So it is the *black* magician who finds the keys to the solution of the problems of belief weighing on the dreamer, the keys that open the way of individuation. The contrast between desert and paradise therefore signifies isolation as contrasted with individuation, or the becoming of the self.

This part of the dream is a remarkable paraphrase of the Oxyrhynchus sayings of Jesus,[38] in which the way to the kingdom of heaven is pointed out by animals, and where we find the admonition: "Therefore know yourselves, for you are the city, and the city is the kingdom." It is also a paraphrase of the serpent of paradise who persuaded our first parents to sin, and who finally leads to the redemption of mankind through the Son of God. As we know, this causal nexus gave rise to the Ophitic identification of the serpent with the *Sōtēr* (Saviour). The black horse and the black magician are half-evil elements whose relativity with respect to good is hinted at in the exchange of garments. The two magicians are, indeed, two aspects of the *wise old man,* the superior master and teacher, the archetype of the spirit, who symbolizes the pre-existent meaning hidden in the chaos of life. He is the father of the soul, and yet the soul, in some miraculous manner, is also his virgin mother, for which reason he was called by the alchemists the "first son of the mother." The black magician and the black horse correspond to the descent into darkness in the dreams mentioned earlier.

What an unbearably hard lesson for a young student of theology! Fortunately he was not in the least aware that the father of all prophets had spoken to him in the dream and placed a great secret almost within his grasp. One marvels at the inappropriateness of such occurrences. Why this prodigality? But I have to admit that we do not know how this dream affected the student in the long run, and I must emphasize that to me, at least, the dream had a very great deal to say. It was not allowed to get lost, even though the dreamer did not understand it.

The old man in this dream is obviously trying to show how good and evil function together, presumably as an answer to the still unresolved moral conflict in the Christian psyche. With this peculiar relativization of opposites we find ourselves approaching nearer to the ideas of the East, to the *nirdvandva* of Hindu philosophy, the freedom from opposites, which is shown as a possible way of solving the conflict through reconciliation. How perilously fraught with meaning this Eastern relativity of good and evil is, can be seen from the Indian aphoristic

[37] Cf. the motif of the "old king" in alchemy. *Psychology and Alchemy (Coll. Works,* Vol. 12), pp. 313 ff.

[38] Cf. James, *The Aprocryphal New Testament,* pp. 27 f.

question: "Who takes longer to reach perfection, the man who loves God, or the man who hates him?" And the answer is: "He who loves God takes seven reincarnations to reach perfection, and he who hates God takes only three, for he who hates God will think of him more than he who loves him." Freedom from opposites presupposes their functional equivalence, and this offends our Christian feelings. Nonetheless, as our dream example shows, the balanced co-operation of moral opposites is a natural truth which has been recognized just as naturally by the East. The clearest example of this is to be found in Taoist philosophy. But in the Christian tradition, too, there are various sayings that come very close to this standpoint. I need only remind you of the parable of the unjust steward.

Our dream is by no means unique in this respect, for the tendency to relativize opposites is a notable peculiarity of the unconscious. One must immediately add, however, that this is true only in cases of exaggerated moral sensibility; in other cases the unconscious can insist just as inexorably on the irreconcilability of the opposites. As a rule, the standpoint of the unconscious is relative to the conscious attitude. We can probably say, therefore, that our dream presupposes the specific beliefs and doubts of a theological consciousness of Protestant persuasion. This limits the statement of the dream to a definite set of problems. But even with this paring down of its validity the dream clearly demonstrates the superiority of its standpoint. Fittingly enough, it expresses its meaning in the opinion and voice of a wise magician, who goes back in direct line to the figure of the medicine man in primitive society. He is, like the anima, an immortal demon that pierces the chaotic darknesses of brute life with the light of meaning. He is the enlightener, the master and teacher, a psychopomp whose personification even Nietzsche, that breaker of tablets, could not escape—for he had called up his reincarnation in Zarathustra, the lofty spirit of an almost Homeric age, as the carrier and mouthpiece of his own "Dionysian" enlightenment and ecstasy. For him God was dead, but the driving demon of wisdom became as it were his bodily double. He himself says:

> Then one was changed to two
> And Zarathustra passed me by.

Zarathustra is more for Nietzsche than a poetic figure; he is an involuntary confession, a testament. Nietzsche too had lost his way in the darkness of a life that turned its back upon God and Christianity, and that is why there came to him the revealer and enlightener, the speaking fountainhead of his soul. Here is the source of the hieratic language of *Zarathustra*, for that is the style of this archetype.

Modern man, in experiencing this archetype, comes to know that most ancient form of thinking as an autonomous activity whose object he is. Hermes Trismegistus or the Thoth of Hermetic literature, Orpheus, the Poimandres (shepherd of men) and his near relation the Poimen of Hermes,[39] are other formulations of the same experience. If the name "Lucifer" were not prejudiced,

[39] Reitzenstein interprets the "Shepherd" of Hermas as a Christian rejoinder to the Poimandres writings.

it would be a very suitable one for this archetype. But I have been content to call it the *archetype of the wise old man,* or *of meaning.* Like all archetypes it has a positive and a negative aspect, though I do not want to enter into this here. The reader will find a detailed exposition of the two-facedness of the wise old man in "The Phenomenology of the Spirit in Fairytales."

The three archetypes so far discussed—the shadow, the anima, and the wise old man—are of a kind that can be directly experienced in personified form. In the foregoing I tried to indicate the general psychological conditions in which such an experience arises. But what I conveyed were only abstract generalizations. One could, or rather one should, really give a description of the process as it occurs in immediate experience. In the course of this process the archetypes appear as active personalities in dreams and fantasies. But the process itself involves another class of archetypes which one would call the *archetypes of transformation.* They are not personalities, but are typical situations, places, ways and means, that symbolize the kind of transformation in question. Like the personalities, these archetypes are true and genuine symbols that cannot be exhaustively interpreted, either as signs or as allegories. They are genuine symbols precisely because they are ambiguous, full of half-glimpsed meanings, and in the last resort inexhaustible. The ground principles, the *archai,* of the unconscious are indescribable because of their wealth of reference, although in themselves recognizable. The discriminating intellect naturally keeps on trying to establish their singleness of meaning and thus misses the essential point; for what we can above all establish as the one thing consistent with their nature is their *manifold meaning,* their almost limitless wealth of reference, which makes any unilateral formulation impossible. Besides this, they are in principle paradoxical, just as for the alchemists the spirit was conceived as *"senex et iuvenis simul"*—an old man and a youth at once.

If one wants to form a picture of the symbolic process, the series of pictures found in alchemy are good examples, though the symbols they contain are for the most part traditional despite their often obscure origin and significance. An excellent Eastern example is the Tantric *chakra* system,[40] or the mystical nerve system of Chinese yoga.[41] It also seems as if the set of pictures in the Tarot cards were distantly descended from the archetypes of transformation, a view that has been confirmed for me in a very enlightening lecture by Professor Bernoulli.[42]

The symbolic process is an experience *in images and of images.* Its development usually shows an enantiodromian structure like the text of the *I Ching,* and so presents a rhythm of negative and positive, loss and gain, dark and light. Its beginning is almost invariably characterized by one's getting stuck in a blind alley or in some impossible situation; and its goal is, broadly speaking, illumination or higher consciousness, by means of which the initial situation is

[40] Arthur Avalon, *The Serpent Power* (London, 1919).

[41] Erwin Rousselle, "Seelische Führung im lebenden Taoismus," *Eranos-Jahrbuch 1933,* pp. 135 ff.

[42] R. Bernoulli, "Zur Symbolik geometrischer Figuren und Zahlen," *Eranos-Jahrbuch 1934,* pp. 397 ff.

overcome on a higher level. As regards the time factor, the process may be compressed into a single dream or into a short moment of experience, or it may extend over months and years, depending on the nature of the initial situation, the person involved in the process, and the goal to be reached. The wealth of symbols naturally varies enormously from case to case. Although everything is experienced in image form, i.e., symbolically, it is by no means a question of fictitious dangers but of very real risks upon which the fate of a whole life may depend. The chief danger is that of succumbing to the fascinating influence of the archetypes, and this is most likely to happen when the archetypal images are not made conscious. If there is already a predisposition to psychosis, it may even happen that the archetypal figures, which are endowed with a certain autonomy anyway on account of their natural numinosity, will escape from conscious control altogether and become completely independent, thus producing the phenomena of possession. In the case of an anima-possession, for instance, the patient will want to change himself into a woman through self-castration, or he is afraid that something of the sort will be done to him by force. The best-known example of this is Schreber's *Memoirs of My Nervous Illness*. Patients often discover a whole anima mythology with numerous archaic motifs. A case of this kind was published some time ago by Nelken.[43] Another patient has described his experiences himself and commented on them in a book.[44] I mention these examples because there are still people who think that the archetypes are subjective chimeras of my own brain.

The things that come to light brutally in insanity remain hidden in the background in neurosis, but they continue to influence consciousness none the less. When, therefore, the analysis penetrates the background of conscious phenomena, it discovers the same archetypal figures that activate the deliriums of psychotics. Finally, there is any amount of literary and historical evidence to prove that in the case of these archetypes we are dealing with normal types of fantasy that occur practically everywhere and not with the monstrous products of insanity. The pathological element does not lie in the existence of these ideas, but in the dissociation of consciousness that can no longer control the unconscious. In all cases of dissociation it is therefore necessary to integrate the unconscious into consciousness. This is a synthetic process which I have termed the "individuation process."

As a matter of fact, this process follows the natural course of life—a life in which the individual becomes what he always was. Because man has consciousness, a development of this kind does not run very smoothly; often it is varied and disturbed, because consciousness deviates again and again from its archetypal, instinctual foundation and finds itself in opposition to it. There then arises the need for a synthesis of the two positions. This amounts to psychotherapy even on the primitive level, where it takes the form of restitution ceremonies. As examples I would mention the identification of the Australian aborigines with their ancestors in the *alcheringa* period, identification with the

[43] "Analytische Beobachtungen über Phantasien eines Schizophrenen," *Jahrbuch für psychoanalytische und psychopathologische Forschungen* (Leipzig), IV (1912), pp. 504 ff.

[44] John Custance, *Wisdom, Madness, and Folly* (New York, 1951).

"sons of the sun" among the Pueblos of Taos, the Helios apotheosis in the Isis mysteries, and so on. Accordingly, the therapeutic method of complex psychology consists on the one hand in making as fully conscious as possible the constellated unconscious contents, and on the other hand in sythetizing them with consciousness through the act of recognition. Since, however, civilized man possesses a high degree of dissociability and makes continual use of it in order to avoid every possible risk, it is by no means a foregone conclusion that recognition will be followed by the appropriate action. On the contrary, we have to reckon with the singular ineffectiveness of recognition and must therefore insist on a meaningful application of it. Recognition by itself does not as a rule do this nor does it imply, as such, any moral strength. In these cases it becomes very clear how much the cure of neurosis is a moral problem.

As the archetypes, like all numinous contents, are relatively autonomous, they cannot be integrated simply by rational means, but require a dialectical procedure, a real coming to terms with them, often conducted by the patient in dialogue form, so that, without knowing it, he puts into effect the alchemical definition of the *meditatio*: "an inner colloquy with one's good angel."[45] Usually the process runs a dramatic course, with many ups and downs. It expresses itself in, or is accompanied by, dream symbols that are related to the *"représentations collectives,"* which, in the form of mythological motifs, have portrayed psychic processes of transformation since the earliest times.[46]

In the short space of a lecture I must content myself with giving only a few examples of archetypes. I have chosen the ones that play the chief part in an analysis of the masculine psyche, and have tried to give you some idea of the transformation process in which they appear. Since this lecture was first published, the figures of the shadow, anima, and wise old man, together with the corresponding figures of the feminine unconscious, have been dealt with in greater detail in my contributions to the symbolism of the self,[47] and the individuation process in its relation to alchemical symbolism has also been subjected to closer investigation.[48]

---

[45] Ruland, *Lexicon alchemiae* (Frankfurt a. M., 1612).

[46] Cf. *Symbols of Transformation.*

[47] *Aion* (*Coll. Works*, Vol. 9, pt. II).

[48] *Psychology and Alchemy.*

The Archetypes of Literature

NORTHROP FRYE

Every organized body of knowledge can be learned progressively; and experience shows that there is also something progressive about the learning of literature. Our opening sentence has already got us into a semantic difficulty. Physics is an organized body of knowledge about nature, and a student of it says that he is learning physics, not that he is learning nature. Art, like nature, is the subject of a systematic study, and has to be distinguished from the study itself, which is criticism. It is therefore impossible to "learn literature": one learns about it in a certain way, but what one learns, transitively, is the criticism of literature. Similarly, the difficulty often felt in "teaching literature" arises from the fact that it cannot be done: the criticism of literature is all that can be directly taught. So while no one expects literature itself to behave like a science, there is surely no reason why criticism, as a sytematic and organized study, should not be, at least partly, a science. Not a "pure" or "exact" science, perhaps, but these phrases form part of a nineteenth century cosmology which is no longer with us. Criticism deals with the arts and may well be something of an art itself, but it does not follow that it must be unsystematic. If it is to be related to the sciences too, it does not follow that it must be deprived of the graces of culture.

Certainly criticism as we find it in learned journals and scholarly monographs has every characteristic of a science. Evidence is examined scientifically; previous authorities are used scientifically; fields are investigated scientifically; texts are edited scientifically. Prosody is scientific in structure; so is phonetics; so is philology. And yet in studying this kind of critical science the student becomes aware of a centrifugal movement carrying him away from literature. He finds that literature is the central division of the "humanities," flanked on

233

one side by history and on the other by philosophy. Criticism so far ranks only as a subdivision of literature; and hence, for the systematic mental organization of the subject, the student has to turn to the conceptual framework of the historian for events, and to that of the philosopher for ideas. Even the more centrally placed critical sciences, such as textual editing, seem to be part of a "background" that recedes into history or some other non-literary field. The thought suggests itself that the ancillary critical disciplines may be related to a central expanding pattern of systematic comprehension which has not yet been established, but which, if it were established, would prevent them from being centrifugal. If such a pattern exists, then criticism would be to art what philosophy is to wisdom and history to action.

Most of the central area of criticism is at present, and doubtless always will be, the area of commentary. But the commentators have little sense, unlike the researchers, of being contained within some sort of scientific discipline: they are chiefly engaged, in the words of the gospel hymn, in brightening the corner where they are. If we attempt to get a more comprehensive idea of what criticism is about, we find ourselves wandering over quaking bogs of generalities, judicious pronouncements of value, reflective comments, perorations to works of research, and other consequences of taking the large view. But this part of the critical field is so full of pseudo-propositions, sonorous nonsense that contains no truth and no falsehood, that it obviously exists only because criticism, like nature, prefers a waste space to an empty one.

The term "pseudo-proposition" may imply some sort of logical positivist attitude on my own part. But I would not confuse the significant proposition with the factual one; nor should I consider it advisable to muddle the study of literature with a schizophrenic dichotomy between subjective-emotional and objective-descriptive aspects of meaning, considering that in order to produce any literary meaning at all one has to ignore this dichotomy. I say only that the principles by which one can distinguish a significant from a meaningless statement in criticism are not clearly defined. Our first step, therefore, is to recognize and get rid of meaningless criticism: that is, talking about literature in a way that cannot help to build up a systematic structure of knowledge. Casual value-judgments belong not to criticism but to the history of taste, and reflect, at best, only the social and psychological compulsions which prompted their utterance. All judgments in which the values are not based on literary experience but are sentimental or derived from religious or political prejudice may be regarded as casual. Sentimental judgments are usually based either on non-existent categories or antitheses ("Shakespeare studied life, Milton books") or on a visceral reaction to the writer's personality. The literary chit-chat which makes the reputations of poets boom and crash in an imaginary stock exchange is pseudo-criticism. That wealthy investor Mr. Eliot, after dumping Milton on the market, is now buying him again; Donne has probably reached his peak and will begin to taper off; Tennyson may be in for a slight flutter but the Shelley stocks are still bearish. This sort of thing cannot be part of any systematic study, for a systematic study can only progress: whatever dithers or vacillates or reacts is merely leisure-class conversation.

We next meet a more serious group of critics who say: the foreground of criticism is the impact of literature on the reader. Let us, then, keep the study of literature centripetal, and base the learning process on a structural analysis of the literary work itself. The texture of any great work of art is complex and ambiguous, and in unravelling the complexities we may take in as much history and philosophy as we please, if the subject of our study remains at the center. If it does not, we may find that in our anxiety to write about literature we have forgotten how to read it.

The only weakness in this approach is that it is conceived primarily as the antithesis of centrifugal or "background" criticism, and so lands us in a somewhat unreal dilemma, like the conflict of internal and external relations in philosophy. Antitheses are usually resolved, not by picking one side and refuting the other, or by making eclectic choices between them, but by trying to get past the antithetical way of stating the problem. It is right that the first effort of critical apprehension should take the form of a rhetorical or structural analysis of a work of art. But a purely structural approach has the same limitation in criticism that it has in biology. In itself it is simply a discreet series of analyses based on the mere existence of the literary structure, without developing any explanation of how the structure came to be what it was and what its nearest relatives are. Structural analysis brings rhetoric back to criticism, but we need a new poetics as well, and the attempt to construct a new poetics out of rhetoric alone can hardly avoid a mere complication of rhetorical terms into a sterile jargon. I suggest that what is at present missing from literary criticism is a co-ordinating principle, a central hypothesis which, like the theory of evolution in biology, will see the phenomena it deals with as parts of a whole. Such a principle, though it would retain the centripetal perspective of structural analysis, would try to give the same perspective to other kinds of criticism too.

The first postulate of this hypothesis is the same as that of any science: the assumption of total coherence. The assumption refers to the science, not to what it deals with. A belief in an order of nature is an inference from the intelligibility of the natural sciences; and if the natural sciences ever completely demonstrated the order of nature they would presumably exhaust their subject. Criticism, as a science, is totally intelligible; literature, as the subject of a science, is, so far as we know, an inexhaustible source of new critical discoveries, and would be even if new works of literature ceased to be written. If so, then the search for a limiting principle in literature in order to discourage the development of criticism is mistaken. The assertion that the critic should not look for more in a poem than the poet may safely be assumed to have been conscious of putting there is a common form of what may be called the fallacy of premature teleology. It corresponds to the assertion that a natural phenomenon is as it is because Providence in its inscrutable wisdom made it so.

Simple as the assumption appears, it takes a long time for a science to discover that it is in fact a totally intelligible body of knowledge. Until it makes this discovery it has not been born as an individual science, but remains an embryo within the body of some other subject. The birth of physics from "natural philosophy" and of sociology from "moral philosophy" will illustrate the process. It is also very approximately true that the modern sciences have developed in the order of their closeness to mathematics. Thus physics and astronomy assumed their modern form in the Renaissance, chemistry in the eighteenth century, biology in the nineteenth, and the social sciences in the twentieth. If systematic criticism, then, is developing only in our day, the fact is at least not an anachronism.

We are now looking for classifying principles lying in an area between two points that we have fixed. The first of these is the preliminary effort of criticism, the structural analysis of the work of art. The second is the assumption that there is such a subject as criticism, and that it makes, or could make, complete sense. We may next proceed inductively from structural analysis, associating the data we collect and trying to see larger patterns in them. Or we may proceed deductively, with the consequences that follow from postulating the unity of criticism. It is clear, of course, that neither procedure will work indefinitely without correction from the other. Pure induction will get us lost in haphazard guessing; pure deduction will lead to inflexible and over-simplified pigeon-holing. Let us now attempt a few tentative steps in each direction, beginning with the inductive one.

II

The unity of a work of art, the basis of structural analysis, has not been produced solely by the unconditioned will of the artist, for the artist is only its efficient cause: it has form, and consequently a formal cause. The fact that revision is possible, that the poet makes changes not because he likes them better but because they are better, means that poems, like poets, are born and not made. The poet's task is to deliver the poem in as uninjured a state as possible, and if the poem is alive, it is equally anxious to be rid of him, and screams to be cut loose from his private memories and associations, his desire for self-expression, and all the other navel-strings and feeding tubes of his ego. The critic takes over where the poet leaves off, and criticism can hardly do without a kind of literary psychology connecting the poet with the poem. Part of this may be a psychological study of the poet, though this is useful chiefly in analysing the failures in his expression, the things in him which are still attached to his work. More important is the fact that every poet has his private mythology, his own spectroscopic band or peculiar formation of symbols, of much of which he is quite unconscious. In works with characters of their own, such as dramas and novels, the same psychological analysis may be extended to the interplay of characters, though of course literary psychology would analyse the behavior of such characters only in relation to literary convention.

There is still before us the problem of the formal cause of the poem, a problem deeply involved with the question of genres. We cannot say much about genres, for criticism does not know much about them. A good many critical efforts to grapple with such words as "novel" or "epic" are chiefly interesting as examples of the psychology of rumor. Two conceptions of the genre, however, are obviously fallacious, and as they are opposite extremes, the truth must lie somewhere between them. One is the pseudo-Platonic conception of genres as existing prior to and independently of creation, which confuses them with mere conventions of form like the sonnet. The other is that pseudo-biological conception of them as evolving species which turns up in so many surveys of the "development" of this or that form.

We next inquire for the origin of the genre, and turn first of all to the social conditions and cultural demands which produced it—in other words to the material cause of the work of art. This leads us into literary history, which differs from ordinary history in that its containing categories, "Gothic," "Baroque," "Romantic," and the like are cultural categories, of little use to the ordinary historian. Most literary history does not get as far as these categories, but even so we know more about it than about most kinds of critical scholarship. The historian treats literature and philosophy historically; the philosopher treats history and literature philosophically; and the so-called "history of ideas" approach marks the beginning of an attempt to treat history and philosophy from the point of view of an autonomous criticism.

But still we feel there is something missing. We say that every poet has his own peculiar formation of images. But when so many poets use so many of the same images, surely there are much bigger critical problems involved than biographical ones. As Mr. Auden's brilliant essay *The Enchafèd Flood* shows, an important symbol like the sea cannot remain within the poetry of Shelley or Keats or Coleridge: it is bound to expand over many poets into an archetypal symbol of literature. And if the genre has a historical origin, why does the genre of drama emerge from medieval religion in a way so strikingly similar to the way it emerged from Greek religion centuries before? This is a problem of structure rather than origin, and suggests that there may be archetypes of genres as well as of images.

It is clear that criticism cannot be systematic unless there is a quality in literature which enables it to be so, an order of words corresponding to the order of nature in the natural sciences. An archetype should be not only a unifying category of criticism, but itself a part of a total form, and it leads us at once to the question of what sort of total form criticism can see in literature. Our survey of critical techniques has taken us as far as literary history. Total literary history moves from the primitive to the sophisticated, and here we glimpse the possibility of seeing literature as a complication of a relatively restricted and simple group of formulas that can be studied in primitive culture. If so, then the search for archetypes is a kind of literary anthropology, concerned with the way that literature is informed by pre-literary categories such as ritual, myth and folktale. We next realize that the relation between these categories and literature is by no means purely one of descent, as we find them reappearing in the greatest classics—in fact there seems to be a general tendency on the part of great classics to revert to them. This coincides with a feeling that we have all had: that the study of mediocre works of art, however energetic, obstinately remains a random and peripheral form of critical experience, whereas the profound masterpiece seems to draw us to a point at which we can see an enormous number of converging patterns of significance. Here we begin to wonder if we cannot see literature, not only as complicating itself in time, but as spread out in conceptual space from some unseen center.

This inductive movement towards the archetype is a process of backing up, as it were, from structural analysis, as we back up from a painting if we want to see composition instead of brushwork. In the foreground of the grave-digger scene in *Hamlet*, for instance, is an intricate verbal texture, ranging from the puns of the first clown to the *danse macabre* of the Yorick soliloquy, which we study in the printed text. One step back, and we are in the Wilson Knight and Spurgeon group of critics, listening to the steady rain of images of corruption and decay. Here too, as the sense of the place of this scene in the whole play begins to dawn on us, we are in the network of psychological relationships which were the main interest of Bradley. But after all, we say, we are forgetting the genre: *Hamlet* is a play, and an Elizabethan play. So we take another step back into the Stoll and Shaw group and see the scene conventionally as part of its dramatic context. One step more, and we can begin to glimpse the archetype of the scene, as the hero's *Liebestod* and first unequivocal declaration of his love, his struggle with Laertes and the sealing of his own fate, and the sudden sobering of his mood that marks the transition to the final scene, all take shape around a leap into and return from the grave that has so weirdly yawned open on the stage.

At each stage of understanding this scene we are dependent on a certain kind of scholarly organization. We need first an editor to clean up the text for us, then the rhetorician and philologist, then the literary psychologist. We cannot study the genre without the help of the literary social historian, the literary philosopher and the student of the "history of ideas," and for the archetype we need a literary anthropologist. But now that we have got our central pattern of criticism established, all these interests are seen as converging on literary criticism instead of receding from it into psychology and history and the rest. In particular, the literary anthropologist who chases the source of the Hamlet legend from the pre-Shakespeare play to Saxo, and from Saxo to nature-myths, is not running away from Shakespeare: he is drawing closer to the archetypal form which Shakespeare recreated. A minor result of our new perspective is that contradictions among critics, and assertions that this and not that critical approach is the right one, show a remarkable tendency to dissolve into unreality. Let us now see what we can get from the deductive end.

III

Some arts move in time, like music; others are presented in space, like painting. In both cases the organizing principle is recurrence, which is called rhythm when it is temporal and pattern when it is spatial. Thus we speak of the rhythm of music and the pattern of painting; but later, to show off our sophistication, we may begin to speak of the rhythm of painting and the pattern of music. In other words, all arts may be conceived both temporally and spatially.

The score of a musical composition may be studied all at once; a picture may be seen as the track of an intricate dance of the eye. Literature seems to be intermediate between music and painting: its words form rhythms which approach a musical sequence of sounds at one of its boundaries, and form patterns which approach the hieroglyphic or pictorial image at the other. The attempts to get as near to these boundaries as possible form the main body of what is called experimental writing. We may call the rhythm of literature the narrative, and the pattern, the simultaneous mental grasp of the verbal structure, the meaning or significance. We hear or listen to a narrative, but when we grasp a writer's total pattern we "see" what he means.

The criticism of literature is much more hampered by the representational fallacy than even the criticism of painting. That is why we are apt to think of narrative as a sequential representation of events in an outside "life," and of meaning as a reflection of some external "idea." Properly used as critical terms, an author's narrative is his linear movement; his meaning is the integrity of his completed form. Similarly an image is not merely a verbal replica of an external object, but any unit of a verbal structure seen as part of a total pattern or rhythm. Even the letters an author spells his words with form part of his imagery, though only in special cases (such as alliteration) would they call for critical notice. Narrative and meaning thus become respectively, to borrow musical terms, the melodic and harmonic contexts of the imagery.

Rhythm, or recurrent movement, is deeply founded on the natural cycle, and everything in nature that we think of as having some analogy with works of art, like the flower or the bird's song, grows out of a profound synchronization between an organism and the rhythms of its environment, especially that of the solar year. With animals some expressions of synchronization, like the mating dances of birds, could almost be called rituals. But in human life a ritual seems to be something of a voluntary effort (hence the magical element in it) to recapture a lost rapport with the natural cycle. A farmer must harvest his crop at a certain time of year, but because this is involuntary, harvesting itself is not precisely a ritual. It is the deliberate expression of a will to synchronize human and natural energies at that time which produces the harvest songs, harvest sacrifices and harvest folk customs that we call rituals. In ritual, then, we may find the origin of narrative, a ritual being a temporal sequence of acts in which the conscious meaning or significance is latent: it can be seen by an observer, but is largely concealed from the participators themselves. The pull of ritual is toward pure narrative, which, if there could be such a thing, would be automatic and unconscious repetition. We should notice too the regular tendency of ritual to become encyclopedic. All the important recurrences in nature, the day, the phases of the moon, the seasons and solstices of the year, the crises of existence from birth to death, get rituals attached to them, and most of the higher religions are equipped with a definitive total body of rituals suggestive, if we may put it so, of the entire range of potentially significant actions in human life.

Patterns of imagery, on the other hand, or fragments of significance, are oracular in origin, and derive from the epiphanic moment, the flash of instantaneous comprehension with no direct reference to time, the importance of which is indicated by Cassirer in *Language and Myth*. By the time we get them, in the form of proverbs, riddles, commandments and etiological folktales, there is already a considerable element of narrative in them. They too are encyclopedic in tendency, building up a total structure of significance, or doctrine, from random and empiric fragments. And just as pure narrative would be unconscious act, so pure significance would be an incommunicable state of consciousness, for communication begins by constructing narrative.

The myth is the central informing power that gives archetypal significance to the ritual and archetypal narrative to the oracle. Hence the myth *is* the archetype, though it might be convenient to say myth only when referring to narrative, and archetype when speaking of significance. In the solar cycle of the day, the seasonal cycle of the year, and the organic cycle of human life, there is a single pattern of significance, out of which myth constructs a central narrative around a figure who is partly the sun, partly vegetative fertility and partly a god or archetypal human being. The crucial importance of this myth has been forced on literary critics by Jung and Frazer in particular, but the several books now available on it are not always systematic in their approach, for which reason I supply the following table of its phases:

1.   The dawn, spring and birth phase. Myths of the birth of the hero, of revival and resurrection, of creation and (because the four phases are a cycle) of the defeat of the powers of darkness, winter and death. Subordinate characters: the father and the mother. The archetype of romance and of most dithyrambic and rhapsodic poetry.

2.   The zenith, summer, and marriage or triumph phase. Myths of apotheosis, of the sacred marriage, and of entering into Paradise. Subordinate characters: the companion and the bride. The archetype of comedy, pastoral and idyll.

3.   The sunset, autumn and death phase. Myths of fall, of the dying god, of violent death and sacrifice and of the isolation of the hero. Subordinate characters: the traitor and the siren. The archetype of tragedy and elegy.

4.   The darkness, winter and dissolution phase. Myths of the triumph of these powers; myths of floods and the return of chaos, of the defeat of the hero, and Götterdämmerung myths. Subordinate characters: the ogre and the witch. The archetype of satire (see, for instance, the conclusion of *The Dunciad*).

The quest of the hero also tends to assimilate the oracular and random verbal structures, as we can see when we watch the chaos of local legends that results from prophetic epiphanies consolidating into a narrative mythology of departmental gods. In most of the higher religions this in turn has become the same central quest-myth that emerges from ritual, as the Messiah myth became the narrative structure of the oracles of Judaism. A local flood may beget a folktale by accident, but a comparison of flood stories will show how quickly such tales become examples of the myth of dissolution. Finally, the tendency of both ritual and epiphany to become encyclopedic is realized in the definitive body of myth which constitutes the sacred scriptures of religions. These sacred scriptures are consequently the first documents that the literary critic has to study to gain a comprehensive view of his subject. After he has understood their structure, then he can descend from archetypes to genres, and see how the drama emerges from the ritual side of myth and lyric from the epiphanic or fragmented side, while the epic carries on the central encyclopedic structure.

Some words of caution and encouragement are necessary before literary criticism has clearly staked out its boundaries in these fields. It is part of the critic's business to show how all literary genres are derived from the quest-myth, but the derivation is a logical one within the science of criticism: the quest-myth will constitute the first chapter of whatever future handbooks of criticism may be written that will be based on enough organized critical knowledge to call themselves "introductions" or "outlines" and still be able to live up to their titles. It is only when we try to expound the derivation chronologically that we find ourselves writing pseudo-prehistorical fictions and theories of mythological contract. Again, because psychology and anthropology are more highly developed sciences, the critic who deals with this kind of material is bound to appear, for some time, a dilettante of those subjects. These two phases of criticism are largely undeveloped in comparison with literary history and rhetoric, the reason being the later development of the sciences they are related to. But the fascination which *The Golden Bough* and Jung's book on libido symbols have for literary critics is not based on dilettantism, but on the fact that these books are primarily studies in literary criticism, and very important ones.

In any case the critic who is studying the principles of literary form has a quite different interest from the psychologist's concern with states of mind or the anthropologist's with social institutions. For instance: the mental response to narrative is mainly passive; to significance mainly active. From this fact Ruth Benedict's *Patterns of Culture* develops a distinction between "Apollonian" cultures based on obedience to ritual and "Dionysiac" ones based on a tense exposure of the prophetic mind to epiphany. The critic would tend rather to note how popular literature which appeals to the inertia of the untrained mind puts a heavy emphasis on narrative values, whereas a sophisticated attempt to disrupt the connection between the poet and his environment produces the Rimbaud type of *illumination*, Joyce's solitary epiphanies, and Baudelaire's conception of nature as a source of oracles. Also how literature, as it develops from the primitive to the self-conscious, shows a gradual shift of the poet's attention from narrative to significant values, this shift of attention being the basis of Schiller's distinction between naive and sentimental poetry.

The relation of criticism to religion, when they deal with the same documents, is more complicated. In criticism, as in history, the divine is always treated as a human artifact. God for the critic, whether he finds him in *Paradise Lost* or the Bible, is a character in a human story; and for the critic all epiphanies are explained, not in terms of the riddle of a possessing god or devil, but as mental phenomena closely associated in their origin with dreams. This once established, it is then necessary to say that nothing in criticism or art compels the critic to take the attitude of ordinary waking consciousness towards the dream or the god. Art deals not with the real but with the conceivable; and criticism, though it will eventually have to have some theory of conceivability, can never be justified in trying to develop, much less assume, any theory of actuality. It is necessary to understand this before our next and final point can be made.

We have identified the central myth of literature, in its narrative aspect, with the quest-myth. Now if we wish to see this central myth as a pattern of meaning also, we have to start with the workings of the subconscious where the epiphany originates, in other words in the dream. The human cycle of waking and dreaming corresponds closely to the natural cycle of light and darkness, and it is perhaps in this correspondence that all imaginative life begins. The correspondence is largely an antithesis: it is in daylight that man is really in the power of darkness, a prey to frustration and weakness; it is in the darkness of nature that the "libido" or conquering heroic self awakes. Hence art, which Plato called a dream for awakened minds, seems to have as its final cause the resolution of the antithesis, the mingling of the sun and the hero, the realizing of a world in which the inner desire and the outward circumstance coincide. This is the same goal, of course, that the attempt to combine human and natural power in ritual has. The social function of the arts, therefore, seems to be closely connected with visualizing the goal of work in human life. So in terms of significance, the central myth of art must be the vision of the end of social effort, the innocent world of fulfilled desires, the free human society. Once this is understood, the integral place of criticism among the other social sciences, in interpreting and systematizing the vision of the artist, will be easier to see. It is at this point that we can see how religious conceptions of the final cause of human effort are as relevant as any others to criticism.

The importance of the god or hero in the myth lies in the fact that such characters, who are conceived in human likeness and yet have more power over nature, gradually build up the vision of an omnipotent personal community beyond an indifferent nature. It is this community which the hero regularly enters in his apotheosis. The world of this apotheosis thus begins to pull away from the rotary cycle of the quest in which all triumph is temporary. Hence if we look at the quest-myth as a pattern of imagery, we see the hero's quest first of all in terms of its fulfilment. This gives us our central pattern of archetypal images, the vision of innocence which sees the world in terms of total human intelligibility. It corresponds to, and is usually found in the form of, the vision of the unfallen world or heaven in religion. We may call it the comic vision of life, in contrast to the tragic vision, which sees the quest only in the form of its ordained cycle.

We conclude with a second table of contents, in which we shall attempt to set forth the central pattern of the comic and tragic visions. One essential principle of archetypal criticism is that the individual and the universal forms of an image are identical, the reasons being too complicated for us just now. We proceed according to the general plan of the game of Twenty Questions, or, if we prefer, of the Great Chain of Being:

1. In the comic vision the *human* world is a community, or a hero who represents the wish-fulfilment of the reader. The archetype of images of symposium, communion, order, friendship and love. In the tragic vision the human

world is a tyranny or anarchy, or an individual or isolated man, the leader with his back to his followers, the bullying giant of romance, the deserted or betrayed hero. Marriage or some equivalent consummation belongs to the comic vision; the harlot, witch and other varieties of Jung's "terrible mother" belong to the tragic one. All divine, heroic, angelic or other superhuman communities follow the human pattern.

2. In the comic vision the *animal* world is a community of domesticated animals, usually a flock of sheep, or a lamb, or one of the gentler birds, usually a dove. The archetype of pastoral images. In the tragic vision the animal world is seen in terms of beasts and birds of prey, wolves, vultures, serpents, dragons and the like.

3. In the comic vision the *vegetable* world is a garden, grove or park, or a tree of life, or a rose or lotus. The archetype of Arcadian images, such as that of Marvell's green world or of Shakespeare's forest comedies. In the tragic vision it is a sinister forest like the one in *Comus* or at the opening of the *Inferno* or a heath or wilderness, or a tree of death.

4. In the comic vision the *mineral* world is a city, or one building or temple, or one stone, normally a glowing precious stone—in fact the whole comic series, especially the tree, can be conceived as luminous or fiery. The archetype of geometrical images: the "starlit dome" belongs here. In the tragic vision the mineral world is seen in terms of deserts, rocks and ruins, or of sinister geometrical images like the cross.

5. In the comic vision the *unformed* world is a river, traditionally fourfold, which influenced the Renaissance image of the temperate body with its four humors. In the tragic vision this world usually becomes the sea, as the narrative myth of dissolution is so often a flood myth. The combination of the sea and beast images gives us the leviathan and similar water-monsters.

Obvious as this table looks, a great variety of poetic images and forms will be found to fit it. Yeats's "Sailing to Byzantium," to take a famous example of the comic vision at random, has the city, the tree, the bird, the community of sages, the geometrical gyre and the detachment from the cyclic world. It is, of course, only the general comic or tragic context that determines the interpretation of any symbol: this is obvious with relatively neutral archetypes like the island, which may be Prospero's island or Circe's.

Our tables are, of course, not only elementary but grossly over-simplified, just as our inductive approach to the archetype was a mere hunch. The important point is not the deficiencies of either procedure, taken by itself, but the fact that, somewhere and somehow, the two are clearly going to meet in the middle. And if they do meet, the ground plan of a systematic and comprehensive development of criticism has been established.

Notes on the Study of Myth

RICHARD CHASE

For twenty years or more there has been a general feeling that creative literature should be brought closer to myth. The resources of naturalism, aestheticism and symbolism have come to seem insufficient for modern literature, and these disciplines have been superseded, or at least modified, by the search for myth. I say "the search for myth" because the new mythological literature—the work of Eliot, Yeats, Mann, Joyce, Toynbee, Freud and others—has been able to make only a few tentative steps. I should like to say at the outset that I agree with the general opinion: our creative literature *should* be brought closer to myth.

In this short essay I do not intend to offer a theory of myth but only to suggest some restrictions on such a theory. These days the word "myth" is thrown about as cavalierly as is any word which the cultural climate envelops with glamor and charges with an emotional voltage. It is a powerful word, but not precise. Let me set down some of the more serious remarks about myth which I have encountered recently. In an essay on Mann and his use of myth (*Partisan Review*, V, June–July, 1938) and in a subsequent controversy with James Burnham, William Troy wrote that myth is "a mode of cognition," that "myth, like science, is at once a method and a body of ordered experience." We need a new myth, he wrote in effect, to replace the narrow and now harmful nineteenth century world-view of science and progress; especially as a method of criticizing and creating literature is myth far superior to science. In retrospect, Troy's account of myth seems gratifyingly sensitive, but it was excessively metaphysical. His loose phraseology allowed Burnham to leap in with the accusation that Troy, and Mann, were proposing that we "revert" to a primitive dogma or absolute world-view which would smother science. Burnham held that science was the best weapon with which to attack those basic dilemmas of modern culture posed by Mann himself. More recently Mark Schorer, in the *Kenyon Review* (Autumn, 1942) wrote that "a myth is a large controlling image ... which gives philosophic meaning to the facts of ordinary life." Myth, he says, is the "indispensable substructure" of poetry, an opinion which I take it he shares with T. S. Eliot. Joseph Campbell, in his appendix to the recent edition of *Grimm's Fairy Tales,* supposes that myth is a system of metaphysics: it is a "revelation of transcendental mysteries"; it is "symbolic of the spiritual norm for Man the Microcosm." These are ideas which at least have the advantage of being as old as the Stoics, or older. Finally, the surrealist Jacques B. Brunius, writing in the Spring, 1945, *Partisan Review,* tells us that "the creation of a modern myth coincides with the problem of knowledge," and he contrasts the modern myth which he hopes to see created with the "myths" of "Egypto-Graeco-Roman paganism," Christianity and contemporary Statism. I do not propose to criticize these writers separately—they are all suggestive in varying degrees. But I do feel that one ought to object to the assumption they all explicitly or implicitly make: namely, *that myth is philosophy—that it is a system of metaphysical or symbolic thought, that it is a theology, a body of dogma, or a world-view, that it is in direct opposition to science, is indeed the other side of the scientific coin.* To make these assumptions, or any one of them, is to make of myth something it has never been; to make them is to commandeer the word "myth" and apply it to something for which there are more exact, though less fashionable words. To make them is to burden myth with a task it cannot by itself perform. If we persist in this interpretation we are bound for another huge disappointment: "myth" will become as empty a word as some of those for which we now substitute it. Our pretensions will have to be more modest, our conclusions more tentative if there is to be any pungency in our understanding and use of myth.

The fact is that the simplest meaning of the Greek word "myth" is the right one: *a myth is a story, myth is narrative or poetic literature.* It need be no more philosophic than any other kind of literature. Myth is therefore art and must be studied as such. Myth is a mode of cognition, a system of thought, a way of life, only as art is. It can be opposed to science only as art is opposed to science. There is no question of one defeating the other. They are complementary and fulfill different needs. The romantic fear that science may destroy myth betrays an acquiescence in the misinterpretation of myth which science sometimes gives us: namely, that it is frivolous or delicate nonsense. There are no eras in recorded history when science has banished myth: though there *are* eras when human thought in general has become superficial. When science is psychologically adequate, it can be shown to have much in common with myth. The best modern proof of this is Freud's reassertion of the natural validity of myth.[1]

The definition of myth as art will be disappointing only to those who refuse

[1] Nothing could more palpably suggest the complementary functions myth and science may assume than the fact that Freud became a myth-maker and a profound student of myth *reluctantly*. His scientific temperament rebelled at every step; yet it forced him into the realm of myth. Jung, for whom mythology is a welcome escape from the rigors of science, is, compared with Freud, a vaporous and fruitless mythologist. (When I speak of Freud as a mythologist, I do not refer to the arbitrary collection of symbols which he erroneously supposed to be common to myths and dreams; I refer rather to his treatment of psychic forces and his reconstructions of the tensions, displacements, and conceptualizations which make images in both myths and dreams.)

to grant art a primary function and efficacy in human thought but must always make it dependent on something else—theological dogma, religion, the State, economics, science. Myth is not the "indispensable substructure" of poetry. Poetry is the indispensable substructure of myth. Myth is a less inclusive category than poetry. Poetry *becomes* myth when it performs a certain function, an idea which Vico entertained and one which, as I shall at least hint, is abundantly affirmed by modern anthropology.

The Relevance of Primitive Myth. We often confuse myth with those hypostatized versions of myth which have come down to us in European literature, "mummified in priestly wisdom," says Malinowski, and "enshrined in the indestructible but lifeless repository of dead religions." We have thus gained the impression that myth is more systematic, less naïve and functional than it is. Those writers who tell us that myth is a system of recondite symbols, that it is a pseudo-scientific explanation of nature or that it describes the sun and the moon, reaffirm this impression. We must study myth as it works in primitive society, before it is overlaid with interpretation.

In primitive culture myth is a relatively clearly definable activity instead of being diffused and obscured by other activities as it is in our culture. Nevertheless we usually overestimate the difference between primitive culture and our own. It is perhaps trite to observe that we are more like primitive men than we once thought, but not so trite to observe that primitive men are more like *us* than we once thought. Only one specific point can be made here: The idea of a primitive "mythopoeic age" in which all thought was mystic or symbolic and in which all literature was equally and completely mythical must be abandoned. All the primitive peoples who have been studied by anthropologists have treated a part of their experience matter-of-factly, just as we do. Primitive thought is in some ways *more* mythical than civilized thought. But the psychoanalyst's analogy with the development of the individual does not hold. We do not simply "revert" to an outgrown stage of fantasy by trying to make our literature more mythical. This is also a problem of maturity, of living better in the present, and of going on to the future. All cultures are capable of making myth. We study primitive culture because it clarifies certain psychological processes of concentration and revivification upon which depends our proceeding into the future.

Vico tells us that he thought of myth as a clear, deep river which in modern times flows into the ocean but retains its purity for a certain distance before being swallowed up. We should rather think of myth as a river which flows eternally; sometimes it is clear and deep but sometimes it becomes shallow and muddy by having to flow over broad flatlands.

Myth and Religion. If we mean by "religion" the whole magico-religious complex of primitive culture then myth is indeed closely allied with religion. If on the other hand we mean moral theism or dogmatic theology, or even a pantheon of gods, myth must be recognized as the enemy of religion. The clear-cut, powerful god, the celestial abstraction, the theological synthesis have always been subverted by the humanizing leaven of myth. The gods of myth, as Herbert Spencer observed, are always "running down from Olympus." The grandiose

South Seas and Greek myths about the sky and the earth being separated by their divine sons are not religious philosophy—they are tales of men tearing their parents apart.

Myth and Magic. Myth is much more akin to the naïve assumptions and techniques of magic than to religion. Magic does not of itself imagine discrete spirits or deities, but only efficacious preternatural forces residing in objects, animals and men, which can be manipulated by human compulsion. Myth should be thought of as a dramatic picturization of magical forces as they clash interact or harmonize with each other.

Myth and Folktale. The traditional idea that myths were primeval philosophies of nature and that the folktales of wonderful animals and birds, magical objects, lost children, young heroes, enchanted forests and so on were degenerate or misread popular versions of the myths was accepted down to the last years of the nineteenth century. The theory of evolution, on the other hand, led to the conclusion that myths had developed out of folktales in accordance with the general evolutionary process. The American anthropologists accept neither of these views. In the writings of Boas, for example, we learn that the folktale is a permanent and universal form of literature and that what are usually called myths are to be thought of as folktales which have been elaborated upon by specially gifted individuals. Several formal distinctions have been made between myth and folktale; but these distinctions are almost completely confounded by the literature of primitive peoples as it actually exists. Primitive literature should be thought of primarily as folktale; once this has been grasped we are in a position to observe that folktales have sometimes been remodeled by story-tellers of religious or philosophic temperament. By far the most useful definition of myth is one which cuts across formal distinctions and says, Myth is any kind of literature which functions in a certain way to the fulfilment of certain ends.

Some Functions of Myth. In what follows I shall try to do two things at once: show how literature becomes myth in primitive culture and suggest how our literature, especially our poetry, may become mythical. Obviously I shall have to leave several large questions unanswered. What I say is suggestion only.

Myth must always discover and accept preternatural forces; it must always reaffirm the efficacy of the preternatural and insulate it from the ordinary world. Here a note of definition: the word "supernatural" is often used in discussions of myth, sometimes with the necessary qualifications, oftener without. But there are at least two objections to "supernatural": it implies a philosophical distinction between two realms of being which are unknown to the myth-maker and it has certain misleading theological overtones. I therefore use the word "preternatural," by which I mean to indicate no more or less than is conveyed by the Melanesian word *mana*; whatever has impersonal magic force or potency and is therefore extraordinarily beautiful, terrible, dangerous, awful, wonderful, uncanny or marvelous has *mana* and is, in our sense of the word, preternatural. Myth shows us reality set afire with our own emotions. In this sense myths do not show us what is *less* than ordinarily natural; they show us what is *more* than ordinarily natural. This function may be regarded as a given fact which holds true of all myth and of much poetry. But not all literature which deals with the preternatural is myth.

Literature becomes mythical by suffusing the natural with preternatural force toward certain ends, by capturing the impersonal forces of the world and directing them toward the fulfilment of certain emotional needs. Within this broad definition, we may notice three functions of myth.

1. In his *Myth in Primitive Psychology* Malinowski discusses especially those serious primitive tales which include statements about the origin of man or which comment on his rituals and social institutions. These commonly invoke what the savage conceives as a primeval period of the world. This was a time of wonderful magic; it is a special projection into the past of the preternatural forces which in other stories (particularly those usually labelled folktales) are represented as ever present and capable of effective interference in the life of man. The serious myth, says Malinowski, is "a narrative resurrection of a primeval reality." This primeval reality is for the moment more relevant to human problems than the reality of the ordinary world; and the myths are told in order to preserve the meaningfulness and purposefulness of social customs and institutions. They "come into play when rite, ceremony, or a social or moral rule demands justification, warrant of antiquity, reality, and sanctity." There can be no doubt that these myths sometimes have the efficacy of dogma. But unlike dogma they are plastic and dynamic. They look to the present and the future. As Malinowski says, they are made *ad hoc* and are "constantly regenerated." No one deduces a way of life from the myths; they are not a canon of behavior or thought. The way of life is given; the myths are life grown literary.

The myths discussed by Malinowski, however, have mostly social and moral functions. Myths, both serious and playful, have a more purely psychological function.

2. Our culture provides innumerable substitutes for what William James called "the pungent sense of effective reality," the sense of "the possibilities of nature." Much of primitive man's life—like much of ours—is spent in apathy and routine; yet primitive man is capable of a precise and dynamic attention which we can equal only with great difficulty. Primitive culture, writes Goldenweiser, is "dynamic and vibrant"; it has to be, like any other organism for which survival is a perpetual ordeal. Our society allows us to let the world run down, grow cold and inoperative, without exposing ourselves to danger. But to primitive man a vibrant sense of present reality is vitally necessary. Paul Radin shows in his *Primitive Man as Philosopher* that to the savage reality is pragmatic. The world is not a museum of objects or a textbook of science; it is a theatre of dynamic activities, of richly mysterious powers, of ends accomplished by forces analogous to human emotions and subject to partial control by magic compulsion. To most savages, gods and spirits exist only in an end accomplished; the spirits become brightly real or fade into impersonality as a desired effect is more or less successfully brought about. The world becomes vibrant in an end accomplished: as Radin says, the savage's world then becomes "a blaze of reality."

The idea of discrete spirits inhabiting and motivating objects is not primary as E. B. Tylor and Herbert Spencer thought; it is secondary and does not take into account the universal practice of magic. To the savage, *mana* or preter-natural power is impersonal; he apprehends it as an immediate quality of things, just as color, sound, size, shape and motion are immediate qualities. As the savage envelops the world in his own emotions, things assume dramatic qualities: they are, in the words of Dewey, "poignant, tragic, beautiful, hum-orous, settled, disturbed, comfortable, annoying, barren, harsh, consoling, splendid, fearful; are such immediately and in their own right and behalf." Magic, and all the benefits it is supposed to bring, depends upon this fusion of power, quality and object: without it "things fall apart"; the world becomes chaotic and dangerous when it can no longer be enveloped in the tissue of human emotion. When objects and qualities become efficacious by being fused with power, they are subject to the compulsive techniques of magic. Besides being a compulsive technique—a pseudo-science as Frazer says—magic is obviously an aesthetic activity. Magic is immediately available to art, and art to magic. Primitive literature is shot through with magic and we may regard it as mythical when it fortifies the magical view of things, when it reaffirms the vibrant dynamism of the world, when it fortifies the ego with the impression that there is a magically potent brilliancy in the world. Myth is not vaporous, abstract, or unreal; it is a "blaze of reality."

3.   Like other kinds of literature, myth performs the cathartic function of dramatizing the clashes and harmonies of life in a social and natural environ-ment. But myth can be understood as the aesthetic leaven which heals or makes tolerable those deep neurotic disturbances which in primitive culture are occasioned by the clashing attitudes of magic and religion. This collision of forces, as Radin points out in his *Primitive Religion,* is partly the result of the priest's struggle to achieve a dominant economic position. Coincident with his war upon the people is his war against magic. For magic is the prerogative of mankind in general; it exalts human power; it places the world and the gods at the disposal of mankind. The priest's task is to transmute magic into religion, to overcome the subjectivism on which magic depends, to present spirits and gods as clearly conceived objective beings, to transfer magical power to the gods and make men obeisant before them. Mythology is full of the tensions created by this universal struggle, and many myths may be said to array the propaganda of men, animals, and magical beings against the propaganda of the gods. But art is constructive where life is destructive. Myth keeps the dilemma operative and resolves the contesting forces into useful experience.

Stated in somewhat abstract terms, magic, as Radin says, is the coercion of the objective world by the ego; religion is the coercion of the ego by the objective world, or by the powers and beings in the objective world. Now I suggest that when literature brings these opposing forces together so that they interact coercively toward a common end, literature has become mythical. This interpretation of myth, as it seems to me, is less immediately valuable to us than are the two interpretations I have offered above; it requires more thorough translation before it can be applied to our own problems. Yet the war between magic and religion still goes on, though sometimes under different names. Certain terms in which this "cathartic function" of myth might be restated will doubtless occur to any student of Freud.

Myths and Paramyths. I am aware that what has been said here cannot fully elucidate those processes of amalgamation by which the symbols, images, concepts and personified beings of myth are made—though a complete elaboration of what I have said would lead us a long way in that direction.

I am aware too that no complete account of myth can be undertaken without wider references to human needs and aspirations than those I have chosen here. The method of pragmatic naturalism seems to me the only fruitful method of studying myth—yet that method leaves us, as it often does, with the feeling that we have made art too resolutely functional, too outward looking, too optimistic. Psychoanalysis may be misleading as psychology, but "the pleasure principle" and the desperate "instincts" of sex and death give myth a dramatic richness unknown to contemporary pragmatism, or at least not yet assimilated by it.

I do not mean, either, to reduce the latitude of reinterpretation unduly. Those ever recurring writers who find the study of primitive thought somehow degrading or irrelevant are right at least when they say that the tales of the folk are often vague, dull or childish. We must be free, as was the primitive intellectual (who may be studied in Radin's *Primitive Man as Philosopher*), so to interpret a myth that it comes alive for us in the moral and intellectual context of our culture—as we have in our time interpreted the myths of Oedipus, Joseph and Philoctetes. This may require symbolism or allegory, certainly conscious intelligence. But we cannot assume a symbol, an allegory or a concept to be the same as the myth itself, or to be the only interpretation of the myth. Apart from the dictates of parochial cultural necessity, there remain constant human needs against which we must measure the adequacy of our interpretations.

Myth has often been philosophical, frequently in advanced cultures, less frequently in primitive cultures. We should not care, for example, to ignore the philosophical aspects of the Oedipus, Joseph or Philoctetes myths or of the myths which we find in the poems of Eliot or Yeats. These myths offer us patterns of feeling and thought. But we are likely to find in them not philosophy but (as Eliot says) the "emotional equivalent" of philosophy. We may be sure at least that the myth is never philosophical without being something else. Myth is, in the phrase of Renan, "simultaneous humanity."

And we have to remember that all myths begin with the apprehension of some marvellous activity or potentiality. Magic and literature meet in myth. An unusual stone, a strange animal, a witch doctor have *mana* for the savage just as do Oedipus for Sophocles or Freud, Joseph for Mann, the "great tomb-haunter" for Yeats, or Mme Sosostris for Eliot. Those concepts, allegories, symbols and theologies which are loosely called mythical are so only so long as they are still faithful to the emotional complexity of literature; for only literature can perform the mythical function of preserving and giving significance to the sensation of *mana*. Once disinherited from their literary matrix concepts are not, properly speaking, myths. I propose (following Herder) disinherited "mythical ideas" called *paramyths*.

Poetry as Myth. A myth is not "a large controlling image." The future of mythical poetry does not depend upon reconciling poetry with an image. It depends rather upon making of poetry something it is always striving against human bias and superficiality to become. The poetical imagination when it attains any consistent fire and efficacy is always displacing the texture of the mind into the external world so that it becomes a theater of preternatural forces. A certain control and direction given the poetical emotions, and poetry, as it always has, becomes mythical.

Poetry, Myth, and Reality

PHILIP WHEELWRIGHT

Poetry suffers today from at once too high and too low an appraisal. We burden Shakespeare with flatteries which his contemporaries would have reserved for royalty or for the ancients, but there is reason to believe that modern theater audiences are insensitive to much in his plays that the rowdier but more perceptive frequenters of the Globe Theater took in as an expected part of the entertainment. Charged language, language of associative complexity, is a rarity on the stage or in the cinema today, and when it occurs it is likely to embarrass by its artiness, its rather too evident snob appeal. We read poetry as a special discipline, becoming scholarly about it or ecstatic about it according to our profession, temperament and mood, but we deprecate its intrusion into the sober business of everyday living. Poetry seems to most of us something to be set upon a pedestal and left there, like one of those chaste heroines of medieval romance, high and dry.

Why is there this impoverishment of response toward poetry in present-day society? The question may be one of the most important we can ask, for it concerns not poetry and poetic response alone, but by implication the general sickness of our contemporary world. The symptoms, though diverse, are connected; and I suspect we shall not understand why great poetry is no longer written in an age which endows innumerable lecturers to talk about poetry, unless we also understand why it is that we must let our fellow-countrymen starve in an era of productive plenty, and why as Americans we spent twenty years professing our love of peace and democracy while helping to finance dictatorships and throttle democracies on three continents, and why as Christians we think it proper to build imposing churches while treating God as something out of last year's Sunday supplement. The question of poetry's status in the present-day world is interrelated with such questions as these, and it seems to me that we cannot adequately understand any one of the questions except in a perspective that catches at least the outlines of the others. The needed perspective is to my mind a mytho-religious one, without any of the claptrap sometimes associated with either word; for it involves a rediscovery of the original and essentially unchangeable conditions of human insight and human blessedness. The aim of this lecture is to indicate the nature of that perspective and to discover its latent presence in some of the great poetry of past times.

Suppose we represent the dimensions of human experience, very tentatively, by means of a diagram—where the horizontal line *E–P* represents the dimension of secular experience, *empirical* experience as I think we may call it without redundancy; of that trafficking with things, relations and ideas that makes up

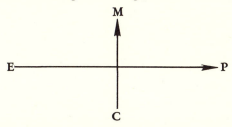

our everyday commonsense world. It has two poles: outwardly there are the phenomena (*P*) that constitute our physical universe; these are spacelike, are interrelated by causal laws, and are the proper object of scientific inquiry. At the other pole of this horizontal axis stands the ego (*E*) which knows the phenomena—partly as a spectator and partly no doubt as a contributor to their connection and significance. The major philosophical movements of the past three centuries owe their character and their limitations to the stress, I think the undue stress, which they have put upon the horizontal axis. Descartes made the additional mistake of hypostatizing *E* and *P*, establishing the thinking self and the extended world of things over against each other as distinct substances; he "cut the universe in two with a hatchet," as Hegel said, separating it into two absolutely alien spheres, thought without extension and extension without thought: thereby settling the direction, perhaps the doom, of modern philosophy. Granted that the Cartesian bifurcation was immensely fruitful for the subsequent development of natural science, the benefit was purely one of conceptual efficiency, not of interpretive fulness. The general result was to alienate nature from man by denuding it of human significance, and thereby deprive man of his natural sense of continuity with the environing world, leaving him to face the Absolute alone. To this stark confrontation the Cartesian man brings a single talisman—pure reason, which, rightly used, can answer all questions, solve all mysteries, illumine every dark cranny in the universal scheme. All truth becomes to the unobstructed reason as clear and indubitable as the truth of an arithmetical sum. A child who performs an arithmetical sum correctly—so Descartes declares—knows the utmost, with respect to that sum, that the human mind, and by implication God's mind, can ever discover.

Analogously a physicist, by confining himself to clear and distinct ideas, may come to know the utmost, with respect to any given problem, that can possibly be known; and this would be true, on Cartesian principles, even of a psychologist or a theologian or a student of any field whatever who adhered to properly rational methods. Athene springs full-born from the head of Zeus; or to use a more modern simile, wisdom consists in a sort of klieg-light brilliance rather than in adjusting one's eyes to the chiaroscuro of the familiar world. For the familiar world—here is its essential defect to a rationalist like Descartes—has a past, it develops, is time-burdened, and draws much of its meaning from shared tradition; while to Descartes' view tradition, except so far as reason can justify it, is superstition, loyalties to the past are servile, and the philosopher should be like an architect who tears down the lovable old houses and crooked streets of a medieval town in order to erect a symmetrical city where no one can lose his way. Thus in this rationalistic philosophy of Descartes we have, close to its modern source, the deadliest of all heresies. It is the sin, or, if you prefer, the delusion, of intellectual pride, a re-enactment of Adam's fall and of the building of Bab-el, and it leads in our time to the fallacy of hoping for a future without organically remembering a past, the imbecility of trying to build history out of an unhistorical present.

The influence of Descartes' dualistic rationalism has been far-flung. In subsequent philosophy, although various parts of his doctrine became modified or rejected, the Cartesian way of conceiving human experience, as an individual ego able by its own powers to know the world of phenomena confronting it, played a decisive role. British empiricists and positivists in particular, from Locke through Hume and Mill right down to Bertrand Russell and a majority of professional philosophers in our own day, have differed from one another not in any doubt as to the self-sufficiency of the horizontal axis of experience but in their particular ways of distinguishing or connecting or distributing the emphasis between the ego and its objects. Today the horizontal philosophy has reached its clearest and most intractable expression in the related doctrines of behaviorism, instrumentalism, and semantic positivism: behaviorism, which reduces the human mind to what can be experimentally observed of its bodily behavior; instrumentalism, which reduces the meaning of any concept to that set of experimental operations by which the denotation of the concept could be objectively shown; and semantic positivism, which aims at a one-to-one correspondence between units of language and the sets or types of objects and events which such language-units denote. These three doctrines, which may be grouped under the general name of positivistic materialism, have acquired great prestige in our time. Every honest and sane intellectual must, I believe, come to grips with them: must recognize both that they are the logically inescapable outcome and expression of our secular way of life, and that they are utterly disastrous. The only truth on this basis is experimental truth, structures built out of the common denominators of human experience; religious truth and poetic truth are dismissed as fictions, as misnomers. Religion ceases to have more than a tentative and subjective validity: it expresses the yearnings and fears and awestruck impotence of human minds with respect to events and

sequences in the external world which up to a given stage of human development have eluded scientific explanation and experimental control. Poetry,
likewise, has no truth-value that is distinctive to it as poetry. It contains, on
the one hand, a "subject" (in Matthew Arnold's sense), a "scenario," a literal
meaning, which could be expressed without essential loss in the language of
science; and beyond this there is only the pleasurable decoration and emotional
heightening which the form and evocative language of the poem bestows. The
poet is not in any sense a seer or a prophet; he is simply, in the jargon of
advertising, an effective layout man. Science has thus become the Great
Dictator, to whom the spiritual republics of religion and poetry are yielding up
their autonomy in bloodless defeat. There is no help for it within the purely
horizontal perspective of human experience: if we see the world only as patterns
of phenomena, our wisdom will be confined to such truths as phenomena can
furnish. And this situation is very barren and very unpromising, not only for
religion and for poetry, but for expanding love and the sense of *radical significance*
which are at the root of both.

Now my belief is that the problem as posited exclusively in terms of the
horizontal consciousness is an unnatural problem, an intellectual monstrosity
which leads away from, rather than toward, the greater and more enduring
truths. No genuine religious teacher, and with the lone exception of Lucretius
no great poet, has ever sought truth in exclusively empirical terms; and I must
say I find deeper truths, richer and more relevant truths, in the mysticism of
Lao-tse and Jesus, in the dramatic suggestiveness of Aeschylus and Shakespeare,
than in the impersonal experiments of scientists or the voluminous literalism of
scholars. How then are we to validate, and in what terms are we to discuss, the
transempirical factor in truth which is presupposed in all religion and in all
the profounder sort of poetry?

The thing required of us, I believe, if we are to escape the blind alley of
empirical positivism, is a proper understanding of myth, and of mythical
consciousness. It is the habit of secular thought to dismiss myth either as pure
fiction, a set of fairy-tales with which the human race in childhood frittered
away its time; or else as allegory—that is, as a roundabout and inexact way of
expressing truths about physical and human nature which could be expressed
just as pertinently and much more accurately by the language of science. On
either interpretation myth becomes regarded as an archaism, a barren survival,
with no function of its own which cannot be served more efficiently by more
up-to-date language and methods; a kind of fiction that should be renounced
as completely as possible by the serious truth-seeker. What I want to stress is
that this secular, positivistic attitude toward myth appears to me quite inadequate to explain the facts—I mean, of course, the salient, the really interesting
aspect of the facts. It ignores or deprecates that haunting awareness of transcendental forces peering through the cracks of the visible universe, that is the
very essence of myth. It blandly overlooks the possibility, which to Aeschylus,
Dante, Shakespeare and many others was an axiom of assured faith, that myth
may have a non-exchangeable semantic function of its own—that myth may
express visions of truth to which the procedures of the scientists are grossly

irrelevant; that the mythical consciousness, in short (to exploit a convenient mathematical metaphor) may be a dimension of experience cutting across the empirical dimension as an independent variable.

In the foregoing diagram I have represented the mythico-religious dimension of human experience by a vertical line C–M cutting across the horizontal axis E–P.

C represents the community mind, which is to myth more or less what the individual mind is to science; and the upper pole M represents Mystery, of which the community mind is darkly aware. Thus the semantic arrow points from C to M, as it points from E to P. This double relation should not be conceived too rigidly: scientific truth is admittedly established by some degree of social cooperation, and mythical truth is apprehended and given form by individuals. Nevertheless the distinction is basically sound. Myth is the expression of a profound sense of togetherness—a togetherness not merely upon the plane of intellect, as is primarily the case among fellow-scientists, but a togetherness of feeling and of action and of wholeness of living. Such togetherness must have, moreover, a history. Community mind is nothing so sporadic as the mass mind of a modern lynching party or a wave of war hysteria, nor even is it found to any considerable degree in a trade union. In such manifestations as these the collective mind possesses little or no significant pattern, for it has had no time to mature. It creates not myths but merely ideologies—an ideology being a sort of parvenu myth which expresses not the interests of the group as a cooperative organism but the interests of each member of the group reflected and repeated in each other member: to this extent it lacks also a transcendental reference. A mass cannot create myths, for it has had no real history. Myths are the expression of a community mind which has enjoyed long natural growth, so that the sense of togetherness becomes patterned and semantically significant. A patterned sense of togetherness develops its proper rhythms in ceremony and prayer, dance and song; and just as the micro-rhythms of the eye project themselves as a visible world of trees and stones, and as the micro-rhythms of the ear project themselves as an audible world of outer sounds, so the larger rhythms of community life project themselves as a sense of enveloping Mystery. In cultures where the mythico-religious consciousness has developed freely, this sense of mystery tinges all cognition: whether called *mana* as by the Melanesians, or *wakonda* as by the Sioux Indians, or *brahma* as by the early Aryan invaders of India, there is felt to be a mysterious Other, a spirit or breath in the world, which is more real, more awful, and in the higher religions more reverenceable than the visible and obvious particulars of experience, while at the same time it may manifest or embody itself in persons, things, words and acts in unforeseeable ways. Sometimes this basic Mystery becomes dispersed and personified into a polytheism of gods and daemons, sometimes concentrated and exalted into a single majestic God. Whatever its eventual form, it appears to express on the one hand man's primordial way of knowing, before the individual has separated himself with clear critical awareness from the group; and on the other hand an indispensable element in the cognitive activity of every vital culture, primitive or civilized. What I am arguing, in short, is not merely that the consciousness which arises from group-life and group-memories is the original matrix of individual consciousness—that much is a sociological truism—but that when the consciousness of individuals separates itself too utterly from the sustaining warmth of the common myth-consciousness, the dissociated consciousness becomes in time unoriented and sterile, fit for neither great poetry nor great wisdom nor great deeds.

What concerns the student of poetry most directly is the relation of myth to speech, the characteristic forms in which the mythical consciousness finds utterance. Shelley declared truly that "in the infancy of society every author is a poet, because language itself is poetry"; and, we may add, the reason why primitive language is poetry lies in the fact that it is the spontaneous expression of a consciousness so largely, in our sense, mythical. There are two outstanding respects in which primitive language, and especially spoken language, tends to be poetic, or at any rate to have a natural kinship with poetry: first, in its manner of utterance, its rhythms and euphonies; second, in its manner of reference, in the delicacy and associative fulness with which it refers to various aspects of the all-encompassing Mystery. In short, primitive speech—for I am dealing here with language that is meant to be spoken—employs both rhythm and metaphor. The reasons for the possession of these characteristics by primitive speech are doubtless clear from the foregoing description of the mythical consciousness. Primitive speech is a more direct expression of the community mind than speech that has grown sophisticated, and rhythm is the vehicle by which the sense of community is projected and carried through time. Rhythm has furthermore a magical function: for since the primitive community mind is not limited to a society of actual living persons but embraces also the ghosts of ancestors and the souls of things in the environing world, the rhythms of gesture and speech are felt to include and to exert a binding effect not only upon men but, when conducted under auspicious conditions, upon ghosts, gods, and nature; which is the essence of magic. Such language thus possesses a naturally evocative quality: it is felt as having a tendency to endow the world with the qualities which it declares to be there. The metaphorical character of primitive language, on the other hand, consists in its tendency to be rather manifoldly allusive: it can be so, because of the varied associations with which communication within a closed society has gradually become charged; and it has a semantic necessity of being so, because only in language having multiple reference can the full, manifold, and paradoxical character of the primordial Mystery find fit expression. Owing to such referential plenitude the language of primitives tends to employ paradox freely: it makes use of statements contradicting each other and of statements contradicting an experimentally accepted situation; for the Mystery which it tries to express cannot be narrowed down to logical categories.

The island of Fiji furnishes a particularly interesting illustration of uses to which primitive poetry can be put. When a Fijian dies, the legend is that his ghost spends three days traversing the fifty-mile path that leads from the principal Fijian city to the sacred mountain Naukavadra, situated on the western coast of the isle. This mountain has a ledge overlooking the sea, called Nai-thombo-thombo, "the jumping-off place," from which the departing ghost hurls itself down and swims to a distant paradise beyond the sunset, where it rejoins its ancestors. Before the final immersion, however, the ghost on arriving at the sacred mountain is received hospitably in a cave by the ghosts of ancient hero-ancestors, guardians of the tribe's morality and well-being. After a feast, partly cannibal, has been eaten in common and ancient tribal lays have been sung, the newcomer finds his spiritual eyes awakened, and realizing for the first time that death has befallen him he is overwhelmed with grief. To the accompaniment of native instruments, addressing the ancestors he chants these words:

> My Lords! In evil fashion are we buried,
> Buried staring up into heaven,
> We see the scud flying over the sky,
> We are worn out with the feet tramping on us.

> Our ribs, the rafters of our house, are torn asunder,
> The eyes with which we gazed on one another are destroyed,
> The nose with which we kissed has fallen in,
> The breast with which we embraced is ruined,
> The mouth with which we laughed at one another has decayed,
> The teeth with which we bit have showered down.
> Gone is the hand that threw the tinka stick.
> The testes have rolled away.

> Hark to the lament of the mosquito!
> It is well that *he* should die and pass onward.
> But alas for my ear that he has devoured.

> Hark to the lament of the fly!
> It is well that *he* should die and pass onward.
> But alas! he has stolen the eye from which I drank.

> Hark to the lament of the black ant!
> It is well that *he* should die and pass onward.
> But alas for my whale's-tooth[1] that he has devoured.

The dead man's meeting with the ancestors takes place on the third day after death, and is followed by the leap into the sea and the passage over into the afterworld. Thus far we are in the realm of myth. Parallel to the myth-pattern is a behavior-pattern which is traditional with the survivors. On the third day they bury the now putrefying corpse, and while doing so they chant ceremonially the same songs that the dead man hears and sings in the cave at Mt. Naukavadra. Evidently the cause-effect relation involved is complex. Sociological analysis will regard the belief as a fictional projection which has the function of explaining and justifying the tribal burial processes; while to the survivors, on the other hand, the matter appears in reverse, their ceremonies being designed to annotate, and by imitative magic to assist, the dead one's

---

[1] Whale's-tooth: the phallus; also used (in its literal sense) as a symbol of wealth and medium of exchange.

situation. In any case the dirge I have just quoted serves by its strongly marked rhythms, inescapable even in translation, to establish a sense of widened community, whereby, for the duration of the ceremony at least, the chanting survivors, the recently deceased, and the ancient ancestor-gods are brought into a strongly felt and tersely articulated togetherness. Such expressions of a widened community-sense, paced in the tribal calendar according to the occurrence of emotionally significant events like births and deaths, puberty, marriage, and war, are the most vitalizing forces in tribal cultural life.

In ancient Egypt a similar phenomenon was current, although in Egyptian death chants the magical element is more explicit. The Pyramid Texts—those ancient inscriptions dating from the fourth millennium B.C. which are found on the inner walls of the pyramid tombs—are records of the royal chants by which bands of faithful subjects, led ceremonially by the high priests, helped the Pharaoh whom they were burying there to secure immortal divinity. Here, in part, is one of the noblest of these texts:

> The flier flies from earth to sky.
> Upward he soars like a heron,
> Upward he leaps like a grasshopper,
> Kissing the sky like a hawk.
>
> Crowned with the headdress of the sun-god,
> Wearing the hawk's plumage,
> Upward he flies to join his brothers the gods.
> Joyously we behold him.
>
> Now we give back your heart, Osiris.
> Now we give back your feet, Osiris.
> Now we give back your arms, Osiris.
>
> Flying aloft like a bird,
> He settles down like a beetle
> On a seat in the ship of the sun-god.
> Now he rows your ship across the sky, O Glowing One!
>
> Now he brings your ship to land, O Glowing One!
> And when again you ascend out of the horizon,
> He will be there with staff in hand,
> The navigator of your ship, O Glowing One!
>
> The primordial gods, the ancient nine, are dazzled,
> The Lords of Forms are shaken with terror
> As he breaks the metallic sky asunder.
> Older than the Great One, he issues commands.
> Eternity is set before him,
> Discernment is placed at his feet,
> The horizon is given to his keeping.
>
> The sky is darkened, the stars rain down,

The bones of the earth-god tremble
When this one steps forth as a god
Devouring his fathers and mothers,
With the sacred serpents on his forehead.

Men and gods he devours.
His sky-dwelling servants prepare the cooking-pots,
Wiping them out with the legs of their women.
The gods are cooked for him piece by piece
In the cooking-pots of the sky at evening.

Cracking the backbones he eats the spinal marrow,
He swallows the hearts and lungs of the Wise Ones.
Their wisdom and their strength has passed into his belly.
Their godhood is within him.

The community-sense expressed in this hymn has a definite but again complex pattern. On the plane of earthly actuality the celebrants feel their union in a shared joy at the heavenly prowess of their dead king. On the transcendental plane, the plane of myth, there is another sort of union—an identification of the dead king with Osiris, god of periodic and perpetual rebirth, and with Ra the sun god. Although a reverent distinction is observed between the worshippers and the "Osirified One," the exalted king-god whose deification they celebrate, nevertheless the surviving community enjoys a vicarious participation in godhood, since the Pharaoh is felt to be still the worshippers' representative and the symbol of their communal solidarity as he had been on earth. That sense of mystical community, in Egypt as elsewhere, found its natural expression in a type of poetry characterized by marked rhythms and transcendental imagery, which are the esthetic correlates of the lower and upper poles of myth-consciousness.

Thus the logic of myth proceeds on different assumptions from the logic of science and of secular realism, and moves by different laws. Attempts to deal with myth by the methods of science fall inevitably short of the mark. While objective methods of inquiry can trace the occasions of myth, the conditions under which it may flourish, they are quite incapable of understanding the mythical consciousness itself. For science and myth are basically incommensurate ways of experiencing, and science cannot "explain" myth without explaining it away. Its explanations are not interpretative but pragmatically reductive. The questions which science poses about myth are never quite relevant, for the questions essential to myth are patterned on a different syntax. Always in scientific thinking there is the implicit assumption of an "either-or" situation. Is the Pharaoh identical with Osiris after death or is he not? If so, and if all the Pharaohs who ruled before him share the identity, it follows (by the logic of science) that they must be identical with each other; and in that case why are they buried and worshipped individually? Moreover, if identification with Osiris is the soul's final attainment, as the Pyramid Texts indicate, why is the corpse mummified as if to preserve symbolically, and perhaps magically, just this individual to whom the body had once belonged? Such questions as these do not admit of any logically clear answer, and it is important for the understanding both of myth and of poetry to see why they do not. Science seeks clarity of an outward, publicly recognizable kind; it can regard mysteries as but materials for its particular techniques of clarification. By scientific logic a thing is either A or B and not both; or, if both, its double character must mean either that the thing is complex and can be dissociated into A and B as its elements, or else that A and B share a common quality K which with sufficient care is susceptible of exact description. The tendency of science is always to think in terms of mechanical models—structures analyzable into parts which, added up, remake the originals. Mechanical operations do work in that way, but wholeness of experience does not, and myth is an expression of whole experiences that whole men have known and felt.

Passing from primitive poetry to the poetry of more civilized eras, we find that while a greater proportion of the poem is contributed by the genius of some individual poet, yet in those poems which carry the signature of greatness, myth still plays a prominent and usually a more deliberate role. Myth is invaluable to the poet, furnishing as it does a background of familiar reference by which the sensibilities of the poet and his readers are oriented and so brought into pro-founder communication than would otherwise have been possible. The ways in which myth is poetically employed, and the effects gained by its employment, depend not only upon the artistry of the individual poet but also upon the general attitude toward myth in the age in which he has the good or bad luck to be born. He may be born, like Aeschylus or Dante, in a period when a substantial body of myths enjoys wide acceptance as literally true: his greatest poems in such a case will be poetic intensifications and elaborations of some of those myths. He may be born, like Virgil or Shakespeare, at a time when a more sophisticated attitude toward myths is beginning to set in but before it has made such headway as to drain the myths of all vitality: the poet will then employ his myths thematically, breaking them up and redistributing their elements as may best suit his esthetic purpose. Or he may be born, finally, in an age like our own, in the late afternoon of a culture, when the myths that once moved men to great deeds now survive as antiquarian curiosities: such a poet will feel himself to be living in a cultural wasteland, his materials will be fragmentary and unpromis-ing, and while he may prove an ingenious renovator of ruined monuments or a resourceful practitioner of metajournalism, his contribution as a poet—the contribution of a whole man who speaks powerfully to whole men—will be small.

Aeschylus, the first great dramatic poet of the West, exemplifies the early condition of civilized poetry in its relation to myth. In his time the chorus of dancing priests, which probably stemmed from ancient religious rituals associa-ted with Dionysus and the grain-goddess Demeter, had become partly secular-ized, until, although the religious background was still a vital part of the whole show and amply familiar to the playgoing Greeks, the predominant purpose of the great dramatic festivals had insensibly slipped from worship to entertainment. The spectators, who in an earlier age had no doubt participated in the ritualistic dance, were now become relatively immunized: their function is to sit still and at proper times to applaud and perhaps even to chant in unison some of the choric refrains—a practice apparently indicated by the closing exhortation of *The Eumenides*. But atavistically they are still religious celebrants, being led in their observances by the band of rhythmically chanting priests, which has now become the tragic chorus; their emotions pulsate synchronically with those which the chorus expresses by word and gesture, and their acceptance of the dramatic situations which unfold themselves is largely governed by this dramatic communion.

The characteristic problem of Aeschylean drama is human guilt and its consequences. In the Greek mind two conceptions of destiny and of guilt interplayed: the Olympian and the chthonic. According to the former conception man's cardinal guilt was *hybris,* pride, which consisted in trying to overstep the boundary that separated man's ordained lot from that of the blessed and deathless gods, while virtue consisted in observing due measure, remaining loyal to one's destined station in life, and especially to one's condition of earth-bound mortal manhood. The Olympian conception was thus at bottom *spacelike,* a matter of observing boundaries, limits and middle paths: indeed, in Hesiod's *Works and Days* it is particularized, in what may have been its original form, as an admonition to till one's own soil and not trespass on one's neighbor's. The chthonic conception, on the other hand, related guilt to the earth (*chthôn*), which became infectiously polluted when innocent blood was spilled, and to the vengeful ancestor ghosts who, living within the earth, were offended by actions that weakened the power and prestige, or violated the moral code, of the tribe or nation to which they still in a manner belonged. Thus the ghost of King Darius, in *The Persians,* returns from the underworld to berate his royal son for leading the Persian host into a disastrous war; and thus too the three Furies (originally snakes and still wearing snaky locks at the beginning of *The Eumenides*) haunt Orestes for his crime of matricide; and thus again in Sophocles' *Oedipus Rex* a plague has fallen on the land and cannot be removed until the unwitting murder and incest have been brought to light and expiated. In all these cases the dominant motif is the rhythmic succession of guilt and expiation, which at once expresses the ingrained Greek sense of a rhythmically pulsating nature in which moral qualities like physical ones undergo seasonal alteration, while at the same time it provides a forceful and intelligible form into which tragic drama can be moulded. There is a clear sense, therefore, in which the chthonic conception of guilt tends to be *timelike,* a matter of working out the patterned destiny of an individual or family or city or nation.

Clearly the chthonic conception of destiny lends itself to representation most readily through the time-charged medium of tragic drama, the Olympian conception through the relatively static medium of the epic. The distinction is a shifting one, however: in the sculpturally conceived *Prometheus Bound* the Olympian conception appears to predominate, while in that one great surviving trilogy, the *Oresteia* the chthonic theme of guilt and retribution is intertwined with Olympian imagery, until in the end both elements are sublimated in a magnificent patriotic finale, by which the dramatic community-sense is explicitly secularized. Nevertheless it is worth noting that in the *Oresteia,* which without much dispute may stand as his greatest work, Aeschylus is more respectful and attaches greater dramatic and moral importance to chthonic than to Olympian ideas. He dismisses gravely the Olympian myth that the gods envy human prosperity, while the chthonic myth of the inheritance of guilt haunts him right through to the end, and motivates the long tortured struggle that constitutes the three dramas. Again, in the final play of the trilogy, although Apollo is strangely ridiculed, the Furies are treated with exaggerated respect, as powers who must be placated and even reverenced since they are the life-germ of Athenian moral and political life. All in all, the time-myth, as Nietzsche's *The Birth of Tragedy* explosively demonstrates, is at the core of Greek as of every other vital culture, and when its rhythms become weakened or vulgarized the culture grows senile.

Magic, which has played so large and so explicit a role in primitive poetry, appears in Aeschylean drama in sublimated form. For what is magic but operation through a direct emotional congruence established between the operator and his object? The dramatist no longer operates like the primitive magician upon gods and daemons and unnamed mysterious forces of the outer world. His magic is turned, at least to a very large degree, upon the responsive feelings of his audience. We still speak today of a dramatist's "magic," but the compliment is usually vapid. In Greek tragedy the word was applicable more literally, as through the medium of rhythmic chants with musical and choreographic accompaniment, behind which lay the common heritage of mythological background that found stylized expression in plot and imagery, the vast throng that packed the City Dionysia was brought for a few hours into significant emotional unity. Aristotle has noted the katharsis of pity and terror which takes place on such occasions, but they do not exhaust the emotional effect. Deeper than they and deeper than any conscious recognition is the communally felt, ceremonially induced emotion of religious awe, by which the Greek spectators in a miraculous bubble of time are caught up and momentarily identified with the transcendental forces that envelop them and impregnate their culture.

Shakespeare was of course a more eclectic mythologer. As a master-dramatist he could adapt expertly to poetic and dramatic uses the myths that colored the popular consciousness of his time. And yet there is in Shakespeare's mythical consciousness a deep-lying unity, which becomes gradually visible as we trace in their varied expressions what I suggest are the two Shakespearean key-myths—the myth of love and the myth of divine and earthly governance. Every play that Shakespeare wrote shows a large concern with one or the other and usually both of these themes—if not in plot, at least in imagery and allusion.

The love myth enjoys a varied and imagistically ally colored career in its earlier expressions—*Venus and Adonis,* the Sonnets, such comedies as *Love's Labour's Lost,* and culminating in *Romeo and Juliet,* as represented here, although often strikingly realistic—

> He wrings her nose, he strikes her on the cheeks,
> He bends her fingers, holds her pulses hard, . . .

is much more than a transient phenomenon of human experience. Unlike the anarchy of lust, love is a harmony, a sweet concord, a transcendently heard music; and Venus' consuming passion for Adonis strikes the reader as sufficiently redeemed and justified by its harmonization with the universal passion that throbs through nature. Venus' desire, allied by pedigree with the high concerns of the gods, becomes merged in the poem with such natural manifestations as the strong-necked stallion who breaks rein on espying a young breeding mare:

> Imperiously he leaps, he neighs, he bounds,
> And now his woven girths he breaks asunder;
> The bearing earth with his hard hoof he wounds,
> Whose hollow womb resounds like heaven's thunder;
>   The iron bit he crusheth 'tween his teeth,
>   Controlling what he was controlled with.
>
> His ears up-prick'd; his braided hanging mane
> Upon his compass'd crest now stand on end;
> His nostrils drink the air, and forth again,
> As from a furnace, vapors doth he send;
>   His eye, which scornfully glisters like fire,
>   Shows his hot courage and his high desire.

The sexual and procreative imagery of these stanzas needs no underlining. But the important thing is that love and procreation are joined—here by imagery as later, in the Sonnets, by explicit statement:

> And nothing 'gainst Time's scythe can make defence
> Save breed, to brave him when he takes thee hence.

This couplet introduces the villain of the love-myth: Time, who devours like a cormorant all of this present breath's endeavors. Or rather, all save one. For through the medium of art man can rise above his mortal existence, and making himself the heir of all eternity can bate the scythe's keen edge.

> Yet do thy worst, old Time; despite thy wrong,
> My love shall in my verse ever live young.

Poetry and music uphold the immortality of love in all Shakespeare's plays; love's frailty or perversion is announced by jangling discordant rhythms, with the frequent imagistic accompaniment of tempests as indicative of discord in nature.

The myth of universal governance, divine and earthly, has its double source in Christianity and in Elizabethan patriotic consciousness; like the love-myth it expresses a harmony that joins mankind with divinity and with ordered nature.

The heavens themselves, the planets, and this center
Observe degree, priority, and place.
　　　　　　　. . . But when the planets
In evil mixture to disorder wander,
What plagues and what portents! what mutiny!
What raging of the sea! shaking of earth!
Commotion in the winds! Frights, changes, horrors,
Divert and crack, rend and deracinate
The unity and married calm of states
Quite from their fixture.

These plagues and portents, tempests and deracinations, symbolize the inverse side of the governance-myth: they accompany—at first in verbal imagery, then later in actual stage-presentation—not only the regicide of a Caesar and a Duncan, but the insurrections of man's inner state which are always the most crucial motivation of Shakespearean tragedy. The myth of governance affirms "degree, priority and place" at once in the political order, in nature, in the soul of man, and in the divine government of the world; now one, now another of these aspects is given foremost emphasis, and at times the last of them is denied, according to the contextual requirements of the individual drama. But in the king-god imagery of *Richard II,* in the allegorical overtones of *Measure for Measure* and *The Tempest,* in the demonology of *Macbeth,* and most subtly of all in the tragic katharsis of *King Lear,* the unity is reaffirmed: earthly and divine government, the order of nature, and the nobility of man are brought again and again into symbolic and always somewhat incomplete identification.

Running through and giving form to the other mythical material, there is, in the greater achievements of Shakespeare, the myth of tragedy itself. This myth, which attains increasingly full realization in Shakespeare's successive experiments with tragedy up to and including *Lear,* finally receives brief explicit utterance in Edmund's cry:

The wheel is come full circle; I am here.

We today have lost this sense of cyclical fulness and therewith of transcendental significance in human affairs; accordingly we no longer produce great tragedy, because we no longer believe in the tragic myth. In its place we have substituted the shabbier myth of comedy, which Shakespeare utilized for a time and then, when it had lost its power to move him dramatically, unleashed his contempt by expressing it as the title of one of his worst and weakest plays, "All's Well That Ends Well." This wretched quarter-truth is exploited in most of the novels and nearly all of the movies of our day—no longer as healthy comedy merely, but decked out with false sentimentality in the trappings that once belonged to tragedy. Our failure in tragic intuition, our substitution for it of bathos and business practicality in loose-wedded conjunction, is not least among the disastrous factors of the contemporary world.

These considerations of the rôle of myth in great poetry of the past may throw some light upon the predicament of the poet and the unpromising estate of poetry in our non-mythological present. The poet of today—and by that I mean the poetic impetus in all of us today—is profoundly inhibited by the dearth of shared consciousness of myth. Our current motivating ideas are not myths but ideologies, lacking transcendental significance. This loss of myth-consciousness I believe to be the most devastating loss that humanity can suffer; for as I have argued, myth-consciousness is the bond that unites men both with one another and with the unplumbed Mystery from which mankind is sprung, and without reference to which the radical significance of things goes to pot. Now a world bereft of radical significance is not long tolerated; it leaves men radically unstable, so that they will seize at any myth or pseudo-myth that is offered. There have been ages of scepticism in the past, and they have always succumbed in time to new periods of belief, sometimes of violent fanaticism. It appears to me historically probable that whether we like it or not, our own present philosophy of liberal democratic scepticism will be succeeded within the next generation, perhaps sooner, by a recrudescence of myth-consciousness in America, although we can only dimly foresee what form that consciousness will take. Probably it will include a strong consciousness of America and the American destiny, but the important question is whether it will include something more—whether America will become a genuine symbol or merely a dogma. The myth of the nation must be shot through with a larger, trans-cendent mythological consciousness, or it lacks sanctity and in the long run will not satisfy the deeper human cravings. But we have to reckon with the possibility that this development will not take place at once. History does serve human needs, but not on the table d'hôte plan; the preparations are slow and we have to expect a certain amount of bungling in the kitchen. Perhaps our immediate prospect is one of darkness, and waiting, and wholesale liquidation of much that has seemed indispensable to us, spiritual as well as material. We do not know what is to come; we can only try to learn what we must do. I suspect we must be like starving men who keep a little from their meager store to plant it in the ground for a future crop. The poetry of our time doesn't matter much, it is a last echo of something important that was alive long ago. What matters is the myth-consciousness of the next generations, the spiritual seed that we plant in our children; their loves and insights and incubating sense of significant community. On that depend the possibilities of future greatness—in poetry and in everything else.

Psychology and Form

KENNETH BURKE

It is not until the fourth scene of the first act that Hamlet confronts the ghost of his father. As soon as the situation has been made clear, the audience has been, consciously or unconsciously, waiting for this ghost to appear, while in the fourth scene this moment has been definitely promised. For earlier in the play Hamlet had arranged to come to the platform at night with Horatio to meet the ghost, and it is now night, he is with Horatio and Marcellus, and they are standing on the platform. Hamlet asks Horatio the hour.

> Hor. I think it lacks of twelve.
>
> Mar. No, it is struck.
>
> Hor. Indeed? I heard it not: then it draws near the season
> Wherein the spirit held his wont to walk.

Promptly hereafter there is a sound off-stage. "A flourish of trumpets, and ordnance shot off within." Hamlet's friends have established the hour as twelve. It is time for the ghost. Sounds off-stage, and of course it is not the ghost. It is, rather, the sound of the king's carousal, for the king "keeps wassail." A tricky and useful detail. We have been waiting for a ghost, and get, startlingly, a blare of trumpets. And, once the trumpets are silent, we feel how desolate are these three men waiting for a ghost, on a bare "platform," feel it by this sudden juxtaposition of an imagined scene of lights and merriment. But the trumpets announcing a carousal have suggested a subject of conversation. In the darkness Hamlet discusses the excessive drinking of his countrymen. He points out that it tends to harm their reputation abroad, since, he argues, this one showy vice makes their virtues "in the general censure take corruption." And for this

267

reason, although he himself is a native of this place, he does not approve of the custom. Indeed, there in the gloom he is talking very intelligently on these matters, and Horatio answers, "Look, my Lord, it comes." All this time we had been waiting for a ghost, and it comes at the one moment which was not pointing towards it. This ghost, so assiduously prepared for, is yet a surprise. And now that the ghost has come, we are waiting for something further. Program: a speech from Hamlet. Hamlet must confront the ghost. Here again Shakespeare can feed well upon the use of contrast for his effects. Hamlet has just been talking in a sober, rather argumentative manner—but now the flood-gates are un-loosed:

> Angels and ministers of grace defend us!
> Be thou a spirit of health or goblin damn'd,
> Bring with thee airs from heaven or blasts from hell . . .

and the transition from the matter-of-fact to the grandiose, the full-throated and full-voweled, is a second burst of trumpets, perhaps more effective than the first, since it is the rich fulfillment of a promise. Yet this satisfaction in turn becomes an allurement, an itch for further developments. At first desiring solely to see Hamlet confront the ghost, we now want Hamlet to learn from the ghost the details of the murder—which are, however, with shrewdness and husbandry, reserved for "Scene V—Another part of the Platform."

I have gone into this scene at some length, since it illustrates so perfectly the relationship between psychology and form, and so aptly indicates how the one is to be defined in terms of the other. That is, the psychology here is not the psychology of the *hero,* but the psychology of the *audience.* And by that distinction, form would be the psychology of the audience. Or, seen from another angle, form is the creation of an appetite in the mind of the auditor, and the adequate satisfying of that appetite. This satisfaction—so complicated is the human mechanism—at times involves a temporary set of frustrations, but in the end these frustrations prove to be simply a more involved kind of satisfaction, and furthermore serve to make the satisfaction of fulfillment more intense. If, in a work of art, the poet says something, let us say, about a meeting, writes in such a way that we desire to observe that meeting, and then, if he places that meeting before us—that is form. While obviously, that is also the psychology of the audience, since it involves desires and their appeasements.

The seeming breach between form and subject-matter, between technique and psychology, which has taken place in the last century is the result, it seems to me, of scientific criteria being unconsciously introduced into matters of purely esthetic judgment. The flourishing of science has been so vigorous that we have not yet had time to make a spiritual readjustment adequate to the changes in our resources of material and knowledge. There are disorders of the social system which are caused solely by our undigested wealth (the basic disorder being, perhaps, the phenomenon of overproduction: to remedy this, instead of having all workers employed on half time, we have half working full time and the other half idle, so that whereas overproduction could be the greatest reward of applied science, it has been, up to now, the most menacing condition our modern civilization has had to face). It would be absurd to suppose that such social disorders would not be paralleled by disorders of culture and taste, especially since science is so pronouncedly a spiritual factor. So that we are, owing to the sudden wealth science has thrown upon us, all *nouveaux-riches* in matters of culture, and most poignantly in that field where lack of native firmness is most readily exposed, in matters of esthetic judgment.

One of the most striking derangements of taste which science has temporarily thrown upon us involves the understanding of psychology in art. Psychology has become a body of information (which is precisely what psychology in science should be, or must be). And similarly, in art, we tend to look for psychology as the purveying of information. Thus, a contemporary writer has objected to Joyce's *Ulysses* on the ground that there are more psychoanalytic data available in Freud. (How much more drastically he might, by the same system, have destroyed Homer's *Odyssey*!) To his objection it was answered that one might, similarly, denounce Cézanne's trees in favor of state forestry bulletins. Yet are not Cézanne's landscapes themselves tainted with the psychology of information? Has he not, by perception, *pointed out* how one object lies against another, *indicated* what takes place between two colors (which is the psychology of science, and is less successful in the medium of art than in that of science, since in art such processes are at best implicit, whereas in science they are so readily made explicit)? Is Cézanne not, to that extent, a state forestry bulletin, except that he tells what goes on in the eye instead of on the tree? And do not the true values of his work lie elsewhere—and precisely in what I distinguish as the psychology of form?

Thus, the great influx of information has led the artist also to lay his emphasis on the giving of information—with the result that art tends more and more to substitute the psychology of the hero (the subject) for the psychology of the audience. Under such an attitude, when form is preserved it is preserved as an annex, a luxury, or, as some feel, a downright affectation. It remains, though sluggish, like the human appendix, for occasional demands are still made upon it; but its true vigor is gone, since it is no longer organically required. Proposition: The hypertrophy of the psychology of information is accompanied by the corresponding atrophy of the psychology of form.

In information, the matter is intrinsically interesting. And by intrinsically interesting I do not necessarily mean intrinsically valuable, as witness the intrinsic interest of backyard gossip or the most casual newspaper items. In art, at least the art of the great ages (Aeschlus, Shakespeare, Racine), the matter is interesting by means of an extrinsic use, a function. Consider, for instance, the speech of Mark Antony, the "Brutus is an honourable man." Imagine in the same place a very competently developed thesis on human conduct, with statistics, intelligence tests, definitions; imagine it as the finest thing of the sort ever written, and as really being at the roots of an understanding of Brutus. Obviously, the play would simply stop until Antony had finished. For in the case of Antony's speech, the value lies in the fact that his words are shaping the future of the audience's desires, not the desires of the Roman populace, but the desires of the pit. This is the psychology of form as distinguished from the psychology of information.

The distinction is, of course, absolutely true only in its nonexistent extremes. Hamlet's advice to the players, for instance, has little of the quality which distinguishes Antony's speech. It is, rather, intrinsically interesting, although one could very easily prove how the play would benefit by some such delay at this point, and that anything which made this delay possible without violating the consistency of the subject would have, in this, its formal justification. It would, furthermore, be absurd to rule intrinsic interest out of literature. I wish simply to have it restored to its properly minor position, seen as merely one out of many possible elements of style. Goethe's prose, often poorly imagined or neutral in its line-for-line texture, especially in the treatment of romantic episode—perhaps he felt that the romantic episode in itself was enough?—is strengthened into a style possessing affirmative virtues by his rich use of aphorism. But this is, after all, but one of many possible facets of appeal. In some places, notably in *Wilhelm Meisters Lehrjahre* when Wilhelm's friends disclose the documents they have been collecting about his life unbeknown to him, the aphorisms are almost rousing in their efficacy, since they involve the story. But as a rule the appeal of aphorism is intrinsic: that is, it satisfies without being functionally related to the context.[1] Also, to return to the matter of Hamlet, it must be observed that the style in this passage is no mere "information-giving" style; in its alacrity, its development, it really makes this one fragment into a kind of miniature plot.

One reason why music can stand repetition so much more sturdily than correspondingly good prose is because music, of all the arts, is by its nature least suited to the psychology of information, and has remained closer to the psychology of form. Here form cannot atrophy. Every dissonant chord cries for its solution, and whether the musician resolves or refuses to resolve this dissonance into the chord which the body cries for, he is dealing in human appetites. Correspondingly good prose, however, more prone to the temptations of pure information, cannot so much bear repetition since the esthetic value of information is lost once that information is imparted. If one returns to such a work again it is purely because, in the chaos of modern life, he has been able to forget it. With a desire, on the other hand, its recovery is as agreeable as its discovery. One can memorize the dialogue between Hamlet and Guildenstern, where Hamlet gives Guildenstern the pipe to play on. For, once the speech is known, its repetition adds a new element to compensate for the loss of novelty. We cannot take a recurrent pleasure in the new (in information) but we can in the natural (in form). Already, at the moment when Hamlet is holding out the pipe to Guildenstern and asking him to play upon it, we "gloat over" Hamlet's

[1] Similarly, the epigram of Racine is "pure art," because it usually serves to formulate or clarify some situation within the play itself. In Goethe the epigram is most often of independent validity, as in *Die Wahlverwandtschaften,* where the ideas of Ottilie's diary are obviously carried over boldly from the author's notebook. In Shakespeare we have the union of extrinsic and intrinsic epigram, the epigram growing out of its context and yet valuable independent of its context.

triumphal descent upon Guildenstern, when, after Guildenstern has, under increasing embarrassment, protested three times that he cannot play the instrument, Hamlet launches the retort for which all this was preparation:

> Why, look you now, how unworthy a thing you make of me. You would play upon me, you would seem to know my stops; you would pluck out the heart of my mystery; you would sound me from my lowest note to the top of my compass; and there is much music, excellent voice, in this little organ, yet cannot you make it speak. 'Sblood, do you think I am easier to be played on than a pipe? Call me what instrument you will, though you can fret me, you cannot play upon me.[2]

In the opening lines we hear the promise of the close, and thus feel the emotional curve more keenly than at first reading. Whereas in most modern art this element is underemphasized. It gives us the gossip of a plot, a plot which too often has for its value the mere fact that we do not know its outcome.[3]

Music, then, fitted less than any other art for imparting information, deals minutely in frustrations and fulfillments of desire,[4] and for that reason more often gives us those curves of emotion which, because they are natural, can bear repetition without loss. It is for this reason that music, like folk tales, is most capable of lulling us to sleep. A lullaby is a melody which comes quickly to rest, where the obstacles are easily overcome—and this is precisely the parallel to those waking dreams of struggle and conquest which (especially during childhood) we permit ourselves when falling asleep or when trying to induce sleep. Folk tales are just such waking dreams. Thus it is right that art should be called a "waking dream." The only difficulty with this definition (indicated by Charles Baudouin in his *Psychoanalysis and Aesthetics,* a very valuable study of Verhaeren) is that today we understand it to mean art as a waking dream for the artist. Modern criticism, and psychoanalysis in particular, is too prone to define the essence of art in terms of the artist's weaknesses. It is, rather, the audience which dreams, while the artist oversees the conditions which determine this dream. He is the manipulator of blood, brains, heart, and bowels which, while we sleep, dictate the mold of our desires. This is, of course, the real meaning of artistic felicity—an exaltation at the correctness

[2] One might indicate still further appropriateness here. As Hamlet finishes his speech, Polonius enters, and Hamlet turns to him, "God bless you, sir!" Thus, the plot is continued (for Polonius is always the promise of action) and a full stop is avoided: the embarrassment laid upon Rosencrantz and Guildenstern is not laid upon the audience.

[3] Yet modern music has gone far in the attempt to renounce this aspect of itself. Its dissonances become static, demanding no particular resolution. And whereas an unfinished modulation by a classic musician occasions positive dissatisfaction, the refusal to resolve a dissonance in modern music does not dissatisfy us, but irritates or stimulates. Thus, "energy" takes the place of style.

[4] Suspense is the least complex kind of anticipation, as surprise is the least complex kind of fulfillment.

of the procedure, so that we enjoy the steady march of doom in a Racinian tragedy with exactly the same equipment as that which produces our delight with Benedick's "Peace! I'll stop your mouth. (*Kisses her*)" which terminates the imbroglio of *Much Ado About Nothing*.

The methods of maintaining interest which are most natural to the psychology of information (as it is applied to works of pure art) are surprise and suspense. The method most natural to the psychology of form is eloquence. For this reason the great ages of Aeschylus, Shakespeare, and Racine, dealing as they did with material which was more or less a matter of common knowledge so that the broad outlines of the plot were known in advance (while it is the broad outlines which are usually exploited to secure surprise and suspense), developed formal excellence, or eloquence, as the basis of appeal in their work.

Not that there is any difference in kind between the classic method and the method of the cheapest contemporary melodrama. The drama, more than any other form, must never lose sight of its audience: here the failure to satisfy the proper requirements is most disastrous. And since certain contemporary work is successful, it follows that rudimentary laws of composition are being complied with. The distinction is one of intensity rather than of kind. The contemporary audience hears the lines of a play or novel with the same equipment as it brings to reading the lines of its daily paper. It is content to have facts placed before it in some more or less adequate sequence. Eloquence is the minimizing of this interest in fact, *per se,* so that the "more or less adequate sequence" of their presentation must be relied on to a much greater extent. Thus, those elements of surprise and suspense are subtilized, carried down into the writing of a line or a sentence, until in all its smallest details the work bristles with disclosures, contrasts, restatements with a difference, ellipses, images, aphorism, volume, sound-values, in short all that complex wealth of minutiae which in their line-for-line aspect we call style and in their broader outlines we call form.

As a striking instance of a modern play with potentialities in which the intensity of eloquence is missing, I might cite a recent success, Capek's *R. U. R.* Here, in a melodrama which was often astonishing in the rightness of its technical procedure, when the author was finished he had written nothing but the scenario for a play by Shakespeare. It was a play in which the author produced time and again the opportunity, the demand, for eloquence, only to move on. (At other times, the most successful moments, he utilized the modern discovery of silence, writing moments wherein words could not possibly serve but to detract from the effect: this we might call the "flowering" of information.) The Adam and Even scene of the last act, a "commission" which the Shakespeare of the comedies would have loved to fill, was in the verbal barrenness of Capek's play something shameless to the point of blushing. The Robot, turned human, prompted by the dawn of love to see his first sunrise, or hear the first bird-call, and forced merely to say, "Oh, see the sunrise," or, "Hear the pretty birds"—here one could do nothing but wring his hands at the absence of that esthetic mold which produced the overslung "speeches" of *Romeo and Juliet*.

Suspense is the concern over the possible outcome of some specific detail of plot rather than for general qualities. Thus, "Will A marry B or C?" is suspense.

In *Macbeth,* the turn from the murder scene to the porter scene is a much less literal channel of development. Here the presence of one quality calls forth the demand for another, rather than one tangible incident of plot awaking an interest in some other possible tangible incident of plot. To illustrate more fully, if an author managed over a certain number of his pages to produce a feeling of sultriness, or oppression, in the reader, this would unconsciously awaken in the reader the desire for a cold, fresh north wind—and thus some aspect of a north wind would be effective if called forth by some aspect of stuffiness. A good example of this is to be found in a contemporary poem, T. S. Eliot's *The Waste Land,* where the vulgar, oppressively trivial conversation in the public house calls forth in the poet a memory of a line from Shakespeare. These slobs in a public house, after a desolately low-visioned conversation, are now forced by closing time to leave the saloon. They say good-night. And suddenly the poet, feeling his release, drops into another good-night, a good-night with *désinvolture,* a good-night out of what was, within the conditions of the poem at least, a graceful and irrecoverable past.

> "Well that Sunday Albert was home, they had a hot gammon,
>   And they asked me in to dinner, to get the beauty of it hot"—
>   [at this point the bartender interrupts: it is closing time]
> "Goonight Bill. Goonight Lou. Goonight May. Goonight. Ta ta.
>   Goonight. Goonight.
>   Good-night, ladies, good-night, sweet ladies, good-night, good-night."

There is much more to be said on these lines, which I have shortened somewhat in quotation to make my issue clearer. But I simply wish to point out here that this transition is a bold juxtaposition of one quality created by another, an association in ideas which, if not logical, is nevertheless emotionally natural. In the case of *Macbeth,* similarly, it would be absurd to say that the audience, after the murder scene, wants a porter scene. But the audience does want the quality which this porter particularizes. The dramatist might, conceivably, have introduced some entirely different character or event in this place, provided only that the event produced the same quality of relationship and contrast (grotesque seriousness followed by grotesque buffoonery). One of the most beautiful and satisfactory "forms" of this sort is to be found in Baudelaire's "Femmes Damnées," where the poet, after describing the business of a Lesbian seduction, turns to the full oratory of his apostrophe:

> *Descendez, descendez, lamentables victimes,*
> *Descendez le chemin de l'enfer éternel . . .*

while the stylistic efficacy of this transition contains a richness which transcends all moral (or unmoral) sophistication: the efficacy of appropriateness, of exactly the natural curve in treatment. Here is morality even for the godless, since it is a morality of art, being justified, if for no other reason, by its paralleling of that staleness, that disquieting loss of purpose, which must have followed the procedure of the two characters, the *femmes damnées* themselves, a remorse which, perhaps only physical in its origin, nevertheless becomes psychic.[5]

But to return, we have made three terms synonymous: form, psychology, and eloquence. And eloquence thereby becomes the essence of art, while pity, tragedy, sweetness, humor, in short all the emotions which we experience in life proper, as non-artists, are simply the material on which eloquence may feed. The arousing of pity, for instance, is not the central purpose of art, although it may be an adjunct of artistic effectiveness. One can feel pity much more keenly at the sight of some actual misfortune—and it would be a great mistake to see art merely as a weak representation of some actual experience.[6] That artists today are content to write under such an esthetic accounts in part for the inferior position which art holds in the community. Art, at least in the great periods when it has flowered, was the conversion, or transcendence, of emotion into eloquence, and was thus a factor added to life. I am reminded of St. Augustine's caricature of the theatre: that whereas we do not dare to wish people unhappy, we do want to feel sorry for them, and therefore turn to plays so that we can feel sorry although no real misery is involved. One might apply the parallel interpretation to the modern delight in happy endings, and say that we turn to art to indulge our humanitarianism in a well-wishing which we do not permit ourselves towards our actual neighbors. Surely the catharsis of art is more complicated than this, and more reputable.

Eloquence itself, as I hope to have established in the instance from *Hamlet* which I have analyzed, is no mere plaster added to a framework of more stable qualities. Eloquence is simply the end of art, and is thus its essence. Even the poorest is eloquent, but in a poor way, with less intensity, until this aspect is obscured by others fattening upon its leanness. Eloquence is not showiness; it is, rather, the result of that desire in the artist to make a work perfect by adapting it in every minute detail to the racial appetites.

The distinction between the psychology of information and the psychology of form involves a definition of esthetic truth. It is here precisely, to combat the deflection which the strength of science has caused to our tastes, that we must examine the essential breach between scientific and artistic truth. Truth in art is not the discovery of facts, not an addition to human knowledge in the scientific sense of the word.[7] It is, rather, the exercise of human propriety, the

[5] As another aspect of the same subject, I could cite many examples from the fairy tale. Consider, for instance, when the hero is to spend the night in a bewitched castle. Obviously, as darkness descends, weird adventures must befall him. His bed rides him through the castle; two halves of a man challenge him to a game of nine-pins played with thigh bones and skulls. Or entirely different incidents may serve instead of these. The quality comes first, the particularization follows.

[6] Could not the Greek public's resistance to Euripides be accounted for in the fact that he, of the three writers of Greek tragedy, betrayed his art, was guilty of esthetic impiety, in that he paid more attention to the arousing of emotion *per se* than to the sublimation of emotion into eloquence?

[7] One of the most striking examples of the encroachment of scientific truth into art is the doctrine of "truth by distortion," whereby one aspect of an object is suppressed the better to emphasize some other aspect; this is, obviously, an attempt to *indicate* by art some fact of knowledge, to make some implicit aspect of an object as explicit as one can by means of the comparatively dumb method of art (dumb, that is, as compared to the perfect ease with which science

formulation of symbols which rigidify our sense of poise and rhythm. Artistic truth is the externalization of taste.[8] I sometimes wonder, for instance, whether the "artificial" speech of John Lyly might perhaps be "truer" than the revelations of Dostoevsky. Certainly at its best, in its feeling for a statement which returns upon itself, which attempts the systole to a diastole, it *could* be much truer than Dostoevsky.[9] And if it is not, it fails not through a mistake of Lyly's esthetic, but because Lyly was a man poor in character whereas Dostoevsky was rich and complex. When Swift, making the women of Brobdingnag enormous, deduces from this discrepancy between their size and Gulliver's that Gulliver could sit astride their nipples, he has written something which is esthetically true, which is, if I may be pardoned, profoundly "proper," as correct in its Euclidean deduction as any corollary in geometry. Given the companions of Ulysses in the cave of Polyphemus, it is true that they would escape clinging to the bellies of the herd let out to pasture. St. Ambrose, detailing the habits of God's creatures, and drawing from them moral maxims for the good of mankind, St. Ambrose in his limping natural history rich in scientific inaccuracies that are at the very heart of emotional rightness, St. Ambrose writes: "Of night-birds, especially the nightingale which hatches her eggs by song; of the owl, the bat, and the cock at cock-crow; in what these may apply to the guidance of our habits," and in the sheer rightness of that program there is the truth of art. In introducing this talk of night-birds, after many pages devoted to other of God's creatures, he says:

> What now! While we have been talking, you will notice how the birds of night have already started fluttering about you, and, in this same fact of warning us to leave off with our discussion, suggest thereby a further to pic—

and this seems to me to contain the best wisdom of which the human frame is

---

can indicate its discoveries). Yet science has already made discoveries in the realm of this "factual truth," this "truth by distortion" which must put to shame any artist who relies on such matter for his effects. Consider, for instance, the motion-picture of a man vaulting. By photographing this process very rapidly, and running the reel very slowly, one has upon the screen the most striking set of factual truths to aid in our understanding of an athlete vaulting. Here, at our leisure, we can observe the contortions of four legs, a head, and a butt. This squirming thing we saw upon the screen showed us an infinity of factual truths anent the balances of an athlete vaulting. We can, from this, observe the marvelous system of balancing which the body provides for itself in the adjustments of moving. Yet, so far as the esthetic truth is concerned, this on the screen was not an athlete, but a squirming thing, a horror, displaying every fact of vaulting except the exhilaration of the act itself.

[8] The procedure of science involves the elimination of taste, employing as a substitute the corrective norm of a pragmatic test, the empirical experiment, which is entirely intellectual. Those who oppose the "intellectualism" of critics like Matthew Arnold are involved in an hilarious blunder, for Arnold's entire approach to the appreciation of art is through delicacies of taste intensified to the extent almost of squeamishness.

[9] As for instance, the "conceit" of Endymion's awakening, when he forgets his own name, yet recalls that of his beloved.

capable, an address, a discourse, which can make our material life seem blatant almost to the point of despair. And when the cock crows, and the thief abandons his traps, and the sun lights up, and we are in every way called back to God by the well-meaning admonition of this bird, here the very blindnesses of religion become the deepest truths of art.

No! in Thunder

LESLIE FIEDLER

THAT the practice of any art at any time is essentially a moral activity I have always believed; indeed, I do not know how to begin to make a book or talk about one without moral commitment. Yet for a long time I tried to keep this secret from myself as well as from others, since in the critical world in which I grew up, a "moralistic approach" to literature was considered not only indecent but faintly comic. Most of my best literary friends, at any rate, considered it strategically advisable to speak of novels and poems *purely* (the adverb is theirs) in terms of diction, structure and point of view, remaining safely inside the realm of the formal. But an author's choice of—or a critic's preference for—one point of view, or type of diction, or kind of structure, or even his emphasis on one of these elements at the expense of the others, involves a judgment of the experience he is rendering; and such a judgment is, implicitly at least, a moral one.

One of the special strengths of modern fiction has been its awareness of the moral dimension of form; and the seminal greatness of Flaubert lies in his willingness to entrust judgment primarily to style: to transform style, in effect, from a social grace to a tool of ethical analysis. The author of *Madame Bovary* seldom comments directly on the social concerns which most deeply vex him; he has, indeed, an almost fanatic resolve *not* to admonish or preach, but his style is his surrogate in this regard. And his style judges—judges Emma and Homais, the clichés of Romanticism and Revolution, the formlessness and falsity of bourgeois life. By the same token, that style judges and condemns, as all serious style continues to judge and condemn, the literature of the market-place and those misguided books dedicated to antistyle.

There are, of course, certain counterfeits of style, quite unlike Flaubert's, which are symptoms of the decay of their world rather than judgments of it; for there can be no neutrality in the area of technique. The form of a book represents either a moral critique of man and society, or a moral surrender. The pseudo-styles—which are called, a little misleadingly, "naturalist" and which have been practiced from the time of Émile Zola to that of James Jones —have represented such capitulations before the collapse of discrimination and sensitivity in the world around them; even as earlier Scott's manly carelessness and Dickens' hasty improvisations represented a retreat from moral engagement, and the ecstatic schoolgirl antistyle of Jack Kerouac projects a more recent sort of cowardice. Such writers as Zola, Jones, and Kerouac are guilty not only of moral weakness but of hypocrisy as well, for they proffer their sloppiness and their submission to the decay of language as tokens of their sincerity and belongingness. To seem "one of the boys" is especially an American temptation, eternally offered and eternally accepted. But it is not only the principled antistylists, populist or Beat, who stand condemned in the court of high art for flagrant immorality, an immorality of form which all their avowed (and guilt-compelled) dedication to quite moral ideas and causes cannot mitigate. Those responsible for books like *Exodus,* or *Advise and Consent,* or whatever improbable contender is currently fighting its way up the best-seller lists, must also be adjudged guilty; since ignorance is no excuse, and good will merely aggravates the crime.

In the realm of fiction, to be inept, whether unwittingly or on purpose, is the single unforgivable sin. To be inept is to lie; and for this, time and the critics grant no pardon. Yet the contemporary audience forgives the liar in art, even adulates him. It knows he is lying, but it needs his lies. In our Do-It-Yourself Age, when no one can really do anything for himself unless provided a kit and instructions, men are plagued by the failure of self-deceit itself, afflicted with a fatal incapacity to believe themselves happy. If happiness is, as Swift insisted, the faculty of being well-deceived, most men can no longer achieve it on their own. They must be lied to every day, and they are willing to pay well for the service.

Our culture is organized around the satisfaction of this demand, and the moral artist, who is the truthteller, is subject (not invariably, but with distressing frequency) to one of two indignities, the first of which is called success, the second failure. Either he is admired, like Faulkner, for the wrong reasons: bought and unread because he is a living "classic" (in the United States, everything is speeded up to a bewildering tempo), his works posthumous before he is laid in the grave; or he is even more enthusiastically bought and *mis*read— like Pasternak, whose *Doctor Zhivago* became the very symbol of being one up on the Russians, or like Nabokov and D. H. Lawrence, the happy authors of once-banned books! Or the moral artist may be condemned out of hand, like Pasternak in Russia or Lawrence in the United States (until only the other day).

The customary charge leveled at the serious writer, until he is ripe for the even more deadly one of being a classic, is that of having written a dirty book. The Russians apparently believe this of all successful American writers who do not sympathize with Soviet objectives; but ironically, the charge is also believed in America of many of the same authors. It is, indeed, part of what has almost assumed the status of a ritual—the standard initiation of the truthteller into the culture of his country, inflicted at the moment when his truth still hurts. One is not startled, perhaps, to discover that Walt Whitman was once called "the dirtiest beast of the age," but it is a little disconcerting to learn that Hawthorne's *The Scarlet Letter* was accused of representing "the beginning of the era of French immorality" in American letters.

Yet it will not do to ignore the difference in the level of hysteria with which such charges were leveled at serious art one hundred years ago and that with which they were made of the first great books in the "modern" tradition at the point when the first of the Great Wars was about to begin. Whatever offense great art has always given and given with particular effect in America seems to have been compounded when, in what is still called, after nearly fifty years, "modern art," that offense was confessed in nonconventional form. Apparently the common man can more easily forgive an attack on home and mother than a flagrant disregard for harmony, or punctuation, or representation. Perhaps it is simply because technical offenses are less easy to overlook or to cancel out by misreading.

I have a clear memory of myself at fourteen or fifteen, struggling for an education in the public libraries of Newark, New Jersey, and having to fight to get Joyce's *A Portrait of the Artist as a Young Man* out of a locked room where it was kept with other dangerous material. Proust's *Remembrance of Things Past* was on the open shelves, but it was no easy matter to get it past the vigilance of a certain librarian who, in her spare time, went through the photography magazines stamping all female nudes three times with the official library stamp (to keep, I suppose, the minds of adolescents pure) and who regarded me as a special challenge. This experience has always seemed to me an archetypal one, my personal myth of The Intellectual Life as Moral Combat; for certainly (to a temperament for which, and in a time when, struggle seemed as necessary as eating) the library became for me an arena in which my morality was pitted against theirs in a war to end all wars! It was not dirty books I was after, I wanted to protest; it was . . . But I did not know how to explain what it was I sought.

Only a long time afterward did I realize that I had been completely misled by the rationalizations of the guardians of the library, that it was not really the "dirtiness," the frank sexuality, of certain novels that irked the censors, but something quite different. Best sellers—in our country at least—have always been books which exploit sex as far as (and a little farther than) contemporary taboos will permit. From *The Monks of Monk Hall* to *Peyton Place* or the latest paperback by Richard S. Prather, the really popular book has talked of sex on the level of broad suggestion; it has spoken the last common language bearing on the last link (as Moravia has argued) between us and the world of nature. It seems to me now that what must be insisted upon is that even a good book can be a popular success if it can be thought of as dirty, like Nabokov's *Lolita* and Faulkner's *Sanctuary*.

No, the problem of the nonacceptance of serious fiction lies elsewhere: in the fact that *to fulfil its essential moral obligation, such fiction must be negative.* There is a dim sense of this in the popular mind, reflected in the over-the-bridge-table charge that certain great books, whatever their merits, are too "morbid" and responded to by the publishers' defensive assurances on the book jackets: "But beneath the shattering events of that book . . . lies a passionate affirmation" or "This is a book of great themes, of life, death and regeneration, of the dignity and triumph of man." Like the more particular religious reassurances of another age, these vaguely pious assertions are rooted in a profound distrust of art itself; and before them I am moved to resentment and anger. I can never read one without remembering a favorite anecdote of my old teacher, William Ellery Leonard, about how, one night in an inn, he had to share a bed with a man whom he had never met before. He felt no qualms until his bedmate kneeled down beside the bed to pray. "At that point," he liked to say, "I grabbed my wallet and ran!" So I before the book whose jacket assures me that the author is committed to affirmation, or love, or a belief in the dignity of man.

Insofar as a work of art is, as art, successful, it performs a negative critical function; for the irony of art in the human situation lies in this: that man—or better, some men—are capable of achieving in works of art a coherence, a unity, a balance, a satisfaction of conflicting impulses which they cannot (but which they desperately long to) achieve in love, family relations, politics. Yet works of art are *about* love, family relations, politics, etc.; and to the degree that these radically imperfect human activities are represented in a perfectly articulated form, they are revealed in all their intolerable inadequacy. The image of man in art, however magnificently portrayed—indeed, precisely when it is most magnificently portrayed—is the image of a failure. There is no way out.

The self-conscious writer, realizing this irony, feels a demand to make explicit the essentially negative view of man implicit in his work insofar as it is art at all. He is driven to make his avowed attitudes and allegiances congruous with the meaning that his techniques cannot help declaring. Especially in recent times, when the obligations of self-consciousness are imposed on us with a rigor unheard of in the past, the writer becomes aware that his Muse is more like the *Daimon* of Socrates (who appeared only to say *No!*) or the God of Job than like any of those white-draped Ladies of the genteel mythologists. The spirit which speaks to him conveys no reassurances or positive revelations; only the terrible message that what his best friends—in newspaper offices, or the pulpit, or Congress—have been, like Job's, telling him is "the thing which is not right." And that spirit addresses him from the whirlwind, directing his attention from himself to those absurd beasts, the Behemoth and the Leviathan.

Demonic, terrible, and negative: this is the Modern Muse—"Bluff'd not a bit by drain-pipe, gasometers, artificial fertilizers," as Walt Whitman had the wit to see; but in his euphoric, comic vision the sense of terror is dissipated. It is to such a writer as James Joyce (who chose for his slogan the device of Satan himself: *Non serviam,* "I will not obey!") or to Henrik Ibsen (whose final words were "On the contrary . . .") or to Whitman's contemporary, Herman Melville, that we must turn for the decisive clue. The secret motto of *Moby Dick* was, Melville once confided: "I baptize you not in the name of the Father, the

Son and the Holy Ghost, but in the name of the Devil." Even better, perhaps, because less theatrically gothic, is the phrase Melville attributes to Bartleby the Scrivener, his portrait of the writer in the modern world—a phrase in which there is already implicit Bartleby's insanity and death: "I would prefer not to." Most explicit of all is the comment in a letter to Hawthorne, in which Melville pretends to describe the essence of his beloved contemporary's art, while in fact revealing the deepest sources of his own:

> There is the grand truth about Nathaniel Hawthorne. He says No! in Thunder; but the Devil himself cannot make him say *yes*. For all men who say *yes*, lie; and all men who say *no*,—why, they are in the happy condition of judicious, unencumbered travelers in Europe; they cross the frontiers into Eternity with nothing but a carpetbag,—that is to say, the Ego.

It pays to be clear about the nature of the "No! in Thunder," which is quite different from certain lesser *no*'s in which a thriving trade is always done: the *no* in newsprint, for instance, and the *no* on manifestoes and petitions. A play written in the 1950's about the Salem witch trials, or a novel of the same period celebrating the revolt of the Maccabees, despite their allegorical intentions, are cheats, exploitations of the pseudo-*no*. Even the attack on slavery in Twain's post-Civil War *Huckleberry Finn*—or, for that matter, in Mrs. Stowe's pre-Civil War *Uncle Tom's Cabin*—like an anti-McCarthyite fiction in the recent past or an excoriation of segregation right now, carry with them a certain air of presumptive self-satisfaction, an assurance of being justified by the future. They are Easy No's, merely disguised *yes*'s, in varying degrees sentimental and righteous; they are *yes*'s by anticipation, tomorrow's *yes*'s. The "No! in Thunder" remains a *no* forever; like the *no* implicit in the whole work of the Marquis de Sade, or the deeper *no* of *Huckleberry Finn*—Huck's *no* to womankind, the family, and organized society, which remains to this very day a *no*.

The "No! in Thunder" is never partisan; it infuriates Our Side as well as Theirs, reveals that all Sides are one, insofar as they are all yea-sayers and hence all liars. There is some evidence that the Hard No is being spoken when the writer seems a traitor to those whom he loves and who have conditioned his very way of responding to the world. When the writer says of precisely the cause that is dearest to him what is always and everywhere the truth about all causes—that it has been imperfectly conceived and inadequately represented, and that it is bound to be betrayed, consciously or unconsciously, by its leading spokesmen—we know that he is approaching an art of real seriousness if not of actual greatness. The thrill we all sense but hesitate to define for ourselves— the thrill of confronting a commitment to truth which transcends all partial allegiances—comes when Dante turns on Florence, Molière on the moderate man, de Sade on reason, Shaw on the socialists, Tolstoy on the reformers, Joyce on Ireland, Faulkner on the South, Graham Greene on the Catholics, Pasternak on the Russians, and Abraham Cahan or Nathanael West on the Jews. What people, what party, what church needs an enemy when it has a great writer in its ranks?

Unless he bites the hand that feeds him, the writer cannot live; and this those who would prefer him dead (so they can erect statues of him) can never understand. I remember Faulkner's coming once, rather improbably, to Missoula, Montana, and getting engaged in conversation with a lady Montanan, who cried out at one point, "Why can't So-and-so write a novel that would do for this part of the world what you've done for Mississippi? He *loves* Montana so!" To which Faulkner, of course, answered (maybe I only dreamed it; it all seems so pat), "To write well about some place, you've got to *hate* it." A pause, and then, "The way a man hates his own wife." But this is scandalous in a way with which the righteous cannot seem to come to terms. Not only the Great Audience but also, and even especially, the Little Elite Audiences demand of the writer its disavowal in the name of a kind of loyalty which is for him death. The first attack on me as a critic ever to appear was launched because I had made some rather drastic qualifying remarks about, I think, Thomas Mann— a small god, at any rate, of the avante garde church to which I was presumably applying for admission. "Aid and comfort to the enemy" was the implicit charge; but this charge the sayer of the Hard No must be willing to face; for he knows that the writer who rejects the negative obligation perishes even as he pleases, perishes though he please only a handful of the very best people— those, for instance, whom he has begun by admiring and whom he never ceases to admire.

It has not always been necessary for the writer to be aware of his denial; his work will do it for him anyhow, if it is honest work. Indeed, at certain periods in the past, it seemed almost better that the writer deceive himself as well as his contemporary audience about his intent: that Dickens, for example, believe himself to be glorifying the purity of woman and the simple heart of the child, while giving us in fact his mad, black-and-white nightmares, in which things live the life of men, and men perform with the lifeless rigidity of things. In the same way, Dostoevsky could think himself the apostle of a revived orthodoxy, and Samuel Richardson considered his essential task the defense of bourgeois virtue. But these days the writer cannot afford to lose for an instant his sense of himself in opposition to the world; let him pretend, however briefly, that his *no* is a *yes,* and he will end up writing *A Fable* or *The Town,* travesties of his own best work.

Naturally, not all writers in our time accept the negative obligation; and, indeed, its rejection separates the purveyor of commodity-fiction from the serious artist in the novel. There are certain pseudo-novels which are, in fact, transitional stages on the way to becoming movies or substitutes for going to the movies; and these books are obliged to be cheerful, positive, affirmative: to sustain the belief in endurance, piety, hard work and a deliberately maintained blessed stupidity. Here is the giveaway! Nothing can, after all, be wholly positive; and even the most affirmative of subnovels (say, *Marjorie Morningstar*) must end by denying something: dirt, disorder, eccentricity, non-conformism, skepticism, intelligence—in short, the negative obligation itself! Conversely, the nay-saying writer is not wholly negative; he is in favor of one thing by definition: telling the truth (*Madame Bovary* will do as the counterexample) and accepting the tragic implications of that truth, the vision of an eternal gap between imagined order and actual chaos.

But it is not enough, in our time, for the serious writer to confess *in general* the inevitable discrepancy between dream and fact, between the best man can imagine and the best he can achieve. The artist must be willing specifically to comment on the defeat of a particular dream. The antiartist, on the other hand, incurs only the most general obligation; despite the particulars in which he apparently deals, he is in fact composing parables, pseudo-myths, to express not wonder and terror but sentimental reassurance. What life refuses, the anti-artist grants: the dying catcher hits a three bagger, and everyone loves him; the coward, at the last moment, finds the courage to fight the segregationist and his hired thugs; the girl in the office takes off her glasses and wins the heart of the boss's playboy son. That these are prefabricated, masturbatory dreams almost everyone (including, I suspect, the authors) would be prepared to admit, yet they do not stir in most of us the moral indignation we feel at the distribution of other habit-forming drugs. They seem more benign than marijuana, which is banned, or tranquilizers, which may soon be sharply regulated; because we accept the fantasies they promote as finally truer than those born of "pot" or happiness pills. Assuring us that man is OK, that men are OK, that we are all— despite our mistakes and the machinations of others—OK, they feed into (at least they do not contradict) the last widely held *Weltanschauung* of the West: the progressive and optimistic, rational and kindly dogma of liberal humanism.

Yet, as some of us are rather disturbedly aware, many if not most of the eminent writers of the twentieth century have found themselves in conflict with this dogma, not always *despite* its nobility, but often because of it. The fact that such otherwise ill-assorted writers as Shaw, Joyce, Faulkner, Yeats, Pound, Eliot, Wyndham Lewis, and Samuel Beckett are arrayed against the liberal tradition indicates that it represents for our age the belief against which the serious artist must define himself, the official "Yea!" to which he must say his private "Nay!" As earlier poets had to say "Nay!" to the fifth-century Greeks' belief that their world was really explicable in terms of the Homeric gods, or the Christians' assumption that their society was Christian, or the Enlightenment's conviction that its passion and politics were finally rational, so the artist today must deny the liberal view of the possibilities of man. But liberalism is essentially different from earlier official faiths, religious or secular, in that its ideal is "openness" rather than orthodoxy; and the writer striving toward the Hard No is likely to discover that his most ardent denial is met with a disconcerting "Yes, yes, though all the same . . ." or "I don't finally agree with you, of course, but still. . . ."

Nietzsche's assertion that God is dead once shook half the world, and Ibsen's attack on marriage left northern Europe trembling, but they find us merely confused or indifferent—or, as we say when confusion and indifference reach their highest pitch, "tolerant." Only an assault on tolerance itself is able to stir us as Goethe's assault on the ban against suicide once stirred his readers.

The very advocacy of adultery, which from the time of the troubadours to that of D. H. Lawrence possessed an almost magic potency to provoke, has now become fashionable and meaningless. The recent redemption of *Lady Chatterley's Lover* in the courts represents not a triumph of literary taste over taboo but a failure of the moral imagination; and Lillian Smith can suggest in her novel *One Hour*, an essentially middlebrow book, that an Episcopalian priest's moment of vision and truth comes when he is in bed with his friend's wife. Who can *épater la bourgeoisie* when the bourgeoisie regards even the grossest scandal as a test of its capacity for understanding and forgiveness?

Yet there is finally a liberal view of man, to deny which is to risk blasphemy: an image of the human situation which persists very like a dogma beneath the undogmatic "openness" of which contemporary society is so proud. This view sees man as the product of a perhaps unplanned but rationally ordered and rationally explicable universe, a product which science can explain, even as it can explain the world which conditions him. The first fictionists who accepted this view of man thought of themselves as protoscientists and of their books as scientific reports on how vice and virtue are produced in the great laboratory of society. Such books, with their blend of rationalism, determinism, and quasi-scientific objectivity, were variously hailed when they appeared as examples of Realism, Naturalism, Verism, etc.; and whatever the inadequacy of their styles, they performed in the beginning the essential function of art, the negative one of provocation and scandal. Novelists like Zola and de Maupassant—in America, even so belated a representative of the school as Dreiser—horrified the genteel by exposing the self-delusions of sentimental Christianity. They soon fell victim to the fallacy of imitative form (realism-naturalism did not *have* to eschew style, as the example of Flaubert should have made clear) and profferred antistyle as evidence of their honesty. But even their very bad writing served temporarily a good cause, exposing the pretensions of academic rhetoric.

Purveyors of the old realistic article still circulate among us (James T. Farrell, for instance, and Nelson Algren), but they tell no truths that are not clichés, and they give no valuable offense. Indeed, they have become indistinguishable from the producers of chic Italian movies and from TV entertainers like Paddy Chayefsky—second-rate artists, purveyors of the scandal of the day before yesterday. The day is gone when the tradition of realism-naturalism was so deeply accepted as *the* mode of serious literature that a mannered and artificial stylist like Hemingway, or an exploiter of backwoods rhetoric and gothic nightmare like Faulkner, had to pretend to be a "naturalist" in order to seem respectable. In the first place, realism-naturalism has become an academy itself, sustaining a triumphant orthodoxy instead of challenging one; and meanwhile certain contraband, smuggled into the presumably objective laboratory report from the beginning, has come to seem more and more essential: political propaganda, heavy-handed symbolism, righteous pornography, and sentimentality.

The latter two especially have assumed a disheartening importance in the standard subforms of post-realism, first clearly defined in the United States in the 1930's: the Popular Front Novel, on the one hand, and Regionalist or

Protest Pornography on the other. John Steinbeck is the father of the first, having established in *The Grapes of Wrath* the prototype of the pious tract disguised as a sociological report, in which the cruel exploiters of labor are contrasted with simple and kindly men who give candy to children, and women of the people who offer their swollen breasts to the starving unemployed. Erskine Caldwell is the founder of the other, having created in *Tobacco Road* a genre capable of providing all the forbidden thrills of a peep show together with the conscientious satisfaction of deploring the state of the (more exotic) poor. It is hard to remember that Caldwell was considered a serious "proletarian" writer before he became a paperback best seller; one reads with surprise the accounts of his current reception in places like Turkey, where he is still regarded as a pattern for "village literature." In this country, his example has occasioned lately only such bootleg high-school literature as Grace Metalious' *Peyton Place*.

Steinbeck's prototype, however, continues to provide inspiration for the prevailing upper middlebrow form of our time: the serious pseudo-novel as practiced by certain not-quite-first-rate authors, committed equally to social conscience and success, and sure that these are not mutually exclusive goals. There is scarcely a moment these days when such authors of the Sentimental Liberal Protest Novel as Irwin Shaw, John Hersey, Budd Schulberg, and James Michener are not fighting for slots on the list of best sellers; since in our time left-of-center politics has become, by virtue of converting all its political content to sentiment, the reigning belief of the educated middle classes. In our genteel age, the class struggle has been translated from a confrontation of workers and bosses on the barricades to a contest between certain invisible or remote exploiters and all the rest of us—a contest in which more tears are shed than blood. The writer dedicated to portraying that struggle is no longer the man in the work shirt rolled to the elbow and open at the neck, but the man ashamed of his gray flannel suit—the searcher out and defender of Victims. For the image of man which possesses the genteel conscience is the image of the Victim: the snubbed Jew, the oppressed Negro, the starving Chinese, the atom-scarred Japanese, the betrayed Hungarian, the misunderstood paraplegic. For each Victim there is an appropriate book, a last indignity: *Gentlemen's Agreement, The Wall, The Bridge at Andau, The Last Pebble, One Hour.* Even the War Novel is recast in the prevailing form, captured, like *The Young Lions,* for piety, protest, and self-pity. In the end, we are left with the sense that wars are fought and armies organized (in representative platoons, with all minorities duly represented) so that the persecuted Jew or tormented Italian can shame his fellows by proving his unforeseen valor in the end.

Having only a single theme, of a rather simple-minded sort, the Sentimental Protestors are driven to eke it out, to conceal its stereo-typical bareness with up-to-date details and topical references. Their eyes are constantly on the headlines; and before the ink is dry, Michener and Hersey are already embarked for the scene of the latest indignity—or at least racing for their typewriters! It is a somewhat comic contest, with the whole reading world breathlessly waiting to discover who will get Little Rock first, who the Puerto Ricans. But what is the ersatz morality which sustains the protest fictionists, from Hersey-Shaw to Jones-Algren, from the soft-sell defenders of the dark-skinned peoples to the tough apologists for maximum security prisoners and minor hoods? It is the theory that the "Little Man" must be defended against the great and powerful, merely because he is little and "wants only to be let alone." Little! Surely no more degrading label has ever been invented for the exploited, none which has so combined pathos and condescension: the little Jew, the little shopkeeper, the little mixed-up kid, the bewildered little pusher of dope, the little pimp trying to establish himself against the competition of the big operators. . . . Against so abject a surrender to sentiment, one wants to cry out in the terrible words of the Old Testament, "Thou shalt not honor the poor man in his cause." But who could be heard over the voices of those storming their book counters for copies of *Exodus* and *Hawaii?*

What, then, of serious literature in our time? What counterimage of man does it proffer? Not, as so often in the past, an image of man struggling (and failing) to fulfill some revealed or inherited view of himself and his destiny; but of man learning that it is the struggle itself which is his definition. In a time when answers are the business of professional answer men (cheats and delusions carefully rehearsed before the show is put on the air), we have been forced to learn that our humanity is dependent not on the answers we hope for but on the questions we are able to ask. Like Job, we are granted no response except from the apparition which tells us it is time to be still, time to know that man is he who asks what man is. And like Melville's "unencumbered travelers," we must be prepared to leave our Encyclopedia Britannicas and Oxford English Dictionaries behind us, to cross the frontiers of Eternity with no baggage except the Ego. This the most serious writers of our day have taught us, insisting that we endure uncertainty, not as a stage on the way to knowledge, but as our essential condition. Now we see as through a glass darkly. There is no "then."

This view of man opens into a world not of melodrama but of ambiguity, not of the polemical but of the problematical. Saul Bellow's *The Victim,* for instance, will survive *Focus, Gentlemen's Agreement, The Professor's Umbrella,* and all the other earnest and humane tracts on anti-Semitism because, despite its title, it is not a protest novel at all. In Bellow's view, both Jew and gentile are simultaneously Victim and Victimizer; he renders their mutual torment in terms of their common desire to discover what it means to be human, their common need to *be* what is human. Our Jewishness or gentileness, Bellow leaves us feeling, is *given*: our humanity is what we must achieve. There is no more room for sentimentality in such a travesty of the liberal Jewish novel than there is in Robert Penn Warren's similar recasting of the political novel, or Malamud's of the novel about baseball, or James Baldwin's of the standard Negro novel, or Mary McCarthy's of fictional protests against the restriction of academic freedom. Reading, say, *All the King's Men,* one need only think of *The Last Hurrah* or *Advise and Consent*—or picking up *The Natural,* one need only recall Mark Harris' *Bang the Drum Slowly*—to realize how we ordinarily lust to be lied to, and how seldom we are granted the privilege of hearing the truth.

Ambiguity is the first resource of the serious novelist, tempted like all the rest of us to clichés of simplicity; but to say that the good novel is ambiguous is not to say that it is difficult and confused (this is optional), merely to insist that it is *about* moral ambiguity and that it cannot betray its theme. I distrust the writer who claims to know black from white, left from right, Hip from Square, Them from Us—no matter which of the sides he chooses. And I distrust especially the characters in whom he embodies his presumable insights. The protagonists of the best recent books are not self-righteous, long-suffering, diminished prigs, who want only to live in peace and are sure they know what peace is. From the most sympathetic to the least, they are troublemakers like their authors, who will not let the world rest until it acknowledges that they exist. We have by now quite a gallery of such types, including Joyce's insufferable Stephen, too stiff-necked to grant his mother's deathbed wish; Kafka's K., guilty as charged though no one knows quite what the charge is; Nathanael West's Miss Lonelyhearts, trying in vain to be the Christ in whom he does not believe; Ralph Ellison's Invisible Man, vainly striving to escape the myth of his color; and Faulkner's Popeye, counterfeiting manhood with a bloody corncob.

The contemporary novel through which such characters stalk—bringing harm to those around them, even as they court destruction for themselves—is terror-ridden, dreadful; but is not humorless. In the midst of Faulkner's grimmest book, *Sanctuary*, a couple of rustics play out a humorous scene in a whorehouse. West's bleakest novel is his funniest, *A Cool Million*, whose title comes from the "Old Saying": "John D. Rockefeller would give a cool million to have a stomach like yours." Kafka, we are told, used to laugh until the tears ran down his cheeks, reading aloud from *Amerika*. Joyce, one sometimes feels, would do anything for a laugh, and Beckett has thought of some things to do which even his master could not imagine; Bellow can be a clown; Mary McCarthy insists on compelling our titters in the midst of our deepest shame; and the British "Angries" have us guffawing like a pack of fools. In this sense, Mark Twain is the true ancestor of the modern writer, and his *Pudd'nhead Wilson* a storehouse of the sort of humor which is not dated by changes of fashion. "*October 12, the Discovery*. It was wonderful to find America, but it would have been more wonderful to miss it." This is our kind of joke, proper to a world in which we may all die laughing—as we like to say.

Such humor is not incompatible with negation, or even terror, for it is not party or factional humor, with which the *in*'s satirize the *out*'s, and the "normal" put the eccentric in their places. It is total humor, through which men laugh not at their foibles but at their essential selves. The vision of man shared by our greatest writers involves an appreciation of his absurdity, and the protagonists of our greatest books are finally neither comic nor tragic but absurd. To the modern writer, the distinction between comedy and tragedy seems as forced and irrelevant as that between hallucination and reality; his world partakes of both, and he would be hard put to it to say where one ends and the other begins. The conventional definitions of the comic and the tragic strike him as simplifications, falsifications of human life, appropriate to a less complex time. To insist that we regard man, even for the space of three acts or five, as *either* horrible or funny; to require us, through four or five hundred pages, *either* to laugh or to cry we find offensive in an age when we can scarcely conceive of wanting to do one without the other. For us, the great works of the past are those which occupy an intermediate position between comedy and tragedy: the *Bacchae* of Euripides, the *Misanthrope* of Molière, Shakespeare's *Measure for Measure*, Ibsen's *An Enemy of the People*, Twain's *Pudd'nhead Wilson*, and Melville's *The Confidence Man*. And the writers of our own time who we most admire—West, Faulkner, and Beckett, among others—pursue a third genre, which suggests that the ludicrous is the source of pity and terror, and that pity and terror themselves are the heart of the ludicrous.

The vision of the truly contemporary writer is that of a world not only absurd but also chaotic and fragmentary. He tries in his work to find techniques for representing a universe in which our perceptions overlap but do not coincide, in which we share chiefly a sense of loneliness: our alienation from whatever things finally are, as well as from other men's awareness of those things and of us. Rapid shifts in point of view; dislocations of syntax and logic; a vividness more like hallucination than photography; the use of parody and slapstick at moments of great seriousness; the exploitation of puns and of the vaudeville of dreams—these experiments characterize much of the best work of recent decades, from Joyce's *Ulysses* through Djuna Barnes's *Nightwood* to Wright Morris' *Field of Vision*, whose winning of the National Book Award so incensed the guardians of middlebrow standards. At the present moment, Morris is almost alone in the United States in his continuing devotion to the themes and techniques of the negative novel. (There is, to be sure, the young novelist John Barth, strangely ignored.) For we have been suffering a general loss of nerve, or a waning of talent, which has persuaded writers of such different origins and generations as Hemingway, Faulkner, Saul Bellow, and Mary McCarthy to pursue affirmation in the place of art—disconcerted, perhaps, as they pass from being ignored to relative degrees of fame and victimized by a perverse sort of *noblesse oblige.*

The unearned euphoria of *Henderson, the Rain King*; the shapeless piety of *A Fable*; the sentimental self-indulgence of *Across the River and into the Trees*; the maudlin falsity of *The Town*; the heavy-handed symbolism and religiosity of *The Old Man and the Sea*, destined from its inception for the pages of *Life*—such failures make over and over the point that the contemporary American writer can abjure negativism only if he is willing to sacrifice truth and art. For major novelists and minor, the pursuit of the positive means stylistic suicide. Language itself decays, and dialogue becomes travesty; character, stereotype; insight, sentiment. The Nobel Prize destined for high-school anthologies requires quite another talent from that demanded by the novel; and the abstract praise of love requires another voice from that which cries *No!* to the most noble temptations, the most defensible lies.

Yet one must not forget, in the face of their recent decline, the successes of Bellow and Hemingway and Faulkner: the terrible impact of *The Victim*, *The Sun Also Rises*, and *The Sound and the Fury*. The last, in particular, remains the exemplary American novel, perhaps the greatest work of fiction produced in the United States in the twentieth century. And it is no accident that its title comes from the bleakest passage in Shakespeare, or that its action begins inside the mind of an idiot. The point is insisted upon bluntly, almost too obviously: life is a tale told by an idiot, full of sound and fury, signifying nothing. Here is the ultimate negation, the Hard No pressed as far as it will go. Yet "nothing" is not quite Faulkner's last word, only the next to the last. In the end, the negativist is no nihilist, for he affirms the void. Having endured a vision of the meaninglessness of existence, he retreats neither into self-pity and aggrieved silence nor into a realm of beautiful lies. He chooses, rather, to render the absurdity which he perceives, to know it and make it known. To know and to render, however, mean to give form; and to give form is to provide the possibility of delight—a delight which does not deny horror but lives at its intolerable heart.

The Myth and Ritual Approach to Shakespearean Tragedy

HERBERT WEISINGER

* * * WHAT I want to do in this paper is to describe the myth and ritual approach to literature as I understand it and to show what new light it can throw on Shakespeare's tragedies, and presumably to illuminate them afresh. For the purposes of this analysis, I take the myth and ritual pattern as fundamental and anterior to tragedy, and I pass Shakespeare's tragedies over this pattern, as tracings over the original drawing, in order to reveal his changes, modifications, and alterations of it; that is to say, I try to distinguish the uniquely Shakespearean from the generally tragic. * * *

Certainly I am not the first to suggest such a correlation; on the contrary, many critics have seen the connection and have in fact gone beyond the tragedies to the later plays in an effort to prove that the pattern of rebirth and reconciliation is fundamental to virtually the whole of Shakespeare's plays. But, while the myth and ritual pattern so used makes, if I may say so, a Christian Olympian out of Shakespeare, it does so only at the expense of the myth and ritual pattern and of the substance of the plays themselves. It is my contention that while the last plays of Shakespeare do indeed carry forward the tragic pattern established in *Hamlet, Othello, King Lear,* and *Macbeth,* they neither heighten nor deepen it but on the contrary reject and even destroy it. In fact, I would go so far as to argue that the tragic pattern in the tragedies themselves is scarcely maintained equally strongly over each of the plays. For, on the basis of a comparison between the myth and ritual pattern as I have described it in *Tragedy and the Paradox of the Fortunate Fall* and the tragedies, I think that Shakespeare's tragic vision, which he was able to sustain but tentatively in *Hamlet,* most fully in

Othello, barely in *King Lear,* and hardly at all in *Macbeth,* failed him altogether in the last plays, and that this failure is manifested by the use of the elements of the myth and ritual pattern as mere machinery, virtually in burlesque fashion, and not as their informing and sustaining spirit. The instinct of the critics in applying the myth and ritual pattern to the plays has been sound, but their superimposition of the pattern on the plays has been inexact and, I suspect, prompted more by religious rather than by critical motives, with the result that both the method and the plays have been falsified.

I

If I begin with some diffidence, it is because I am always acutely aware that the myth and ritual pattern, upon which the myth and ritual approach to literature must be founded, is as uncertain in its origins as it is unrealized in actuality. I have tried to account for the persistence and power of the myth and ritual pattern by retracing it generally to that initial impact of experience which produced the archetypes of belief, and specifically, to the archetype of rebirth as crystallized out of the archetype of belief. Unfortunately no real proof of this process is possible, for the events which generated the primary shock of belief are now too deep and too dim in the racial memory of man to be exhumed by archeological means, though the psychoanalytic probings of Freud have cleared a path through this labyrinth, with reluctant confirmation coming from the anthropologists and classicists. Similarly, we must not forget that there is really no such thing as the myth and ritual pattern *per se*; at best, it is a probable construction of many varieties and variations of a number of beliefs and actions so closely related to each other that it is reasonable to construct—reconstruct would be a misleading word here—an ideal form of the myth and ritual pattern more comprehensive and more realized than any variations of it which we actually possess.

The myth and ritual pattern of the ancient Near East, which is at least six thousand years old, centers in a divine king who was killed annually and who was reborn in the person of his successor. In its later development, the king was not killed, but went through an annual symbolic death and a symbolic rebirth or resurrection. Starting out as a magical rite designed to ensure the success of the crops in climates where the outcome of the struggle between water and drought meant literally the difference between life and death, the pattern was gradually transformed into a religious ritual, designed this time to promote man's salvation, and finally became an ethical conviction, freed now of both its magical and religious ritual practices but still retaining in spiritualized and symbolic form its ancient appeal and emotional certitude. Because it begins with the need to survive, the pattern never loses its force, for it is concerned always with survival, whether physical or spiritual. So far as can be ascertained at present, the pattern had a double growth, one along the lines of the ancient civilizations of the Near East, the Sumerian, the Egyptian, the Babylonian, both South and North, the Palestinian—first with the Canaanites, and then with the Hebrews—and from thence into Christianity; the other along the lines of the island civilizations of the Aegean, from Crete to the mainland of Greece, from thence to Rome, and once more into Christianity, the two streams of development flowing into each other and reinforcing themselves at this crucial juncture.

Despite the differences between the religions of the ancient Near East (as, for example, between those of Egypt and Mesopotamia, and between that of the Hebrews and of the others), nevertheless they all possessed certain significant features of myth and ritual in common. These features, in their turn, stemmed from the common bond of ritual, characteristic (in one form or another) of all together, though, as I have said, none possessed completely all the elements, which varied in some degree from religion to religion. In this single, idealized ritual scheme, the well-being of the community was secured by the regular performance of certain ritual actions in which the king or his equivalent took the leading role. Moreover the king's importance for the community was incalculably increased by the almost universal conviction that the fortunes of the community or state and those of the king were inextricably intermingled; indeed one may go so far as to say that on the well-being of the king depended the well-being of the community as a whole. On the basis of the evidence covering different peoples at different times, we know then that in the ancient Near East there existed a pattern of thought and action which gripped the minds and emotions of those who believed in it so strongly that it was made the basis on which they could apprehend and accept the universe in which they lived. It made possible man's conviction that he could control that universe for his own purposes; and it placed in his hands the lever whereby he could exercise that control.

From an analysis of the extant seasonal rituals, particularly the new year festivals, and from the coronation, initiation, and personal rituals of the ancient Near East, it is possible to make a reconstructed model of the basic ritual form. Essentially the pattern contains these basic elements: 1. the indispensable role of the divine king; 2. the combat between the God and an opposing power; 3. the suffering of the God; 4. the death of the God; 5. the resurrection of the God; 6. the symbolic recreation of the myth of creation; 7. the sacred marriage; 8. the triumphal procession; and 9. the settling of destinies. We must remember, however, that the dying-rising-God theme constitutes but one illustration, so to speak, of the greater cycle of birth, death, and rebirth. The many and various rites connected with birth, with initiation, with marriage, and with death in the case of the individual, as well as the rites concerned with the planting, the harvesting, the new year celebrations, and with the installation ceremonies of the king in the case of the community, all these rites repeat each in its own way the deep-rooted and abiding cycle of death and rebirth. Not only do these rituals *symbolize* the passage from death to life, from one way of life to another, but they are the actual *means* of achieving the changeover; they mark the transition by which—through the processes of separation, regeneration, and the return on a higher level—both the individual and the community are assured their victory over the forces of chaos which are thereby kept under control.

The purpose of these rituals is by enaction to bring about a just order of existence in which God, nature, and man are placed in complete and final rapport with each other; they are both the defence against disorder and the guarantee of order. In the myth and ritual pattern, then, man has devised a mighty weapon by which he keeps at bay, and sometimes even seems to conquer, the hostile forces which endlessly threaten to overpower him. In the early stages of the development of the myth and ritual pattern, however, the best that man could hope for was an uneasy truce between himself and chaos, because the cycle merely returned to its beginnings; the God fought, was defeated, was resurrected, was momentarily triumphant, and thus ensured the well-being of the community for the coming year, but it was inevitable that in the course of the year he would again be defeated and would again have to go through his annual agony. Thus nothing new could be expected nor was anticipated, and year after year man could hope for no more than a temporary gain which he was sure would soon be turned into an inevitable loss. To achieve genuine faith, therefore, was an act of courage difficult and infrequent to attain, and it is no wonder that we detect in the myth and ritual pattern of the ancient Near East before the Hebraic-Christian tradition takes over, too strong a reliance on the mere machinery of ritual, ultimately leading not to faith but to superstition, as well as the melancholy notes of despair and pessimism. But the Hebraic-Christian tradition in the very process of adapting the pattern, transformed it, for by virtue of its unique and tenacious insistence on the mercy and judgment of its transcendent God, it introduced a new and vital element in the pattern, that of the dialectical leap from out of the endless circle on to a different and higher stage of understanding. The crucial moment in this transformation of the myth and ritual pattern comes when man, by himself, undertakes on his own to make the leap; to him remains the decision and his is the responsibility; by making the leap, he makes himself. The Hebraic-Christian tradition utilized the cycle of birth, life, death, and rebirth to conquer chaos and disorder, but it made its unique contribution to the pattern by giving man the possibility of defeating chaos and disorder by a single, supreme act of human will which could wipe them out at one stroke. In so doing it preserved the potency of the pattern and retained its ancient appeal and, at the same time, ensured its continued use by supplying the one element it had hitherto lacked to give it its permanent role as the means whereby man is enabled to live in an indifferent universe; it showed that man can, by himself, transcend that universe.

II

This, then, is the myth and ritual pattern as I understand it. What are its implications for tragedy? To start with, I would suggest that in the myth and ritual pattern we have the seedbed of tragedy, the stuff of which it was ultimately formed. Both the form and content of tragedy, its architecture as well as its ideology, closely parallel the form and content of the myth and ritual pattern. But having said that, I must also say that the myth and ritual pattern and tragedy are not the same. Both share the same shape and the same intent, but they differ significantly in the manner of their creation and in the methods of achieving their purposes. The myth and ritual pattern is the group product of many and different minds groping on many and different levels over long and kaleidoscopic periods of time under the stimulus of motivations quite different from those which produce tragedy. I am not suggesting anything like the formerly accepted communal origin of the ballad, for we know that myth in its form as the complement to ritual must have been devised by the priest-astrologer-magicians of the ancient world. The intent of the myth and ritual pattern is control, its method that of mimetically reproducing the rhythm of birth, death, and birth again to gain that control. But imitation here means, not acting alike, as we think of the term—a parallel and similar yet at the same time a distinct and different attitude and behavior toward the thing imitated—but rather the interpenetration of and union with the imitator, the thing imitated, and the imitation, all three being one and the same thing.

Tragedy, on the other hand, is a creation compounded of conscious craft and conviction. If we describe the myth and ritual pattern as the passage from ignorance to understanding through suffering mimetically and at first hand, then we must describe tragedy as the passage from ignorance to understanding through suffering symbolically and at a distance. To speak of symbolic meaning is already to have made the leap from myth to art. In the myth and ritual pattern, the dying-reborn God-king, the worshippers for whom he suffers, and the action of his agony are identical; in tragedy, the tragic protagonist undergoes his suffering at an aesthetic distance and only vicariously in the minds of his audience. And for that reason does Aristotle tell us that tragedy is an imitation of an action. You participate in a ritual but you are a spectator of a play.

Moreover, tragedy reconstitutes the myth and ritual pattern in terms of its own needs. Of the nine elements which make up the myth and ritual pattern as I have described it, four have been virtually eliminated from tragedy, namely, the actual death of the God, the symbolic recreation of the myth of creation, the sacred marriage, and the triumphal procession; two elements, the indispensable role of the divine king and the settling of destinies, are retained only by implication and play rather ambiguous roles in tragedy; while the remaining three—combat, suffering (with death subsumed), and resurrection—now give tragedy its structure and substance. I have already noted that one of the characteristics of the myth and ritual pattern is its adaptability, its ability to change shape while retaining its potency, and we should therefore not be surprised to find the same process at work in its relation to tragedy. What is revealing, however, is the direction of change, for we find, first, that the theme of the settling of destinies which is the highest point in the myth and ritual pattern—the goal of the struggle, since without it the passion of the God would be in vain, and chaos and disorder would be triumphant—this theme, so elaborately explicated in the ritual practices of the ancient Near East, is no more than implied in tragedy, just as the correspondence between the well-being of the king and the well-being of the community, again so detailed in ritual, is only shadowed forth, as a condition to be aimed at but not to be achieved in reality.

Second, we discover that even greater emphasis is placed on the small moment of doubt in tragedy than in the myth and ritual pattern itself. In the rituals of the ancient Near East, at the point between the death of the God and his resurrection, all action is arrested as the participants fearfully and anxiously wait for the God to be revived. After the din of combat, this quiet moment of doubt and indecision is all the more awful, for there is no assurance that the God will be reborn: "For a small moment have I forsaken thee." "But," continues Isaiah, "with great mercies will I gather thee." It is no wonder that the small moment is followed in the pattern by creation, the sacred marriage, and the triumphal procession as the peoples' expression of joy that the death of the God has not been in vain and that for another year at least: "the earth remaineth, seedtime and harvest, and cold and heat, and summer and winter, and day and night shall not cease."

And, clearly spelling out the implications of the second change made by tragedy in the myth and ritual pattern is the third, the freedom of choice of the tragic protagonist and the responsibility for the consequences of making that choice. For in that small moment of doubt and indecision, when victory and defeat are poised in the balance, only the moral force of man wills him on in action to success. The tragic protagonist acts in the conviction that his action is right, and he accepts the responsibility for that action; for him to do less than that means the loss of his stature as a moral, responsible agent. The tragic occurs when by the fall of a man of strong character we are made aware of something greater than that man or even than mankind; we seem to see a new and truer vision of the universe.

But that vision cannot be bought cheaply. It cannot be bought by blind reliance on the mere machinery of the myth and ritual pattern, and it cannot be bought by fixing the fight, as Handel's librettist fatuously puts it:

> How vain is man who boasts in fight
> The valour of gigantic might,
> And dreams not that a hand unseen
> Directs and guides this weak machine.

Better the indifferent Gods of Lucretius than the busybody *deus ex machina* of Vine Street and Madison Avenue. Only the deliberate moral choice of the tragic protagonist confronted by two equal and opposite forces and fully aware of the consequences of his choice can bring off the victory, and then only at the expense of pain and suffering: "He is despised and rejected of men; a man of sorrows, and acquainted with grief." But suffering can be made bearable only when at the same time it is made part of a rational world order into which it fits and which has an understandable place for it. * * *

Tragedy therefore occurs when the accepted order of things is fundamentally questioned only to be the more triumphantly reaffirmed. It cannot exist where there is no faith; conversely, it cannot exist where there is no doubt; it can exist only in an atmosphere of sceptical faith. The protagonist must be free to choose, and though he chooses wrongly, yet the result of the wrong choice is our own escape and our enlightenment. Yet nothing less than this sacrifice will do, and only the symbolic sacrifice of one who is like us can make possible our atonement for the evil which is within us and for the sins which we are capable of committing. Nevertheless, in western thought, if man is free to choose, in the end he must choose rightly. He is free to choose his salvation, but he is punished for his wrong choice. Man is free, but he is free within the limits set for him by his condition as a man. So great is the emphasis placed on freedom of choice in tragedy that the settling of destinies, which in the myth and ritual pattern is the tangible reward of victory, recedes more and more into the background, and the messianic vision implicit in the settling of destinies is personalized and humanized in tragedy in the form of heightened self-awareness as the end of the tragic agony. In short, what I have been saying is that the myth and ritual pattern pertains to religion which proceeds by assertion, tragedy to literature which proceeds by assessment.

To sum up, then, the structure of tragic form, as derived from the myth and ritual pattern may be diagrammed in this way: the tragic protagonist, in whom is subsumed the well-being of the people and the welfare of the state, engages in conflict with a representation of darkness and evil; a temporary defeat is inflicted on the tragic protagonist, but after shame and suffering he emerges triumphant as the symbol of the victory of light and good over darkness and evil, a victory sanctified by the covenant of the settling of destinies which re-affirms the well-being of the people and the welfare of the state. In the course of the conflict there comes a point where the protagonist and the antagonist appear to merge into a single challenge against the order of God; the evil which the protagonist would not do, he does, and the good which he would, he does not; and in this moment we are made aware that the real protagonist of tragedy is the order of God against which the tragic hero has rebelled. In this manner is the pride, the presumption which is in all of us by virtue of our mixed state as man, symbolized and revealed, and it is this *hybris* which is vicariously purged from us by the suffering of the tragic protagonist. He commits the foul deed which is potentially in us, he challenges the order of God which we would but dare not, he expiates our sin, and what we had hitherto felt we had been forced to accept we now believe of our free will, namely, that the order of God is just and good. Therefore is the tragic protagonist vouchsafed the vision of victory but not its attainment. * * *

III

Seen from this point of view, *Hamlet* is a particularly fascinating example of the relationship between the myth and ritual pattern and tragedy, because it shows within the action of the play itself the development of Shakespeare's awareness of tragedy as a heightened and secularized version of the pattern. Hamlet begins by crying for revenge which is personal and ends by seeking justice which is social. Shakespeare deals with the problem of the play—how shall a son avenge the injustice done his father?—by presenting it to us in four different yet related ways simultaneously, each consistent within its pattern of behavior, yet each overlapping and protruding beyond the other, like the successive superimpositions of the same face seen from different angles in a portrait by Picasso. First, there is Hamlet-Laertes who, incapable of seeking more than revenge, dies unchanged and unfulfilled, no better nor no worse than when he had begun. Then there is Hamlet the Prince, caught midway between revenge and justice, who passes from ignorance to understanding but too late. Third, there is Hamlet-Fortinbras who avenges his father's wrongs by joining the warring kingdoms into a single nation under his able rule. And finally, containing all these Hamlets, is Hamlet the King, idealized by his son into the perfect king whom he must replace. From this dynastic destiny stems Hamlet's ambivalence towards his father: he loves him for the man he wants to be himself and hates him for the King who stands in the way of the Prince and for the father who stands in the way of the son. Seeking his father's murderer, Hamlet finds himself. The same necessity holds Hal and Hamlet alike, but where Hal sees a straight line between his father and himself—"You won it, wore it, kept it, gave it me;/ Then plain and right must my possession be." (*II Henry IV*. IV. v.222–23)—and is therefore sure of himself and of his actions, Hamlet finds himself in a labyrinth whose walls are lined with trick doors and distorting mirrors: "O cursed spite,/ That ever I was born to set it right!"

Hamlet's ambivalence is reflected in the fragmentation of his character; there are as many Hamlets as there are scenes in which he appears, and each person in the play sees a different Hamlet before him. But of the contradictions in his character, two stand out as the major symptoms of his incompleteness. The first is Hamlet's yearning to be able to act, not for the sake of action alone, but rightly, in the clear cause of justice; for while no tragic protagonist acts more frequently and more vigorously than Hamlet, he is more and more perplexed to discover that the more he would do good—that is, cleanse Denmark by avenging his father's death—the more evil he in fact accomplishes; hence his envy of Fortinbras' ability to act resolutely and without equivocation (IV. iv.). Second, though he is nominally a Christian, yet in the moments of sharpest crisis Hamlet turns instead to the consolations of Stoicism: "If it be now, 'tis not to come; if it be not to come, it will be now; if it be not now, yet it will come; the readiness is all. Since no man has aught of what he leaves, what is't to leave betimes?" (V. ii.231–35). And it is not enough: his mission succeeds only by mischance, his cause is still not understood, and with his dying breath he calls on Horatio, the true Stoic, to tell his story to the unsatisfied. Hamlet's vision is still clouded at his death—"Things standing thus unknown"; Horatio's own version of the events is surprisingly but an advertisement for a tragedy by Seneca (V. ii.391–97); and there is something too cold and callous in the way Fortinbras embraces his fortune. In short, the myth and ritual elements have not been completely assimilated into the tragedy: the suffering of the tragic protagonist is neither altogether deserved nor altogether understood by him, the rebirth is not quite inevitable nor necessary, and the settling of destinies in the person of Fortinbras is somewhat forced and mechanical.

The genuine sense of tragic loss is somewhat vulgarized into regret: Hamlet has been too-fascinating.

In *Othello,* Shakespeare mixed his most perfect amalgam of the myth and ritual elements with tragedy. Where in *Hamlet* he was almost too fecund and profusive in characterization—invention inundating integration—in *Othello* he ruthlessly simplified and organized; if *Hamlet* is linear, proceeding by the method of montage and multiple exposure, *Othello* is monolithic and nuclear: the opposites of good and evil in human nature are forcibly split and then fused together in the fire of suffering. By over-valuing human nature, Othello destroys the balance between good and bad which is the condition of man; by undervaluing human nature, Iago brings about the same destruction from the equal and opposite direction. Each in his own way is an incomplete man: where Othello responds emotionally, Iago reasons; where Othello feels that men are better than they are, Iago knows that they are worse; each, in short, believes only what he wants to, and they are alike only in that both lack tolerance and understanding. Othello must be made to realize that the perfect love which he demands—"My life upon her faith!" "And when I love thee not, Chaos is come again."—is nothing more than the perfect hate which Iago practices:

> *Othello.* Now art thou my lieutenant.
> *Iago.* I am your own for ever. (III. iii. 478–79)

If Iago is motivated by pride, will, and individualism, so then is Othello in his own way. Iago is the external symbol of the evil in Othello, for everything that Othello would stand for is negated and reversed in Iago: the subverter of the order of God whose coming is after the working of Satan, the man who rejects principle, and who denies virtue, love, and reputation. To him, ideals are but a mask which conceals the sensuality, the brutality, and the greed for money, power, and sex, which he believes constitute man's true nature.

As the opposites of character in Othello and Iago meet and merge in Act III, scene iii, Othello becomes for the moment Iago: he reverts to paganism and calls on the stars for help, he orders his friend murdered, he spies on and humiliates and at the last repudiates his wife: "She's like a liar, gone to burning hell." But this is for him the bottom of the pit, and by a supreme effort of will he purges the Iago from within him; and in that awful moment of self-awareness, he recreates himself as he might have been, he realizes his potential as a human being. Having by his rashness put the well-being of the people and the welfare of the state in jeopardy, as Brabantio had foretold, perhaps better than he knew—

> Mine's not an idle cause. The Duke himself,
> Or any of my brothers of the state,
> Cannot but feel this wrong as 'twere their own;
> For if such actions may have passage free,
> Bond-slaves and pagans shall our statesmen be. (I. ii. 95–99)

—Othello is inevitably punished. And Iago is defeated by the one force which he is incapable of understanding, the power of principle. What he fails to see is that Othello's love for Desdemona is the symbol of Othello's faith in the goodness and justice of the world. What Othello seeks, therefore, when that faith is called into question, is not revenge, which is Iago's goal, but the cleansing of evil and the reaffirmation of goodness and justice: "It is the cause, my soul." From the depth of his self-awareness, bought at so dear a price, there emerges the theme of the settling of destinies, not embodied in the person of a successor, but filling as it were with its vision the entire stage, the sign of evil purged and the good restored, the image of man in his full stature as responsible man: "Speak of me as I am." "And when man faces destiny," Malraux writes, "destiny ends and man comes into his own."

IV

Both *Hamlet* and *Othello* possess three features in common which by contrast are not present in *Lear* and *Macbeth*. First, both *Hamlet* and *Othello* are for the Elizabethan audience contemporary plays laid in contemporary or nearly contemporary settings. No great historical distance separates them from their audience as it does in *Lear* and *Macbeth*, which are laid in pre-Christian England and Scotland. Second, both *Hamlet* and *Othello* operate within the Christian framework, recognized and apprehended as such by the audience for which they were written. But in *Lear* and *Macbeth* the pagan background is insistent. From the depth of their suffering Lear and Gloucester can appeal no higher than to the heathen gods: "As flies to wanton boys, are we to th' gods,/ They kill us for their sport" (IV. i. 38–39); and Edgar's wisdom is but cold comfort in the Stoic manner: "Bear free and patient thoughts" (IV. vi. 80). In *Macbeth,* the witches play the same role as do the gods in *Lear:*

> But 'tis strange;
> And oftentimes, to win us to our harm,
> The instruments of darkness tell us truths,
> Win us with honest trifles, to betray's
> In deepest consequence. (I. iii. 122–26)

Finally, the theme of the settling of destinies—present directly in *Hamlet* and indirectly in *Othello*—fades away in *Lear* and disappears altogether in *Macbeth*. These changes reveal a significant shift in Shakespeare's use of the myth and ritual pattern and seem to be symptomatic of his increasing inability to bear the burden of the tragic vision. Having confronted the face of evil in *Othello* with an intensity unmatched even by the man staring at Death in Michelangelo's "Last Judgment," and having in the face of that evil been able to reassert the good, Shakespeare seems to have fallen back exhausted, so to speak, the effort of holding off evil weakening with each successive play.

Lear begins with the abdication of responsibility already accomplished; that a king could even contemplate, let alone achieve, the division of his kingdom must have struck an Elizabethan audience with fear and horror. By his own act, Lear deliberately divests himself of power and retains only the trappings of power, which in turn are one by one inexorably stripped from him until he stands naked on the heath in the rain. The waters of heaven give him wisdom, but his insight into the hypocrisy of this great stage of fools comes to him only in his madness, and he realizes at last that clothes—the symbols of his *hybris*—make neither the king nor the man. Having been purged of the pride of place, he sees himself as he is:

> I am a very foolish fond old man,
> Fourscore and upward, not an hour more nor less;
> And, to deal plainly,
> I fear I am not in my perfect mind. (IV. vii. 60–63)

But this moment of illumination, of heightened self-awareness, so like Othello's, occurs not at the end of Act V, where it would be normally expected, but at the end of Act IV. Having said "Pray you now, forget and forgive; I am old and foolish" (IV. vii. 85), what is left for Lear to say? Yet Shakespeare forces the action on to the shambles of the Grand Guignol of Act V, completely cancelling the calming and cleansing effect of the tragic vision already attained with Lear's self-awareness. The play ends not with the hope that this suffering has not been in vain, but with the defeatism of Kent's "All's cheerless, dark, and deadly" and Edgar's "The oldest hath borne most; we that are young/ Shall never see so much, nor live so long." The order of nature has been turned topsy-turvy; the old who cannot bear suffering have endured too much of it; the young who should be able to bear it are too weak.

But at least *Lear* gives us the consolation of the settling of destinies, mis-handled and misplaced as it is. There is none in *Macbeth*. The action of the play begins with the figure of the bloody man and ends with the figure of the dead butcher, and nothing between mitigates the endless horrors of the progression from one to the other. Macbeth accepts the evil promise of the witches' pre-diction because they so neatly match the evil ambition already in him. Nor does his desire for the crown even pretend that it is for the well-being of the people and the welfare of the state, that excuse which gives some color to Bolingbroke's ambition: "I have no spurs/ To prick the sides of my intent," Macbeth confesses to himself, "but only/ Vaulting ambition." The country suffers under Macbeth's iron rule; "Things bad begun make strong themselves by ill" (III. ii. 55), says Macbeth, and Malcolm confirms him:

> I think our country sinks beneath the yoke;
> It weeps, it bleeds; and each new day a gash
> Is added to her wounds. (IV. iii. 39–41)

More—while Malcolm stands behind Macbeth as Fortinbras stands behind Hamlet, can we seriously accept him as the doctor who can "cast/ The water of my land, find her disease,/ And purge it to a sound and pristine health" (V. iii. 50–52)? What are we to make of a potential successor to the throne whose own ambivalence towards himself confounds even his strongest supporter? Is Macduff —are we—really persuaded that Malcolm is in fact capable of exhibiting "The king-becoming graces,/ As justice, verity, temp'rance, stableness,/ Bounty, perseverance, mercy, lowliness,/ Devotion, patience, courage, fortitude" (IV.

iii. 91–94)? Surely his black scruples, coupled with his innocence and inexperi-
ence, bode ill for Scotland, whatever the outcome, so that when at last Malcolm
is hailed King of Scotland, and, like Hal and Fortinbras, emerges as the symbol
of the settling of destinies, our eyes do not see the vision of peace rising from
suffering, and our ears hear only the echo—

> for, from this instant,
> There's nothing serious in mortality.
> All is but toys; renown and grace is dead;
> The wine of life is drawn, and the mere lees
> Is left this vault to brag of. (II. iii. 96–101)

—repeated in the dying close of Macbeth's reply to Seyton. The witches have
indeed triumphed:

> He shall spurn fate, scorn death, and bear
> His hopes 'bove wisdom, grace, and fear;
> And, you all know, security
> Is mortals' chiefest enemy. (III. v. 30–33)

Man's security, for which he has fought so feverishly, the guarantee of rebirth,
has at the very last moment been snatched away from him. Tragedy may be
much more and much different from what I have been suggesting here, but
one thing it cannot be and that is a tale signifying nothing. * * *

VI

The limitations of the subject of this paper prevent me from showing that
the disintegration of the tragic pattern which we have seen take place in the
major tragedies is paralleled in the middle comedies, *Troilus and Cressida, All's
Well That Ends Well,* and *Measure for Measure,* and comes to its culmination in
the four last plays, *Pericles, Cymbeline, The Winter's Tale,* and *The Tempest.*
Nevertheless, I think that the configuration of Shakespeare's thought was for
the most part sympathetically conformable to the shape of the myth and ritual
pattern. Yet having raised the pattern to the heights of its most moving and
significant expression, Shakespeare was unable to hold it there for long. This
does not mean that we must regard him as less than, say, Sophocles or Milton,
neither of whom seems to have given way to doubt, nor does it mean that the
myth and ritual pattern is inadequate either to its purposes or as a means of
elucidating tragedy. On the contrary, the application of the pattern to Shakespeare's plays discriminates between them with nicety, it intensifies our awareness of the unique qualities of the individual plays, and it enables us to respond
to Shakespeare on a most profound level of understanding. Recent critics of
Shakespeare have enjoyed many a laugh at the expense of their predecessors
who labored to box Shakespeare's plays under the neat labels "in the workshop,"
"in the world," "out of the depths," and "on the heights"—to use Dowden's
terms—but I cannot see that they themselves have done anything more than

to say the same thing in perhaps more fashionable language. But the myth and ritual approach converts a Progress into a Calvary.

Shakespeare paid for the cost of the tragic vision by its loss. He looked long and directly into the face of evil. In the end, he shut his eyes. Writing of another artist who found himself in the same dilemma, Sir Kenneth Clark says: "The perfect union of Piero's forms, transcending calculation, rested on confidence in the harmony of creation; and at some point this confidence left him." As it seems to me, at some point Shakespeare too lost his confidence in the harmony of creation. I do not know when Shakespeare reached that point, but I think that it perhaps came at the moment of his greatest expression of faith in the harmony of creation, in *Othello* when he realized that he had left Iago standing alive on the stage. When in the bottommost circle of Hell, Virgil steps aside from Dante and reveals to him that creature fairest once of the sons of light: "Behold now Dis!", the poet is moved to cry out: "This was not life, and yet it was not death." So in the end Iago: "Demand me nothing; what you know, you know./ From this time forth I never will speak word." The rest is silence.

PART 4

Historical Criticism

The determining principle for the "close attention to the text" practice of the Formalist Critic was said to reside in his conviction that the differentia of literary art is precisely its formal use of language designed to create a presentational symbol. Hence his strict attention to the articulation of meaning in literature's presentations. Similarly, the determining principle for the practice of the Historical Critic may be seen to lie in his conviction that literature is also a recreation of the past. The Historical Critic characteristically sees his function as the elucidation of the work in the light of the past. For Hippolyte Taine, generally recognized as the father of the historical method, writing in the middle of the nineteenth century, the function of the Historical Critic was to "recover from the monuments of literature, a knowledge of the manner in which men thought and felt centuries ago."

For the Historical Critic, then, the interpretation of a literary work from the past as if it were a work of the present necessarily constitutes a violation of the integrity of the work. For his focus is at once on what he sees to be the chief value of the work, the formulation of a presentation in the literary mode, not simply of some aspect of man's experience, but of man's experience in the past. That is, he sees his "critical job of work" to be not simply the elucidation of the work but the elucidation of the work in the light of what he regards as its most essential characteristic, its unique quality of pastness. Lionel Trilling, often a lecturer at the New Critics' Kenyon School of Letters, offered the corrective advice to the Formalists as early as 1942 when he pointed out that the fault of the New Critics "is that in their reaction from the historical method they forget that the literary work is ineluctably an historical fact, and, what is more important, that its historicity is a fact in our aesthetic experience." For Trilling, then, the factor of historicity "is part of the *given* of the work," which, he added, "we cannot help but respond to." Trilling's observation is at once the corrective advice that reveals the common ground for both the Formalist and Historical Critic. In the general recognition that the "sense of the past" is *also* part of the subject matter of the work, the Formalist and the Historical Critic, both professing the ultimate aim of elucidating the work, find common ground and intention. Clearly no Formalist Critic would quarrel with Professor Woodhouse's admirable statement of the Historical Critic's intention in his 1950 MLA paper:

For criticism, of whatever school, is a means, not an end; and the test to be applied to it is purely pragmatic: Does it or does it not throw new light on, or minister to an understanding of the work or the author under examination? By that test alone must it stand or fall.

The characteristic practice of the Historical Critic follows from his intention to focus, as Taine announced, on "the condition of race, epoch, circumstance" which produced it. His most immediate concerns then become: (1) *The scholarly attempt to recreate the conditions under which the author worked.* (2) *The characteristic philosophical thought that he sees as a determining force for the literary work produced in that age.* (3) *The literary sources and influences of a work.* (One thinks at once of J. L. Lowes' *The Road to Xanadu*.) (4) *The text.* As Professor Woodhouse has pointed out, "Historical Criticism alone can supply the text on which the New Criticism desires to focus its attention." (5) *The dating of a work.* (6) *The intellectual convictions of the author.* Again Professor Woodhouse's advice to the practicing critic is apt: "Milton's aesthetic patterns rely on a foundation or rather perhaps a framework of conceptual thought, and they cannot be elucidated without reference to it." And in another place, "Milton's thought as thought is very much 'of an age,' and hence susceptible only to historical elucidation." (7) *The biography of the writer.* Here a passage from Taine himself suggests his zeal and conviction for the attention to biography characteristic of the historical method:

> When we have established the parentage of dogma, or the classifications of poems, or the progress of constitutions, or the transformation of idioms, we have only cleared the soil: genuine history is brought into existence only when the historian begins to unravel, across the lapse of time, the living man, toiling, impassioned, entrenched in his customs, with his voice and features, his gestures and his dress, distinct and complete as he from whom we have just parted on the street. Let us endeavor, then, to annihilate as far as possible this great interval of time, which prevents us from seeing our man with our eyes, with the eyes of our head. . . . Let us make the past present: in order to judge of a thing, it must be before us.

And in a passage of remarkable resemblance to this earliest of stated convictions of Historical Criticism, Lionel Trilling writes: "But it is only if we are aware of the reality of the past as past that we can feel it as alive and present."

It is, of course, true that the seemingly extra-literary concerns of the Historical Critic remove the specific analysis of an individual work from the immediate attention of the critic. Indeed the Formalist Critic's main objection is precisely here, that in his preoccupation with such concerns as sources, biography, intellectual milieu, the Historical Critic fails to give adequate attention to the individual work before him. But the objection in the eyes of the

Historical Critic is not vital to what is most fundamental to the historical method. Professor Woodhouse provides an answer which while not refuting the charge places it in a more valid perspective:

> Meanwhile we must notice the common indictment of the Historical Critic, that he allows a consideration of sources and analogues, and of historical influences generally, to distract his attention from the text. This, in so far as it is true, is an example of human weakness, and no necessary concomitant of the historical method; for the very object with which the historical data are brought forward is the elucidation of the text.

Finally for the Historical Critic the insistence of the Formalist Critic that he wishes to bring a free critical sensibility to the interpretation of a work of the past is misguided, producing at best an incomplete account and at worst a distorted one. The Historical Critic would caution the Formalist that the desire to confront the work with a fresh, uninhibited sensibility is admirable enough but that it must be the whole work, the work with its quality of historical pastness present, that the critic of whatever persuasion must confront.

Bibliography

Aaron, Daniel. *Writers on the Left*. New York: Harcourt, Brace and World, Inc., 1961.

Adler, Mortimer. *Poetry and Politics*. Pittsburgh: Duquesne University Press, 1966.

Aldridge, A. O. "Biography in the Interpretation of Poetry." *College English*, XXV (1964), pp. 412–20.

Altick, Richard D. *The Art of Literary Research*. New York: W. W. Norton and Company, Inc., 1963, pp. 3–6, 47–117.

Auerbach, Erich. *Mimesis: The Representation of Reality in Western Literature*. Translated by Willard Trask. Princeton, N.J.: Princeton University Press, 1953.

Bowers, Fredson. *Textual and Literary Criticism*. New York: Cambridge University Press, 1959, pp. 1–34.

Brooks, Van Wyck. *The Writer in America*. New York: Avon Books, 1953.

Bush, Douglas. "My Credo: The Humanist Critic." *Kenyon Review*, XIII (1951), pp. 81–92.

———"The New Criticism: Some Old-Fashioned Queries." *PMLA*, LXIV (1949), pp. 13–21. Note: This article appears in the *second supplement* to the March issue.

Coffman, Stanley K. *Imagism: A Chapter for the History of Modern Poetry*. Norman, Okla. University of Oklahoma Press, 1951.

Cowley, Malcolm, ed. *After the Genteel Tradition: American Writers Since 1910*. New York: W. W. Norton and Company, Inc., 1937.

Daiches, David. "Fiction and Civilization." *The Novel and the Modern World*. Chicago: University of Chicago Press, 1939.

————*Literature and Society*. London: V. Gollancz, Ltd., 1938.

————*Poetry and the Modern World*. Chicago: University of Chicago Press, 1940.

Gardner, Helen. *The Business of Criticism*. Oxford: Clarendon Press, 1959.

Güerard, Albert. *Literature and Society*. Boston: Lothrop, Lee and Shepard Company, 1935.

Hicks, Granville. *The Great Tradition*. New York: Macmillan, 1933. Rev. 1935.

————*et. al. Proletarian Literature in the United States*. New York: International Publishers, 1935.

Jones, Howard Mumford. *History and the Contemporary: Essays in Nineteenth-Century Literature*. Madison: University of Wisconsin Press, 1964.

————"Literary Scholarship and Contemporary Criticism." *The English Journal*, XXIII (1934), pp. 740–58.

Kazin, Alfred. "The Function of Criticism Today." In *Contemporaries*. Boston: Little, Brown and Company, 1962, pp. 494–509.

————*On Native Grounds*. New York: Reynal and Hitchcock, 1942.

Leavis, F. R. "Literature and Society." In *The Common Pursuit*. New York: New York University Press, 1952, pp. 82–94.

Lovejoy, Arthur. *The Great Chain of Being*. Cambridge, Mass.: Harvard University Press, 1936.

Lowes, John L. *The Road to Xanadu: A Study in the Ways of the Imagination*. Boston: Houghton, Miffllin and Co., 1927.

Pottle, F. A. "The New Critics and the Historical Method." *Yale Review*, XLIII (1954), pp. 14–23.

Pritchard, J. P. *Criticism in America*. Norman, Okla.: University of Oklahoma Press, 1956, pp. 231–65.

Rahv, Philip. "Criticism and the Imagination of Alternatives." *Michigan Alumnus Quarterly Review*, LXIII (1956), pp. 7–16.

————"Fiction and the Criticism of Fiction." *Kenyon Review*, XVIII (1956), pp. 276–99.

Robertson, D. W., Jr. "Historical Criticism." In Alan S. Downer, ed., *English Institute Essays: 1950*. New York: Columbia University Press, 1951, pp. 3–31.

Smith, Bernard. *Forces in American Criticism*. New York: Harcourt, Brace and World, Inc., 1939.

Steiner, George. "Marxism and the Literary Critic." *Encounter*, XI (1958), pp. 33–43.

Svendsen, Kester. *Milton and Science*. Cambridge, Mass.: Harvard University Press, 1956.

Thorp, Willard. "The Literary Scholar as Chameleon." In Carroll Camden, ed., *Literary Views: Critical and Historical Essays*. Chicago: University of Chicago Press, 1964, pp. 166–71.

Tillotson, Geoffrey. "The Critic and the Dated Text." *Sewanee Review*, LXVIII (1960), pp. 595–602.

Tindall, William. "Scholarship and Contemporary Literature." *English Institute Annual* (1940), pp. 42–60.

Wellek, Rene. "Literary Theory, Criticism, and History," *Sewanee Review*, LXVIII (1960), pp. 1–19.

————"Periods and Movements in Literary History." *English Institute Annual, 1940*. New York: Columbia University Press, 1941, pp. 73–93.

Whalley, George. "Scholarship and Criticism." *University of Toronto Quarterly*, XXIX (1959–60), pp. 33–45.

Williams, Arnold. "Why Literary Scholarship?" *Centennial Review of Arts and Sciences,* VIII (1964), pp. 278–91.

Williams, Raymond. *Culture and Society, 1780–1950.* New York: Columbia University Press, 1958.

Wilson, Edmund. *Axel's Castle: A Study in the Imaginative Literature of 1870–1930.* New York: Charles Scribner's Sons, 1931, 1947.

——*The Triple Thinkers.* New York: Oxford University Press, 1948, pp. 197–212; 257–70.

Wimsatt, W. K., Jr. "History and Criticism: A Problematic Relationship." *PMLA,* LXVI (1951), pp. 21–31.

Witte, W. "The Sociological Approach to Literature." *Modern Language Review,* XXXVI (1941), pp. 86–94.

From the Introduction to the History of English Literature

HIPPOLYTE-ADOLPHE TAINE

HISTORY has been transformed, within a hundred years in Germany, within sixty years in France, and that by the study of their literatures.

It was perceived that a literary work is not a mere individual play of imagination, the isolated caprice of an excited brain, but a transcript of contemporary manners, a manifestation of a certain kind of mind. It was concluded that we might recover, from the monuments of literature, a knowledge of the manner in which men thought and felt centuries ago. The attempt was made, and it succeeded.

Pondering on these modes of feeling and thought, men decided that they were facts of the highest kind. They saw that these facts bore reference to the most important occurrences, that they explained and were explained by them, that it was necessary thenceforth to give them a rank, and a most important rank, in history. This rank they have received, and from that moment history has undergone a complete change: in its subject matter, its system, its machinery, the appreciation of laws and of causes. It is this change, such as it is and must be, that we shall here endeavor to exhibit.

I

What is your first remark on turning over the great, stiff leaves of a folio, the yellow sheets of a manuscript—a poem, a code of laws, a confession of faith? This, you say, did not come into existence all alone. It is but a mold, like a

History of English Literature. Published in 1863; translated by H. van Laun (Edinburgh, 1871).

fossil shell, an imprint, like one of those shapes embossed in stone by an animal which lived and perished. Under the shell there was an animal, and behind the document there was a man. Why do you study the shell, except to bring before you the animal? So you study the document only to know the man. The shell and the document are lifeless wrecks, valuable only as a clue to the entire and living existence. We must get hold of this existence, endeavor to re-create it. It is a mistake to study the document as if it were isolated. This were to treat things like a simple scholar, to fall into the error of the bibliomaniac. Neither mythology nor languages exist in themselves; but only men, who arrange words and imagery according to the necessities of their organs and the original bent of their intellects. A dogma is nothing in itself; look at the people who have made it—a portrait, for instance, of the sixteenth century, say the stern powerful face of an English archbishop or martyr. Nothing exists except through some individual man; it is this individual with whom we must become acquainted. When we have established the parentage of dogmas, or the classification of poems, or the progress of constitutions, or the transformation of idioms, we have only cleared the soil: genuine history is brought into existence only when the historian begins to unravel, across the lapse of time, the living man, toiling, impassioned, entrenched in his customs, with his voice and features, his gestures and his dress, distinct and complete as he from whom we have just parted in the street. Let us endeavor, then, to annihilate as far as possible this great interval of time, which prevents us from seeing man with our eyes, with the eyes of our head. . . . Let us make the past present: in order to judge of a thing, it must be before us; there is no experience in respect of what is absent. Doubtless this reconstruction is always incomplete; it can produce only incomplete judgments; but that we cannot help. It is better to have an imperfect knowledge than none at all; and there is no other means of acquainting ourselves approximately with the events of other days, than to *see* approximately the men of other days.

This is the first step in history; it was made in Europe at the revival of imagination, toward the close of the last century, by Lessing and Walter Scott; a little later in France, by Chateaubriand, Augustin Thierry, Michelet, and others. And now for the second step.

II

When you consider with your eyes the visible man, what do you look for? The man invisible. The words which enter your ears, the gestures, the motions of his head, the clothes he wears, visible acts and deeds of every kind, are expressions merely; something is revealed beneath them, and that is a soul. An inner man is concealed beneath the outer man; the second does but reveal the first. You look at his house, furniture, dress; and that in order to discover in them the marks of his habits and tastes, the degree of his refinement or rusticity, his extravagance or his economy, his stupidity or his acuteness. You listen to his conversation, and you note the inflections of his voice, the changes in his attitudes; and that in order to judge of his vivacity, his self-forgetfulness or his gaiety, his energy or his constraint. You consider his writings, his artistic productions, his business transactions or political ventures; and that in order to measure the scope and limits of his intelligence, his inventiveness, his coolness, to find out the order, the character, the general force of his ideas, the mode in which he thinks and resolves. All these externals are but avenues converging towards a center; you enter them simply in order to reach that center; and that center is the genuine man, I mean that mass of faculties and feelings which are the inner man. We have reached a new world, which is infinite, because every action which we see involves an infinite association of reasonings, emotions, sensations new and old, which have served to bring it to light, and which, like great rocks deep-seated in the ground, find in it their end and their level. This underworld is a new subject matter, proper to the historian. If his critical education is sufficient, he can lay bare, under every detail of architecture, every stroke in a picture, every phrase in a writing, the special sensation whence detail, stroke, or phrase had issue; he is present at the drama which was enacted in the soul of artist or writer; the choice of a word, the brevity or length of a sentence, the nature of a metaphor, the accent of a verse, the development of an argument—everything is a symbol to him; while his eyes read the text, his soul and mind pursue the continuous development and the ever-changing succession of the emotions and conceptions out of which the text has sprung: in short, he works out its psychology. If you would observe this operation, consider the originator and model of all grand contemporary culture, Goethe, who, before writing *Iphigenia,* employed day after day in making drawings of the most finished statues, and who at last, his eyes filled with the noble forms of ancient scenery, his mind penetrated by the harmonious loveliness of antique life, succeeded in reproducing so exactly in himself the peculiarities of the Greek imagination, that he gives us almost the twin sister of the Antigone of Sophocles, and the goddesses of Phidias. This precise and proved interpretation of past sensations has given to history, in our days, a second birth; hardly anything of the sort was known to the preceding century. They thought men of every race and century were all but identical; the Greek, the barbarian, the Hindoo, the man of the Restoration, and the man of the eighteenth century, as if they had been turned out of a common mould; and all in conformity to a certain abstract conception, which served for the whole human race. They knew men, but not man; they had not penetrated to the soul; they had not seen the infinite diversity and marvellous complexity of souls; they did not know that the moral consti-tuition of a people or an age is as particular and distinct as the physical structure of a family of plants or an order of animals. Now-a-days, history, like zoology, has found its anatomy; and whatever the branch of history to which you devote yourself, philology, linguistic lore, mythology, it is by these means you must strive to produce new fruit. . . . This is the second step; we are in a fair way to its completion. It is the fit work of the contemporary critic. No one has done it so justly and grandly as Sainte-Beuve: in this respect we are all his pupils; his method has revolutionized, in our days, in books, and even in newspapers, every kind of literary, philosophical and religious criticism. From it we must set out in order to begin the further development. I have more than once endeavored to indicate this development; there is here, in my mind, a new path open to history, and I will try to describe it more in detail.

III

When you have observed and noted in man one, two, three, then a multitude of sensations, does this suffice, or does your knowledge appear complete? Is psychology only a series of observations? No; here as elsewhere we must search out the causes after we have collected the facts. No matter if the facts be physical or moral, they all have their causes; there is a cause for ambition, for courage, for truth, as there is for digestion, for muscular movement, for animal heat. Vice and virtue are products, like vitriol and sugar; and every complex phenomenon arises from other more simple phenomena on which it hangs. Let us then seek the simple phenomena for moral qualities; as we seek them for physical qualities; and let us take the first fact that presents itself: for example, religious music, that of a Protestant church. There is an inner cause which has turned the spirit of the faithful toward these grave and monotonous melodies, a cause broader than its effect; I mean the general idea of the true, external worship which man owes to God. It is this which has modeled the architecture of Protestant places of worship, thrown down the statues, removed the pictures, destroyed the ornaments, curtailed the ceremonies, shut up the worshippers in high pews which prevent them from seeing anything, and regulated the thousand details of decoration, posture, and general externals. This again comes from another more general cause, the idea of human conduct in all its comprehensiveness, internal and external, prayers, actions, duties of every kind which man owes to God; it is this which has enthroned the doctrine of grace, lowered the status of the clergy, transformed the sacraments, suppressed various practices, and changed religion from a discipline to a morality. This second idea in its turn depends upon a third still more general, that of moral perfection, such as is met with in the perfect God, the unerring judge, the stern watcher of souls, before whom every soul is sinful, worthy of punishment, incapable of virtue or salvation, except by the power of conscience which He calls forth, and the renewal of heart which He produces. That is the master idea, which consists in erecting duty into an absolute king of human life, and in prostrating all ideal models before a moral model. Here we track the root of man; for to explain this conception it is necessary to consider the race itself, the German and Northman, the structure of his character and mind, his general processes of thought and feeling, the sluggishness and coldness of sensation which prevent his falling easily and headlong under the sway of pleasure, the bluntness of his taste, the irregularity and revolutions of his conception, which arrest in him the birth of fair dispositions and harmonious forms, the disdain of appearances, the desire for truth, the attachment for bare and abstract ideas, which develop in him conscience, at the expense of all else. There the search is at an end; we have arrived at a primitive disposition; at a feature peculiar to all the sensations, and to all the conceptions of a century or a race, at a particularity inseparable from all the motions of his intellect and his heart. Here lie the grand causes, for they are the universal and permanent causes, present at every moment and in every case, everywhere and always acting, indestructible, and finally infallibly supreme, since the accidents which thwart them, being limited and partial, end by yielding to the dull and incessant repetition of their efforts; in such a manner that the general structure of things, and the grand features of events, are their work; and religions, philosophies, poetries, industries, the framework of society and of families, are in fact only the imprints stamped by their seal. . . .

IV

Three different sources contribute to produce this elementary moral state— RACE, SURROUNDINGS, and EPOCH. What we call the race are the innate and hereditary dispositions which man brings with him into the world and which, as a rule, are united with the marked differences in the temperament and structure of the body. They vary with various peoples. There is a natural variety of men, as of oxen and horses, some brave and intelligent, some timid and dependent, some capable of superior conceptions and creations, some reduced to rudimentary ideas and inventions, some more specially fitted to special works, and gifted more richly with particular instincts, as we meet with species of dogs better favored than others—these for coursing, those for fighting, those for hunting, these again for house dogs or shepherds' dogs. We have here a distinct force—so distinct that amidst the vast deviations which the other two motive forces produce in him, one can recognize it still; and a race, like the old Aryans, scattered from the Ganges as far as the Hebrides, settled in every clime, and every stage of civilization, transformed by thirty centuries of revolutions, nevertheless manifests in its languages, religions, literatures, philosophies, the community of blood and of intellect which to this day binds its offshoots together. Different as they are, their parentage is not obliterated; barbarism, culture and grafting, differences of sky and soil, fortunes good and bad, have labored in vain: the great marks of the original model have remained, and we find again the two or three principal lineaments of the primitive stamp under- neath the secondary imprints which time has laid upon them. There is nothing astonishing in this extraordinary tenacity. Although the vastness of the distance lets us but half perceive—and by a doubtful light—the origin of species,[1] the events of history sufficiently illumine the events anterior to history, to explain the almost immovable steadfastness of the primordial marks. When we meet with them, fifteen, twenty, thirty centuries before our era, in an Aryan, an Egyptian, a Chinese, they represent the work of a great many ages, perhaps of several myriads of centuries. For as soon as an animal begins to exist, it has to reconcile itself with its surroundings; it breathes and renews itself, is differently affected according to the variations in air, food, temperature. Different climate and situation bring it various needs and, consequently, a different course of activity; and this, again, a different set of habits; and still again, a different set

---

[1] Darwin, *The Origin of Species*; Prosper Lucas, *De L'hérédité*. [Taine.]

of aptitudes and instincts. Man, forced to accommodate himself to circumstances, contracts a temperament and a character corresponding to them; and his character, like his temperament, is so much more stable, as the external impression is made upon him by more numerous repetitions, and is transmitted to his progeny by a more ancient descent. So that at any moment we may consider the character of a people as an abridgement of all its preceding actions and sensations; that is, as a quantity and as a weight, not infinite,[2] since every-thing in nature is finite, but disproportioned to the rest, and almost impossible to lift, since every moment of an almost infinite past has contributed to increase it, and because, in order to raise the scale, one must place in the opposite scale a still greater number of actions and sensations. Such is the first and richest source of these master faculties from which historical events take their rise; and one sees at the outset that, if it be powerful, it is because this is no simple spring but a kind of lake, a deep reservoir wherein other springs have, for a multitude of centuries, discharged their several streams.

Having thus outlined the interior structure of a race, we must consider the surroundings in which it exists. For man is not alone in the world; nature surrounds him, and his fellow men surround him; accidental and secondary tendencies overlay his primitive tendencies, and physical or social circumstances disturb or confirm the character committed to their charge. Sometimes the climate has had its effect. Though we can follow but obscurely the Aryan peoples from their common fatherland to their final settlements, we can yet assert that the profound differences which are manifest between the German races on the one side, and the Greek and Latin on the other, arise for the most part from the difference between the countries in which they are settled: some in cold moist lands, deep in rugged marshy forests or on the shores of a wild ocean, beset by melancholy or violent sensations, prone to drunkenness and gluttony, bent on a fighting, blood-spilling life; others, again, within the loveliest landscapes, on a bright and pleasant seacoast, enticed to navigation and commerce, exempt from gross cravings of the stomach, inclined from the begin-ning to social ways, to a settled organization of the state, to feelings and dis-positions such as develop the art of oratory, the talent for enjoyment, the inventions of science, letters, arts. . . .

Thus it is with a people as with a plant; the same sap, under the same temperature, and in the same soil, produces, at different steps of its progressive development, different formations, buds, flowers, fruits, seed-vessels, in such a manner that the one which follows must always be preceded by the former, and must spring up from its death. And if now you consider no longer a brief epoch, as our own time, but one of those wide intervals which embrace one or more centuries, like the Middle Ages, or our last classic age, the conclusion will be similar. A certain dominant idea has had sway; men, for two, for five hundred years, have taken to themselves a certain ideal model of man: in the Middle Ages, the knight and the monk; in our classic age, the courtier, the man who speaks well. This creative and universal idea is displayed over the whole field

[2] Spinoza, *Ethics,* Pt. IV, axiom. [Taine.]

of action and thought; and, after covering the world with its involuntarily systematic works, it has faded, it has died away, and lo, a new idea springs up, destined to a like domination, and as manifold creations. And here remember that the second depends in part upon the first, and that the first, uniting its effect with those of national genius and surrounding circumstances, imposes on each new creation its bent and direction. . . .

V

It remains for us to examine how these causes, when applied to a nation or an age, produce their results. As a spring, rising from a height and flowing downwards spreads its streams according to the depth of the descent, stage after stage, until it reaches the lowest level of the soil, so the disposition of intellect or soul impressed on a people by race, circumstances, or epoch, spreads in different proportions and by regular descents, down the diverse orders of facts which make up its civilization. If we arrange the map of a country, starting from the watershed, we find that below this common point the streams are divided into five or six principal basins, then each of these into several secondary basins, and so on, until the whole country with its thousand details is included in the ramifications of this network. So, if we arrange the psychological map of the events and sensations of a human civilization, we find first of all five or six well-defined provinces—religion, art, philosophy, the state, the family, the industries; then in each of these provinces natural departments; and in each of these, smaller territories, until we arrive at the numberless details of life such as may be observed within and around us every day. If now we examine and compare these diverse groups of facts, we find first of all that they are made up of parts, and that all have parts in common. Let us take first the three chief works of human intelligence—religion, art, philosophy. What is a philosophy but a conception of nature and its primordial causes, under the form of abstractions and formularies? What is there at the bottom of a religion or of an art but a conception of this same nature and of these same causes, under form of symbols more or less concise, and personages more or less marked; with this difference, that in the first we believe that they exist, in the second we believe that they do not exist? . . . A civilization forms a body, and its parts are connected with each other like the parts of an organic body. As in an animal, instincts, teeth, limbs, osseous structure, muscular envelope, are mutually connected, so that a change in one produces a corresponding change in the rest, and a clever naturalist can by a process of reasoning reconstruct out of a few fragments almost the whole body; even so in a civilization, religion, philosophy, the organization of the family, literature, the arts, make up a system in which every local change induces a general change, so that an experienced historian, studying some particular part of it, sees in advance and half predicts the character of the rest. There is nothing vague in this interdependence. In the living body the regulator is, first, its tendency to manifest a certain primary type; then its necessity for organs whereby to satisfy its wants, and to be in harmony with itself in order that it may live. In a civilization, the regulator is the presence, in every great human creation, of a productive element, present also in other surrounding creations,—to wit, some faculty, aptitude, disposition, effective and discernible, which, being possessed of its proper character, introduces it into all the operations in which it assists, and, according to its variations, causes all the works in which it co-operates to vary also.

VI

History now attempts, or rather is very near attempting this method of research. The question propounded now-a-days is of this kind. Given a literature, philosophy, society, art, group of arts, what is the moral condition which produced it? what the conditions of race, epoch, circumstance, the most fitted to produce this moral condition? . . . No one has better taught us [than Stendhal] how to open our eyes and see, to see first the men that surround us and the life that is present, then the ancient and authentic documents, to read between the black and white lines of the pages, to recognize beneath the old impression, under the scribbling of a text, the precise sentiment, the movement of ideas, the state of mind in which they were written. In his writings, in Sainte-Beuve, in the German critics, the reader will see all the wealth that may be drawn from a literary work: when the work is rich, and people know how to interpret it, we find there the psychology of a soul, frequently of an age, now and then of a race. In this light, a great poem, a fine novel, the confessions of a superior man, are more instructive than a heap of historians with their histories. I would give fifty volumes of charters and a hundred volumes of state papers for the memoirs of Cellini, the epistles of St. Paul, the table talk of Luther, or the comedies of Aristophanes. In this consists the importance of literary works: they are instructive because they are beautiful; their utility grows with their perfection; and if they furnish documents it is because they are monuments. The more a book brings sentiments into light, the more it is a work of literature; for the proper office of literature is to make sentiments visible. The more a book represents important sentiments, the higher is its place in literature; for it is by representing the mode of being of a whole nation and a whole age that a writer rallies round him the sympathies of an entire age and of an entire nation. That is why, amid the writings which set before our eyes the sentiments of preceding generations, a literature, and notably a grand literature, is incomparably the best. It resembles those admirable apparatuses of extraordinary sensibility by which physicians disentangle and measure the most recondite and delicate changes of a body. Constitutions, religions, do not approach it in importance; the articles of a code of laws and of a creed only show us the spirit roughly and without delicacy. If there are any writings in which politics and dogma are full of life, it is in the eloquent discourses of the pulpit and the tribune, memoirs, unrestrained confessions; and all this belongs to literature: so that, in addition to itself, it has all the advantage of other works. It is then chiefly by the study of literatures that one may construct a moral history, and advance toward the knowledge of psychological laws, from which events spring.

I intend to write the history of a literature, and to seek in it for the psychology of a people: if I have chosen this nation in particular, it is not without a reason. I had to find a people with a grand and complete literature, and this is rare: there are few nations who have, during their whole existence, really thought and written. Among the ancients, the Latin literature is worth nothing at the outset, then it borrowed and became imitative. Among the moderns, German literature does not exist for nearly two centuries.[3] Italian literature and Spanish literature end at the middle of the seventeenth century. Only ancient Greece, modern France and England, offer a complete series of great significant monuments. I have chosen England, because being still living, and subject to direct examination, it may be better studied than a destroyed civilization, of which we retain but the relics, and because, being different from France, it has in the eyes of a Frenchman a more distinct character. Besides, there is a peculiarity in this civilization, that apart from its spontaneous development, it presents a forced deviation, it has suffered the last and most effectual of all conquests, and the three grounds whence it has sprung, race, climate, the Norman invasion, may be observed in its remains with perfect exactness; so that we may examine in this history the two most powerful moving springs of human transformation, natural bent and constraining force, and we may examine them without uncertainty or gap, in a series of authentic and unmutilated memorials.

I have to define these primary springs, to exhibit their gradual effects, to explain how they have ended by bringing to light great political, religious, and literary works, and by developing the recondite mechanism whereby the Saxon barbarian has been transformed into the Englishman of today.

[3] From 1550 to 1750. [Taine.]

The Historical Interpretation of Literature

EDMUND WILSON

I WANT to talk about the historical interpretation of literature—that is, about the interpretation of literature in its social, economic and political aspects.

To begin with, it will be worth while to say something about the kind of criticism which seems to be furthest removed from this. There is a kind of comparative criticism which tends to be non-historical. The essays of T. S. Eliot, which have had such an immense influence in our time, are, for example, fundamentally non-historical. Eliot sees, or tries to see, the whole of literature, so far as he is acquainted with it, spread out before him under the aspect of eternity. He then compares the work of different periods and countries, and tries to draw from it general conclusions about what literature ought to be. He understands, of course, that our point of view in connection with literature changes, and he has what seems to me a very sound conception of the whole body of writing of the past as something to which new works are continually being added, and which is not thereby merely increased in bulk but modified as a whole—so that Sophocles is no longer precisely what he was for Aristotle, or Shakespeare what he was for Ben Jonson or for Dryden or for Dr. Johnson, on account of all the later literature that has intervened between them and us. Yet at every point of this continual accretion, the whole field may be surveyed, as it were, spread out before the critic. The critic tries to see it as God might; he calls the books to a Day of Judgment. And, looking at things in this way, he may arrive at interesting and valuable conclusions which could hardly be reached by approaching them in any other way. Eliot was able to see, for example—what I believe had never been noticed before—that the French Symbolist poetry of the nineteenth century had certain fundamental resemblances to the English poetry of the age of Donne. Another kind of critic would draw certain historical conclusions from these purely aesthetic findings, as the Russian D. S. Mirsky did; but Eliot does not draw them.

Another example of this kind of non-historical criticism, in a somewhat different way and on a somewhat different plane, is the work of the late George Saintsbury. Saintsbury was a connoisseur of wines; he wrote an entertaining book on the subject. And his attitude toward literature, too, was that of the connoisseur. He tastes the authors and tells you about the vintages; he distinguishes the qualities of the various wines. His palate was as fine as could be, and he possessed the great qualification that he knew how to take each book on its own terms without expecting it to be some other book and was thus in a position to appreciate a great variety of kinds of writing. He was a man of strong social prejudices and peculiarly intransigent political views, but, so far as it is humanly possible, he kept them out of his literary criticism. The result is one of the most agreeable and most comprehensive commentaries on literature that have ever been written in English. Most scholars who have read as much as Saintsbury don't have Saintsbury's discriminating taste. Here is a critic who has covered the whole ground like any academic historian, yet whose account of it is not merely a chronology but a record of fastidious enjoyment. Since enjoyment is the only thing he is looking for, he does not need to know the causes of things, and the historical background of literature does not interest him very much.

There is, however, another tradition of criticism which dates from the beginning of the eighteenth century. In the year 1725, the Neapolitan philosopher Vico published *La Scienza Nuova,* a revolutionary work on the philosophy of history, in which he asserted for the first time that the social world was certainly the work of man, and attempted what is, so far as I know, the first social interpretation of a work of literature. This is what Vico says about Homer: "Homer composed the *Iliad* when Greece was young and consequently burning with sublime passions such as pride, anger and vengeance—passions which cannot allow dissimulation and which consort with generosity; so that she then admired Achilles, the hero of force. But, grown old, he composed the *Odyssey,* at a time when the passions of Greece were already somewhat cooled by reflection, which is the mother of prudence—so that she now admired Ulysses, the hero of wisdom. Thus also, in Homer's youth, the Greek people liked cruelty, abuse, savagery, fierceness, ferocity; whereas, when Homer was old, they were already enjoying the luxuries of Alcinoüs, the delights of Calypso, the pleasures of Circe, the songs of the sirens and the pastimes of the suitors, who went no further in aggression and combat than laying siege to the chaste Penelope—all of which practices would appear incompatible with the spirit of the earlier time. The divine Plato is so struck by this difficulty that, in order to solve it, he tells us that Homer had foreseen in inspired vision these dissolute, sickly and disgusting customs. But in this way he makes Homer out to have been but a foolish instructor for Greek civilization, since, however much he may condemn them he is displaying for imitation these corrupt and decadent habits which were not to be adopted till long after the foundation of the nations of Greece, and accelerating the natural course which human events would take by spurring the Greeks on to corruption. Thus it is plain that the Homer of the *Iliad* must have preceded by many years the Homer who wrote the *Odyssey*; and it is plain that the former must belong to the northeastern part of Greece, since he celebrates the Trojan War, which took place in his part of the country, whereas the latter belongs to the southeastern part, since he celebrates Ulysses, who reigned there."

You see that Vico has here explained Homer in terms both of historical period and of geographical origin. The idea that human arts and institutions were to be studied and elucidated as the products of the geographical and climatic conditions in which the people who created them lived, and of the phase of their social development through which they were passing at the moment, made great progress during the eighteenth century. There are traces of it even in Dr. Johnson, that most orthodox and classical of critics—as, for example, when he accounts for certain characteristics of Shakespeare by the relative barbarity of the age in which he lived, pointing out, just as Vico had done, that "nations, like individuals, have their infancy." And by the eighties of the eighteenth century Herder, in his *Ideas on the Philosophy of History*, was writing of poetry that it was a kind of "Proteus among the people, which is always changing its form in response to the languages, manners, and habits, to the temperaments and climates, nay even to the accents of different nations." He said—what could still seem startling even so late as that—that "language was not a divine communication, but something men had produced themselves." In the lectures on the philosophy of history that Hegel delivered in Berlin in 1822–23, he discussed the national literatures as expressions of the societies which had produced them—societies which he conceived as great organisms continually transforming themselves under the influence of a succession of dominant ideas.

In the field of literary criticism, this historical point of view came to its first complete flower in the work of the French critic Taine, in the middle of the nineteenth century. The whole school of historian-critics to which Taine belonged—Michelet, Renan, Sainte-Beuve—had been occupied in interpreting books in terms of their historical origins. But Taine was the first of these to attempt to apply these principles systematically and on a large scale in a work devoted exclusively to literature. In the introduction to his *History of English Literature*, published in 1863, he made his famous pronouncement that works of literature were to be understood as the upshot of three interfusing factors: *the moment, the race and the milieu.* Taine thought he was a scientist and a mechanist, who was examining works of literature from the same point of view as the chemist in experimenting with chemical compounds. But the difference between the critic and the chemist is that the critic cannot first combine his elements and then watch to see what they will do; he can only examine phenomena which have already taken place. The procedure that Taine actually follows is to pretend to set the stage for the experiment by describing the moment, the race and the milieu, and then to say: "such a situation demands such and such a kind of writer." He now goes on to describe the kind of writer that the situation demands, and the reader finds himself at the end confronted with Shakespeare or Milton or Byron or whoever the great figure is—who turns out to prove the accuracy of Taine's prognosis by precisely living up to the description.

There was thus a certain element of imposture in Taine; but it was the rabbits he pulled out that saved him. If he had really been the mechanist that he thought he was, his work on literature would have had little value. The truth was that Taine loved literature for its own sake—he was at his best himself a brilliant artist—and he had very strong moral convictions which give his writing emotional power. His mind, to be sure, was an analytical one, and his analysis, though terribly oversimplified, does have an explanatory value. Yet his work was what we call creative. Whatever he may say about chemical experiments, it is evident when he writes of a great writer that the moment, the race and the milieu have combined, like the three sounds of the chord in Browning's poem about Abt Vogler, to produce not a fourth sound but a star.

To Taine's set of elements was added, dating from the middle of the century, a new element, the economic, which was introduced into the discussion of historical phenomena mainly by Marx and Engels. The non-Marxist critics themselves were at the time already taking into account the influence of the social classes. In his chapters on the Norman conquest of England, Taine shows that the difference between the literatures produced respectively by the Normans and by the Saxons was partly the difference between a ruling class, on the one hand, and a vanquished and oppressed class, on the other. And Michelet, in his volume on the Regency, which was finished the same year that the *History of English Literature* appeared, studies the *Manon Lescaut* of the Abbé Prévost as a document representing the point of view of the small gentry before the French Revolution. But Marx and Engels derived the social classes from the way that people made or got their livings—from what they called the *methods of production*; and they tended to regard these economic processes as fundamental to civilization.

The Dialectical Materialism of Marx and Engels was not really so material-istic as it sounds. There was in it a large element of the Hegelian idealism that Marx and Engels thought they had got rid of. At no time did these two famous materialists take so mechanistic a view of things as Taine began by professing; and their theory of the relation of works of literature to what they called the *economic base* was a good deal less simple than Taine's theory of the moment, the race and the milieu. They thought that art, politics, religion, philosophy and literature belonged to what they called the *superstructure* of human activity; but they saw that the practitioners of these various professions tended also to constitute social groups, and that they were always pulling away from the kind of solidarity based on economic classes in order to establish a professional solidarity of their own. Furthermore, the activities of the superstructure could influence one another, and they could influence the economic base. It may be said of Marx and Engels in general that, contrary to the popular impression, they were tentative, confused and modest when it came down to philosophical first principles, where a materialist like Taine was cocksure. Marx once made an attempt to explain why the poems of Homer were so good when the society that produced them was from his point of view—that is, from the point of view of its industrial development—so primitive; and this gave him a good deal of trouble. If we compare his discussion of this problem with Vico's discussion of Homer, we see that the explanation of literature in terms of a philosophy of social history is becoming, instead of simpler and easier, more difficult and more complex.

Marx and Engels were deeply imbued, moreover, with the German admiration for literature, which they had learned from the age of Goethe. It would never have occurred to either of them that *der Dichter* was not one of the noblest and most beneficent of humankind. When Engels writes about Goethe, he presents him as a man equipped for "practical life," whose career was frustrated by the "misery" of the historical situation in Germany in his time, and reproaches him for allowing himself to lapse into the "cautious, smug and narrow" philistinism of the class from which he came; but Engels regrets this, because it interfered with the development of the "mocking, defiant, world-despising genius," "der geniale Dichter," "der gewaltige Poet," of whom Engels would not even, he says, have asked that he should have been a political liberal if Goethe had not sacrificed to his bourgeois shrinkings his truer esthetic sense. And the great critics who were trained on Marx—Franz Mehring and Bernard Shaw—had all this reverence for the priesthood of literature. Shaw deplores the absence of political philosophy and what he regards as the middle-class snobbery in Shakespeare; but he celebrates Shakespeare's poetry and his dramatic imagination almost as enthusiastically as Swinburne did, describing even those potboiling comedies—*Twelfth Night* and *As You Like It*—the themes of which seem to him most trashy—as "the Crown Jewels of English dramatic poetry." Such a critic may do more for a writer by showing him as a real man dealing with a real world at a definite moment of time than the impressionist critic of Swinburne's type who flourished in the same period of the late nineteenth century. The purely impressionist critic approaches the whole literature as an exhibit of belletristic jewels, and he can only write a rhapsodic catalogue. But when Shaw turned his spotlight on Shakespeare as a figure in the Shavian drama of history, he invested him with a new interest as no other English critic had done.

The insistence that the man of letters should play a political role, the disparagement of works of art in comparison with political action, were thus originally no part of Marxism. They only became associated with it later. This happened by way of Russia, and it was due to special tendencies in that country that date from long before the Revolution or the promulgation of Marxism itself. In Russia there have been very good reasons why the political implications of literature should particularly occupy the critics. The art of Pushkin itself, with its marvelous power of implication, had certainly been partly created by the censorship of Nicholas I, and Pushkin set the tradition for most of the great

Russian writers that followed him. Every play, every poem, every story, must be a parable of which the moral is *implied*. If it were stated, the censor would suppress the book as he tried to do with Pushkin's *Bronze Horseman,* where it was merely a question of the packed implications protruding a little too plainly. Right down through the writings of Chekhov and up almost to the Revolution, the imaginative literature of Russia presents the peculiar paradox of an art that is technically objective and yet charged with social messages. In Russia under the Tsar, it was inevitable that social criticism should lead to political conclusions, because the most urgent need from the point of view of any kind of improvement was to get rid of the tsarist regime. Even the neo-Christian moralist Tolstoy, who pretended to be non-political, was to exert a subversive influence, because his independent preaching was bound to embroil him with the Church, and the Church was an integral part of the tsardom. Tolstoy's pamphlet called *What Is Art?,* in which he throws overboard Shakespeare and a large part of modern literature, including his own novels, in the interest of his intransigent morality, is the example which is most familiar to us of the moralizing Russian criticism; but it was only the most sensational expression of a kind of approach which had been prevalent since Belinsky and Chernyshevsky in the early part of the century. The critics, who were usually journalists writing in exile or for a contraband press, were always tending to demand of the imaginative writers that they should dramatize bolder morals.

Even after the Revolution had destroyed the tsarist government, this state of things did not change. The old habits of censorship persisted in the new socialist society of the Soviets, which was necessarily made up of people who had been stamped by the die of the despotism. We meet here the peculiar phenomenon of a series of literary groups that attempt, one after the other, to obtain official recognition or to make themselves sufficiently powerful to establish themselves as arbiters of literature. Lenin and Trotsky and Lunacharsky had the sense to oppose these attempts; the comrade-dictators of Proletcult or Lef or Rapp would certainly have been just as bad as the Count Benckendorff who made Pushkin miserable, and when the Stalin bureaucracy, after the death of Gorky, got control of this department as of everything else, they instituted a system of repression that made Benckendorff and Nicholas I look like Lorenzo de' Medici. In the meantime, Trotsky, who was Commissar of War but himself a great political writer with an interest in belles-lettres, attempted, in 1924, apropos of one of these movements, to clarify the situation. He wrote a brilliant and valuable book called *Literature and Revolutions,* in which he explained the aims of the government, analyzed the work of the Russian writers, and praised or rebuked the latter as they seemed to him in harmony or at odds with the former. Trotsky is intelligent, sympathetic; it is evident that he is really fond of literature and that he knows that a work of art does not fulfill its function in terms of the formulas of party propaganda. But Mayakovsky, the Soviet poet, whom Trotsky had praised with reservations, expressed himself in a famous joke when he was asked what he thought of Trotsky's book —a pun which implied that a Commissar turned critic was inevitably a Commissar still;[1] and what a foreigner cannot accept in Trotsky is his assumption that it is the duty of the government to take a hand in the direction of literature.

This point of view, indigenous to Russia, has been imported to other countries through the permeation of Communist influence. The Communist press and its literary followers have reflected the control of the Kremlin in all the phases through which it has passed, down to the wholesale imprisonment of Soviet writers which has been taking place since 1935. But it has never been a part of the American system that our Republican or Democratic administration should lay down a political line for the guidance of the national literature. A recent gesture in this direction on the part of Archibald MacLeish, who seemed a little carried away by his position as Librarian of Congress, was anything but cordially received by serious American writers. So long as the United States remains happily a non-totalitarian country, we can very well do without this aspect of the historical criticism of literature.

Another element of a different order has, however, since Marx's time been added to the historical study of the origins of works of literature. I mean the psychoanalysis of Freud. This appears as an extension of something which had already got well started before, which had figured even in Johnson's *Lives of the Poets,* and of which the great exponent has been Sainte-Beuve: the interpretation of works of literature in the light of the personalities behind them. But the Freudians made this interpretation more exact and more systematic. The great example of the psychoanalysis of an artist is Freud's own essay on Leonardo da Vinci; but this has little critical interest: it is an attempt to construct a case history. One of the best examples I know of the application of Freudian analysis to literature is in Van Wyck Brooks' book, *The Ordeal of Mark Twain,* in which Mr. Brooks uses an incident of Mark Twain's boyhood as a key to his whole career. Mr. Brooks has since repudiated the method he resorted to here, on the ground that no one but an analyst can ever know enough about a writer to make a valid psychoanalytic diagnosis. This is true, and it is true of the method that it has led to bad results where the critic has built a Freudian mechanism out of very slender evidence, and then given us merely a romance exploiting the supposed working of this mechanism, in place of an actual study that sticks close to the facts and the documents of the writer's life and work. But I believe that Van Wyck Brooks really had hold of something important when he fixed upon that childhood incident of which Mark Twain gave so vivid an account to his biographer—that scene at the deathbed of his father when his mother had made him promise that he would not break her heart. If it was not one of those crucial happenings that are supposed to determine the complexes of Freud, it has certainly a typical significance in relation to Mark Twain's whole psychology. The stories that people tell about their childhood are likely to be profoundly symbolic even when they have been partly or wholly made up in the light of later experience. And the attitudes, the compulsions, the emotional

---

[1] *The first pancake lies like a narkom* . . . (people's commissar)—a parody of the Russian saying, . . . *The first pancake lies like a lump.*

"patterns" that recur in the work of a writer are of great interest to the historical critic.

These attitudes and patterns are embedded in the community and the historical moment, and they may indicate its ideals and its diseases as the cell shows the condition of the tissue. The recent scientific experimentation in the combining of Freudian with Marxist method and of psychoanalysis with anthropology, has had its parallel development in criticism. And there is thus another element added to our equipment for analyzing literary works, and the problem grows still more complex.

The analyst, however, is of course not concerned with the comparative values of his patients any more than the surgeon is. He cannot tell you why the neurotic Dostoevsky produces work of immense value to his fellows while another man with the same neurotic pattern would become a public menace. Freud himself emphatically states in his study of Leonardo that his method can make no attempt to account for Leonardo's genius. The problems of comparative artistic value still remain after we have given attention to the Freudian psychological factor just as they do after we have given attention to the Marxist economic factor and to the racial and geographical factors. No matter how thoroughly and searchingly we may have scrutinized works of literature from the historical and biographical points of view, we must be ready to attempt to estimate, in some such way as Saintsbury and Eliot do, the relative degrees of success attained by the products of the various periods and the various personalities. We must be able to tell good from bad, the first-rate from the second-rate. We shall not otherwise write literary criticism at all, but merely social or political history as reflected in literary texts, or psychological case histories from past eras, or, to take the historical point of view in its simplest and most academic form, merely chronologies of books that have been published.

And now how, in these matters of literary art, do we tell the good art from the bad? Norman Kemp Smith, the Kantian philosopher, whose courses I was fortunate enough to take at Princeton twenty-five years ago, used to tell us that this recognition was based primarily on an emotional reaction. For purposes of practical criticism this is a safe assumption on which to proceed. It is possible to discriminate in a variety of ways the elements that in any given department go to make a successful work of literature. Different schools have at different times demanded different things of literature: *unity, symmetry, universality, originality, vision, inspiration, strangeness, suggestiveness, improving morality, socialist realism,* etc. But you could have any set of these qualities that any school of writing has called for and still not have a good play, a good novel, a good poem, a good history. If you identify the essence of good literature with any one of these elements or with any combination of them, you simply shift the emotional reaction to the recognition of the element or elements. Or if you add to your other demands the demand that the writer must have *talent,* you simply shift this recognition to the talent. Once people find some grounds of agreement in the coincidence of their emotional reactions to books, they may be able to discuss these elements profitably; but if they do not have this basic agreement, the discussion will make no sense.

But how, you may ask, can we identify this élite who know what they are talking about? Well, it can only be said of them that they are self-appointed and self-perpetuating, and that they will compel you to accept their authority. Imposters may try to put themselves over, but these quacks will not last. The implied position of the people who know about literature (as is also the case in every other art) is simply that they know what they know, and that they are determined to impose their opinions by main force of eloquence or assertion on the people who do not know. This is not a question, of course, of professional workers in literature—such as editors, professors and critics, who very often have no real understanding of the products with which they deal—but of readers of all kinds in all walks of life. There are moments when a first-rate writer, unrecognized or out of fashion with the official chalkers-up for the market, may find his support in the demand for his work of an appreciative cultivated public.

But what is the cause of this emotional reaction which is the critic's divining rod? This question has long been a subject of study by the branch of philosophy called esthetics, and it has recently been made a subject of scientific experimentation. Both these lines of inquiry are likely to be prejudiced in the eyes of the literary critic by the fact that the inquiries are sometimes conducted by persons who are obviously deficient in literary feeling or taste. Yet one should not deny the possibility that something of value might result from the speculations and explorations of men of acute minds who take as their given data the esthetic emotions of other men.

Almost everybody interested in literature has tried to explain to himself the nature of these emotions that register our approval of artistic works; and I of course have my own explanation.

In my view, all our intellectual activity, in whatever field it takes place, is an attempt to give a meaning to our experience—that is, to make life more practicable; for by understanding things we make it easier to survive and get around among them. The mathematician Euclid, working in a convention of abstractions, shows us relations between the distances of our unwieldy and cluttered-up environment upon which we are able to count. A drama of Sophocles also indicates relations between the various human impulses, which appear so confused and dangerous, and it brings out a certain justice of Fate— that is to say, of the way in which the interaction of these impulses is seen in the long run to work out—upon which we can also depend. The kinship, from this point of view, of the purposes of science and art appears very clearly in the case of the Greeks, because not only do both Euclid and Sophocles satisfy us by making patterns, but they make much the same kind of patterns. Euclid's *Elements* takes simple theorems and by a series of logical operations builds them up to a climax in the square on the hypotenuse. A typical drama of Sophocles develops in a similar way.

Some writers (as well as some scientists) have a different kind of explicit message beyond the reassurance implicit in the mere feat of understanding life or of moulding the harmony of artistic form. Not content with such an achievement as that of Sophocles—who has one of his choruses tell us that it is better not to be born, but who, by representing life as noble and based on law, makes its tragedy easier to bear—such writers attempt, like Plato, to think out and recommend a procedure for turning it into something better. But other departments of literature—lyric poetry such as Sappho's, for example—have *less* philosophical content than Sophocles. A lyric gives us nothing but a pattern imposed on the expression of a feeling; but this pattern of metrical quantities and of consonants and vowels that balance has the effect of reducing the feeling, however unruly or painful it may seem when we experience it in the course of our lives, to something orderly, symmetrical and pleasing; and it also relates this feeling to the more impressive scheme, works it into the larger texture, of the body of poetic art. The discord has been resolved, the anomaly subjected to discipline. And this control of his emotion by the poet has the effect at second-hand of making it easier for the reader to manage his own emotions. (Why certain sounds and rhythms gratify us more than others, and how they are connected with the themes and ideas that they are chosen as appropriate for conveying, are questions that may be passed on to the scientist.)

And this brings us back again to the historical point of view. The experience of mankind on the earth is always changing as man develops and has to deal with new combinations of elements; and the writer who is to be anything more than an echo of his predecessors must always find expression for something which has never yet been expressed, must master a new set of phenomena which has never yet been mastered. With each such victory of the human intellect, whether in history, in philosophy or in poetry, we experience a deep satisfaction: we have been cured of some ache of disorder, relieved of some oppressive burden of uncomprehended events.

This relief that brings the sense of power, and, with the sense of power, joy, is the positive emotion which tells us that we have encountered a first-rate piece of literature. But stay! you may at this point warn: are not people often solaced and exhilarated by literature of the trashiest kind? They are: crude and limited people do certainly feel some such emotion in connection with work that is limited and crude. The man who is more highly organized and has a wider intellectual range will feel it in connection with work that is finer and more complex. The difference between the emotion of the more highly organized man and the emotion of the less highly organized one is a matter of mere graduation. You sometimes discover books—the novels of John Steinbeck, for example—that seem to mark precisely the borderline between work that is definitely superior and work that is definitely bad. When I was speaking a little while back of the genuine connoisseurs who establish the standards of taste, I meant, of course, the people who can distinguish Grade A and who prefer it to the other grades.

The Historical Criticism of Milton*

A. S. P. WOODHOUSE

As I understand the assignment given to me, it is to suggest a definition and defence of Historical Criticism as applied to Milton, while Mr. Brooks is to tell us how the New Criticism (as it is called) would deal with the poet. So short a time has elapsed since Mr. Eliot took down the sign reading "No Thoroughfare," and directing an elaborate detour around Milton, that Mr. Brooks enjoys, I imagine, a freedom from embarrassing examples, which I can only envy. Again, he has at command a growing body of theory; for the New Critics have been concerned to provide their own dialectic, whereas historical students of literature have tended to work by a silent instinct of accumulation like the bee. Obviously, no one can hope to supply in a thirty-minute paper a theory of Historical Criticism, though I shall try to set down a few points towards the formation of such a theory. Nor is it any part of my purpose to attack the New Criticism in its theory or practice. First, because I do not know enough about it, being indeed somewhat in the case of Lord Monboddo. ("Have you read my last book?" asked Lord Kames. "No, my lord," said Monboddo; "I can't read as fast as you can write.") But secondly (and seriously) because we have had enough, I think, of mutual recrimination, and it is time for each side to make plain, without polemics, what it can do for the elucidation of Milton, in the hope that students who care more for literature than for labels may find something of use to them in both schools. For criticism, of whatever school, is a means, not an end; and the test to be applied to it is purely pragmatic: Does it or does it not throw new light on, or minister to an understanding of, the work

---

* This paper was read before the Milton Group of the Modern Language Association of America on 28 December 1950. It was followed by a paper on "Milton and Critical Re-estimates" by Cleanth Brooks. —ED.

or the author under examination? By that test alone it must stand or fall.

I will commence by drawing a distinction between historical criticism and historical research. The latter is concerned with the amassing and ordering of historical facts; the former, with an application of the results to the interpretation of a work or an author, which is the proper business of all criticism. In practice, of course, the two activities are often fruitfully combined, but the distinction is nevertheless valid and necessary. With historical research as such I shall not be directly concerned. But since it is clearly instrumental to historical criticism, its utility will inevitably follow from the utility of historical criticism if that is established.

Now, the common possession of all schools of criticism is the text; and where they differ is in the method which they adopt in interpreting this common possession. It is the boast of the New Criticism that it concentrates all its attention upon the text and applies to it a purely aesthetic analysis, waiving every extraneous consideration. And this we may concede to be admirable, so far as it goes. But the really difficult questions remain: What considerations are indeed extraneous, or rather, what considerations are really germane? And how far does aesthetic pattern, the object of analysis, itself involve materials which are utilized by the poetic process, but in no sense originated by it? To these questions we shall return; for they are fundamental. Meanwhile we must notice the common indictment of the Historical Critic, that he allows a consideration of sources and analogues, and of historical influences generally, to distract his attention from the text. This, in so far as it is true, is an example of human weakness, and no necessary concomitant of historical method; for the very object with which the historical data are brought forward is the elucidation of the text. But finally, under the heading of text, it is to be observed that Historical Criticism (though not every historical critic) is concerned with the text in a way in which the New Criticism is not. The establishment of the true text is the business, not merely of historical research, but of historical criticism: it demands an application of the results of historical research to this particular problem, by the critical intelligence. Of the work in progress by Professor Harris Fletcher and others, I am not competent to speak in detail. I do not know whether it has yet resulted in determinations of comparable critical importance to those reached in the very different problem of Shakespeare's text—determinations like Professor Dover Wilson's that what Hamlet really said was, "O that this too, too *sullied* flesh would melt." Whether it has or not, no one will deny that the establishment of the true text is an essential task, without which neither historical elucidation nor aesthetic analysis can proceed with safety. Here, then, is the first department of Historical Criticism, and its first claim to be regarded as indispensable. It alone can supply the text on which the New Criticism desires to focus all its attention.

With the text established, a wide field of investigation and critical decision opens out. The starting point is the text of the individual poems, but the sum of the decisions reached should yield a critical estimate of Milton the poet. So far (if I am not mistaken) the New Criticism has largely confined itself to the individual poem (and to the shorter and more purely lyric examples thereof) and has looked on, not to the character of the particular poet, but rather to the nature of poetry in general, as its larger objective. Herein it differs sharply from Historical Criticism, whose procedure is to examine all the author's poems, of whatever length and kind, and thus to advance from the individual poem (the primary concern of all criticism) to the whole body of his work. Let us compromise by taking as our starting point a poem of middle length and remind ourselves how Historical Criticism would deal—indeed has dealt—with *Samson Agonistes.*

Now, it is perfectly possible to attempt an analysis of the aesthetic pattern of *Samson Agonistes,* and to such an analysis every critic must come. The question is whether or not the analysis shall be undertaken in the light of certain historical facts. *Samson Agonistes* is Milton's deliberate effort to write a classical tragedy on a Hebrew-Christian subject (that is, an Old Testament subject as interpreted by Christianity); and to the Historical Critic this fact immediately suggests two considerations as by no means extraneous: "Milton's Debt to Greek Tragedy in *Samson Agonistes*" (to adopt the actual title of Professor W. R. Parker's book), and "Milton's Samson and the Christian Tradition" (to adopt the title of Professor F. M. Krouse's). The latter makes us aware of the various choices in interpretation and emphasis which previous commentary had placed at Milton's disposal; the former fixes our attention on his detailed imitation of the Greek tragic form. Neither seeks to lead us away from Milton's text, but at most to postpone our consideration of it till the relevant information is acquired. And both entail at the end, and indeed during the whole process, an effort of critical interpretation. It is interpretation undertaken from a particular point of view, and so can hardly even pretend to finality. But if the history of criticism demonstrates anything it is that "final interpretations" are an illusion. Criticism cannot escape from the general rhythm of human thought which prescribes its passage from thesis to antithesis to synthesis, which is itself a new thesis. Every "final interpretation" turns out to be the last but one. In certain ways the critical efforts of Parker and Krouse correct each other, simply by virtue of their different points of view. The correction of former critics is a role often assigned to Historical Criticism—particularly of course the correction of the daydreams of the Impressionist—and it is a role assumed with some degree of zest. It should not, however, be mistaken for the primary role. Historical Criticism is not merely negative in function. If it can correct errors, it can also suggest new and fruitful ways of looking at the poem under examination. Two of these are illustrated in the books to which we have referred.

There are doubtless other relevant considerations. Besides the poem, the subject, and the traditional form, there is also the poet. It was *Milton* who undertook to write a classical tragedy on the Hebrew-Christian subject of Samson, and we know a good deal about this man Milton beside the fact, never to be forgotten, that he was a poet. Upon those who would dismiss as irrelevant every consideration of Milton the man, his extra-aesthetic experience, the drama of his own life, a heavy burden of proof must rest. Now here, confessedly, we are on ground doubly debatable; for many Historical Critics draw back from the assumed presence of Milton in his works, as the "autobiographical fallacy" or the "personal heresy." The reaction against Masson's heavy-handed interpretation, and particularly his reading of *Samson Agonistes* as concealed autobiography and political allegory, is understandable enough, and no doubt salutary. But that Milton's state of mind when he undertook the tragedy had no bearing upon the work which he produced remains a proposition far more difficult to establish than is its opposite. It is interesting to notice how much Professors Hanford and Parker, in their recent writings on *Samson*, have modified their former position; and yet more significant to observe how this issue of quite fundamental importance has been brought up again for debate in connection with the effort of Professor Parker, Professor A. H. Gilbert, and others, to determine a highly controversial matter of fact, namely, the date at which *Samson Agonistes* was probably written. This is very often the way of Historical Criticism: it attacks a question of fact and finds itself confronted by a question of interpretation. The remaining problems of chronology are unlikely now to be solved by a new discovery of external evidence (that is, simply by a process of historical research). They are much more likely to demand the weighing of internal evidence (that is, an exercise of historical criticism). It would be patently absurd to consider all the evidence except that afforded by the poem itself. But to read the internal evidence aright the critic must know the whole body of his author's work. He must be able to compare the undated poem with every other, and especially with those whose dates are known; he must have formed to himself a clear notion of the probable pattern of the poet's career, and be alert to see where in that pattern the undated poem finds its most natural place; and only in relation to the poet's practice in his other poems can the critical question with which we started be answered, namely, the degree to which, not *any* poet's, but *this* poet's, extra-aesthetic experience enters into his poetry. A tentative answer to that question is essential before one can determine the nature and limits of the internal evidence with which one has to deal. In the light of Milton's practice in other poems, is it more probable that the inescapable parallels between Milton's Samson and Milton himself after the Restoration are conscious and dependent on the poet's situation and state of mind when he wrote, or that they are merely coincidental and without value as evidence?

But the answer given to this question has implications far beyond the problem of the date of *Samson Agonistes*. The question may serve therefore to conduct us to some further observations on Historical Criticism as it applies to other poems; and, first, to an observation on method. The degree to which Milton's extra-aesthetic experience enters into his poems is a question which can be approached only by means of hypothesis. That it enters in its plentitude, that it enters not at all, that it enters in certain degree and under certain conditions: each of these is an hypothesis, and to be subjected to the appropriate tests. Does the hypothesis run counter to any known evidence? Does it, then, cover all the phenomena? Is it the simplest hypothesis that will do so? The answer to these questions will dictate its acceptance, its abandonment, or its modification. Every time the hypothesis satisfactorily explains a poem, and every time it is found to have provided in advance for new evidence as this appears, the hypothesis has in effect received experimental verification. Every historical critic must form, for example, some hypothetical scheme of Milton's early development. I had the advantage (if I may be pardoned one personal reference) of forming mine with Dr. E. M. W. Tillyard's important argument on the date of *L'Allegro* and *Il Penseroso* before me, but Professor Parker's equally important argument on the date of the sonnet "How soon hath Time" came later. To find the hypothetical pattern fortified by his conclusion was to verify the hypothesis, and also, I think, to add an argument in favour of the conclusion itself. Hypothesis, then, is an indispensable instrument of Historical Criticism.

I have indicated that there is some dispute among historical critics as to the degree, and the manner, in which Milton's extra-aesthetic experience, including his thought, enters into his various poems. The results are worth examining.

Those who deny that such experience enters into his poetry at all, greatly restrict the range of Historical Criticism (as did Mr. Stoll in his treatment of Shakespeare). They reduce it to a consideration of the poems with reference to their genres and to the traditional patterns and conventions which Milton adopted, with perhaps some attention to the intellectual commonplaces of the age, but with none to Milton's more individual and distinctive ideas. That illuminating criticism may be achieved on this narrow basis need not be denied. It is illustrated, for example, in Mr. B. Rajan's admirable *Paradise Lost and the Seventeenth-century Reader*. But such criticism, by restricting itself virtually to aesthetic analysis, approaches as near as Historical Criticism well may to the concerns and methods of the New Criticism. As a device for isolating certain features of Milton's poetry this is legitimate enough. It becomes dangerous only when erected into a dogma, whose effect is to prejudge the character and the historical relations of his poetry; and when it seeks to rule out as irrelevant all those studies of Milton's life and thought, and of his religious and intellectual background,[1] which, existing in their own right, may still claim to be heard before we pass final judgment on the poet—before, indeed, we can pretend fully to understand any one of his poems.

On this, as on other subjects, Historical Criticism should, it seems, preserve an open mind, till the facts suggest an hypothesis to be tested and, in the light of this testing, to be accepted, rejected or modified. The denial of any important relation between Milton's extra-aesthetic experience and a particular poem is a perfectly possible outcome of this process. For example, it seems evident that *Arcades* neither embodies nor even finds its starting point in any important extra-aesthetic experience intellectual or emotional. It takes its rise simply from the invitation to provide the text for a simple entertainment in honour of the Dowager Countess of Derby and from Milton's election of the masque form and the pastoral note. *Arcades* is a pure, and a singularly effective, example of aesthetic patterning, entirely adequate to its occasion and purpose, and carrying no overtones from Milton's life unless for a moment in the exquisite "Nymphs and shepherds dance no more." This view of the poem can be verified in different ways, and among others by observing the use to which Milton puts a

---

[1] Those of William Haller, Arthur Barker, Merritt Y. Hughes, Arnold Williams, and a host of others.

favourite image, that of the music of the spheres. Whenever this image occurs elsewhere it bears an ethical and religious reference and becomes the vehicle of Milton's youthful idealism. The one exception is *Arcades:* there it is bent solely to the purpose of compliment and achieves a purely aesthetic effect with none of the overtones that it habitually carries. So much for *Arcades.* But nothing could justify an historical critic in a blanket denial of relation between Milton's poetry as a whole and his extra-aesthetic experience save an examination of his work poem by poem, undertaken with a full knowledge of his life, thought, and background. Such an examination would presently entail a comparison of *Arcades* and *Comus*, and this could not fail to bring home to the critic the wide difference between them, first in general effect, and then, on more detailed perusal, in argument and image, and in the extent to which the character of the poem can be accounted for by its occasion and avowed purpose, and by the genre in which Milton has chosen to work. Whatever is not to be accounted for by these considerations must seek its explanation elsewhere, and here the hypothesis of a relation to Milton's extra-aesthetic experience presents itself. We need go no farther. For indeed the assertion that Milton's poetry in general bears no ascertainable relation to his extra-aesthetic experience is not a result of such painstaking examination at all. It is a dogma, an assumption respecting the nature of poetry, which the critic is applying or misapplying to Milton.

Now, a sense of poetry as something *sui generis* is as necessary to the Historical Critic as to any other, and if he lacks this sense he had better betake himself to some other occupation; for he will reduce poetry to a mere document and a document whose language he cannot read. But what does the proposition, that poetry is *sui generis*, mean? It certainly does not mean that all poems are alike; for that is a notion dissipated by half an hour with any anthology, or by the simple confronting of *Arcades* and *Comus*. Poems are endlessly various. But they have certain qualities in common, two of which we may specify. First, whatever the subject, the poem develops it by means of—that is, under the form of—an aesthetic pattern. And, secondly, whatever its starting point in extra-aesthetic experience, the poem is never a mere record of that experience. On the contrary, it is the realization of a new experience: or (to put it in another way) the poem *is* the experience which it records. And it is with this experience —this poem—that the critic *qua* critic is concerned, an experience of which the aesthetic pattern holds the key.

But when these common characteristics of poetry *qua* poetry are recognized, there still remains the vast difference between poem and poem, and between one poet and another. And the differentiating qualities are as much a part of the poem, or of the body of poetry, as are the common characteristics. With these differentiating qualities, the Historical Critic is likewise concerned; and he is not content merely to observe them: he wants to know why they are there. Why is *Comus* so different from *Arcades*, or *Lycidas* from the *Epitaphium Damonis?* Why is *Paradise Lost* so different from the *Aeneid*, or *Samson Agonistes* from *Oedipus at Colonus?* Why do Milton's poems in their effect add up to something so different from Spenser's, or Donne's, or Dryden's, or Wordsworth's? No one,

I suppose, will deny that these are important questions or that they fall legitimately within the critic's field of inquiry. For to recognize that complete and final answers are impossible is no reason for discarding such partial answers as can be found. And no one will imagine that these answers can be reached by any other method than the historical or without constant reference to Milton's text. One brief example will suffice. No doubt *Paradise Lost* differs from the *Aeneid* because one was written by Milton, the other by Virgil. But the answer in that form is unmanageable and unproductive—is, in fact, no answer at all. The question requires to be broken down into its parts, and of these some are certainly answerable. It is obvious, for example, that an important difference depends upon Milton's Christian subject-matter, and his Christian attitude, which entail marked adaptations of the traditional epic form; so that we are led back immediately from the poem's pattern to its subject-matter, and from the subject-matter to the poet's belief or thought, in order to account for differences in pattern and effect. This is the sort of question that can be dealt with by the Historical Critic, and by no one else.

Apart, however, from the comparative study, Historical Criticism has a vast field of inquiry open to it. *Paradise Lost* is not only a classical epic (and thus comparable with the *Aeneid*): it is also a Christian theodicy (whose avowed purpose is to "assert Eternal Providence And justify the ways of God to men") and a philosophical poem (with a view of man and of the cosmic order to present). In these aspects also it takes its place in history, and is fully understandable only in relation to history.

Though as an activity poetry is indeed *sui generis*, the particular view which the poet takes of the nature and end of poetry, and especially of his own poetry, has an immense effect on what he writes. But his view of poetry depends in part on his view of life. Behind every philosophy of art there lies a philosophy of life. In a poet like Milton who consistently asserts or assumes the closest relation between his art and life, every shaping experience, every idea embraced, will, or at least may, have its bearing on his poetry. For example, why was Milton able to adopt with such singular literalness the idea that the Christian poet was indeed inspired? Because he read the conventional idea of the inspired poet in the light of the Christian conviction, reinforced by the Reformation, that every believer is inspired. Why did he not proceed to the romantic conclusion, that learning, thought, and conscious artistry are, then, superfluous, are even an impediment? Because he also inherited the Renaissance tradition of learned poetry and conscious art, because (like his fellows) he incorporated the Roman ideal of the orator in his conception of the poet, and because he adopted the Platonic view of reason, which made the flash of intuitive insight the result and the reward of patient thought, not something opposed to it. By his whole conception of poetry, with its ethical and religious as well as aesthetic end, Milton is led to embody in many of his poems his most searching thoughts and his profoundest convictions. It is not by their form alone, any more than by their content alone, that these poems seek "to imbreed and cherish . . . the seeds of virtue, to allay the pertubations of the mind, and set the affections in right tune." But indeed the dichotomy and the problem are of our making, not Milton's, as every historical student knows or may come to know.

Thus Milton's thought enters deeply into his poetry. The cosmology of the *De Doctrina Christiana* is (by grace of the epic tradition) embodied in *Paradise Lost* and adapted to the purpose of the poem. The doctrine of free will is central in Milton's reading of the action and in his whole effort to justify the ways of God to men, and thus is doubly essential to the poem. His view of the nature and function of Christ, argued at length in the *De Doctrina,* shapes and colours the two poems in which he is a central figure. In *Paradise Regained* this very question is the poem's secondary theme—until the end, when it becomes primary. And that this transition might be effected Milton chose the order of temptations in St. Luke. Thus the theological content conditions the pattern of the poem. And this is characteristic of Milton. Whatever may be said of some other poets, Milton's aesthetic patterns rely on a foundation, or rather perhaps a framework, of conceptual thought, and they cannot be elucidated without reference to it. This is already true in the Nativity Ode, and it is still true in *Paradise Regained.* Milton's thought as thought is very much "of an age," and hence susceptible only of historical elucidation. Somehow it is transmuted into poetry which is "for all time." It is for the critic to explain as best he can how this miracle is performed.

Mr. Cleanth Brooks has complained[2] that for Professor Maurice Kelley, in *This Great Argument,* "the problem of exegesis is almost amusingly simple." In the *De Doctrina* you discover what Milton's ideas were: you then explain *Paradise Lost,* that "tangled and difficult poetic document, by means of the explicit prose statement." But, Mr. Brooks continues, Mr. Kelley's argument rests on two assumptions: first, "that the Milton who wrote the *Christian Doctrine* was precisely and at all points the same man who composed *Paradise Lost*" (and this assumption Mr. Brooks surprisingly concedes); secondly, it involves "the further and much more dangerous assumption that Milton was able to say in *Paradise Lost* exactly what he intended to say, and that what he supposed he had put into the poem is actually to be found there" (and this assumption Mr. Brooks peremptorily denies).

Now, I am equally astonished at the concession of the first assumption and the denial of the second. For it seems to me that to deny to Milton a knowledge of what he was doing in *Paradise Lost* and, after it was written, a knowledge of what he had done, runs counter to all the evidence of self-possession and deliberation as distinguishing marks of Milton, which the long study of his artistry has accumulated. It appears, further, to open the way for every aberration of romantic criticism. But to me it seems equally clear that the Milton who wrote the *De Doctrina* was *not* the same as the Milton who composed *Paradise Lost.* The one was Milton the thinker and controversialist; the other, Milton the thinker *and poet.* In this statement, I am not committing myself to that most absurd of dichotomies—the one adopted by Hilaire Belloc in what must surely be (among many strong competitors) the worst book on Milton ever written. I do not mean that the thinker and the poet bear no relation to each other. Far

---

[2] In his "Criticism and Literary History," *Sewanee Rev.,* LV (1947), 199–222.

from it. I am simply recognizing the indubitable fact that poetry differs from prose, and thought in poetry from thought in prose. In the more controversial parts of the *De Doctrina* Milton is arguing a case; much of his effort goes to demolishing the case of his opponents, and the animation of the work has much in common with that of Milton's other controversial prose. His concern is with theology—not with religious, and certainly not with aesthetic, experience. He fits his thought to a theological scheme, not to a vision of existence. But in the two epics argument gives place to vision, and negation to affirmation—to an affirmation, that is, of the residuum of positive faith by which Milton lived. In the *De Doctrina* Milton argues the case for monism (I will not call it materialism). In *Paradise Lost* he embodies the doctrine in his vision of creation. In the *De Doctrina* he argues the case for an Arian or semi-Arian view of Christ. In *Paradise Lost* he realizes, and makes us realize, how entirely for him this view is compatible with the impulse of worship:

> Hail, Son of God, Saviour of Men, thy Name
> Shall be the copious matter of my song
> Henceforth, and never shall my harp thy praise
> Forget, nor from thy Father's praise disjoin.

Paradise Regained is the fulfilment of this promise, and there (as we have said) the secondary theme of Christ's divinity becomes at the end primary, when, abating nothing of his Arianism, the poet reaffirms the doctrine (and fulfils the promise) of *Paradise Lost:*

> True Image of the Father, whether throned
> In the bosom of bliss and light of light
> Conceiving, or remote from Heaven, enshrined
> In earthly tabernacle and human form—

everywhere and always, the Son is the true Image of the Father. And Milton, I infer, was enabled, not to reach this position, but to realize its full implications, by the aid of poetry. For whatever his limitations, he has this indispensable mark of the religious poet: his aesthetic experience and his religious are not two things, but one. And the poem is not a record of experience: it *is* the experience. It is not a record of thought: it is compacted of those

> thoughts that voluntary move
> Harmonious numbers,

and that reach full realization only in them.

Poetry, it seems clear, has two aspects, a temporal and a permanent. It is the reproach of Historical Criticism that it is sunk in the temporal and in the relativism that pertains thereto; and sometimes no doubt the charge is well founded. But one does not get rid of the temporal by ignoring it; and to pretend to do so often means no more than the introduction of a new relativism: one reads the poem in relation to one's own age instead of to the poet's. Milton has suffered and Donne has benefited by this new and usually concealed relativism. But to speak of a temporal aspect of poetry, and a permanent, is not sufficiently precise. It is the miracle of poetry that it makes of the temporal something permanent. And if one would understand how this is done, and even in some instances be sure that it is done, one must know the temporal conditions in which it is essayed.

The contemporary audience always enjoys two advantages: an intuitive and comprehensive grasp of the potentialities and limits of the genre in which the poet is working, so that it does not ask for the impossible, and an immediate recognition of the frame of reference within which his ideas move. Much of the misunderstanding of *Comus* springs from a failure to grasp the potentialities and limits of the masque form (with which confessedly Milton takes great liberties) and of Spenserian allegory. Much misunderstanding also arises from a failure to recognize the distinction and the relation of the two orders of nature and of grace, which furnish the poem's frame of reference. The sense of these things three centuries have almost completely destroyed, and they can be restored only by painful historical study. But, when restored, they do not merely serve to correct errors of interpretation or to crowd out the false assumptions which will always fill the vacuum when true assumptions are lacking: they also give us a new vantage point from which to attempt our analysis of the poem's pattern. For the function of Historical Criticism is not simply to act as a corrective: it can suggest new and productive ways of looking at the poem.

And this, as it seems to me, holds the best promise of some alliance between Historical Criticism and the New Criticism. They need each other. Certainly we historical critics have something to learn from the method of analysis employed by the New Criticism: from the method, for example, of Mr. Brooks's essay on *L'Allegro* and *Il Penseroso*.[3] Perhaps too, the New Critics may sometimes

---

[3] "The Light Symbolism in 'L'Allegro-Il Penseroso,'" in *The Well Wrought Urn* (1947), pp. 47–61. I remarked above, "Whatever may be said of other poets, Milton's aesthetic patterns rely on a foundation, or rather perhaps a framework, of conceptual thought, and they cannot be elucidated without reference to it." This suggests a reservation which must not be overlooked. The method of analysis employed by the New Criticism appears to consist of a frontal attack on the imagery of the poem, with little or no attention to its theme as presented in action or argument. Applied to imagist verse, this method, corresponding to the intention of the poet, will yield whatever is to be discovered. Applied to poetry such as Milton's, it will, by itself, yield only results which, however valuable, are secondary and supplemental. This limitation, as it seems to me, is illustrated both in Mr. Brooks's essay on *L'Allegro* and *Il Penseroso* and in the part of his paper dealing with the image of "the *fruit* of the tree of Knowledge" in *Paradise Lost*. For, Dr. Tillyard to the contrary notwithstanding, the theme of *L'Allegro* and *Il Penseroso* is not day and night, but two contrasting ways of life, or two moods, as the titles indicate; day and night enter the poems because of the temporal sequence in which Milton has found his structural pattern; the images of light and darkness do not reveal the theme, but they support and supplement it. And so with "the *fruit* of the tree of Knowledge": everything that Mr. Brooks says of it may well be true, and (if true) illuminating. (Indeed an historical critic would find confirmation in Bacon's "philosophy of fruits," with which Milton must have been familiar.) But the suggestions conveyed by this image—one among many—are secondary and supplemental to Milton's theme of the Fall and his central interpretation thereof. The role of imagery in Milton would appear to be twofold: to *support* the main theme presented in action or argument, but also to *supplement* it by other and not inconsistent suggestions, and thereby to give the poem that density and richness of suggestion which differentiates it from any mere summary of its theme, as revealed through action, argument, or structural pattern. When this relation is recognized, the technique of the New Criticism in exploring Milton's imagery seems to me of the highest value, and exemplary.

gather suggestions from the findings of Historical Criticism. No doubt we shall continue to disagree, and our remarks about each other will have a certain tonic bitterness. But we are all, I assume, concerned with truth, if not with finality. And I cannot help recalling two principles which Newman invoked in another and more solemn context: "Truth cannot contradict truth"; but "truth often seems to contradict truth." And the inference surely is obvious: that we should be patient one with another.

University of Toronto

Bibliography and the Novelistic Fallacy

BRUCE HARKNESS

It is a truth universally acknowledged, that a critic intent upon analysis and interpretation, must be in want of a good text. It is also universally acknowledged that we live in an age of criticism, indeed of "new criticism"—which means that we as critics are dedicated to a very close reading of the text. Sometimes, it is true, that critical principle leads to abuses. The symbol-hunting, the ambiguity-spinning become wonders to behold. As one objector has put it, "nose to nose, the critic confronts writer and, astonished, discovers himself."[1] Nonetheless, the principle of close reading is held central by us all. Immediately that one contemplates novel criticism, however, an oddity appears: the last thing we find in a discussion by a new critic is some analysis of the actual text.

The modern critic is apt to be entirely indifferent to the textual problems of a novel. He is all too prone to examine rigorously a faulty text. As Gordon Ray and others have pointed out, even the Great Cham of British Criticism errs in this respect. F. R. Leavis defends the early Henry James in *The Great Tradition:* "Let me insist, then, at once, . . . that his [James's] 'first attempt at a novel,' *Roderick Hudson* (1874), in spite of its reputation, is a very distinguished book that deserves permanent currency—much more so than many novels passing as classics." Professor Ray adds that "Mr. Leavis goes on to quote three long paragraphs to illustrate the novel's 'sustained maturity of theme and treatment. . . .' These remarks are amply warranted by the passage that Mr. Leavis cites. But unhappily he has quoted, not the text of the first edition of 1877 [while carefully dating it from the time of composition to make it appear all

---

[1] Marvin Mudrick, "Conrad and the Terms of Modern Criticism," *Hudson Review*, VI (1954), 421.

the more precocious], which is simple enough, but that of the New York edition of 1907, revised in James's intricate later manner. "This leaves him," concludes Leavis's critic, "in the position of having proved at length what nobody would think of denying, that James's writing at the age of sixty-four has all the characteristics of maturity."[2]

Unhappily, few of us can afford to laugh at the poor new critic. We all know the truth that we must have a good text, but most of us do not act upon it. A commonplace? Yes, and unfortunately, I have only that commonplace to urge; but I claim good company. Jane Austen, with whom I started, recognized that *Pride and Prejudice* had no profoundly new meaning. She ironically developed upon commonplaces: don't act on first impressions; don't interfere in your best friend's love affair; don't ignore your younger daughters. My point is that, ironically, everyone ignores the bibliographical study of the novel. People who would consider it terribly bad form to slight the textual study of a play or poem —or even doggerel—commit bibliographical nonsense when handed a novel. It seems that the novel just doesn't count. A key error in many studies of the novel is simply this, that the novel is unconsciously considered a different order of thing from poetry—a poem's text must be approached seriously. I shall illustrate by mentioning the sins of editors, reprinters, publishers, scholars, and, alas, bibliographers. Then, after discussing a few of the many reasons for this bibliographical heresy, I shall turn to my main illustration of the need for textual bibliography, *The Great Gatsby*.

I

A list of representative errors, by no means exhaustive, by sound men whom I admire in all other respects will make clear how faulty the texts of novels are, and how little we care. A good editor has put *The Nigger of the "Narcissus"* in *The Portable Conrad*, an excellent volume the introductions to which contain some of the best Conrad criticism. But what, one may wonder, is the copy-text for *The Nigger*? A search through the book discloses two references, the less vague of which reads as follows: "It is from the editions published and copyrighted by the latter [Doubleday and Company] that the texts reproduced in this volume have been drawn" (p. 758).

After a spot of searching the reader can discover for himself that the copy-text for *The Nigger of the "Narcissus"* is not the collected English edition, which as is well known was Conrad's major concern. The copy-text was an early American publication, which Conrad habitually did not supervise. The new critic immediately asks, does it make any difference?

The collected English edition was, as one might suspect with an author who was constantly revising, changed in many ways. This final version cuts down Conrad's intrusive "philosophizing," and corrects Donkin's cockney accent,

---

[2] Gordon N. Ray, "The Importance of Original Editions," in *Nineteenth-Century English Books*, by Gordon N. Ray, Carl Weber, and John Carter (1952), p. 22. See also "Henry James Reprints," *TLS* 5 Feb. 1949, p. 96.

among other shifts.[3] I yield to no man in my admiration for Conrad, but if he has a fault, it lies in that adjectival "philosophy" which is admired by some, charitably overlooked by others, and condemned by a few as pipe-sucking old seadog-talk. Surely the following, from the early part of Chapter Four, is inappropriate in the mouth of the sailor-narrator: "Through the perfect wisdom of its grace [the sea's] they [seamen] are not permitted to meditate at ease upon the complicated and acrid savour of existence, lest they should remember and, perchance, regret the reward of a cup of inspiring bitterness, tasted so often, and so often withdrawn before their stiffening but reluctant lips. They must without pause justify their life. . . ." Most of this passage, and much similar sententiousness, were cut by Conrad from the collected English text; but they all stand in *The Portable Conrad*.

As for the class of books known loosely as "reprints," I suppose that no one expects a good text for twenty-five or thirty-five cents. These books I am not concerned with, but the more serious paperbacks, obviously intended for use in colleges, are sometimes faulty. For example, Rinehart Editions' copy of *Pride and Prejudice* reprints Chapman's excellent text—but suppresses the indication of three volume construction by numbering the chapters serially throughout.[4] Though three volumes are mentioned in the introduction, this misprinting of such a tightly constructed novel can only be regretted, for the effect on the college reader must be odd.

What of the publisher of more expensive novels? It can easily be seen that errors are not limited to the paperback field. Consider, for example, the one-volume Scribner edition of James's *The Wings of the Dove*, dated 1945 or 1946. Here is no scrimping for paperback costs, but the book is not what one would think. It is not a reprint of the famous New York edition; it is another, unacknowledged impression of the 1902 first American edition, dressed up with a new-set New York preface—an odd procedure the reason for which is not apparent. The publisher nowhere tells the reader that this is like some wines—an old text with a new preface. Yet one line of print would have made the matter clear. It is only by his own efforts of collation of the preface and the text itself that the reader knows where he is.[5]

[3] C. S. Evans of the editorial department of Heinemann wrote Conrad on 2 Sept. 1920 about Donkin's inconsistent dialect: "I have queried the spelling of 'Hymposed,' " and so on. (See *Life and Letters* [London: Heinemann, 1927], II, 247–48, for the exchange with Evans.) J. D. Gordan in *Joseph Conrad: The Making of a Novelist* (1940), p. 139 and passim, discusses many of the revisions of the text.

It might be possible to defend the use of an early text for *The Nigger*, but no reason is given in *The Portable Conrad*.

[4] Though I cannot pretend to have examined them all, I know of only one independently produced paperback novel with good textual apparatus. This is Rinehart Editions' *Lord Jim*, which contains a collation of the four main texts. Riverside's *Pride and Prejudice* has a good text, but again Chapman's edition lies behind it. There must be, I am sure, many more good texts beside *Lord Jim* in the higher class of paperbacks, and even in the cheaper ones. But what publishers draw them to our attention, and what publisher doesn't (apparently) feel that a properly edited paperback novel will frighten away the common reader by its appearance?

[5] Furthermore, it would be difficult to defend the choice of first-edition text, as one might for *The Nigger of the "Narcissus,"* or *Roderick Hudson*, since James was writing in his intricate manner by 1902.

To turn to the errors of scholarship, take F. O. Matthiessen's lengthy appreciation of Melville's phrase "soiled fish of the sea" in *White-Jacket*. Melville's narrator says of himself, after he had fallen into the sea, "I wondered whether I was yet dead or still dying. But of a sudden some fashionless form brushed my side—some inert, soiled fish of the sea; the thrill of being alive again tingled. . . ." This section Matthiessen acclaims as being imagery of the "sort that was to become peculiarly Melville's . . . hardly anyone but Melville could have created the shudder that results from calling this frightening vagueness some '*soiled* fish of the sea'!" Then follows a discussion of the metaphysical conceit and its moral and psychological implications.

As has been pointed out, the genius in this shuddering case of imagery is not Melville, who wrote *coiled* fish, not *soiled* fish. "Coiled fish" stands in the first editions of *White-Jacket,* and to an unknown Constable printer should go the laurels for soiling the page with a typographical error.[6]

Matthiessen's error does not concern me now, but it does concern me that the scholar who first caught the mistake has a strange but perhaps understandable attitude toward textual matters. Recognizing that such an error "in the proper context" might have promulgated a "false conception," the scholar feels that the slip does not actually matter in Melville's case. Furthermore, he feels that Matthiessen's position is essentially sound—he was merely the victim of "an unlucky error." While sympathizing with common sense and professional etiquette, one may still wonder, however, how many such slips in illustration are allowable. Could the critic, if challenged, produce as many sound illustrations as one would like? Does not Matthiessen, in his categorizing of conceits, virtually admit that this particular kind is rare in *White-Jacket?*

When we look at the texts of novels from the other way, how many good editions of novelists do we have? How do they compare with the poets? We know a good bit about the bibliographies of Scott, Trollope, Meredith, but those of Dickens, Thackeray, Conrad, Hawthorne, and many more are completely out of date.[7] How many collected editions can be put on the same shelf with Chapman's 1923 Jane Austen? "We have virtually no edited texts of Victorian novelists," says Mrs. Tillotson in the introduction of *Novels of the Eighteen-Forties* (1954). How slowly we move, if at all.

Take Hardy for example. In 1946 Carl Weber said that "many scholars have apparently made no attempt to gain access to Hardy's definitive texts." In March, 1957, a scholar can complain that "As late as November 1956, sixty full years after the publication of the book, the only edition of *Jude* printed in the United States took no account of either of the two revisions which Hardy gave the novel. . . . The New Harper's Modern Classics edition . . . [however] is *almost* identical with that of the definitive 1912 'Wessex Edition.' "[8] One is hardly surprised that Professor Weber is the editor.

[6] See J. W. Nichol, "Melville's 'Soiled Fish of the Sea,' " *AL,* XXI (1949), 338–39.

[7] See John Carter, *op. cit.,* p. 53 and passim; reasons for the lack of bibliographical study are also discussed.

[8] Robert C. Slack, "The Text of Hardy's *Jude the Obscure,*" *N-CF,* XI (1957), 275. Italics added.

Sixty years is a long time, but American literature is no better off. *Moby-Dick,* our greatest novel, presents no problem of copy-text. Yet more than 100 years went by after publication before we had what a recent scholar called the "first serious reprint," by Hendricks House. Before that, the careful reader did not even know, for example, the punctuation of the famous "Know ye, now, Bulkington?" passage. But how good is this reprint? The same scholar—not the editor—asks us to consider it a definitive edition. His reasons? It contains only 108 compositor's errors and twenty silent emendations.[9] Would anyone make such a claim for a volume of poems?

So much for editors, publishers, scholars. The sins of the bibliographer are mainly those of omission. For well-known reasons he tends to slight 19th- and 20th-century books in general, and in consequence most novels.[10]

The critic therefore needs convincing that novels should be approached bibliographically. The critic appreciates the sullied-solid-sallied argument about Shakespeare, but not that of 108 typos for *Moby-Dick.* A false word in a sonnet may change a fifth of its meaning; the punctuation at the end of the "Ode on a Grecian Urn" can be considered crucial to the meaning of the whole poem; but who, the critic argues from bulk, can stand the prospect of collating 700 pages of Dickens to find a few dozen misplaced commas? Like the "soiled fish" reading of *White-Jacket,* a few mistakes seriously damage neither novel nor criticism. They are swallowed up in the vast bulk of the novel, which by and large (and excepting a few well-known oddities such as *Tender is the Night* in which case one must be sure which text one is attacking) is decently printed and generally trustworthy. The critic feels that a mistake here or there in the text is immaterial. "It doesn't *really* alter my interpretation," is the standard phrase.

This attitude has long since been defeated by bibliographers for all genres except the novel. One wonders indeed, if the critic would be willing to make his plea more logical. Could not the attitude be extended to some formula for trustworthiness versus error? It ought not to be difficult to arrive at a proportion expressing the number of errors per page, exceeding which a novel could be condemned as poorly printed.

Amid bad reasoning, there is some truth to the critic's defence against bibliography. The argument can be shifted from the ground of a novel's size and a reader's energy to the aesthetic nature of the novel. The critic is certainly right in maintaining that novels are more loosely constructed, even the best of them, than poems or short stories. The effects of a novel are built through countless small touches, and the loss of one or two—whether by error in text or inattention in reading—is immaterial. Putting aside the counter claim that this truth is damaging to the critical and crucial premise of close reading, surely

[9] William T. Hutchinson, "A Definitive Edition of *Moby-Dick,*" *AL,* XXV (1954), 472–78.

[10] See Fredson Bowers, *Principles of Bibliographica' Description* (1949), p. 356 ff, for a discussion of these reasons on the part of the bibliographer. One should admit, furthermore, that the non-professional bibliographers, the scholarly readers and editors, may have reasons which are indefensible, but are nevertheless *reasons.* I daresay one would be shocked to know how many trained men feel today that novels aren't really "literature"; or that modern printing is either perfect or too complicated ever to be fathomed.

all is a matter of degree. And what is more, the theory applies mainly to character portrayal. If we fail to recognize Collins as a fawning ass on one page, we will certainly see him aright on another.

That much must be granted the critic. In other concerns, however, the novel may not be repetitive. To give just one illustration: F. Scott Fitzgerald's *Last Tycoon* as published in unfinished form contains a boy whom the reader should compare to the "villain" of the piece, Brady (or Bradogue as he was called in an earlier draft). In Fitzgerald's directions to himself left in his MSS, he says "Dan [the boy] bears, in some form of speech, a faint resemblance to Bradogue. This must be subtly done and not look too much like a parable or moral lesson, still the impression must be conveyed, but be careful to convey it *once* and not rub it in. If the reader misses it, let it go—don't repeat."[11]

My last and painful reason why virtually no one is concerned with the texts of novels is this: most bibliographers are also university teachers and many of them suffer from schizophrenia. I do not refer to that familiar disease which makes us scholars by day and diaper washers by night, but that split in the man between Graduate Seminar number 520 in Bibliography and Freshman "Intro. to Fic.," 109. How many of us make bibliographical truths part of our daily lives or attempt to inspire our graduate students so to do? In this respect many bibliographers are like socialists and Christians: walking arguments from the weakness of the cause.

Let me give one or two illustrations from experience. Not very long ago I sat in a staff meeting while we worried over a sentence of Conrad's introduction to *Victory* in the Modern Library edition. The sentence contained the odd phrase "adaptable cloth," used about mankind. It made no sense until it was finally pointed out that "adap-table" was divided at the end of the line in both American collected edition and reprint—a domestically minded compositor was talking about a table cloth, while Conrad was saying that Man is "wonderfully adaptable both by his power of endurance and in his capacity for detachment." And our silly discussion had gone on despite long teaching, and one's natural suspicion of the cheaper reprints that perforce must be used in college classes.

More seriously, consider Dickens' *Great Expectations,* taught to freshmen at many universities, by staffs composed of men nearly all of whom have been required to "take" bibliography. Yet how many of these teachers have turned to the facts of serial publication to explain the figure of Orlick, extremely puzzling by critical standards alone? One immediately sees that Orlick's attack on Mrs. Joe, which ultimately causes her death, is used by Dickens to pep up a three instalment sequence the main purpose of which is simply to let Pip age. This sequence would have been too dull, too insistent on domestic scenes round the hearth while Pip gradually withdraws from Joe, were it not for the Orlick subplot.[12] The novel apparently had to have thirty-six weekly units, and Dickens

---

[11] F. Scott Fitzgerald, *The Last Tycoon,* in *Three Novels* (1953), p. 157. Italics added.

[12] See instalments 8, 9, 10 (Chapters XII and XIII, XIV and XV, XVI and XVII). The Pip-Magwitch strand is early developed as much as can be without giving away the plot. Pip loves Estella early, but is apprenticed back to Joe by the beginning of Chapter XIII. The glad

therefore could not simply skip this period of Pip's life. The figure of Orlick may not be critically acceptable, but he is at least understandable when one views him in the light of publishing history.

I am also indicting myself for not understanding this point; for it was not many months ago that I looked up the weekly issues of *All the Year Round* and now have far more detail than, as the saying goes, "the short space of this article will permit the discussion of." I was derelict in my duty partly because life is short and bibliography is long, but also partly because I unconsciously resented the editor of my paperback *Great Expectations* whose job I was having to do.

For I am more familiar with the schizophrenia than most people, though mine takes a different form. With critics I am apt to claim to be a bibliographer; among bibliographers, I proclaim myself a critic.

The critic, one must recognize, can argue on aesthetic grounds against working on the texts of novels. He can produce the *tu quoque* argument. And he can say that the bibliographer neglects *what* he is working on. Of 244 articles on textual bibliography in the *Studies in Bibliography* list for 1954, only three were related to novels.[13] "What has the bibliographer been doing?" asks the new critic.

It may be that under the aspect of eternity George Sandys' *Ovid* is more important than Conrad's *Nostromo* or Melville's *Moby-Dick,* but it would be hard to convince the novel critic of that.

II

For these reasons I have chosen F. Scott Fitzgerald's *The Great Gatsby* as my main illustration. It brings out nearly all my points: inconsistent editing,

tidings of Great Expectations don't come until instalment 11. Without Orlick, more than four chapters would have to deal with domestic bliss and withdrawal. Orlick is introduced and attacks Mrs. Joe, all in the ninth instalment.

At the other end of the book a similar situation obtains. The reconciliation with Miss Havisham comes in instalment 30; that with Joe is brief enough not to be needed until after instalment 33. Estella is not brought in until the end. Instalments 31, 32, 33 are needed, therefore, to make the 36 weekly unit structure complete—but they cannot all contain the secret plan to get Magwitch downstream. The reader cannot go boating with Pip, Startop, and Herbert for two entire instalments before the disastrous attempt to get Magwitch out of the country; so instalment 32 is devoted to Orlick's attempt to kill Pip.

In other words, serial publication took Dickens to melodrama, but not quite in the crude form that one's unsubstantiated suspicions would indicate.

[13] There are, it is encouraging to note, signs of change. In the last year or two, one has the feeling that perhaps six or eight articles appeared on the texts of 19th- or 20th-century novels. For example, see Linton Massey, "Notes on the Unrevised Galleys of Faulkner's *Sanctuary*," *SB*, VIII (1956), 195–208; or Matthew J. Bruccoli, "A Collation of F. Scott Fitzgerald's *This Side of Paradise*," *SB*, IX (1957): 263–65. The latter article is especially interesting in pointing out changes between impressions of editions.

Having mentioned Dickens, I must add that Mrs. Tillotson has followed up her remark (*Novels of the Eighteen-Forties*) that we have no Victorian texts, and "no means, short of doing the work ourselves, of discovering how (and why) the original edition differed from the text we read." I refer of course to John Butt and Kathleen Tillotson, *Dickens at Work* (1957); on the importance of part publication, it deals mainly with novels other than *Great Expectations*. While it also illustrates how long it takes for a general appreciation of the importance of bibliographical facts to culminate in a specific study, the book makes my comments on Dickens, so to speak, unspeakable.

an unknown or unidentified text, a publisher who is good but vague, important errors in an important book, schizophrenia in the bibliographer-teacher. Not only is *Gatsby* a fine novel, but it is taught so often because it contains many of the basic themes of American literature: West versus East; the search for value; the American dream; crime and society; and in young Jim Gatz's "General Resolves," it even reaches back to Ben Franklin and Poor Richard.

How many know, however, what they have been teaching?

The Great Gatsby exists in print in three main versions: the first edition, beginning in April, 1925; a new edition in the volume with *The Last Tycoon* and certain stories, beginning in 1941; and a sub-edition of the latter text in the Modern Standard Authors series (*Three Novels*) together with *Tender is the Night* and *The Last Tycoon*, beginning in 1953.[14] Though *Gatsby* in the *Three Novels* version is another impression of *The Last Tycoon* plates I call it a sub-edition because *Gatsby's* position is different, coming first in the volume, and there are many changes in the text.[15]

So far as I know, the only available information about the text of *Gatsby* is buried in the notes to Arthur Mizener's *The Far Side of Paradise*. Mizener says that Fitzgerald found a misprint in the first edition: the future Nick Carraway speaks of at the end of the novel should be "orgiastic," not "orgastic":[16]

It was one of the few proof errors in the book [adds Mizener], perhaps

[14] The first edition has had three impressions: April, 1925, August, 1925, and August, 1942. I have collated three copies of the first impression, including Fitzgerald's personally corrected volume now located at Princeton. The August, 1942, impression I have not examined. I would like to record here my special thanks to Lawrence D. Stewart of Beverly Hills, California, for most kindly checking my collation against his copy of the rare second impression.

The second edition of *Gatsby* is that printed with *The Last Tycoon* and certain stories, as supervised by Edmund Wilson. It uses as copy-text the August, 1925, first edition. I have collated three impressions, 1941, 1945, 1948.

The sub-edition of *Gatsby*, as printed with *Tender is the Night* and *The Last Tycoon*, in the *Three Novels* volume, has been collated in three impressions, 1953, 1956, 1957.

The parent company, Scribner's, has permitted several reprints, which I have not examined thoroughly. There is also a recent (1957), third edition of *Gatsby*, by Scribner's, a paperback, called "Student's Edition."

I shall refer to these editions of *Gatsby* by the short but obvious forms of *First*, *Last Tycoon* or *LT*, *Three Novels* or *TN*, *Student's Edition* or *SE*. For convenience I shall give the line in a page reference by a simple decimal; as TN 31.30, for *Three Novels*, p. 31, line 30.

[Professor Matthew J. Bruccoli in "A Further Note on the First Printing of *The Great Gatsby*," *SB*, XVI (1963), 244, reports that a collation of his privately owned copy of the August, 1942, printing "reveals that there are no fresh corrections or revisions in the third printing. . . . However, this collation did turn up a second-printing correction Prof. Harkness missed: 211.7–8 Union Street station] Union Station." B.H.]

[15] My thanks are due to Princeton University Library for permitting me to examine both Fitzgerald's own copy of *Gatsby* and the surviving manuscripts. Doubtless I should add that since my special concern is the printed texts, I did not rigorously collate the mass of MS, TS, and galleys.

I would like also to thank Wallace O. Meyer of Scribner's, Harold Ober, Edmund Wilson, Malcolm Cowley, and Dan C. Piper for their advice and for patiently answering my queries about the changes in the texts.

[16] The comment is a trifle misleading, because the reading "orgastic" stands in MS, galleys, and first edition. Perhaps this is another example of Fitzgerald's well-known weakness in matters of spelling, grammar, and so on; at any rate, it can hardly be called a "proof error."

because Scribner's worked harder over *Gatsby* than over Fitzgerald's earlier books, perhaps because [Ring] Lardner read the final proofs. The only other proof error Fitzgerald found was the reading of "eternal" for "external" on p. 58 [of the first edition]. . . . Edmund Wilson's reprint in his edition of *The Last Tycoon* corrects all it could without access to Fitzgerald's personally corrected copy.[17]

Let us couple these comments with Matthew Bruccoli's interesting article on Fitzgerald's *This Side of Paradise*. Bruccoli is surprised that thirty-one errors are corrected in later impressions of the novel. He concludes that "the first printing was an inexcusably sloppy job," although Fitzgerald was himself in part responsible for the difficulty. We might infer two things, therefore: far fewer errors in *Gatsby's* first edition, and a correction of the word "eternal," in *The Last Tycoon*.

Not so. The correction to "external" is not made in the second impression of the first edition, nor in any impression of *Last Tycoon* (202.2,TN 38.2). Though there are only four changes from the first to second impression of the first edition, there are no less than twenty-seven changes between *First* and *Last Tycoon*. Between *First* and the 1953 *Three Novels*, there are more than 125 changes. Of these changes about fifty are quite meaningless. They change "to-morrow" with a hyphen to "tomorrow," for example. Or they change "Beale Street Blues" to *Beale Street Blues*. This class of change will not be commented upon nor included in statistics, except to add that the publisher was not at all consistent in making such alterations.[18]

There are, in other words, 75 changes of moment between the first edition and *Three Novels*—forty-four more than in *This Side of Paradise*. Many of them are more important. Of the changes the August, 1925, first edition brought, the most important was the substitution of the word "echolalia" for "chatter" in the phrase "the chatter of the garden" (*First* 60 line 16).[19]

But we must remember that *Last Tycoon* and *Three Novels* are both posthumous, and that of the twenty-seven changes from *First* to LT, twelve are clearly errors, seven are dubious improvements, and only eight are clearly

[17] Arthur Mizener, *The Far Side of Paradise* (1951), p. 336, n. 22. Mizener points up the generally sad fate of Fitzgerald's texts by mentioning that the reprints of The Modern Library, New Directions, Bantam (first edition), and Grosset and Dunlap all have the word "orgastic." One therefore assumes they reprint the first edition, though at least the Modern Library reprints the second impression. The later Bantam edition and *The Portable Fitzgerald* both use the faulty *Last Tycoon* as copy-text.

[18] See, for example, the word "today," in LT, p. 280 line 36 and TN p. 116 line 36; but "to-day" (as in *First,* p. 184 lines 7 and 10) is kept three lines later—LT p. 281.1, TN p. 117.1. In addition to forty-two such changes, there are six more which are nearly as minor: the word "sombre" is changed to "somber"; "armistice" to "Armistice," as examples. All these, and the change in the spelling of a name (Wolfshiem to Wolfsheim) which was usually but not always wrong in the first edition, are not included in my statistics.

[19] See LT 203.4 and TN 39.4. The other changes in the August, 1925, *First* are as follows: April, 1925: it's driver (p. 165.16) August, 1925: its driver. April: some distance away (p. 165.29) August: some distance away. April: sick in tired (p. 205.9 & 10) August: sickantired. All four are, presumably, authorial.

better readings. Of them all, the word "orgiastic," apparently, alone has the author's authority. What's more, the sub-edition *Three Novels* retains all but two of these bad changes. An example of an error begun in LT and continued in TN occurs on page 209.6 of *First* (296.8 of LT and 132.8 of TN). The sentence of Nick's, "It just shows you." is dropped from the text, thereby making the punctuation wrong and leading the reader to confuse speakers.

Between *First* and *Three Novels* the changes are of several kinds. In addition to the fifty or so "meaningless" changes, there are (*a*) fifteen changes of spelling, including six that change the meaning of a word and others that affect dialect; (*b*) seventeen changes in punctuation, including quotation marks, paragraph indication, and so on; (*c*) six incorrect omissions of a word or sentence or other details; (*d*) six proper deletions of a word or more; (*e*) thirty-one substantive changes—the substitution of a word or the addition of a phrase or sentence. For instance, Gatsby is transferred from the Sixteenth to the Seventh Infantry during the war. (See *First* 57.17, LT 201.12, TN 37.12.)

For when we turn to *Three Novels* we must move out of the camp of strict bibliography into the field of its important ally, publishing history. Fitzgerald's own copy of the first impression, with pencilled notes in the margins, is now located at the Princeton University Library and was used to make the sub-edition.

Of the seventy-five changes between *First* and *TN*, thirty-eight are with Fitzgerald's sanction and thirty-seven are without. Most of the thirty-seven changes not recommended by Fitzgerald are "corrections" made by a publisher's staff editor or by Malcolm Cowley, who supervised the sub-edition. However, some of this group are clearly errors, many of them having crept into the text by way of the *Last Tycoon* version. The noteworthy thing is that no reader knows the authority for *any* of the changes. The sub-edition itself does not even announce that it takes into account Fitzgerald's marginal comments—which, one would have supposed, would have been good business as well as good scholarship.

Furthermore, some of the thirty-eight "sanctioned" changes were only queried by Fitzgerald: no actual rewording was directed. An example is the phrase "lyric again in." Fitzgerald questioned "again" and the editor dropped it. But in five instances of Fitzgerald's questioning a word, no change was made —as, for example, Fitzgerald was unhappy to note that he had used the word "turbulent" twice in the first chapter.[20] There is also one instance in which Fitzgerald expressly asked for a change that was not made. At *First,* 50.1, Fitzgerald corrected "an amusement park" to "amusement parks," but the later version does not record the request (TN 32.32).

On the whole, one can say this, therefore: that about sixty of the changes from *First* to *Three Novels* are proper. That is, they either have the author's authority or are stylistic or grammatical improvements or are immaterial. I speak just now as a devil's advocate—a critic with a jaundiced eye toward bibliography. He would call the deletion of a comma from a short compound

[20] See "lyric again in," *First* 62.17, LT 204.12; "lyric in," TN 40.12. Cf. "turbulent," *First* 20.17, LT 178.25, TN 14.25; "turbulence," *First* 7.28, LT 171.3, TN 7.3.

sentence "immaterial," though it was not done by the author.[21] I am trying, in other words, to make the text sound as good as I can. Problems arise, however, from the fact that awkward readings sometimes come from purely typographical errors, sometimes from editor's decision, and sometimes from Fitzgerald's own notes. Everyone would accept such changes as "an Adam study" for "an Adam's study," (*First* 110.26, LT 233.30, TN 69.30); but by the same token few critics will be pleased by a Fitzgerald marginal correction reading "common knowledge to the turgid sub or suppressed journalism of 1902," instead of "common property of the turgid journalism of 1902" (*First* 120.11, TN 76.5).

We are left then with fifteen or sixteen errors begun or continued in *Three Novels*, errors which I trust even the newest of new critics would accept as having some degree of importance. That degree of course varies. The dedication "Once again, to Zelda," is left off, for example. Dialectical words are falsely made standard English, or half-doctored-up, as in this sentence where the word in *First* was "appendicitus": "You'd of thought she had my appendicitis out" (*First* 37.4, LT 188.37, TN 24.37). Sentences start without a capital[22] or end without a period[23] or are dropped altogether.[24] Quotation marks appear or disappear[25] and awkward readings come from nowhere. To illustrate that last: on page 149.10 of *First* Nick says that "the giant eyes of Doctor T. J. Eckleburg kept their vigil, but I perceived, after a moment, that other eyes were regarding us with peculiar intensity from less than twenty feet away." The eyes are Myrtle Wilson's but in *Three Novels* 95.1 (and LT 259.1) the sentence is confused when "the" is added without any reference and "from" and "with peculiar intensity" are dropped: "the giant eyes of Doctor T. J. Eckleburg kept their vigil, but I perceived, after a moment that *the* other eyes were regarding us less than twenty feet away" (italics added). Another dubious change is this: a joking slip or drunken mistake by Daisy is corrected—"Biloxi, Tennessee" becomes academically placed in its proper governmental locality.[26] One hardly needs to add that none of these changes have Fitzgerald's sanction.

The biggest errors, critically speaking, are ones that also occur in *Last Tycoon*. The principle of order in *The Great Gatsby* is a simple one: Nick Carraway, the narrator, tells his story wildly out of chronological order, but *in the*

[21] See *First*, 35.21: Her eyebrows had been plucked and then drawn on again at a more rakish angle, but the efforts of nature. . . . LT 188.7 and TN 24.7 remove the comma.

[22] *First* 111.14 and LT 234.5 When I try . . . TN 70.6 when I try . . .

[23] *First* 115.25 generating on the air. So LT 236.33. TN 72.33 generating on the air.

[24] The sentence "It just shows you," mentioned above as an error begun in LT.

[25] *First* 141.6, LT 253.38, TN 89.38. Tom Buchanan is speaking, and by closing a paragraph with quote marks, LT and TN give the reader the momentary impression that the next sentence and paragraph beginning "Come outside . . ." is by someone else.
First 139.26, LT 253.7, TN 89.7 represent the obverse. "The bles-sed pre-cious. . . . spoken by Daisy loses the quotation mark in LT and TN.

[26] See *First* 153.8, LT 261.14, TN 97.14. TN alone reads "Biloxi, Mississippi." I realize that the line can be interpreted in other ways, that for example, Fitzgerald wished an obviously fictional town. But I cannot agree that Fitzgerald was so ignorant of Southern geography as to put the city in the wrong state. I am all the more certain that Fitzgerald meant it as a joke because there is other geographical wordplay in the same scene, and it is only four pages earlier that Tom snorts that Gatsby must have been an Oxford man—"Oxford, New Mexico."

order that he learned it—with one exception.[27] The first half of the book is concerned with the development of the outsiders' illusions about Jay Gatsby— he is "nephew to Von Hindenburg," and so on (TN 47). The second half is a penetration in depth of Gatsby's illusion itself. The shift in the theme of the book is marked by the one major sequence which Nick gives the reader out of the order in which he himself learned it. I refer to the Dan Cody episode from Gatsby's early days.[28]

Now the most important structural unit in the book below the chapter is the intra-chapter break signified by a white space left on the page.[29] In *Last Tycoon* and *Three Novels* four of these important indications of structure are suppressed.[30] Oddly enough, it is the one following the Dan Cody story that is the first one missing. The detail that divides the book into its two structural elements is botched.

In the *Three Novels* version of *Gatsby*, then, we have a book quite well printed—surprisingly so when we look at the galley proofs. They are filled with changes—with page after page added in longhand, with whole galleys deleted or rearranged. (I would estimate that one-fifth of the book was written after the galley stage.) And we have a book that tries to take into account the author's latest stylistic revisions. Unfortunately, it is also a book that has far too many errors.

Perhaps this is the place to mention the third Scribner edition of *Gatsby*, the paperback Student's Edition, which uses TN as copy-text. Have matters been improved? Some have, but more errors have been added. There are twelve changes from TN to SE: it makes two distinct improvements, including the replacement of the dedication; but it adds three places in which intra-chapter breaks are suppressed.[31] The other changes are "immaterial" typographical

[27] The statement is not quite accurate: there are one or two other violations of this order, minor ones very late in the book. For example, the giving of Michaelis's testimony, p. 124 of TN is apparently after the scene on pp. 119 ff.

[28] The scene was, in the manuscript, at the place where it is referred to in the chapter now numbered VIII, p. 112 of TN. Fitzgerald then changed it to its present position, ending at TN 76, LT 241, *First* 121—Chapter VI.

[29] Since I have mentioned Conrad so often, it might not be amiss to add Conrad's name to the list of influences mentioned by Cowley in the introduction to *Three Novels*. (See Fitzgerald's introduction to the Modern Library *Gatsby* and *The Crack-Up* for his interest in Conrad.) The time scheme of *Gatsby* is, of course, Conradian, as well as the narrator. And there are quite a few passages that echo Conrad—the closing section on the old Dutch sailors' feelings in New York might be a twist on parts of "Heart of Darkness." "In the abortive sorrows and short-winded elations of men," p. 4 of TN's *Gatsby*, is just one of the verbal echoes of Conrad. More pertinently, the intra-chapter break was a device very much used by the older author. For a detailed examination of this relationship, see R. W. Stallman, "Conrad and *The Great Gatsby*," *TCL*, I (1955), 5–12.

[30] See *First* 121.26, LT 240 foot, TN 76 foot; *First* 163.26, LT 267 foot, TN 103 foot; *First* 192.16, LT 285 foot, TN 121 foot; *First* 214.21, LT 299.21, TN 135.21. In all but the last of these the break in the page comes at the turn-over of the page and, unfortunately, no space was left for it.

[31] For the suppressed intra-chapter breaks, see TN 126.31 and SE 167.26; TN 132.24 and SE 175.19; TN 136.24 and SE 181.7. The other improvement is at TN 89.7 and SE 117.3, where SE returns to *First* to get the quotation marks of "The bles-sed . . ." as spoken by Daisy, correctly once more. SE 175.1 does not restore Nick's sentence "It just shows you." but it does "correct" the quotation marks that were wrong in the preceding sentence in TN 132.9.

errors such as "turned to be," instead of "turned to me" (SE 71.17 and TN 54.20) and "*police*," instead of "pol*ice*" (SE 27.27 and TN 22.19).

I hope it is clear, then, that *Three Novels* represents the best present text of *Gatsby*. No doubt it and the Student's Edition will be the ones most used in colleges for some time. It should also be clear that in *Three Novels*, we have this kind of book:

1. A book which nowhere gives the reader the authority for seventy-five changes, all of them posthumously printed.
2. One which fails to make use of all of Fitzgerald's corrections.
3. One which contains thirty-seven changes which Fitzgerald did not authorize —some of which are of most dubious value.
4. A book which contains at least fifteen quite bad readings, one of which is of the highest structural importance.

So, armed with this mixed blessing, or with the worse one of *Last Tycoon*, or worst of all, with a reprint by another publisher which has none of Fitzgerald's corrections and additions, many students unwittingly face the next semester with the prairie squints. Only a nonexistent, eclectic text, combining the best of the August, 1925, first edition and the *Three Novels* text of *The Great Gatsby* would be proper.[32]

Could we not as critics pay more attention to Bibliography, and we as Bibliographers to criticism? Can not we somehow insist that editing actually be done—instead of the practice of putting a fancy introduction on a poor text? Can not we have sound texts reproduced and publisher's history stated by the editor? Can not we know *what it is* we have in our hands? For it is simply a fallacy that the novel does not count.

---

[32] I should add that the collation of these three editions has of course not been reproduced in full here—and there are several places in the text that call for emendation though there are no changes between editions. For example, Tom brings the car to a dusty spot under Wilson's sign. (So in *First* 147 and TN 93.23 and SE 123.7). Should it be a dusty stop?

[The discussions of the readings "orgastic/orgiastic" above illustrate another common difficulty, but one not developed in this article: the problem of conflicting authorial evidence. The change of "orgiastic" in the Princeton copy is the only revision there made not by rewriting but by printer's mark. One is puzzled to account for the difference.

On January 24, 1925, furthermore, Fitzgerald wrote Maxwell Perkins: "It's deliberate. 'Orgastic' is the adjective for 'orgasm' and it expresses exactly the intended ecstasy." See *The Letters of F. Scott Fitzgerald*, ed. Andrew Turnbull (1963), p. 175.

In short, the making of a "proper" text would be enormously complicated, requiring not only thorough examination of all editions and printings, but of proofs and manuscripts—and even these would not lead to certainty. Emendation and resolution of conflicting authorial evidence would be necessary. B. H.]

Historicism Once More

ROY HARVEY PEARCE

"Por el examen de su conciencia histórica penetran [los hombres] en su intra-historia y se hallan de veras. . . ."

—MIGUEL DE UNAMUNO
En torno al casticismo

"If one can really penetrate the life of another age, one is penetrating the life of one's own. . . ."

—T. S. ELIOT
Introduction to Ezra Pound's *Selected Poems*

EARLY in Georg Simmel's great *Sociology*, there is an excursus into a question fundamental to the general inquiry which that book undertakes. The excursus is called "How Is Society Possible?" And it might well furnish us a paradigm for initiating still another inquiry into the theory of literature and criticism. How, indeed, is literature possible? Such a question is entailed by another, one which it has been our particular compulsion to ask in this Critical Age: what is literature? But, like Simmel, we may find that it is one which we can ask properly only if we at the same time ask one which it entails. Thus: how is it possible that literature should be what it is?

Consider how, asking only what literature is, we find ourselves regularly confronted by answers set in terms of a series of either/or propositions—critical purism *v.* critical pragmatism, the autonomous *v.* the instrumental, the individual *v.* the societal, the poet *v.* the period, foregrounding *v.* automatization, texture *v.* structure . . . and finally, art *v.* life. Those who confront us with such propositions, of course, most often strive to show how one element of a given proposition is resolved into the other, so to achieve that "higher" synthesis which is marked by tension, ambiguity, irony, and the like. But, asking how it is possible that literature should be what it is, I wonder if such a synthesis is achievable, or even desirable. Might it not be that the function of the literary work is to show us that such a synthesis is, in fact, impossible of achievement; that there is a constant and necessary dialectical opposition between the very categories we would synthesize; that in a realization of this opposition lies our fullest and richest sense of the quality of high art and, beyond that, of our sense of the highest possibilities of ourselves as critical readers?

Here I think of another of our either/or propositions: literature *v.* history. And I wonder if it is not the case that literature is possible precisely as it is because it is in its very nature a way, perhaps the most profound, of comprehending that dialectical opposition which characterizes our knowledge of ourselves in our history; and that that opposition is one which subsumes all those I have noted above. Thus, the proposition should read: history (*our* history) via literature. If this is so, then we shall have again to develop a kind of criticism which is, by definition, a form of historical understanding.

In point of fact, we are doing so. We move toward a kind of criticism which is historical in not the usual sense of the term. For we have regularly used it to refer to the historical placement and elucidation of the literary work. This "new" historical criticism would go somewhat further and establish between ourselves and the literary work a direct, existential relationship. This is, I take it, essentially a form of what is usually called historicism.[1] Hence my title. This

---

[1] There is an annoying semantic problem here, of course: What, actually, does "historicism" mean? What kind of critical philosophy of history does it entail? The question centers on the kind of relativism which the historicist assumes. It is my own sense that positivistically minded historians have adopted the term as a means of supporting an illimitable relativism, although they would surely be uncomfortable to discover that this can easily lead them to the kind of idealistic view of history expounded by, say, a Croce. On the other hand, it would seem that "historicism" can be expounded as having always settled itself upon the bedrock of a "universal" theory of human nature. If the latter is the case, then there is no necessity for qualifying "historicism" with "existentialist," as, following the example of some recent Hispanists in particular, I am tempted to do. The best brief account that I know of the problems here involved is Friedrich Meinecke's "Values and Causalities in History," as translated in Fritz Stern's *The Varieties of History* (New York, 1956), pp. 268–288. See also Rudolf Bultmann's 1957 Gifford Lectures *History and Eschatology* (Edinburgh, 1957), especially pp. 140–142. [My understanding of "historicism," I would add in 1969, is confirmed by the following account of the thought of Leopold Ranke, from whom all modern historicism is said to flow, in Gerhard Ritter's "Scientific History, Contemporary History, and Political Science," *History and Theory*, I (1961), 264–265:

Ranke's objectivity, which became the model of all scientific history, has been all too often misinterpreted as mere neutrality. Granted, he declined to act as judge of the past but declared that he only wanted to report it "as it really happened." In contemplation of the grand drama of world history he wanted most to "blot out his self"—not, however, to stand by as the disinterested observer but rather to be able to dissolve completely in the reliving of the awesome events. Not neutral indifference but the opposite—the most intimate, enthusiastic participation, the strongest involvement in the course of events and in the inexhaustible complexity of their manifestations—is the spiritual posture in which he confronts world history. In the last analysis his objectivity stems thus from the universality of his conception of history. He keeps himself free (at least in principle, that is, insofar as is at all possible for a human being) from all commitment to any particular interests, to any particular intellectual currents, to any historical epochs —even from commitment to his own fatherland, to his own religion, to his own times. Not only are all epochs for him equally "immediate to God" (in his famous phrase), but likewise all nations and ultimately also all great movements and trends of the human spirit which have become historically significant. Scientific history, so understood, is fundamentally unlimited in

historicism assumes that the past, by virtue of its very pastness, becomes an aspect of the present. In effect, a literary work carries the past into the present— and not just as a monument endowed with the sort of factuality from which we may infer its previous mode of existence, but rather as a somehow "living" thing from whose particularity of form we may apprehend that existence and to a significant degree share in it.

I grant at the outset that the historicist critic as I have envisaged him would not have been able or inclined to compile an *NED*, do a critical text of *Beowulf*, initiate a *Variorum Shakespeare*, travel the *Road to Xanadu*, or, for that matter, fully determine the fateful tensions and paradoxes of "The Rape of the Lock" or calculate precisely the component of the personal and impersonal in "Lycidas." Moreover, I freely admit that such jobs still need doing and are being done, though, I suspect, more and more rarely and with increasingly diminishing returns, I assume, in short, that our relation to our literature has changed as we have changed, that the needs accruing from that relation have changed too, and that the changes point us toward what can most accurately be called historicism. In turn, as they come up, the relevant questions are: how has this taken place? what does it mean that it should take place? what does it mean to be, shall we say, a "critical historicist" instead of an "historical critic"?

Now, this historicist tendency in our criticism is by no means a unique or isolated phenomenon, not just another specialized product of the scholar-critic's specialism. Quite the contrary. It can best be understood as one of the most complex and sophisticated aspects of a problem that now generally tries our soul—that of the nature and the import of our sense of the past. We recognize that at the most the past has done much to make us what we are and has given us much of what we have—our modes of hope, aspiration, and responsibility. And at the very least, we recognize that the past is the one thing we cannot change, that it is *just there*, absolutely given. Our problem is to understand it, which should mean to accept it—which is *not* to say approve of it. Whether with a Frank Yerby we play with libidinal fantasies about the past; or, with a Bruce Catton we lose ourselves in its sheer factuality; or with a Robert Penn Warren we conceive of its chief protagonists as a series of Adams, in whose fall/ we have sinnéd all—however we look toward the past, we cannot free ourselves from the fact that it is somehow here, now, built into our sense of our time. Our sense of our time seems these days inevitably, with ever-increasing

its quest for knowledge. It by no means restricts its choice of material in the manner which is often set as an ideal today: to choose out of the past only that which has continued up to the present, that which is important for our immediate self-understanding Its fundamental aim is rather to illuminate the entire cosmos of human cultural strivings and thereby to enlarge our little selves into the unmeasured, thus meeting a deep and genuine need of the human spirit. Ranke once formulated its highest aim thus in a letter: "To understand and capture all the deeds and sorrows of this wild, passionate, violent, good, noble, peaceful, of this sullied and pure creature that we are ourselves, in their genesis and in their configuration." It must be understood that this is not a question of a kind of historical anthropology, of exhibiting what has always been the same in human nature, but rather of the opposite: to bring to light the inexhaustible variety of the potentialities that man possesses in the struggle with his fate to create his civilization.]

intensity, to involve a sense of the past. And literary criticism is answering to that sense too.

Our criticism and the scholarship that buttresses it are certainly now mature enough to assume the burden that our culture has forced upon it: not only to see literature in history, but to see history in literature; to understand that the art of reading a poem is an act of at once appropriating and being appropriated by its history; to declare that a poem is an expression of the highest humanistic import, as it is an expression of a man whose very humanity is defined both by the fact that he is a man and that he is a man in a particular place and at a particular time. When will our criticism fully assume this burden? When it understands that it has already begun to do so, or at least recognized that it needs must do so. The immediate task is to describe the conditions of doing so. How is historicism possible? How is criticism possible?

I

The problem of history, to be sure, has been central to the formalist criticism which gives our age one of its names. But it has been a problem stated in such a way as to obscure the terms and conditions of its solution. There is, for instance, the great example of "Tradition and the Individual Talent," with its insistence that the poet is he for whom history, or at least the history of literature, is totally and immediately available. If the tendency of that notable essay was to imply somehow that the poet was a prophet through whom history spoke, Eliot corrected it in his many brilliant essays of formal explicatory analysis, essays in which his interest was the way a poet "uses" the history which he is given to know better than the ordinary run of men. Yet the problem of history *qua* history, of what part history itself has in the meaning of poems, has always been present in Eliot's thinking about literature. It is there particularly when he speaks, as he so often does, of the poet's concern for "language."

"We may say," he writes in "The Social Function of Poetry," "that the duty of the poet, as poet, is only indirectly to his people; his direct duty is to his *language,* first to preserve, and second to extend and improve. . . ." This is, as I shall maintain, an auspicious beginning, since it is on the consideration of the poet's relation to his language that there must be centered any examination of his relation to history; for language must be for the poet the principal vehicle for history; through language history gets into literature. But here, as elsewhere, Eliot goes not much beyond this sentence. And of course, when, as poet, he most starkly confronts the problem of language, he does so as a Christian for whom the problem of history, and thus the problem of language, is resolved in the dogma of the Word. The dogma may or may not be correct; as far as Eliot's religious commitments are concerned, one must grant that it is so. But there remains the problem of how a reader who is not of Eliot's persuasion can be brought to grant that it is so. There remains the problem of how Eliot's dogmatic view of language (and history) can be made convincing to a reader who is concerned not so much to agree or disagree with him but to understand him.

There remains, in short, the problem of understanding in what sense Eliot's views, as his poems project them, are themselves segments of history—not only his history, but also ours as his poems may make it ours.

I instance the views of Eliot here as being seminal for that formalist criticism which has helped many of us to learn how to read. Language is a primary concern of all that criticism; but almost always it is a curiously non-historical language, overripe with its accumulated load of meanings, which it is the poet's obligation to preserve, extend, and improve and the critic's to explicate and perhaps to generalize. In their formalist *vade mecum, Theory of Literature,* Mr. Wellek and Mr. Warren distribute most forms of historical study among the various levels of that Hell they call "The Extrinsic Approach." They do, however, detach from historical scholarship the study of the language of poetry and admit it to that Better World they call "The Intrinsic Approach"—yet only under the name "Style and Stylistics." And even here they take a dim view of stylistic study when it goes beyond the descriptively formalist. Such work, they write, "often assumes that true, or great, art must be based on experience, *Erlebnis.* . . ." (Is this to say: poetry is an experience but is not based on one?) And, of course, since history is merely a record of human experience, for Mr. Wellek and Mr. Warren it would seem to follow that if we attempt to know literature as a phenomenon in history and ourselves as readers thereby also bound up in that history, we must necessarily founder on historical reductionism.

The prime assumption is that the historical study of literature is necessarily reductionist. Going on this assumption, the formalist critic can do no more than make obeisance to the power of the language with which the poet must work and then hasten on to see how the work has been carried out. Thus it is significant, I think, that in his recent statesmanlike summation of the doctrines of those whom he calls the *New Apologists for Poetry,* Mr. Murray Krieger repeatedly is obliged to point out that, although the New Critics have given us a quite powerful and fairly consistent theory of the author's role in the creative process, they have never been able to deal adequately with the role of language in that process. He writes, for example: "Clearly, then, . . . language must be considered as a formative factor in the complex process of creation. I must say that the poet's original idea for his work, no matter how clearly thought out and complete he thinks it is, undergoes such radical transformations as language goes creatively to work upon it that the finished poem, in its full internal relations, is far removed from what the author thought he had when he began. . . ."[2]

---

[2] *The New Apologists for Poetry* (Minneapolis, 1956), p. 23; and cf. pp. 73–74, 97–98. It should be noted also that Mr. Krieger, in "A Note on the Objectivity of Value," pp. 158–163, defends the possibility of "objectivism" in value-theory as against extreme "historical relativism." He fully acknowledges the fact that literary conventions and the like are "historically relative" and indicates that his Apologists, or some of them, do also. But he does not go on to discuss the possible implications for the nature of the literary work and the realization of its intrinsic values which derive from such "objectivism." Once more, he limits himself to elucidating the poetics of his Apologists. And this is only proper. I think, therefore, that had he pursued the subject further, he might well have reached conclusions of the sort I come to in this paper. Which is another way of claiming that the sort of historicism (which I take to be akin to his "objectivism")

Now, Mr. Krieger nowhere specifies exactly what he means by "language." At the most he seems to mean, as so often with the New Critics on whom his study centers, "medium." And therein lies, for both the New Critics and him who is their apologist, the large difficulty. For "medium" carries with it in much New Critical (and other) aesthetic thinking a kind of mystique: something (its power as "symbol"?) in the medium, in language, works in such a way as to make for that sort of creative resistance to the artist's initial intuition which *must* contribute much to the production of the achieved literary work. Surely, the logic is essentially analogical: language (for all its power as "symbol") is like the stone, or clay, or paint with which the artist works. But, and herein lies the difficulty, the analogy holds only minimally. For language is obviously freighted with values to a degree and in a way which plastic substances are not.[3] This is, indeed, of the essence of its power to symbolize. Language above all communicates values; and by "values" I mean both feelings of desirability and obligation and their negatives, and the very modes and forms by which those feelings and their negatives are expressed. (Perhaps it would be better to say values and valuations.) To reach this belief, one need not go so far as to accept as linguistic orthodoxy the theses of Benjamin Lee Whorf. Still, reading someone like Whorf might at least have a heuristic value, if only because it would serve to remind us that literature can never be as "pure" (i.e. freed of mundanely determined value-forces) as we, well instructed by Mr. Krieger's Apologists, might like it to be.

Mr. Krieger, then, can find among the New Critics, whom of course he studies in their own terms, no adequate account for this ("the linguistic") side of the creative process; he must make do with what he and his Critics have. But if he wished to move beyond his Critics' terms and categories (as he does not), he could well talk about language in its historical-cultural aspect. For it is in relation to its culture that language has its initial and minimal symbolizing power. Language is, as we regularly say, a system of symbols whereby, in great part, culture is historically transmitted. The values projected by a language (whether in a poem or any other form of expression) are not just initially and minimally, but also residually, the values of the culture whose language it is. Indeed, it is the force of this residual power which, in the making of a poem, gives to language a creative power analogous to the poet's. The power is ulti-

---

expounded here develops necessarily out of formalist New Critical poetics when it is considered in relation to the historicist theory of culture assumed in this essay. [Mr. Krieger's "objectivism" has entailed for him a conception of the use of language in poetry whereby it is dissociated from its historical matrix yet continues to refer to it. He would, as he says, explicitly affirm the "miraculous power of poetry" and insists that I and others are wrong in accepting the common-sense view, developed in much modern linguistic theory, that the language of poetry remains the language of ordinary discourse, but with an intensification of those aspects of usage (metaphor, meter, etc.) which make for fictionality. See his *A Window to Criticism* (Princeton, 1964), pp. 1–70.]

[3] Plastic substances as media (and also musical tones?) indeed could, at least theoretically, be held to be analogous to language as medium. For surely the historically definable conventions as to "suitable" uses of those media in the fine arts must have some significance for artist and beholder, critical and uncritical. But here again the analogy is minimal and of not much use to the theorist or critic. Mr. Krieger, however (footnote, p. 68), believes differently.

mately that of the poet's culture as, through its historical development, it has made the world in, about, and for which he writes. The study of language, thus, is a form of the historical study of culture. So that in the end, Mr Krieger's remark about the New Critics' concern with "language" is one about their concern with history. But it remains a concern limited by their strangely unsophisticated conception of language—unsophisticated because it is a conception set by an assurance that the historical dimension of language is not finally relevant to the meaning and import of the literary work. We come, then, to a version of the complaint regularly set forth by antagonists of Mr. Krieger's Apologists: that they are inadequate as historians and therefore, in all their brilliance, incomplete as critics.

Still, I should say that in general the antagonists have not argued their case well enough. True, they have caught the Apologists in a number of factual errors. But for the most part they themselves have either conceived of history as being merely a "setting" for literary works and then have tacitly admitted that it is much more interesting to study the setting than the works; or they have so confused works with setting that the works have become for them just dim spots on the historical horizon—so dim that it doesn't seem to be worthwhile to distinguish one from another; so dim that critical explication is at best an adventure in uncontrolled impressionism. From such (at their extremes) antiquarianism and reductionism the New Apologists set out to rescue us, and in great part did, but only at the expense of tearing the literary work out of its historical-cultural context and putting it entirely in ours. Although this was a desperate measure taken to save the literary work from the disappearance into context which seemed to threaten, it was nonetheless one that now appears a little prideful and comports strangely with the Apologists' vaunted sense of order, continuity, and tradition. The Apologists respected language, yet do not seem to have wanted really to understand just what it was they respected. Perhaps, in order to do what they did, they could not afford to want to do so. Perhaps their great success could be achieved only at the expense of this, their great failure. Precisely because they succeeded, it seems to me, we can see wherein they failed; we may even avoid such failure ourselves. This is *our* chance—or one of our chances—for success. I daresay that this is a task set for us by our situation at our moment in history.

Studying language, we study history. We study history, so that we can study language. (There are other ways to do so, of course, as there are other institutions which make for the historical continuity of culture; but this one is our major concern, because it is our artists'.) Studying history, we study culture. Studying a culture, we study its poetry. Studying its poetry, we study its language. The system is one and whole. If it is closed, that is because it encloses us. And even though we may prefer to work within any one of its segments, we must not confuse the segment with the whole. Nor must we forget how and to what purpose the other segments exist.[4]

[4] Cf. Allen Tate's remarks, at the end of his "The Man of Letters In the Modern World" (1952): "It is the duty of the man of letters to supervise the culture of language, to which the rest of culture is subordinate, and to warn us when our language is ceasing to forward the ends

It is not enough to protest, as have many of the New Apologists, that they regularly go to the *NED* or that they can read *The Great Chain of Being* too. This is to yield to the conception of history as "setting." For the questions immediately arise: to what critical use are the *NED* and *The Great Chain of Being* to be put? What happens to the historical-cultural ambiance of a word when it gets into a poem? Is the ambiance somehow left behind? Does it survive, but as entirely transformed? This last would seem to be the New Critic's answer. But it is an unsatisfactory answer; for it would do away with history as by a transformative fiat. Hence the historical critic, meditating Mr. Krieger's argument, would take the matter one step further and ask: to what degree is language, or culture, or history, qualitatively *in*, existentially *in*, a literary work? By virtue of being there, what does it do? Then: in what sense do we, as we read critically, actually engage ourselves to the language, the culture, the history, which is there? If language, as we must say, has an active, creative role in the making of the literary work, then the effect of that work on us must be in some part the effect of language—of the specific values with which it is charged and of the form which values took, and so of the period in which those values had their existence. Somehow, it would seem to follow, we are made to be vitally committed to those aspects of the period out of which the literary work has come. Somehow, we have come to be relativists of a sort—historicists, that is to say—which above all the New Criticism would seem to want us not to be.[5]

proper to man. The end of social man is communion in time through love, which is beyond time." Mr. Tate's man of letters, like Mr. Eliot's, seems not to be subject to the claims and demands of history as it is conceived in this essay. But this is so only because he has committed himself to a religion which subsumes the historical under the ahistorical. Thus a difficulty arises in some of Mr. Tate's criticism when, for example, viewing Poe and Emily Dickinson, *sub specie aeternitatis*, he cannot grant them any life except that which is of transcendentally immediate significance to him. The net result is to fail to see such poets whole and to be a victim of what the historicist might call the eschatological fallacy.

[5] The New Critical treatment of the implications for literary criticism of Professor Lovejoy's work is a useful, because extreme, instance of its anti-historicism. More than once (most influentially by René Wellek and Austin Warren, *Theory of Literature* [New York, 1949], p. 109) there have been quoted, out of context, the following words from the introductory chapter of *The Great Chain of Being*: "... the ideas in serious reflective literature are, of course, in great part philosophical ideas in dilution. ..." The rest of the sentence is significantly left unquoted; indeed, there is usually no indication that the sentence does not end here. The rest of it reads: "—to change the figure, growths from seed scattered by great philosophic systems which themselves, perhaps, have ceased to be." Thus Professor Lovejoy would appear to be saying that although he, as an "analytic" historian of ideas, is interested in his work only in the ideas themselves, they nonetheless, when present in literary structures, are involved in "growths" which are quite obviously, as the language indicates, somehow different from and not reducible to the "seed" in which they originated. That Professor Lovejoy means such an interpretation to be put on his words is clearly indicated in a couple of sentences he quotes approvingly from Whitehead toward the end of the paragraph in which the supposedly heretical initial statement about "dilution" occurs: "... it is in literature that the concrete outlook of humanity receives its expression. Accordingly, it is to literature that we must look, particularly in its more concrete forms, if we hope to discover the inward thoughts of a generation." My point is that, misinterpreting Professor Lovejoy's assertion as they have characteristically done, the New Critics have cut themselves off from a possible way of developing a sense of the past, a way which in itself would let them more fully evoke that concreteness and particularity which they insist is primary in the quality of a literary work.

We may not go all the way with historicism as it has usually been defined; but our way of thinking has been fatefully conditioned by a kind of thinking so close to historicism that we must use it as a means of defining our own position. For classically historicism holds (and I quote here a "neutral" definition, that of Maurice Mandelbaum in his *Problem of Historical Knowledge*) "that . . . every set of cultural values [is] relative to the age in which it is dominant."[6] (The question here, of course, is the meaning of "relative." If it means "relative to nothing but," we would balk and say "relative to, among other things. . . ." But it is not entirely clear that the classical historicist would push us into balking thus.) Insofar as language creates, the fact of creation is inextricable from the point in time of creation; and insofar as we know a literary work, we know, among other things, its time. Not—and this is the main point—as exotic information, as something totally apart from our time, but as something which, as we know it, is at once of its time and ours. Pastness in a literary work is an aspect—a vital, authentic aspect, a *sine qua non*—of presentness. The work of art may well live forever as the creation of a man like other men before and after him. But an integral part of its life, of its formal quality, will derive from the fact that it was created at a time, and for and of a time. Thus, and only thus, is literature possible. Thus, and only thus, does it become what it is.

II

We must, therefore, consider the literary work as it is a kind of statement which can never be dissociated from either the time in which it was made or the time in which it is known: i.e. when the work was written or when it was (or is) read. Let us say of a literary work that it is a form of a conditional contrary-to-fact statement of the order: "If there had been such a person as X, living in a specified situation, etc., he would have acted in this way." The literary work is thus, as we say, not "true"; it consists of a series of hypothetical situations, imagined and motivated in such a way that, within their confines, we can accept as necessary the actions and responses into which the situations— and the imagined human beings in them—are made to issue. What primarily interests us in "created" situations of this sort is, of course, not their inevitable relevance to factuality, but their possibility: their resonance with our deepest sense of ourselves. And it is this interest in possibility which lets us willingly suspend our ordinary disbelief in such imagined situations and accordingly assent to them as fully as an artist can compel us to. In effect, we compact with him to go as far as he can take us into the realm of human possibility. Indeed, we say that what differentiates him from most of us is his possession of a superior degree both of awareness of such possibility and of ability to express that possibility in language and all the formal, constructivist means which language

---

[6] *The Problem of Historical Knowledge* (New York, 1938), p. 89. This is meant to categorize statements like the following from Karl Mannheim ("Historicism" [1924], *Essays on the Sociology of Knowledge*, trans. P. Kocskeméti [New York, 1952], p. 86): "The first approach to a historic mode of thought and living lies . . . in the ability to experience every segment of the spiritual-intellectual world as in a state of flux and growth."

bears within itself. This is what we mean when we speak of a writer's sensibility.

I am aware that to put such a complex and parlous matter so briefly is to run the risk of oversimplification. Nonetheless, I think that what I have said is, so far as the task I have set myself is concerned, not only correct but adequate. For it takes us into the heart of our matter: if the literary statement is contrary-to-fact and if, further, it defines the conditions under which the facts might have been otherwise, i.e. "true to life," then its attraction and power for us must lie in the fullness of the definition. For a literary work does, indeed, define the conditions of our existence as it *might* have been: which is to say—if we will look as profoundly into our situation as the literary work would have us—as it is. So far as our lives have meaning, we are what we aspire to be—what the literary work tells us we might have been, under the conditions which would have made such an existence possible. In literature, then, we believe in our own historical, existential possibility as the writer's use of language defines it.

Such belief is what I have previously called, borrowing a phrase from Américo Castro, a "commitment to a vital possibility." And at this point *a fortiori*, we must take into account the specific moment in history at which the work was made. For the language of the work is bound to that moment, as are all the substantial compositional elements which the language is made to render. In assenting to the actions and responses developed in the literary work—and, moreover, in being satisfied, by virtue of the hold the formal structure of the work may have on us, to look at it in and of itself—we likewise assent to the beliefs and the values which those actions and responses manifest. That the assent is an as-if assent (to a conditional contrary-to-fact statement) makes all the difference. The difference is that, moving toward such an assent, we are fully prepared to take into our purview, as a vital human possibility, all the historically definable forms of life in which that possibility is made operative. Such an assent entails no "practical" decision and consequent action on our part. For it is grounded on the crucial fact that the past world realized for us is a possible world, not a real one, however much it may seem like that real past world of which we can learn in historical works. Knowing this, now thereby freed to conceive of the past world not as one which did happen but as one which could have happened, we do indeed commit ourselves to its vital possibility. In this way literature "teaches" us.

It is, I should say, this as-if commitment which obliges us to conceive of the literary work as necessarily at once of its time and ours. For although the form of the commitment is defined by the modes of possibility manifested in the work, still the object of the commitment—that toward which our awareness of possibility draws us—is that portion of the past which constitutes the concrete and infinitely particularized substance of the work. *Hamlet* is not true, we declare, but it is true to life. Reading the play, we assent to the possibility that a man could have been like this one, at this time, in this place. That to which it is true is the sense of possibility which is at once ours and a Shakespeare's (or ours as a Shakespeare, in all his creative genius, can evoke it in us), but which we can realize only as a Shakespeare can make it charge a particular Eliza-bethan situation with the life of art. What is true of *Hamlet* is true of a poem written an instant ago. Criticism is thus a form of historical study—perhaps the purest of historicisms.

This point or a point quite close to it has been made before, of course—most handsomely, so far as my reading goes, by Lionel Trilling in his essay, "The Sense of the Past." But the tendency has been to think of Mr. Trilling's essay and the criticism which it has generated as being, somehow, apart from that of the proper New Critics. My point is that it is not apart from their work, but that it grows out of their work, and necessarily. But then, if we can deduce an editorial principle from the kind of criticism filling our quarterlies and journals, we can find evidence of a need to go beyond anti-historicist formalist criticism into something more truly responsive to our need for a criticism which will take into account what Mr. Krieger calls the creative role of language—and what I have ventured to define further as the creative role of historically determinate culture.

I mean here the criticism of those whom I shall call the New Mythographers, I cannot, of course, go into the perilous ramifications of mythographic criticism. What I wish to point out is something quite simple: that our New Mythographers have been concerned to go beyond textual explication and to locate in literary works some substantial center whereby such works may be realized as specifically cultural products. It is as though they had sensed the need to demonstrate how the literary work, by virtue of its activity as literary work, has historical import. They would account for its informing and assent-commanding power by pointing to something beyond (or antecedent to) the creative act of the author. And they point not to language, or culture, or history (for these entities are for them too large, inchoate, and amorphous) but to myth. As to the source of that mythic power: well, therein lies the tremendous range of their interests and commitments—from, say, the frankly theistic, proto-religious criticism of Philip Wheelwright to, say, the frankly naturalistic, proto-anthropological criticism of Stanley Hyman, and beyond. And further, the senior New Critics themselves—Mr. Ransom, Mr. Tate, and Mr. Brooks, for example—have as often as not had recourse to the concept of myth when they have come up against the necessity of accounting somehow for such informing power in literary works as they could not trace in the exquisitely creative manipulations of the author. In fact where the Old Critic has had recourse to history—to sources, background, and biography—the New Critic has had recourse to myth.[7] He has seen clearly that insofar as language (to use Mr.

---

[7] Thus the attraction—or should one say the felt authenticity—for the New Critic of Christian myth, which is *par excellence* that myth which would completely absorb history into itself and has thereby been taken to transcend it. Objecting to Douglas Bush's kind of historical criticism and Leslie Fielder's extreme mythographic criticism—both of which yield, in his view, to the temptation "to find in literature a support for religion or perhaps a surrogate for religion"—Cleanth Brooks points out that "it is no accident that so many of the formalist critics either hold, or are sympathetic to, an orthodox Christian faith" ("A Note on the Limits of 'History' and the Limits of 'Criticism.'" *Sewanee Review*, LXI [1953], 129–135). Mr. Brooks, in the historicist view, is perfectly right in his desire to avoid both "ersatz religion" and "ersatz poetry." But he offers, so far as my reading of his work goes, no adequate account of the quite obvious historical otherness of poetry, because, one supposes, being a good Christian, he cannot conceive of a component of otherness as radical as that which the historicist would discover in the literary work. Saying

Krieger's term again) is creative, its power cannot be located in the manifold of the sort of social and intellectual history which has been the standard fare of so much Old Criticism. Nonetheless, he has been unable on the one hand to define clearly his sense of myth in its relationship to the hard details of historical evolution; or on the other hand, to generalize his sense of myth into a theory which would account for the sheer plenitude of that evolution—its quality of constant change, activity, and transformation, of vertiginously comprehensive fulness. He has failed, I would say, to take into account the very historicity of history. Mythographic criticism, then, on this analysis, is a proto-historicism generated by the New Critic's deep need not to be frozen into methodological orthodoxy. But, as so often happens, the means to avoid orthodoxy have themselves become orthodox. And the life of literature, which as teachers and critics we would evoke, is said to be compressed into so many archetypes and rituals whose secrets we must unlock if we are to show how they touch with their charismatic power the author in the act of making his work. *Where* those archetypes and rituals are, and *how* they are—this question thus far has not been amenable to historical study, as it should be, but only to psycho-analytic and theological exegesis. Looking to see whither it has gone, we see only the withering away of the New Criticism into the New Mythography.

The Elder Statesmen of our New Criticism were so concerned to save litera-ture from historical study—and one of the lessons of *my* life, in any case, is that it had to be done and they have done it—that they tended to hold suspect anything that smacked of relativistic historicism. Yet, if we are only willing to look into our situation deeply enough, we can see that this has been their share of one of the ills of our culture, the fear of history itself. And we can see that the New Mythography has been an attempt to cure that ill by fiat. Moreover, so intent have we been on doing our job as we have been taught to do it, we are hardly aware of other relevant approaches to our problem: for example, the

---

this, however, the historicist must add that Mr. Brooks's way with history and its existential actualities is not the only way for the Christian. Another way is that of William F. Lynch, S. J., in his "Theology and Imagination," *Thought,* xxix (1955), 529–554. Father Lynch writes, for example: ". . . the order of belief called Christology is a belief in the capacity of the human, and the actual, if we imagine and live through it, to lead somewhere. The essential meaning of Christ is that He rejected the way of tricks and magic and power and quick infinities as redeeming ways and chose instead to walk through the mysteries of man (thus I refer to the actualities of man and all the stages of human life) as a way into God. Thus all Christians talk about the 'mysteries of Christ' but they do not talk enough about the mysteries, I mean the realities, of man—through which He, Christ, walked and imagined as a path to freedom and the infinite. It is easy enough to believe in the virtue of infinities, but it is hard to trust in the finite and the actual as a way to them. A properly understood Christology should provide the theological energy required for that penetration for which we no longer seem to have the heart or the energy. I do not say that Christology must get into the poem or the symbol, but what we may call the Christic act, the act of athletic and confident penetration of limit, of the actual, and the human, can again become the model and energizer for the poetic imagination and for the total act and attitude of any human culture. What other firmer *quid credas* could there be for the poet or for popular culture?" A little later Father Lynch says, "And we may briefly define the men of belief as those who, with every concomitant obligation, believe in and possess *historical* symbols." In short, Father Lynch's Christology holds inseparably in view history and man, and his eschatology is such that, so far as literature and the arts are concerned, it teaches man to trust in the finite and the actual.

iconological studies (however different one from the other) of Panofsky and of Gombrich and others of their groups, or closer to home, to the criticism, primarily in Romance Literature, of that part of the so-called New Stylistics which we in this country know mainly in Erich Auerbach's *Mimesis* and a cornucopia of essays by Leo Spitzer. Here we see a tendency to take language, culture, and history with a degree and kind of seriousness that we have got used to thinking is impossible. Thus, in *Mimesis,* Mr. Auerbach would show us precisely how the life of language—all that makes for Style—in a given series of works is a manifestation of the very reality principle of the culture in which they had their origin. In effect, the author is not so much agent as carrier; his genius inheres in the fact that he is sensitive to the creative possibilities latent in his culture, to be realized only in his art. Now, we might object that criticism of the sort which *Mimesis* typifies does not do enough to comprehend the creative genius of the author in his art. But at the same time we might well admit that our criticism correspondingly has not done enough to comprehend the creative genius of language in *its* art. I instance the work of Spitzer and Auerbach here, of course, not to expound it, but because it exemplifies a significant sort of critical study which moves in a direction other than the one in which we now tend generally to be moving—or better, which moves in a direction in which we seem to want to move. Indeed, I think that in some notable cases we *are* moving in that direction.[8]

We are doing so when, as historical critics, we write of Shakespeare (as has J. V. Cunningham), or Donne (as has Rosemond Tuve), or Wordsworth (as has Josephine Miles), or Keats (as has Earl Wasserman), or Defoe (as has Ian Watt), or Cooper (as has Henry Nash Smith), or seventeenth-century prose style (as have George Williamson and Jackson Cope), or the nineteenth-century American compulsion toward the symbolic mode (as has Charles Feidelson), in such a way as to evoke our subjects "as they actually happened"—to use the much maligned (and much misinterpreted) historicist battle cry.

---

[8] René Wellek has most notably set himself against our moving in that direction. See, for example, his *History of Modern Criticism* (New Haven, 1955), I, 183ff.; his discussion of Auerbach's *Mimesis, Kenyon Review,* XVI (1954), 299–307; and his memorial note on Auerbach, *Comparative Literature,* x (1958), 93–94. In his and Mr. Warren's *Theory of Literature* (New York, 1949), p. 157, Mr. Wellek dismisses cultural relativism of the sort I am expounding by quoting Troeltsch: "All relativism is ultimately defeated by the recognition [in Troeltsch's words] that 'the Absolute is in the relative, though not finally and fully in it.' " But it is my understanding that these words of Troeltsch's are consonant with his doctrine of "value-relativity," a mode of what Mr. Wellek elsewhere calls "perspectivism." Meinecke quotes Troeltsch as saying "Value-relativity is not relativism, anarchy, accident, arbitrariness. It signifies rather a fusion of the factual and normative, which is ever moving and newly created and cannot, therefore, be determined universally and timelessly." On this Meinecke comments: "Value-relativity, in other words, is nothing other than individuality in the historical sense. It is the unique and intrinsically valuable imprint of an unknown absolute—for this kind of absolute will be acknowledged by faith as the creative ground of all values—upon that which is relative and bound to time and nature" ("Values and Causalities in History," p. 283). The task of the critic, it would follow, is to expound literature as something "ever moving and newly created" even as it is "bound to time and nature." His faith will be in man's ability to sense in himself (however ultimately derived) "the creative ground of all values." [As of 1968, Mr. Wellek's views were best summed up in his Olympian refutation of Auerbach's—to me irrefutable—arguments for the historicist position. See his 1960 essay, "Literary Theory, Criticism, and History," in his *Concepts of Criticism* (New Haven, 1963), pp. 1–20.]

Doing so, we strive to see how the very wholeness of a work of art is a product not only of an author's own creative activity but of the creative potential of his culture. Mr. Cunningham is spokesman for them all when he writes in his *Woe or Wonder: The Emotional Effect of Shakespearean Tragedy*: ". . . our purpose in the study of literature, and particularly in the historical study of literature, and particularly in the historical interpretation of texts, is not in the ordinary sense to further the understanding of ourselves. It is rather to enable us to see how we could think and feel otherwise than we do. It is to erect a larger context of experience within which we may define and understand our own by attending to the disparity between it and the experience of others."[9]

[9] [*Woe or Wonder* (1951) is reprinted in Mr. Cunningham's *Tradition and Poetic Structure* (Denver, 1960). The quotation is from p. 141.]

The Sense of the Past

LIONELL TRILLING

In recent years the study of literature in our universities has again and again been called into question, chiefly on the ground that what is being studied is not so much literature itself as the history of literature. John Jay Chapman was perhaps the first to state the case against the literary scholars when in 1927 he denounced the "archaeological, quasi-scientific, and documentary study of the fine arts" because, as he said, it endeavored "to express the fluid universe of many emotions in terms drawn from the study of the physical sciences." And since Chapman wrote, the issue in the universities has been clearly drawn in the form of an opposition of "criticism" to "scholarship." Criticism has been the aggressor, and its assault upon scholarship has been successful almost in proportion to the spiritedness with which it has been made; at the present time, although the archaeological and quasi-scientific and documentary study of literature is still the dominant one in our universities, it is clear to everyone that scholarship is on the defensive and is ready to share the rule with its antagonist.

This revision of the academic polity can be regarded only with satisfaction. The world seems to become less and less responsive to literature; we can even observe that literature is becoming something like an object of suspicion, and it is possible to say of the historical study of literature that its very existence is an evidence of this mistrust. De Quincey's categories of *knowledge* and *power* are most pertinent here; the traditional scholarship, in so far as it takes literature to be chiefly an object of knowledge, denies or obscures that active power by which literature is truly defined. All sorts of studies are properly ancillary to the study of literature. For example, the study of the intellectual conditions in which a work of literature was made is not only legitimate but sometimes even necessary to our perception of its power. Yet when Professor Lovejoy in his influential book, *The Great Chain of Being,* tells us that for the study of the history of ideas a really dead writer is better than one whose works are still enjoyed, we naturally pull up short and wonder if we are not in danger of becoming like the Edinburgh body-snatchers who *saw to it* that there were enough cadavers for study in the medical school.

Criticism made its attack on the historians of literature in the name of literature as power. The attack was the fiercer because literary history had all too faithfully followed the lead of social and political history, which, having given up its traditional connection with literature, had allied itself with the physical sciences of the nineteenth century and had adopted the assumption of these sciences that the world was reflected with perfect literalness in the will-less mind of the observer. The new history had many successes and it taught literary study what it had itself learned, that in an age of science prestige is to be gained by approximating the methods of science. Of these methods the most notable and most adaptable was the investigation of genesis, of how the work of art came into being. I am not concerned to show that the study of genesis is harmful to the right experience of the work of art: I do not believe it is. Indeed, I am inclined to suppose that whenever the genetic method is attacked we ought to suspect that special intersts are being defended. So far is it from being true that the genetic method is in itself inimical to the work of art, that the very opposite is so; a work of art, or any human thing, studied in its genesis can take on an added value. Still, the genetic method can easily be vulgarized, and when it is used in its vulgar form, it can indeed reduce the value of a thing; in much genetic study the implication is clear that to the scholar the work of art is nothing but its conditions.

One of the attractions of the genetic study of art is that it seems to offer a high degree of certainty. Aristotle tells us that every study has its own degree of certainty and that the well-trained man accepts that degree and does not look for a greater one. We may add that there are different kinds as well as different degrees of certainty, and we can say that the great mistake of the scientific-historical scholarship is that it looks for a degree and kind of certainty that literature does not need and cannot allow.

The error that is made by literary scholars when they seek for a certainty analogous with the certainty of science has been so often remarked that at this date little more need be said of it. Up to a point the scientific study of art is legitimate and fruitful; the great thing is that we should recognize the terminal point and not try to push beyond it, that we should not expect that the scientific study of, say, literature will necessarily assure us of the experience of literature; and if we wish as teachers to help others to the experience of literature, we cannot do so by imparting the fruits of our scientific study. What the partisans of the so-called New Criticism revolted against was the scientific notion of the fact as transferred in a literal way to the study of literature. They wished to restore autonomy to the work of art, to see it as the agent of power rather than as the object of knowledge.

The faults of these critics we know. Perhaps their chief fault they share with scientific-historical scholars themselves—they try too hard. No less than the scholars, the critics fall into an error that Chapman denounced, the great modern illusion "that anything whatever . . . can be discovered through hard intellectual work and concentration." We often feel of them that they make the elucidation of poetic ambiguity or irony a kind of intellectual calisthenic ritual. Still, we can forgive them their strenuousness, remembering that something has happened to our relation with language which seems to require that we make methodical and explicit what was once immediate and unformulated.

But there is another fault of the New Critics of which we must take notice. It is that in their reaction from the historical method they forget that the literary work is ineluctably a historical fact, and, what is more important, that its historicity is a fact in our aesthetic experience. Literature, we may say, must in some sense always be an historical study, for literature is an historical art. It is historical in three separate senses.

In the old days the poet was supposed to be himself an historian, a reliable chronicler of events. Thucydides said that he was likely to be an inaccurate historian, but Aristotle said that he was more accurate, because more general, than any mere annalist; and we, following Aristotle, suppose that a large part of literature is properly historical, the recording and interpreting of personal, national, and cosmological events.

Then literature is historical in the sense that it is necessarily aware of its own past. It is not always consciously aware of this past, but it is always practically aware of it. The work of any poet exists by reason of its connection with past work, both in continuation and in divergence, and what we call his originality is simply his special relation to tradition. The point has been fully developed by T. S. Eliot in his well-known essay "Tradition and the Individual Talent." And Mr. Eliot reminds us how each poet's relation to tradition changes tradition itself, so that the history of literature is never quiet for long and is never merely an additive kind of growth. Each new age makes the pattern over again, forgetting what was once dominant, finding new affinities; we read any work within a kaleidoscope of historical elements.

And in one more sense literature is historical, and it is with this sense that I am here chiefly concerned. In the existence of every work of literature of the past, its historicity, its *pastness*, is a factor of great importance. In certain cultures the pastness of a work of art gives it an extra-aesthetic authority which is incorporated into its aesthetic power. But even in our own culture with its ambivalent feeling about tradition, there inheres in a work of art of the past a certain quality, an element of its aesthetic existence, which we can identify as its pastness. Side by side with the formal elements of the work, and modifying these elements, there is the element of history, which, in any complete aesthetic analysis, must be taken into account.

The New Critics exercised their early characteristic method almost exclusively upon lyric poetry, a genre in which the historical element, although of course present, is less obtrusive than in the long poem, the novel, and the drama. But even in the lyric poem the factor of historicity is part of the aesthetic experience; it is not merely a negative condition of the other elements, such as prosody or diction, which, if they are old enough, are likely to be insufficiently understood—it is itself a positive aesthetic factor with positive and pleasurable relations to the other aesthetic factors. It is a part of the *given* of the work, which we cannot help but respond to. The New Critics imply that this situation *should* not exist, but it cannot help existing, and we have to take it into account.

We are creatures of time, we are creatures of the historical sense, not only as men have always been put in a new way since the time of Walter Scott. Possibly this may be for the worse; we would perhaps be stronger if we believed that Now contained all things, and that we in our barbarian moment were all that had ever been. Without the sense of the past we might be more certain, less weighted down and apprehensive. We might also be less generous, and certainly we would be less aware. In any case, we have the sense of the past and must live with it, and by it.

And we must read our literature by it. Try as we will, we cannot be like Partridge at the play, wholly without the historical sense. The leap of the imagination which an audience makes when it responds to *Hamlet* is enormous, and it requires a comprehensive, although not necessarily a highly instructed sense of the past. This sense does not, for most artistic purposes, need to be highly instructed; it can consist largely of the firm belief that there really is such a thing as the past.

In the New Critics' refusal to take critical account of the historicity of a work there is, one understands, the impulse to make the work of the past more immediate and more real, to deny that between Now and Then there is any essential difference, the spirit of man being one and continuous. But it is only if we are aware of the reality of the past as past that we can feel it as alive and present. If, for example, we try to make Shakespeare literally contemporaneous, we make him monstrous. He is contemporaneous only if we know how much a man of his own age he was; he is relevant to us only if we see his distance from us. Or to take a poet closer to us in actual time, Wordsworth's Immortality Ode is acceptable to us only when it is understood to have been written at a certain past moment; if it had appeared much later than it did, if it were offered to us now as a contemporary work, we would not admire it; and the same is true of *The Prelude,* which of all works of the Romantic Movement is closest to our present interest. In the pastness of these works lies the assurance of their validity and relevance.

The question is always arising: What is the real poem? Is it the poem we now perceive? Is it the poem the author consciously intended? Is it the poem the author intended and his first readers read? Well, it is all these things, depending on the state of our knowledge. But in addition the poem is the poem as it has existed in history, as it has lived its life from Then to Now, as it is a thing which submits itself to one kind of perception in one age and another kind of perception in another age, as it exerts in each age a different kind of power. This makes it a thing we can never wholly understand—other things too, of course, help to make it that—and the mystery, the unreachable part of the poem, is one of its aesthetic elements.

To suppose that we can think like men of another time is as much of an illusion as to suppose that we can think in a wholly different way. But it is the first illusion that is exemplified in the attitude of the anti-historical critics. In the admirable poetry textbook of Cleanth Brooks and Robert Penn Warren, the authors disclaim all historical intention. Their purpose being what it is, they are right to do so, but I wonder if they are right in never asking in their aesthetic analysis the question: What effect is created by our knowledge that the language of a particular poem is not such as would be uttered by a poet writing now? To read a poem of even a hundred years ago requires as much translation of its historical circumstance as of its metaphors. This the trained and gifted critic is likely to forget; his own historical sense is often so deeply ingrained that he is not wholly conscious of it, and sometimes, for reasons of his own, he prefers to keep it merely implicit. Yet whether or not it is made conscious and explicit, the historical sense is one of the aesthetic and critical faculties.

What more apposite reminder of this can we have than the early impulse of the New Critics themselves to discover all poetic virtue in the poetry of the seventeenth century, the impulse, only lately modified, to find the essence of poetic error in the poetry of Romanticism? Their having given rein to this impulse is certainly not illegitimate. They were doing what we all do, what we all must and even should do: they were involving their aesthetics with certain cultural preferences, they were implying choices in religion, metaphysics, politics, manners. And in so far as they were doing this by showing a preference for a particular period of the past, which they brought into comparison with the present, they were exercising their historical sense. We cannot question their preference itself; we can only question the mere implicitness of their historical sense, their attitude of making the historical sense irrelevant to their aesthetic.

But if the historical sense is always with us, it must, for just that reason, be refined and made more exact. We have, that is, to open our minds to the whole question of what we mean when we speak of causation in culture. Hume, who so shook our notions of causation in the physical sciences, raises some interesting questions of causation in culture. "There is no subject," he says, "in which we must proceed with more caution than in tracing the history of the arts and sciences; lest we assign causes which never existed and reduce what is merely contingent to stable and universal principles." The cultivators of the arts, he goes on to say, are always few in number and their minds are delicate and "easily perverted." "Chance, therefore, or secret and unknown causes must have great influence on the rise and progress of all refined arts." But there is one fact, he continues, which gives us the license to speculate—this is the fact that the choice spirits arise from and are related to the mass of the people of their time. "The question, therefore, is not altogether concerning the taste, genius, and spirit of a few, but concerning those of a whole people; and may, therefore, be accounted for, in some measure, by general causes and principles." This gives us our charter to engage in cultural history and cultural criticism, but we must see that it is a charter to deal with a mystery.

The refinement of our historical sense chiefly means that we keep it properly complicated. History, like science and art, involves abstraction: we abstract certain events from others and we make this particular abstraction with an end in view, we make it to serve some purpose of our will. Try as we may, we cannot, as we write history, escape our purposiveness. Nor, indeed, should we try to escape, for purpose and meaning are the same thing. But in pursuing our purpose, in making our abstractions, we must be aware of what we are doing; we ought to have it fully in mind that our abstraction is not perfectly equivalent to the infinite complication of events from which we have abstracted. I should like to suggest a few ways in which those of us who are literary scholars can give to our notion of history an appropriate complication.

It ought to be for us a real question whether, and in what way, human nature is always the same. I do not mean that we ought to settle this question before we get to work, but only that we insist to ourselves that the question is a real one. What we certainly know has changed is the *expression* of human nature, and we must keep before our minds the problem of the relation which expression bears to feeling. E. E. Stoll, the well-known Shakespearean critic, has settled the matter out of hand by announcing the essential difference between what he calls "convention" and what he calls "life," and he insists that the two may have no truck with each other, that we cannot say of Shakespeare that he is psychologically or philosophically acute because these are terms we use of "life," whereas Shakespeare was dealing only with "convention." This has the virtue of suggesting how important is the relation of "convention" to "life," but it misses the point that "life" is always expressed through "convention" and in a sense always *is* "convention," and that convention has meaning only because of the intentions of life. Professor Stoll seems to go on the assumption that Shakespeare's audiences were conscious of convention; they were aware of it, but certainly not conscious of it; what they were conscious of was life, into which they made an instantaneous translation of all that took place on the stage. The problem of the interplay between the emotion and the convention which is available for it, and the reciprocal influence they exert on each other, is a very difficult one, and I scarcely even state its complexities, let alone pretend to solve them. But the problem with its difficulties should be admitted, and simplicity of solution should always be regarded as a sign of failure.

A very important step forward in the complication of our sense of the past was made when Whitehead and after him Lovejoy taught us to look not for the expressed but for the assumed ideas of an age, what Whitehead describes as the "assumptions which appear so obvious that people do not know that they are assuming them because no other way of putting things has ever occurred to them."

But a regression was made when Professor Lovejoy, in that influential book of his, assured us that "the ideas in serious reflective literature are, of course, in great part philosophical ideas in dilution." To go fully into the error of this common belief would need more time than we have now at our disposal. It is part of our suspiciousness of literature that we undertake thus to make it a dependent art. Certainly we must question the assumption which gives the priority in ideas to the philosopher and sees the movement of thought as always from the systematic thinker, who thinks up the ideas in, presumably, a cultural vacuum, to the poet who "uses" the ideas "in dilution." We must question this even if it means a reconstruction of what we mean by "ideas."

And this leads to another matter about which we may not be simple, the relation of the poet to his environment. The poet, it is true, is an effect of environment, but we must remember that he is no less a cause. He may be used as the barometer, but let us not forget that he is also part of the weather. We have been too easily satisfied by a merely elementary meaning of environment; we have been content with a simple quantitative implication of the word, taking a large and literally environing thing to be always the environment of a smaller thing. In a concert room the audience and its attitude are of course the environment of the performer, but also the performer and his music make the environment of the audience. In a family the parents are no doubt the chief factors in the environment of the child; but also the child is a factor in the environment of the parents and himself conditions the actions of his parents toward him.

Corollary to this question of environment is the question of influence, the influence which one writer is said to have had on another. In its historical meaning, from which we take our present use, *influence* was a word intended to express a mystery. It means a flowing-in, but not as a tributary river flows into the main stream at a certain observable point; historically the image is an astrological one and the meanings which the Oxford Dictionary gives all suggest "producing effects by *insensible* or *invisible* means"—"the infusion of any kind of divine, spiritual, moral, immaterial, or *secret* power or principle." Before the idea of influence we ought to be far more puzzled than we are; if we find it hard to be puzzled enough, we may contrive to induce the proper state of uncertainty by turning the word upon ourselves, asking, "What have been the influences that made me the person I am, and to whom would I entrust the task of truly discovering what they were?"

Yet another thing that we have not understood with sufficient complication is the nature of ideas in their relation to the conditions of their development and in relation to their transmission. Too often we conceive of an idea as being like the baton that is handed from runner to runner in a relay race. But an idea as a transmissible thing is rather like the sentence that in the parlor game is whispered about in a circle; the point of the game is the amusement that comes when the last version is compared with the original. As for the origin of ideas, we ought to remember that an idea is the formulation of a response to a situation; so, too, is the modification of an existing idea. Since the situations in which people or cultures find themselves are limited in number, and since the possible responses are also limited, ideas certainly do have a tendency to recur, and because people think habitually ideas also have a tendency to persist when the situation which called them forth is no longer present; so that ideas do have a certain limited autonomy, and sometimes the appearance of a complete autonomy. From this there has grown up the belief in the actual perfect autonomy of ideas. It is supposed that ideas think themselves, create themselves and their descendants, have a life independent of the thinker and the situation. And from this we are often led to conclude that ideas, systematic ideas, are directly responsible for events.

A similar feeling is prevalent among our intellectual classes in relation to words. Semantics is not now the lively concern that it was a few years ago, but the mythology of what we may call political semantics has become established in our intellectual life, the belief that we are betrayed by words, that words push us around against our will. "The tyranny of words" became a popular phrase and is still in use, and the semanticists offer us an easier world and freedom from war if only we assert our independence from words. But nearly a century ago Dickens said that he was tired of hearing about "the tyranny of words" (he used that phrase); he was, he said, less concerned with the way words abuse us than with the way we abuse words. It is not words that make our troubles, but our own wills. Words cannot control us unless we desire to be controlled by them. And the same is true of the control of systematic ideas. We have come to believe that some ideas can betray us, other save us. The educated classes are learning to blame ideas for our troubles, rather than blaming what is a very different thing—our own bad thinking. This is the great vice of academicism, that it is concerned with ideas rather than with thinking, and nowadays the errors of academicism do not stay in the academy; they make their way into the world, and what begins as a failure of perception among intellectual specialists finds its fulfillment in policy and action.

In time of war, when two different cultures, or two extreme modifications of the same culture, confront each other with force, this belief in the autonomy of ideas becomes especially strong and therefore especially clear. In any modern war there is likely to be involved a conflict of ideas which is in part factitious but which is largely genuine. But this conflict of ideas, genuine as it may be, suggests to both sides the necessity of believing in the fixed, immutable nature of the ideas to which each side owes allegiance. What gods were to the ancients at war, ideas are to us. Thus, in the last war, an eminent American professor of philosophy won wide praise for demonstrating that Nazism was to be understood as the inevitable outcome of the ideas of Schopenhauer and Nietzsche, while the virtues of American democracy were to be explained by tracing a direct line of descent from Plato and the Athenian polity. Or consider a few sentences from a biography of Byron, written when, not so long ago, the culture of Nazism was at its height. The author, a truly admirable English biographer, is making an estimate of the effort of the Romantic Movement upon our time. He concludes that the Romantic Movement failed. Well, we have all heard that before, and perhaps it is true, although I for one know less and less what it means. Indeed, I know less and less what is meant by the ascription of failure to any movement in literature. All movements fail, and perhaps the Romantic Movement failed more than most because it attempted more than most; possibly it attempted too much. To say that a literary movement failed seems to suggest a peculiar view of both literature and history; it implies that literature ought to settle something for good and all, that life ought to be progressively completed. And according to our author, not only did the Romantic Movement fail—it left a terrible legacy:

Nationalism was essentially a Romantic movement, and from nationalism springs the half-baked racial theorist with his romantic belief in the superiority of "Aryan" blood and his romantic distrust of the use of reason. So far-reaching were the effects of the Romantic Revival that they still persist in shapes under which they are no longer recognized. . . . For Romantic literature appeals to that strain of anarchism which inhabits a dark corner of every human mind and is continually advancing the charms of extinction against the claims of life—the beauty of all that is fragmentary and youthful and half-formed as opposed to the compact achievement of adult genius.

It is of course easy enough to reduce the argument to absurdity—we have only to ask why Germany and not ourselves responded so fiercely to the romantic ideas which, if they be indeed the romantic ideas, were certainly available to everybody. The failure of logic is not however what concerns us, but rather what the logic is intended to serve: the belief that ideas generate events, that they have an autonomous existence, and that they can seize upon the minds of some men and control their actions independently of circumstance and will.

Needless to say, these violations of historical principle require a violation of historical fact. The Schopenhauer and the Nietzsche of the first explanation have no real reference to two nineteenth-century philosophers of the same names; the Plato is imaginary, the Athens out of a storybook, and no attempt is made to reconcile this fanciful Athens with the opinion of the real Athens held by the real Plato. As for the second explanation, how are we to connect anarchism, and hostility to the claims of life, and the fragmentary, and the immature, and the half-formed, with Kant, or Goethe, or Wordsworth, or Beethoven, or Berlioz, or Delacroix? And how from these men, who *are* Romanticism, dare we derive the iron rigidity and the desperate centralization which the New Order of the Nazis involved, or the systematic cruelty or the elaborate scientism with which the racial doctrine was implicated?

The two books to which I refer are of course in themselves harmless and I don't wish to put upon them a weight which they should not properly be made to bear. But they do suggest something of the low estate into which history has fallen among our educated classes, and they are of a piece with the depreciation of the claims of history which a good many literary people nowadays make, a depreciation which has had the effect of leading young students of literature, particularly the more gifted ones, to incline more and more to resist historical considerations, justifying themselves, as it is natural they should, by pointing to the dullness and deadness and falsifications which have resulted from the historical study of literature. Our resistance to history is no doubt ultimately to be accounted for by nothing less than the whole nature of our life today. It was said by Nietzsche—the real one, not the lay figure of cultural propaganda—that the historical sense was an actual faculty of the mind, "a sixth sense," and that the credit for the recognition of its status must go to the nineteenth century. What was uniquely esteemed by the nineteenth century is not likely to stand in high favor with us: our coldness to historical thought may in part be explained by our feeling that it is precisely the past that caused all our troubles, the nineteenth century being the most blameworthy of all the culpable centuries. Karl Marx, for whom history was indeed a sixth sense, expressed what has come to be the secret hope of our time, that man's life in politics, which is to say, man's life in history, shall come to an end. History, as we now understand it, envisions its own extinction—that is really what we nowadays mean by "progress"—and with all the passion of a desire kept secret even from ourselves, we yearn to elect a way of life which shall be satisfactory once and for all, time without end, and we do not want to be reminded by the past of the considerable possibility that our present is but perpetuating mistakes and failures and instituting new troubles.

And yet, when we come to think about it, the chances are all in favor of our having to go on making our choices and so of making our mistakes. History, in its meaning of a continuum of events, is not really likely to come to an end. There may therefore be some value in bringing explicitly to mind what part in culture is played by history in its other meaning of an ordering and understanding of the continuum of events. There is no one who is better able to inform us on this point than Nietzsche. We can perhaps listen to him with the more patience because he himself would have had considerable sympathy for our impatience with history, for although he thought that the historical sense brought certain virtues, making men "unpretentious, unselfish, modest, brave, habituated to self-control and self-renunciation," he also thought that it prevented them from having the ability to respond to the very highest and noblest developments of culture, making them suspicious of what is wholly completed and fully matured. This ambivalent view of the historical sense gives him a certain authority when he defines what the historical sense is and does. It is, he said, "the capacity for divining quickly the order of the rank of the valuation according to which a people, a community, or an individual has lived." In the case of a people or of a community, the valuations are those which are expressed not only by the gross institutional facts of their life, what Nietzsche called "the operating forces," but also and more significantly by their morals and manners, by their philosophy and art. And the historical sense, he goes on to say, is "the 'divining instinct' for the relationships of these valuations, for the relation of the valuations to the operating forces." The historical sense, that is, is to be understood as the critical sense, as the sense which life uses to test itself. And since there never was a time when the instinct for divining—and "quickly"!—the order of rank of cultural expressions was so much needed, our growing estrangement from history must be understood as the sign of our desperation.

Nietzsche's own capacity for quickly divining the order of rank of cultural things was, when he was at his best, more acute than that of any other man of his time or since. If we look for the explanation of his acuity, we find it in the fact that it never occurred to him to separate his historical sense from his sense of art. They were not two senses but one. And the merit of his definition of the historical sense, especially when it is taken in conjunction with the example of himself, is that it speaks to the historian and to the student of art as if they were one person. To that person Nietzsche's definition prescribes that culture be studied and judged as life's continuous evaluation of itself, the evaluation being understood as never finding full expression in the "operating forces" of a culture, but as never finding expression at all without reference to these gross, institutional facts.

The Backgrounds of "The Dead"

RICHARD ELLMAN

> The silent cock shall crow at last. The west shall shake
> the east awake. Walk while ye have the night for morn,
> lightbreakfastbringer. . . .
>
> —*Finnegans Wake* (473)

THE stay in Rome had seemed purposeless, but during it Joyce became aware of the change in his attitude toward Ireland and so toward the world. He embodied his new perceptions in "The Dead." The story, which was the culmination of a long waiting history, began to take shape in Rome, but was not set down until he left the city. The pressure of hints, sudden insights, and old memories rose in his mind until, like King Midas's barber, he was compelled to speech.

Although the story dealt mainly with three generations of his family in Dublin, it drew also upon an incident in Galway in 1903. There Michael ("Sonny") Bodkin courted Nora Barnacle; but he contracted tuberculosis and had to be confined to bed. Shortly afterwards Nora resolved to go to Dublin, and Bodkin stole out of his sickroom, in spite of the rainy weather, to sing to her under an apple tree and bid her goodbye. In Dublin Nora soon learned that Bodkin was dead, and when she met Joyce she was first attracted to him, as she told a sister, because he resembled Sonny Bodkin.[1]

Joyce's habit of ferreting out details had made him conduct minute interrogations of Nora even before their departure from Dublin. He was disconcerted by the fact that young men before him had interested her. He did not much like to know that her heart was still moved, even in pity, by the recollection of the boy who had loved her. The notion of being in some sense in rivalry with a dead man buried in the little cemetery at Oughterard was one that came

---

[1] Letter to me from Mrs. Kathleen Barnacle Griffin.

easily, and gallingly, to a man of Joyce's jealous disposition. It was one source of his complaint to his Aunt Josephine Murray that Nora persisted in regarding him as quite similar to other men she had known.

A few months after expressing this annoyance, while Joyce and Nora Barnacle were living in Trieste in 1905, Joyce received another impulsion toward "The Dead." In a letter Stanislaus happened to mention attending a concert of Plunket Greene, the Irish baritone, which included one of Thomas Moore's *Irish Melodies* called "O, Ye Dead!"[2] The song, a dialogue of living and dead, was eerie enough, but what impressed Stanislaus was that Greene rendered the second stanza, in which the dead answer the living, as if they were whimpering for the bodied existence they could no longer enjoy:

> It is true, it is true, we are shadows cold and wan;
> And the fair and the brave whom we loved on earth are gone;
> > But still thus ev'n in death,
> > So sweet the living breath
> Of the fields and the flow'rs in our youth we wandered o'er,
> > That ere, condemn'd, we go
> > To freeze, 'mid Hecla's snow,
> We would taste it awhile, and think we live once more!

James was interested and asked Stanislaus to send the words, which he learned to sing himself. His feelings about his wife's dead lover found a dramatic counterpart in the jealousy of the dead for the living in Moore's song: it would seem that the living and the dead are jealous of each other. Another aspect of the rivalry is suggested in *Ulysses,* where Stephen cries out to his mother's ghost, whose "glazing eyes, staring out of death, to shake and bend my soul, . . . to strike me down," he cannot put out of mind: "No, mother. Let me be and let me live."[3] That the dead do not stay buried is, in fact, a theme of Joyce from the beginning to the end of his work; Finnegan is not the only corpse to be resurrected.

In Rome the obtrusiveness of the dead affected what he thought of Dublin, the equally Catholic city he had abandoned, a city as prehensile of its ruins, visible and invisible. His head was filled with a sense of the too successful encroachment of the dead upon the living city; there was a disrupting parallel in the way that Dublin, buried behind him, was haunting his thoughts. In *Ulysses* the theme was to be reconstituted, in more horrid form, in the mind of Stephen, who sees corpses rising from their graves like vampires to deprive the living of joy. The bridebed, the childbed, and the bed of death are bound together, and death "comes, pale vampire, through storm his eyes, his bat sails bloodying the sea, mouth to her mouth's kiss."[4] We can be at the same time in death as well as in life.[5]

[2] S. Joyce, 'The Background to "Dubliners," ' *Listener,* li (March 25, 1954), 526-7.

[3] *Ulysses,* p. 12 (8).

[4] Ibid. p. 48 (44).

[5] The converse of this theme appears in *Ulysses* (113 [107]), when Bloom, walking in Glasnevin, thinks, "They are not going to get me this innings. Warm beds: warm fullblooded life."

By February 11, 1907, after six months in Rome, Joyce knew in general what story he must write. Some of his difficulty in beginning it was due, as he said himself, to the riot in Dublin over *The Playboy of the Western World*. Synge had followed the advice of Yeats that Joyce had rejected, to find his inspiration in the Irish folk, and had gone to the Aran Islands. This old issue finds small echoes in the story. The nationalistic Miss Ivors tries to persuade Gabriel to go to Aran (where Synge's *Riders to the Sea* is set), and when he refuses twits him for his lack of patriotic feeling. Though Gabriel thinks of defending the autonomy of art and its indifference to politics, he knows such a defense would be pretentious, and only musters up the remark that he is sick of his own country. But the issue is far from settled for him.

"The Dead" begins with a party and ends with a corpse, so entwining "funferal" and "funeral" as in the wake of Finnegan. That he began with a party was due, at least in part, to Joyce's feeling that the rest of the stories in *Dubliners* had not completed his picture of the city. In a letter of September 25, 1906, he had written his brother from Rome to say that some elements of Dublin had been left out of his stories: "I have not reproduced its ingenuous insularity and its hospitality, the latter 'virtue' so far as I can see does not exist elsewhere in Europe." He allowed a little of this warmth to enter "The Dead." In his speech at the Christmas party Gabriel Conroy explicitly commends Ireland for this very virtue of hospitality, though his expression of the idea is distinctly after-dinner: "I feel more strongly with every recurring year that our country has no tradition which does it so much honour and which it should guard so jealously as that of its hospitality. It is a tradition that is unique as far as my experience goes (and I have visited not a few places abroad) among the modern nations." This was Joyce's oblique way, in language that mocked his own, of beginning the task of making amends.

The selection of details for "The Dead" shows Joyce making those choices which, while masterly, suggest the preoccupations that mastered him. Once he had determined to represent an Irish party, the choice of the Misses Morkans' as its location was easy enough. He had already reserved for *Stephen Hero* a Christmas party at his own house, a party which was also to be clouded by a discussion of a dead man. The other festive occasions of his childhood were associated with his hospitable great-aunts Mrs. Callanan and Mrs. Lyons, and Mrs. Callanan's daughter Mary Ellen, at their house at 15 Usher's Island, which was also known as the "Misses Flynn school." [6] There every year the Joyces who were old enough would go, and John Joyce carved the goose and made the speech. Stanislaus Joyce says that the speech of Gabriel Conroy in "The Dead" is a good imitation of his father's oratorical style. [7]

In Joyce's story Mrs. Callanan and Mrs. Lyons, the Misses Flynn, become the spinster ladies, the Misses Morkan, and Mary Ellen Callanan becomes Mary Jane. Most of the other party guests were also reconstituted from Joyce's

[6] Interview with Mrs. May Joyce Monaghan, 1953.

[7] He excepts the quotation from Browning, but even this was quite within the scope of the man who could quote Vergil when lending money to his son.

recollections. Mrs. Lyons had a son Freddy, who kept a Christmas card shop in Grafton Street.[8] Joyce introduces him as Freddy Malins, and situates his shop in the less fashionable Henry Street, perhaps to make him need that sovereign Gabriel lent him. Another relative of Joyce's mother, a first cousin, married a Protestant named Mervyn Archdale Browne, who combined the profession of music teacher with that of agent for a burglary insurance company. Joyce keeps him in "The Dead" under his own name. Bartell d'Arcy, the hoarse singer in the story, was based upon Barton M'Guckin, the leading tenor in the Carl Rosa Opera Company. There were other tenors, such as John McCormack, whom Joyce might have used, but he needed one who was unsuccessful and uneasy about himself; and his father's often-told anecdote about M'Guckin's lack of confidence furnished him with just such a singer as he intended Bartell d'Arcy to be.

The making of his hero, Gabriel Conroy, was more complicated. The root situation, of jealousy for his wife's dead lover, was of course Joyce's. The man who is murdered, D. H. Lawrence has one of his characters say, desires to be murdered;[9] some temperaments demand the feeling that their friends and sweethearts will deceive them. Joyce's conversation often returned to the word "betrayal,"[10] and the entangled innocents whom he uses for his heroes are all aspects of his conception of himself. Though Gabriel is less impressive than Joyce's other heroes, Stephen, Bloom, Richard Rowan, or Earwicker, he belongs to their distinguished, put-upon company.

There are several specific points at which Joyce attributes his own experiences to Gabriel. The letter which Gabriel remembers having written to Gretta Conroy early in their courtship is one of these; from it Gabriel quotes to himself the sentiment, "Why is it that words like these seem to me so dull and cold? Is it because there is no word tender enough to be your name?" These sentences are taken almost directly from a letter Joyce wrote to Nora in 1904.[11] It was also Joyce, of course, who wrote book reviews, just as Gabriel Conroy does, for the *Daily Express*. Since the *Daily Express* was pro-English, he had probably been teased for writing for it during his frequent visits to the house of David Sheehy, M.P. One of the Sheehy daughters, Kathleen, may well have been the model for Miss Ivors, for she wore that austere bodice and sported the same patriotic pin.[12] In Gretta's old sweetheart, in Gabriel's letter, in the book reviews and the discussion of them, as well as in the physical image of Gabriel with hair parted in the middle and rimmed glasses, Joyce drew directly upon his own life.

His father was also deeply involved in the story. Stanislaus Joyce recalls that when the Joyce children were too young to bring along to the Misses Flynns' party, their father and mother sometimes left them with a governess

---

[8] Idem.

[9] Birkin in *Women in Love*.

[10] Information from Professor Joseph Prescott.

[11] At Cornell.

[12] Interview with Mrs. Mary Sheehy Kettle, 1953.

and stayed at a Dublin hotel overnight instead of returning to their house in Bray.[13] Gabriel and Gretta do this too. Gabriel's quarrels with his mother also suggest John Joyce's quarrels with his mother, who never accepted her son's marriage to a woman of lower station. But John Joyce's personality was not like Gabriel's; he had no doubts of himself, in the midst of many failures he was full of self-esteem. He had the same unshakable confidence as his son James. For Gabriel's personality there is among Joyce's friends another model.[14] This was Constantine Curran, sometimes nicknamed "Cautious Con." He is a more distinguished man than Joyce allows, but Joyce was building upon, and no doubt distorting, his memories of Curran as a very young man. That he has Curran partly in mind is suggested by the fact that he calls Gabriel's brother by Curran's first name Constantine, and makes Gabriel's brother, like Curran's, a priest.[15] Curran has the same high color and nervous, disquieted manner as Gabriel, and like Gabriel he has traveled to the continent and has cultivated cosmopolitan interests. Curran, like Conroy, married a woman who was not a Dubliner, though she came from only as far west as Limerick. In other respects he is quite different. Gabriel was made mostly out of Curran, Joyce's father, and Joyce himself. Probably Joyce knew there was a publican on Howth named Gabriel Conroy; or, as Gerhard Friedrich has proposed,[16] he may have borrowed the name from the title of a Bret Harte novel. But the character, if not the name, was of his own compounding.[17]

Joyce now had his people, his party, and something of its development. In the festive setting, upon which the snow keeps offering a different perspective until, as W. Y. Tindall suggests,[19] the snow itself changes, he develops Gabriel's private tremors, his sense of inadequacy, his uncomfortable insistence on his small pretensions. From the beginning he is vulnerable; his well-meant and even generous overtures are regularly checked. The servant girl punctures his blithe assumption that everyone is happily in love and on the way to the altar. He is not sure enough of himself to put out of his head the slurs he has received long ago; so in spite of his uxorious attitude towards Gretta he is a little ashamed of her having come from the west of Ireland. He cannot bear to think of his dead mother's remark that Gretta was "country cute," and when Miss Ivors says of Gretta, "She's from Connacht, isn't she?" Gabriel answers shortly, "Her people are." He has rescued her from that bog. Miss Ivors's suggestion, a true Gaelic Leaguer's, that he spend his holiday in the Irish-speaking Aran Islands (in the

[13] My Brother's Keeper, p. 38 (58).

[14] Interview with S. Joyce, 1953.

[15] Suggested to me by Professor Vivian Mercier.

[16] Gerhard Friedrich, 'Bret Harte as a Source for James Joyce's "The Dead," ' Philological Quarterly, xxxiii (Oct. 1954), pp. 442-4.

[17] The name of Conroy's wife Gretta was borrowed from another friend, Gretta (actually Margaret) Cousins, the wife of James H. Cousins. Since Joyce mentioned in a letter at the same time that he was meditating "The Dead," the danger of becoming "a patient Cousins,"[18] this family was evidently on his mind.

[18] Letter to S. Joyce, Feb. 1907.

[19] W. Y. Tindall, The Literary Symbol (New York, 1955), p. 227.

west) upsets him; it is the element in his wife's past that he wishes to forget During most of the story, the west of Ireland is connected in Gabriel's mind with a dark and rather painful primitivism, an aspect of his country which he has steadily abjured by going off to the continent. The west is savagery; to the east and south lie people who drink wine and wear galoshes.

Gabriel has been made uneasy about this attitude, but he clings to it defiantly until the ending. Unknown to him, it is being challenged by the song, "The Lass of Aughrim." Aughrim is a little village in the west not far from Galway. The song has a special relevance; in it a woman who has been seduced and abandoned by Lord Gregory comes with her baby in the rain to beg for admission to his house. It brings together the peasant mother and the civilized seducer, but Gabriel does not listen to the words; he only watches his wife listening. Joyce had heard this ballad from Nora; perhaps he considered also using Tom Moore's "O, Ye Dead" in the story, but if so he must have seen that "The Lass of Aughrim" would connect more subtly with the west and with Michael Furey's visit in the rain to Gretta. But the notion of using a song at all may well have come to him as the result of the excitement generated in him by Moore's song.

And now Gabriel and Gretta go to the Hotel Gresham, Gabriel fired by his living wife and Gretta drained by the memory of her dead lover. He learns for the first time of the young man in Galway, whose name Joyce has deftly altered from Sonny or Michael Bodkin to Michael Furey. The new name suggests, like the contrast of the militant Michael and the amiable Gabriel, that violent passion is in her Galway past, not in her Dublin present. Gabriel tries to cut Michael Furey down. "What was he?" he asks, confident that his own profession of language teacher (which of course he shared with Joyce) is superior; but she replies, "He was in the gasworks," as if this profession was as good as any other. Then Gabriel tries again, "And what did he die of so young, Gretta? Consumption, was it?" He hopes to register the usual expressions of pity, but Gretta silences and terrifies him by her answer, "I think he died for me."[20] Since Joyce has already made clear that Michael Furey was tubercular, this answer of Gretta has a fine ambiguity. It asserts the egoism of passion, and unconsciously defies Gabriel's reasonable question.

Now Gabriel begins to succumb to his wife's dead lover, and becomes a pilgrim to emotional intensities outside of his own experience. From a biographical point of view, these final pages compose one of Joyce's several tributes to his wife's artless integrity. Nora Barnacle, in spite of her defects of education, was independent, unself-conscious, instinctively right. Gabriel acknowledges the same coherence in his own wife, and he recognizes in the west of Ireland, in Michael Furey, a passion he has himself always lacked. "Better pass boldly into that other world, in the full glory of some passion, than fade and wither dismally with age," Joyce makes Gabriel think. Then comes that strange

[20] Adaline Glasheen has discovered here an echo of Yeats's nationalistic play, *Cathleen ni Houlihan* (1902), where the old woman who symbolizes Ireland sings a song of "yellow-haired Donough that was hanged in Galway." When she is asked, "What was it brought him to his death?" she replies, "He died for love of me; many a man has died for love of me."[21]

[21] I am indebted to Mrs. Glasheen for pointing this out to me.

sentence in the final paragraph: "The time had come for him to set out on his journey westward." The cliché runs that journeys westward are towards death, but the west has taken on a special meaning in the story. Gretta Conroy's west is the place where life had been lived simply and passionately. The context and phrasing of the sentence suggest that Gabriel is on the edge of sleep, and half-consciously accepts what he has hitherto scorned, the possibility of an actual trip to Connaught. What the sentence affirms, at last, on the level of feeling, is the west, the priimtive, untutored, impulsive country from which Gabriel had felt himself alienated before; in the story, the west is paradoxically linked also with the past and the dead. It is like Aunt Julia Morkan who, though ignorant, old, grey-skinned, and stupified, seizes in her song at the party "the excitement of swift and secure flight."

The tone of the sentence, "The time had come for him to set out on his journey westward," is somewhat resigned. It suggests a concession, a relinquishment, and Gabriel is conceding and relinquishing a good deal—his sense of the importance of civilized thinking, of continental tastes, of all those tepid but nice distinctions on which he has prided himself. The bubble of his self-possession is pricked; he no longer possesses himself, and not to possess oneself is in a way a kind of death. It is a self-abandonment not unlike Furey's, and through Gabriel's mind runs the imagery of Calvary. He imagines the snow on the cemetery at Oughterard, lying "thickly drifted on the crooked crosses and headstones, on the spears of the little gate, on the barren thorns." He thinks of Michael Furey who, Gretta has said, died for her, and envies him his sacrifice for another kind of love than Christ's. To some extent Gabriel too is dying for her, in giving up what he has most valued in himself, all that holds him apart from the simpler people at the party. He feels close to Gretta through sympathy if not through love; now they are both past youth, beauty, and passion; he feels close also to her dead lover, another lamb burnt on her altar, though she too is burnt now; he feels no resentment, only pity. In his own sacrifice of himself he is conscious of a melancholy unity between the living and the dead.

Gabriel, who has been sick of his own country, finds himself drawn inevitably into a silent tribute to it of much more consequence than his spoken tribute to the party. He has had illusions of the rightness of a way of life that should be outside of Ireland; but through this experience with his wife he grants a kind of bondage, of acceptance, even of admiration to a part of the country and a way of life that are most Irish. Ireland is shown to be stronger, more intense than he. At the end of *A Portrait of the Artist,* too, Stephen Dedalus, who has been so resolutely opposed to nationalism, makes a similar concession when he interprets his departure from Ireland as an attempt to forge a conscience for his race.

Joyce did not invent the incidents that conclude his story, the second honeymoon of Gabriel and Gretta which ends so badly. His method of composition was very like T. S. Eliot's, the imaginative absorption of stray material. The method did not please Joyce very much because he considered it not imaginative enough, but it was the only way he could work. He borrowed the ending for "The Dead" from another book. In that book a bridal couple receive, on their wedding night, a message that a young woman whom the husband jilted has just committed suicide. The news holds them apart, she asks him not to kiss her, and both are tormented by remorse. The wife, her marriage unconsummated, falls off at last to sleep, and her husband goes to the window and looks out at "the melancholy greyness of the dawn." For the first time he recognizes, with the force of a revelation, that his life is a failure, and that his wife lacks the passion of the girl who has killed herself. He resolves that, since he is not worthy of any more momentous career, he will try at least to make her happy. Here surely is the situation that Joyce so adroitly recomposed. The dead lover who comes between the lovers, the sense of the husband's failure, the acceptance of mediocrity, the resolve to be at all events sympathetic, all come from the other book. But Joyce transforms them. For example, he allows Gretta to kiss her husband, but without desire, and rarefies the situation by having it arise not from a suicide but from a memory of young love. The book Joyce was borrowing from was one that nobody reads any more, George Moore's *Vain Fortune;* but Joyce read it,[22] and in his youthful essay, "The Day of the Rabblement," overpraised it as "fine, original work."[23]

Moore said nothing about snow, however. No one can know how Joyce conceived the joining of Gabriel's final experience with the snow. But his fondness for a background of this kind is also illustrated by his use of the fireplace in "Ivy Day," of the streetlamps in "Two Gallants," and of the river in *Finnegans Wake.* It does not seem that the snow can be death, as so many have said, for it falls on living and dead alike, and for death to fall on the dead is a simple redundancy of which Joyce would not have been guilty. For snow to be "general all over Ireland" is of course unusual in that country. The fine description: "It was falling on every part of the dark central plain, on the treeless hills, falling softly upon the Bog of Allen and, farther westward, softly falling into the dark mutinous Shannon waves," is probably borrowed by Joyce from a famous simile in the twelfth book of the Iliad, which Thoreau translates:[24] "The snowflakes fall thick and fast on a winter's day. The winds are lulled, and the snow falls incessant, covering the tops of the mountains, and the hills, and the plains where the lotus-tree grows, and the cultivated fields, and they are falling by the inlets and shores of the foaming sea, but are silently dissolved by the waves." But Homer was simply describing the thickness of the arrows in the battle of the Greeks and Trojans; and while Joyce seems to copy his topographical details, he uses the image here chiefly for a similar sense of crowding and quiet pressure. Where Homer speaks of the waves silently dissolving the snow, Joyce adds the final detail of "the mutinous Shannon waves" which suggests the "Furey" quality of the west. The snow that falls upon Gabriel, Gretta, and Michael Furey, upon the Misses Morkan, upon the dead singers and the living, is mutuality, a sense of their connection with each other, a sense that none has his being alone. The partygoers prefer dead singers to living ones, the wife prefers a dead lover to a live lover.

[22] He evidently refreshed his memory of it when writing "The Dead," for his copy of *Vain Fortune,* now at Yale, bears the date "March 1907."

[23] *Critical Writings,* p. 83.

[24] Professor Walter B. Rideout kindly called my attention to the similarity of these passages.

The snow does not stand alone in the story. It is part of the complex imagery that includes heat and cold air, fire, and rain, as well as snow. The relations of these are not simple. During the party the living people, their festivities, and all human society seem contrasted with the cold outside, as in the warmth of Gabriel's hand on the cold pane. But this warmth is felt by Gabriel as stuffy and confining, and the cold outside is repeatedly connected with what is fragrant and fresh. The cold, in this sense of piercing intensity, culminates in the picture of Michael Furey in the rain and darkness of the Galway night.

Another warmth is involved in "The Dead." In Gabriel's memory of his own love for Gretta, he recalls incidents in his love's history as stars, burning with pure and distant intensity, and recalls moments of his passion for her as having the fire of stars. The irony of this image is that the sharp and beautiful experience was, though he has not known it until this night, incomplete. There is a telling metaphor: he remembers a moment of happiness, standing with Gretta in the cold, looking in through a window at a man making bottles in a roaring furnace, and suddenly calling out to the man, "Is the fire hot?" The question sums up his naïve deprivation; if the man at the furnace had heard the question, his answer, thinks Gabriel, might have been rude; so the revelation on this night is rude to Gabriel's whole being. On this night he acknowledges that love must be a feeling which he has never fully had.

Gabriel is not utterly deprived. Throughout the story there is affection for this man who, without the sharpest, most passionate perceptions, is yet generous and considerate. The intense and the moderate can meet; intensity bursts out and declines, and the moderated can admire and pity it, and share the fate that moves both types of mankind towards age and death. The furthest point of love of which Gabriel is capable is past. Furey's passion is past because of his sudden death. Gretta is perhaps the most pitiful, in that knowing Furey's passion, and being of his kind, she does not die but lives to wane in Gabriel's way; on this night she too is fatigued, not beautiful, her clothes lie crumpled beside her. The snow seems to share in this decline; viewed from inside at the party, it is desirable, unattainable, just as at his first knowledge of Michael Furey, Gabriel envies him. At the end as the partygoers walk to the cab the snow is slushy and in patches, and then, seen from the window of the hotel room, it belongs to all men, it is general, mutual. Under its canopy, all human beings, whatever their degrees of intensity, fall into union. The mutuality is that all men feel and lose feeling, all interact, all warrant the sympathy that Gabriel now extends to Furey, to Gretta, to himself, even to old Aunt Julia.

In its lyrical, melancholy acceptance of all that life and death offer, "The Dead" is a linchpin in Joyce's work. There is that basic situation of cuckoldry, real or putative, which is to be found throughout. There is the special Joycean collation of specific detail raised to rhythmical intensity. The final purport of the story, the mutual dependency of living and dead, is something that he meditated a good deal from his early youth. He had expressed it first in his essay on Mangan in 1902, when he spoke already of the union in the great memory of death along with life;[25] even then he had begun to learn like Gabriel that we are all Romes, our new edifices reared beside, and even joined with,

[25] *Critical Writings,* p. 83.

ancient monuments. In *Dubliners* he developed this idea. The interrelationship of dead and living is the theme of the first story in *Dubliners* as well as of the last; it is also the theme of "A Painful Case," but an even closer parallel to "The Dead" is the story, "Ivy Day in the Committee Room." This was in one sense an answer to his university friends who mocked his remark that death is the most beautiful form of life by saying that absence is the highest form of presence. Joyce did not think either idea absurd. What binds "Ivy Day" to "The Dead" is that in both stories the central agitation derives from a character who never appears, who is dead, absent. Joyce wrote Stanislaus that Anatole France had given him the idea for both stories.[26] There may be other sources in France's works, but a possible one is "The Procurator of Judaea." In it Pontius Pilate reminisces with a friend about the days when he was procurator in Judaea, and describes the events of his time with Roman reason, calm, and elegance. Never once does he, or his friend, mention the person we expect him to discuss, the founder of Christianity, until at the end the friend asks if Pontius Pilate happens to remember someone of the name of Jesus, from Nazareth, and the veteran administrator replies, "Jesus? Jesus of Nazareth? I cannot call him to mind." The story is overshadowed by the person whom Pilate does not recall; without him the story would not exist. Joyce uses a similar method in "Ivy Day" with Parnell and in "The Dead" with Michael Furey.

In *Ulysses* the climactic episode, *Circe,* whirls to a sepulchral close in the same juxtaposition of living and dead, the ghost of his mother confronting Stephen, and the ghost of his son confronting Bloom. But Joyce's greatest triumph in asserting the intimacy of living and dead was to be the close of *Finnegans Wake.* Here Anna Livia Plurabelle, the river of life, flows toward the sea, which is death; the fresh water passes into the salt, a bitter ending. Yet it is also a return to her father, the sea, that produces the cloud which makes the river, and her father is also her husband, to whom she gives herself as a bride to her groom. Anna Livia is going back to her father, as Gabriel journeys westward in feeling to the roots of his fatherland; like him, she is sad and weary. To him the Shannon waves are dark and mutinous, and to her the sea is cold and mad. In *Finnegans Wake* Anna Livia's union is not only with love but with death; like Gabriel she seems to swoon away.

That Joyce at the age of twenty-five and -six should have written this story ought not to seem odd. Young writers reach their greatest eloquence in dwelling upon the horrors of middle age and what follows it. But beyond this proclivity which he shared with others, Joyce had a special reason for writing the story of "The Dead" in 1906 and 1907. In his own mind he had thoroughly justified his flight from Ireland, but he had not decided the question of where he would fly *to.* In Trieste and Rome he had learned what he had unlearned in Dublin, to be a Dubliner. As he had written his brother from Rome with some astonishment, he felt humiliated when anyone attacked his "impoverished country."[27] "The Dead" is his first song of exile.

---

[26] Letter to S. Joyce, Feb. 11, 1907.
[27] Letter to S. Joyce, Sept. 25, 1906.

Macbeth, King James, and The Bible

JANE H. JACK

Macbeth is the swiftest and most concise of Shakespeare's tragedies: the action is concentrated to an exceptional degree in the thoughts and actions of the protagonist: the vivid strands of imagery, forming into bold and simple patterns, maintain a perfect balance with the other elements in the dramatic whole. More than any other of the tragedies it seems the result of "one swift act of the poet's mind." Two features of its probable history make this unity of effect surprising: first, editors seem to agree that the text has been subjected to some cutting and interpolation: and secondly, the play is to a considerable extent an *occasional* piece, shot through with compliments to the reigning monarch. It is no doubt because he feels that the latter hypothesis is inconsistent with the unity of the play that its most recent editor, Professor Kenneth Muir,[1] regards it with disfavour and suspicion. I wish to suggest that earlier editors were better advised, in accepting the fact that James exerted a considerable influence on *Macbeth*: and my thesis is that so far from being a handicap which Shakespeare had to surmount, the writings of the King were a positive help to him as he wrote the play.

Professor Muir is surely right when he insists that "the imperial theme," the mention of "touching" for scrofula, and the advocacy of prenuptial chastity were not dragged into the play "as irrelevant flattery":[2] there is not a line in the play which is irrelevant to Shakespeare's illumination of his tragic theme. If critics who discover passages in other men's books which seem to have influenced Shakespeare are misled into suggesting that he was less original than has been thought, or into maintaining that he was deflected from his true purpose by

[1] In the New Arden edition, London, 1951. My quotations are from this edition.

[2] P. lxii.

subsidiary intentions, then Professor Muir is justified in his attitude of suspicion. But this is not inevitable. On the contrary, a knowledge of the books which Shakespeare read may help us to guard against an interpretation of the play unduly coloured by developments in politics, morality, psychology or theology which have taken place since Shakespeare's time. The works of James are part of the "background" of the tragedy of *Macbeth*. Their uniformly Hebraic and Christian quality serves to illuminate that part of the common Jacobean stock of knowledge and ideas which is most relevant to the interpretation of *Macbeth*. Shakespeare found the story of Macbeth and the witches in Holinshed: in the works of James, and in the books of the Bible to which James constantly refers, he found many suggestions which helped him to turn this tale of ambition, "supernatural soliciting," regicide and tyranny into a tragedy of extraordinary economy and unity. Far from merely echoing here and there the political and daemonological notions of the King, Shakespeare, as I hope to show, found in his works many fertile seeds of inspiration for the expression of the deepest themes of the tragedy.

In view of the work which has been done on the sources[3] of *Macbeth* it is scarcely necessary to show that Shakespeare would have access to James' principal works as they were published or reissued. Interest in the character and tastes of the new king must have mounted steadily as the court moved about England avoiding the Plague and the coronation was repeatedly postponed.[4] The *Basilikon Doron* appeared in 1603:[5] as well as the official Edinburgh edition four London editions appeared in the same year, which also saw the publication at Cambridge of a paraphrase of the work in Latin and English by William Willymat.[6] In this same year there appeared two London editions of the *Daemonologie* based on the Edinburgh edition of 1597.[7] Lastly, there was published in 1603 an English edition of a sermon by James which has been overlooked by commentators on the King's influence on *Macbeth:* this was *A Fruitfull Meditation, Containing A plaine and easie Exposition, or laying open of the 7. 8. 9. & 10. verses of the 20. chap. of the Reuelation, in forme & maner of a Sermon.*[8]

The evidence so far brought forward to demonstrate the influence of James on *Macbeth* has tended to draw attention to the political or the daemonological elements in the tragedy. A knowledge of James' opinion of usurping tyrants has led to an interpretation of *Macbeth* as a study in tyranny: the King's interest in daemonology has persuaded commentators to consider *Macbeth* as Shakespeare's contribution to the debate on witchcraft and necromancy. But these,

[3] These are most fully dealt with in J. W. Draper, "Macbeth as a Compliment to James I," *Englische Studien*, 1937-8, pp. 207 *et seq.* and by Henry N. Paul. *The Royal Play of Macbeth*, The Macmillan Company, New York, 1950.

[4] See *The Plague in Shakespeare's England*, F. P. Wilson, Oxford, 1927.

[5] Waldegrave, 1603. *Reprinted in Publications of the Scottish Text Society*: Third Series; (16) 1942, ed. James Craigie. All my quotations from the *Basilikon Doron* are from this edition.

[6] *A Princes Looking Glasse*, Cambridge, 1603.

[7] Waldegrave, 1597. Reprinted in Bodley Head Quartos IX. All my quotations from the *Daemonologie* are from this reprint.

[8] Imprinted first in Scottish at Edinburgh, by *Henry Charteris*, 1588. And now newly reprinted for *Iohn Harrison*, . . . 1603. My quotations are from this edition.

together with other topics common to James' works and *Macbeth*, are only subordinate elements in the tragedy. The problem is not to account for their presence by reference to James but to explain how they are fused into a unity and made to support and illuminate Shakespeare's meaning in the tragedy as a whole. It is, therefore, interesting that James' works themselves reveal a remarkable unity. The books of 1603 are rather a bid for the title "Defender of the Faith" than for a name as an original theorist in the field of politics or the occult. The topics discussed range over a wide field: the thought is invariably developed within an elaborate framework of Hebraic and Christian references. It is this background which is important for our understanding of *Macbeth*. While I wish to point out, for the sake of balance, some old and new parallels between James' opinions and interests and *Macbeth*, my main purpose is to draw attention to the influence exerted on *Macbeth* by the strong theological bias of James' mind and by his constant references to particular places in the Old and New Testaments.

It is interesting to note that James deals with Henry's "duty towards God as a Christian" in the First Book of the *Basilikon Doron*, considering his duty as a king only in the Second Book. He was deeply interested in the problem of evil and in the functions of conscience and prayer. The overmastering theme both of the *Daemonologie* and the sermon on *Revelation* is that the kingdom of evil lies very close to Christendom. Indeed, in the sermon he is of the opinion that his own times are the "latter dayes" in which, according to the prophecy of St. Paul, the Devil is let loose until the Day of Judgment. The *Daemonologie* was written to prove "that such assaultes of Sathan are most certainly practized."[9] It is not merely human weakness that endangers the soul, but the direct attack of well-armed agents of Hell. In the *Basilikon Doron* James enlarges on the topic that only faith, a good conscience and the gift of prayer form adequate protection against the assaults of the Devil. The stakes for which this battle is waged are eternal felicity as against eternal damnation. "Remember therefore in all your actions, of the great accounte that ye are one day to make," Henry is entreated, "in all the deyes of your life euer learning to dye, and liuing euerie day as it were your last. . . . And therefore, I woulde not haue you to pray with the Papistes, to bee preserued from suddaine death, but that God will giue you grace so to liue, as ye may euerie houre of your life be readie for death."[10] Religion is the only bulwark against the Devil: faith is the nourisher and quickener of Religion:[11] and conscience is the "conseruer of Religion."[12] Faith is to be maintained by prayer. ("Use often to pray when ye are quyetest.")[13] Conscience, which is "a great torture to the wicked," must be preserved from the two diseases of "leaprosie" and "supersition." "By a leaprouse conscience I meane *a cauterized conscience* as Paul calleth it, become senselesse of sinne—as King Dauid's was after his murther & adultery."[14]

[9] *Daemonologie*, p. xi.

[10] *Basilikon Doron*, p. 45. Cf. *Macbeth* IV, iii, 109–11. ". . . the Queen that bore thee, Oft'ner upon her knees than on her feet, Died every day she liv'd."

[11] *Ibid.*, p. 37.   [12] *Ibid.*, p. 41.

[13] *Ibid.*, p. 39.   [14] *Ibid.*, p. 43.

When, in the Second Book of the *Basilikon Doron*, James deals briefly with tyranny—the greatest evil into which a king, as a king, can fall—he deals almost exclusively with its religious implications, emphasising that it is a heinous sin which will be punished by endless pains hereafter. In a general way he adduces prudential arguments against tyranny which are much the same as those which Macbeth enumerates as practical deterrents from the murder of Duncan: ". . . a Tyrannes miserable & infamous life, armeth in end his own subjects to become his burreaux."[15]

But in these cases,[16]
We still have judgment here; that we but teach
Bloody instructions, which, being taught, return
To plague th'inventor.

But it is the reckoning that must be paid, "at the houre of our death, or at the great day of judgement"[17] that James chooses to stress in this and the other most impressive parts of the *Basilikon Doron*.

James' concern with evil, his conception of life as a war between Grace and the Devil and his intimate knowledge of Scripture lead him naturally into the use of the symbolism of light and darkness. Images of light recur with powerful effect wherever he speaks of good kings: "Remember then, that this glistering worldly glorie of Kings, is giuen them by God, to teache them to preasse so to glister & shine before their people, in al works of sanctification & righteousness, that their persons as brighte lampes of godlines and vertue may, going in & out before their people, giue light to all their steppes."[18] James' hatred of secrecy and hypocrisy, of things which are other than they seem, is particularly evident throughout his works. The first public edition of the *Basilikon Doron* opens in this way: "*Charitable Reader, it is one of the golden sentences, whiche Christ our Sauiour vttered to his Apostles, that there is* nothing so couered, that shall not be reuealed, neither so hid, that shall not be knowne: and whatsoever they haue spoken in darknesse should be heard in the light."[19] This reference to St. Luke's Gospel is typical of the way in which James gave gravity to his subject and enriched his literary style by a wealth of Scriptural allusions.

The *Basilikon Doron*, together with the *Daemonologie* and the sermon on *Revelation* which place an even greater emphasis on the attacks of the Devil and the precariousness of Christendom, must have established James in the minds of his new subjects as a man at once deeply religious and profoundly pessimistic.

Shakespeare clearly took care that nothing in *Macbeth* should run counter to James' political views.[20] But these views are traditional and old-fashioned

---

[15] *Basilikon Doron*, p. 57.

[17] *Basilikon Doron*, p. 43.

[19] *Ibid.*, p. 12.

[16] *Macbeth*, I, vii, 7 *et seq.*

[18] *Basilikon Doron*, p. 27.

[20] Most of these have been pointed out by Draper and Paul. Neither notices James' advice on "indifferent things": ". . . as Kings vse oft to eate publicklie, it is meete and honorable that ye also doe so, . . . to eschewe the opinion that he loue not to haunt companie, whiche is one of

and had already been worked out dramatically by Shakespeare in the course of the history plays: it is much more likely that it was what was more original and idiosyncratic in the writings of James that would leave the deepest impression on Shakespeare: the sombre, archaic style with its strong Biblical overtones, the emphasis on death and on the extreme precariousness of Christendom, the constant references to the stories of Old Testament kings and, in particular, to *Jeremiah*, *Kings* and *Chronicles*.

Macbeth is a play about evil which is given dramatic shape by the story of the deterioration in sin of a man who has yielded up his soul to the devil. The nature of evil, its power and pervasiveness, is thrown into relief by a vivid pattern of references to Scripture. Like *Hamlet*, though much more explicitly, this play is set in Christendom: what is more, the values of Christianity predominate in *Macbeth*. The scene at the court of the saintly Edward the Confessor is the most sustainedly and explicitly Christian in the tragedy. It is not, however, isolated: just when the power of evil is about to be overcome the tone and vocabulary of this scene reaffirm the spirit in which the drama of Macbeth has been unfolded. When, after the first part of the witches' prophecy has been fulfilled, Banquo ejaculates "What! can the Devil speak true?",[21] he means the Devil of Christian orthodoxy.

> . . . What thou wouldst highly.[22]
> That wouldst thou holily,

Lady Macbeth reflects as she apostrophises her husband. She prays that "Heaven" will not frustrate her plans.[23] Macbeth speaks of his readiness to "jump the life to come" and imagines Duncan's virtues arousing "heaven's Cherubins" and angels with Biblical trumpets.[24] When he returns from the murder he is tortured by the incident in the grooms' chamber:

> One cried, "God bless us!" and, "Amen," the other,[25]
> As they had seen me with these hangman's hands.
> List'ning their fear, I could not say, "Amen,"
> When they did say, "God bless us."
>
> .   .   .   .
>
> But wherefore could I not pronounce "Amen"?
> I had most need of blessing, and "Amen"
> Stuck in my throat.

Duncan is described, in Old Testament phrase, as "the Lord's anointed Temple."[26] Banquo declares, "In the great hand of God I stand";[27] and the

the markes of a Tyrant." (*Basilikon Doron*, p. 165) Macbeth's reign of lonely tyranny is begun with an attempt to hold a feast which is first interrupted by the murderers' report ("It is no waies comelie to dispatche affaires, or to be pensiue at meate: but keepe then an open & cheerefull countenance." *Basilikon Doron*, p. 169) and finally abandoned.

[21] I, iii, 106.

[22] I, v, 19–20.

[23] I, v, 52.

[24] I, vii, 7 *et seq.*

[25] II, ii, 26 *et seq.*

[26] II, iii, 68.

[27] II, iii, 130.

old man says to Ross and Macduff, "God's benison go with you."[28] When Macbeth is urging on the murderers of Banquo, he asks them:

> Are you so gospell'd[29]
> To pray for this good man, and for his issue,
> Whose heavy hand hath bow'd you to the grave,
> And beggar'd yours for ever?

Macduff goes to England "to pray the holy King" for help, "with Him above/ To ratify the work."[30] Lennox prays:

> . . . Some holy Angel[31]
> Fly to the court of England, and unfold
> His message ere he come, that a swift blessing
> May soon return to this our suffering country
> Under a hand accurs'd!

and is answered, "I'll send my prayers with him."[32] Lady Macbeth is more in need of "the divine than the physician,"[33] and the amazed doctor adds, "God, God forgive us all!" Young Siward, killed in the battle, is "God's soldier," and the play ends with Malcolm's invocation of "the grace of Grace."[34]

The explicitly Christian quality of *Macbeth,* the fact that it is an imaginative exploration of evil in Biblical terms, is the key to the tragedy. At one level the plot is a story of regicide, usurpation and tyranny—a theme dear to the mind of James. But it is in the verse, and not in anything that can be isolated from it, that *Macbeth* exists and some overlooked preoccupations of James, as they are reflected in the language and the imagery, confirm the judgment that the plot was conceived in relation to sources which are not primarily political. Macbeth's story is told less in terms of English history and the (recently overworked) notion of order and degree, than in the spirit of the Old Testament histories of kings whose reigns are characterised as good or evil according to their allegiance to false prophets or the true God. An evil reign is consequent not only upon the turning away of the king from the law of God but on his failure to acknowledge the supremacy of the true God as the one source of truth. The punishment for false allegiance involves the whole people and is directly ascribed to God's angry intervention or the withdrawing of his protection. There are two elements in *Macbeth* on which James' directives to the Old Testament and his pessimistic sermon on *Revelation* throw light: Macbeth's motive for the murder of Duncan and the completeness of Scotland's descent into hell on earth after Macbeth's accession.

It is because *Macbeth* is less a story of regicide and tyranny than of the war

---

[28] II, iv, 40.

[29] III, i, 87–90.

[30] III, vi, 30 and 32–3.

[31] III, vi, 45 *et seq.*

[32] III, vi, 49.

[33] V, i, 71. Cf. II, *Chronicles,* xvi, 12. Asa, who has defied God is stricken with a disease: "Yet in his disease he sought not to the Lord, but to the physicians."

[34] V, ix, 38.

between the forces of evil and supernatural good that Shakespeare does not avail himself of any of the excuses for Macbeth's murder of Duncan which he found in Holinshed. This has not been understood by those critics who complain that Macbeth's action has no sufficient motive. Macbeth's "motive," in the sense that is dramatically relevant, is his ill-placed trust in the prophecies of the weird sisters which is consequent upon his spiritual unpreparedness for strong temptation.

The significance of the witches is apparent to the reader of the *Daemonologie*. They are not irresistible, but they are strong enough to overpower a man of weak faith. "It is most certaine, that God will not permit him [the Devil] so to deceiue his own: but only such as first wilfully deceiues themselves, by running vnto him, whome God then suffers to fall in their owne snares, and justlie permittes them to be illuded with great efficacy of deceit, because they would not beleeue the trueth."[35] It is apparent to Banquo from the first that, in listening to the witches, Macbeth is listening to the Devil: this is acknowledged by Macbeth himself at the end. He seeks out the weird sisters in order to learn the future "by the worst means." It is important to remember that, in the *Basilikon Doron*, James' general recommendation to merciful judgment is modified in respect to a number of crimes: the first of these is witchcraft, the second "wilfull murther."[36] Later Henry is warned of the danger of soothsayers: "Consult therefore with no Necromancier nor false Prophet, vpon the successe of your warres; remembring on king *Saules* miserable end: but keepe your hand clene of all Suth-sayers, according to the command in the Lawe of God, dilated by *Ieremie*."[37]

This warning forms a point of contact between the *Daemonologie* and the *Basilikon Doron*, for an early part of the former work is devoted to a long discussion of Saul's crime. Indeed the story of *Macbeth* is deepened in import if we remember Saul and God's commands and threats in *Jeremiah*.

Thus saith the Lord of hostes, Heare not the wordes of the Prophets that prophecie vnto you, and teache you vanitie: thei speake the vision of their owne heart & not out of the mouth of the Lord.
Thei saie vnto them that despise me. The Lord hath said, Ye shal haue peace: & thei saie vnto euerie one that walketh after the stubbernes of his owne heart, No euil shal come vpon you.[38]

Compare Macbeth's words to Macduff:

> The spirits that know[39]
> All mortal consequence have pronounc'd me thus:
> "Fear not, Macbeth...."

Macbeth's crime here is the same as Saul's, and his end is the same. When his head was borne in impaled on a pole at the end of the play the audience

---

[35] *Daemonologie*, p. 4.   [36] *Basilikon Doron*, p. 65.   [37] *Ibid.*, p. 99.

[38] *Jeremiah*, xxiii, 16–17. All my quotations from the Bible are from the Geneva version.

[39] V, iii, 4–6.

could not have failed to be reminded of I *Samuel*, xxxi, 9: "And they cut of his head, and stripped him out of his armour, and sent into the land of the Philisims on euerie side, that they shulde publish it. . . ."

The play opens with the witches and their plan to approach Macbeth. When part of the prophecy has been fulfilled Banquo muses:

> That, trusted home,[40]
> Might yet enkindle you unto the crown,
> Besides the Thane of Cawdor. But 'tis strange:
> And oftentimes, to win us to our harm,
> The instruments of Darkness tell us truths;
> Win us with honest trifles, to betray's
> In deepest consequence.

Much of Lady Macbeth's strength is derived from her faith in the witches' prophecy: to her "fate and metaphysical aid"[41] seem to have set Macbeth on the road to the throne.[42] Macbeth's downfall is sealed by his seeking out of the weird sisters in Act IV; "for by the Deuils meanes, *can neuer the Deuill be casten out*."[43] Like Saul, Macbeth hears from the witches the confirmation of what he most fears. The crisis of the story is the victory of the witches: the resolution of the story is the judgment passed on Macbeth at the end—the same judgment that is passed on Saul: "So Saul dyed for his transgression, that he committed against the Lord, *euen* against the worde of the Lord, which he kept not, and in that he soght and asked consel of a familiar spirit."[44]

The murder of Duncan is an overt act of evil. Its significance is illuminated by numerous references to the Bible. The murder itself is described in terms drawn from another part of the story of Saul. David, we remember, refrains from killing Saul when he is delivered into his hands: "The Lord kepe me from doing that thing vnto my master the Lords Anointed, to lay mine hand vpon him: for he is the Anointed of the Lord."[45]

> Most sacrilegious Murther hath broke ope[46]
> The Lord's anointed Temple, and stole thence
> The life o'th' building!

These are the terms in which Macbeth had failed to realise the projected murder

---

[40] I, iii, 120–6.   [41] I, v, 29.

[42] It is possible that another famous Old Testament story, that of Naboth's Vineyard, lay behind Shakespeare's conception of the character of Lady Macbeth. Jezebel is the archetype of a wife who engineers a murder to further a husband's ambition. It is Lady Macbeth who suggests the incrimination of the grooms, as Jezebel arranged for the false accusation of Naboth. Lady Macbeth recalls Jezebel particularly in Act III, ii, when she asks Macbeth to be "bright and jovial" and replies to his reference to Banquo and Fleance, "But in them Nature's copy's not eterne." Cf. I *Kings*, xxi. 7: ". . . eat bread, and be of good chere, I wil giue thee the vineyard of Naboth the Izreelite."

[43] *Daemonologie*, p. 49.

[44] *Chronicles*, x. 13. "A familiar spirit" is glossed in the Geneva version as "witche and sorceresse."

[45] I, *Samuel*, xxiv, 7.   [46] II, iii, 68–70.

of Duncan. *Macbeth* is a study not only of regicide and tyranny but of a damned soul, of a man who, having destroyed his own conscience, is capable of acting in defiance of the restraints both of human nature and religion. It is significant that we first see Macbeth as a bright ornament of the society of which he is part. He is "brave Macbeth," "valiant cousin! worthy gentleman!", and he is rewarded by falling heir to the title of a thane who has betrayed his king. For a brief space two Thanes of Cawdor live in the kingdom, one dishonoured and a traitor, the other "noble Macbeth." This scene is followed immediately by Macbeth's encounter with the witches, his amazed reception of their prophecies and Banquo's apprehension that the Devil has spoken the truth as to Cawdor and that the rest of the prophecy must be regarded as a treacherous temptation to murder. A few lines later Macbeth speaks the word "murther." But he continues in his character as one of the figures in the "plenteous joys" of Duncan. He is not in Shakespeare, as he is in Holinshed, by nature cruel and unnatural. He is kind, seeming to Lady Macbeth "too full o' th' milk of human kindness." We accept his own evaluation of himself as one who practises the virtues which become a man. But in these early scenes in which the instruments of evil brood over Duncan's gratitude and contentment we are made aware of a distinction between the virtues which become a man and those which become a Christian. In the first great soliloquy we listen to a man dismayed by the thought of the worldly risks he may take and by the idea of the social laws of kinship, fidelity and hospitality which he is tempted to break, but who begins his self-debate with the categorical statement that he is prepared to "jump the life to come." Assailed by the strong temptation of ambition and a superstitious willingness to pay attention to the prophecies of the sisters, he chooses to fight down his conscientious scruples without reference to higher laws than those of the world. Before the murder he can oppose no other argument to his wife's prompting than that he wishes to enjoy the "golden opinions" which he has lately won from all sorts of people. Immediately after the murder, with dreadful irony, he is tormented by the knowledge that he was unable to say "Amen" to the grooms' prayer. He is quite free from any perverted desire to do evil for its own sake: he cannot hate even the man who stands in the way of his ambitious desires. The conceptions of duty, honour, even pity, have meaning for him. But he is incapable of opposing to the temptations of the instruments of darkness anything more than prudential fears and a natural disinclination to kill a virtuous old man. The presence of the witches at the beginning of the play is a device which gives evil and good a transcendental position in the tragedy. Although the *Daemonologie* and other contemporary treatises on witchcraft have been used by Shakespeare to give colour to the witches, it is the wider significance of the echoes of Old Testament conflicts between false prophets and the true God which reinforce the meaning of the tragedy. The witches represent the opposite of the holiness and grace which their presence in the play itself calls into the mind.

Far from being an irrelevant interpolation, the scenes at Edward's court pick up threads which have already run throughout the tragedy, explicitly and by implication. The story of Saul lies behind several passages in the play, and

Malcolm's long altercation with Macduff recalls in part the history of Saul and David. Saul, having hunted David down, is met with the words, "Wherefore giuest thou an eare to mēs wordes, that say, Beholde, Dauid sketh euil against thee? . . . Vnderstand and se, that there is nether euil nor wickednes in me, nether haue I sinned against thee. . . . The Lord be iudge betwene thee & me."[47]

> But God above[48]
> Deal between thee and me!

While it is possible that Shakespeare, in working up these scenes from Holinshed, remembered James' advice to Henry to help foreign princes in their trouble and to be suspicious of reports, the function of this scene is to arm Malcolm with a more than merely legal right to the throne and to invest him and his army with the supernatural brightness of holiness. David also lived in a foreign country to escape the wrath of a tyrant, and ascended his throne as the result of the defeat of that tyrant by a foreign army. The contrast drawn between Scotland groaning under the accursed hand of Macbeth and the court of England where "sundry blessings" proclaim the king "full of grace" emphasises the contrast already indicated in Biblical terms between evil and good. In the early part of the play evil triumphs in the heart of a man naturally good but empty of grace. Without these implications the tragedy of *Macbeth* loses much of its import: it is not merely about a man who succumbs to evil: its subject is Evil itself.

The problem of Scotland's immediate descent into terrible miseries at Macbeth's accession is only a problem at the prose level, and is readily explained if we consider the tragedy as a poetic exploration of evil. The miseries of Scotland, as they are reported to Malcolm, seem impossibly extensive:

> Each new morn,[49]
> New widows howl, new orphans cry: new sorrows
> Strike heaven on the face.

We are never told, as we are in Holinshed, what Macbeth has done to cause this horror, or what his motives were. James had himself pointed out that a tyrant, however bloody, knows that it is in his own interest to administer justice and accept some, at least, of the responsibilities of kingship. These descriptions in *Macbeth* read more like accounts of the havoc wrought by what we call "acts of God" than by one brief reign of tyranny. That is precisely what they are. Evil has made its entrance into the land by Macbeth's action: the centre of the play is the presentation of Shakespeare's vision of evil in dramatic terms. Macbeth himself speaks the prelude:

> Had I but died an hour before this chance,[50]
> I had liv'd a blessed time; for, from this instant,
> There's nothing serious in mortality;

---

[47] I *Samuel*, xxiv, 10–12.

[48] IV, iii, 120–1. This phrase does not occur in the account in Holinshed.

[49] IV, iii, 4–6.   [50] II, iii, 91–6.

All is but toys: renown, and grace, is dead;
The wine of life is drawn, and the mere lees
Is left this vault to brag of.

". . . Of all Bookes the holy Scripture is the most necessary for the instruction of a Christian, and of al the Scriptures, the Booke of the *Reuelation* is most meete for this our last age, as a Prophesie of the latter time."[51] So James begins his "fruitful meditation," and I believe that Shakespeare leant heavily on *Revelation* and James' commentary on it for the expression of his imaginative apprehension of overwhelming evil. Although the "meditation" refers back and forth over the whole Book, it is a commentary on four verses in the twentieth chapter:

And when the thousand yeres are expired, Satan shal be losed out of his prison. And shal go out to deceiue the people, which are in the foure quarters of the earth: *euen* Gog and Magog, to gather them together to battel, whose number *is* as the sand of the sea.

And they went vp into the plaine of the earth, & compassed the tents of the Saintes about, and the bleoued citie: but fyre came downe from God out of heuen, & deuoured them.

And the deuil that deceiued them, was cast into a lake of fvre & brimstone, where the beast and the false prophet shal be tormented euen day and night for euermore.[52]

James paraphrases this: "Sathan . . . shall at last breake forth again loose, and for a space rage in the earth more than euer before: but shall in the end bee ouercome and confounded for euer."[53] The space in which Satan is unleashed is an exact analogy of Macbeth's reign in Scotland. Macbeth becomes the Devil:

Not in the legions[54]
Of horrid Hell can come a devil more damn'd
In evils, to top Macbeth.

No-one in Scotland has the moral strength or the integrity to oppose him: everyone is paralysed and tainted in some way by the pervasive evil. Lady Macduff describes their plight in words which form the obverse of the Christian belief, "Perfect love casteth out fear":

All is the fear, and nothing is the love;[55]

"For as al that do good, are inspired of God thereto . . ." James comments in his sermon, "so all that doe euill, are inspired by sathan, and doe vtter the same in dyuers degrees, according as that vncleane spirite taketh possession in them, and by diuers obiects and meanes, allureth them to doe his will, some by ambition, some by enuie, some by malice, & some by feare, . . ."[56] Ambition,

---

[51] *A Fruitful Meditation*, p. [A 6 r].　　[52] XX, 7–10.
[53] P. [A 6 v].　　[54] IV, iii, 56–8.
[55] IV, ii, 12.　　[56] P. [A S r].

envy and malice inspired the murder of Duncan, Banquo and Macduff's family: it is fear that led Macduff to desert his wife and children.

> His flight was madness: when our actions do not,[57]
> Our fears do make us traitors.

It is interesting to note that *Revelation* is particularly rich in images depicting the withdrawal of Grace. The truth which James saw most clearly enforced in the Book is that human nature alone is pitifully weak in the face of evil. "We are enformed that the wicked are euer the greatest part of the world. And therefore our Maister saith. *Many are called, fewe chosen: And againe, Wide is the waye that leadeth to destruction, and many enter thereat: But narrowe is the waye that leadeth to life, and few enter thereat.*"[58] In two prose passages Shakespeare builds these concepts into the fabric of his tragedy: "I had thought to have let in some of all professions, that go the primrose way to th' everlasting bonfire."[59] And later, "Then the liars and swearers are fools; for there are liars and swearers enow to beat the honest men, and hang up them."[60] Not only are the natural virtues of Macbeth powerless alone against temptation. The evil which enters his world by the gate of his own castle requires more than human goodness to combat it.

Miss Spurgeon has noted that there are in *Macbeth* numerous suggestions of vast space. "Another image or idea which runs through *Macbeth* is the reverberation of sound echoing over vast regions, even into the limitless spaces beyond the confines of the world."[61] These cosmic suggestions, which occur in all the more imaginative parts of the tragedy, are not confined to sound. The words

> here,[62]
> But here, upon this bank and shoal of time,

place the situation in the light of eternity, in the vast space of the world viewed, as it is in *Revelation,* from heaven to hell. There are suggestions of the Day of Judgment. Duncan's sons are told to look on "The great doom's image!":

> As from your graves rise up, and walk like sprites.[63]

Compare *Revelation*:

And the sea gaue vp her dead, which were in her, and death and hell deliuered vp the dead, which were in them:[64]

In Ross's speech to the old man after the murder there are numerous Biblical overtones:

> Ha! good Father,[65]
> Thou seest the heavens, as troubled with man's act,
> Threatens his bloody stage: by th'clock 'tis day,

---

[57] IV, ii, 3–4.

[58] P. 0B 5 v7.

[59] II, iii, 19–21.

[60] IV, ii, 55–7.

[61] Caroline Spurgeon, *Shakespeare's Imagery*, pp. 324–355.

[62] I, vii, 5–6

[63] II, iii, 80

[64] *Revelation*, XX, 13.

[65] II, iv, 4–9.

> And yet dark night strangles the travelling lamp.
> Is't night's predominance, or the day's shame,
> That darkness does the face of earth entomb,
> When living light should kiss it?

Duncan is given all the characteristics of a martyr,[66] and this idea of the connection between the unnatural dark and guilt, between the shedding of innocent blood and the withdrawal of light and grace, is strongly reminiscent of God's threats and punishments throughout the Bible, culminating in the prophetic descriptions which are given symbolical expression in *Revelation*:

And the fourthe Angel blewe the trumpet, and the third parte of the sunne was smitten, & the third parte of the moone, and the third parte of the starres, so that the third parte of them was darkened: and the day *was smitten*, that the third parte of it colde not shine, and likewise the night.[67]

Earlier, before the murder, strange phenomena have been noticed:

> The night has been unruly: where we lay,[68]
> Our chimneys were blown down; and, as they say,
> Lamentings heard i' th'air; strange screams of death,
> And, prophesying with accents terrible
> Of dire combustion, and confus'd events,
> New hatch'd to the'woeful time, the obscure bird
> Clamour'd the livelong night: some say, the earth
> Was feverous, and did shake.

This may be compared with:

And there were voyces, and thundrings, and lightnings, & there was a great earthquake. [69]

These are echoed again in the tragedy in Macbeth's terrible invocation of the forces of destruction. He conjures the witches to answer him,

> Though you untie the winds, and let them fight
> Against the Churches.

If this is considered against the visions in *Revelation* it takes on a new quality of horror. Macbeth does not single out the churches because their high towers are ready victims for high winds. In *Revelation* the angels hold back the winds of destruction until the faithful have been marked with a seal.

And after that, I sawe foure Angels stād on ye foure corners of the earth, holding the foure windes of the earth, that the windes shulde not blowe on the earth, nether on the sea, nether on anie tre.

And I saw another Angel . . . and he cryed with a loude voyce to the foure

---

[66] "Thy royal father/Was a most sainted King." IV, iii, 108–9.

[67] VIII, 12.   [68] II, iii, 55–62.

[69] XVI, 18.

Angels to whome power was giuen to hurt the earth, and the Sea, saying, Hurt ye not the earth, nether the sea, nether the trees, til we haue sealed ye seruants of our God in their foreheades.[70]

In this speech Macbeth aligns himself with the Devil: he would turn the wrath of the Day of Judgment against the saints, the earth, the sea and the trees:

> Though you untie the winds, and let them fight[71]
> Against the Churches; though the yesty waves
> Confound and swallow navigation up;
> Though bladed corn be lodg'd, and trees blown down.

Macbeth's own fate is the fate of the damned: "O! full of scorpions is my mind, dear wife!"[72] recalls "the paine that cometh of a scorpion,"[73] and his longing for death—"I 'gin to be aweary of the sun,/ And wish th' estate o' th'world were now undone"[74]—is a reminiscence of: "Therefore in those daies shal men seke death, and shal not finde it, and shal desire to dye, and death shal flee from them."[75] At this point Macbeth is still thinking of death as the peaceful sleep which he knows Duncan enjoys.

> After life's fitful fever he sleeps well;[76]
> Treason has done his worst: nor steel, nor poison,
> Malice domestic, foreign levy, nothing
> Can touch him further!

This forecast of the evils which Duncan is spared harks back to many accounts of death in the Old Testament, perhaps that of Josiah in particular:
Beholde therefore, I wil gather thee to thy fathers, and thou shalt be put in thy graue in peace, and thine eyes shal not se all the euil, which I wil bring vpon this place.[77]

No imagery in *Macbeth* is more powerful or more characteristic than the imagery of blood. In earlier plays Shakespeare had made use of references to blood to lend atmosphere to tragic events. In *Macbeth* the influence of James' allusions both to the Old Testament and to *Revelation* may be seen in the greater logic and subtlety of this kind of imagery. When Macbeth cries:

> Will all great Neptune's ocean wash this blood[78]
> Clean from my hand? No, this my hand will rather
> The multitudinous seas incarnadine,
> Making the green one red,

a passage in *Revelation* may have been in Shakespeare's mind as he thought of Duncan's blood on Macbeth's hands staining the whole sea:

And the secōd Angel powred out his vial vpon the sea, and it became as the blood of a dead man.[79]

---

[70] VII, i. [71] IV, i, 51–5. [72] III, ii, 36.

[73] *Revelation* IX, v. [74] V, vii, 49–50. [75] *Revelation*, IX, vi.

[76] III, ii, 22–26. [77] II, *Kings*, xxii, 20. [78] II, ii, 59–62.

[79] XVI, iii-

As I have already suggested, Duncan is given many of the characteristics of a martyr: in several passages of *Revelation* the blood of martyrs is associated with punishment through blood.

And the thirde Angel powred out his uial upon the riuers & fountaines of waters, and they became blood.

And I heard the Angel of the waters say, Lord, thou art just, Which art, and Which wast, and Holie, because thou hast judged these things.

For they shed the blood of the Saintes, and Prophets, and therefore hast thou giuen them blood to drink.[80]

So Macbeth and Lady Macbeth are haunted by blood: "It will have blood: they say blood will have blood";[81] and again: "Here's the smell of the blood still."[82]

In a recent study of the imagery of *Macbeth*[83] the recurrence of references to children, and the place of infancy in the great soliloquies, have been singled out for discussion. The wonderful and puzzling image,

> And Pity, like a naked new-born babe,[84]
> Striding the blast,

demands an elucidation which will demonstrate its relation to the rest of the poem. But there is a principle unifying the imagery of *Macbeth* which lies outside the words and action of the tragedy itself, in the sources, in the fields of knowledge open both to Shakespeare and his audience. I do not think that a contemporary audience could have failed to be struck by Macbeth's increasing similarity to Herod as the tragedy progressed: surely the Book of *Revelation* was much in Shakespeare's mind as he wrote the play. Here is how Herod appears in that Book:

And she was with childe and cryed trauailing in birth, and was pained readie to be deliuered.

And there appeared another wonder in heauen: for beholde, a great red dragon. . . .

And the dragon stode before the woman, which was readie to be deliuered, to deuoure her childe when she had broght it forthe.

So she broght forthe a man childe . . . : and her sonne was taken vp vnto God and to this throne.[85]

Surely it is this passage which explains the transition from the concept of a pitiful, helpless babe to that of a power striding the blast.

The child-imagery which is so noticeable in *Macbeth* often recalls the Christ-

---

[80] XVI, iv.   [81] III, iv, 121.   [82] V, i, 48.

[83] *The Naked Babe and the Cloak of Manliness*, in *The Well Wrought Urn*, by Cleanth Brooks, Reynal and Hitchcock, 1947.

[84] I, vii, 21–2.   [85] XII, 2–5.

child and the Slaughter of the Innocents, as it does here. Macbeth resembles Herod in that he can kill other children, but not the particular child or children that represent Good (as opposed to his own Evil). Fleance escapes: Duncan's son lives on to march against him. When Banquo's descendants pass before his eyes, Macbeth's words,

> Upon my head they plac'd a fruitless crown,
> And put a barren sceptre in my gripe,
> Thence to be wrench'd with an unlineal hand,
> No son of mine succeeding[86]

are, in a sense, a description of the curse that has been laid upon him. Knowing that no son can succeed him, he cannot enjoy his own "sovereign sway and masterdom." This is part of the web of evil which is spun round him by the avenging forces of supernatural good.

Henry N. Paul has pointed out that in Macbeth's bitterness, as he watches the vision of Banquo's descendants, there is an oblique implied compliment to James' pride in his lineage. I have tried to show that it is because James possessed a mind rich in Old Testament history that the play presents so rich a poetic unity. Macbeth's reaction to the vision of Banquo's issue forms a last phrase in the story of a man who has defied God by placing his trust in daemonic powers. A passage in *Jeremiah* (a book particularly recommended by James) is relevant:

Thus saith the Lord, Write this man destitute of *children*, a man that shal not prosper in his dayes: for there shal be no man of his sede that shal prosper and sit vpon the throne of Dauid, or beare rule any more in Iudah.[87]

It is noteworthy that this curse in *Jeremiah* is directed against those guilty of Macbeth's initial sin, that of listening to false prophets. What links the *Basilikon Doron* to the *Daemonologie,* and both of these to the sermon on *Revelation,* is a common preoccupation with false prophecy and with God's power to abandon the world at will to the Devil. This same thread binds the elements in *Macbeth* into a unity. The scene depicting Banquo's descendants perfectly exemplifies the nature of James' influence on the tragedy: superficially the words are a compliment to the king, but in the dramatic context, spoken by the agents of the witches, they are a powerful reminder to the audience of Biblical descriptions of the evil of listening to false prophets and of the fulfilled horrors of the wrath of God.

[86] III, i, 60–3.   [87] XXII, 30.

PART 5

Interdisciplinary Criticism

Among the most exciting of the new voices in criticism are the Interdisciplinary Critics, whose foundations lie in the intellectual discoveries of the various disciplines, primarily in the variety of insights offered by recent developments in the social sciences. In a general way, Interdisciplinary Criticism is simply what the name suggests, a criticism based on the belief that a work of literature is best examined from the viewpoint of a variety of disciplines. A poem may be read strictly as a work of art, in accord with this or that theory of art, and meanings in the poem may be discovered; but it will be profitable to study that same poem through the discipline of history, philosophy, political science, psychology, sociology, anthropology, theology, or whatever approach the poem itself seems to call for. The approaches suggested, of course, will become more specific at the moment of work—Platonic Idealism rather than philosophy, the theory of decay in the eighteenth century rather than political science, and so on.

Such a broad definition might lead one to conclude that any good critic is interdisciplinary, and in a sense this is true. Very few critics would reject an insight into a poem merely because the insight was associated with a rival school; and not even the New Critic—academic rumor to the contrary—believes that the poem should be severed from its cultural context. In addition, several movements and fields of study could be included under this single heading. Certainly, the approach called "intellectual history" or "history of ideas" is interdisciplinary. American Studies is interdisciplinary. Anthropologists and folklorists, by the very nature of the materials they work with, must use a variety of disciplines. Art critics and film critics often move intelligently from one discipline to another. Comparative literature, even when restricted to literary studies, is at least a cousin. Events in history may prompt a movement that is relevant to a definition, the socio-economic criticism of the 1930's, for example, or the political criticism of the 1960's. And since variety need not be an invitation to write superficially, a literary critic who always works from a single viewpoint, like psychology, may be an Interdisciplinary Critic who recognizes the difficulty of mastering several fields of knowledge and chooses to concentrate on two of them.

Though necessary to an understanding of Interdisciplinary Criticism, generalizations like those above raise more questions than they answer. The student inevitably—and understandably—will ask if we are not talking about eclecticism and just calling it something else. But the best of Interdisciplinary Critics do not accept eclecticism, which implies a philosophical looseness or relativism that is anathema to the *discipline* of *interdisciplinarian*. And thus we reach what is, I think, the central question: how is it that the Interdisciplinary Critic is both anti-philosophy (his rejection of any single philosophy) and philosophical (his rejection of eclecticism)? Why is he willing to dwell for a time and with respect in the house of Plato and then, without looking back or feeling disloyal, move with equal devotion to the house of Aristotle or Freud or Sartre or Taine?

If variety is the watchword, any single answer is to be approached with suspicion; but the Interdisciplinary Critic does tend to believe that some philosophies are ontologically sound, not descriptive merely, that a given philosophy may achieve insight into the nature of a reality which exists objectively. At the same time, he believes that this objective reality which stands still for observation and analysis will not stand still for very long. It will reveal only a part of its nature and then slip away, escaping the lense of any single system of philosophy or criticism. So he is philosophically oriented in the sense that he believes a given theory can provide a schema for valid insights into what objectively *is*. Yet he is anti-philosophy in his suspicion of any single theory or system.

It is this skepticism which makes him reluctant to construct a master theory that would provide the standard by which he decides that one idea is objective while another is not, that a given theory has this or that validity but the following limitations, or, most important, the standard by which he decides which ontological home he will defend on which occasion. Thus he prefers methodology to theory and politely refuses the names of all the philosophical families that admire his scholarly, if occasional, devotion to their cause and would like to claim him as kinfolks.

To recognize is not to define, but perhaps the most reliable badge of identification for the Interdisciplinary Critic is his ability to trace a meaning even when it appears in alien garb. He is not the kind of critic who finds Freudian symbols or Christ figures or existential overtones in everything he reads. His belief, rather, is that validity is common property. Any legitimate insight in Freud is an insight into what exists and may therefore be discovered by writers who have never read Freud. The corollary is that all signs—when not grounded ontologically—will point in the wrong direction. The Kantian-based transcendentalism of Ralph Waldo Emerson, for example, just might not have any meaningful connection with the archetypally-based transcendentalism of John Steinbeck. The purpose, always, is to understand the subject at hand, and the method is characterized by an ability to recognize the philosophical home of an idea or image whether it comes in proper uniform, in disguise, or in mixed allegiance.

A school of criticism so broad, so careful about the theories of others and yet so skeptical of its own theorizing, may not be a school at all. In practice many who contribute riches to the field are themselves lacking in mobility. Their single lense may offer an important contribution to understanding, and the discoverer may be unwilling to move away from his success. But the Interdisciplinary Critic—the partisan with a single fresh slant and the philosopher–critic with a variety of lenses—has established a character; and it is a character of remarkable distinction. In books like *The Great Chain of Being, The American Renaissance,* and *The Mirror and the Lamp,* it becomes clear that a poem, like history, may have objective integrity and yet be various in a way that astonishes the eye and confounds both the relativist and the dogmatist.

Bibliography

Aaron, Daniel. *Writers on the Left.* New York: Harcourt, Brace and World, Inc., 1961.

Adler, Mortimer. *Poetry and Politics.* Pittsburgh: Duquesne University Press, 1966.

Balázs, Bela. *Theory of the Film.* London: Dobson Books Ltd., 1952.

Basler, Roy P. *Sex, Symbolism, and Psychology in Literature.* New Brunswick, N.J.: Rutgers University Press, 1948.

Bluestone, George. *Novels Into Film.* Berkeley: University of California Press, 1957.

Bobker, Lee R. *Elements of Film.* New York: Harcourt, Brace and Jovanovich, Inc., 1969.

Boorstein, Daniel J. *The Image; or, What Happened to the American Dream.* New York: Atheneum Publishers, 1962.

Brooks, Van Wyck. *America's Coming-of-Age.* New York: Doubleday Anchor Books, 1958.

Brown, Norman O. *Life Against Death.* Middletown, Conn.: Wesleyan University Press, 1959.

Browne, Louis *et. al.,* eds. *Challenges in American Culture.* Bowling Green, Ohio: Bowling Green University Popular Press, 1970.

Caillois, Roger. *Man, Play, and Games.* Translated by Meyer Barash. New York: Free Press of Glencoe, 1961.

Fischer, Ernst. *The Necessity of Art: A Marxist Approach.* Baltimore, Ind.: Penguin Books, Inc., 1963.

Fishwick, Marshall *et. al.* "In Depth—Black Popular Culture." *Journal of Popular Culture,* IV (1971), pp. 638–718.

Flores, Angel, ed. *Literature and Marxism.* New York: Critics Group, 1938.

Freud, Sigmund. *On Creativity and the Unconscious.* New York: Harper and Row Publishers, Inc., 1958.

———*On Dreams.* Translated by James Strachey. New York: W. W. Norton and Company, Inc., 1952, 1962.

Guérard, Albert. *Literature and Society.* Boston: Lothrop, Lee and Shepard Company, 1935.

Guttmann, Allen. *The Conservative Tradition in America.* New York: Oxford University Press, 1967.

Hassan, Ihab. *The Literature of Silence: Henry Miller and Samuel Beckett*. New York: Random House, 1967.

Hoffman, Frederick J. *Freudianism and the Literary Mind*. New York: Grove Press, Inc., 1959.

Hofstadter, Richard. *Anti-Intellectualism in American Life*. New York: Alfred A. Knopf and Random House, 1963.

Huizinga, Johan. *Homo Ludens: A Study of the Play Element in Culture*. Boston: Beacon Press, 1955.

Hyman, Stanley Edgar. *The Tangled Bank: Darwin, Marx, Frazer, and Freud as Imaginative Writers*. New York: Atheneum Publishers, 1962.

Jakobson, R. "Concluding Statement: Linguistics and Poetics." In Thomas A. Sebeok, ed., *Style in Language*. Cambridge, Mass.: Technology Press of M.I.T., 1960.

Jones, Ernest. *Hamlet and Oedipus*. Garden City, N.Y.: Doubleday and Company, Inc., 1954.

Kauffmann, Stanley. *A World on Film*. New York: Harper and Row Publishers, 1966.

Kepes, Gyorgy, ed. *The Nature and Art of Motion*. New York: George Braziller, 1965.

Kwiat, Joseph J. and Mary C. Turpie, eds. *Studies in American Culture*. Minneapolis, Minn.: University of Minnesota Press, 1960.

Lemon, Lee T. *The Partial Critics*. New York: Oxford University Press, 1965.

Lesser, Simon O. *Fiction and the Unconscious*. Boston: Beacon Press, 1957.

Levi-Strauss, Claude. *The Savage Mind*. Chicago: University of Chicago Press, 1966.

Lowenthall, Leo. *Literature, Popular Culture, and Society*. Englewood Cliffs, N.J.: Prentice-Hall, Inc., 1961.

MacCann, Richard Dyer. *A Montage of Theories*. New York: E. P. Dutton and Company Inc., 1966.

Macdonald, Dwight. *Against the American Grain*. New York: Random House Inc., 1962.

McLoughlin, William G. "Pietism and the American Character." *American Quarterly*, XVII (1965), pp. 163–86.

Marcus, Fred H., ed. *Film and Literature: Contrasts in Media*. Scranton: Chandler Publishing Company, 1971.

Marx, Leo. *The Machine in the Garden*. New York: Oxford University Press, 1964.

Mead, Margaret. *And Keep Your Powder Dry: An Anthropologist Looks at America*. New York: William Morrow, 1965 (new, expanded ed.).

Merideth, Robert, ed. *American Studies: Essays on Theory and Method*. Columbus, Ohio: Charles E. Merrill Publishing Company, 1968.

Miller, Elizabeth and Mary Fisher, eds. *Negro in America: A Bibliography*. Cambridge, Mass.: Harvard University Press, 1970.

Muller, Herbert J. *Science and Criticism*. New York: George Braziller, Inc., 1956.

Nash, Roderick. *Wilderness and the American Mind*. New Haven, Conn.: Yale University Press, 1967.

Potter, David. *People of Plenty*. Chicago: University of Chicago Press, 1954.

Redding, Saunders. "The Black Revolution in American Studies." *American Studies*, IX (1970), pp. 3–10.

Richardson, Robert. *Literature and Film*. Bloomington, Ind.: Indiana University Press, 1969.

Riesman, David *et. al. The Lonely Crowd: A Study of the Changing American Character*. New Haven, Conn.: Yale University Press, 1950 (revised).

Rischin, Moses, ed. *The American Gospel of Success*. Chicago: Quadruple Books, 1965.

Samuels, Charles Thomas. *A Casebook on Film*. New York: Van Nostrand Reinhold Company, 1970.

Scott, Nathan A. Jr. *The Broken Center: Studies in the Theological Horizon of Modern Literature*. New Haven, Conn.: Yale University Press, 1968.

Sklar, Robert. "American Studies and the Realities of America." *American Quarterly*, XXII, Part Two (1970), pp. 597–605.

Sontag, Susan. *Against Interpretation*. New York: Dell Publishing Company, Inc., 1966. *Styles of Radical Will*. New York: Dell Publishing Company, Inc., 1969.

Spiller, Robert E. "Value and Method in American Studies." In *The Third Dimension: Studies in Literary History*. New York: Macmillan, 1965.

Stallknecht, N. P. and Horst Frenz, eds. *Comparative Literature: Method and Perspective*. Carbondale: Southern Illinois University Press, 1961, 1971.

Swados, Harvey, ed. *The American Writer and the Great Depression*. New York: The Bobbs-Merrill Company, Inc., 1966.

Witte, W. "The Sociological Approach to Literature." *Modern Language Review*, XXXVI (1941), pp. 86–94.

Wyllie, Irvin G. *The Self-Made Man in America: The Myth of Rags to Riches*. New Brunswick, N.J.: Rutgers University Press, 1954.

Literature and Covert Culture

BERNARD BOWRON, LEO MARX, AND ARNOLD ROSE

This essay is an experiment in collaboration between scholars associated with literary studies and with sociology. Its authors had the privilege of a year's close association in an American Studies faculty ("Technology and American Culture") at the University of Minnesota.

By covert culture we refer to traits of culture rarely acknowledged by those who possess them. In any society men tend to ignore or repress certain commonly learned attitudes and behavior patterns, much as an individual may ignore or repress certain personal experiences or motives. In the case of covert culture, the repressed traits are more or less common to members of a society, and they probably are transmitted in the same informal ways that the basic elements of the overt culture are transmitted. The covert traits are not more "true" or "real" than the overt traits; they are equally representative of people's attitudes and behaviors. The distinction lies in the degree of acknowledgment (to self and to others) and the degree of repression. If one were to suggest to a representative member of a society that his behavior, or that of his community, exhibits a particular characteristic of covert culture, he might be expected to scoff at the idea, even to reject it heatedly. Public responses to the Kinsey report are a case in point. Similarly, Americans might deny the evidence of their disguised hostility toward machine technology which we present in this essay.

How then is covert culture recognized? We may assume we are in the presence of covert culture when we note a recurrent pattern of inconsistent or seemingly illogical behavior.[1] When most people in a given society or subsociety persist in acting inconsistently, when they resist with emotion any attempts to reconcile their actions with their expressed beliefs, and when they persist in this behavior over an extended period of time, then presumably we are dealing with covert culture. For obvious reasons, however, it is difficult to study covert culture. And in a heterogeneous society like our own, where variations in behavior are relatively common, it is unlikely that much of our culture long remains covert. On the other hand, the little that does may be of the greatest importance in certain emotionally charged areas of behavior, such as racial or sexual relations or religion.

At this point it might be well to indicate what covert culture is not. In the first place, it is not a complete culture that exists beneath the surface of the overt culture and "really" directs people's attitudes and behavior. It consists, rather, of parts of culture that happen to be seriously inconsistent with other parts of culture and so get driven underground.

Second, behavior in conformity with covert culture is not the same as alienation from culture (or "anomie," to use Durkheim's term). Covert elements of culture are just as much a part of culture as are overt elements. To be sure, behavior in conformity with an aspect of covert culture will strike an observer as inconsistent with a parallel aspect of overt culture. But we do not mean to imply that every obvious inconsistency in behavior is a result of such a disparity. Many forms of inconsistent behavior have nothing to do with covert culture. They result from the individual's efforts to adhere to elements within the covert culture which are at bottom incompatible. In such cases, where a person acts out more or less commonplace contradictions of his culture, the disharmony is not so great as in cases where the contradiction is repressed or, as we say, covert. In any event, logical incompatibility between two elements of culture is, obviously enough, more likely to occur in a society that embraces heterogeneous traditions, or in a society that is changing rapidly.

Third, covert culture is not a subculture. We are all familiar with the different roles a person plays in the various groups to which he belongs: contrast the behavior of the adolescent in his family and in his peer group. But, while members of each group are, in this case, shocked or scornfully amused by behavior in the other group, they recognize each other's existence and—in a sense—regard the discrepancies as natural and even desirable. The adolescent himself is aware of the disparity in his roles, whether or not it creates a conflict for him. Even the subculture of a minority group (such as, for example, the Mennonites or Jews) is in no way to be equated with covert culture. This is a different culture from the dominant one, practiced by a small section of the society, and while it may be deliberately hidden from the majority, its deviations from the dominant culture are quite well known and apparent to those living

---

[1] This technique for observing covert culture has been presented in Arnold M. Rose, *Theory and Method in the Social Sciences* (Minneapolis: University of Minnesota Press, 1954), Chap. 21, "Popular Logic in the Study of Covert Culture." Some elements of covert culture in the United States are suggested in this chapter.

in both the minority group and the larger society. Sociologists call those living in two societies "marginal men"; they are understood to be fairly rare in any society. Covert culture traits, on the contrary, are exhibited by the large majority of persons in a society if not by all of them.

But it may be asked how covert culture is learned, if it is unacknowledged and secret. The question, however, implies that the transmission of *overt* culture is deliberate and rational. Actually, only a small part of the education of the young in the overt culture of a society is deliberate. While the child learns through language or other symbols such as gestures, most of the process is very subtle. As Hickman and Kuhn point out: "Few, if any, fathers or mothers take their children aside and say, in effect, 'I will now tell you what I know,' 'I will now tell you what you ought to know and believe,' or 'I will now tell you about our society and our culture.' Any conversations of this general nature could have relatively little over-all influence on the child's attitudes. 'Attitudes are caught, not taught.' "[2] This is true for both overt and covert culture. The difference lies not in manner of learning, but in the degree of the adult's awareness of the cues he is providing, or in the degree of his willingness to acknowledge the cues when they are called to his attention. One characteristic of this learning process is that the child picks up the cues of the covert culture, but at first does not know that they are "secret." He proudly displays the just learned trait openly in behavior or speech, and then the parent is shocked. This negative reaction—coming once or several times—now teaches the child that he must "forget" and "deny" this part of what he has recently learned from the parent. It should be pointed out, however, that the difference between covert and overt culture is a relative matter; some aspects of covert culture are talked over by intimate friends, as it were "over the back fence." Adults "teach" other adults some aspects of covert culture just as they teach children other aspects.

Those who are probably in the best position to study a society's covert traits are observers who come to it with the perspective of an alien culture. Hence anthropologists and perceptive foreign travelers have until now provided much of the evidence of covert culture. The anthropologists have most frequently analyzed the concept itself.[3] This would suggest that the concept is most useful when direct impressions of a living culture are available. The study of covert culture does not at first thought seem possible through the analysis of written documents; hence the concept seems irrelevant to the study of past societies

[2] C. Addison Hickman and Manford H. Kuhn, *Individuals, Groups, and Economic Behavior* (New York: Dryden Press, 1946), p. 30.

[3] The anthropologists have concerned themselves more with the tendency of culture to form patterns or systems covertly rather than with the relationship of covert culture to behavior. See, for example, Edward Sapir, "The Unconscious Patterning of Behavior in Society," in E. S. Dummer, ed., *The Unconscious: A Symposium* (New York: Alfred A. Knopf, 1928); Clyde Kluckhohn, "Patterning as Exemplified in Navaho Culture," in L. Spier, A. I. Hallowell, and S. S. Newman, eds., *Language, Culture and Personality: Essays in Memory of Edward Sapir* (Menasha, Wis.: Sapir Memorial Publication Fund, 1941), pp. 109–128; Laura Thompson, "Attitudes and Acculturation," *American Anthropologist*, L (April–June 1948), 200–215. A few sociologists also have worked with the concept of covert culture: F. Stuart Chapin, "Latent Culture Patterns of the Unseen World of Social Reality," *American Journal of Sociology*, XL (July 1934), 61–68; Robert K. Merton, *Social Theory and Social Structure* (Glencoe, Ill.: The Free Press, 1949), pp. 21–81.

about which we have few other sources of evidence. It is our purpose here to suggest a means of uncovering elements of covert culture through the analysis of written, and particularly literary, evidence.

Now, to be sure, there is nothing new about the idea of studying literature as a source of information about culture. Historians have been doing it for a long time. When allowances are made for shifts in style and taste, the manifest content of literature may be assumed to reflect important characteristics of culture. But what about covert culture? Since we assume, to begin with, that most members of a society do not care to be reminded that they exhibit traits of covert culture, it follows that the writer who seeks a sizable audience will not knowingly portray them. On the other hand, popular literature may be studied for what it betrays as well as what it depicts. In other words, it may be approached as a projection of covert culture. Such an approach to the arts is well established in several areas. Psychologists have for some time been using graphic and lingual expression to get at the unconscious associations of individuals. Of these projective tests, the Rorschach, TAT, and Word Association Test are perhaps the best known. Similarly, literature widely accepted by the public, or a significant segment of the public, may provide an avenue to the unstated ideas of a society. Of course the Freudians and Jungians have studied literature, but not precisely in the way we are suggesting. They have sought recurring popular themes in the classics as projections of what they consider to be universal instincts or complexes. They are concerned with the traits common to virtually all men. What we are concerned with, on the other hand, is a technique for dealing with certain distinctive characteristics of a particular culture located in time and place.[4]

The projective component of written documents is chiefly to be found in imagery and metaphor, using metaphor in the broadest sense to include all the more common figurative modes of expression. When a writer uses such analogizing devices, in which the analogy is either explicit or implicit, he is in effect revealing a pattern of association which can only be partly conscious. That is to say, no matter how many reasons he may acknowledge for selecting a particular figure of speech, the fact remains that he selects it from a virtually infinite range of possibilities. Therefore no degree of deliberate calculation can fully explain his choice. For example, why does an author choose a machine to express menace; why not a storm or an earthquake? We are of course not concerned here with idiosyncratic quirks of personality. Our interest is limited to images and metaphors which recur frequently in the written expression of a particular society. We do not have in mind the mere cliché or faddish expression,

---

[4] Although the Freudians have characteristically been most concerned with universal rather than particular cultural traits, Freud himself did suggest the possibility of inquiries along the line of this essay. "The analogy between the process of cultural evolution and the path of individual development may be carried further in an important respect. It can be maintained that the community, too, develops a super-ego, under whose influence cultural evolution proceeds. It would be an enticing task for an authority on human systems of culture to work out this analogy in specific cases." *Civilization and Its Discontents*, trans. Joan Riviere, 3rd ed. (London: Hogarth Press, 1946), p. 136.

but rather the metaphor *repeatedly used in varying language* to describe similar phenomena.[5] We shall provide an example below.

First, however, a word must be said about our apparent tendency to favor the more stereotyped modes of expression. It is true that the more unreflective the creative process, the more useful the work may be as a projection of the psyche, so to speak, of the entire society. But this is not to say that we underestimate the value of less hackneyed literary modes. We assume that written documents are distributed along a spectrum from the most stereotyped or conventional at one end to the most original and perceptive at the other. The great writer is a sensitive observer, and needless to say he does not merely project his culture. On the contrary, often he consciously reveals covert elements that less perceptive artists ignore; moreover, he sometimes reveals them precisely by turning stereotypes inside out. Hence this distinction between overt and covert culture should not seem completely unfamiliar to students of literature. Indeed, it is in some respects akin to a recurrent literary motif, the paradoxical relation between "appearance" and "reality." Not that there is an exact equivalence between the two sets of terms. When a writer indicates the presence of a "reality" hidden beneath "appearances" he usually intends more than we do by covert culture. Nevertheless he often includes an awareness of covert traits. For example, Shakespeare has Lear become aware of covert traits of culture; Cervantes, on the other hand, deliberately makes Don Quixote oblivious of them. In *King Lear* the discrepancy between overt and covert generates a tragic view of life; in *Don Quixote* it is the essence of comedy. In both works, however, the reader's illumination comes at least in part from the author's revelation of the disparity between what we have called overt and covert culture. That disparity is, however, but one aspect of the paradox of appearance and reality.

For an illustration of the use of written documents to reveal covert patterns, consider American culture during the onset of industrialism before the Civil War. Here, as most historians testify, was a society wholeheartedly committed to the idea of progress. This was an era of unprecedented expansion, social mobility, and optimism. In the newspapers, magazines, and orations of the time we find countless celebrations of the new technology as emblematic of man's increasing dominion over nature. Take, as an example, a minister's address to the New York Mechanics' Institute in 1841. In expounding his theme ("Improvement of the Mechanic Arts"), the Reverend Mr. Williamson employed many commonplaces of the hour. The mechanic arts, he said,

> . . . change the face of nature itself, and cause the desolate and solitary place to be glad and blossom as the rose—the mountains are levelled—the crooked is made strait [*sic*] and the rough plain—the ascending vapor is arrested in

[5] While popular clichés have some interest for the social scientist, they are to be thought of as habits of speech (e.g., "pretty as a picture") rather than as unconsciously selected projections of covert culture, so that mere recurrence of metaphor is not a sufficient criterion. What is to be sought is a metaphor or image that is expressed recurrently in *varying* language and used to describe the same set of phenomena.

its upward course and converted into a power that well nigh enables us to laugh at distance and space—the broad Atlantic has become, as it were, a narrow lake. . . . And still the course is onward, and we even threaten to seize upon the forked lightning, and pluck from the faithful magnet a power, that shall render useless the canvass [*sic*] of the mariner and achieve a yet mightier triumph over the obstacles that space has interposed to the intercourse of man with his fellow-man . . . much of human happiness depends upon the cultivation of these arts . . . without them, man is but a helpless child, exposed to ten thousand dangers and difficulties, that he cannot control; but with them, he is strong, and can rule in majesty over that mighty empire which God has given him.[6]

To say that this rhetoric embodies certain dominant values of the culture is not to deny that there also were outspoken critics of technological innovation. There were. But they constituted a relatively small minority. Some spoke for the slavery interest or the emergent labor movement, others for various religious sects or utopian reform groups. By and large, however, Americans at this time enthusiastically endorsed the new machine power, and even more enthusiastically applied it. Many of the respected leaders of society, men like Daniel Webster and Edward Everett, paid homage to technology in language indistinguishable from Mr. Williamson's. On the basis of much written evidence, therefore, one might conclude that American culture, leaving aside a few groups of partially alienated people, exhibited only approval of industrialization.

But that is not quite the whole story. To be sure, it describes the dominant overt response to mechanization, but it fails to account for a certain contrary undertone that any close student of the period recognizes. To be more specific, in examining a large sample of reactions to technological change in this period, we discover some which defy simple classification. Here, for instance, is an article by James H. Lanman on "Railroads in the United States," which appeared in Hunt's *Merchants' Magazine* in 1840.[7] In accordance with the spirit of this journal of commerce, the writer presents an affirmative survey of the advance of steam power in America. He regards "productive enterprise" as the distinguishing feature of American culture, and he praises the new machines as "the triumphs of our own age, the laurels of mechanical philosophy, of untrammelled mind, and a liberal commerce!" He finds railroads particularly inspiring; so far as he is concerned "it is clear that all patriotic and right-minded men have concurred in the propriety of their construction." If we confine attention to Mr. Lanman's manifest opinions, we have no reason to distinguish him from such ebullient devotees of progress as the Reverend Mr. Williamson.

[6] Rev. Bro. I. D. Williamson, *The Covenant and Official Magazine of the Grand Lodge of the United States,* I (June 1842), 275–281. The original lecture was delivered on November 18, 1841. A survey of responses to industrialization was made possible by a grant from the Graduate School, University of Minnesota, and by the research assistance of Dr. Donald Houghton.

[7] James H. Lanman, "Railroads in the United States," *Merchants' Magazine,* III (October 1840), 273–295.

Nevertheless a more searching examination of this article uncovers a curious anomaly. In spite of the writer's evident effort to enlist support for the new power, he repeatedly invokes images which convey less than full confidence in the benign influence of machines. Steamships and railroads are "iron monsters," "dragons of mightier power, with iron muscles that never tire, breathing smoke and flame through their blackened lungs, feeding upon wood and water, out-running the race horse. . . ." Elsewhere Mr. Lanman is eager to allay fear of railroad accidents. Therefore he carefully evaluates statistics on deaths and injuries. He finds the results clearly favorable to railroads as compared with travel on "common roads." At the same time, however, he describes a train "leaping forward like some black monster, upon its iron path, by the light of the fire and smoke which it vomits forth."

In contrast to the explicit theme of the piece, these images associate machines with the destructive and the repulsive. They communicate an unmistakable sense of anxiety and menace. Without more evidence, of course, we cannot prove that the writer actually was uneasy about the new power. By themselves these images prove nothing. But the fact is that we can produce many other examples of the same kind. Moreover, and this seems to us a most telling point, when we turn to these alienated writers who consciously try to arouse fear of machines, we find them deliberately choosing the same images. Robert Owen, for example, describes the new technology as a power "which neither eats nor drinks, and faints not by over-exertion, brought into direct competition with flesh and blood." "Who is there," he asks, "to check this mighty monster that is now allowed to stalk the earth . . .?"[8] It was in this period that a kind of machine created in a writer's imagination entered the language as the prototype of terror and the demoniacal—Frankenstein's monster. A final example of the simultaneous attraction and fearfulness of the locomotive, with distinct Oedipal overtones, is provided by this doggerel:

> Big iron horse with lifted head,
> Panting beneath the station shed,
> You are my dearest dream come true;—
> I love my Dad; I worship you!

> Your noble heart is filled with fire,
> For all your toil you never tire,
> And though you're saddled-up in steel,
> Somewhere, inside, I *know* you feel.

> All night in dreams when you pass by,
> You breathe out stars that fill the sky,
> And now, when all my dreams are true,
> I hardly dare come close to you.[9]

[8] *New Harmony Gazette*, II (August 8, 1927), 347. Owen's words are from an address delivered to the Franklin Institute on June 27, 1827.

[9] Benjamin R. C. Low, "The Little Boy to the Locomotive," in David L. Cohn, *The Good Old Days* (New York: Simon and Schuster, 1940), p. 188.

To sum up, we conclude that expressions of the overt culture do not provide an adequate conception of the American response to industrialization. From them we get the familiar picture of a confident, optimistic public and a few small dissident groups. But the concept of covert culture makes possible a somewhat different hypothesis. When we analyze the imagery employed even by those who professed approval of technological change, we discover evidence of widespread if largely unacknowledged doubt, fear, and hostility.[10] It is not necessary to our present purpose to account in detail for this phenomenon. Suffice it to suggest that American culture at this time also embraced a set of values and meanings inherently antithetic to the new technological power. This was a time, as everyone knows, when Americans tended to celebrate the "natural" as against the "artificial." At all levels of culture, from the relatively abstruse speculations of Emerson to the popular gift books, from Cooper's novels to the paintings of the Hudson River School, Americans affirmed values and meanings said to reside in nature. Natural process, that is, was conceived as containing the key, barely concealed, to all human problems. Needless to say, this belief was not peculiar to America. But as a consequence of the unique American geography—the actual presence of the wilderness—it did seem particularly relevant to this country. As Perry Miller has pointed out, what the European romantic dreamed the American actually experienced.[11] Now the progress of technology hardly was reconcilable, at least in the long run, with the sanctity of the natural order. For the use of power machines implied that nature was a neutral if not hostile force that men needed to dominate. This view was in obvious contradiction with the idea that man's felicity depended upon the ordering of life in passive accommodation to spontaneous operations of nature.

We are suggesting, though here we can hardly demonstrate, that this conflict of values, when unacknowledged, may have been an important source of the anxiety revealed by the imagery to which we have called attention.[12] This is not to identify approval of technological progress with overt culture, and hostility with covert. What is covert here results from the impulse to adhere (simultaneously) to logically incompatible values. In other words, it is the awareness of the contradiction that is repressed and that gives rise to the covert traits (in this case *unacknowledged* fear and hostility) revealed in imagery. Thus it is worth noting that Lanman, the writer who praised locomotives even as he called them monsters, also praised the "steam screw" which, he said, "should

---

[10] It is possible that people betrayed their fear of the machine in casual conversation. But this source of information usually is not available to sociologists, much less to historians. If the sociologist asks people directly about their attitudes toward machines, he is likely to get "rational" answers about how much labor they save, how they provide products and services previously not available, and so on.

[11] Perry Miller, "The Romantic Dilemma in American Nationalism and the Concept of Nature," *Harvard Theological Review*, xlviii (October 1955), 239–253.

[12] It is interesting that as early as 1881 Dr George Miller Beard, an American physician, related the anxiety of Americans to the new technology His pioneering work, *American Nervousness, Its Causes and Consequences* (New York: G. P. Putnam's, 1881), was taken seriously by Freud. See Philip P. Wiener, "G. M. Beard and Freud on 'American Nervousness,'" *Journal of the History of Ideas*, xvii (April 1956), 269–274.

tear up by the roots the present monarchs of the forest, and open the ample bosom of the soil to the genial beams of the fertilizing sun." Recall that the writer speaks for a culture passionately devoted to nature—to Bryant's lyric view that "the groves were God's first temples." Is it surprising that he felt impelled to compare machines to terrible monsters? In any event, the disparity between the feelings latent in his images and the manifest optimism of his theme is highly suggestive. It gives some clue to the correspondence between this writer's strangely mixed feelings and the recurrent, if largely unexpressed, pattern of inconsistency in the culture of nineteenth-century America.

This interpretation, finally, is borne out by the work of the more sensitive and perceptive writers of the age. When we turn, for example, to Cooper, Thoreau, Hawthorne, and Melville we find a reiterated expression of precisely those contradictory meanings the typical magazine writers did not acknowledge. What is more, the great writers in many cases employed the same or similar imagery to get at these conflicts. But with an important difference. When Lanman called a machine a monster he was scarcely aware of what he was doing. We know this because he fails to take into account the negative response to technological change that is the unmistakable burden of his imagery. In other words, his conscious theme expresses one viewpoint and his images another. There is a marked disparity between thought and feeling here. Either the writer is unaware of the contradiction or he is unable to find words capable of expressing it. In either event, this is not what happens in the work of a talented and disciplined artist.

When we look closely at the way Thoreau or Hawthorne handles the same material the difference quickly becomes apparent. In *Walden,* for example, or in Hawthorne's "The Celestial Railroad," we find a deliberate effort to complicate the significance of America's favorite symbol of progress. Here the machine is invested with ambiguous meaning, not because the writers have an inherent passion for ambiguity, but rather because no other interpretation would have seemed adequate.[13] Given the conditions of life in nineteenth-century America, the entire pattern of the culture, the new machine power was bound to represent contrary possibilities. No doubt everyone in some degree sensed the ambiguity. But only a few were able to express it. Among them were the serious writers who made it their business to convey as much of the meaning of experience as possible. Hence it is no accident that they so often employ machine imagery in opposition to various emblems of nature. This device served to express precisely the contradiction that Lanman felt but that he did not fully recognize

[13] We agree with Henry G. Fairbanks who, in a recent article, disagrees with scholars who regard Hawthorne as a doctrinaire and romantic opponent of science and technology. But, like the writers he criticizes, Mr. Fairbanks tends to misconstrue Hawthorne's aim in mentioning machines at all. Hawthorne was not concerned to convey his opinions about the new technology, but rather to express its meaning, often ambiguous, within the larger pattern of human experience. In doing so, as we have tried to indicate, he revealed contradictions characteristic of American culture generally. See "Hawthorne and the Machine Age," *American Literature,* xxviii (May 1956), 155–164. For a somewhat different method of interpreting the response of American writers to the onset of industrialism see, for example, Leo Marx, "The Machine in the Garden," *New England Quarterly,* xxix (March 1956), 27–42; "The Pilot and the Passenger: Landscape Conventions and the Style of *Huckleberry Finn,*" *American Literature,* xxviii (May 1956), 129–146.

or express. What we are saying is that the skilled writer confirms the presence of those covert traits of culture which unreflective and untrained writers merely betray. When the two kinds of evidence fit, as they do here, we feel confident that we have uncovered a disparity between covert and overt culture.

Repressed traits and attitudes of former periods need not be a closed book. Dead men answer no poll-takers, but they have left an extensive written record of their underground cultures. This record may be deciphered. One indispensable key is the analysis of systems of imagery and metaphor in diverse popular writings and in works of formal literary art. The sociologist need not regard this method of study as an exclusive possession of the literary scholars who originally developed it. Used with care and discrimination, it is equally available to him.

Such collaboration between literary and sociological scholarship is, fortunately, a two-way street. At least it should be. For the concept of covert culture, in turn, offers a rewarding approach to literary studies. This point cannot be developed here. But it is surely implicit in what has been said about formal literature's significant confirmation of the existence of culture traits that are only revealed inadvertently in popular modes of expression. Critics concerned with the devious ways in which a society nurtures its men of letters cannot afford to neglect the existence of covert culture and the writer's responses to it. Here is a major source of those tensions that give a work of literary art its structure, its irony, and its stylistic signature.

Psycho-Analysis and Criticism

HERBERT READ

ANY attempt to raise literary criticism above the vague level of emotional appreciation through the incorporation of scientific elements is sure to meet with opposition, not only from the great majority of critics, who depend on their emotions, but also from more serious people who imagine that the prescribed boundaries of decent critical activity are being broken down. To the former set we can only present our weapons; with the latter we must reason, and our task is all the more difficult for the lack, in England, of any scientific tradition. Our critics have, as a rule, resorted to nothing more distant from their subject than common-sense. Perhaps the only successful attempt of a more ranging kind was that of Coleridge, who did consciously strive to give literary criticism the rank of a mental science by relating it to what he called "the technical process of philosophy." Unfortunately, what this technical process amounted to in Coleridge's day was a very innate kind of metaphysical speculation, speculation rather dim across an interval of more than a hundred years. We have become more empirical, and the general effect of the growth of science has been to discredit transcendental reasoning altogether.[1] Traditional criticism, therefore, in so far as it can claim to be fundamental, is a structure whose very foundations have perished, and if we are to save it from becoming the province of emotional dictators, we must hasten to relate it to those systems of knowledge which have to a great extent replaced transcendental philosophy. Physics, demanding as it does such impressive modifications of aspect and attitude, provides the most general background for all subsidiary efforts, but for the

---

[1] I imply "in the general mind." That empirical science can ever dispense with all aprioristic processes is a vulgar error to which the general tenour of this book is opposed.

literary critic psychology gains an intimate importance because it is so directly concerned with the material origins of art.

The critic, in approaching psychology, will not be altogether disinterested: he will merely raid it in the interests of what he conceives to be another science, literary criticism. This science—if it is permissible to call it a science—really covers a very wide field indeed. It is the valuation, by some standard, of the worth of literature. You may say that the standard is always a very definitely aesthetic one, but I find it impossible to define aesthetics without bringing in questions of value which are, when you have seen all their implications, social or ethical in nature. There is no danger, therefore (or very little danger), in the direction of a too inclusive conception of the critic's function: danger, and death, is rather to be found in the narrow drift of technical research, the analysis of the *means* of expression and so on. But it is a proper complaint against literary criticism in general that it has reached no agreed definition of its boundaries, and until it does it has no serious claim to be considered as a science. It is only because I want to distinguish one kind of literary criticism from another, even as you distinguish astronomy from astrology, or chemistry from alchemy, that I resort to a pretence of science. That distinction established, there is no need to carry the pretence any further: it is not necessary, I mean, to simulate the vocabularies of science.

Another consideration meets us at the outset of this inquiry, and the more one realizes it the more it appears to put the whole utility of our discussion in doubt. I mean the very obvious difference in the subject-matter of our two sciences: psychology is concerned with the processes of mental activity, literary criticism with the product. The psychologist only analyses the product to arrive at the process: art is, from this point of view, as significant as any other expression of mentality. But of no more significance: its significance does not correspond to its value as literature. The psychologist is indifferent to literary values (too often, alas, even in his own work), and may even definitely deplore them, especially when they represent the trimming of subjective phantasies under the influence of some objective standard or tradition. But in any case the psychologist has found and will always find a large body of material in the imaginative literature of all epochs: that side of the question is so obvious that I shall pay no more attention to it. But whether in the nature of things it is possible for such psychology to add anything positive to the principles of literary criticism is more in doubt. Analysis involves the reduction of the symbol to its origins, and once the symbol is in this way dissolved, it is of no aesthetic significance: art is art as symbol, not as sign. Alfred Adler, whom I have found, for my purpose, one of the most suggestive of the psycho-analytical school, has recognized this, pointing out that *"the attraction of a work of art arises from its synthesis, and that the analysis of science profanes and destroys this synthesis."*[2] This is perhaps *too* respectful an attitude; there is no need to make a mystery of art. But it is an easy and an unprofitable task to translate into crude terms of sexual phantasy a poem like William Blake's "I saw a Chapel all of Gold." One might as well

[2] *Individual Psychology*, English edition, 1924, p. 268.

confess that the impossibility of avoiding such a translation is a serious defect in the psychological critic; for him the naïve acceptance of such a poem is impossible; here at least there is no beauty without mystery. Luckily for the critic, few poets are so artless as Blake, and meaning and intelligence tend to be remote in the degree that they are profound.[3]

I have perhaps laid sufficient emphasis on the general limitations of the psychological method in criticism. Before I begin with my main task, which is to explore the uses of psycho-analysis to literary criticism, let me deal with one of its misuses. It perhaps concerns literature rather than criticism, but we must all realize by now that no good artist exists who is not, at every point of his career, firstly a good critic. The work of art emerges within a radiation of critical perceptions. But, criticism apart, the author who imagines that he can start from psycho-analysis and arrive at art is making a complete mistake. No literature, not even a novel, can arise out of a schematic understanding of the phenomena of life. Art has only one origin—experience. Art is itself a schematic construction; an order imposed on the chaos of life. As such it has its own delicate and individual laws. But to conceive art as the illustration of science, or even as the embodiment in tangible fiction of aprioristic views of the universe, is surely a final sort of degradation, a use of the imagination more finally discredited than any it is possible to think of.

That is not to say that the study of psycho-analysis is entirely without object for the would-be novelist or poet. It might at least help him to realize, more quickly and more reasonably than the normal man would realize from his own experience, such facts as the subjectivity of love,[4] and the general law of determinism in which all our emotions and ideals are bound. Again, the novelist cannot in his plot ignore with impunity what we might now call the psycho-analytical probabilities. Then surely, it might be said, the examination of such probabilities is an opportunity for the critic well versed in psycho-analysis. But it does not follow. Here, admittedly, is the opportunity of the psycho-analyst, straying from his strict domain, eager to show what fools these artists be. But the literary critic will ignore this obvious use of psycho-analysis, if only for the sufficient reason that to a critic of any worth these psychological defects in a work of the imagination will appear as literary defects. You cannot write well— you cannot, as we say, "create" your atmosphere—without a "germ of the real." Any psychological unreality will, in the end, be apparent in some insincerity of style or method.

In the endeavour to discover the critical utility of psycho-analysis I will, merely for dialectical reasons, formulate three questions.

---

[3] When this remoteness occurs, as in the case of Shakespeare's *Hamlet,* then I think it inevitably follows that any explanation that psychology can offer for the complicated strands of poetic creation tends to quicken our general sensibility. Reasoning and mechanism do not lose their value because we follow step by step the process of their operation; and I think a poetic process is exactly analogous. It is where you have, not a dynamic process, but a static symbol, that analysis is without any critical significance, and may be positively destructive of the aesthetic effect. I shall return to this point in dealing with Dr. Ernest Jones's study of *Hamlet.*

[4] *Cf.* Jacques Rivière, "Notes on a Possible Generalisation of the Theories of Freud" (*The Criterion,* Vol. i, no. iv, pp. 344–5).

    I. What general function does psycho-analysis give to literature?

    II. How does psycho-analysis explain the process of poetic creation or inspiration?

    III. Does psycho-analysis cause us to extend in any way the functions of criticism?

I ask the first question, apart from its intrinsic interest, to make sure from both points of view—that of psycho-analysis and that of criticism—that we have the same subject-matter in mind. I ask the second question—again apart from its intrinsic interest—to make sure that we have a common conception of what "creative" literature is. We can then, without fear of misconstruction, deal with the third question—which is the question I have all the time been leading up to.

To most questions in psycho-analysis there are three answers—those respectively of Freud, Jung, and Adler—and as a mere expropriator in this territory I take the liberty to lift my material from whichever quarter suits me best. Perhaps in this matter of the general function of literature Jung is the only one of the three to work out a theory in any detail. Freud and Adler do not seem to press the question beyond its individual aspect, to which I shall come in my second question. Jung's theory springs from that general principle of contrasted attitudes which is really the characteristic method of his psychology—the contrasted attitudes which he calls introversion and extraversion, a fundamental division of the self which may be traced in every activity and which we may variously paraphrase as the opposition between subject and object, between thought and feeling, between idea and thing. Now Jung's theory is that living reality is never the exclusive product of one or the other of these contrasted attitudes, but only of a specific vital activity which unites them, bridges the gulf between them, giving intensity to sense-perception and effective force to the idea. This specific activity he calls *phantasy*, and he describes it as a perpetually creative act. "It is the creative activity whence issue the solutions to all unanswerable questions; it is the mother of all possibilities, in which, too, the inner and the outer worlds, like all psychological antitheses, are joined in living union."[5] Jung further differentiates *active* and *passive* phantasy—the latter a morbid state which we need not stop to consider here. Active phantasy he describes as owing its existence "to the propensity of the conscious attitude for taking up the indications or fragments of relatively lightly-toned unconscious associations, and developing them into complete plasticity by association with parallel elements."[6] Now although Jung remarks that this active phantasy is "the principal attribute of the artistic mentality," he nowhere seems to have pressed home the conclusions which are surely latent in his theory, namely, that the poetic function is nothing else but this active phantasy in its more-than-individual aspect. The poet, in fact, is one who is capable of creating phantasies of more than individual use—phantasies, as we should say, of

[5] *Psychological Types*, English edition, London, 1923, p. 69.
[6] *Ibid.*, p. 574.

universal appeal. Thus art has for psycho-analysis the general function of resolving into one uniform flow of life all that springs from the inner well of primordial images and instinctive feelings, and all that springs from the outer mechanism of actuality—doing this, not only for the artist himself, from whose own need the phantasy is born, but also, by suggestion and by symbol, for all who come to participate in his imaginative work.

And here at last the processes of psycho-analysis and literary criticism run together. "Whether the actual social validity of the symbol," says Jung, "is more general or more restricted depends upon the quality or vital capacity of the creative individuality. The more abnormal the individual, *i.e.*, the less his general fitness for life, the more limited will be the common social value of the symbols he produces, although their value may be absolute for the individuality in question."[7] Now "the social validity of the symbol" is a phrase which I confess I would willingly annex for literary criticism, for it is to some such concept that any thorough critical activity leads us, and though I think the "symbol" in literature (we should never call it that) is something more precise, more deliberate, something more intelligent than the normal unconscious symbol of psychology, yet, if psycho-analysis can help us to test its social validity, then it can in this respect be of some use to literary criticism.

I come to the individual aspect: do we gain any further light from the psycho-analysis of the creative mind? How does the modern psychologist define inspiration, and does his definition bear any correspondence to our critical concepts? It is the general problem of the psychology of genius and far too big a field to explore in any detail here. But it will, I think, be worth while to examine one or two relevant aspects of the question. I think that in the mind of every artist (though I think particularly of the literary artist) there are two contrary tendencies. In one direction he is impelled to shuffle off conscious control and sink back into his primitive mind, where he knows he can find a fresh elemental imagery, a rich though incoherent phantasy. It is the disjointed fortuitous world of dreams—day-dreams. In the other direction he is impelled to establish strong affective tendencies—ideals of moral beauty, of plastic form, of order and architecture. These resolve themselves into some kind of unity and form the goal towards which, consciously or unconsciously, the artist's life is formed. You get the harmony of perfect art when the two forces achieve a balance. I think this is all a matter of psychological observation, but it has a direct bearing on what we may call the central problem of literary criticism— I mean the question of romanticism and classicism. There is, therefore, a peculiar echo of reality in these words of André Gide, written from a purely literary standpoint, in reply to an inquiry on Classicism:

> It is important to remember that the struggle between classicism and romanticism also exists inside each mind. And it is from this very struggle that the work is born; the classic work of art relates the triumph of order and measure over an inner romanticism. And the wilder the riot to be tamed

[7] *Op. cit.*, p. 380.

the more beautiful your work will be. If the thing is orderly in its inception, the work will be cold and without interest.[8]

It is this riot within that we ordinarily call inspiration, and a good deal of attention has been devoted to its description by modern psychologists. By some it is assumed to be a function of the unconscious mind, which is credited with autonomous activity, with powers of incubation and elaboration. Most people will be familiar with Poincaré's account of his own experiences in mathematical discovery (*Science et méthode,* chap. iii), where he describes how some sudden illumination would come to him after a period during which conscious application to the problem had been abandoned. Poincaré attributed these sudden illuminations to the unconscious workings of the mind, but he did not really advance any proof of his hypothesis, and I do not think the idea is any longer entertained by psychologists. Modern psychologists explain sudden illumination or inspiration rather as due solely to a fortuitous entry into activity of ideas which are immediately associated and seized upon in their happy combination,[9] and this theory is, I think, entirely satisfactory as an explanation of poetic inspiration. It will not, perhaps, satisfy the poets themselves, who all, like Blake, imagine that they take down from the dictation of angels. But we are none of us very exact in the description of our own emotional states. What really happens may perhaps be described in the following way: you have in the first place the prevailing affectivity, the latent ideal of form or thought; what forms this ideal, what brings it into being, I shall explain in a moment. You have, next, the bringing into activity fortuitously of some image or memory which until the moment of inspiration had lain latent in the unconscious mind; this fortuitous image is as it were criticized by the excited interest; it is selected or rejected; and if selected it is developed and transformed by the ever prevalent affectivity. If the affective tendency is suddenly and strongly roused, then you get a state of emotion, bringing with it an intensity of awareness to all the images and ideas that follow in the wake of the first fortuitous image. This is the state of ecstasy. Images seem to leap from their hiding-places all fully equipped for the service of the ideal or affective tendency. But even in this state of animation or ecstasy I believe that a good deal of selection and rejection of images still goes on. However, normally a creative act occurs when the exact word or image is found. And the full creative process is but a summation of many of these primary creative moments.

If this be a correct description of the process of poetic creation—and it is based both on my reading of psychology and on the analysis of my own putative experiences—then the part that may be played by suggestion or self-hypnosis

---

[8] "Il importe de considérer que la lutte entre classicisme et romantisme existe aussi bien à l'intérieur de chaque esprit. Et c'est de cette lutte même que doit naître l'oeuvre; l'oeuvre d'art classique raconte le triomphe de l'ordre et de la mesure sur le romantisme intérieur. L'oeuvre est d'autant plus belle que la chose soumise était d'abord plus révoltée. Si la matière est soumise par avance l'oeuvre est froide et sans intérêt."—Réponse à une enquête de la Renaissance sur le classicisme, 8 Janvier 1921 (*Morceaux Choisis,* p. 453).

[9] *Cf.* E. Rignano, *The Psychology of Reasoning.* London, 1923, p. 129.

in the encouragement of such states is obviously considerable, and I think that in time a complete technique of inspiration may be evolved. That this will result in a vast increase in the number of poets need not be feared, for nothing ever comes out of the unconscious mind that has not previously been consciously elaborated or sensibly felt: the product of the unconscious mind will always strictly correspond with the quality of the conscious mind, and dull intellects will find as ever that there is no short cut to genius.

It will be observed that there is nothing essential or peculiar in this description of the creative process: it is just what occurs in any man's mind when he is suddenly endowed with a "bright idea." Where then must we seek for an explanation of the abnormality of the artist? Obviously, I think, in the nature of the ideal or affective tendency to which his whole creative life is subservient. And for an explanation of this I return to the psychoanalysis.

Freud and his disciples would trace back the formation of the abnormal mentality of the artist to the period of infancy. "Analysis of this aspiration" (for ideal beauty), says Dr. Ernest Jones, "reveals that the chief source of its stimuli is not so much a primary impulse as a reaction, a rebellion against the coarser and more repellent aspects of material existence, one which psychogenetically arises from the reaction of the young child against its original excremental interests."[10] The repression of such tabooed interests may indeed contribute to the details of aesthetic activity, but this particular hypothesis seems far too limited in conception, and far too poorly supported by facts to account for the variety and profundity of aesthetic expression in general. The less specialized theory of Adler seems to offer a clearer explanation. According to the principles of "individual psychology," "every neurosis can be understood as an attempt to free oneself from a feeling of inferiority in order to gain a feeling of superiority."[11] The feeling of inferiority usually arises in the family circle, and the compensatory feeling of superiority is usually a phantasy so absurd in its high-set goal of godlikeness that it remains in the unconscious; it is repressed by the communal standards of logic, sympathy, and co-operation. This buried sense of superiority is present in most of us, but the artist takes the goal of godlikeness seriously and is compelled to flee from real life and compromise to seek a life within life;[12] and he is an artist in virtue of the form and ideal perfection which he can give to this inner life. The neurotic fails to create a formal phantasy, and lapses into some degree of chaos. Now it is worth observing, as a confirmation of the general truth of this theory, that the most general period for the formation of the superiority-complex coincides with the most general period for the outburst of the poetic impulse. I mean the time of the awakening of the adolescent sexual instincts, the time of the withdrawal of parental protection, the period of intense conflict between instinctive desires and social control. I think there can be no doubt that the artist is born of this conflict. Freud himself lends support to this view. He says: The artist "is one

[10] *Essays in Applied Psycho-Analysis*, 1923, p. 262.

[11] Alfred Adler, *The Practice and Theory of Individual Psychology*, English edition. London, 1924, p. 23.

[12] *Cf.* Adler, *op. cit.*, p. 8.

who is urged on by instinctive needs which are too clamorous; he longs to attain to honour, power, riches, fame, and the love of woman; but he lacks the means of achieving these gratifications. So, like any other with an unsatisfied longing, he turns away from reality, and transfers all his interest, and all his libido too, on to the creation of his wishes in the life of phantasy." And Freud goes on to explain how the artist can, by the expression and elaboration of his phantasies, give them the impersonality and universality of art and make them communicable and desirable to others—"and then he has won—through his phantasy—what before he could only win in phantasy: honour, power, and the love of woman."[13]

The essential point to notice is that psycho-analysis seems to show that the artist is initially by tendency a neurotic, but that in becoming an artist he as it were escapes the ultimate fate of his tendency and through art finds his way back to reality. I think it will be seen now where psycho-analysis can be of some assistance to the critic—namely, in the verification of the reality of the sublimation of any given neurotic tendency. The psycho-analyst should be able to divide sharply for us, in any given artistic or pseudo-artistic expression, the real and the neurotic. There is much in literature that is on the border-line of reality: it would be useful for the critic to be able to determine by some scientific process the exact course of this borderline. But again I would suggest that in all probability the critic could determine this border-line by general critical principles; but psycho-analysis might be a shorter path to the test; and in any case it would supply collateral evidence of a very satisfactory kind. Psycho-analysis finds in art a system of symbols, representing a hidden reality, and by analysis it can testify to the purposive genuineness of the symbols; it can also testify to the faithfulness, the richness, and the range of the mind behind the symbol.

There still remains the third question that I propounded: Does psycho-analysis modify in any way our conception of the critic's function? The clear difference in subject-matter, already defined, makes it unlikely that we shall find any fundamental influence. It is merely a question of what kind of attitude, among the many possible to the critic within the strict limits of his function, psycho-analysis will stress. It does not, so far as I can see, amount to anything very definite—anything more precise than a general admonition to tolerance. Human activities are shown to be so inter-related, so productive of unrealized compensations, that any narrowly confined application of energy and intelligence results in a distortion of reality. Hence the futility of a purely categorical criticism—which may be illustrated by reference to "the Hamlet problem." During the past two hundred years an extensive body of criticism has accumulated around Shakespeare's cryptic masterpiece. The difficulty, for the critics, is to account within the canons of art for Hamlet's hesitancy in seeking to revenge his father's murder. Dr. Ernest Jones has given a fairly complete summary,[14] which I will summarize still further, of all the various theories advanced at

---

[13] Sigm. Freud, *Introductory Lectures on Psycho-Analysis*, English edition. London, 1922, pp. 314–15.

[14] *Essays in Applied Psycho-Analysis*, 1923, pp. 1–98, "The Problem of Hamlet."

different times. There are two main points of view: one, that of Goethe and Coleridge, finds a sufficient explanation of the inconsistencies of the play in the temperament of Hamlet, whom they regard as a noble nature, but one incapable of decisive action of any kind—"without that energy of the soul which constitutes the hero," as Goethe expresses it. The second point of view sees a sufficient explanation in the difficulty of the task that Hamlet is called upon to perform. Both these theories have been decisively refuted, time and time again, from the very facts of the play, and finally criticism has manoeuvred itself into a paradoxical position, boldly asserting that the tragedy is in its essence "inexplicable, incoherent, and incongruous." This is the position taken up with so much force by Mr. J. M. Robertson. "Robertson's thesis" (I quote from Dr. Jones's summary) "is that Shakespeare, finding in the old play 'an action that to his time discounting sense was one of unexplained delay, elaborated that aspect of the hero as he did every other,' 'finally missing artistic consistency simply because consistency was absolutely excluded by the material'; he concludes that Hamlet is 'not finally an intelligible drama as it stands,' that 'the play cannot be explained from within' and that 'no jugglery can do away with the fact that the construction is incoherent, and the hero perforce an enigma, the snare of idolatrous criticism.' " All this can be said, and said intelligently, and with a convincing absence of emotional prejudice. But it leaves us curiously dissatisfied. We cannot dismiss so easily the personal intensity of expression throughout the play, and such intensity, such *consistent* intensity, gives the play a unity which the old academic criticism has failed to perceive. It seems that here is a case of an instrument not large enough, or not exact enough, to measure the material in hand.

And where literary criticism fails to account for its problem, what can psycho-analysis do? Dr. Jones has shown that it will claim to do a great deal, and he has elaborated in his study of Hamlet a psychological explanation of the peculiar problems of the play. He sees in Hamlet's vacillation the workings of a typical "complex"—the Oedipus complex, as it is called by the psychoanalysts. That is to say, the mental peculiarities of Hamlet, expressed throughout the play with such vividness and actuality, can be explained as the consequences of "repressed" infantile incestuous wishes, stirred into activity by the death of the father and the appearance of a rival, Claudius. With the use of this hypothesis Dr. Jones can explain, and explain very plausibly, all the difficulties and incoherences of the action; and he finds in the play such an exact delineation and such a rich wealth of detail that he cannot but conclude that in writing *Hamlet* Shakespeare was giving expression to a conflict passing through his own mind. There is a certain amount of biographical confirmation of this further hypothesis in the circumstances of the composition of the play, but not facts enough, alas, to be of much use to any solution of the problem.

It would be interesting to follow this application of psycho-analysis to literary criticism into further detail, but perhaps I have indicated enough of Dr. Jones's theory and method to show the possibilities of this new approach to the problems of literature. Whether Dr. Jones's explanation is tenable or not, it does provide what is at present the only way out of a critical impasse, and for that reason alone it merits serious consideration. At the very least it points to a defect in our critical methods, for the failure of literary criticism to deal with *Hamlet* is largely due to its approach to the problem along too narrow a front: we must always be prepared for literature refusing to fit into our critical categories. Criticism is a process of crystallization, of the discovery and elaboration of general concepts; but we must be prepared for the voyage of discovery leading us into strange and unfamiliar tracts of the human mind.

That is one way in which psycho-analysis supplies a corrective to the narrowness of criticism. I find still another, tending to the same end. I have referred before to the eternal opposition of the classic and the romantic: to this blind difference under the influence of which even the best of critics race into untenable dogmatisms. Can psycho-analysis resolve this difficult conflict and supply us with a common standpoint?

I think it can—particularly the psycho-analysis associated with the name of Jung. Jung has devoted his best work to the analysis of psychological types. As I have mentioned before, he distinguishes between two fundamental types, the extraverted and the introverted, determined according to whether the general mental energy of the individual is directed outwards to the visible, actual world, or inward to the world of thought and imagery. These two fundamental types are further subdivided into types determined by the functions of thinking, feeling, sensation, and intuition, but the psychological types so determined do not form hard-and-fast categories into which the whole of humanity can be classified: they are merely indications of extensive divisions which merge one into another. But in our particular sphere they do supply a scientific basis for the description of literary types. You will find, for example, that the romantic artist always expresses some function of the extraverted attitude, whilst the classic artist always expresses some function of the introverted attitude. Now this suggests that the critic, like the psychologist, should take up a position above the conflict, and although his own psychological state may lead him to sympathize with one school or the other, yet as a scientific critic he must no longer be content with a dog-in-the-manger attitude. Again, he must broaden the basis of his criticism: he must see the romantic and classic elements in literature as the natural expression of a biological opposition in human nature. It is not sufficient to treat the matter one way or the other as a question of intellectual fallacy; it is a question, for the individual, of natural necessity; and criticism must finally, for its general basis, resort to some criterion above the individual.

I would like to indicate, in conclusion, what I think might be a fruitful direction for further work in the application of psycho-analysis to literature. Recent theories explain memory, and indeed most of the characteristics of mind, on a basis of physiological "traces" left by experience. Experience may be individual or collective, and what happens individually must also happen collectively, and those instincts and experiences incidental to the struggle for adaptation and existence leave their traces on the mind when, and in so far as, it functions collectively. The accretion of innumerable traces ensures a set response to environment. A given physical structure of the brain results in certain inevitable forms of thought, and these Jung, following Burckhardt, calls primordial images. Such images eventually crystallize as myths and religions,[15] and psychology has already devoted a good deal of attention to the relation of such myths and religions to the unconscious processes of which they are the expression. Sometimes these collective ideas or primordial images find expression in literature, which, from an evolutionary point of view, has been regarded as a rational mythology.[16] Jung quotes from a letter of Burckhardt's these very suggestive sentences:

> What you are destined to find in *Faust*, that you will find by intuition. *Faust* is nothing else than pure and legitimate myth, a great primitive conception, so to speak, in which everyone can divine in his own way his own nature and destiny. Allow me to make a comparison: What would the ancient Greeks have said had a commentator interposed himself between them and the Oedipus legend? There was a chord of the Oedipus legend in every Greek which longed to be touched directly and respond in its own way. And thus it is with the German nation and *Faust*.[17]

This train of thought, allied to what we know of the possibilities of psychoanalysis in dealing with myths, seems to suggest the further possibility of relating the types actualized by the poetic imagination to their origin in the root-images of the community. In this way criticism would possess still another basic reality on which it could ground the imaginative hypotheses of art. Whether criticism, under the guidance of psycho-analysis, could go still further and indicate the needs of the collective mind, is perhaps too venturesome a suggestion to make. But with the advance of reason we have lost the main historic content of the collective mind: the symbols of religion are no longer effective because they are no longer unconscious. We still, however, retain structural features of the mind that cry for definite satisfaction. The modern world is uneasy because it is the expression of an unappeased hunger. We need some unanimity to focus the vague desires that exist in the collective mind. Will the psychologist unite with the critic to define and to solve this problem?

---

[15] This process, however, should not be held to exclude the possibility of the specific origin of myths. The opposition recently created between psycho-analysts and ethnologists of the Manchester school is largely fictitious. The origin of the myth may be a plain event devoid of psychological significance: the elaboration of this event into a mythical structure, often over a period of many years, even centuries, may all the same be a process for which we should seek an explanation in psychology.

[16] *Cf.* Th. Ribot, *Essai sur l'Imagination Créatrice*, Paris, 1900, p. 114: "La Littérature est une mythologie déchue et rationalisée."

[17] C. G. Jung, *Psychology of the Unconscious*, English edition, 1918, p. 490.

Faith and Art in a World Awry

NATHAN A. SCOTT, JR.

WHAT is in view when I speak of a theology of the imagination, is not anything so grandiose as might require to be spoken of as a "Christian philosophy of art." It is true, of course, that in the theological forum today one sometimes overhears expressions of confidence in the possibility and imperativeness of developing what is called by some a Christian philosophy of art. And though I shall not here attempt fully to explicate the theological grounds from which my own reservations about this kind of project stem, I do want, at least, to say flatly that I do not conceive it to be the business of the Christian, of the man whom Kierkegaard called "the knight of faith," to bully the world into granting its suffrage to some special system of propositions of his own invention. For he does not come into this world from another world like a *deus ex machina,* with a marvelous formula that can unlock all the entanglements of human culture. No, he lives in the historical order like all his fellows: the resource on which he relies is simply that particular hope and confidence to which he is given access in this world by reason of what he knows God to have done for this world. And, having this resource, his single vocation is to live, as did Jesus the Lord, in solicitude for, and in openness to, the men to whom he is related by the particular moment in history in which he happens to stand.

The Christian scholar faces the same world that is faced by all other men; and I believe it is outrageous arrogance for him to assume that his faith provides him with some sort of privileged perspective by means of which he can integrate internally the various fields of culture and then assign to each its proper place is some tidily comprehensive arrangement that will be a Christian map of the modern mind. Indeed, for him even to attempt to produce some special *speculum mentis* for his brethren in the faith is for him profoundly to misunderstand the nature of the intellectual situation in which he must today do his work. And, here, surely the endless multiplication of metaphors based on the I-Thou

430

philosophy of Martin Buber is something which witnesses to a deep and pervasive intuition among the most sensitive men of our age that the fragmentation of modern intellectual life commits us irrevocably to an ethos of encounter and to the stance of attentiveness and listening. It is, I take it, the recognition of precisely this that lies behind Roger Hazelton's recent definition of what the theological enterprise must entail in our time. He turns to the physiological image of the systole and diastole of the human heart and suggests that the work of the Christian theologian is, in a way, analogous to the alternate expansions and contractions of the heart. "There are times," he says, "when Christian faith has to turn inward upon itself, asking what is authentically and ultimately its own kind of truth. Then theology becomes an essay in self-discovery and self-definition." But then there are other times when "it becomes imperative for theologians to move out into the world again, on the basis of this self-understanding, seeking out and coming to grips with those modes of truth from which earlier they had strategically withdrawn." And Dr. Hazelton is alert to the fact that it is into this second phase that the theological community is moving. Nor does he see the reasons for this as being wholly cultural in character, for he takes careful cognizance of what it is in the nature of Christian faith itself that requires the attitude of attentiveness and listening to the world of culture. "Living within the circle of faith," he says, "involves the most drastic sort of exposure to unwelcome experience and unfamiliar truth. It finds charity and hope to be not simply moral but also intellectual virtues."[1]

So it would seem to behoove the Christian in his intellectual existence not to segregate himself from anyone and not to suppose that he has been given exclusive charge of the truth about any segment of human reality. In other words, he had better not come prancing into the forums of our cultural life with a Christian system of aesthetics or with a Christian system of psychology or with a Christian system of anything else. For the world is one, the same for the Christian as for all other men of whatever persuasion: if Christ is truly the *Logos*, then He is witnessed to in all apprehensions of truth, whether they occur within a framework of Christian concern or not. And, this being the case, the Christian theologian will not be in a hurry to sponsor any particular system as necessarily *the* Christian way of ordering the data in a given field of inquiry. For he will understand that the fundamental issue for Christian thought pertains not to any conceptual structure but rather, as Ronald Gregor Smith of Glasgow has said, to the question "Whence do we receive?"[2] So, then, instead of attempting to put forward anything that might be called a Christian philosophy of art, it may well be that at present the more fruitful task for the Christian humanist is the more modest task of clearly discerning what in fact the function of art truly is and how it touches the kind of imagination of reality that is distinctively Christian.

Now, in attempting to define what it is the ultimate office of art to do, it is important to avoid at least one of the answers which has continually recurred

[1] Roger Hazelton, *New Accents in Contemporary Theology* (New York, Harper, 1960), pp. 11–12.

[2] Ronald Gregor Smith, "A Theological Perspective of the Secular," *The Christian Scholar*, **43** (1960), 14.

in the history of aesthetics; and this is the doctrine which, in one way or another, asserts that a work of art is an expression of the artist's subjectivity, or, as it has often been put, of his emotion. The perennial attractiveness of this doctrine is, doubtless, in large part a result of the fact that we know both the creative process and the aesthetic experience to be suffused with emotion; and when a work of art is of unquestioned greatness, it does indeed very often stem from and elicit emotion of the intensest sort. But, however much emotion may be a factor both in the act of artistic creation and in the act of aesthetic appreciation, the fact remains that, finally, all emotionalist theories of art are both internally illogical and essentially untrue to the experience that we actually have when we are in the presence of a work of art that is capable of deeply engaging the imagination. The emotionalist theory is internally illogical, because it succeeds in doing precisely what it is unreasonable to expect an aesthetic theory to do—namely, to dissolve itself into some field of discourse that is not aesthetical but something else. That is to say, in viewing the work of art as significant because of what it tells us about the emotional condition of the artist, an expressionist aesthetic is always tending to convert aesthetics into a branch of psychology and thus to destroy the vital nerve of its own integrity as an independent field of humanistic inquiry. I speak of the emotionalist theory of art as untrue to our profoundest aesthetic experience because I am convinced that this is an experience which we deem to be of such high importance not at all by reason of any information it conveys about the artist, for what is exhilarating in our encounter with an authentic work of art is always the clarification and deepening we feel in our perception of the realities that constitute our world-environment. The aesthetic experience might be said always to involve an experience of what Paul Tillich calls "the shock of being,"[3] and this may be why Jacques Maritain tells us that, "Poetry is ontology."

Of course, when Maritain speaks of poetry as ontology, he does not intend to imply that the operation which the poet performs is identical, in its kind or agency, with the operation that is performed by a philosopher. For, unlike the philosopher, the poet does not deal with *generalizations* about anything at all: his mode of statement, as Susanne Langer says in *Feeling and Form*, is a "non-discursive" mode. He does not discourse, for example, about the mortality of the human creature with the funereal air of a young parson: no, Shakespeare simply says:

> Golden lads and girls all must,
> As chimney-sweepers, come to dust.

Nor does he talk about the internal complications of the mind in the labored, discursive manner of the academic psychologist: no, Hopkins tells us:

> O the mind, mind has mountains; cliffs of fall
> Frightful, sheer, no-man-fathomed. Hold them cheap
> May who ne'er hung there. Nor does long our small
> Durance deal with that steep or deep.

[3] See Paul Tillich, *The Protestant Era* (1948), p. 85; also *Systematic Theology, 1* (1951), pp. 110–15, 163; both published by the University of Chicago Press.

In short, the poet's purpose is to reveal to us the stark irrevocability of things as they are. And "things" is the word we must use, for it is with things that the poetic transaction is carried on, since, as I suspect, it is in things that Being has its location. It is the poet's habit to be fascinated with *the singular*—with the particular event, the unrepeatable experience, the unique reality. "The texture of poetry is of actual things," says Hugh McCarron in his fine little book *Realization*. And we should not forget that Homer dealt with the ocean and Wordsworth with the farmland and Gerard Manley Hopkins with "the dearest freshness deep down things." So, too, has the imagination of all true poets been captured by things, by that which is *other than* the human mind. Indeed, it is "the wonder and mystery of art," as it is also of religion in the last analysis, that it "is the revelation of something 'wholly other' by which the inexpressible loneliness of thinking is broken and enriched."

Poetry does not, characteristically, handle universals: instead, as H. D. Lewis has remarked, it "uncovers for us the character of particular things in the starkness and strangeness of their being what they are."[4] And this is why the scientist, and the philosopher who conceives of philosophy as a handmaiden of science, tend to view the poet with misgivings, for the poet remains incorrigibly devoted to celebrating that rich complexity of the singular which always resists domestication within the abstract systems of scientific and philosophic ideas. We have long said that poetry's great gift to man is an affair of *katharsis,* and it may well be that that experience involves, fundamentally, the profound relief that is to be had when we succeed in gaining such release from the prison of the mind as enables us simply to contemplate the intractable givenness of reality, as this objectiveness transcends all our scientific and philosophic propositions about it, and our efforts at poetic evocation of it, making its majesty known through what Hegel called the "concrete universal."

Now, of course, modern aestheticians since Kant have often said something quite different about art—namely (as A. C. Bradley put it), that "its nature is to be not a part, nor yet a copy, of the real world . . . but to be a world by itself, independent, complete, autonomous." And this too is true. Indeed, here we come upon what is perhaps the central paradox that art presents. For, on the one hand, we must never forget that it does establish a world of its own, and, as Bradley said, "to possess it fully, you must enter that world, conform to its laws, and ignore for the time the beliefs, aims, and particular conditions which belong to you in the other world of reality."[5] On the other hand, it is equally true (and true perhaps in a very much larger order of magnitude) that the greatest and most vital art always drives us beyond itself and makes us contemplate anew, with a shock of discovery, the permanence and glory and strangeness of the circumambient world. Its purpose is to stir and quicken within us an awareness of realities that impinge upon us from beyond ourselves. It wants, as it were, to make all things new, in order that we might marvel at the sheer thereness of them, at the fact that they exist in one way rather than in a thousand other

---

[4] Lewis, *Morals and Revelation*, pp. 241, 212.

[5] A. C. Bradley, *Oxford Lectures on Poetry* (London, Macmillan, 1909), p. 5.

possible ways. "To know facts as facts in the ordinary way has, indeed, no particular power or worth. But," H. D. Lewis says, "a quickening of our awareness of the irrevocability by which a thing is what it is has such power, and it is . . . the very soul of art."[6] For the poet, as Marianne Moore puts it, is a "literalist of the imagination" who presents "for inspection 'imaginary gardens with real toads in them.' " That is, although he creates a kind of fiction, it is a fiction intended to be a vehicle by means of which there may be conveyed to us a haunting sense of some otherness in reality which impinges upon us and with which we must risk a confrontation.

Now I wonder if it is not precisely this sense of otherness in reality to which religious faith itself conduces. Gregor Smith tells us that our ultimate theological concern has to do with what is not ourselves, with what we "do not and never can possess at all," with what comes to us "all the time from beyond."[7] And this is indeed the import of vital religion. Becket, in Eliot's *Murder in the Cathedral*, says at one point:

> Only
> The fool, fixed in his folly, may think
> He can turn the wheel on which he turns.

And it is some such realization as this that all great religion promotes: it brings us news of a reality beyond all the extremities of human thought and calculation, and it speaks of a world which moves to "a rhythm which is neither the strophe nor the antistrophe of our mortal music."[8] So, though a certain kind of Philistine hostility to the arts may sometimes be expressed under the guise of having religion's sanction, the truth of the matter is that both art and religious faith share a common intention to summon us into the presence of what is other than, and transcendent to, the human mind; and, in this, they provide each other with a kind of mutual confirmation.

But, in the particular kind of faith that Christianity entails, it is not simply sheer otherness that is confronted, however much the early teachings of Karl Barth may have seemed to represent this as being the Christian's situation. For, in the world of Christian experience, the otherness which confronts and which challenges man becomes luminously transparent in the incarnate Word of God which was Jesus Christ Himself. Which is to say that, for the Christian imagination, the ultimate reality—which is the reality of God—is disclosed in the person and in the life of Jesus Christ. And this means that, when human life is understood within the terms of the Christian faith, the primary axiom of all thought henceforward becomes the premise that what it is important for man to know about the meaning of his existence is made manifest in Jesus the Lord. In Him all Christian reflection finds its basic fulcrum, for He is the transparent center and focus of that disturbing otherness which surrounds us and pursues us and requires of us an appropriate acknowledgment.

[6] Lewis, pp. 241, 242.

[7] Smith, p. 15.

[8] M. Chaning-Pearce, *The Terrible Crystal* (New York, Oxford University Press, 1941), p. 143.

There is no one to whom I have been more indebted for deepening my understanding of this central reality of Christian faith than to Dietrich Bonhoeffer. Above all else, what I owe to Bonhoeffer is the realization that what we meet in Jesus Christ is not the old metaphysical riddle of how the two natures, the divine and the human, could co-inhere in one person. Nor should it be supposed that Bonhoeffer's refusal to fidget over this ancient puzzle was the result of any intellectual indolence which made him want to find excuses for evading the hard, exacting labor of reading the history of Christian theology. Indeed, it was just as a result of the most careful study of the theological tradition that he reached a conclusion the revolutionary consequences of which for Christian thought in our time are only beginning to be felt. His conclusion was that on this one point the tradition has often been woefully misguided: for, said he, what we meet in Jesus Christ is not a metaphysical enigma but the simple fact of a human life that was totally pledged in responsibility for others, a life indeed so concentrated in the selflessness of its concern for all other life that it had the consequence of disclosing to the community of faith the tremendous fact that in His life the essential structure of all life had been revealed. And to this essential structure of responsible life as bound to man and to God Bonhoeffer applied the term "deputyship." For this, he declared, is the form that life takes when it is lived responsibly: one person or one group of persons acts *for* another: when a "father acts for the children, working for them, caring for them, interceding, fighting and suffering for them . . . in a real sense he is their deputy." Indeed, whenever and wherever life surrenders itself in obedience to the needs and claims of other life, there you have deputyship. And here, said Bonhoeffer, is the essential truth about Jesus Christ, that He "lived in deputyship for us as the incarnate Son of God," and, since "His living, His action and His dying was deputyship," in Him we have "the responsible person *par excellence*": "in Him there is fulfilled what the living, the action and the suffering of men ought to be."[9]

When Paul in his *Epistle to the Philippians* (1:21) tells us that "to me to live is Christ," he is simply saying, both for himself and for other men, that, insofar as we do truly live, we live in and through Christ, for He *is* life. That is, life is deputyship, or—as it was put by the Jewish thinker Martin Buber, who had a remarkable gift for expressing a sense of reality deeply akin to the Christian— real life is "meeting."[10] This is what Christ reveals the fundamental form of reality to be. And faith, as Bonhoeffer taught us to understand, is not so much believing difficult propositions about ghostly things as it is life lived in "correspondence" with the form that Christ disclosed reality to have: the real man, as he liked to say, is "the man for others."

Now I have spoken of the dimension of otherness into which we are brought by both art and religious faith. But, as I have said, in the Christian apprehension of reality, this is an otherness whose essential character is disclosed in the person and in the life of Jesus Christ. For in Him the Christian imagination beholds the fundamental form of reality—which, adopting a central term of

[9] Bonhoeffer, *Ethics*, pp. 194–95.

[10] See Martin Buber, *I and Thou*, trans. Ronald Gregor Smith (Edinburgh, Clark, 1937).

the late Charles Williams, we may call "exchange,"[11] or, following Martin Buber, meeting; or which we may call deputyship or, as Dietrich Bonhoeffer sometimes spoke of it, "life together."

When, however, we move from any authentically Christian account of life to that which is recorded in the representative art and literature of our period, it becomes immediately apparent that here a quite different form of reality is presented as normative in human experience. Not life together, but life fractured and broken into isolateness and solitude and loneliness: this is the reality which makes up the special kind of pathos that we meet in the most characteristic art of our time.

From the painting of this century one recalls, for example—and inevitably— those great Cubist canvases of the early Picasso in which the human image is either shattered utterly or is forsaken altogether for the pastiche of newspaper clippings and odd bits of junk extracted from some scrap heap. Or, there are those dreadful and wonderfully fascinating double-faced images which he was painting in the nineteen-thirties and which figure forth the awful dragons of the inner life that must be captured in us all. And, then, there is that beautiful and horrible immensity in black and white and gray, the *Guernica* mural, which brings to a kind of climax the scenes of disorder which the artists of our time have painted; it is a canvas which is ostensibly about a particular moment in the modern agony but which, once we have really confronted it, makes us know that it is about the whole eschatological furnace of our age. It has some-times been said that what is most essential in Picasso is a "taste for paroxysm," but, in a way, this seems also to be what is most essential in such men as Kokoschka and Beckmann and Rouault, who were his contemporaries, and in the later generation of Pollock and de Kooning, whose vision is felt with especial immediacy at the present time. Indeed, these and many others have often been navigators negotiating a voyage that has skirted most narrowly the brink of the chaos which has threatened to overwhelm us all.

And not only have our painters fought battles with the dragons of the inner life, but so too have our poets and our novelists and dramatists. The age has been rife with nervous disorder and panic, with exile and excruciating anxieties. And it should therefore be no occasion of surprise when these are the themes that we encounter in our literature. Here is a sentence, for example, from a novel, *On This Side Nothing,* by the English writer, Alex Comfort, and it takes us immediately into the ethos which the representative writers of our age have been exploring: "I saw the same fear in her face that I should have felt if a stranger called at night, the world-wide twentieth-century fear which one sees wherever one knocks unexpectedly at any door." This is the face of the con-temporary hero, whether one encounters him in the plays of Beckett and Ionesco, or in the novels of Faulkner and Camus, or in the poetry of Penn Warren and Gottfried Benn. Here and there, to be sure, there have been a few writers— like Eliot and Edith Sitwell of the older generation, or Auden and Christopher Fry of the middle generation, or Robert Lowell of a still younger group—who

[11] See Charles Williams, *The Image of the City—And Other Essays* (London, Oxford University Press, 1958), Sec. V.

found sustenance in a traditional faith. But by far the great majority of those on the contemporary scene who exemplify our period-style are writers who live in much the same ambiance as that with which we associate the great classic moderns, Kafka and Pound and Joyce and Hemingway. For the fundamental form of the human reality, as they report upon it, is that of disruption and anxiety and nostalgia and loneliness.

When, therefore, the Christian community faces the whole body of testimony issuing from much of the great art of the modern period, it is confronted by a diametrical opposition between the form of reality that it knows to be the true norm of human existence and that which tends generally to be cited by the artists of our time. Yet surely it would be a great mistake for churchmen simply to reject this testimony and to withdraw into the stiff, imperious certitudes of those theologians who write systems of Church dogmatics and who expatiate on the divine-human encounter. Indeed, were this to be the prevailing Christian response to the modern movement in art, nothing would more tellingly indicate that ours is today a Church which has forgotten the Cross and all that it implies for Christian participation in the life of culture. For if, in the words of Charles Gore, the Church is an "extension and perpetuation of the Incarnation in the world"[12] (and the formula has, I suppose, at best a limited usefulness), then its relation to the world must be wholly governed by God's relation to the world, as this was disclosed in Christ Himself, and most especially in His Crucifixion. In other words, the Church is the community that lives under the Cross—it is the community which knows the fundamental form of reality to be that of deputyship, of living and acting for others. It is also, of course, the community in which there is knowledge of the "last things,"—of the fact that the final and ultimate word to be pronounced on the human situation is that man shall be justified by grace and faith alone. But, when it seeks the kind of profound identification with the world that the message of the Crucifixion demands, it may then, for the very sake of the ultimate truth about human existence, choose not to speak about last things but rather to open itself up to what Dietrich Bonhoeffer called "the things which go before the last things"—those difficult "penultimate" experiences of humanity which are the real *preparatio* for the Gospel of Jesus Christ.[13] Indeed, the Christian community should never fail to heed Bonhoeffer's wise warning against speaking of the last things too soon. "I don't think it is Christian," he said, "to want to get to the New Testament too soon and too directly."[14] And what he meant is simply that if the Christian community closets itself in safety away from what is broken and problematic in human life then the ultimate message of the Gospel will never be grasped in its *relevance* to man's deepest predicaments. Christ's coming in grace is, to be sure, the very last thing, but we shall perceive the power and the apposite-

---

[12] Charles Gore, *The Incarnation of the Son of God* (London, John Murray, 1891), p. 219. The formula is of limited usefulness because, though it does a rough kind of justice to the doctrine of the Mystical Body, it very seriously fails to make adequate provision for the possibility of the Church itself falling under judgment.

[13] See Bonhoeffer, *Ethics*, pp. 84–91.

[14] Bonhoeffer, *Letters*, p. 50.

ness of this ultimacy only insofar as we remain attentive to everything that is penultimate in the human story.

Therefore, on the particular frontier of culture which is here in view, the task of those who are custodians of the Christian faith in our time is not, I think, to invent something called a Christian *philosophy* of art, and thus to add to the Babel of conflicting philosophies which so much oppresses us today. We shall want, I should think, a vigorous Christian criticism in the various fields of art, and there are signs, particularly in the field of literature, that this is an effort which is beginning to be undertaken with intelligence and discrimination —and we shall want to search after something like a theology of the imagination. But a Christian philosophy of art, in the sense of a systematic phenomenology of aesthetic facts which consistently proceeds from Christian presuppositions, is not to be expected from anyone on the theological scene today of whom I have any knowledge; and I suspect that there are difficult jurisdictional questions of a theoretical order that may, in principle, rule out even the possibility of such a project. But, were it theoretically possible and were it something which we might reasonably expect the best theological intelligence of our day in time to deliver, I should still, from a strategic standpoint, question its real value at this particular juncture in our cultural life. For that which is most needed, I believe, is for theological interpreters to keep the Church alive to what in the nature of its own faith requires it to be attentive to all the somber reports and prophecies and maledictions that the arts in our time are uttering. And, if this effort is attended with success, so that the Christian community does really appear once again to be a community of deputyship, of those who are for others, then it may well be that the artist may be persuaded to move beyond what is penultimate to the things that are really the last things.

The Science of the Concrete

CLAUDE LEVI-STRAUSS

I AM not however commending a return to the popular belief (although it has some validity in its own narrow context) according to which magic is a timid and stuttering form of science. One deprives oneself of all means of understanding magical thought if one tries to reduce it to a moment or stage in technical and scientific evolution. Like a shadow moving ahead of its owner it is in a sense complete in itself, and as finished and coherent in its immateriality as the substantial being which it precedes. Magical thought is not to be regarded as a beginning, a rudiment, a sketch, a part of a whole which has not yet materialized. It forms a well-articulated system, and is in this respect independent of that other system which constitutes science, except for the purely formal analogy which brings them together and makes the former a sort of metaphorical expression of the latter. It is therefore better, instead of contrasting magic and science, to compare them as two parallel modes of acquiring knowledge. Their theoretical and practical results differ in value, for it is true that science is more successful than magic from this point of view, although magic foreshadows science in that it is sometimes also successful. Both science and magic however require the same sort of mental operations and they differ not so much in kind as in the different types of phenomena to which they are applied.

These relations are a consequence of the objective conditions in which magic and scientific knowledge appeared. The history of the latter is short enough for us to know a good deal about it. But the fact that modern science dates back only a few centuries raises a problem which ethnologists have not sufficiently pondered. The Neolithic Paradox would be a suitable name for it.

It was in neolithic times that man's mastery of the great arts of civilization—

of pottery, weaving, agriculture and the domestication of animals—became firmly established. No one today would any longer think of attributing these enormous advances to the fortuitous accumulation of a series of chance discoveries or believe them to have been revealed by the passive perception of certain natural phenomena.[1]

Each of these techniques assumes centuries of active and methodical observation, of bold hypotheses tested by means of endlessly repeated experiments. A biologist remarks on the rapidity with which plants from the New World have been acclimatized in the Philippines and adopted and named by the natives. In many cases they seem even to have rediscovered their medicinal uses, uses identical with those traditional in Mexico. Fox's interpretation is this:

> ... plants with bitter leaves or stems are commonly used in the Philippines for stomach disorders. If an introduced plant is found to have this characteristic, it will be quickly utilized. The fact that many Philippine groups, such as the Pinatubo Negritos, constantly experiment with plants hastens the process of the recognition of the potential usefulness, as defined by the culture, of the introduced flora (R. B. Fox, pp. 212–13).

To transform a weed into a cultivated plant, a wild beast into a domestic animal, to produce, in either of these, nutritious or technologically useful properties which were originally completely absent or could only be guessed at; to make stout, water-tight pottery out of clay which is friable and unstable, liable to pulverize or crack (which, however, is possible only if from a large number of organic and inorganic materials, the one most suitable for refining it is selected, and also the appropriate fuel, the temperature and duration of firing and the effective degree of oxidation); to work out techniques, often long and complex, which permit cultivation without soil or alternatively without water; to change toxic roots or seeds into foodstuffs or again to use their poison for hunting, war or ritual—there is no doubt that all these achievements required a genuinely scientific attitude, sustained and watchful interest and a desire for knowledge for its own sake. For only a small proportion of observations and experiments (which must be assumed to have been primarily inspired by a desire for knowledge) could have yielded practical and immediately useful results. There is no need to dwell on the working of bronze and iron and of precious metals or even the simple working of copper ore by hammering which preceded metallurgy by several thousand years, and even at that stage they all demand a very high level of technical proficiency.

[1] An attempt has been made to discover what would happen if copper ore had accidentally found its way into a furnace: complex and varied experiments have shown that nothing happens at all. The simplest method of obtaining metallic copper which could be discovered consisted in subjecting finely ground malachite to intense heat in a pottery dish crowned with an inverted clay pot. This, the sole result, restricts the play of chance to the confines of the kiln of some potter specializing in glazed ware (Coghlan).

Neolithic, or early historical, man was therefore the heir of a long scientific tradition. However, had he, as well as all his predecessors, been inspired by exactly the same spirit as that of our own time, it would be impossible to understand how he could have come to a halt and how several thousand years of stagnation have intervened between the neolithic revolution and modern science like a level plain between ascents. There is only one solution to the paradox, namely, that there are two distinct modes of scientific thought. These are certainly not a function of different stages of development of the human mind but rather of two strategic levels at which nature is accessible to scientific enquiry: one roughly adapted to that of perception and the imagination: the other at a remove from it. It is as if the necessary connections which are the object of all science, neolithic or modern, could be arrived at by two different routes, one very close to, and the other more remote from, sensible intuition.

Any classification is superior to chaos and even a classification at the level of sensible properties is a step towards rational ordering. It is legitimate, in classifying fruits into relatively heavy and relatively light, to begin by separating the apples from the pears even though shape, colour and taste are unconnected with weight and volume. This is because the larger apples are easier to distinguish from the smaller if the apples are not still mixed with fruit of different features. This example already shows that classification has its advantages even at the level of aesthetic perception.

For the rest, and in spite of the fact there is no necessary connection between sensible qualities and properties, there is very often at least an empirical connection between them, and the generalization of this relation may be rewarding from the theoretical and practical point of view for a very long time even if it has no foundation in reason. Not all poisonous juices are burning or bitter nor is everything which is burning and bitter poisonous. Nevertheless, nature is so constituted that it is more advantageous if thought and action proceed as though this aesthetically satisfying equivalence also corresponded to objective reality. It seems probable, for reasons which are not relevant here, that species possessing some remarkable characteristics, say, of shape, colour or smell give the observer what might be called a 'right pending disproof' to postulate that these visible characteristics are the sign of equally singular, but concealed, properties. To treat the relation between the two as itself sensible (regarding a seed in the form of a tooth as a safeguard against snake bites, yellow juices as a cure for bilious troubles, etc.) is of more value provisionally than indifference to any connection. For even a heterogeneous and arbitrary classification preserves the richness and diversity of the collection of facts it makes. The decision that everything must be taken account of facilitates the creation of a 'memory bank'.

It is moreover a fact that particular results, to the achievement of which methods of this kind were able to lead, were essential to enable man to assail nature from a different angle. Myths and rites are far from being, as has often been held, the product of man's 'myth-making faculty',[2] turning its back on

---

[2] The phrase is from Bergson, *op. cit.*, 'fonction fabulatrice' (trans. note).

reality. Their principal value is indeed to preserve until the present time the remains of methods of observation and reflection which were (and no doubt still are) precisely adapted to discoveries of a certain type: those which nature authorised from the starting point of a speculative organization and exploitation of the sensible world in sensible terms. This science of the concrete was necessarily restricted by its essence to results other than those destined to be achieved by the exact natural sciences but it was no less scientific and its results no less genuine. They were secured ten thousand years earlier and still remain at the basis of our own civilization.

There still exists among ourselves an activity which on the technical plane gives us quite a good understanding of what a science we prefer to call 'prior' rather than 'primitive', could have been on the plane of speculation. This is what is commonly called 'bricolage' in French. In its old sense the verb 'bricoler' applied to ball games and billiards, to hunting, shooting and riding. It was however always used with reference to some extraneous movement: a ball rebounding, a dog straying or a horse swerving from its direct course to avoid an obstacle. And in our own time the 'bricoleur' is still someone who works with his hands and uses devious means compared to those of a craftsman.[3] The characteristic feature of mythical thought is that it expresses itself by means of a heterogeneous repertoire which, even if extensive, is nevertheless limited. It has to use this repertoire, however, whatever the task in hand because it has nothing else at its disposal. Mythical thought is therefore a kind of intellectual 'bricolage'—which explains the relation which can be perceived between the two.

Like 'bricolage' on the technical plane, mythical reflection can reach brilliant unforeseen results on the intellectual plane. Conversely, attention has often been drawn to the mytho-poetical nature of 'bricolage' on the plane of so-called 'raw' or 'naive' art, in architectural follies like the villa of Cheval the postman or the stage sets of Georges Méliès, or, again, in the case immortalized by Dickens in *Great Expectations* but no doubt originally inspired by observation, of Mr. Wemmick's suburban 'castle' with its miniature drawbridge, its cannon firing at nine o'clock, its bed of salad and cucumbers, thanks to which its occupants could withstand a siege if necessary . . . .

The analogy is worth pursuing since it helps us to see the real relations between the two types of scientific knowledge we have distinguished. The 'bricoleur' is adept at performing a large number of diverse tasks; but, unlike the engineer, he does not subordinate each of them to the availability of raw materials and tools conceived and procured for the purpose of the project. His universe of instruments is closed and the rules of his game are always to make do with 'whatever is at hand', that is to say with a set of tools and materials which is always finite and is also heterogeneous because what it contains bears

---

[3] The 'bricoleur' has no precise equivalent in English. He is a man who undertakes odd jobs and is a Jack of all trades or a kind of professional do-it-yourself man, but, as the text makes clear, he is of a different standing from, for instance, the English 'odd job man' or handyman (trans note).

no relation to the current project, or indeed to any particular project, but is the contingent result of all the occasions there have been to renew or enrich the stock or to maintain it with the remains of previous constructions or destructions. The set of the 'bricoleur's' means cannot therefore be defined in terms of a project (which would presuppose besides, that, as in the case of the engineer, there were, at least in theory, as many sets of tools and materials or 'instrumental sets', as there are different kinds of projects). It is to be defined only by its potential use or, putting this another way and in the language of the 'bricoleur' himself, because the elements are collected or retained on the principle that 'they may always come in handy'. Such elements are specialized up to a point, sufficiently for the 'bricoleur' not to need the equipment and knowledge of all trades and professions, but not enough for each of them to have only one definite and determinate use. They each represent a set of actual and possible relations; they are 'operators' but they can be used for any operations of the same type.

The elements of mythical thought similarly lie half-way between percepts and concepts. It would be impossible to separate percepts from the concrete situations in which they appeared, while recourse to concepts would require that thought could, at least provisionally, put its projects (to use Husserl's expression) 'in brackets'. Now, there is an intermediary between images and concepts, namely signs. For signs can always be defined in the way introduced by Saussure in the case of the particular category of linguistic signs, that is, as a link between images and concepts. In the union thus brought about, images and concepts play the part of the signifying and signified respectively.

Signs resemble images in being concrete entities but they resemble concepts in their powers of reference. Neither concepts nor signs relate exclusively to themselves; either may be substituted for something else. Concepts, however, have an unlimited capacity in this respect, while signs have not. The example of the 'bricoleur' helps to bring out the differences and similarities. Consider him at work and excited by his project. His first practical step is retrospective. He has to turn back to an already existent set made up of tools and materials, to consider or reconsider what it contains and, finally and above all, to engage in a sort of dialogue with it and, before choosing between them, to index the possible answers which the whole set can offer to his problem. He interrogates all the heterogeneous objects of which his treasury[4] is composed to discover what each of them could 'signify' and so contribute to the definition of a set which has yet to materialize but which will ultimately differ from the instrumental set only in the internal disposition of its parts. A particular cube of oak could be a wedge to make up for the inadequate length of a plank of pine or it could be a pedestal—which would allow the grain and polish of the old wood to show to advantage. In one case it will serve as extension, in the other as material. But the possibilities always remain limited by the particular history of each piece and by those of its features which are already determined by the use for which it was originally intended or the modifications it has undergone

---

[4] Cf. 'Treasury of ideas' as Hubert and Mauss so aptly describe magic (2, p. 136).

for other purposes. The elements which the 'bricoleur' collects and uses are 'pre-constrained' like the constitutive units of myth, the possible combinations of which are restricted by the fact that they are drawn from the language where they already possess a sense which sets a limit on their freedom of manoeuvre (Lévi-Strauss, 5, p. 35). And the decision as to what to put in each place also depends on the possibility of putting a different element there instead, so that each choice which is made will involve a complete reorganization of the structure, which will never be the same as one vaguely imagined nor as some other which might have been preferred to it.

The engineer no doubt also cross-examines his resources. The existence of an 'interlocutor' is in his case due to the fact that his means, power and knowledge are never unlimited and that in this negative form he meets resistance with which he has to come to terms. It might be said that the engineer questions the universe, while the 'bricoleur' addresses himself to a collection of oddments left over from human endeavours, that is, only a sub-set of the culture. Again, Information Theory shows that it is possible, and often useful, to reduce the physicists' approaches to a sort of dialogue with nature. This would make the distinction we are trying to draw less clearcut. There remains however a difference even if one takes into account the fact that the scientist never carries on a dialogue with nature pure and simple but rather with a particular relationship between nature and culture definable in terms of his particular period and civilization and the material means at his disposal. He is no more able than the 'bricoleur' to do whatever he wishes when he is presented with a given task. He too has to begin by making a catalogue of a previously determined set consisting of theoretical and practical knowledge, of technical means, which restrict the possible solutions.

The difference is therefore less absolute than it might appear. It remains a real one, however, in that the engineer is always trying to make his way out of and go beyond the constraints imposed by a particular state of civilization while the 'bricoleur' by inclination or necessity always remains within them. This is another way of saying that the engineer works by means of concepts and the 'bricoleur' by means of signs. The sets which each employs are at different distances from the poles on the axis of opposition between nature and culture. One way indeed in which signs can be opposed to concepts is that whereas concepts aim to be wholly transparent with respect to reality, signs allow and even require the interposing and incorporation of a certain amount of human culture into reality. Signs, in Peirce's vigorous phrase 'address somebody'.

Both the scientist and 'bricoleur' might therefore be said to be constantly on the look out for 'messages'. Those which the 'bricoleur' collects are, however, ones which have to some extent been transmitted in advance—like the commercial codes which are summaries of the past experience of the trade and so allow any new situation to be met economically, provided that it belongs to the same class as some earlier one. The scientist, on the other hand, whether he is an engineer or a physicist, is always on the look out for *that other message* which might be wrested from an interlocutor in spite of his reticence in pronouncing on questions whose answers have not been rehearsed. Concepts thus appear like operators *opening up* the set being worked with and signification like the operator of its *reorganization,* which neither extends nor renews it and limits itself to obtaining the group of its transformations.

Images cannot be ideas but they can play the part of signs or, to be more precise, co-exist with ideas in signs and, if ideas are not yet present, they can keep their future place open for them and make its contours apparent negatively. Images are fixed, linked in a single way to the mental act which accompanies them. Signs, and images which have acquired significance, may still lack comprehension; unlike concepts, they do not yet possess simultaneous and theoretically unlimited relations with other entities of the same kind. They are however already *permutable,* that is, capable of standing in successive relations with other entities—although with only a limited number and, as we have seen, only on the condition that they always form a system in which an alteration which affects one element automatically affects all the others. On this plane logicians' 'extension' and 'intension' are not two distinct and complementary aspects but one and the same thing. One understands then how mythical thought can be capable of generalizing and so be scientific, even though it is still entangled in imagery. It too works by analogies and comparisons even though its creations, like those of the 'bricoleur', always really consist of a new arrangement of elements, the nature of which is unaffected by whether they figure in the instrumental set or in the final arrangement (these being the same, apart from the internal disposition of their parts): 'it would seem that mytho-logical worlds have been built up, only to be shattered again, and that new worlds were built from the fragments' (Boas I, p. 18). Penetrating as this com-ment is, it nevertheless fails to take into account that in the continual recon-struction from the same materials, it is always earlier ends which are called upon to play the part of means: the signified changes into the signifying and vice versa.

This formula, which could serve as a definition of 'bricolage', explains how an implicit inventory or conception of the total means available must be made in the case of mythical thought also, so that a result can be defined which will always be a compromise between the structure of the instrumental set and that of the project. Once it materializes the project will therefore inevitably be at a remove from the initial aim (which was moreover a mere sketch), a pheno-menon which the surrealists have felicitously called 'objective hazard'. Further, the 'bricoleur' also, and indeed principally, derives his poetry from the fact that he does not confine himself to accomplishment and execution: he 'speaks' not only *with* things, as we have already seen, but also through the medium of things: giving an account of his personality and life by the choices he makes between the limited possibilities. The 'bricoleur' may not ever complete his purpose but he always puts something of himself into it.

Mythical thought appears to be an intellectual form of 'bricolage' in this sense also. Science as a whole is based on the distinction between the contingent and the necessary, this being also what distinguishes event and structure. The qualities it claimed at its outset as peculiarly scientific were precisely those which formed no part of living experience and remained outside and, as it were, unrelated to events. This is the significance of the notion of primary qualities. Now, the characteristic feature of mythical thought, as of 'bricolage' on the practical plane, is that it builds up structured sets, not directly with other structured sets[5] but by using the remains and debris of events: in French 'des bribes et des morceaux', or odds and ends in English, fossilized evidence of the history of an individual or a society. The relation between the diachronic and the synchronic is therefore in a sense reversed. Mythical thought, that 'bricoleur', builds up structures by fitting together events, or rather the remains of events,[6] while science, 'in operation' simply by virtue of coming into being, creates its means and results in the form of events, thanks to the structures which it is constantly elaborating and which are its hypotheses and theories. But it is important not to make the mistake of thinking that these are two stages or phases in the evolution of knowledge. Both approaches are equally valid. Physics and chemistry are already striving to become qualitative again, that is, to account also for secondary qualities which when they have been explained will in their turn become means of explanation. And biology may perhaps be marking time waiting for this before it can itself explain life. Mythical thought for its part is imprisoned in the events and experiences which it never tires of ordering and re-ordering in its search to find them a meaning. But it also acts as a liberator by its protest against the idea that anything can be meaningless with which science at first resigned itself to a compromise.

The problem of art has been touched on several times in the foregoing discussion, and it is worth showing briefly how, from this point of view, art lies half-way between scientific knowledge and mythical or magical thought. It is common knowledge that the artist is both something of a scientist and of a 'bricoleur'. By his craftsmanship he constructs a material object which is also an object of knowledge. We have already distinguished the scientist and the 'bricoleur' by the inverse functions which they assign to events and structures as ends and means, the scientist creating events (changing the world) by means of structures and the 'bricoleur' creating structures by means of events. This is imprecise in this crude form but our analysis makes it possible for us to refine it. Let us . . . look at this portrait of a woman by Clouet and consider the reason for the very profound aesthetic emotion which is, apparently inexplicably, aroused by the highly realistic, thread by thread, reproduction of a lace collar . . . .

The choice of this example is not accidental. Clouet is known to have liked to paint at less than life-size. His paintings are therefore, like Japanese gardens, miniature vehicles and ships in bottles, what in the 'bricoleur's' language are called 'small-scale models' or 'miniatures'. Now, the question arises whether the small-scale model or miniature, which is also the 'masterpiece' of the journeyman may not in fact be the universal type of the work of art. All mini-

---

[5] Mythical thought builds structured sets by means of a structured set, namely, language. But it is not at the structural level that it makes use of it: it builds ideological castles out of the debris of what was once a social discourse.

[6] 'Bricolage' also works with 'secondary' qualities, i.e. 'second hand'.

atures seem to have intrinsic aesthetic quality—and from what should they draw this constant virtue if not from the dimensions themselves?—and conversely the vast majority of works of art are small-scale. It might be thought that this characteristic is principally a matter of economy in materials and means, and one might appeal in support of this theory to works which are incontestably artistic but also on a grand scale. We have to be clear about definitions. The paintings of the Sistine Chapel are a small-scale model in spite of their imposing dimensions, since the theme which they depict is the End of Time. The same is true of the cosmic symbolism of religious monuments. Further, we may ask whether the aesthetic effect, say, of an equestrian statue which is larger than life derives from its enlargement of a man to the size of a rock or whether it is not rather due to the fact that it restores what is at first from a distance seen as a rock to the proportions of a man. Finally even 'natural size' implies a reduction of scale since graphic or plastic transposition always involves giving up certain dimensions of the object: volume in painting, colour, smell, tactile impressions in sculpture and the temporal dimension in both cases since the whole work represented is apprehended at a single moment in time.

What is the virtue of reduction either of scale or in the number of properties? It seems to result from a sort of reversal in the process of understanding. To understand a real object in its totality we always tend to work from its parts. The resistance it offers us is overcome by dividing it. Reduction in scale reverses this situation. Being smaller, the object as a whole seems less formidable. By being quantitatively diminished, it seems to us qualitatively simplified. More exactly, this quantitative transposition extends and diversifies our power over a homologue of the thing, and by means of it the latter can be grasped, assessed and apprehended at a glance. A child's doll is no longer an enemy, a rival or even an interlocutor. In it and through it a person is made into a subject. In the case of miniatures, in contrast to what happens when we try to understand an object or living creature of real dimensions, knowledge of the whole precedes knowledge of the parts. And even if this is an illusion, the point of the procedure is to create or sustain the illusion, which gratifies the intelligence and gives rise to a sense of pleasure which can already be called aesthetic on these grounds alone.

I have so far only considered matters of scale which, as we have just seen, imply a dialectical relation between size (i.e. quantity) and quality. But miniatures have a further feature. They are 'man made' and, what is more, made by hand. They are therefore not just projections or passive homologues of the object: they constitute a real experiment with it. Now the model being an artefact, it is possible to understand how it is made and this understanding of the method of construction adds a supplementary dimension. As we have already seen in the case of 'bricolage', and the example of 'styles' of painters shows that the same is true in art, there are several solutions to the same problem. The choice of one solution involves a modification of the result to which another solution would have led, and the observer is in effect presented with the general picture of these permutations at the same time as the particular solution offered. He is thereby transformed into an active participant without even being aware of it. Merely by contemplating it he is, as it were, put in possession of other possible forms of the same work; and in a confused way, he feels himself to be their creator with more right than the creator himself because the latter abandoned them in excluding them from his creation. And these forms are so many further perspectives opening out on to the work which has been realized. In other words, the intrinsic value of a small-scale model is that it compensates for the renunciation of sensible dimensions by the acquisition of intelligible dimensions.

Let us now return to the lace collar in Clouet's picture. Everything that has been said applies in this case, for the procedure necessary to represent it as a projection, in a particular space, of properties whose sensible dimensions are fewer and smaller than that of the object is exactly the reverse of that which science would have employed had it proposed, in accordance with its function, to produce (instead of reproducing) not only a new, instead of an already known, piece of lace but also real lace instead of a picture of lace. Science would have worked on the real scale but by means of inventing a loom, while art works on a diminished scale to produce an image homologous with the object. The former approach is of a metonymical order, it replaces one thing by another thing, an effect by its cause, while the latter is of a metaphorical order.

This is not all. For if it is true that the relation of priority between structure and event is exactly the opposite in science and "bricolage", then it is clear that art has an intermediate position from this point of view as well. Even if, as we have shown, the depiction of a lace collar in miniature demands an intimate knowledge of its morphology and technique of manufacture (and had it been a question of the representation of people or animals we should have said: of anatomy and physical attitudes), it is not just a diagram or blueprint. It manages to synthesize these intrinsic properties with properties which depend on a spatial and temporal context. The final product is the lace collar exactly as it is but so that at the same time its appearance is affected by the particular perspective. This accentuates some parts and conceals others, whose existence however still influences the rest through the contrast between its whiteness and the colour of the other clothes, the reflection of the pearly neck it encircles and that of the sky on a particular day and at a particular time of day. The appearance of the lace collar is also affected by whether it indicates casual or formal dress, is worn, either new or previously used, either freshly ironed or creased, by an ordinary woman or a queen, whose physiognomy confirms, contradicts or qualifies her status in a particular social class, society, part of the world and period of history. . . . The painter is always mid-way between design and anecdote, and his genius consists in uniting internal and external knowledge, a "being" and a "becoming", in producing with his brush an object which does not exist as such and which he is nevertheless able to create on his canvas. This is a nicely balanced synthesis of one or more artificial and natural structures and one or more natural and social events. The aesthetic emotion is the result of this union between the structural order and the order of events, which is brought about within a thing created by man and so also in effect by the observer who discovers the possibility of such a union through the work of art.

Several points are suggested by this analysis. In the first place, the analysis helps us to see why we are inclined to think of myths both as systems of abstract relations and as objects of aesthetic contemplation. The creative act which gives rise to myths is in fact exactly the reverse of that which gives rise to works of art. In the case of works of art, the starting point is a set of one or more objects and one or more events which aesthetic creation unifies by revealing a common structure. Myths travel the same road but start from the other end. They use a structure to produce what is itself an object consisting of a set of events (for all myths tell a story). Art thus proceeds from a set (object + event) to the *discovery* of its structure. Myth starts from a structure by means of which it *constructs* a set (object + event).

The first point tempts one to generalize the theory. The second might seem to lead to a restriction of it. For we may ask whether it is in fact the case that works of art are always an integration of structure and event. This does not on the face of it seem to be true for instance of the cedarwood Tlingit club, used to kill fish, which I have in front of me on my bookshelf (Plate 2). The artist who carved it in the form of a sea monster intended the body of the implement to be fused with the body of the animal and the handle with its tail, and that the anatomical proportions, taken from a fabulous creature, should be such that the object could *be* the cruel animal slaying helpless victims, at the same time as an easily handled, balanced and efficient fishing utensil. Everything about this implement—which is also a superb work of art—seems to be a matter of structure: its mythical symbolism as well as its practical function. More accurately, the object, its function and its symbolism seem to be inextricably bound up with each other and to form a closed system in which there is no place for events. The monster's position, appearance and expression owe nothing to the historical circumstances in which the artist saw it, in the flesh or in a dream, or conceived the idea of it. It is rather as if its immutable being were finally fixed in the wood whose fine grain allows the reproduction of all its aspects and in the use for which its empirical form seems to pre-determine it. And all this applies equally to the other products of primitive art: an African statue or a Melanesian mask. . . . So it looks as if we have defined only one local and historical form of aesthetic creation and not its fundamental properties or those by means of which its intelligible relations with other forms of creation can be described.

We have only to widen our explanation to overcome this difficulty. What, with reference to a picture of Clouet's, was provisionally defined as an event or set of events now appears under a broader heading: events in this sense are only one mode of the contingent whose integration (perceived as necessary) into a structure gives rise to the aesthetic emotion. This is so whatever the type of art in question. Depending on the style, place and period the contingent plays a part in three different ways or at three distinct points in artistic creation (or in all of them). It may play a part in the occasion for the work or in the execution of the work or in the purpose for which it is intended. It is only in the first case that it takes the form of an event properly speaking, that is, of contingency exterior and prior to the creative act. The artist perceives it from without as an attitude, an expression, a light effect or a situation, whose sensible and intellectual relations to the structure of the object affected by these modalities he grasps and incorporates in his work. But the contingent can also play an intrinsic part in the course of execution itself, in the size or shape of the piece of wood the sculptor lays hands on, in the direction and quality of its grain, in the imperfections of his tools, in the resistance which his materials or project offer to the work in the course of its accomplishment, in the unforeseeable incidents arising during work. Finally, the contingent can be extrinsic as in the first case but posterior, instead of anterior, to the act of creation. This is the case whenever the work is destined for a specific end, since the artist will construct it with a view to its potential condition and successive uses in the future and so will put himself, consciously or unconsciously, in the place of the person for whose use it is intended.

The process of artistic creation therefore consists in trying to communicate (within the immutable framework of a mutual confrontation of structure and accident) either with the *model* or with the *materials* or with the future *user* as the case may be, according to which of these the artist particularly looks to for his directions while he is at work. Each case roughly corresponds to a readily identifiable form of art: the first to the plastic arts of the West, the second to so-called primitive or early art and the third to the applied arts. But it would be an oversimplification to take these identifications very strictly. All forms of art allow all three aspects and they are only distinguished from one another by the relative proportion of each. Even the most academic of painters comes up against problems of execution, for example. All the so-called primitive arts can be called applied in a double sense: first, because many of their productions are technical objects and, secondly, because even those which seem most divorced from practical preoccupations have a definite purpose. Finally, as we know, implements lend themselves to disinterested contemplation even among ourselves.

With these reservations, it is easy to show that the three aspects are functionally related and that the predominance of any one of them leaves less or no place for the others. So-called professional painting is, or believes itself to be, quite free so far as both execution and purposes are concerned. Its best examples display a complete mastery of technical difficulties—which, indeed, can be considered to have been completely overcome since Van der Weyden; the problems which painters have set themselves since then amount to little more than a game of technical refinement. In the extreme case it is as though, given his canvas, paints and brushes, the painter were able to do exactly what he pleased. On the other hand, he also tries to make his work into an object independent of anything contingent, of value in itself and for itself. This is indeed what the formula of the "easel picture" implies. Freed from the contingent both with regard to execution and purpose professional painting can, then, bring it to bear upon the occasion of the work, and indeed if this account is correct it is bound to do so. Professional painting can therefore be defined as "genre" painting if the sense of this expression is considerably widened. For, from the very general viewpoint we are taking, the attempt of a portrait painter

—even of a Rembrandt—to recapture on his canvas his model's most revealing expression or secret thoughts belongs to the same genre as that of a painter like Detaille, whose compositions reproduce the hour and order of battle and the number and disposition of the buttons distinguishing the uniforms of each Arm. To use a disrespectful analogy, "opportunity makes the thief"[7] in either case. The relative proportions of the three aspects are reversed in the applied arts. In these, first place is given to purpose and execution, contingent factors playing an approximately equal part in each, in the examples we consider the most "pure", at the same time the occasion of the work plays no part. This can be seen from the fact that a wine cup or goblet, a piece of basket work or a fabric seems to us perfect when its practical value manifestly transcends time and corresponds wholly to its functions for men of different periods and civilizations. If the difficulties of execution are entirely mastered, as is the case when it is entrusted to machines, the purpose can become more and more precise and specific and applied art is transformed into industrial art. We call it peasant or folk art if the reverse is the case. Finally, primitive art is the opposite of professional or academic art. Professional or academic art internalizes execution (which it has, or believes itself to have, mastered) and purpose ("art for art's sake" being an end in itself). As a result, it is impelled to externalize the occasion (which it requires the model to provide) and the latter thus becomes a part of the signified. Primitive art, on the other hand, internalizes the occasion (since the supernatural beings which it delights in representing have a reality which is timeless and independent of circumstances) and it externalizes execution and purpose which thus become a part of the signifying.

On a different plane we therefore find once more this dialogue with the materials and means of execution by which we defined "bricolage". The essential problem for the philosophy of art is to know whether the artist regards them as interlocutors or not. No doubt they are always regarded as such, although least of all in art which is too professional and most of all in the raw or naive art which verges on "bricolage", to the detriment of structure in both cases. No form of art is, however, worthy of the name if it allows itself to come entirely under the sway of extraneous contingencies, whether of occasion or purpose. If it did so it would rate as an icon (supplementary to the model) or as an implement (complementary with the material worked). Even the most professional art succeeds in moving us only if it arrests in time this dissipation of the contingent in favour of the pretext and incorporates it in the work, thereby investing it with the dignity of being an object in its own right. In so far as early art, primitive art and the "primitive" periods of professional painting are the only ones which do not date, they owe it to this dedication of the accidental to the service of execution and so to the use, which they try to make complete, of the raw datum as the empirical material of something meaningful.[8]

---

[7] In the original: "l'occasion fait le larron" (trans. note).

[8] Pursuing this analysis, one might define non-representational painting by two features. One, which it has in common with "easel" painting, consists in a total rejection of the contingency of purpose: the picture is not made for a particular use. The other feature characteristic of non-representational painting is its methodical exploitation of the contingency of execution, which is

It is necessary to add that the balance between structure and event, necessity and contingency, the internal and external is a precarious one. It is constantly threatened by forces which act in one direction or the other according to fluctuations in fashion, style or general social conditions. From this point of view, it would seem that impressionism and cubism are not so much two successive stages in the development of painting as partners in the same enterprise, which, although not exact contemporaries, nevertheless collaborated by complementary distortions to prolong a mode of expression whose very existence, as we are better able to appreciate today, was seriously threatened. The intermittent fashion for "collages", originating when craftsmanship was dying, could not for its part be anything but the transposition of "bricolage" into the realms of contemplation. Finally, the stress on the event can also break away at certain times through greater emphasis either on transient social phenomena (as in the case of Greuze at the end of the eighteenth century or with socialist realism) or on transient natural, or even meteorological, phenomena (impressionism) at the expense of structure, "structure" here being understood as "structure of the same level", for the possibility of the structural aspect being re-established elsewhere on a new plane is not ruled out.

claimed to afford the external pretext or occasion of the picture. Non-representational painting adopts "styles" as "subjects". It claims to give a concrete representation of the formal conditions of all painting.

The Aesthetics of Silence

SUSAN SONTAG

1

EVERY era has to reinvent the project of "spirituality" for itself. (Spirituality = plans, terminologies, ideas of deportment aimed at resolving the painful structural contradictions inherent in the human situation, at the completion of human consciousness, at transcendence.)

In the modern era, one of the most active metaphors for the spiritual project is "art." The activities of the painter, the musician, the poet, the dancer, once they were grouped together under that generic name (a relatively recent move), have proved a particularly adaptable site on which to stage the formal dramas besetting consciousness, each individual work of art being a more or less astute paradigm for regulating or reconciling these contradictions. Of course, the site needs continual refurbishing. Whatever goal is set for art eventually proves restrictive, matched against the widest goals of consciousness. Art, itself a form of mystification, endures a succession of crises of demystification; older artistic goals are assailed and, ostensibly, replaced; outworn maps of consciousness are redrawn. But what supplies all these crises with their energy—an energy held in common, so to speak—is the very unification of numerous, quite disparate activities into a single genus. At the moment when "art" comes into being, the modern period of art begins. From then on, any of the activities therein subsumed becomes a profoundly *problematic* activity, all of whose procedures and, ultimately, whose very right to exist can be called into question.

From the promotion of the arts into "art" comes the leading myth about art, that of the absoluteness of the artist's activity. In its first, more unreflective version, the myth treated art as an *expression* of human consciousness, conscious-

453

ness seeking to know itself. (The evaluative standards generated by this version of the myth were fairly easily arrived at: some expressions were more complete, more ennobling, more informative, richer than others.) The later version of the myth posits a more complex, tragic relation of art to consciousness. Denying that art is mere expression, the later myth rather relates art to the mind's need or capacity for self-estrangement. Art is no longer understood as consciousness expressing and therefore, implicitly, affirming itself. Art is not consciousness per se, but rather its antidote—evolved from within consciousness itself. (The evaluative standards generated by this version of the myth proved much harder to get at.)

The newer myth, derived from a post-psychological conception of consciousness, installs within the activity of art many of the paradoxes involved in attaining an absolute state of being described by the great religious mystics. As the activity of the mystic must end in a *via negativa*, a theology of God's absence, a craving for the cloud of unknowing beyond knowledge and for the silence beyond speech, so art must tend toward anti-art, the elimination of the "subject" (the "object," the "image"), the substitution by chance for intention, and the pursuit of silence.

In the early, linear version of art's relation to consciousness, a struggle was discerned between the "spiritual" integrity of the creative impulses and the distracting "materiality" of ordinary life, which throws up so many obstacles in the path of authentic sublimation. But the newer version, in which art is part of a dialectical transaction with consciousness, poses a deeper, more frustrating conflict. The "spirit" seeking embodiment in art clashes with the "material" character of art itself. Art is unmasked as gratuitous, and the very concreteness of the artist's tools (and, particularly in the case of language, their historicity) appears as a trap. Practiced in a world furnished with second-hand perceptions, and specifically confounded by the treachery of words, the artist's activity is cursed with mediacy. Art becomes the enemy of the artist, for it denies him the realization—the transcendence—he desires.

Therefore, art comes to be considered something to be overthrown. A new element enters the individual artwork and becomes constitutive of it: the appeal (tacit or overt) for its own abolition—and, ultimately, for the abolition of art itself.

2

The scene changes to an empty room.

Rimbaud has gone to Abyssinia to make his fortune in the slave trade. Wittgenstein, after a period as a village schoolteacher, has chosen menial work as a hospital orderly. Duchamp has turned to chess. Accompanying these exemplary renunciations of a vocation, each man has declared that he regards his previous achievements in poetry, philosophy, or art as trifling, of no importance.

But the choice of permanent silence doesn't negate their work. On the contrary, it imparts retroactively an added power and authority to what was broken off—disavowal of the work becoming a new source of its validity, a certificate of unchallengeable seriousness. That seriousness consists in not regarding art (or philosophy practiced as an art form: Wittgenstein) as something whose seriousness lasts forever, an "end," a permanent vehicle for spiritual ambition. The truly serious attitude is one that regards art as a "means" to something that can perhaps be achieved only by abandoning art; judged more impatiently, art is a false way or (the word of the Dada artist Jacques Vaché) a stupidity.

Though no longer a confession, art is more than ever a deliverance, an exercise in asceticism. Through it, the artist becomes purified—of himself and, eventually, of his art. The artist (if not art itself) is still engaged in a progress toward "the good." But whereas formerly the artist's good was mastery of and fulfillment in his art, now the highest good for the artist is to reach the point where those goals of excellence become insignificant to him, emotionally and ethically, and he is more satisfied by being silent than by finding a voice in art. Silence in this sense, as termination, proposes a mood of ultimacy antithetical to the mood informing the self-conscious artist's traditional serious use of silence (beautifully described by Valéry and Rilke): as a zone of meditation, preparation for spiritual ripening, an ordeal that ends in gaining the right to speak.

So far as he is serious, the artist is continually tempted to sever the dialogue he has with an audience. Silence is the furthest extension of that reluctance to communicate, that ambivalence about making contact with the audience which is a leading motif of modern art, with its tireless commitment to the "new" and/or the "esoteric." Silence is the artist's ultimate other-worldly gesture: by silence, he frees himself from servile bondage to the world, which appears as patron, client, consumer, antagonist, arbiter, and distorter of his work.

Still, one cannot fail to perceive in this renunciation of "society" a highly social gesture. The cues for the artist's eventual liberation from the need to practice his vocation come from observing his fellow artists and measuring himself against them. An exemplary decision of this sort can be made only after the artist has demonstrated that he possesses genius and exercised that genius authoritatively. Once he has surpassed his peers by the standards which he acknowledges, his pride has only one place left to go. For, to be a victim of the craving for silence is to be, in still a further sense, superior to everyone else. It suggests that the artist has had the wit to ask more questions than other people, and that he possesses stronger nerves and higher standards of excellence. (That the artist *can* persevere in the interrogation of his art until he or it is exhausted scarcely needs proving. As René Char has written, "No bird has the heart to sing in a thicket of questions.")

3

The exemplary modern artist's choice of silence is rarely carried to this point of final simplification, so that he becomes literally silent. More typically, he continues speaking, but in a manner that his audience can't hear. Most valuable art in our time has been experienced by audiences as a move into silence (or unintelligibility or invisibility or inaudibility); a dismantling of the artist's competence, his responsible sense of vocation—and therefore as an aggression against them.

Modern art's chronic habit of displeasing, provoking, or frustrating its audience can be regarded as a limited, vicarious participation in the ideal of silence which has been elevated as a major standard of "seriousness" in contemporary aesthetics.

But it is also a contradictory form of participation in the ideal of silence. It is contradictory not only because the artist continues making works of art, but also because the isolation of the work from its audience never lasts. With the passage of time and the intervention of newer, more difficult works, the artist's transgression becomes ingratiating, eventually legitimate. Goethe accused Kleist of having written his plays for an "invisible theatre." But eventually the invisible theatre becomes "visible." The ugly and discordant and senseless become "beautiful." The history of art is a sequence of successful transgressions.

The characteristic aim of modern art, to be *unacceptable* to its audience, inversely states the unacceptability to the artist of the very presence of an audience—audience in the modern sense, an assembly of voyeuristic spectators. At least since Nietzsche observed in *The Birth of Tragedy* that an audience of spectators as we know it, those present whom the actors ignore, was unknown to the Greeks, a good deal of contemporary art seems moved by the desire to eliminate the audience from art, an enterprise that often presents itself as an attempt to eliminate "art" altogether. (In favor of "life"?)

Committed to the idea that the power of art is located in its power to *negate*, the ultimate weapon in the artist's inconsistent war with his audience is to verge closer and closer to silence. The sensory or conceptual gap between the artist and his audience, the space of the missing or ruptured dialogue, can also constitute the grounds for an ascetic affirmation. Beckett speaks of "my dream of an art unresentful of its insuperable indigence and too proud for the farce of giving and receiving." But there is no abolishing a minimal transaction, a minimal exchange of gifts—just as there is no talented and rigorous asceticism that, whatever its intention, doesn't produce a gain (rather than a loss) in the capacity for pleasure.

And none of the aggressions committed intentionally or inadvertently by modern artists has succeeded in either abolishing the audience or transforming it into something else, a community engaged in a common activity. They cannot. As long as art is understood and valued as an "absolute" activity, it will be a separate, elitist one. Elites presuppose masses. So far as the best art defines itself by essentially "priestly" aims, it presupposes and confirms the existence of a relatively passive, never fully initiated, voyeuristic laity that is regularly convoked to watch, listen, read, or hear—and then sent away.

The most the artist can do is to modify the different terms in this situation vis-à-vis the audience and himself. To discuss the idea of silence in art is to discuss the various alternatives within this essentially unalterable situation.

4

How literally does silence figure in art?

Silence exists as a *decision*—in the exemplary suicide of the artist (Kleist, Lautréamont), who thereby testifies that he has gone "too far"; and in the already cited model renunciations by the artist of his vocation.

Silence also exists as a *punishment*—self-punishment, in the exemplary madness of artists (Hölderlin, Artaud) who demonstrate that sanity itself may be the price of trespassing the accepted frontiers of consciousness; and, of course, in penalties (ranging from censorship and physical destruction of artworks to fines, exile, prison for the artist) meted out by "society" for the artist's spiritual nonconformity or subversion of the group sensibility.

Silence doesn't exist in a literal sense, however, as the *experience* of an audience. It would mean that the spectator was aware of no stimulus or that he was unable to make a response. But this can't happen; nor can it even be induced programmatically. The non-awareness of any stimulus, the inability to make a response, can result only from a defective presence on the part of the spectator, or a misunderstanding of his own reactions (misled by restrictive ideas about what would be a "relevant" response). As long as audiences, by definition, consist of sentient beings in a "situation," it is impossible for them to have no response at all.

Nor can silence, in its literal state, exist as the *property* of an artwork—even of works like Duchamp's readymades or Cage's *4'33"*, in which the artist has ostentatiously done no more to satisfy any established criteria of art than set the object in a gallery or situate the performance on a concert stage. There is no neutral surface, no neutral discourse, no neutral theme, no neutral form. Something is neutral only with respect to something else—like an intention or an expectation. As a property of the work of art itself, silence can exist only in a cooked or non-literal sense. (Put otherwise: if a work exists at all, its silence is only one element in it.) Instead of raw or achieved silence, one finds various moves in the direction of an ever receding horizon of silence—moves which, by definition, can never be fully consummated. One result is a type of art that many people characterize pejoratively as dumb, depressed, acquiescent, cold. But these privative qualities exist in a context of the artist's objective intention, which is always discernible. Cultivating the metaphoric silence suggested by conventionally lifeless subjects (as in much of Pop Art) and constructing "minimal" forms that seem to lack emotional resonance are in themselves vigorous, often tonic choices.

And, finally, even without imputing objective intentions to the artwork, there remains the inescapable truth about perception: the positivity of all experience at every moment of it. As Cage has insisted, "There is no such thing as silence. Something is always happening that makes a sound." (Cage has described how, even in a soundless chamber, he still heard two things: his heartbeat and the coursing of the blood in his head.) Similarly, there is no such thing as empty space. As long as a human eye is looking, there is always something to see. To look at something which is "empty" is still to be looking, still to be seeing something—if only the ghosts of one's own expectations. In order to perceive fullness, one must retain an acute sense of the emptiness which marks it off; conversely, in order to perceive emptiness, one must apprehend other zones of the world as full. (In *Through the Looking Glass,* Alice comes upon a shop "that seemed to be full of all manner of curious things—but the oddest part of it all was that whenever she looked hard at any shelf, to make out exactly what it had on it, that particular shelf was always quite empty, though the others round it were crowded full as they could hold.")

"Silence" never ceases to imply its opposite and to depend on its presence: just as there can't be "up" without "down" or "left" without "right," so one must acknowledge a surrounding environment of sound or language in order to recognize silence. Not only does silence exist in a world full of speech and other sounds, but any given silence has its identity as a stretch of time being perforated by sound. (Thus, much of the beauty of Harpo Marx's muteness derives from his being surrounded by manic talkers.)

A genuine emptiness, a pure silence are not feasible—either conceptually or in fact. If only because the artwork exists in a world furnished with many other things, the artist who creates silence or emptiness must produce something dialectical: a full void, an enriching emptiness, a resonating or eloquent silence. Silence remains, inescapably, a form of speech (in many instances, of complaint or indictment) and an element in a dialogue.

5

Programs for a radical reduction of means and effects in art—including the ultimate demand for the renunciation of art itself—can't be taken at face value, undialectically. Silence and allied ideas (like emptiness, reduction, the "zero degree") are boundary notions with a very complex set of uses, leading terms of a particular spiritual and cultural rhetoric. To describe silence as a rhetorical term is, of course, not to condemn this rhetoric as fraudulent or in bad faith. In my opinion, the myths of silence and emptiness are about as nourishing and viable as might be devised in an "unwholesome" time—which is, of necessity, a time in which "unwholesome" psychic states furnish the energies for most superior work in the arts. Yet one can't deny the pathos of these myths.

This pathos appears in the fact that the idea of silence allows, essentially, only two types of valuable development. Either it is taken to the point of utter self-negation (as art) or else it is practiced in a form that is heroically, ingeniously inconsistent.

6

The art of our time is noisy with appeals for silence.

A coquettish, even cheerful nihilism. One recognizes the imperative of silence, but goes on speaking anyway. Discovering that one has nothing to say, one seeks a way to say *that.*

Beckett has expressed the wish that art would renounce all further projects for disturbing matters on "the plane of the feasible," that art would retire, "weary of puny exploits, weary of pretending to be able, of being able, of doing a little better the same old thing, of going further along a dreary road." The alternative is an art consisting of "the expression that there is nothing to express, nothing from which to express, no power to express, no desire to express, together with the obligation to express." From where does this obligation derive? The very aesthetics of the death wish seems to make of that wish something incorrigibly lively.

Apollinaire says, "J'ai fait des gestes blancs parmi les solitudes." But he *is* making gestures.

Since the artist can't embrace silence literally and remain an artist, what the rhetoric of silence indicates is a determination to pursue his activity more deviously than before. One way is indicated by Breton's notion of the "full margin." The artist is enjoined to devote himself to filling up the periphery of the art space, leaving the central area of usage blank. Art becomes privative, anemic—as suggested by the title of Duchamp's only effort at film-making, "Anemic Cinema," a work from 1924–26. Beckett projects the idea of an "impoverished painting," painting which is "authentically fruitless, incapable of any image whatsoever." Jerzy Grotowski's manifesto for his Theatre Laboratory in Poland is called "Plea for a Poor Theatre." These programs for art's impoverishment must not be understood simply as terroristic admonitions to audiences, but rather as strategies for improving the audience's experience. The notions of silence, emptiness, and reduction sketch out new prescriptions for looking, hearing, etc.—which either promote a more immediate, sensuous experience of art or confront the artwork in a more conscious, conceptual way.

7

Consider the connection between the mandate for a reduction of means and effects in art, whose horizon is silence, and the faculty of attention. In one of its aspects, art is a technique for focusing attention, for teaching skills of attention. (While the whole of the human environment might be so described—as a pedagogic instrument—this description particularly applies to works of art.) The history of the arts is tantamount to the discovery and formulation of a repertory of objects on which to lavish attention. One could trace exactly and in order how the eye of art has panned over our environment, "naming," making its limited selection of things which people then become aware of as significant, pleasurable, complex entities. (Oscar Wilde pointed out that people didn't see fogs before certain nineteenth-century poets and painters taught them how to; and surely, no one saw as much of the variety and subtlety of the human face before the era of the movies.)

Once the artist's task seemed to be simply that of opening up new areas and objects of attention. That task is still acknowledged, but it has become problematic. The very faculty of attention has come into question, and been subjected to more rigorous standards. As Jasper Johns says: "Already it's a great deal to see anything *clearly*, for we don't see *anything* clearly."

Perhaps the quality of the attention one brings to bear on something will be better (less contaminated, less distracted), the less one is offered. Furnished with impoverished art, purged by silence, one might then be able to begin to transcend the frustrating selectivity of attention, with its inevitable distortions of experience. Ideally, one should be able to pay attention to everything.

The tendency is toward less and less. But never has "less" so ostentatiously advanced itself as "more."

In the light of the current myth, in which art aims to become a "total experience," soliciting total attention, the strategies of impoverishment and reduction indicate the most exalted ambition art could adopt. Underneath what looks like a strenuous modesty, if not actual debility, is to be discerned an energetic secular blasphemy: the wish to attain the unfettered, unselective, total consciousness of "God."

8

Language seems a privileged metaphor for expressing the mediated character of art-making and the artwork. On the one hand, speech is both an immaterial medium (compared with, say, images) and a human activity with an apparently essential stake in the project of transcendence, of moving beyond the singular and contingent (all words being abstractions, only roughly based on or making reference to concrete particulars). On the other hand, language is the most impure, the most contaminated, the most exhausted of all the materials out of which art is made.

This dual character of language—its abstractness, and its "fallenness" in history—serves as a microcosm of the unhappy character of the arts today. Art is so far along the labyrinthine pathways of the project of transcendence that one can hardly conceive of it turning back, short of the most drastic and punitive "cultural revolution." Yet at the same time, art is foundering in the debilitating tide of what once seemed the crowning achievement of European thought: secular historical consciousness. In little more than two centuries, the consciousness of history has transformed itself from a liberation, an opening of doors, blessed enlightenment, into an almost insupportable burden of self-consciousness. It's scarcely possible for the artist to write a word (or render an image or make a gesture) that doesn't remind him of something already achieved.

As Nietzsche says: "Our pre-eminence: we live in the age of comparison, we can verify as has never been verified before." Therefore "we enjoy differently, we suffer differently: our instinctive activity is to compare an unheard number of things."

Up to a point, the community and historicity of the artist's means are implicit in the very fact of intersubjectivity: each person is a being-in-a-world. But today, particularly in the arts using language, this normal state of affairs is felt as an extraordinary, wearying problem.

Language is experienced not merely as something shared but as something corrupted, weighed down by historical accumulation. Thus, for each conscious artist, the creation of a work means dealing with two potentially antagonistic domains of meaning and their relationships. One is his own meaning (or lack of it); the other is the set of second-order meanings that both extend his own language and encumber, compromise, and adulterate it. The artist ends by choosing between two inherently limiting alternatives, forced to take a position that is either servile or insolent. Either he flatters or appeases his audience, giving them what they already know, or he commits an aggression against his audience, giving them what they don't want.

Modern art thus transmits in full the alienation produced by historical consciousness. Whatever the artist does is in (usually conscious) alignment with something else already done, producing a compulsion to be continually checking his situation, his own stance against those of his predecessors and contemporaries. To compensate for this ignominious enslavement to history, the artist exalts himself with the dream of a wholly ahistorical, and therefore unalienated, art.

9

Art that is "silent" constitutes one approach to this visionary, ahistorical condition.

Consider the difference between *looking* and *staring*. A look is voluntary; it is also mobile, rising and falling in intensity as its foci of interest are taken up and then exhausted. A stare has, essentially, the character of a compulsion; it is steady, unmodulated, "fixed."

Traditional art invites a look. Art that is silent engenders a stare. Silent art allows—at least in principle—no release from attention, because there has never, in principle, been any soliciting of it. A stare is perhaps as far from history, as close to eternity, as contemporary art can get.

10

Silence is a metaphor for a cleansed, non-interfering vision, appropriate to artworks that are unresponsive before being seen, unviolable in their essential integrity by human scrutiny. The spectator would approach art as he does a landscape. A landscape doesn't demand from the spectator his "understanding," his imputations of significance, his anxieties and sympathies; it demands, rather, his absence, it asks that he not add anything to *it*. Contemplation, strictly speaking, entails self-forgetfulness on the part of the spectator: an object worthy of contemplation is one which, in effect, annihilates the perceiving subject.

Toward such an ideal plenitude to which the audience can add nothing, analogous to the aesthetic relation to nature, a great deal of contemporary art aspires—through various strategies of blandness, of reduction, of deindividuation, of alogicality. In principle, the audience may not even add its thought.

All objects, rightly perceived, are already full. This is what Cage must mean when, after explaining that there is no such thing as silence because something is always happening that makes a sound, he adds, "No one can have an idea once he starts really listening."

Plenitude—experiencing all the space as filled, so that ideas cannot enter—means impenetrability. A person who becomes silent becomes opaque for the other; somebody's silence opens up an array of possibilities for interpreting that silence, for imputing speech to it.

The way in which this opaqueness induces spiritual vertigo is the theme of Bergman's *Persona*. The actress's deliberate silence has two aspects: Considered as a decision apparently relating to herself, the refusal to speak is apparently the form she has given to the wish for ethical purity; but it is also, as behavior, a means of power, a species of sadism, a virtually inviolable position of strength from which she manipulates and confounds her nurse-companion, who is charged with the burden of talking.

But the opaqueness of silence can be conceived more positively, as free from anxiety. For Keats, the silence of the Grecian urn is a locus of spiritual nourishment: "unheard" melodies endure, whereas those that pipe to "the sensual ear" decay. Silence is equated with arresting time ("slow time"). One can stare endlessly at the Grecian urn. Eternity, in the argument of Keats' poem, is the only interesting stimulus to thought and also the sole occasion for coming to the end of mental activity, which means interminable, unanswered questions ("Thou, silent form, dost tease us out of thought/ As doth eternity"), in order to arrive at a final equation of ideas ("Beauty is truth, truth beauty") which is both absolutely vacuous and completely full. Keats' poem quite logically ends in a statement that will seem, if the reader hasn't followed his argument, like empty wisdom, a banality. As time, or history, is the medium of definite, determinate thought, the silence of eternity prepares for a thought beyond thought, which must appear from the perspective of traditional thinking and the familiar uses of the mind as no thought at all—though it may rather be the emblem of new, "difficult" thinking.

11

Behind the appeals for silence lies the wish for a perceptual and cultural clean slate. And, in its hortatory and ambitious version, the advocacy of silence expresses a mythic project of total liberation. What's envisaged is nothing less than the liberation of the artist from himself, of art from the particular artwork, of art from history, of spirit from matter, of the mind from its perceptual and intellectual limitations.

As some people know now, there are ways of thinking that we don't know about. Nothing could be more important or precious than that knowledge, however unborn. The sense of urgency, the spiritual restlessness it engenders, cannot be appeased, and continues to fuel the radical art of this century. Through its advocacy of silence and reduction, art commits an act of violence upon itself, turning art into a species of auto-manipulation, of conjuring—trying to bring these new ways of thinking to birth.

Silence is a strategy for the transvaluation of art, art itself being the herald of an anticipated radical transvaluation of human values. But the success of this strategy must mean its eventual abandonment, or at least its significan, modification.

Silence is a prophecy, one which the artist's actions can be understood as attempting both to fulfill and to reverse.

As language points to its own transcendence in silence, silence points to its own transcendence—to a speech beyond silence.

But can the whole enterprise become an act of bad faith if the artist knows *this*, too?

12

A famous quotation: "Everything that can be thought at all can be thought clearly. Everything that can be said at all can be said clearly. But not everything that can be thought can be said."

Notice that Wittgenstein, with his scrupulous avoidance of the psychological issue, doesn't ask why, when, and in what circumstances someone would *want* to put into words "everything that can be thought" (even if he could), or even to utter (whether clearly or not) "everything that could be said."

13

Of everything that's said, one can ask: *why?* (Including: why should I say *that?* And: why should I say anything at all?)

Moreover, strictly speaking, nothing that's *said* is true. (Though a person can *be* the truth, one can't ever say it.)

Still, things that are said can sometimes be helpful—which is what people ordinarily mean when they regard something *said* as being true. Speech can enlighten, relieve, confuse, exalt, infect, antagonize, gratify, grieve, stun, animate. While language is regularly used to inspire to action, some verbal statements, either written or oral, are themselves the performing of an action (as in promising, swearing, bequeathing). Another use of speech, if anything more common than that of provoking actions, is to provoke further speech. But speech can silence, too. This indeed is how it must be: without the polarity of silence, the whole system of language would fail. And beyond its generic function as the dialectical opposite of speech, silence—like speech—also has more specific, less inevitable uses.

One use for silence: certifying the absence or renunciation of thought. Silence is often employed as a magical or mimetic procedure in repressive social relationships, as in the Jesuit regulations about speaking to superiors and in the disciplining of children. (This should not be confused with the practice of certain monastic disciplines, such as the Trappist order, in which silence is both an ascetic act and bears witness to the condition of being perfectly "full."

Another, apparently opposed, use for silence: certifying the completion of thought. In the words of Karl Jaspers, "He who has the final answers can no longer speak to the other, breaking off genuine communication for the sake of what he believes in."

Still another use for silence: providing time for the continuing or exploring of thought. Notably, speech closes off thought. (An example: the enterprise of criticism, in which there seems no way for a critic not to assert that a given artist is *this*, he's *that*, etc.) But if one decides an issue isn't closed, it's not. This is presumably the rationale behind the voluntary experiments in silence that some contemporary spiritual athletes, like Buckminster Fuller, have undertaken, and the element of wisdom in the otherwise mainly authoritarian, philistine silence of the orthodox, Freudian psychoanalyst. Silence keeps things "open."

Still another use for silence: furnishing or aiding speech to attain its maximum integrity or seriousness. Everyone has experienced how, when punctuated by long silences, words weigh more; they become almost palpable. Or how, when one talks less, one begins feeling more fully one's physical presence in a given space. Silence undermines "bad speech," by which I mean dissociated speech—speech dissociated from the body (and, therefore, from feeling), speech not organically informed by the sensuous presence and concrete particularity of the speaker and by the individual occasion for using language. Unmoored from the body, speech deteriorates. It becomes false, inane, ignoble, weightless. Silence can inhibit or counteract this tendency, providing a kind of ballast, monitoring and even correcting language when it becomes inauthentic.

Given these perils to the authenticity of language (which doesn't depend on the character of any isolated statement or even group of statements, but on the relation of speaker, utterance, and situation), the imaginary project of saying clearly "everything that can be said" suggested by Wittgenstein's remarks looks fearfully complicated. (How much time would one have? Would one have to speak quickly?) The philosopher's hypothetical universe of clear speech (which assigns to silence only "that whereof one cannot speak") would seem to be a moralist's, or a psychiatrist's, nightmare—at the least a place no one should lightheartedly enter. Is there anyone who *wants* to say "everything that could be said"? The psychologically plausible answer would seem to be no. But yes is plausible, too—as a rising ideal of modern culture. Isn't that what many people *do* want today—to say everything that can be said? But this aim cannot be maintained without inner conflict. In part inspired by the spread of the ideals of psychotherapy, people are yearning to say "everything" (thereby, among other results, further undermining the crumbling distinction between public and private endeavors, between information and secrets). But in an overpopulated world being connected by global electronic communication and jet travel at a pace too rapid and violent for an organically sound person to assimilate without shock, people are also suffering from a revulsion at any further proliferation of speech and images. Such different factors as the unlimited "technological reproduction" and near universal diffusion of printed language and speech as well as images (from "news" to "art objects"), and the degeneration of public language within the realms of politics and advertising and entertainment, have produced, especially among the better-educated inhabitants of modern mass society, a devaluation of language. (I should argue, contrary to McLuhan, that a devaluation of the power and credibility of images has taken place no less profound than, and essentially similar to, that afflicting language.) And, as the prestige of language falls, that of silence rises.

I am alluding, at this point, to the sociological context of the contemporary ambivalence toward language. The matter, of course, goes much deeper than this. In addition to the specific sociological determinants, one must recognize the operation of something like a perennial discontent with language that has been formulated in each of the major civilizations of the Orient and Occident, whenever thought reaches a certain high, *excruciating* order of complexity and spiritual seriousness.

Traditionally, it has been through the religious vocabulary, with its meta-absolutes of "sacred" and "profane," "human" and "divine," that the dis-affection with language itself has been charted. In particular, the antecedents of art's dilemmas and strategies are to be found in the radical wing of the mystic-al tradition. (Cf., among Christian texts, the *Mystica Theologia* of Dionysius the Areopagite, the anonymous *Cloud of Unknowing,* the writings of Jakob Boehme and Meister Eckhart; and parallels in Zen, Taoist, and Sufi texts.) The mystical tradition has always recognized, in Norman Brown's phrase, "the neurotic character of language." (According to Boehme, Adam spoke a language differ-ent from all known languages. It was "sensual speech," the unmediated expres-sive instrument of the senses, proper to beings integrally part of sensuous nature —that is, still employed by all the animals except that sick animal, man. This, which Boehme calls the only "natural language," the sole language free from distortion and illusion, is what man will speak again when he recovers paradise.) But in our time, the most striking developments of such ideas have been made by artists (and certain psychotherapists) rather than by the timid legatees of the religious traditions.

Explicitly in revolt against what is deemed the desiccated, categorized life of the ordinary mind, the artist issues his own call for a revision of language. A good deal of contemporary art is moved by this quest for a consciousness purified of contaminated language and, in some versions, of the distortions produced by conceiving the world exclusively in conventional verbal (in their debased sense, "rational" or "logical") terms. Art itself becomes a kind of counterviolence, seeking to loosen the grip upon consciousness of the habits of lifeless, static verbalization, presenting models of "sensual speech."

If anything, the volume of discontent has been turned up since the arts inherited the problem of language from religious discourse. It's not just that words, ultimately, are inadequate to the highest aims of consciousness; or even that they get in the way. Art expresses a double discontent. We lack words, and we have too many of them. It raises two complaints about language. Words are too crude. And words are also too busy—inviting a hyperactivity of consciousness that is not only dysfunctional, in terms of human capacities of feeling and acting, but actively deadens the mind and blunts the senses.

Language is demoted to the status of an event. Something takes place in time, a voice speaking which points to the before and to what comes after an utterance: silence. Silence, then, is both the precondition of speech and the result or aim of properly directed speech. On this model, the artist's activity is the creating or establishing of silence; the efficacious artwork leaves silence in its wake. Silence, administered by the artist, is part of a program of perceptual and cultural therapy, often on the model of shock therapy rather than of persuasion. Even if the artist's medium is words, he can share in this task: language can be employed to check language, to express muteness. Mallarmé thought it was the job of poetry, using words, to clean up our word-clogged reality—by creating silences around things. Art must mount a full-scale attack on language itself, by means of language and its surrogates, on behalf of the standard of silence.

14

In the end, the radical critique of consciousness (first delineated by the mystical tradition, now administered by unorthodox psychotherapy and high modernist art) always lays the blame on language. Consciousness, experienced as a burden, is conceived of as the memory of all the words that have ever been said.

Krishnamurti claims that we must give up psychological, as distinct from factual, memory. Otherwise, we keep filling up the new with the old, closing off experience by hooking each experience onto the last.

We must destroy continuity (which is insured by psychological memory), by going to the *end* of each emotion or thought.

And after the end, what supervenes (for a while) is silence.

15

In his Fourth Duino Elegy, Rilke gives a metaphoric statement of the problem of language and recommends a procedure for approaching as near the horizon of silence as he considers feasible. A prerequisite of "emptying out" is to be able to perceive what one is "full of," what words and mechanical gestures one is stuffed with, like a doll; only then, in polar confrontation with the doll, does the "angel" appear, a figure representing an equally inhuman though "higher" possibility, that of an entirely unmediated, translinguistic apprehension. Neither doll nor angel, human beings remain situated within the kingdom of language. But for nature, then things, then other people, then the textures of ordinary life to be experienced from a stance other than the crippled one of mere spectatorship, language must regain its chastity. As Rilke describes it in the Ninth Elegy, the redemption of language (which is to say, the redemption of the world through its interiorization in consciousness) is a long, infinitely arduous task.

Human beings are so "fallen" that they must start with the simplest linguistic act: the naming of things. Perhaps no more than this minimal function can be preserved from the general corruption of discourse. Language may very well have to remain within a permanent state of reduction. Though perhaps, when this spiritual exercise of confining language to naming is perfected, it may be possible to pass on to other, more ambitious uses of language, nothing must be attempted which will allow consciousness to become reestranged from itself.

For Rilke the overcoming of the alienation of consciousness is conceivable; and not, as in the radical myths of the mystics, through transcending language altogether. It suffices to cut back drastically the scope and use of language. A tremendous spiritual preparation (the contrary of "alienation") is required for this deceptively simple act of naming. It is nothing less than the scouring and harmonious sharpening of the senses (the very opposite of such violent projects, with roughly the same end and informed by the same hostility to verbal-rational culture, as "systematically deranging the senses").

Rilke's remedy lies halfway between exploiting the numbness of language as a gross, fully installed cultural institution and yielding to the suicidal vertigo of pure silence. But this middle ground of reducing language to naming can be claimed in quite another way than his. Contrast the benign nominalism proposed by Rilke (and proposed and practiced by Francis Ponge) with the brutal nominalism adopted by many other artists. The more familiar recourse of modern art to the aesthetics of the inventory is not made—as in Rilke—with an eye to "humanizing" things, but rather to confirming their inhumanity, their impersonality, their indifference to and separateness from human concerns. (Examples of the "inhumane" preoccupation with naming: Roussel's *Impressions of Africa*; the silk-screen paintings and early films of Andy Warhol; the early novels of Robbe-Grillet, which attempt to confine the function of language to bare physical description and location.)

Rilke and Ponge assume that there *are* priorities: rich as opposed to vacuous objects, events with a certain allure. (This is the incentive for trying to peel back language, allowing the "things" themselves to speak.) More decisively, they assume that if there are states of false (language-clogged) consciousness, there are also authentic states of consciousness—which it's the function of art to promote. The alternative view denies the traditional hierarchies of interest and meaning, in which some things have more "significance" than others. The distinction between true and false experience, true and false consciousness is also denied: in principle, one should desire to pay attention to everything. It's this view, most elegantly formulated by Cage though its practice is found everywhere, that leads to the art of the inventory, the catalogue, surfaces; also "chance." The function of art isn't to sanction any specific experience, except the state of being open to the multiplicity of experience—which ends in practice by a decided stress on things usually considered trivial or unimportant.

The attachment of contemporary art to the "minimal" narrative principle of the catalogue or inventory seems almost to parody the capitalist world-view, in which the environment is atomized into "items" (a category embracing things and persons, works of art and natural organisms), and in which every item is a commodity—that is, a discrete, portable object. A general leveling of value is encouraged in the art of inventory, which is itself only one of the possible approaches to an ideally uninflected discourse. Traditionally, the effects of an artwork have been unevenly distributed, to induce in the audience a certain sequence of experience: first arousing, then manipulating, and eventually fulfilling emotional expectations. What is proposed now is a discourse without emphases in this traditional sense. (Again, the principle of the stare as opposed to the look.)

Such art could also be described as establishing great "distance" (between spectator and art object, between the spectator and his emotions). But, psychologically, distance often is linked with the most intense state of feeling, in which the coolness or impersonality with which something is treated measures the insatiable interest that thing has for us. The distance that a great deal of "antihumanist" art proposes is actually equivalent to obsession—an aspect of the involvement in "things" of which the "humanist" nominalism of Rilke has no intimation.

16

"There is something strange in the acts of writing and speaking," Novalis wrote in 1799. "The ridiculous and amazing mistake people make is to believe they use words in relation to things. They are unaware of the nature of language—which is to be its own and only concern, making it so fertile and splendid a mystery. When someone talks just for the sake of talking he is saying the most original and truthful thing he can say."

Novalis' statement may help explain an apparent paradox: that in the era of the widespread advocacy of art's silence, an increasing number of works of art babble. Verbosity and repetitiveness are particularly noticeable in the temporal arts of prose fiction, music, film, and dance, many of which cultivate a kind of ontological stammer—facilitated by their refusal of the incentives for a clean, anti-redundant discourse supplied by linear, beginning-middle-and-end construction. But actually, there's no contradiction. For the contemporary appeal for silence has never indicated merely a hostile dismissal of language. It also signifies a very high estimate of language—of its powers, of its past health, and of the current dangers it poses to a free consciousness. From this intense and ambivalent valuation proceeds the impulse for a discourse that appears both irrepressible (and, in principle, interminable) and strangely inarticulate, painfully reduced. Discernible in the fictions of Stein, Burroughs, and Beckett is the subliminal idea that it might be possible to out-talk language, or to talk oneself into silence.

This is not a very promising strategy, considering what results might reasonably be anticipated from it. But perhaps not so odd, when one observes how often the aesthetic of silence appears alongside a barely controlled abhorrence of the void.

Accommodating these two contrary impulses may produce the need to fill up all the spaces with objects of slight emotional weight or with large areas of barely modulated color or evenly detailed objects, or to spin a discourse with as few possible inflections, emotive variations, and risings and fallings of emphasis. These procedures seem analogous to the behavior of an obsessional neurotic warding off a danger. The acts of such a person must be repeated in the identical form, because the danger remains the same; and they must be repeated endlessly, because the danger never seems to go away. But the emotional fires feeding the art-discourse analogous to obsessionalism may be turned down so low one can almost forget they're there. Then all that's left to the ear is a kind of steady hum or drone. What's left to the eye is the neat filling of a space with things, or, more accurately, the patient transcription of the surface detail of things.

In this view, the "silence" of things, images, and words is a prerequisite for their proliferation. Were they endowed with a more potent, individual charge, each of the various elements of the artwork would claim more psychic space and then their total number might have to be reduced.

17

Sometimes the accusation against language is not directed against all of language but only against the written word. Thus Tristan Tzara urged the burning of all books and libraries to bring about a new era of oral legends. And McLuhan, as everyone knows, makes the sharpest distinction between written language (which exists in "visual space") and oral speech (which exists in "auditory space"), praising the psychic and cultural advantages of the latter as the basis for sensibility.

If written language is singled out as the culprit, what will be sought is not so much the reduction as the metamorphosis of language into something looser, more intuitive, less organized and inflected, non-linear (in McLuhan's terminology) and—noticeably—more verbose. But, of course, it is just these qualities that characterize many of the great prose narratives of our time. Joyce, Stein, Gadda, Laura Riding, Beckett, and Burroughs employ a language whose norms and energies come from oral speech, with its circular repetitive movements and essentially first-person voice.

"Speaking for the sake of speaking is the formula of deliverance," Novalis said. (Deliverance from what? From speaking? From art?)

In my opinion, Novalis has succinctly described the proper approach of the writer to language and offered the basic criterion for literature as an art. But to what extent oral speech is the privileged model for the speech of literature as an art is still an open question.

18

A corollary of the growth of this conception of art's language as autonomous and self-sufficient (and, in the end, self-reflective) is a decline in "meaning" as traditionally sought in works of art. "Speaking for the sake of speaking" forces us to relocate the meaning of linguistic or para-linguistic statements. We are led to abandon meaning (in the sense of references to entities outside the artwork) as the criterion for the language of art in favor of "use." (Wittgenstein's famous thesis, "the meaning is the use," can and should be rigorously applied to art.)

"Meaning" partially or totally converted into "use" is the secret behind the widespread strategy of *literalness,* a major development of the aesthetics of silence. A variant on this: hidden literality, exemplified by such different writers as Kafka and Beckett. The narratives of Kafka and Beckett seem puzzling because they appear to invite the reader to ascribe high-powered symbolic and allegorical meanings to them and, at the same time, repel such ascriptions. Yet when the narrative is examined, it discloses no more than what it literally means. The power of their language derives precisely from the fact that the meaning is so bare.

The effect of such bareness is often a kind of anxiety—like the anxiety produced when familiar things aren't in their place or playing their accustomed role. One may be made as anxious by unexpected literalness as by the Surrealists' "disturbing" objects and unexpected scale and condition of objects conjoined in an imaginary landscape. Whatever is wholly mysterious is at once both psychically relieving and anxiety-provoking. (A perfect machine for agitating this pair of contrary emotions: the Bosch drawing in a Dutch museum that shows trees furnished with two ears at the sides of their trunks, as if they were listening to the forest, while the forest floor is strewn with eyes.) Before a fully conscious work of art, one feels something like the mixture of anxiety, detachment, pruriency, and relief that a physically sound person feels when he glimpses an amputee. Beckett speaks favorably of a work of art which would be a "total object, complete with missing parts, instead of partial object, Question of degree."

But exactly what is a totality and what constitutes completeness in art (or anything else)? That problem is, in principle, unresolvable. Whatever way a work of art is, it could have been—could be—different. The necessity of *these* parts in this order is never given; it is conferred.

The refusal to admit this essential contingency (or openness) is what inspires the audience's will to confirm the closedness of a work by interpreting it, and what creates the feeling common among reflective artists and critics that the artwork is always somehow in arrears of or inadequate to its "subject." But unless one is committed to the idea that art "expresses" something, these procedures and attitudes are far from inevitable.

19

This tenacious concept of art as "expression" has given rise to the most common, and dubious, version of the notion of silence—which invokes the idea of "the ineffable." The theory supposes that the province of art is "the beautiful," which implies effects of unspeakableness, indescribability, ineffability. Indeed, the search to express the inexpressible is taken as the very criterion of art; and sometimes becomes the occasion for a strict—and to my mind untenable—distinction between prose literature and poetry. It is from this position that Valéry advanced his famous argument (repeated in a quite different context by Sartre) that the novel is not, strictly speaking, an art form at all. His reason is that since the aim of prose is to communicate, the use of language in prose is perfectly straightforward. Poetry, being an art, should have quite different aims: to express an experience which is essentially ineffable; using language to express muteness. In contrast to prose writers, poets are engaged in subverting their own instrument and seeking to pass beyond it.

This theory, so far as it assumes that art is concerned with beauty, is not very interesting. (Modern aesthetics is crippled by its dependence upon this essentially vacant concept. As if art were "about" beauty, as science is "about" truth!) But even if the theory dispenses with the notion of beauty, there is still a more serious objection. The view that expressing the ineffable is an essential function of poetry (considered as a paradigm of all the arts) is naïvely unhistorical. The ineffable, while surely a perennial category of consciousness, has certainly not always made its home in the arts. Its traditional shelter was in religious discourse and, secondarily (as Plato relates in his 7th Epistle), in philosophy. The fact that contemporary artists are concerned with silence—and, therefore, in one extension, with the ineffable—must be understood historically, as a consequence of the prevailing contemporary myth of the "absoluteness" of art. The value placed on silence doesn't arise by virtue of the *nature* of art, but derives from the contemporary ascription of certain "absolute" qualities to the art object and to the activity of the artist.

The extent to which art *is* involved with the ineffable is more specific, as well as contemporary: art, in the modern conception, is always connected with systematic transgressions of a formal sort. The systematic violation of older formal conventions practiced by modern artists gives their work a certain aura of the unspeakable—for instance, as the audience uneasily senses the negative presence of what else could be, but isn't being, said; and as any "statement" made in an aggressively new or difficult form tends to seem equivocal or merely vacant. But these features of ineffability must not be acknowledged at the expense of one's awareness of the positivity of the work of art. Contemporary art, no matter how much it has defined itself by a taste for negation, can still be analyzed as a set of assertions of a formal kind.

For instance, each work of art gives us a form or paradigm or model of *knowing* something, an epistemology. But viewed as a spiritual project, a vehicle of aspirations toward an absolute, what any work of art supplies is a specific model for meta-social or meta-ethical *tact*, a standard of decorum. Each art-work indicates the unity of certain preferences about what can and cannot be said (or represented). At the same time that it may make a tacit proposal for upsetting previously consecrated rulings on what can be said (or represented), it issues its own set of limits.

20

Contemporary artists advocate silence in two styles: loud and soft.

The loud style is a function of the unstable antithesis of "plenum" and "void." The sensuous, ecstatic, translinguistic apprehension of the plenum is notoriously fragile: in a terrible, almost instantaneous plunge it can collapse into the void of negative silence. With all its awareness of risk-taking (the hazards of spiritual nausea, even of madness), this advocacy of silence tends to be frenetic and overgeneralizing. It is also frequently apocalyptic and must endure the indignity of all apocalyptic thinking: namely, to prophesy the end, to see the day come, to outlive it, and then to set a new date for the incineration of consciousness and the definitive pollution of language and exhaustion of the possibilities of art-discourse.

The other way of talking about silence is more cautious. Basically, it presents itself as an extension of a main feature of traditional classicism: the concern with modes of propriety, with standards of seemliness. Silence is only "reticence" stepped up to the nth degree. Of course, in the translation of this concern from the matrix of traditional classical art, the tone has changed—from didactic seriousness to ironic open-mindedness. But while the clamorous style of proclaiming the rhetoric of silence may seem more passionate, its more subdued advocates (like Cage, Johns) are saying something equally drastic. They are reacting to the same idea of art's absolute aspirations (by programmatic disavowals of art); they share the same disdain for the "meanings" established by bourgeois-rationalist culture, indeed for culture itself in the familiar sense. What is voiced by the Futurists, some of the Dada artists, and Burroughs as a harsh despair and perverse vision of apocalypse is no less serious for being proclaimed in a polite voice and as a sequence of playful affirmations. Indeed, it could be argued that silence is likely to remain a viable notion for modern art and consciousness only if deployed with a considerable, near systematic irony.

21

It is in the nature of all spiritual projects to tend to consume themselves—exhausting their own sense, the very meaning of the terms in which they are couched. (This is why "spirituality" must be continually reinvented.) All genuinely ultimate projects of consciousness eventually become projects for the unraveling of thought itself.

Art conceived as a spiritual project is no exception. As an abstracted and fragmented replica of the positive nihilism expounded by the radical religious myths, the serious art of our time has moved increasingly toward the most excruciating inflections of consciousness. Conceivably, irony is the only feasible counterweight to this grave use of art as the arena for the ordeal of consciousness. The present prospect is that artists will go on abolishing art, only to resurrect it in a more retracted version. As long as art bears up under the pressure of chronic interrogation, it would seem desirable that some of the questions have a certain playful quality.

But this prospect depends, perhaps, on the viability of irony itself.

From Socrates on, there are countless witnesses to the value of irony for the private individual: as a complex, serious method of seeking and holding one's truth, and as a means of saving one's sanity. But as irony becomes the good taste of what is, after all, an essentially collective activity—the making of art—it may prove less serviceable.

One need not judge as categorically as Nietzsche, who thought the spread of irony throughout a culture signified the floodtide of decadence and the approaching end of that culture's vitality and powers. In the post-political, electronically connected cosmopolis in which all serious modern artists have taken out premature citizenship, certain organic connections between culture and "thinking" (and art is certainly now, mainly, a form of thinking) appear to have been broken, so that Nietzsche's diagnosis may need to be modified. But if irony has more positive resources than Nietzsche acknowledged, there still remains a question as to how far the resources of irony can be stretched. It seems unlikely that the possibilities of continually undermining one's assumptions can go on unfolding indefinitely into the future, without being eventually checked by despair or by a laugh that leaves one without any breath at all.

Film as Environment

ANTHONY SCHILLACI

THE better we understand how young people view film, the more we have to revise our notion of what film is. Seen through young eyes, film is destroying conventions almost as quickly as they can be formulated. Whether the favored director is "young" like Richard Lester, Roman Polanski, and Arthur Penn, or "old" like Kubrick, Fellini, and Buñuel, he must be a practicing cinematic anarchist to catch the eye of the young. If we're looking for the young audience between sixteen and twenty-four, which accounts for 48 per cent of the box office today, we will find they're on a trip, whether in a Yellow Submarine or on a Space Odyssey. A brief prayer muttered for Rosemary's Baby and they're careening down a dirt road with Bonnie and Clyde, the exhaust spitting banjo sounds, or sitting next to The Graduate as he races across the Bay Bridge after his love. The company they keep is fast; Belle de Jour, Petulia, and Joanna are not exactly a sedentary crowd. Hyped up on large doses of *Rowan and Martin's Laugh-In*, and *Mission: Impossible*, they are ready for anything that an evolving film idiom can throw on the screen. And what moves them must have the pace, novelty, style, and spontaneity of a television commercial.

All of this sounds as if the script is by McLuhan. Nevertheless, it is borne out by the experience of teaching contemporary film to university juniors and seniors, staging film festivals for late teens and early adults, and talking to literally hundreds of people about movies. The phenomenon may be interesting, and even verifiable, but what makes it important is its significance for the future of film art. The young have discovered that film is an environment which you put on, demanding a different kind of structure, a different mode of attention than any other art. Their hunger is for mind-expanding experience and simultaneity, and their art is film.

Occasionally a young director gives us a glimpse of the new world of film as environmental art. The optical exercise known as *Flicker* came on like a karate chop to the eyes at Lincoln Center's Film Seminar three years ago. One half-hour of white light flashing at varied frequency, accompanied by a deafening sound track designed to infuriate, describes the screen, but not what happened to the audience. As strangers turned to ask if it was a put-on, if they had forgotten to put film in the projector, they noticed that the flickering light fragmented their motions, stylizing them like the actions of a silent movie. In minutes, the entire audience was on its feet, acting out spontaneous pantomimes for one another, no one looking at the flashing screen. The happening precipitated by *Flicker* could be called the film of the future, but it was actually an anti-environment that gives us an insight into the past. By abstracting totally from content, the director demonstrated that the film is in the audience which acts out personal and public dramas as the screen turns it on. The delight of this experience opened up the notion of film as an environmental art.

Critics have noted the trend which leaves story line and character development strewn along the highways of film history like the corpses in Godard's *Weekend*. The same critics have not, in general, recognized that the growing option for nonlinear, unstructured experiences that leave out sequence, motivation, and "argument" is a vote for film as environment. Young people turn to film for a time-space environment in which beautiful things happen to them. The screen has, in a sense, less and less to do with what explodes in the audience. This new scene could mean either that film is plunging toward irrelevant stimulation, or that there is a new and unprecedented level of participation and involvement in young audiences. I prefer to think the latter is the case. Young people want to talk about Ben's hang-up, why Rosemary stayed with the baby, or what it feels like to be in the electronic hands of a computer like Hal. They do not forget the film the minute they walk out of the theater.

The attention given the new style of film goes beyond stimulation to real involvement. A generation with eyes fixed on the rearview mirror tended to give film the same attention required for reading—that is, turning off all the senses except the eyes. Film became almost as private as reading, and little reaction to the total audience was experienced. As the Hollywood dream factory cranked out self-contained worlds of fantasy, audiences entered them with confidence that nothing even vaguely related to real life would trouble their reveries. As long as one came and left in the middle of the film, it was relatively non-involving as environment. When television brought the image into the living room, people gave it "movie attention," hushing everyone who entered the sacred presence of the tube as they would a film patron who talked during a movie. One was not allowed to speak, even during commercials. It took post-literate man to teach us how to use television as environment, as a moving image on the wall to which one may give total or peripheral attention as he wishes. The child who had TV as a baby-sitter does not turn off all his senses, but walks about the room carrying on a multiplicity of actions and relationships, his attention a special reward for the cleverness of the pitchman, or the skill of the artist. He is king, and not captive. . . .

The new multisensory involvement with film as total environment has been primary in destroying literary values in film. Their decline is not merely farewell to an understandable but unwelcome dependence; it means the emergence of a new identity for film. The diminished role of dialogue is a case in point. The difference between *Star Trek* and *Mission: Impossible* marks the trend toward self-explanatory images that need no dialogue. Take an audio tape of these two popular TV shows, as we did in a recent study, and it will reveal that while *Mission: Impossible* is completely unintelligible without images, *Star Trek* is simply an illustrated radio serial, complete on the level of sound. It has all the characteristics of radio's golden age: actions explained, immediate identification of character by voice alone, and even organ music to squeeze the proper emotion or end the episode. Like *Star Trek,* the old film was frequently a talking picture. . . . It was the films of Fellini and Bergman, with their subtitles, that convinced us there had been too many words. Approximately one-third of the dialogue is omitted in subtitled versions of these films, with no discernible damage—and some improvement—of the original.

More than dialogue, however, has been jettisoned. Other literary values, such as sequential narrative, dramatic choice, and plot are in a state of advanced atrophy, rapidly becoming vestigial organs on the body of film art as young people have their say. *Petulia* has no "story," unless one laboriously pieces together the interaction between the delightful arch-kook and the newly divorced surgeon, in which case it is nothing more than an encounter. The story line wouldn't make a ripple if it were not scrambled and fragmented into an experience that explodes from a free-floating present into both past and future simultaneously. *Petulia* is like some views of the universe which represent the ancient past of events whose light is just now reaching us simultaneously with the future of our galaxy, returning from the curve of outer space. Many films succeed by virtue of what they leave out. *2001: A Space Odyssey* is such a film, its muted understatement creating gaps in the action that invite our inquiry. Only a square viewer wants to know where the black monolith came from and where it is going. For most of the young viewers to whom I have spoken, it is just there. *Last Year at Marienbad* made the clock as limply shapeless as one of Salvador Dali's watches, while $8\frac{1}{2}$ came to life on the strength of free associations eagerly grasped by young audiences. The effect of such films is a series of open-ended impressions, freely evoked and enjoyed, strongly inviting inquiry and involvement. In short, film is freed to work as environment, something which does not simply contain, but shapes people, tilting the balance of their faculties, radically altering their perceptions, and ultimately their views of self and all reality. Perhaps one sense of the symptomatic word "grooving," which applies to both sight and sound environments, is that a new mode of attention—multisensory, total, and simultaneous—has arrived. When you "groove," you do not analyze, follow an argument, or separate sensations; rather, you are massaged into a feeling of heightened life and consciousness.

If young people look at film this way, it is in spite of the school, a fact which says once more with emphasis that education is taking place outside the classroom walls. The "discovery" that television commercials are the most exciting and creative part of today's programming is old news to the young. Commercials are a crash course in speed-viewing, their intensified sensations challenging the viewer to synthesize impressions at an ever increasing rate. The result is short films like one produced at UCLA, presenting 3,000 years of art in three minutes. *God is Dog Spelled Backwards* takes you from the cave paintings of Lascaux to the latest abstractions, with some images remaining on the screen a mere twenty-fourth of a second! The young experience the film, however, not as confusing, but as exuberantly and audaciously alive. They feel joy of recognition, exhilaration at the intense concentration necessary (one blink encompasses a century of art), and awe at the 180-second review of every aspect of the human condition. Intended as a put-on, the film becomes a three-minute commercial for man. This hunger for overload is fed by the television commercial, with its nervous jump cuts demolishing continuity, and its lazy dissolves blurring time-space boundaries. Whether the young are viewing film "through" television, or simply through their increased capacity for information and sensation (a skill which makes most schooling a bore), the result is the same—film becomes the primary environment in which the hunger to know through experience is satisfied.

Hidden within this unarticulated preference of the young is a quiet tribute to film as the art that humanizes change. In its beginnings, the cinema was celebrated as the art that mirrored reality in its functional dynamism. And although the early vision predictably gave way to misuse of the medium, today the significance of the filmic experience of change stubbornly emerges again. Instead of prematurely stabilizing change, film celebrates it. The cinema can inject life into historical events by the photo-scan, in which camera movement and editing liberate the vitality of images from the past. *City of Gold,* a short documentary by the National Film Board of Canada, takes us by zoom and cut into the very life of the Klondike gold rush, enabling us to savor the past as an experience.

Education increasingly means developing the ability to live humanly in the technological culture by changing with it. Film is forever spinning out intensifications of the environment which make it visible and livable. The ability to control motion through its coordinates of time and space makes film a creative agent in change. Not only does film reflect the time-space continuum of contemporary physics, but it can manipulate artistically those dimensions of motion which we find most problematic. The actuality of the medium, its here-and-now impact, reflects how completely the present tense has swallowed up both past and future. Freudian psychology dissolves history by making the past something we live; accelerated change warps the future by bringing it so close that we can't conceive it as "ahead" of us. An art which creates its own space, and can move time forward and back, can humanize change by conditioning us to live comfortably immersed in its fluctuations.

On the level of form, then, perhaps the young are tuned in to film for "telling it like it is" in a sense deeper than that of fidelity to the event. It is film's accurate reflection of a society and of human life totally in flux that makes it the liberating art of the time. We live our lives more like Guido in *8½*—

spinners of fantasies, victims of events, the products of mysterious associations—
than we do like Maria in *The Sound of Music,* with a strange destiny guiding our
every step. Instead of resisting change and bottling it, film intensifies the experience of change, humanizing it in the process. What makes the ending of *The
Graduate* "true" to young people is not that Ben has rescued his girl from the
Establishment, but that he did it without a complete plan for the future. The
film may fail under analysis, but it is extraordinarily coherent as experience, as
I learned in conversations about it with the young. The same accurate reflection
of the day may be said of the deep space relativity of *2001,* the frantic pace of
Petulia, or the melodramatic plotting of *Rosemary's Baby.* Whether this limitless
capacity for change within the creative limits of art has sober implications for
the future raises the next (and larger) question of what young people look for
and get out of film.

When the question of film content is raised, the example of *Flicker* and other
films cited may seem to indicate that young people favor as little substance as
possible in their film experiences. A casual glance at popular drive-in fare would
confirm this opinion quickly. Nevertheless, their attitude toward "what films
are about" evidences a young, developing sensitivity to challenging comments
on what it means to be human. The young are digging the strong humanism
of the current film renaissance and allowing its currents to carry them to a level
deeper than that reached by previous generations. One might almost say that
young people are going to the film-maker's work for values that they have
looked for in vain from the social, political, or religious establishments. This
reaction, which has made film modern man's morality play, has not been carefully analyzed, but the present state of evidence invites our inquiry.

As far as the "point" of films is concerned, young people will resist a pack-
aged view, but will welcome a problematic one. The cry, "Please, I'd rather
do it myself!" should be taken to heart by the film-maker. It is better to use
understatement in order to score a personal discovery by the viewer. Such a
discovery of an idea is a major part of our delight in the experience of film art.
A frequent answer to a recent survey question indicated that a young man takes
his girl to the movies so that they will have something important to talk about.
It is not a matter of pitting film discussion against "making out," but of
recognizing that a rare and precious revelation of self to the other is often occasioned by a good film. The young feel this experience as growth, expanded
vitality, more integral possession of one's self with the consequent freedom to
go out to others more easily and more effectively.

Very little of the business of being human happens by instinct, and so we
need every form of education that enlightens or accelerates that process. While
young people do not go to films for an instant humanization course, a strong
part of the pleasure they take in excellent films does just this. Whether through
a connaturality of the medium described earlier, or because of a freer viewpoint,
young audiences frequently get more out of films than their mentors. It is not
so much a matter of seeing more films, but of seeing more in a film. The film-
as-escape attitude belongs to an age when the young were not yet born; and

the film-as-threat syndrome has little meaning for the sixteen to twenty-four group. . . . A typical irrelevance that causes youthful wonder is the elderly matron's complaint that *Bonnie and Clyde* would teach bad driving habits to the young.

The performance of youthful audiences in discussions of contemporary film indicates their freedom from the judgmental screen which blurs so many films for other generations. In speaking of *Bonnie and Clyde,* late high school kids and young adults do not dwell upon the career of crime or the irregularity of the sexual relationship, but upon other things. The development of their love fascinates young people, because Clyde shows he knows Bonnie better than she knows herself. Although he resists her aggressive sexual advances, he knows and appreciates her as a person. It is the sincerity of their growing love that overcomes his impotence, and the relationship between this achievement and their diminished interest in crime is not lost on the young audience. The reversal of the "sleep together now, get acquainted later" approach is significant here. These are only a few of the nuances that sensitive ears and eyes pick up beneath the gunfire and banjo-plucking. Similarly, out of the chaotic impressions of *Petulia,* patterns are perceived. Young people note the contrasts between Petulia's kooky, chaotic life, and the over-controlled precision of the surgeon's existence. The drama is that they both come away a little different for their encounter. Instead of a stale moral judgment on their actions, one finds open-ended receptivity to the personal development of the characters.

Youth in search of identity is often presented as a ridiculous spectacle, a generation of Kierkegaards plaintively asking each other: "Who am I?" Nevertheless, the quest is real and is couched in terms of a hunger for experience. SDS or LSD, McCarthy buttons or yippie fashions, it is all experimentation in identity, trying on experiences to see if they fit. The plea is to stop the world, not so that they can get off, but so they can get a handle on it. To grasp each experience, to suck it dry of substance, and to grow in that process is behind the desire to be "turned on." But of all the lurid and bizarre routes taken by young people, the one that draws least comment is that of the film experience. More people have had their minds expanded by films than by LSD. Just as all art nudges man into the sublime and vicarious experience of the whole range of the human condition, film does so with a uniquely characteristic totality and involvement.

Ben, *The Graduate,* is suffocating under his parents' aspirations, a form of drowning which every young person has felt in some way. But the film mirrors their alienation in filmic terms, by changes in focus, by the metaphors of conveyor belt sidewalk and swimming pool, better than any moralist could say it. The satirical portraits of the parents may be broad and unsubtle, but the predicament is real and compelling. This is why the young demand no assurances that Ben and the girl will live happily ever after, it is enough that he jarred himself loose from the sick apathy and languid sexual experimentation with Mrs. Robinson to go after one thing, one person that he wanted for himself, and not for others. Incidentally, those who are not busy judging the morality of the hotel scenes will note that sex doesn't communicate without love. Some may even note that Ben is using sex to strike at his parents—not a bad thing for the young (or their parents) to know.

Emotional maturity is never painless and seldom permanent, but it can become a bonus from viewing good films because it occurs there not as taught but experienced. Values communicated by film are interiorized and become a part of oneself, not simply an extension of the womb that parents and educators use to shield the young from the world. Colin Smith, in *The Loneliness of the Long Distance Runner,* IS youth, not because he did it to the Establishment, but because he is trying to be his own man and not sweat his guts out for another. The profound point of learning who you are in the experience of freedom, as Colin did in running, is not lost on the young who think about this film a little. Some speak of Col's tragedy as a failure to realize he could have won the race for himself, and not for the governor of the Borstal. Self-destruction through spite, the pitfalls of a self-justifying freedom, and the sterility of bland protest are real problems that emerge from the film. The values that appeal most are the invisible ones that move a person to act because "it's me" (part of one's identity), and not because of "them." Because they have become an object of discovery and not of imposition, such values tend to make morality indistinguishable from self-awareness.

It should be made clear, however, that it is not merely the content, but the mode of involvement in the film experience that makes its humanism effective. In terms of "message," much of contemporary film reflects the social and human concerns that Bob Dylan, the Beatles, Simon and Garfunkel, and Joan Baez communicate. But the words of their songs often conceal the radical nature of the music in which they appear. The direct emotional appeal of the sound of "Eleanor Rigby," "Give a Damn," "I Am a Rock," or "Mr. Businessman" communicates before we have the words deciphered. Films with honest human concern, similarly, change audiences as much by their style as their message. *Elvira Madigan's* overpowering portrait of a hopeless love, *A Thousand Clowns'* image of nonconformity, *Zorba's* vitality, and *Morgan's* tragedy are not so much the content of the images as the outcome of their cinematic logic. If these films change us, it is because we have done it to ourselves by opening ourselves to their experiences.

Expo 67 audiences were charmed by the Czech Kinoautomat in which their vote determined the course of comic events in a film. Once again, we find here not a peek into the future, but an insight into all film experience. In one way or another, we vote on each film's progress. The passive way is to patronize dishonest or cynical films, for our box-office ballot determines the selection of properties for years to come. We have been voting this way for superficial emotions, sterile plots, and happy endings for a generation. But we vote more actively and subtly by willing the very direction of a film through identification with the character, or absorption into the action. The viewer makes a private or social commitment in film experience. He invests a portion of himself in the action, and if he is changed, it is because he has activated his own dreams. What happens on the screen, as in the case of *Flicker,* is the catalyst for the value systems, emotional responses, and the indirect actions which are the byproducts of a good film. Film invites young people to be part of the action by making the relationships which take the work beyond a mere succession of images. The reason why young people grow through their art is that they supply the associations that merely begin on the screen but do not end there. When parents and educators become aware of this, their own efforts at fostering maturity may be less frantic, and more effective.

It is not only the films that please and delight which appeal to the young, but also those which trouble and accuse by bringing our fears into the open. The new audience for documentary films highlights a new way of looking at film as an escape *into* reality. From *The War Game* to *Warrendale*, from *The Titicut Follies'* to *Battle of Algiers*, young audiences are relishing the film's ability to document the present in terms of strong social relevance. *Portrait of Jason* is more than a voyeuristic peek into the psyche of a male whore; it is a metaphor for the black man's history in America, and this is what young people see in that film. Even the most strident dissenters will appreciate the ambiguities of *The Anderson Platoon*, which leaves us without anyone to hate, because it is not about Marines and Vietcong, but about men like ourselves. In these as in other films, the social content is intimately wed to the film experience, and together they form a new outlook. Ultimately, we may have to change our views on what film art is about.

The foregoing analysis of how young people look at film will appear to some to constitute a simplistic eulogy to youth. For this reason, we may temper our optimism by a hard look at real problems with this generation. There is a desperate need for education. Although they cannot all be structured, none of the better youthful attitudes or responses described came about by chance. Mere screening of films, for example, whether they be classics or trash, does little good. Colleges can become places where the young are taught hypocrisy, being told they "should" like Fellini, Bergman, Antonioni, or Godard. They can accept these film-makers just as uncritically as their parents adulated movie stars. Unless there is encouragement to reflect on film experience, its impact can be minimal and fleeting. Most of the responses I have mentioned came from students who were well into the habit of discussing film. These discussions are best when they flow from the natural desire we have to communicate our feelings about a film. Nonverbalization, the reluctance to betray by treacherous abstractions the ineffable experience of the film, arises at this point. Real as it is, there must be found some middle ground between a suffocatingly detailed dissection of a film, and the noncommunicative exclamation, "like WOW!" Reflecting on one's experience is an integral part of making that experience part of one's self. Furthermore, one can see an almost immediate carry-over to other film experiences from each film discussed.

A problem more crucial than lack of reflection is the poverty of critical perspective. The young can plunge into their personal version of the *auteur* theory and make a fad or fetish out of certain films and directors. Roman Polanski has made some bad films, that is, films which do not reflect his own experience and feelings honestly as did *Knife in the Water*. Fascinating as

Rosemary's Baby is, it suffers from an uncertain relationship of the director to his work. Some directors are adulated for peripheral or irrelevant reasons. Joseph Losey is a good film-maker, not because of a cynical preoccupation with evil, but because, like Hitchcock and Pinter, he makes us less certain of our virtue. And Buñuel, far from being a cheerful anarchist attacking church and society with abandon, is a careful surgeon, excising with camera the growths of degenerate myth on the cancerous culture.

In their own work, young people can celebrate bad film-making as "honest" and voyeuristic films as "mature." Criticism of poor films is not "putting down" the director for doing his own thing, especially if his thing is trite, dishonest, or so personal that it has no meaning accessible to others. Criticism means taking a stand on the basis of who you are. The current preference of spoof over satire is not just another instance of cool over hot, but is symptomatic of a noncritical stance. *Dr. Strangelove* makes comic absurdity out of the cold war from a certain conviction about what mature political action should be. The *Laugh-In* has no convictions but a lot of opinions. If it is accused of favoring an idea or cause, it will refute the charge by ridiculing what it holds. The cynical, sophisticated noninvolvement of the "won't vote" movement in the recent election has its counterpart in film viewing.

A question that should perhaps have been asked earlier is: Why should we be concerned with asking how young people look at film? Tired reasons, citing *Time's* Man of the Year, the under-twenty-five generation, or the youth-quake menace of *Wild in the Streets* (they'll be taking over!) are not appropriate here. Anyone who is interested in the direction taken by cinema, and its continued vitality in the current renaissance of the art, will have to take the young into account as the major shaping force on the medium. If the age group from sixteen to twenty-four accounts for 48 per cent of the box office, it means that this eight-year period determines the success or failure of most films. Fortunately, there has not yet appeared a formula for capturing this audience. *Variety* described the youth market as a booby trap for the industry, citing the surprise success of sleepers such as *Bonnie and Clyde* and *The Graduate,* as well as the supposed youth-appeal failures (*Half a Sixpence, Poor Cow, Here We Go Round the Mulberry Bush*). The list may suggest a higher level of young taste than producers are willing to admit. In any case, if the young have influenced the medium this far, we cannot ignore the fact. It is for this reason that we are encouraged to speculate on the future in the form of two developments revolutionizing the young approach to film: student film-making and multi-media experiences.

More and more, the answer to how young people look at film is "through the lens of a camera." In coming years, it will be youth as film-maker, and not simply as audience, that will spur the evolution of the cinema. Students want a piece of the action, whether in running a university, the country, or the world; in terms of our question, this means making films. There is a strong resonance between film-making and the increasingly sophisticated film experience. Young people delighted by a television commercial are tempted to say: "I could do that!" Considering the cost and artistry of some commercials, this is a pretty naïve statement, but it doesn't stop the young from taking out their father's Super-8 or buying an old Bolex to tell their story on film. Today, anyone can make a film. Although Robert Flaherty's longed-for parousia, when film is as cheap as paper, has not yet arrived, the art has come into the reach of almost everyone. The Young Film-Makers Conference held by Fordham University last February drew 1,200 people, 740 of them student film-makers below college age. On a few weeks' notice, some 120 films were submitted for screening. Kids flew in from Richmond, California, and bussed in from Louisville, Kentucky, with twenty-seven states and Canada represented. Numbers, however, do not tell the story. One of the notable directors and actors present sized up the scene by saying: "My God, I'm standing here in the middle of a revolution!" It was the quality of the films that caused Eli Wallach to remark, only half in jest, that some day he'd be working for one of these film-makers. The young look at film as potential or actual film-makers, and this fact raises participation to an unprecedented critical level. The phenomenon also removes the last residue of passive audience participation from the Golden Forties box-office bonanza.

Foolhardy though it may be, one can predict that the new interest in film will take the direction of multi-media experimentation. Expo 67, it seems, is *now*. Our new and growing capacity to absorb images and synthesize sounds demands a simultaneity that cannot be met by traditional forms of film-making. The response so far has been the half-hearted multiple screens of *The Thomas Crown Affair*, not part of the conception of the film, but inserted as fancy dressing. The object of multiple images is not so much to condense actions as to create an environment such as the Ontario pavilion film, *A Place to Stand*. My own students have begun to relegate location shots such as street scenes or mood sequences to peripheral attention on side screens and walls, while the action takes place on the main screen . . . .

The young look at film is a revolutionary one, motivated more by love of the medium than hatred of the Establishment. In a sense, the new taste is liberating film for a free exploration of its potential, especially in the area of humanizing change. The hunger for a relativity of time and space will extend to morality, producing films that explore problems rather than package solutions. Nevertheless, the very intensity of young involvement gives promise of profound changes in the youth audience as people themselves to the reality of the medium. Whether as young film-maker or multi-media entrepreneur, the young will have their say. If we take the time to cultivate their perspective, we may learn an interesting view of the future of media, and a fascinating way to stay alive.

Hamlet: The Psycho-analytical Solution

ERNEST JONES

We are compelled then to take the position that there is some cause for Hamlet's vacillation which has not yet been fathomed. If this lies neither in his incapacity for action in general, nor in the inordinate difficulty of the particular task in question, then it must of necessity lie in the third possibility—namely, in some special feature of the task that renders it repugnant to him. This conclusion, that Hamlet at heart does not want to carry out the task, seems so obvious that it is hard to see how any open-minded reader of the play could avoid making it.[1] Some of the direct evidence for it furnished in the play will presently be brought forward when we discuss the problem of the cause of the repugnance, but it will first be necessary to mention some of the views that have been expressed on the subject.

The first writer clearly to recognize that Hamlet was a man not baffled in his endeavours but struggling in an internal conflict was Ulrici,[2] in 1839. The details of Ulrici's hypothesis, which like Klein's originated in the Hegelian views of morality, are not easy to follow, but the essence of it is the contention that Hamlet gravely doubted the moral legitimacy of revenge. He was thus plunged into a struggle between his natural tendency to avenge his father and his highly developed ethical and Christian views, which forbade the indulging of this instinctive desire. This hypothesis has been further developed on moral, ethical,

---

[1] Anyone who doubts this conclusion is recommended to read Loening's convincing chapter (XII), "Hamlet's Verhalten gegen seine Aufgabe".

[2] Ulrici: *Shakespeare's dramatische Kunst; Geschichte und Charakteristik des Shakespeare'schen Dramas,* 1839.

and religious planes by Tolman,[3] Arndt,[4] Egan,[5] Wright,[6] Liebau,[7] Mézières,[8] Gerth,[9] Baumgart,[10] Robertson,[11] and Ford.[12] Von Berger[13] says that the task laid on him is beneath Hamlet's dignity: "He is too wise and too noble for this pernicious world." Foss[14] thinks that the motive for Hamlet's delay is to gain time so as to think out how he can sinlessly commit a great sin; his conscience tells him it was wrong even to think of assassination, and that what he should do was to denounce Claudius. Kohler[15] ingeniously transferred the conflict to the sphere of jurisprudence, maintaining that Hamlet represented a type in advance of his time in recognizing the superiority of legal punishment over private revenge or family vendetta and was thus a fighter in the van of progress; he writes:[16] "Hamlet is a corner-stone in the evolution of law and morality." A similar view has been developed by Rubinstein.[17] This special pleading has been effectually refuted by Loening[18] and Fuld;[19] it is contradicted by all historical considerations. Finally, Schipper,[20] Gelber,[21] and, more recently, Stoll[22] have suggested that the conflict was a purely intellectual one, Hamlet being unable to satisfy himself of the adequacy or reliability of the Ghost's evidence. In his interesting work Figgis combines these views by insisting that the play is a tragedy of honour, Hamlet's main instinct: "In striking at the King without a full assurance of his guilt, was to him not only to strike at the legal monarch of the realm, but also to seem as though he was seizing a pretext to strike for the throne, he being the next in succession":[23] "What seems like indecision in the early portion of the play is really the honourable desire not

---

[3] Tolman: "A View of the Views about 'Hamlet'," *Publications of the Modern Language Association of America*, 1898, p. 155.

[4] Wilhelm Arndt: "Hamlet, der Christ," *Die Zukunft*, 1896, S. 275.

[5] M. F. Egan: "The Puzzle of Hamlet" in *The Ghost in Hamlet and Other Essays*, 1906.

[6] W. B. Wright: "Hamlet," *Atlantic Monthly*, 1902, p. 686.

[7] Liebau: *Studien über William Shakespeares Trauerspiel Hamlet*. Date not stated.

[8] Mézières: *Shakespeare, ses oeuvres et ses critiques*, 1860.

[9] Gerth: *op. cit.*

[10] Baumgart: *op. cit.*

[11] J. M. Robertson: *Montaigne and Shakespeare*, 1897, p. 129.

[12] Ford: *Shakespeare's Hamlet: A New Theory*, 1900.

[13] A. von Berger: "Hamlet" in *Dramaturgische Vorträge*, 1890.

[14] G. R. Foss: *What the Author Meant*, 1932, p. 13.

[15] Kohler: *Shakespeare vor dem Forum der Jurisprudenz*, 1883; and *Zur Lehre von der Blutrache*, 1885. See also *Zeitschrift für vergleichende Rechtswissenschaft*, Bd. V, S. 330.

[16] Kohler: *Shakespeare etc.; op. cit.*, S. 189.

[17] Rubinstein: *Hamlet als Neurastheniker*, 1896.

[18] Loening: *Zeitschrift für die gesamte Strafrechtswissenschaft*, Bd. V, S. 191.

[19] Fuld: "Shakespeare und die Blutrache," *Dramaturgische Blätter und Bühnen-Rundschau*, 1888, Nr. 44.

[20] Schipper: *Shakespeare's Hamlet; ästhetische Erläuterung des Hamlet*, 1862.

[21] Gelber: *Shakespeare'sche Probleme, Plan und Einheit im Hamlet*, 1891.

[22] Stoll: *op. cit.* (1919).

[23] Figgis: *op. cit.*, p. 213.

to let his mere hatred of the King prick him into a capital action against an innocent man, to prove that the apparition of his father was no heated fantasy, and, above all, not to take action till he was assured that his action would not involve his mother."[24]

The obvious question that one puts to the upholders of any of the hypotheses just mentioned is: why did Hamlet in his monologues give us no indication whatsoever of the nature of the conflict in his mind? As we shall presently note, he gave several pretended excuses for his hesitancy, but never once did he hint at any doubt about what his duty was in the matter. He was always clear enough about what he *ought* to do; the conflict in his mind ranged about the question why he couldn't bring himself to do it. If Hamlet had at any time been asked whether it was right for him to kill his uncle, or whether he really intended to do so, no one can seriously doubt what his instant answer would have been. Throughout the play we see his mind irrevocably made up on the desirability of a given course of action, which he fully accepts as being his bounden duty; indeed, he would have resented the mere insinuation of doubt on this point as an untrue slur on his filial piety. Ulrici, Baumgart, and Kohler try to meet this difficulty by assuming that the ethical objection to personal revenge was never clearly present to Hamlet's mind; it was a deep and undeveloped feeling which had not fully dawned. I would agree that only in some such way as this can the difficulty be logically met, and further that in recognizing Hamlet's non-consciousness of the cause of his repugnance to his task we are nearing the core of the mystery. In fact Hamlet tells us so himself in so many words (in his bitter cry—Act IV, Sc. 3—*I do not know why*, etc.). But an insurmountable obstacle in the way of accepting any of the causes of repugnance suggested above is that the nature of them is such that a keen and introspective thinker, as Hamlet was, would infallibly have recognized some indication of their presence, and would have openly debated them instead of deceiving himself with a number of false pretexts in the way we shall presently recall. Loening[25] well states this in the sentence: "If it had been a question of a conflict between the duty of revenge imposed from without and an inner *moral* or *juristic* counter-impulse, this discord and its cause *must* have been brought into the region of reflection in a man so capable of thought, and so accustomed to it, as Hamlet was."

In spite of this difficulty the hint of an approaching solution encourages us to pursue more closely the argument at that point. The hypothesis just stated may be correct up to a certain stage and then have failed for lack of special knowledge to guide it further. Thus Hamlet's hesitancy may have been due to an internal conflict between the impulse to fulfil his task on the one hand and some special cause of repugnance to it on the other; further, the explanation of his not disclosing this cause of repugnance may be that he was not conscious of its nature; and yet the cause may be one that doesn't happen to have been considered by any of the upholders of this hypothesis. In other words, the first two stages in the argument may be correct, but not the third. This is the view

[24] *Idem: op. cit.*, p. 232.

[25] Loening: *Die Hamlet-Tragödie Shakespeares*, 1893, S. 78.

that will now be developed, but before dealing with the third stage of the argument it is first necessary to establish the probability of the first two—namely, that Hamlet's hesitancy was due to some special cause of repugnance for his task and that he was unaware of the nature of this repugnance.

A preliminary obstruction to this line of thought, based on some common prejudices on the subject of mental dynamics, may first be considered. If Hamlet was not aware of the nature of his inhibition, doubt may be felt concerning the possibility of our penetrating to it. This pessimistic thought was expressed by Baumgart[26] as follows: "What hinders Hamlet in his revenge is for him himself a problem and *therefore* it must remain a problem for us all." Fortunately for our investigation, however, psycho-analytic studies have demonstrated beyond doubt that mental trends hidden from the subject himself may come to external expression in ways that reveal their nature to a trained observer, so that the possibility of success is not to be thus excluded. Loening[27] has further objected to this hypothesis that the poet himself has not disclosed this hidden mental trend, or even given any indication of it. The first part of his objection is certainly true—otherwise there would be no problem to discuss, but we shall presently see that the second is by no means true. It may be asked: why has the poet not put in a clearer light the mental trend we are trying to discover? Strange as it may appear, the answer is probably the same as with Hamlet himself—namely, he could not because he was unaware of its nature. We shall later deal with this question in connection with the relation of the poet to the play.

As Trench well says:[28] "We find it hard, with Shakespeare's help, to understand Hamlet: even Shakespeare, perhaps, found it hard to understand him: Hamlet himself finds it impossible to understand himself. Better able than other men to read the hearts and motives of others, he is yet quite unable to read his own." I know of no more authentic statement than this in the whole literature on the Hamlet problem. But, if the motive of the play is so obscure, to what can we attribute its powerful effect on the audience, since, as Kohler[29] asks, "Who has ever seen Hamlet and not felt the fearful conflict that moves the soul of the hero?" This can only be because the hero's conflict finds its echo in a similar inner conflict in the mind of the hearer, and the more intense is this already present conflict the greater is the effect of the drama.[30] Again, it is certain that the hearer himself does not know the inner cause of the conflict in his own mind, but experiences only the outer manifestations of it. So we reach the apparent paradox that the hero, the poet, and the audience are all profoundly moved by feelings due to a conflict of the source of which they are unaware.

The fact, however, that such a conclusion should appear paradoxical is in

---

[26] Baumgart: *op. cit.*, S. 48.

[27] Loening: *op. cit.*, S. 78, 79.

[28] Trench: *op. cit.*, p. 115.

[29] Kohler: *Shakespeare vor dem Forum der Jurisprudenz*, 1883, S. 195.

[30] It need hardly be said that the play, like most others, appeals to its audience in a number of different respects. We are here considering only the main appeal, the central conflict in the tragedy.

itself a censure on popular ignorance of the actual workings of the human mind, and before undertaking to sustain the assertions made in the preceding paragraph it will first be necessary to make a few observations on the prevailing views of motive and conduct in general. The new science of clinical psychology stands nowhere in sharper contrast to the older attitudes towards mental functioning than on this very matter. Whereas the generally accepted view of man's mind, usually implicit and frequently explicit in psychological writings and elsewhere, regards it as an interplay of various processes that are for the most part known to the subject, or are at all events accessible to careful introspection on his part, the analytic methods of clinical psychology have on the contrary decisively proved that a far greater number of these processes than is commonly surmised arises from origins that he never even suspects. Man's belief that he is a self-conscious animal, alive to the desires that impel or inhibit his actions, is the last stronghold of that anthropomorphic and anthropocentric outlook on life which has so long dominated his philosophy, his theology, and, above all, his psychology. In other words, the tendency to take man at his own valuation is rarely resisted, and we assume that the surest way of finding out why a person commits a given act is simply to ask him, relying on the knowledge that he, as we ourselves would in a like circumstance, will feel certain of the answer and will almost infallibly provide a plausible reason for his conduct. Special objective methods of penetrating into the more obscure mental processes, however, disclose the most formidable obstacles in the way of this direct introspective route, and reveal powers of self-deception in the human mind to which a limit has yet to be found. If I may quote from a former paper:[31] "We are beginning to see man not as the smooth, self-acting agent he pretends to be, but as he really is, a creature only dimly conscious of the various influences that mould his thought and action, and blindly resisting with all the means at his command the forces that are making for a higher and fuller consciousness."

That Hamlet is suffering from an internal conflict the essential nature of which is inaccessible to his introspection is evidenced by the following considerations. Throughout the play we have the clearest picture of a man who sees his duty plain before him, but who shirks it at every opportunity and suffers in consequence the most intense remorse. To paraphrase Sir James Paget's well-known description of hysterical paralysis: Hamlet's advocates say he cannot do his duty, his detractors say he will not, whereas the truth is that he cannot will. Further than this, the deficient will-power is localized to the one question of killing his uncle; it is what may be termed a *specific aboulia*. Now instances of such specific aboulias in real life invariably prove, when analyzed, to be due to an unconscious repulsion against the act that cannot be performed (or else against something closely associated with the act, so that the idea of the act becomes also involved in the repulsion). In other words, whenever a person cannot bring himself to do something that every conscious consideration tells him he should do—and which he may have the strongest conscious desire to do—it is always because there is some hidden reason why a part of him doesn't

---

[31] "Rationalization in Every Day Life", *Journal of Abnormal Psychology*, 1908, p. 168.

want to do it; this reason he will not own to himself and is only dimly if at all aware of. That is exactly the case with Hamlet. Time and again he works himself up, points out to himself his obvious duty, with the cruelest self-reproaches lashes himself to agonies of remorse—and once more falls away into inaction. He eagerly seizes at every excuse for occupying himself with any other matter than the performance of his duty—even in the last scene of the last act entering on the distraction of a quite irrelevant fencing-match with a man who he must know wants to kill him, an eventuality that would put an end to all hope of fulfilling his task: just as on a lesser plane a person faced with a distasteful task, e.g. writing a difficult letter, will whittle away his time in arranging, tidying, and fidgeting with any little occupation that may serve as a pretext for procrastination. Bradley[32] even goes so far as to make out a case for the view that Hamlet's self-accusation of "bestial oblivion" is to be taken in a literal sense, his unconscious detestation of his task being so intense as to enable him actually to forget it for periods.

Highly significant is the fact that the grounds Hamlet gives for his hesitancy are grounds none of which will stand any serious consideration, and which continually change from one time to another. One moment he pretends he is too cowardly to perform the deed, at another he questions the truthfulness of the ghost, at another—when the opportunity presents itself in its naked form— he thinks the time is unsuited, it would be better to wait till the King was at some evil act and then to kill him, and so on. They have each of them, it is true, a certain plausibility—so much so that some writers have accepted them at face value; but surely no pretext would be of any use if it were not plausible. As Madariaga[33] truly says: "The argument that the reasons given by Hamlet not to kill the king at prayers are cogent is irrelevant. For the man who wants to procrastinate cogent arguments are more valuable than mere pretext." Take, for instance, the matter of the credibility of the ghost. There exists an extensive and very interesting literature concerning Elizabethan beliefs in supernatural visitation. It was doubtless a burning topic, a focal point of the controversies about the conflicting theologies of the age, and moreover, affecting the practical question of how to treat witches. But there is no evidence of Hamlet (or Shakespeare!) being specially interested in theology, and from the moment when the ghost confirms the slumbering suspicion in his mind ("O, my prophetic soul! My uncle!") his intuition must indubitably have convinced him of the ghost's veridical nature. He never really doubted the villainy of his uncle.

When a man gives at different times a different reason for his conduct it is safe to infer that, whether consciously or not, he is concealing the true reason. Wetz,[34] discussing a similar problem in reference to Iago, truly observes: "Nothing proves so well how false are the motives with which Iago tries to persuade himself as *the constant change in these motives*." We can therefore safely dismiss all the alleged motives that Hamlet propounds, as being more or less

---

[32] Bradley: *op. cit.*, pp. 125, 126, 410, 411.

[33] Madariaga: *op. cit.*, p. 98.

[34] Wetz: *Shakespeare vom Standpunkt der vergleichenden Litteraturgeschichte*, 1890, Bd. I, S. 186.

successful attempts on his part to blind himself with self-deception. Loening's[35] summing-up of them is not too emphatic when he says: "They are all mutually contradictory; *they are one and all false pretexts.*" The alleged motives excellently illustrate the psychological mechanisms of evasion and rationalization I have elsewhere described.[36] It is not necessary, however, to discuss them here individually, for Loening has with the greatest perspicacity done this in full detail and has effectually demonstrated how utterly untenable they all are.[37]

Still, in his moments of self-reproach Hamlet sees clearly enough the recalcitrancy of his conduct and renews his efforts to achieve action. It is noticeable how his outbursts of remorse are evoked by external happenings which bring back to his mind that which he would so gladly forget, and which, according to Bradley, he does at times forget: particularly effective in this respect are incidents that contrast with his own conduct, as when the player is so moved over the fate of Hecuba (Act II, Sc. 2), or when Fortinbras takes the field and "finds quarrel in a straw when honour's at the stake" (Act IV, Sc. 4). On the former occasion, stung by the monstrous way in which the player pours out his feeling at the thought of Hecuba, he arraigns himself in words which surely should effectually dispose of the view that he has any doubt where his duty lies.

> What's Hecuba to him, or he to Hecuba,
> That he should weep for her? What would he do,
> Had he the motive and the cue for passion
> That I have? He would drown the stage with tears
> And cleave the general ear with horrid speech,
> Make mad the guilty and appal the free,
> Confound the ignorant, and amaze indeed
> The very faculties of eyes and ears; yet I,
> A dull and muddy-mettled rascal, peak
> Like John-a-dreams, unpregnant of my cause,[38]
> And can say nothing; no, not for a king,
> Upon whose property and most dear life
> A damn'd defeat was made: Am I a coward?
> Who calls me villain, breaks my pate across,
> Plucks off my beard and blows it in my face,
> Tweaks me by the nose, gives me the lie i' the throat
> As deep as to the lungs? Who does me this?
> Ha, 'swounds, I should take it: for it cannot be
> But I am pigeon-liver'd, and lack gall
> To make oppression bitter, or ere this
> I should ha' fatted all the region kites

[35] Loening: *op. cit.*, S. 245.

[36] *op. cit.*, p. 161.

[37] See especially his analysis of Hamlet's pretext for non-action in the prayer scene: *op. cit.*, S. 240–2.

[38] How the essence of the situation is conveyed in these four words.

> With this slave's offal. Bloody, bawdy villain!
> Remorseless, treacherous, lecherous, kindless villain!
> O, vengeance!
> Why, what an ass am I! This is most brave,
> That I, the son of a dear father murder'd,
> *Prompted to my revenge by heaven and hell,*
> Must like a whore unpack my heart with words,
> And fall a-cursing like a very drab;
> A scullion![39]

The readiness with which his guilty conscience is stirred into activity is again evidenced on the second appearance of the Ghost, when Hamlet cries,

> Do you not come your tardy son to chide,
> That lapsed in time and passion lets go by
> Th'important acting of your dread command?
> O, say!

The Ghost at once confirms this misgiving by answering,

> Do not forget! this visitation
> Is but to whet thy almost blunted purpose.

In short, the whole picture presented by Hamlet, his deep depression, the hopeless note in his attitude towards the world and towards the value of life, his dread of death,[40] his repeated reference to bad dreams, his self-accusations, his desperate efforts to get away from the thoughts of his duty, and his vain attempts to find an excuse for his procrastination: all this unequivocally points to a *tortured conscience,* to some hidden ground for shirking his task, a ground which he dare not or cannot avow to himself. We have, therefore, to take up the argument again at this point, and to seek for some evidence that may serve to bring to light the hidden counter-motive.

The extensive experience of the psycho-analytic researches carried out by Freud and his school during the past half-century has amply demonstrated that certain kinds of mental processes show a greater tendency to be inaccessible to consciousness (put technically, to be "repressed") than others. In other words, it is harder for a person to realize the existence in his mind of some mental trends than it is of others. In order, therefore, to gain a proper perspective it is necessary briefly to inquire into the relative frequency with which various sets of mental processes are "repressed". Experience shows that this can be correlated with the degree of compatibility of these various sets with the ideals

---

[39] Dover Wilson considers this a misprint for "stallion".

[40] Tieck (*Dramaturgische Blätter*, II, 1826) saw in Hamlet's cowardly fear of death a chief reason for his hesitancy in executing his vengeance. How well Shakespeare understood what this fear was like may be inferred from Claudio's words in *Measure for Measure:*

> The weariest and most loathed worldly life
> That age, ache, penury and imprisonment
> Can lay on nature is a paradise
> To what we fear of death.

and standards accepted by the conscious ego; the less compatible they are with these the more likely are they to be "repressed". As the standards acceptable to consciousness are in considerable measure derived from the immediate environment, one may formulate the following generalization: those processes are most likely to be "repressed" by the individual which are most disapproved of by the particular circle of society to whose influence he has chiefly been subjected during the period when his character was being formed. Biologically stated, this law would run: "That which is unacceptable to the herd becomes unacceptable to the individual member", it being understood that the term herd is intended here in the sense of the particular circle defined above, which is by no means necessarily the community at large. It is for this reason that moral, social, ethical, or religious tendencies are seldom "repressed," for, since the individual originally received them from his herd, they can hardly ever come into conflict with the dicta of the latter. This merely says that a man cannot be ashamed of that which he respects; the apparent exceptions to this rule need not be here explained.

The language used in the previous paragraph will have indicated that by the term "repression" we denote an active dynamic process. Thoughts that are "repressed" are actively kept from consciousness by a definite force and with the expenditure of more or less mental effort, though the person concerned is rarely aware of this. Further, what is thus kept from consciousness typically possesses an energy of its own; hence our frequent use of such expressions as "trend," "tendency," etc. A little consideration of the genetic aspects of the matter will make it comprehensible that the trends most likely to be "repressed" are those belonging to what are called the innate impulses, as contrasted with secondarily acquired ones. Loening[41] seems very discerningly to have grasped this, for, in commenting on a remark of Kohler's to the effect that "where a feeling impels us to action or to omission, it is replete with a hundred reasons—with reasons that are as light as soap-bubbles, but which through self-deception appear to us as highly respectable and compelling motives, because they are hugely magnified in the (concave) mirror of our own feeling," he writes: "But this does not hold good, as Kohler and others believe, when we are impelled by *moral* feelings of which reason *approves* (for these we admit to ourselves, they need no excuse), only for feelings that arise from our *natural man,* those the gratification of which is *opposed by our reason.*" It only remains to add the obvious corollary that, as the herd unquestionably selects from the "natural" instincts the sexual one on which to lay its heaviest ban, so it is the various psycho-sexual trends that are most often "repressed" by the individual. We have here the explanation of the clinical experience that the more intense and the more obscure is a given case of deep mental conflict the more certainly will it be found on adequate analysis to centre about a sexual problem. On the surface, of course, this does not appear so, for, by means of various psychological defensive mechanisms, the depression, doubt, despair, and other manifestations of the conflict are transferred on to more tolerable and permissible topics, such as anxiety about

---

[41] Loening: *op. cit.,* S. 245, 246.

worldly success or failure, about immortality and the salvation of the soul, philosophical considerations about the value of life, the future of the world, and so on.

Bearing these considerations in mind, let us return to Hamlet. It should now be evident that the conflict hypotheses discussed above, which see Hamlet's conscious impulse towards revenge inhibited by an unconscious misgiving of a highly ethical kind, are based on ignorance of what actually happens in real life, since misgivings of this order belong in fact to the more conscious layers of the mind rather than to the deeper, unconscious ones. Hamlet's intense self-study would speedily have made him aware of any such misgivings and, although he might subsequently have ignored them, it would almost certainly have been by the aid of some process of rationalization which would have enabled him to deceive himself into believing that they were ill-founded; he would in any case have remained conscious of the nature of them. We have therefore to invert these hypotheses and realize—as his words so often indicate—that the positive striving for vengeance, the pious task laid on him by his father, was to him the moral and social one, the one approved of by his consciousness, and that the "repressed" inhibiting striving against the act of vengeance arose in some hidden source connected with his more personal, natural instincts. The former striving has already been considered, and indeed is manifest in every speech in which Hamlet debates the matter: the second is, from its nature, more obscure and has next to be investigated.

This is perhaps most easily done by inquiring more intently into Hamlet's precise attitude towards the object of his vengeance, Claudius, and towards the crimes that have to be avenged. These are two: Claudius' incest with the Queen,[42] and his murder of his brother. Now it is of great importance to note the profound difference in Hamlet's attitude towards these two crimes. Intellectually of course he abhors both, but there can be no question as to which arouses in him the deeper loathing. Whereas the murder of his father evokes in him indignation and a plain recognition of his obvious duty to avenge it, his mother's guilty conduct awakes in him the intensest horror. Furnivall[43] remarks, in speaking of the Queen, "Her disgraceful adultery and incest, and treason to his noble father's memory, Hamlet has felt in his inmost soul. Compared to their ingrain die, Claudius' murder of his father—notwithstanding all his protestations—is only a skin-deep stain."

Now, in trying to define Hamlet's attitude towards his uncle we have to guard against assuming off-hand that this is a simple one of mere execration, for there is a possibility of complexity arising in the following way: The uncle has not merely committed *each* crime, he has committed *both* crimes, a distinction of considerable importance, since the *combination* of crimes allows the admittance of a new factor, produced by the possible inter-relation of the two, which may prevent the result from being simply one of summation. In addition, it has

[42] Had this relationship not counted as incestuous, then Queen Elizabeth would have had no right to the throne; she would have been a bastard, Katherine of Aragon being still alive at her birth.

[43] Furnivall: Introduction to the "Leopold" Shakespeare, p. 72.

to be borne in mind that the perpetrator of the crimes is a relative, and an exceedingly near relative. The possible inter-relationship of the crimes, and the fact that the author of them is an actual member of the family, give scope for a confusion in their influence on Hamlet's mind which may be the cause of the very obscurity we are seeking to clarify.

Let us first pursue further the effect on Hamlet of his mother's misconduct. Before he even knows with any certitude, however much he may suspect it, that his father has been murdered he is in the deepest depression, and evidently on account of this misconduct. The connection between the two is unmistakable in the monologue in Act I, Sc. 2, in reference to which Furnivall[44] writes: "One must insist on this, that before any revelation of his father's murder is made to Hamlet, before any burden of revenging that murder is laid upon him, he thinks of suicide as a welcome means of escape from this fair world of God's, made abominable to his diseased and weak imagination by his mother's lust, and the dishonour done by her to his father's memory."

> O that this too too solid[45] flesh would melt,
> Thaw and resolve itself into a dew,
> Or that the Everlasting had not fix'd
> His canon 'gainst self-slaughter, O God, God,
> How weary, stale, flat, and unprofitable
> Seem to me all the uses of this world!
> Fie on 't, O fie, 'tis an unweeded garden
> That grows to seed, things rank and gross in nature
> Possess it merely, that it should come to this,
> But two months dead, nay, not so much, not two,
> So excellent a king; that was to this
> Hyperion to a satyr, so loving to my mother,
> That he might not beteem the winds of heaven
> Visit her face too roughly—heaven and earth
> Must I remember? why, she would hang on him
> As if increase of appetite had grown
> By what it fed on, and yet within a month,
> Let me not think on 't; frailty thy name is woman!
> A little month or ere those shoes were old
> With which she follow'd my poor father's body
> Like Niobe all tears, why she, even she—
> O God, a beast that wants discourse of reason
> Would have mourn'd longer—married with my uncle,
> My father's brother, but no more like my father
> Than I to Hercules, within a month,
> Ere yet the salt of most unrighteous tears

[44] Furnivall: *op. cit.*, p. 70.

[45] Dover Wilson (*Times Literary Supplement*, May 16, 1908) brings forward excellent reasons for thinking that this word is a misprint for "sullied," I use the Shakespearean punctuation he has restored.

> Had left the flushing in her galled eyes,
> She married. O most wicked speed . . . to post
> With such dexterity to incestuous sheets!
> It is not, nor it cannot come to good,
> But break my heart, for I must hold my tongue.

According to Bradley,[46] Hamlet's melancholic disgust at life was the cause of his aversion from "any kind of decided action." His explanation of the whole problem of Hamlet is "the moral shock of the sudden ghastly disclosure of his mother's true nature,"[47] and he regards the effect of this shock, as depicted in the play, as fully comprehensible. He says:[48] "Is it possible to conceive an experience more desolating to a man such as we have seen Hamlet to be; and is its result anything but perfectly natural? It brings bewildered horror, then loathing, then despair of human nature. His whole mind is poisoned . . . A nature morally blunter would have felt even so dreadful a revelation less keenly. A slower and more limited and positive mind might not have extended so widely through the world the disgust and disbelief that have entered it."

But we can rest satisfied with this seemingly adequate explanation of Hamlet's weariness of life only if we accept unquestioningly the conventional standards of the causes of deep emotion. Many years ago Connolly,[49] a well-known psychiatrist, pointed out the disproportion here existing between cause and effect, and gave as his opinion that Hamlet's reaction to his mother's marriage indicated in itself a mental instability, "a predisposition to actual unsoundness;" he writes: "The circumstances are not such as would at once turn a healthy mind to the contemplation of suicide, the last resource of those whose reason has been overwhelmed by calamity and despair." In T. S. Eliot's[50] opinion, also, Hamlet's emotion is in *excess* of the facts as they appear, and he specially contrasts it with Gertrude's negative and insignificant personality. Wihan[51] attributes the exaggerated effect of his misfortunes to Hamlet's "Masslosigkeit" (lack of moderation), which is displayed in every direction. We have unveiled only the exciting cause, not the predisposing cause. The very fact that Hamlet is apparently content with the explanation arouses our misgiving, for, as will presently be expounded, from the very nature of the emotion he cannot be aware of the true cause of it. If we ask, not what ought to produce such soul-paralysing grief and distaste for life, but what in actual fact does produce it, we are compelled to go beyond this explanation and seek for some deeper cause. In real life speedy second marriages occur commonly enough without leading to any such result as is here depicted, and when we see them followed by this result we invariably find, if the opportunity for an analysis of the subject's mind presents itself, that there is some other and more hidden reason why the event

---

[46] Bradley: *op. cit.*, p. 122.

[47] *Idem: op. cit.*, p. 117.

[48] *Idem: op. cit.*, p. 119.

[49] Connolly: *A Study of Hamlet*, 1863, pp. 22, 23.

[50] T S Eliot: *loc. cit.*

[51] J. Wihan: "Die Hamletfrage", in *Leipziger Beiträge zur englischen Philogie*, 1921, S. 89.

is followed by this inordinately great effect. The reason always is that the event has awakened to increased activity mental processes that have been "repressed" from the subject's consciousness. His mind has been specially prepared for the catastrophe by previous mental processes with which those directly resulting from the event have entered into association. This is perhaps what Furnivall means when he speaks of the world being made abominable to Hamlet's "diseased imagination." In short, the special nature of the reaction presupposes some special feature in the mental predisposition. Bradley himself has to qualify his hypothesis by inserting the words "to a man such as we have seen Hamlet to be."

We come at this point to the vexed question of Hamlet's sanity, about which so many controversies have raged. Dover Wilson[52] authoritatively writes: "I agree with Loening, Bradley and others that Shakespeare meant us to imagine Hamlet as suffering from some kind of mental disorder throughout the play." The question is what kind of mental disorder and what is its significance dramatically and psychologically. The matter is complicated by Hamlet's frequently displaying simulation (the Antic Disposition),[53] and it has been asked whether this is to conceal his real mental disturbance or cunningly to conceal his purposes in coping with the practical problems of this task? This is a topic that presently will be considered at some length, but there can be few who regard it as a comprehensive statement of Hamlet's mental state. As T. S. Eliot[54] has neatly expressed it, "Hamlet's 'madness' is less than madness and more than feigned."

But what of the mental disorder itself? In the past this little problem in clinical diagnosis seems to have greatly exercised psychiatrists. Some of them, e.g. Thierisch,[55] Sigismund,[56] Stenger,[57] and many others, have simply held that Hamlet was insane, without particularizing the form of insanity. Rosner[58] labelled Hamlet as a hysteroneurasthenic, an opinion contradicted by Rubinstein[59] and Landmann.[60] Most, however, including Kellog,[61] de Boismon,[62] Heuse,[63] Nicholson,[64] and others, have committed themselves to the view that Hamlet was suffering from melancholia, though there are not failing psychia-

---

[52] Dover Wilson: *What Happens* etc., p. 217.

[53] Cp. R. Alexander: "Hamlet, the Classical Malingerer," *Medical Journal and Record*, Sept. 4, 1929, p. 287.

[54] T. S. Eliot: *Selected Essays*, 1932, p. 146.

[55] Thierisch: *Nord und Süd*, 1878, Bd. VI.

[56] Sigismund: *Jahrbuch der Deutschen Shakespeare-Gesellschaft*, 1879, Jahrg. XVI.

[57] E. Stenger: *Der Hamlet Charakter. Eine psychiatrische Shakespeare-Studie*, 1883.

[58] Rosner: *Shakespeare's Hamlet im Lichte der Neuropathologie*, 1895.

[59] Rubinstein: *op. cit.*

[60] Landmann: *Zeitschrift für Psychologie*, 1896, Bd. XI.

[61] Kellog: *Shakespeare's Delineation of Insanity*, 1868.

[62] De Boismon: *Annales médico-psychologiques*, 1868, 4e série, 12e fasc.

[63] Heuse: *Jahrbuch der deutschen Shakespeare-Gesellschaft*, 1876, Jahrg. XIII.

[64] Nicholson: *Transactions of the New Shakespeare Society*, 1880–5, Part II.

trists, e.g. Ominus,[65] who reject this. Schücking[66] attributes the delay in his action to Hamlet's being paralysed by melancholia. Laehr[67] has a particularly ingenious hypothesis which maintains that Shakespeare, having taken over the Ghost episode from the earlier play, was obliged to depict Hamlet as a melancholiac because this was theatrically the most presentable form of insanity in which hallucinations occur. Long ago Dowden made it seem probable that Shakespeare had made use of an important study of melancholia by Timothe Bright,[68] but, although he may have adapted a few phrases to his own use, the clinical picture of Hamlet differs notably from that delineated by Bright.

More to the point is the actual account given in the play by the King, the Queen, Ophelia, and above all, Polonius.[69] In his description, for example, we note—if the Elizabethan language is translated into modern English—the symptoms of dejection, refusal of food, insomnia, crazy behaviour, fits of delirium, and finally of raving madness; Hamlet's poignant parting words to Polonius ("except my life", etc.) cannot mean other than a craving for death. These are undoubtedly suggestive of certain forms of melancholia, and the likeness to manic-depressive insanity, of which melancholia is now known to be but a part, is completed by the occurrence of attacks of great excitement that would nowadays be called "hypomanic", of which Dover Wilson[70] counts no fewer than eight. This modern diagnosis has indeed been suggested, e.g. by Brock,[71] Somerville,[72] and others. Nevertheless, the rapid and startling oscillations between intense excitement and profound depression do not accord with the accepted picture of this disorder, and if I had to describe such a condition as Hamlet's in clinical terms—which I am not particularly inclined to—it would have to be as a severe case of hysteria on a cyclothymic basis.

All this, however, is of academic interest only. What we are essentially concerned with is the psychological understanding of the dramatic effect produced by Hamlet's personality and behaviour. That effect would be quite other were the central figure in the play to represent merely a "case of insanity." When that happens, as with Ophelia, such a person passes beyond our ken, is in a sense no more human, whereas Hamlet successfully claims our interest and sympathy to the very end. Shakespeare certainly never intended us to regard Hamlet as insane, so that the "mind o'erthrown" must have some other meaning than its literal one. Robert Bridges[73] has described the matter with exquisite delicacy:

---

[65] Ominus: *Revue des Deux Mondes*, 1876, 3e sér., 14e fasc.

[66] Schücking: *Character Problems in Shakespeare's Plays*, 1922, p. 162.

[67] Laehr: *Die Darstellung krankhafter Geisteszustände in Shakespeare's Dramas*, 1898, S. 179, etc.

[68] Timothe Bright: *A Treatise of Melancholia*, 1586.

[69] Act 2, Sc. 2. "Fell into a sadness," etc.

[70] Dover Wilson: *op. cit.*, p. 213.

[71] J. H. E. Brock: *The Dramatic Purpose of Hamlet*, 1935.

[72] H. Somerville: *Madness in Shakespearean Tragedy*, 1929.

[73] Robert Bridges: *The Testament of Beauty*, I. 577.

> Hamlet himself would never have been aught to us, or we
> To Hamlet, wer't not for the artful balance whereby
> Shakespeare so gingerly put his sanity in doubt
> Without the while confounding his Reason.

I would suggest that in this Shakespeare's extraordinary powers of observation and penetration granted him a degree of insight that it has taken the world three subsequent centuries to reach. Until our generation (and even now in the juristic sphere) a dividing line separated the sane and responsible from the irresponsible insane. It is now becoming more and more widely recognized that much of mankind lives in an intermediate and unhappy state charged with what Dover Wilson[74] well calls "that sense of frustration, futility and human inadequacy which is the burden of the whole symphony" and of which Hamlet is the supreme example in literature. This intermediate plight, in the toils of which perhaps the greater part of mankind struggles and suffers, is given the name of psychoneurosis, and long ago the genius of Shakespeare depicted it for us with faultless insight.

Extensive studies of the past half century, inspired by Freud, have taught us that a psychoneurosis means a state of mind where the person is unduly, and often painfully, driven or thwarted by the "unconscious" part of his mind, that buried part that was once the infant's mind and still lives on side by side with the adult mentality that has developed out of it and should have taken its place. It signifies *internal* mental conflict. We have here the reason why it is impossible to discuss intelligently the state of mind of anyone suffering from a psychoneurosis, whether the description is of a living person or an imagined one, without correlating the manifestations with what must have operated in his infancy and is *still operating*. That is what I propose to attempt here.

For some deep-seated reason, which is to him unacceptable, Hamlet is plunged into anguish at the thought of his father being replaced in his mother's affections by someone else. It is as if his devotion to his mother had made him so jealous for her affection that he had found it hard enough to share this even with his father and could not endure to share it with still another man. Against this thought, however, suggestive as it is, may be urged three objections. First, if it were in itself a full statement of the matter, Hamlet would have been aware of the jealousy, whereas we have concluded that the mental process we are seeking is hidden from him. Secondly, we see in it no evidence of the arousing of an old and forgotten memory. And, thirdly, Hamlet is being deprived by Claudius of no greater share in the Queen's affection than he had been by his own father, for the two brothers made exactly similar claims in this respect— namely, those of a loved husband. The last-named objection, however, leads us to the heart of the situation. How if, in fact, Hamlet had in years gone by, as a child, bitterly resented having had to share his mother's affection even with his own father, had regarded him as a rival, and had secretly wished him out of the way so that he might enjoy undisputed and undisturbed the mono- poly of that affection? If such thoughts had been present in his mind in child-

---

[74] Dover Wilson: *op. cit.*, p. 261.

hood days they evidently would have been "repressed," and all traces of them obliterated, by filial piety and other educative influences. The actual realization of his early wish in the death of his father at the hands of a jealous rival would then have stimulated into activity these "repressed" memories, which would have produced, in the form of depression and other suffering, an obscure aftermath of his childhood's conflict. This is at all events the mechanism that is actually found in the real Hamlets who are investigated psychologically.[75]

The explanation, therefore, of the delay and self-frustration exhibited in the endeavour to fulfil his father's demand for vengeance is that to Hamlet the thought of incest and parricide combined is too intolerable to be borne. One part of him tries to carry out the task, the other flinches inexorably from the thought of it. How fain would he blot it out in that "bestial oblivion" which unfortunately for him his conscience condemns. He is torn and tortured in an insoluble inner conflict.

[75] See, for instance, Wulf Sachs: *Black Hamlet*, 1937.